RUSSIA AND REFORM

THIS BOOK IS INSCRIBED

TO

JAMES RICHMOND PATON

RUSSIA AND REFORM

BY

BERNARD PARES, M.A.

HYPERION PRESS, INC.
WESTPORT, CONNECTICUT

Library of Congress Cataloging in Publication Data

Pares, Sir Bernard, 1867-1949.
    Russia and reform.

    Reprint of the 1907 ed. published by A. Constable,
London.
    1. Russia—Politics and government. 2. Russia—
Social conditions. I. Title.
DK40.P32 1973   309.1'47.'08   73-849
ISBN 0-88355-046-6

Published in 1907
by Archibald Constable & Co., Ltd., London, England

First Hyperion reprint edition 1973

Library of Congress Catalogue Number 73-849

ISBN 0-88355-046-6

Printed in the United States of America

PREFACE.

In this book I try to summarise the chief things which Englishmen ought to know, if they wish to form an intelligent judgment
of what is now taking place in Russia. We have arrived at one
of the most critical turning-points in Russian history, but present
events are the crisis of a long and dramatic story. Without an
acquaintance with the beginning of the chapter which is now in
progress, we cannot hope to understand the end.

The chief political differences in Russia are themselves the
result of a great moral conflict between the instincts of two
schools. Of course there are many kinds of Slavophils and also
many kinds of Westernisers, and there is hardly any Russian of
the one creed who has not in him the elements of the other ; but
the main difference is so important, that I have made it the
foundation of the plan of this book. I have not tried to write a
history of modern Russia; but I have sketched the chief features
of her development as a people and as a State, and have tried to
catch the significance of the main points at issue between the
Government and the people. In the first part, I deal chiefly with
the Slavophil tradition, which is summed up in the three words,
" Tsar, Church, and People; " only I naturally put the people first,
because they were there first. In the second part, I trace the
origins and the gradual growth of what is called in Russia " the
Intelligence," that is, the educated class. Next, I study those
many changes in Russian life which resulted from the reforms of
Alexander II., and which tended to show that the gap between the
old instincts and the new intelligent consciousness was gradually
being bridged over. Lastly, I give a sketch of the present movement for liberation, of many of the chief events of which I was
an eye-witness. I carry the story up to the elections for the
second Duma.

As yet no full statement of fact can be made on most of these subjects; but, even if all the details are not accessible, it is essential for the understanding of Russia that we should try to form our power of judgment, by putting into what seems their proper proportion the different elements of the story. This process has to submit itself to a hard test. Our conclusions are constantly being confirmed or refuted by events themselves; and, in the course of several years, I, like my Russian friends, have had to modify my estimate time after time, before I could believe that the general statement which I should make would square with the details of fact, and would commend itself as consequent and reasonable to men of various views in Russia.

It is quite impossible for any one man to make an adequate study of all the chief aspects of Russian life. It has rather been my object to suggest to future students some of the many important and fascinating questions which demand special study. The history, the literature, the geography, the economy, of Russia might each absorb the interest of a number of genuine students. Russia has for a long time been almost the chief factor of our foreign policy; her Imperial importance challenges our attention; her industrial future cannot be a matter of indifference to us.

The difficulties of a political study of Russia are very great. The abnormal bias of the Government against all publicity has long made it very difficult for Russian writers to deal adequately and objectively even with some of the most innocent statistics. There also exists amongst the educated class a spirit of antagonism to the Government which often diminishes the value, not only of such publications as may have evaded the censorship, but even of the most simple statement of fact made in private conversation. I have therefore found it necessary to sometimes confine myself to that which I could see for myself or learn at first hand from those persons who were best qualified to inform me on a given point, checking their statements by what I was able to gather from others. This, of course, meant that I had to select certain typical districts for investigation. The answers to my questions were recorded as soon as possible after I received them. I also had many talks with the chief leaders of the different political parties, and it may be assumed that, in the latter part of the book, I am often summarising the statements made to me by the persons chiefly concerned. For the accuracy of my reports, however, I must myself take all responsibility. I am aware that many errors of detail must have crept in; but I took the greatest pains to make sure that I was not misunderstanding my informants on any point of major importance.

The average English reader has had but few opportunities of gaining even an elementary knowledge of Russia. It is therefore a country in which the less scrupulous of journalists are peculiarly at home. There are correspondents, occupying highly responsible positions, who have confessed to me that they cannot speak or understand Russian. These men are at the mercy of their interpreters, who are in some cases revolutionary propagandists. One correspondent, according to his own account, wrote his Russian news in London, using a handbook of Russian telegraph stations in order to avoid dating a despatch from a place where no such station existed. Of course, by no means all of our correspondents are of this kind. For instance, Dr. E. J. Dillon, Mr. Maurice Baring, Mr. H. W. Williams, Mr. V. E. Marsden, and Mr. J. McGowan all know the country and the language well, and can speak with authority on political events; and this list of names is, of course, not exhaustive. But there has been enough bad work, and it has been widely enough circulated, to popularise the most wrong-headed conceptions of the country and people. For this reason, a writer on Russia has to begin by creating an atmosphere for his reader; and I have preferred to do this by making much of my book, especially in the two last parts, something like a transcript of selected statements of Russians themselves. This must be my excuse for the number of repetitions; it seemed that a statement already reported acquired a new value when applied to a fresh district or repeated by a person of a different class or of opposite political views. Much, too, of what I have quoted is meant to be illustrative rather of the speaker than of the subject about which he is talking.

I should fill several pages if I recorded the names of all the Russians who have helped me in my study. No Englishman who knows anything about Russia will need to be told that I received throughout and, almost without exception, from everyone far more active co-operation than I had any right to ask for; and the ideal of hospitality in Russia is broader and deeper than any that I have met with elsewhere. I am indebted to those officials who secured for me the permission of the Government to see all that I wanted to see, to those Governors and local officials who everywhere facilitated my investigations, to the Heads of all those institutions which I had occasion to visit, and to the many private persons who gave me unstinted help. I am specially indebted for assistance and personal kindness to Mr. M. Alpheráki, Mr. A. Bashmakóff, Mr. S. Syromátnikoff, Professor P. Vinográdoff, Professor S. Múromtseff, Mr. I. Petrunkyévich, Professor P. Milyukóff, Mr. N. Astroff, Mr. M. Margulies, and Mr. A. Aládin ; and I have also to acknowledge much help from Mr. V. Issáyeff, Mr. V. Yanchevetsky, and Mr. A. Fedoróvich, and also from my colleagues, Mr. H. W. Williams and Mr. S. N. Harper. Mr. E. A. Dixon most kindly assisted me in the reading of the proofs and offered many useful suggestions. He also undertook the compilation of the index.

March 1, 1907.

CONTENTS.

PART I.—TSAR, CHURCH, AND PEOPLE.

CHAPTER I.

A HISTORICAL SKETCH.

CHAPTER II.

REFORM AND REACTION, 1854—1904.

x

CONTENTS.

CHAPTER III.

THE CLASS SYSTEM.

The Merchants and Townsmen—Vastness of Russia—The Great Plains and Forests—Roads and Inns—Villages—The Peasants—The Village Community —A Village Meeting—A Cantonal Meeting—Family Life—Partitions— Provincial Types—Costume—Rural Superstitions—Music and Folk Songs— Feast Days—Origins of the Gentry—Effect of the Emancipation on the Country Gentry—Class Organisation—The Marshal of the Gentry—Russian Country Houses—Life of the Country Gentry .   .   .   *pp.* **89—126**

CHAPTER IV.

THE CHURCH.

The Orthodox Church—Clerical Seminaries—Psalm-singers and School Teachers—Deacons and Priests—The Holy Synod—Diocesan Government— Mr. Pobyedonóstseff—Obscurantism—Count Tolstoy and John of Kronstadt —St. Seraphim—The Trinity Monastery—An Archimandrite—A Monk—The Old Believers—The Milk-drinkers—A Rural Dean—Country Priests— Town Priests—Religion of the Peasants—Feast of Michael of Good Faith
pp. **127—153**

CHAPTER V.

ADMINISTRATION AND OFFICIALS.

The Ministries—Overlapping and Dualism of Control—The Political Police —Provincial Governors—Governor's Chancellery—Government Adminis- tration—"Governor's Presences"—Chamber of Control—Military Service and Conscription—Governments, Districts, Stations, Cantons—Town and Country Police—The Land Captains—A Town Policeman—A Police Cor- poral—Police Captains—A Police Colonel—A Governor on Revision—Auto- cracy and the Bureaucratic System .   .   .   .   .   *pp.* **154—178**

PART II.—THE "INTELLIGENCE."

CHAPTER VI.

ORIGINS OF THE "INTELLIGENCE"—PUBLIC INSTRUCTION.

Dogmas of the French Revolution—Their Effect on the Russian "Intelli- gence"—Isolation of Russia—Reforms of Peter the Great—Influence of Germany and France—Imitative Character of Russian Culture—The Univer- sity of Moscow—Catherine II. and Alexander I.—Reaction after 1812—The

CONTENTS.   xi

CHAPTER VII.

THE LITERATURE.

CHAPTER VIII.

THE PRESS AND THE CENSORSHIP.

CHAPTER IX.

LIVES OF THE INTELLIGENTS—THE REVOLUTIONARIES.

PART III.—BRIDGING THE GAP.

CHAPTER X.

LAW AND THE ADMINISTRATION.

CHAPTER XI.

THE ZEMSTVA AND TOWN COUNCILS.

CHAPTER XII.

THE PROGRESS OF THE PEASANTS.

CHAPTER XIII.

THE PEASANT IN TOWN—FACTORY LIFE.

PART IV.

CHAPTER XIV.

A SKETCH OF THE LIBERATION MOVEMENT.

I. The Claim for the "Freedoms" and a National Assembly.

II. The Claim for Ministerial Responsibility.

ERRATUM.

On page 87, margin, *for* "Nov. 16—19, 1904," *read* "Nov. 19—21, 1904."

RUSSIA AND REFORM.

PART I.—TSAR, CHURCH AND PEOPLE.

CHAPTER I.

A HISTORICAL SKETCH.

I.—RUSSIA AND THE EAST.

IT is the map of Russia that gives us the first and the most informing suggestions as to the destinies of the Russian people. Herodotus, who visited the northern shores of the Black Sea, tells us that the inhabitants of these shores lead that kind of life which has been marked out for them by the character of their country, and his words stand in the forefront of the great "History of Russia" by Solovyéff.

Russia is a land of difficulties; she lies between Europe and Asia, and is not sharply divided from either; if anything, the line of marshes which once separated her from Europe was the more definite boundary. Asia and Europe are terms of which the historical significance is more important than the political. The word Europe implies a certain kind of civilisation, a mass of moral traditions, at one time covering only the Greek world and now extending far beyond the oceans. Europe has grown larger and larger; her growth was a victory of civilisation; but from time to time, when the vitality of the peoples entrusted with her mission was not equal to the task of conquest, the expansion of the civilised world proceeded on lines of far greater difficulty. The enervated peoples of this world were attacked in their turn by invaders from outside. The great nursery from which the invading peoples came was, by the nature of things, Asia. Discontent with a poor soil or with a hard life drove whole tribes and nations afield, and some vague instinct made them seek the road which would bring them into those happier lands which were the nests of civilisation. It was the same instinct that urged the great tribes of the interior towards the seas. At such a period all that we call Europe would seem for the time to be submerged; but the new invaders of the Pale, after their first work of destruction, gradually came more and more closely under the influence of the traditions which they had disturbed; and, bringing a new vitality into a worn-out world, they themselves became in turn the adherents and extenders of civilisation. In this great and often-repeated struggle between East and West, Russia was by her very position marked out for a field of battle. Here the conflict took the most vast and momentous dimensions. Yet Russia was far more than a simple stage in a line of march. If she had been only that, she would probably have disappeared from the map. But the Russian people had a strong character of their own. In no part of the world is the instinct of brotherhood and solidarity more developed; they clung by instinct to their national and moral independence. It was this that saved them from their dangers, and the very length of their sufferings and of their training qualified them for a great future.

> " By lasting out the strokes of fate,
>   In trials long they learned to feel
>   Their inborn strength : as hammers weight
>   Will splinter glass but temper steel." [1]

In the north the soil is poor; the excellent black land of the south lay mostly outside the Russian Empire until the eighteenth century. In fact, this black land was a source of constant danger to Russia; it produced crops without much labour, and was therefore the favourite high road of invaders from Asia. Yet, if the fruitful south could be joined to the wooded north, the two would prove to be only complementary to each other. Till then Russia had to live in a state of flux; her triumph, to be effective, had to be complete.

The climate immobilises the labourer for a great part of the year. The violent spring and autumn break up the roads and

---

[1] Pushkin : Poltáva

cause regular interruptions in the sequence of work. Yet the very similarity of climate all over these vast plains suggested the political unity which was to come.

There were always the greatest potentialities in the rivers of Russia. The chief of them flow eastward and southward, and these were therefore the lines along which Russian history would naturally travel. In the Volga and the Kama, Russia possessed a direct road to Siberia, and the lower Volga connected her with Central Asia. The Dnyépr directed her towards Constantinople.

A poor soil and a hard climate meant a thin population—plenty of land, but few hands to work it. This helps to explain why estates came to be reckoned, not by the number of acres, but by the number of " souls." Later the peasants, the real property, came to be fastened to the soil.

The Slavs do not seem adapted by nature for these conditions. They are a people of feeling and fancy, reminding one of the Kelts, but more permanent in their moods, more serious and earnest in them, and therefore less quick of recovery. Feeling, by itself, seems a poor weapon to meet the tedious and recurring difficulties of Russia. No Slav race, except one, has made much out of its existence as a nation, and that one is a blend. Russia, at the beginning of its history, was largely peopled by tribes of more directly Asiatic origin, stolid and persevering Finns; these blended with Slavs to form the Great Russians, who are at once the most eastern of Slavs and the most successful. The Little Russians are more lively and less stable; the White Russians have less vigour and enterprise. It is the Great Russians who have made Russian history; they have been adapted, almost against nature and by long habit, to the character of the country in which they live, but the contrast between them and it is still visible enough. The happy instinctive character of clever children, so open, so kindly and so attractive, still remains; but the interludes of depression or idleness are longer than is normal. Yet often, at the very bottom of all, persists the steadiness of patient purpose : only without hurry—which seems to be useless under the prevailing conditions—and without any captious blaming of Providence, which is thought to be absurd. In Russia one has no right to expect that everything should run smoothly.

There are certain instincts which run all through Russian history; in every country where they exist together, they are sure to make a great people.

First, there is the instinct of order. The turbulent Slavs of Lake Ilmen knew what they needed. "Our land is great and rich," they said to the Varanger chiefs, "but order there 862. is none; come and rule over us." So began the Russian Empire, a thousand years ago, and over and over again since then Russia has invited education from abroad—now from Constantinople, now from Italy and Germany, now from Holland and England, now from France, but always from what was for her the West. Her relations with the West were always curiously two-fold. The doors were either locked fast against attack or thrown wide open for instruction.

The new "grand principality" thus established wore from the first an air of empire, the empire of the rivers, that is, of the roads. Its ambition at once answered to the great one-907. ness of the country: Kieff was soon added to Novgorod, and Constantinople was attacked for the first time. Yet in the presence of such great unconquered distances—of forest, plain and marsh—local government was the first need, and it seemed inevitable that the country should be divided into little kindred States. Not many years before we had had seven kingdoms in little England alone. But Russia had leaped at once to the great principle. By a curious plan she kept her hold on it. The reigning family was large, and Russia was ruled by a multitude of brothers and cousins. The eldest was the senior and was Grand Prince in Kieff. When he died, each prince "went up one," so that the ruler of Novgorod in the north might at any time become the prince of the frontier capital in the south. Thus the principle of family unity and allegiance preserved the unity of interests in the Empire. We see, at the same time, the beginnings of a governing caste.

Russia, as always militant against great dangers, has had many frontier capitals; the capital has had the post of honour closest to the enemy—Moscow as against the Tartars, St. Petersburg as against the Swedes. Some day, perhaps, Constantinople will be another such. The point is chosen or chooses itself, less as the centre of the nation than as the concentration of the national energy and purpose.

Each prince had round him an army of liege companions, the beginnings of the aristocracy. They gave him service and he gave them land; but they held it as his gift, and the coming of a new prince meant the gathering of a new band of Boyars. Thus the aristocracy could not easily become independent of State service.

The second great instinct is faith in Christianity and championship of it. Russia became Christian by the choice of her prince, Vladímir. He felt the insufficiency of his old gods, sent to inquire into other religions, and picked that which pleased 972— him best. He chose the Orthodoxy of Constantinople, 1015. possibly because of its sense of awe and for the reverence to imperial authority which it taught. He did not beg his baptism : he conquered it by defeating the Greeks; and it was the exercise of his will which converted his subjects.

Thus early began a direct connection with Constantinople, which has never ceased. Russia got from thence not only Greek Christianity, Greek sacred books and Greek saints, but also a tradition, which came to be her greatest honour and responsibility when the invasion of the Turks made her the chief champion of the faith against the East.

The Greek missionaries and their Russian followers were real educators of Russia. By their austerity and absolute abnegation of worldly interests, they shone as indeed lights in a dark place. Nothing is more simple reading and in the highest sense moral than their story. One feels at once what the Christian tradition of the West might have been without that intrusion of political ambitions which mars the Papacy. These monks were, for Russia, rather a constant standard of effort, a tradition of a better world worth trying for—a tradition which has never been wholly or even generally lost. The instinct of reverence for that real sanctity which illumined their lives passed as a permanent inheritance into princes and people. In reading Vladímir Mono- mach's testament, we almost seem to recognise our own 1125. King Alfred. There has hardly been one Russian Tsar who did not pay his tribute to religion, whether by pretence of observance or, as far more often, by real reverence and piety. Amongst the people there are and always have been men and women who, without seeking any kind of ordination and without ever

thinking of separating themselves from the national Church, have
set themselves to do some difficult exploit for their special salvation.
Such persons ordinarily court no attention. One may go bare-
footed and wear heavy chains beneath his clothes. The Russian
word for such exploits may be translated as "moving onwards."
It is a gospel of effort. Many will walk extraordinary distances
to collect money for the beautifying of a village church, and sums
so collected are practically never known to go astray.

All the highest offices in the Church can only be held by monks.
Thus the missionary character of the Church as a whole is preserved, and its leaders are less likely to compromise with what I have
heard described from an English pulpit as "our legitimate comforts." Yet the Church is by no means separated from the married
morality of the country: the country priests, who must marry
before their appointment, set the best example in this matter.
The Church is in very close touch both with the Government and
with the people; it is probably the best link between the two.
On the other hand, a comparison with the clergy of the West has
always shown up the backwardness of Russia in instruction and
in culture.

The third great principle of Russian history is the life and
labour of the Russian people. Here again there are long halts
in front of stubborn difficulties—difficulties so great, that all the
first vigorous attempts to turn the flank of them prove futile.
But the great salvation of Russia is her strong family unity;
there is unquestionably something great, living and self-existent
in her, or there would have been no struggle at all. This great
army, always and before all things insisting on remaining an
army, moves by the rule of the pace of the slowest, and thus,
as nothing short of complete conquest can be contemplated, there
are long periods when victory seems to be altogether impossible;
the baffled forces make leisurely and uncertain essays on this side
or on that, or else sit down in despair in front of their enemy.
The position, the character of the country imposed this solidarity
on the Russian people; they were always surrounded by great
common dangers; a Russian could not sink, so to speak, into the
interests of private life, after the manner of the Germans, and
content himself with assuring, by limited and detailed effort, his
own personal well-being. Public life, of their Church and of

their nation, was a necessity to them; for otherwise even the rude beginnings of their individual prosperity would be swept away.

What makes the story of Russia so fascinating is this—that, taken as a whole, she was always only just a little more than equal to her immense difficulties. It was the constant versatile inexhaustible vitality of the people, always fresh in fancy, but always broken to patience, that made success possible. It is this varied mass of humour, good-hearted patience and quaint resource which has given the body to Russian history.

The great distances of Russia, comparatively unpeopled, called for civilisation, especially to eastwards; and we have to understand that, from the very first, the Russians were a colonising people, especially on that side; I have already mentioned the eastward direction of the rivers. The story is one of the great unwritten narratives of battles against the land. The Russians, like others of the more Eastern peoples, easily change their habitations; often enough the stress of events has obliged them to do so. The Slavs followed the Germans when the Germans were driven westwards into the old Roman Empire. The first Russian Empire was itself little more than a road, consisting of that great water-way which ran from the Baltic to Constantinople. The Russians, as born travellers, were indeed, from the very first, born borrowers, —in a sense born to cosmopolitanism. They took their ruling race from the Baltic and their system of Church and State from Constantinople. At first, not so very much more than the through roads were in the hands of the Government, as is still the case in many parts of Siberia. But the stream of Russian energy went on flowing, and the wilderness was conquered step by step.

There were great centres which the reigning family held less tightly than others. This, amidst the constant changes of princes, was inevitable. Novgorod was a great town living on travel and trade, and therefore full of the spirit of enterprise. It was only the " second seat," and the rough energy of its people made this seat undesirable for princes. It was left almost to govern itself, and generally made its own bargain with its rulers. In many cases, in the virile language of the annalists, it " saluted them and showed them the way out." Such towns supply the needed tradition of town self-government in the history of the Russian people.

The family system of joint-government proved to be only a first sketch of a plan, not suited to meet great dangers. The princes got to quarrelling about their respective appanages, and their enmities were brutal and hereditary. Just at this 1224— time descended upon Russia one of those avalanches 40. which seem to wipe out the past. The Tartars came ravaging through Russia; hardly one important town escaped. When Russia had buried her countless dead, she found herself under a foreign yoke.

This domination lasted for more than two hundred years. For a long time, it seemed to be hopelessly and permanently invincible by the sheer weight of numbers. It was sheer numbers 1240— that had made the conquest; there had been no lack 1480. of chivalry or of noble deaths on the Russian side, nor did Russia now lie easy under the yoke. At least one glorious premature attempt at liberation was made by the united people under Demetrius of the Don; but his great victory was followed almost immediately by the taking and sacking of his capital. The load of physical force was too heavy, and it lay on Russia too long.

This domination was alien, unprofitable, and miserable. The Tartars founded nothing of themselves. They were greedy and hateful oppressors. The Russians were themselves inevitably degraded by the unclean connection. Despair came to be almost an instinct with them.

Yet in reality their hold on life never showed itself more clearly than now. The old easy days of the reckless princes were gone; there remained the possibility of building up a new system by tension and effort; the political instinct became more of a general necessity. In this work the Church was to the fore. Holy men, such as the hermit Sergius, still held up the standard of aloofness from an evil world; they also broke new ground for Russia by colonising and conquering more of the wilderness. The places made sacred by their labours became the 1380. fastnesses of national spirit, even of national defiance. Sergius blessed Demetrius before his campaign, and even sent two of his young monks to fight for Russia. In the Church, there was unity of authority before it existed in the **Circa** State; the Metropolitans chose this time for moving **1330.** their seat to the new centre of Russian life, Moscow, and did everything to secure for Moscow a national dictatorship against the national danger.

We have to understand that this new tradition of dictatorship was inevitable and to be desired. I do not discuss whether a nation must save its independence before it can develop its corporate life; I assume that it must. We ourselves may have been able, during long intervals, to think that our own independence could never be really endangered, and may have almost ceased to think of ourselves as militant personalities engaged in a struggle for life; but this is the gospel of the undisturbed, and is at variance with the ordinary laws of life. We can afford to be generous and impersonal so long as we are seated on the wealth of the world. The Russian had his back arched on the ground and had to wrestle.

It was under such conditions that the Russian autocracy was developed. In time of war, though we may all be of different opinions as to detail, and though any one of us may be right, we must have a general: otherwise the enemy will march round and over us, whilst we are still discussing on the principle of "one man, one vote," and whilst the last and perhaps deciding member of "the public" is still being educated up to just the right opinion. It is not without reason that emperor means general.

This dictatorship was distinctively national. The Church had to save itself, so had the nation; and both were really represented by the Grand Princes of Moscow. Moscow grew up as the incarnate tradition of this dictatorship.

The details of the policy of Moscow were various and often much more than questionable; there runs all through it the sense of self-interest and self-preservation. The beginnings of it are all found in a previous attempt by a prince of Suzdal; these methods were consistently followed up by Moscow, and became a tradition.

First the prince must secure peace and power. He is careful with money, and thus becomes more rich than the neighbouring Russian princes. He avoids all hopeless defiance of the lordship of the suzerain Tartar. But the Tartars are lazy in peace-time,

and govern Russia by a deputy—by a Russian. The rich prince
of Moscow outbids his brother princes and secures this office.
As deputy for the Tartars, he often quarrels with his Russian
neighbours, and has the help of the Tartars to conquer them.
These Tartars see that his government brings in to them more
money than they could themselves extort, and they are beginning
to quarrel amongst themselves, and see no more. The success of
Moscow attracts population; people, in these plains, change their
homes easily. Boyars desert their failing masters; it is their
ancient right to do so. Peasants come to live in rich and
peaceful Muscovy. But, in Russia, the land gets its chief value
from the number of its inhabitants. Thus Moscow establishes a
kind of economic predominance over her rivals.

Moscow has opportunities of position. She is between the
three waterways, running eastward, westward, and northward.
She stands between the forests of the north and the good soil of
the south. She is herself neither north nor south, and must
make a bid for the unity of all Russia.

All this the Church was quick to see. The Metropolitan came
to live at Moscow; the Grand Prince became his "eldest son"
and protector.

Moscow still did everything to avoid direct collision with the
Tartars; she fought their battles and acted as their executioner.
The worst things that have been said against diplomacy as an
art were sometimes true of the diplomacy of Moscow.

When the noble Demetrius made his great attempt to shake off
the yoke, he appeared, for the first time, to be rather the ruler of a
nation than the chief of a coalition. His victory cost
1380. him so many of his best men that Russia was almost
depleted of her captains of war. The time was not yet
come; but this only proved the wisdom of Moscow's previous
self-restraint, and at the same time the enterprise of Demetrius
convinced everyone that Moscow was the true champion of Church
and nation. The end of the foreign domination seemed to be in
sight, especially as the dissensions of the Tartars were breaking
them up into hostile kingdoms. In Russia, on the contrary, the
minor princes, though never all at once deprived of all rights,
were gradually relegated to the position first of "younger
brothers" and then of "sons" and "dependents." The first

and most strict limitation was that which debarred them from any direct political relations with the Tartars. By treaty they engaged themselves "not to know the Horde." It was a national need that dictated their dependence. Meanwhile, in each new treaty between Russian princes, the titles of the Grand Prince grew in dignity and pomp. From the first Russia had held to the family system of government. The greatness of Moscow depended on the personal leadership of an acknowledged father. On no subject has the Russian Government been at all times more tender than on what is called the "diminution" of this title.

A time of quarrels follows in Russia, but it shows up the completeness of the change. Almost the whole of a long reign is filled with civil wars; yet no one outside the Moscow dynasty makes a bid for supremacy; the question lies between the son and the brother of the last prince of Moscow. The old tradition of the brother's succession has, up to this point, prevailed. But the Church sees where the interests of order lie and strongly takes the side of the son.

Its *protégé*, Basil, called the Sightless, was blinded by his cousin in the course of this struggle; yet he triumphed in the end and lived on to old age. His son, John the Great, a seldom seen but terrible figure, looms larger over Russia than **1425—** any of his predecessors. The victory had been won; he **65.** was born to the fruits of it; all that he had to do was to reap these fruits. His pride rose to the measure of his position. The feel of his presence was communicated from the chief servants around him, all over his empire and beyond its frontiers. Everywhere was felt the impression of an anointed mysterious and irresistible purpose, choosing its own ways, conscious of its own power, resting on the vastness of the country and the number of its people, on the long patience and simple faith of the nation. It was as if somehow Russia lay couched beneath his throne.

This was a reign of great accomplishment in many fields, and the autocracy finally became a part of the hereditary instincts of the nation. Novgorod had been a centre of life and enterprise for all the north of Russia. She had broken new ground right up to the Urals. But the parties in the town had become so factious that sometimes whole days were spent in riot and fighting in the streets and on the bridge. Then, too, Novgorod fed herself by her trade, richly enough in times of peace, but only with difficulty when the Prince of Moscow cut off the supplies which came from the great "hinterland." The story of Novgorod's quarrels with Moscow was generally that of a famine and a submission. Novgorod was a purely Russian town, but in the times of division she had played the part of the "free lance," and had been able to set off one neighbouring prince against another. Half republic, half principality, she represented the free popular instinct in Russian history, but times and systems were become too strong for her. In despair she turned towards a foreign power, Lithuania, the enemy of Russia and of the Russian Church. Few stories will strike more fear than that of John's reduction of Novgorod; you never seem to see him or hear him **1478—** till the end, but you often enough hear about him. **95.** Novgorod may be said to have been paralysed and stricken down by a well-grounded instinct of fatality. She fell by degrees, but finally. Autocracy was supreme in Russia.

It was in John's reign that the Tartar domination, long little more than nominal, quite faded away. The final credit is due, not to John, but to the Church and the people. It was a great ecclesiastic who by his pure religious patriotism and **1480.** stinging reproaches practically compelled John to march against the Tartars. We have not many years to wait for the beginning of the long counter-stroke. When John's grandson took Kazán and celebrated his conquest amidst a general fervour of converting zeal, the first step was taken in that march which was to carry Russia to the shores of the Pacific.

Constantinople had fallen to the Turks. The Pope seems to have thought that as Russia had now no intact religious centre to look to for guidance, a little flattery might bring her **1453.** into the fold of the Western Church. He planned a Russo-Greek marriage between John and the niece of the last Greek Emperor, who had fallen fighting on the walls of his capital. He cannot have known what instincts and what hopes he was flattering. The Russians had been dreaming of Constantinople since the Russian Empire began: the dream is woven into their most homely country poetry. They had flatly refused to accept the agreement of their representative at the Council of Florence to the union of the two Churches, and had chased him out in shame. Long before, Alexander **1251.** Nevsky, replying to an offer of religious instruction from the West, had said, "We know quite as much about it as you do." John then accepted the Greek bride, and with her a new title to the championship of the Greek Church and the succession to its headship; and when the Papal legate seemed likely to introduce the Latin cross into Moscow, the Metropolitan said in plain terms to the Grand Prince, "My son, if he comes in with it at one gate, I, your father, go out at the other."

John's grandson, John the Terrible, turned autocracy **1533—** into a definite system. It is largely to him that we owe **84.** the tradition of a great host of officials. Yet it could not be said that the instinct of his people was all against him in this work.

John the Terrible was the pupil of his own terror before he taught terror to his nobles and even to his people. His was no coarse, brutal nature; his faults were those of a clever, quick sensibility. He fought a merciless battle for a principle which had come to be identified with the person of the prince—namely, the unity of the nation. In this sense his work for Russia was more than valuable—it was necessary.

As a child-sovereign he saw the nobles lead the rabble into his palace and murder his friends. Treated with the utmost neglect in private, he yet noticed the respect paid to him on public occasions, and thus got to know that some virtue of tradition was in him. Wise and learned beyond his years and his people, he had the energy to strike a sudden blow for freedom. At the age of thirteen he seemed to have made himself absolute; but four years later the palace was again invaded and some of his blood-relations were killed. The Government of the nobles was always worse in Russia than that of the one trained and titled autocrat. National feeling rallied to the bold boy, who **1547.** returned to Moscow on his own terms and governed ably and well. But he could not now trust the nobles, and chose his ministers from the more obscure. While he was supposed to be dying he heard even these favourites dividing his succession. He did not die, and henceforth trusted only to agents who would

depend absolutely upon him. He divided his subjects into those
who were neutral, and those who were bound to him beyond all
ties of family by a specially terrible oath. With the help of these
last he crushed out all opposition in blood.

John conquered Kazán. The back of the Tartars was broken,
and Astrakhan fell to him almost of itself. But "order" was
the motto and the mission of Russia, and order was very
1552. hard to establish amongst the broken and disorderly
masses of various races which different invasions had
left stranded all down the banks of the Volga. Here there was
no rival principle to fight against the Government, unless the
instinct of untrammelled licence in the robber can be called a
principle; and Russia's work was here a work of civilisation, that
is, of turning the natural man into a member of a great community. In the forefront of this work stood the convents, which
broke up new land, developed peace and trade, and spread a
religion which we may make bold to call far superior to anything
which it replaced. The great through-waterway was necessary
to Russia; yet caravans could never travel down it without very
large escorts. Pioneers of the people were engaged in this work
of advance more actively than the Government itself. It was by
the victory of such pioneers that John received the
1582-4. submission of a part of Siberia. Russia had pushed
forward to east and south, but a last relic of the
Golden Horde, the separate kingdom of Crimea, still blocked
her from the Black Sea, and kept the splendid black soil
of the south in suspense of cultivation. The southern frontiers still had to be militant. They were held by the natural
advance-guard of the Russian Church and people, the Cossacks.
These men of adventure were in many ways like most of our
colonists; they were those who had not lived in peace with the
Government—those who wanted elbow-room; their numbers
were recruited less by birth than by the accession of new
wanderers, driven by Government severity in the van of the
Government advance, but united generally by the ties of Russian
blood and instincts, and almost always by devotion to the
Orthodox Church. They were happy as living from raids on
their natural enemies the Tartars and later, the Turks. John
even made an attempt to break through to the Black Sea, but

this plan was complicated by others; he was not strong enough for all-round success, and so all his various plans of advance, for the time, failed together.

To sum up : Russia had always with her the long and painful responsibility of being on the frontier between Europe and Asia. But then, too, she always had her own strong national existence, her family instinct of unity, her loyalty to her Church, of which she was become the champion. The East had imposed on her the necessity of a national dictatorship, but was already breaking up before her persistency. But, if she was to teach the East, she was also bound to learn from the West. This was the more difficult task of the two.

II.—RUSSIA AND THE WEST.

Along the south-eastern coast of the Baltic lived a group of tribes distantly akin to the Russians, and including the Prussians, Zhmuds, Courlanders, Lithuanians and Letts. The east coast of the Baltic, from the north of Finland to Revel, and including the district in which St. Petersburg now stands, was occupied by Finnish tribes, of which the southernmost were the Esthonians. These blocked off Russia from the Western Seas.

The Letts and the Esthonians are deeply hostile to each other by race and by instinct. Their animosity alone still serves as a natural frontier between them.

Upon these coasts descended Germans: traders, missionaries, and finally an Order of crusading knights, shortly followed by another such Order further westwards. These two Orders were later united. Germany was at this time **Circa** hopelessly entangled with Italian affairs, and therefore **1180.** still hopelessly divided; but this eastward movement was a natural advance, made by private enterprise in the cause of western civilisation.

These Germans founded great trading towns which joined the Hansa league; they, by the argument of the sword, converted the Letts and Esthonians to Western Christianity; they built great castles for the control of these aliens, for only the towns were wholly theirs, not the country. They then set about quarrelling amongst themselves. Yet in arms, arts, and personal enterprise they were much superior to the Russians, with whom they were almost always at war. There was no natural geographical or racial frontier between them and Russia, for many Finnish tribes were subject to the Russians.

The Lithuanians, in their heathen forests, heard of the German successes, and got rid of their divisions just in time to make a desperate stroke for freedom and even for empire. They held off the Germans by war or intrigue, twice pretending to adopt **1240—** Christianity in order to take away from the crusaders **1430.** their reason for being there. They had four great rulers[1] (the three last in succession), each of whom was cunning, unscrupulous, untiring, and able. By a counter-stroke of the energy which was originally aroused in them by their struggle with the Germans, they were able to conquer the White Russians and Little Russians, who lay to the south of them, and thus cut their way, not indeed to the Baltic, but to the Black Sea. Their subjects, then, were mostly foreigners, and the White Russian dialect was even their official language.

Meanwhile Russia was still struggling for her existence against the Tartars; and Moscow, without any other recognised claim than that of partial success, was bidding for the headship of Russia. One can imagine to what an extent the rise of Lithuania complicated the difficulties of Moscow. There were now two claimants for the headship, and Lithuania was the stronger of the two; she had also advantages of position, for she was not equally exposed to the violence of the Tartars; she was better placed for learning from the West those arts of organisation which might increase her strength as a State, and she was able to prevent the teachers of these arts from getting through to Russia. The West, then, instead of coming in peace to civilise Russia, appeared to Moscow in the guise of a hostile power armed for conquest. Lithuania tried to split the religious unity of Russia by establishing a new Metropolitan at old Kieff, the former Russian capital, which she had conquered. Yet everything was unreal in the Lithuanian claim; she was not really a Russian power. Kieff was hers, but was not her capital or her centre of life.

Moscow was indeed the new centre of Russia, but she was new,

---

[1] Mindovg, Gedimin, Olgerd, Vitovt.

and had to prove her claim by her vitality. There were many conflicts with Lithuania, who joined sometimes with the Tartars against her and sometimes with the smaller Russian States, such as Tver and Novgorod. There were comparatively few pitched battles, both sides being in more or less equal balance. This was to the profit of Moscow, who, as being of sounder substance, had everything to gain from time. But there was always the subtle war of intrigue, and the proscripts of each court were welcomed at the other. This meant that there were two Russias, and that Russian princes had their choice of service. They might easily prefer the looser master.

Yet both these countries, Muscovy and Lithuania, were peopled mainly by Russians, adherents of the Greek Church; and every-thing seemed to point to their ultimate union, when an artificial development, in keeping with the artificial character of Lithuania, diverted the course of history.

To westward, behind Lithuania, were the Poles. This people has been brilliantly described as a "nation on horseback"; the description applies only to the ruling classes of Poland, for they alone politically constituted the nation. While Russia was still centred round her western capital, Kieff, and before the Tartars and Lithuanians had cut her connection with the West, Russians and Poles had often been in contact of alliance or war. At that time somewhat similar political conditions prevailed in both countries; in language and in blood they were closely enough allied, but there was this fateful difference—that Eastern Chris-tianity was part of the very soul of Russian nationality, and that the Poles took their civilisation and their religion from Western Europe.

The "nation on horseback" had its strong national pride, not a pride in discipline and unity such as the hard tutorship of the Tartars was teaching to Moscow, but a pride in common liberties which were really liberties of licence, because exercised at the expense of the king on the one side and of a whole subject class on the other. While other nations developed themselves out of this primitive state, the Polish nobles succeeded in stereotyping it more and more as time went on. The king, in order to bolster himself up against the tyranny of the great nobles, accorded equal rights of licence to all the smaller gentry as well. The ties of race and language, of common privileges, of a narrow exclusive " society," could unite the Polish nobles for glorious national defence or perhaps for one campaign of attack ; but national organisation was impossible. Cut off from its ballast—the infantry of the people—the nation on horseback played with history, much as our own full-blooded nobles did under the Lancastrians and Yorkists.

Thus their civilisation, though much in advance of that of the Russians, had something fictitious about it. There was not that foundation of work and character on which civilisation must be built. The religion came from over the frontier, not once for all, but by regular instalments ; its influence was much too militant and political. The alphabet was Latin ; the official tongue was Latin. The nobles wore better arms than the Russians, and knew more about war ; but there was no middle class except foreigners,—Germans and Jews. The Jews came to manage nearly all the estates of the happy-go-lucky nobles, and that, too, on a system of quick profits for themselves. Thus there was not, in Poland, that back-bone which could sustain a long national struggle.

To a young girl, Hedwig, was left the heritage of the Polish throne. There was instituted the usual search for a political husband. The young lady, who had certainly given her heart already and perhaps her hand too,[1] was anyhow looked upon as officially a spinster. The Polish nobles, and still more their Roman Catholic directors, were fascinated by a scheme that suggests the motto of Austria : " Bella gerant alii ; tu, felix Austria, nube." " Lucky Poland " was to annex, without a blow, to herself and to Latin Christendom the whole of Lithuania. Hedwig and the Polish crown were offered to Yagailo (Jagellon), Prince of Lithuania, on condition of the conversion of himself and his country. The bargain was carried out, Hedwig being

1386. persuaded to make a saint of herself by a repulsive marriage. The Lithuanians, the alien conquerors of White Russia, were themselves still in large part heathens. They were officially converted ; the majority of their subjects, who were Orthodox Russians, found themselves handed over to a Roman Catholic power.

---

[1] There is some evidence of a marriage between Hedwig and William of Austria.

In this bargain both parties expected to gain without effort by a kind of trick, and so both sides were disappointed. Meanwhile, the Russia of Muscovy saw its difficulties infinitely increased. Lithuania still struggled for many years to assert her independence, but eventually fell into a close political union with Poland. Polish nobles secured important **1569.** posts and great estates in Lithuania. The Orthodox peasants of White Russia learnt the habit of subjection. In spite of persecutions they held closely to their religion, and the Union later had to be completed by the religious bargain known as the " Unia," by which many of the Orthodox White **1595.** Russians acknowledged the purely nominal headship of the Pope, and received in return a promise of toleration. The Polish settlers were aliens amongst their new peasants, and dealt with them chiefly through their agents, the Jews ; some even mortgaged to the Jews the Orthodox churches of their peasants, so that the Jew could ask his own price when the keys were wanted to open the doors for Christian service. Muscovy was now the champion of Orthodoxy and of Russian nationality ; but in her quarrels with Lithuania, the political weight of Poland was henceforth always against her.

John the Terrible had too many enemies to carry any of his plans of advance right through. He attacked the Germans of the Baltic and sought election to the throne of Poland. The rival eventually preferred to him was Bathory, an **1576.** able general, who, on his election, made a coalition of all the enemies of Russia. John was foiled at every point. He had already met with many other disillusions, and was now fully earning the name which he bears in history. His eldest son he killed in a fit of anger, and the rest of his life was a round of alternate mortifications and excesses. His second son who succeeded him —a monk rather than a prince—died childless. His third son was murdered in childhood. The direct line of Rurik was extinct.

The murder of little Demetrius can be traced almost with certainty to the machinations of a Tartar-born lieutenant of John. This man, Borís Godunóff is the Richard III. of Russian history. Boris now got himself elected Tsar; **1598.** but in a few years the rumour went about that Demetrius was still alive and about to march on his inheritance from the side

of Poland. In Russia, where the great distances and the thinness
of population favour ignorance, rumour has always been the most
ordinary channel of news; and rumour is always hard to refute.
It was never difficult for a Pretender living in one part of
Russia to claim to be some one who was personally known only
in some other part. It seems that a young monk had fled
from Moscow to Lithuania; he entered the service of a Polish
noble, and later, during a feigned illness, declared himself to be
the rightful heir to Russia. Warlike nobles gathered round him,
the Latin priests intrigued with him for the future
1605. conversion of Russia, King Sigismund gave his indirect
support, and the false Demetrius marched on Moscow.
Borís died at his approach. The Pretender was accepted as
Tsar.

But no religious bargain was possible. In Russia the very
merits of the Westerniser were counted as faults. Within a year
he was surrounded in his palace by an angry crowd, driven to
jump from one of the back windows, and dispatched where he
fell. His body, we are told, was burnt, and the ashes fired from
a cannon in the direction of Poland.

Moscow chose as Tsar an old noble, descended, by a side line,
from Rurik. This Tsar Basil was broken and shifty. In more
than one part of Russia rose a new false Demetrius, and the
number of these Pretenders does not seem to have awakened any
sense of humour. On the contrary, even the sane man would
have taken the joke seriously; for you cannot laugh, when nearly
every one has lost his senses. The real issue was obvious and
serious enough. The natural forces of disorder which are in
every man's heart had risen in a reaction against the tight hold
of the old autocracy. The system seemed to be breaking
up, and thousands of men were willing to fish in the troubled
waters of chaos. The movement was directed against all government, and it certainly did nothing to recommend such movements to Russia for the future. All the painful efforts of the
past to draw the country from its native disorder were now
being squandered in a desperate licence, which raised every
man's hand against his weaker neighbour. The wild riot
centred round one of the Pretenders, a brigand chief who established himself at Túshino, near Moscow. The Moscow nobles

A HISTORICAL SKETCH. 21

intrigued with him. The various robber bands overran the country, and made their own profit. The Polish chiefs with their bands of retainers were at the very heart of Russia, and their dubious and insincere king was preparing to lead in his army, with that cry for order which the Russians were later to carry into Poland. The Poles, then, had their chance first, but of the cause of order they were unworthy and inadequate champions; they had no home basis to stand upon and to act from.

Even this danger was not the last of Russia's difficulties. Russia was always and justly feared by her Western neighbours, and their way of keeping her in check was always to push her back from those Western influences which might make her morally more their equal. The Germans of the Baltic had offered education only at the price of independence; more than that, they had in time of peace detained on their way the teachers of the Western arts whom Russia had called to her help. But the Crusading Orders decayed and died out; the Reformation made this district Protestant; and, when **1582.** John the Terrible failed to break a way through to the Baltic, the old German territory became subject, part to the Poles and part to the Swedes.

The Swedes, from the time of their early conquest of Finland, had always been in contact with the Russians. They had led a Latin crusade into North Russia, and had been defeated on the Neva by the hero of the **1240.** Russian church, Prince Alexander Nevsky. They now blocked Russia from the sea as Poland blocked her from the West, and in this time of confusion they even occupied for a time one of the most Russian of Russian towns, Novgorod the Great. The old Tsar Basil bought from them by concessions a dubious help; his brilliant nephew, Skopin, thus set free to face the Polish partisans, won a series of victories over them, but suddenly died. Some put down his death to the jealousy of his uncle; and it was not long before Tsar Basil was deposed and handed over to the Poles. Moscow seemed to have no other choice than that of either accepting the brigand of Túshino or making some kind of arrangement with the Poles. By the first alternative she would have legitimised

disorder pure and simple, and her nobles closed with the second.
But they tried to make their conditions : they chose as
1610. Tsar, not the Polish king, but the Polish crown prince,
who had yet to secure his way to the Polish throne by
election. Polish troops were now the garrison of Moscow.

But King Sigismund wanted to be Tsar himself; he also
meant to use the occasion to conquer what he could of Russia
for the absolute possession of Poland. He imprisoned the
ambassadors sent to him, and continued to besiege Smolensk.

Russia had no Tsar of her own to save her. Her greater
nobles seemed to be all corrupt and self-seeking. If she had
wished to abandon the old autocratic system, she had but to sit
still and watch it die. And yet she did exactly the opposite;
she faced all sacrifices to re-establish the old national and
religious dictatorship because she cared for it, because, after all,
the sense of solidarity, of standing together, was the first and
most valued instinct of the Russian people. And what was it
that did this for Russia? Precisely that force which was so con-
spicuously lacking in Poland when her time of trouble came—the
force of popular instinct as pervading the Russian Church and
the humbler and steadier of the Russian people.

It is a story of thousands, such as history can hardly
write and seldom attempts. There were " men of God," " men
moving forwards," who came out of their life-long cells to say
that at least they had still a Church and a country. Skopin
had sought the blessings of such men before attempting what was
apparently impossible. The true wounded of the nation, the
robbed or maimed fugitives, driven by stress of violence from their
daily work, were gathered and comforted by the simple and holy
Dionysius and his monks of the Trinity Monastery. From this
fastness of the Church and the nation, which had kept
1608— out the Pole Sapieha during sixteen months of siege,
10. went forth letters to the Russian people, couched in
the simplest and straightest language, and calling on
all to forget their individual safety and to march on the enemies
of Russia. Such letters arrived in distant Nizhny
1611. Novgorod. Minin, a butcher, took the lead there, and a
general sacrifice of valuables was made to the holy cause.
The instinct of discipline sought a leader among the gentry and

discovered the wounded but willing champion Pozharsky. The great national host rolled on Moscow. Even the disorderly Cossacks felt bound to help. The Polish garrison was driven to surrender before the slow Sigismund could relieve it; and, after solemnly humiliating themselves before their God, the deputies of all Russia, the often-cited historic National Assembly, chose for their Tsar, not any powerful intriguer, but a young lad whose only antecedents were those of a tradition of suffering patriotism, Michael Románoff. A band of **1613.** Poles marched to seize this lad on his country estate, but a peasant, Susánin, led them astray into the recesses of a wild marsh and gave his life to save his Tsar. The boy whom Susánin saved, the first of the Románoffs, was to be the grandfather of Peter the Great.

In the reigns of Michael and his son Alexis, the Poles were pressed back until even Smolensk was recovered. Both these Tsars owed much to the counsels of great statesmen of the Church—Michael to his father, the Patriarch Philaret, one of the imprisoned ambassadors of Smolensk, and Alexis to his friend Nikon, a bold and masterful man, who forced Church Reform upon Russia. The Patriarchate had, significantly enough, been established just before the temporary **1589.** failure of Tsardom and the lawless time of troubles; and we have seen what the Church did for the nation amidst the stress of national dangers. At this time Poland, the enemy of the Orthodox Church, pressed back on her foundations, which proved to be all weakness within, was now sinking further and further into anarchy; thus the barrier to education from the West was no longer so effective, and the old Russia began to beautify herself and to instruct herself, to be ready for the great Remodeller who was to come. To the south there were hereditary conflicts between the Cossacks and the Turks, and the Cossacks themselves were drawn into the governmental life of Russia. To the east Russia descended the Volga by regular stages of evangelising, of colonising, and of fortifying, and the lawless robbers of the south-east rose in vain under Razin against the Tsar of Moscow.

A most important social development had been legalised during the reign of Feodor, the last of the direct line of Rurik. Bands of discontented men — ex-soldiers, escaped servants or monks, beggars and robbers—were almost a normal source of trouble in Russia. The battle which the Government was fighting was a battle for order, but its success had always been only gradual, especially amongst the sea of peoples in the south and east. We have seen that the Government had found it necessary to compromise with the restless spirits and to sanction their practical independence in frontier districts as in the case of the Cossacks, thus driving this current of militant energy in the direction where it found its desired conditions of life and could even act as a vigorous advance-guard of Russia. But the evil, fed by every increase of severity in the Government, continued to be great in the interior. This evil was particularly ruinous to the smaller gentry. There was plenty of land, but much of it was of poor quality and required many hands to work it. Migration, as we know, was in the blood, the conditions and the habits of the people. We have seen how the boyars passed from one master to another. The same thing was happening in detail with agriculture. The same appeal of wealth and success induced peasants to leave the poor service of the smaller gentry, and to gather in masses around the richer land-owners. This might well frighten the Government, and, in any case, it reduced almost to nothing the value of the land of the poorer gentry. But the Government was organised on the top of the society, and not independently of it; the smaller gentry held their land for service to the Tsars. They were the natural officers in what was almost the only armed force, the national militia, and their peasants were the soldiers whom they were expected to bring to the field. How could these gentry fulfil their obligations if they lost their peasants? They would have neither means nor men.

Official control was only gradually developed in Russia. The struggle for control was, as we have seen, for a long time if not always, an uphill fight against sheer chaos, and it was the task which the Government had been specially set there to attempt. In fact, the Russian peasant's idea of government was always that it was there because man is sinful. He did not wish to himself have the burden of the responsibility of governing, but he strongly desired that order should be maintained. Godunóff, who was the prime minister of Feodor, had been an agent of John the Terrible, and could not expect an easier time than his master had had. He was logically developing that master's work when he tied the peasants to the estates on which they were working. If his decree could be carried out, the Government would henceforth know where everyone was and who was responsible for the control of each individual subject.

This fastening of the peasants to the soil came late in Russia. It had been a stage in the development of other nations; and such it was in the case of Russia, which had more **Circa** need of order than other countries, and had to fight **1595.** harder and wait longer for it. In Poland, then, serfdom was accepted for the advantage of the gentry, and in Russia it was decreed for the common advantage of the gentry and of the State; yet, whatever the differences in principle, the same selfishness of the unrestrained proprietor was bound to run riot all over Russia too. The local landowner was a small Tsar—that is, a Tsar from whom a broad training and a wide sense of responsibility were not to be expected. The voice of the small people was hushed, and the comparative silence which was thus created left the Government cut off from the guidance of popular instinct, and shut up in the company of courtiers, selfish and intriguing.

The Románoffs at first gave promise of better principles of rule. They owed their throne to public election and to the devotion of the people. They frequently called public assemblies for the discussion of great issues of war and peace. The assemblies made no attempt to extend their powers, and these beginnings faded away, as the Government, right in the main as to great questions, found itself opposed by ignorance and unintelligence in nobles and people alike. The work of reform was therefore left to the autocracy, which, naturally enough, even when it was reforming Russia, was seeking to increase its own power.

The Patriarch Nikon, with the Tsar Alexis behind him, wished to correct some mistakes in the Russian translations of Church books from the Greek; but the people as a whole **1654.** preferred to keep the mistakes. We are reminded of that English bishop who is said to have spoken of the Authorised Version as "the blessed original." The weight of authority carried the day; but a large fraction of the Church refused to be moved.

These men are now called the " Old Believers," and indeed they can claim that the Church changed, and not they. To spell the name of Jesus with the omission of one letter, and to cross oneself with two fingers instead of three, do not seem to be rights worth preserving by martyrdom. Yet the Old Believers did not even wait to be martyred for their cause ; they in many cases martyred themselves, burning themselves alive *en masse*. But we should make a great mistake if we only laughed at the whole matter. The Old Believers were standing out for an instinct strong everywhere, but especially strong in Russia. They wanted, not a universal best plan, but their own plan ; and it was in this very cause of local instinct, of the differences of time and place, of the careful handling of the prejudices of habit, that Russia was later to champion Europe in 1812 and to wreck the system of Napoleon. The Old Believers, just because they were a minority, a militant Church, are now some of the most moral, energetic and prosperous of all the subjects of the Emperor.

Far greater was the shock which local instinct was to suffer from the impact of the will, the intelligence, and the ability of Peter the Great.

Peter was a third son, the child of a second wife. His mother was not of the highest nobility. His eldest brother died after a short reign, and Russia had to choose between the second, who was hardly sound in mind, and Peter, who was still a little boy. At first Peter was preferred, but later it was decided that both were to reign together, while the real power went to Peter's step-sister, Sophia. Through her intrigues, the child Peter, like the child John, saw his mother's relations butchered in his own palace. He was now left to himself, and it was this neglect that enabled him to give himself that free and quick education which, from the first, his instinct had dictated to him. His earliest playthings were ships, and his earliest friends a regiment

1689. of boys whom he trained. Early, like John, he by a sudden stroke established himself in the real possession of his power. His brother remained a cypher.

We must understand that Peter, taking him all round, was himself the instinct of Russia, enlightened and made conscious. It was impossible for Russia to separate the two issues of her relations with the West; she had to educate herself by the West, but she also had to fight the West. The combination of these two conditions was, and still is, imposed upon Russia by ourselves, the Westerners. If the Westerners had not only thought of self-interest and cheap conquest, Russia would have reached far sooner that degree of moral equality with the West which it is the interest of the world that she should attain. But the civilised came always with arms in their hands. Peter, like Vladímir in ancient days, would conquer his education from the West. For him the two issues of victory and civilisation were clearly one. In the wars which follow, we see, not the nation driven on to her knees and fighting blindly for what she somehow felt to be her own, but rather· Russia, in the person of one exceptional man, herself taking the aggressive to conquer something which that man knew to be necessary to her.

It was now Sweden that barred the advance of Russia. We have traced the long tradition of antagonism. Sweden had had a quite exceptional sequence of able rulers. That racial vitality, that concentration of effort to the point of exhaustion, which had given to the Vikings and Varangers an importance out of all proportion to their numbers, were used by Gustav Adolf and his successors to make Sweden something very like a first-class European power. The Baltic is a poor sea ; but Sweden held a ring of territory almost all round it, and it was the sea to which Russia must first gain access, if she was to " open a window upon the West." Nor was Peter in any way fanciful when he sought civilisation by way of the sea ; the sea has always been, and even still is, civilisation's best and most natural road.

Peter's life is curiously typical of the difficulties of Russia. Everything had to be attempted at once, and one danger complicated another. He attacked the Turks in a distant corner of the Black Sea, had a first partial success—to **1695-6.** be cancelled in the last years of his reign—went on his **1697.** travels in the West of Europe, that he might at least educate himself, and was recalled because by so doing he had almost broken the moral link which bound him to his old-fashioned people ; a revolt at home was endangering **1698.** the whole basis of his power. How shall the blind lead the blind ? By will, and of that there was plenty, as the mutinous stryéltsy and the sullen crown prince had to learn.

Peter now set about his deliberate attack upon Sweden. But
Charles XII., who seemed to be but a careless boy encompassed
with enemies, turned out to be a lion at rest. Almost in a moment
Peter's coalition was broken up; Denmark and Poland could
not stand against the impact. At Narva, Peter's dis-

1700. orderly and ignorant army fled in disgraceful rout,
owing escape only to the fewness of the enemy. " Tres
uno contudit ictu ! "[1]

Quick successes, even extending into years, have not counted
against Russia. While Charles, not able to be everywhere, went
off to finish with Poland, Peter learnt the lessons of defeat,
won more and more ground towards the coveted sea-shore,
and even had the magnificent audacity to plant his

1703. new frontier capital (which was this time to face
Europe), on a strip of unhealthy land which he had
raided during Charles's absence. Most towns have been
placed and outlined by Nature herself; but, if there is anything divine in a great purpose, then it is not for nothing
that St. Petersburg carries its prefix of " Saint." This town
grew by the will of one man. Its marshy site was not meant
for a great place of habitation ; faces are pale there—of a
kind of dirty-linen complexion ; there are few, even of Russian
visitors, who do not suffer in health by even a short stay there.
The streets are periodically in danger of inundation. Peter issued
decrees that stone houses should stop building all over the
empire till St. Petersburg had reached a certain size ; also, that the
more considerable of the nobles should be obliged to build stone
houses, and even possess boats in his new capital. The site was
for Russia a quite unnatural centre, less Russian even than
Galicia. The dwellers of the district were not Russians, and the
Russification of Petersburg is still not finally complete. This
great shifting of the centre was not undertaken by a national
instinct, like that which founded Moscow on the eastern frontier.
The Russian people can themselves deal with the questions of
Asia ; they have streamed in that direction of themselves ; but,
in the more difficult conquest of education from the West, they
needed a dictatorship of intelligence. Yet the dictatorship, for
all that, remained national ; Peter, in his strenuous push

[1] The legend on a Swedish medal struck after Narva.

towards the West, and in his stubborn assertion of Russianness was a typical Russian; and the Tsar was a peasant when work was to be done, building, punishing, or saving life with his own hands. His was the vitality of Russia; his impact was limited to no one point. In many a town still stands his little travelling palace, or cottage, full of his own handiwork and surrounded by signs of his industrial enterprise. The chill which killed him was caught while he was saving some drowning peasants, and was made fatal by his bare-headed attendance at a popular Church festival in the depth of winter. As St. Petersburg grew by his will, so it still stands by the instinctive sense of his superiority. That is the significance of the Horseman of Bronze, who still stands pointing to the quays of the Neva.[1] In St. Petersburg the Russians are great only because they follow Peter, only in so far as they realise that they must sacrifice individual comfort in the struggle for a window that looks out upon Europe.

But St. Petersburg had hardly been mapped out, when Peter was called upon to again face his still triumphant enemy, and this time in the heart of Russia. Charles would have no peace while he was still short of Moscow. His splendidly trained and tried army threw itself into the depths of Russia and the depths of a Russian winter—perhaps the severest **1708.** within memory. Leaving the Moscow road, Charles turned to the richer south for stores and for Cossack help. In these expectations he was deceived, but "not even an angel from heaven," as he said, could bring him to retreat. Charles, in one sense, surpassed Napoleon; he did, indeed, struggle through a Russian winter, and was still besieging Poltava, when Peter at last gave him battle. The **1709.** Swedes, as on other fields, made their first victorious rush; but worn out, and with their glorious king disabled, the scanty invaders at last saw the Russians closing in all round them. The snap came; effort broke; Charles fled alone; his army was dissolved or captured; and Peter that night drank to the health of his teachers in war. "Now," he wrote, "the first

---

[1] See Pushkin's poem, "The Bronze Horseman." While he records the devastation and misery caused by a flood in St. Petersburg, the poet turns, from time to time, to the statue of Peter, pointing towards the Neva.

stone for the foundation of St. Petersburg is laid with the help of God."

Sweden was never again dangerous to Russia. St. Petersburg was built; a fleet was launched on the Baltic, which was soon able to even threaten the coasts of Sweden. The Baltic provinces as far as Riga fell into Peter's hands, and the Germans of that district have been from then till now loyal subjects of the Russian Emperors.

Peter had conquered for Russia the right to educate herself in her own way. Russia had saved her individuality, and had at the same time got touch with the civilisation of the West.

As to the East, that question was settling itself. Siberia, thinly peopled and undeveloped, offered practically no resistance to the victorious Russian advance. Siberia was before all things a road, chiefly important by that which it led to. Along this road the Russians had been rapidly pressing forward, passing from one great river to another, and by a system of block-houses, which were to become towns, securing their hold on each in turn. They got their first footing in Asia in 1578, and within sixty years from that date they had already reached the Pacific.

Circa 1635.

III.—Russia and the Western Ideas.

St. Petersburg was the gage of Russia's desire to learn from Europe. She wished to shorten the distance between herself and her teacher, and with this object she tried to displace her own centre and come half of the way. But the strain of this attempt to bridge the gap is very great. Russians are not comfortable in St. Petersburg. On the other side, foreigners who only visit St. Petersburg will see the Government and will not see Russia. Some of them may even think that there is no Russia except the Government.

Peter was all the more autocratic for being a reformer. It was autocracy alone that carried the reforms through. Peter gave himself a liberal education, and certainly, by example and school-ing, did very much to create an intelligent initiative in his people. But free initiative for its own sake was not what he desired; he desired rather to train capable servants for the State; and, as his own best plans met with the most stubborn opposition from the nation, we could hardly have expected anything different. He abolished the Patriarchate, and thus **1700—** destroyed the anomaly of two national heads, one **12.** secular and one religious. He kept the military basis of class distinctions and systematised it in all his institutions. He ordered that precedence in the State should depend, not on birth, but on official rank; so that all the nobles, **1722.** in order to keep their superiority, were forced to work as he himself had done. His mistake was natural to a Government which reforms from above; he grudged Time its work; he wanted ready-made results, machines for Government use. The army of officials became larger; very many of them were foreigners, preferred for efficiency, but not likely to be best in touch with the instincts of the people.

Peter had now facilities for free intercourse with Europe, and he at once set about building new schemes on the new basis. Russian princesses were married to minor princes of Germany, and Russia might later hope to hold a kind of balance in that divided country; it was the German lack of unity that allowed Russia to show her strength to the West so soon. Peter even entered into a wide European coalition against the English Hanoverians and the French Regent. He had succeeded to almost the whole power of Sweden round the Baltic.

After his death came an intermission—a confused period of re-action. First there was the short reign of his widow, who had no real title to the throne. His grandson, **1725.** Peter II., was in the hands of this or that clique of **1727—** courtiers, and, had he lived, might have again made **30.** Moscow his capital. Anna, niece of Peter I., was chosen Empress by the nobles, because they thought that the weakness of her title would force her to leave the real power in their hands.[1] Anna, however, turned out to **1730—** be a born Empress, and chose her own favourites, who **40.** were more tyrannous than any before them. Anna **1741.** extended Russia towards the Black Sea. A daughter of the great Peter, the masculine-minded Elizabeth, obtained the succession, won part of Finland from the Swedes, encouraged

[1] The "constitution" planned by these nobles was no better than t e Polish oligarchy, and cannot be construed into the principles of modern Liberalism.

the beginnings of Russian literature, and took part in a great
German quarrel (the Seven Years' War). Prussia was to be
          partitioned ; and Russia did practically conquer her
1762. share. Her successor, Peter III., reversed her policy
          and gave up his conquests ; but he was soon put out
of the world by his brilliant wife, who ruled as Catherine II.
The gloomy period of cliques and crimes had given to St.
Petersburg traditions as sinister as almost any that stained
Moscow.

Russia had often enough said to the foreigner, " Come and
rule over us " ; but it is amazing that Princess Sophia [1] from tiny
Anhalt-Zerbst should have been a better Russian and more of a
man than any of the able counsellers whom she called round her.
She had more breadth of view, more quick intelligence, and more
strength of purpose than any of them. She gained her position
by deposing and murdering her husband, and her private morality
was throughout her long reign that of the most vigorous and most
depraved manhood ; but, for all that, when she came into the
succession of Peter the Great she came into her own.

We do not read that there was any malice in the abominable
crime which established her in power. We see no signs of
repentance ; she certainly saw in herself a political ability which
justified any means by which she could mount the throne. She
felt that she had the instincts of her new people. For this reason,
her face, as it shows itself to them, is still a beneficent one. She
concentrated in herself all the intelligence of their traditions, when
she was dealing with other countries. Like a true Russian, she
was anything but indifferent to opinion outside, of whose applause
she had her share ; but she was not disturbed by it in the tenacity
of her national purpose.

Her greatest danger was at home. The rough and brutal
          Pugachéff united against the Government all the ordinary
1773. elements of discontent and disorder which so often
          ran wild in the south-west. He raised an enormous
"jacquerie " against the increasingly tight hold of the Government; this kind of peril terrifies rulers out of all their conventional
calm, and is so many-headed as to make the stoutest despair.
But, while almost all her generals lost confidence, Catherine stood

[1] She took the name of Catherine when she was received into the Orthodox
Church on her arrival in Russia.

firm against any kind of concession. The area of devastation and murder was slowly reduced, and Pugachéff was at last deserted, hunted down, taken like a wild beast, and executed.

This was really a victory of Europe over Asia, of order over disorder. Such, too, was Catherine's conquest of Crimea. The good land, which had once been the road **1784.** and camping-ground of Asiatic invaders and so had been lost to all plans of progressive development, was now secured to Europe and to Russia. The Cossacks of the Marches could no longer play off Pole, Turk, or Swede against Russia, and were reduced to settled life and a much stricter obedience. Being still restless and military, they have been employed to police the Russian people. By her appearance in force on the shores of the Black Sea, Russia already dominated Turkey, against whom Rumyántseff and Suvóroff, the two greatest generals of Russian history, won triumph after triumph. From the treaty which ended one war of this reign, Russia was later able to claim a vague right to interfere in Turkish affairs and to champion the Christian subjects of the Sultan. **1774.** Catherine's grandsons bore the significant names of Alexander, Constantine, and Nicholas,[1] which were to be continued in later generations.

Westwards Catherine pushed home the victories of her predecessors. Prussia had held good against plans of partition. Poland, on the other hand, had begun her own destruction when she had admitted first,—foreign candidates to her throne at each new election, next,—foreign bribes, and last,—foreign troops in support of the different candidates. The partition of Poland is in method almost as unclean a piece of work as the destruction of the Rohillas in the same period ; but the cause which it served was infinitely more national. In the first **1772.** partition, Russia won back a people who were really her own by blood, language, and religion—the White Russians. Poland made desperate attempts to be worthy to live. An excellent constitution was made. But the Roman **1791.** Catholic nobles were still for the most part utterly selfish and, by custom, ready to invite foreign help and civil

---

[1] Nicholas the "Wonder Worker" is one of the greatest saints of the Greek Church.

war; there was no national middle-class; the peasants, so far
strangers to questions of Government, were first invited
1772, into public life by the confusing ideas of the French
1793, Revolution. There was much treason, and later much
1795. brave but disunited fighting. The three partitions were
carried through.

A similar attempt on the independence of Sweden was begun,
but French support helped Gustav III. to defeat it.

In Germany, Catherine carried on the system of marriages and
balance. She welcomed the teaching of the West, which, at this
time, happened to be the creed of humanity preached by the
French philosophers; Catherine was one of the many correspondents of Voltaire. But the Liberalism of sovereigns was at this
time more a fad than a conviction; and Catherine, who really
wanted to train a vast *personnel* for Government service, worked,
like Peter, for the creation of an appearance of European results
in the shortest possible time. Yet she did not deceive herself as
to the measure of her admiration for the French; her great con-
vention of representatives of all classes was allowed to
1766—8. "preach maxims which might overturn walls,"[1] but was
dismissed as soon as Catherine had obtained from it
the information which she needed for her own use in administration. It was against serfdom that Pugacheff had fought, and
Catherine, in her triumph over disorder, extended serfdom even
to Little Russia. Like Peter, she was ahead of her people,
and introduced many improvements; but all went to the profit of
autocracy. Most of her law-abiding subjects were grateful to her,
for they knew of no alternative but licence and rapine.

But a new and great danger was developing itself against the
Russian Government. The revolutionary changes carried through
by Peter had admitted a whole flood of Western ideas. Even the
language was threatened by the influx of ill-digested foreign words.
Catherine's chief task then was this—to rule and moderate this
invasion from the West, now favouring and now restricting, and
above all to keep intact her machinery of control by preserving
the system of autocracy. For this very reason every forward step
of participation in Western politics had to be carefully pondered.
Yet Russia had to go forward; her need of education imposed the

---

[1] Letter of Catherine to Voltaire.

necessity of her imperial advance. We have seen that it had been the toughness of her national sense which had given her the power to resist the West in its overbearing schemes of conquest, and to buy her education at a less cost than the loss of her independent existence. So now she had to balance her inferiority of culture against her national power. She was like the schoolboy who is too big for his class and yet too backward. The evil of Peter's work and Catherine's was this—that advance in the cultivation of character at home lingered long behind the advance of prestige and national power abroad; and this circumstance did much to create that fear of Russia in the West which has characterised all subsequent history. But the Russian Government had its own fear; it lived in the midst of a much more serious danger, the danger of the swamping of its authority in the invading sea of Western ideas; and, for the misfortune of Russia, the ideas of the West, when the West first came into close touch with her, were those of the new French "philosophy"—half-truths, confidently asserted as whole truths, and destined to threaten the very principle of authority. These ideas were backed, first, by the conquering charm of French exposition, and later by the irresistible impact of the French nation in arms; and the man who came to lead the French armies was, in spite of his own contempt for "ideologues," the most formidable dogmatist of modern times. Then, too, these half-truths were for Russians very confusing; the Russians very much needed to learn personal initiative, but they needed no return to nature, which meant a return to the chaos of Pugachéff. No wonder that the Russian Government stood for throne and altar during this stormy period; and no wonder that, in the course of time, a gap began to open between the Russian Government and the more intelligent of the Russian people.

In her later years, Catherine had found herself in a position to play a great part in the affairs even of the extreme West. The line of policy which she struck out was instinctive and natural; in the struggle between England and the United States she took up the position of a great chief among the neutrals, ready to resist any general domination, whether on land or on sea. In the following years, Russia had to choose between resisting one or other of two great dominations—that of the French and Napoleon on land, or that of the English on sea. It would have been

hopeless to have resisted both at the same time. There were
many changes of Russian policy, dictated as it generally was by
the personal sentiment or even whims of this or that Russian
sovereign ; yet a certain line of consistency can be traced
throughout. Paul, the son of Catherine, is at first for
1796— universal peace ; this is natural enough in an autocrat of
1801. vague and generous ideas, who wishes to make the most
decisive and the most ideal use of his apparently
unlimited opportunities of doing good. Next, he is all for throne
and altar, and fights with England against France. His general,
Suvóroff, full of what may be called a constitutional antipathy to
the new French and presenting so very many points of resemblance to his great co-worker Nelson, won everywhere as he had
always done, even when almost cheated by his Austrian allies and
cutting a desperate road of retreat through triumphant enemies.
Next, the question of England's sea-power held the scene, and
Paul, looking at the young Napoleon as the restorer of authority
in France, turned against England. But his nobles would not
follow him through all these quick changes, each of which used up
so many men and so much money ; in lesser matters too, Paul had
been altogether too absolute, and further, Russia had not yet so far
developed her own trade as to be able to make herself independent
of English traders. Paul and his policy seemed to be half-
demented. George III., when demented, rested under the shadow
of William Pitt, but a demented autocrat has to be removed ;
removal easily leads to murder ; Paul was killed.

Alexander I. began his reign as a neutral ; he too made
proposals of universal peace. Napoleon could not agree to let
such an initiative pass into the hands of another sovereign ; and
he slighted Alexander's efforts. Thus Russia was our
1805. ally in the year of Trafalgar and Austerlitz. She again
opposed Napoleon when he picked a quarrel with
Prussia, but the Prussian army was practically destroyed at Jena
and Auerstädt ; the English gave only the most trivial help ;
Napoleon formulated his scheme for " defending" the Continent
against our sea power, beat the Russians well at Friedland, and
offered apparently equal terms to their Emperor, namely, the
division of Europe into the Empire of the West and the Empire
of the East. Alexander, won by the revival of an old ambitious

dream and by the fascination of apparent equality with his superior, embraced Napoleon's friendship and welcomed the hostility of England. But he was now almost isolated amongst his own subjects, and even the fate of Paul **1807.** seemed to be not far off from him.[1] His French alliance gave him Finland, which he won without glory and retained by a compromise with its old constitutional rights; the longed-for Danube provinces he could not conquer at all. He stimulated himself to a last emotional effort at friendship when he met Napoleon at Erfurt; but his friend took more and more of the liberties of friendship, treating Alexander's sister with scant courtesy and seizing the land of his relatives—and that for the furtherance of the Continental blockade of England and the ruin of English trade, a scheme which was quite as adverse to the interests of the Russian people as it had been in the days of Paul. In the war against Austria (1809) the Franco-Russian alliance had proved almost worse than fictitious; the breach rapidly widened, and Alexander, throwing himself on to the old instincts and prejudices of his subjects, awaited manfully the shock of the great invasion of 1812.

We have seen no greatness of genius in this story of the policy of the Russian Government, a story of sentiment, ambition, and change of plans. Russia feels her depletion after the robust and triumphant broadness of Catherine and Suvóroff. And we have now been brought back to the years of trial, those fateful years which at the outset of each new century[2] seem to cancel a past of painful effort, and push Russia back into the darkness. In this the year of great appeal to the old instincts of sheer resistance,[3] of appeal to the heart of local life, we see something more than confused and doubtful counsellors and ignorant peasant soldiers. In the handsome and fitful Alexander lives the spirit of Peter, and in devotion to the national autocracy rises everywhere a Minin or a Pozharsky. No simple triumph here for the superior brain and business-like methods of the world's best general,—for

[1] Savary describes the unpopularity of the French alliance in Russia; while ambassador of France, he was hardly received at any house in St. Petersburg except that of the Emperor.

[2] 1611 : the Poles in the Kremlin ; 1707 : Charles XII. in Russia.

[3] "The Russian is self-confident because he knows nothing whatsoever of the matter in hand and does not want to."—L. Tolstoy : "War and Peace."

clear-cut plans and quick marching: the peasants themselves are become a vast uncontrollable factor in the decision, and they have asked for the word which is to tell them when to burn their houses, and leave a desert in front of the invader. With a world alive all round you, there are too many things to be counted, and calculation can no longer be even approximately final.

Let us look at the issues. Clever, conscious Intelligence, with its one plan for the whole world, was marching on Russia, offering its gifts at the unpayable price of national ruin. On the other side stood the blundering instinct of Independence leaning on its antiquated wooden club, Obedience. And yet Russia was after all fighting the battle of local instinct for all Europe.

It was almost impossible to organise the invasion better, yet the invasion should never have been planned at all. Civilisation, when it invaded this country, had to bring with it all that it might need; for here it would find nothing ready to hand. From the Nyémen onwards, a wilderness enveloped the Grand Army, which, as Ségur[1] tells us, for want of something to look at, had to satisfy itself with the contemplation of its own magnificence. The wilderness became more wide and more dense when the frontier of old Russia had been crossed. One sometimes forgets that the demoralisation and destruction of the army began on a gigantic scale almost from the start. To the ignorant, the campaign might seem to be an easy conquest without a battle; but the French felt that they were seizing on nothing, and Napoleon really thought nothing won till he should have brought the Russians to battle.

Yet, even when they were retreating, the Russians morally held the initiative: it was the advancing Napoleon who was on the defensive of attack all through. Their very mediocrity of brains served them; fixed plan they had none; and their conduct was simply the expression of an instinct, multiform yet corporate as of a whole people in arms—exactly what Spain had been able to produce and Germany so far had not. They retreated at first because there was nothing else to do, and later because they could see no better course. Their one general who deserves high military praise, Barclay de Tolly, was never quite certain of himself, and was unintelligible to his

---

[1] " Campagne de Russie."

Emperor, his colleagues and his soldiers. It was, in fact, the soldier's spirit in every man—the spirit of local instinct—that matched the genius of a Napoleon.

The Russians, in their plan of a great redoubt at Drissa, peddled with inferior science of German extraction, but returned in time to the old instinct. Owing to the divisions of their generals, they were close to ruin at Mohilyéff and Smolensk. The old and sacred fortress of Smolensk they defended just long enough to save the army and then burnt, getting away in confusion behind a screen set up by desperate soldierly heroism.

To the French, the details of the Russian conduct of the campaign were unintelligible because unintelligent; yet they had to feel that the negation opposed to them had something behind it which was stronger than the stupidity of a particular general; and this feeling, though it would never quite argue out of countenance their cock-sure self-satisfaction, yet was very effective in making them really more and more doubtful of themselves. Napoleon himself began to contract all the whims and fancies of the isolated tourist, and to look impatiently for the end of his journey. He stopped at Vítebsk; he stopped at Smolensk; he thought of stopping just before Borodinó; but it was the sheer impatience of the traveller that drove him on each time.[1]

Towns such as St. Petersburg are incarnations of a Government, and blows brought home on them may fail to wound the heart of a people. But many towns are great concentrations of country life; they are themselves "country," only more so. Moscow has well been described as the "village-city." The French were looking forward to finding a "town" as opposed to "country"; towns were what they were seeking in this wilderness; but the Russians stood before Moscow, precisely because they could not give up without a special struggle what was for them the very cream of "country." The battlefield of Borodinó, chosen by the Russians (not by the French), proved equal to the historical occasion. The tremendous struggle was typically great—in numbers, in area, in losses both of officers and of men, but most of all in the feel which it leaves of vaguely understood forces of Nature, full of purpose and triumphant over sheer human

---

[1] Witness Ségur's interesting account of Napoleon's behaviour at Vítebsk.

planning. Kutúzoff counts almost for nothing, and Napoleon
for very little. The true heroes are the simple fighters in their
infinite variety of temper—Davoust, Ney, Murat, Caulaincourt;
Barclay, Bagratión, Túchkoff, Kutaisoff,—and these only as
typical of thousands of others. Napoleon found a battlefield
too large even for him; he kept waiting beyond the limits of
daylight for that single moment which was to make possible the
one man's certain and conquering stroke of genius; meanwhile
the battle split up into numberless desperate struggles between
warring personal instincts, an infinity of small commands, the
sea of the heart's efforts instead of the single problem of the
brain. When Napoleon had really won the field, time and space
forbade that he should know it, and the Russians withdrew by
night, leaving no fruit of victory but the dead.

The foreigner, Benningsen, pleaded ostentatiously for another
stand before Moscow, but Kutúzoff, without giving reasons, issued
the order for retreat. All Russia was, by now, an army; the
force which represented her in the field was too much broken to
save her and too valuable to be sacrificed. Moscow could afford
to suffer; for the present was alive with the very spirit that had
created her.

And here, in the fitting scenery—before Moscow—we see the
great world-scheme of Napoleon break up. The tension was
already past sustaining. Ségur tells us that the Frenchmen
before Moscow felt that they were already wonderful beings of
another world. There is no deputation of citizens to flatter and
feed them, for the people are gone, and the Governor too, taking
all the fire-pumps with him. They enter, and the town lights up
in flames all round them. The wind changed from time to time,
but always seemed to blow from that quarter where the fire was
strongest. It blew on the Kremlin and drove Napoleon out of
the city. The Russian army, marching to its new positions on
the south, saw these flames and made a new compact with
death.[1] Alexander heard of them, and pledged himself never to
treat before victory, even if he should be driven out of Europe
into Asia.

Napoleon had won nothing. Moscow, as he said, was not a
military position, but a political one. The game of bluff had

---

[1] See Pushkin's "Ode on Napoleon."

failed; the loss of a capital had had the opposite effect on the Russians to that which he had expected—that was all; and strength was failing, and discipline and assurance too. There was little point in staying on, and the final argument was the news that the Russians were on the French line of communications and were taking the offensive. Napoleon, then, would retreat, but through a country as yet unwasted.

On this new road lay Maloyaroslávets, a little town on a high plateau, which sinks in steep bluffs or gullies to the river in front. The Russians were just in time to block the way at this point; and the French, after a terribly murderous struggle, gave up all hope of carrying the position and turned aside to the old wasted road by which they had come. From this time the Grand Army broke up always faster and faster. It was the country itself that did most of the damage—that is, the Russian winds and snows, frost and thaw, the Russian roads and distances, marshes and gullies. Next dangerous were the implacable Russian peasants; for the French, to loiter was to be lost; the Cossacks, who harried the almost horseless army from all sides and huddled it into a long train of fugitives, were only the military expression of the enmity of the peasants. The Russian army itself only half used its chances, and the Russian generals had the smallest share of all in these last successes. At Krásny and on the Bereziná the French were cut off and ought to have been practically annihilated. Ségur has a right to say that "the Russians came short of their climate." Indeed, the Russian losses were almost as great as those of the French, and were only covered by their ability to bring in new forces—that is, by the fact that they had been attacked in their own country. There is something in Kutúzoff's warning that his men "must not reach the frontier as a pack of vagabonds,"[1] and the warning gained in value as the army passed into White Russia, and later into Poland, where the Russians were by no means at home.

The triumph of the defensive is wonderfully complete and dramatic. It is almost exactly at the chief point of irruption, Kóvno, that the last relics of the main army struggle over the Nyémen; and the last Frenchman left fighting on its banks is not a general, but the prince of soldiers and the real hero of the

[1] Bogdanóvich, "History of the Patriotic War," Vol. III., p. 141.

retreat—Ney, dishevelled and with blood-shot eyes, but to the
last robust and whole-hearted.

All through, it is the triumph of local spirit, and the terribly
convincing proof of the limitations of brain-power. The startling
lesson was for all Europe, which of late, more than ever, lived a
corporate life and had common questions to solve. Thus the
single supreme event, which in reality only proved that Napoleon
had gone too far, was exaggerated and turned into a kind of complete gospel. Russia had been the instrument of Napoleon's first
overthrow ; her military power was soon to be taken for granted
as a positive aggressive and ruling force, and the moral ideas
which she represented claimed to be a constructive system, fit to
take the place of what they seemed to have overthrown. This is
the real beginning of that period which is named from "the Holy
Alliance."[1] We see this reactionary mood (it is a mood rather
than a principle) beginning in the Grand Army itself during the
campaign : even the French historians become emotional, melodramatic and fatalistic, when they reach the story of the fire of
Moscow. Europe took the Russians at above their own valua-
tion. Europeans seemed ready to become second-hand Russians.
Yet the mind, the civilisation of the West, had not been proved
useless ; it had only received a lesson by which it might profit for
further successes, and it had already begun its great counter-
stroke on the Russian people itself.

Thus the contrast which we have noticed in Russian history
has, at this point, become extraordinarily greater. Russia, taken
as a unit of government, has achieved a kind of moral conquest
over her European difficulties. France, the very heart of the
West, has to accept her as a component part of a common whole.
Much more than that, she seems for the time to be the force
which exercises the greatest control over Europe. The Russian
Government has rested on the old instincts of a giant people.
Those vague instincts represent themselves, to an eye half tired
of definitions, as a whole system of new principles triumphant
over the mental genius which recently ruled Europe ; and such
a system seems in keeping with the mood of reaction which now
generally prevails. Thus Europe, for a time, thinks of copying
Russia, which means that Russia hinders the education of

---

[1] The policing of peoples by their sovereigns in common.

Europe. But Europe no longer actively hinders the education of Russia. It is Russia herself who, in the defence of her own system or want of system, will accentuate all the old restrictions on the entry of European thought; for the Western ideas now seem to be a danger to Russia herself. All Russians have had to interest themselves in national affairs in 1812. That public interest will live when the material danger which threatened from outside is gone. There will come the inevitable question, "What had we to learn from them?" There will spring up groups of thinkers, of writers, of propagandists; and the Russian Government, pledged to reaction both in Europe and at home, will find a deeper gulf opening out between itself and its more intelligent subjects.

The strength of Russia is, in the main, defensive. The Russian Government might still be representative, at home, of the great mass of the people; but it could not really and permanently dominate Europe. This becomes clear at once in the sequel. Russia did nothing wonderful in 1813. Prussia, when the forces of Alexander crossed the frontier, rose for her freedom against the French; but Napoleon, with a new and raw army, beat both Russians and Prussians together at **1813—** Lützen and at Bautzen. The Austrians and Swedes **4.** join in against him; the Saxons betray him on the field of battle; and at Leipzig he goes down amidst a sea of enemies. The glory of 1814 is practically all his. It is chiefly the pettiness, insignificance, and greed of the new rulers of Europe that give Napoleon his second short-lived chance in 1815.

It is to be noticed that the time of Russian predominance is marked by a series of congresses, of meetings between sovereigns. These meetings were useful to Russia, as comparatively the newcomer, for they associated her more definitely with Europe. Also the task of the Russian Government was two-fold—to extend the political influence of Russia, and to keep a check on movements which might endanger the whole artificial supremacy of reaction in Europe; and thus it was necessary to unite Governments in a police-ring as against peoples. Congresses of sovereigns were, for this purpose, the natural weapon. Still, by these meetings, Russia again showed her liking for general understandings on a large scale and for frank discussion by Governments of their common difficulties; and the congresses are a part of her contribution towards the development of European unity.

Alexander's mood had been Liberal in the earlier years of his reign. It was now "devôt"[1] and reactionary. But one of his old ideals was that of a frank and generous union between Russia and Poland. The Poles had now no alternative, for the Congress of Vienna had surrendered the majority of them to Alexander. Much of Poland had been ruled by the Napoleonic system and laws; the serfs had been freed. Alexander took the additional title of Tsar of Poland (his Russian title was "Emperor"), and granted a constitution. Here was an example of Russia's new difficulty. The Poles, for national reasons, wanted more than Alexander could consistently give,[2] and the Russians could not see why Poland should have liberties denied to themselves. Inside Alexander's empire was begun the debate between intellect, culture, and initiative on the one side, and the old instincts of simple allegiance on the other. Russian Liberals, from this time onward, might perhaps unite with Poles for common objects— that is, against their common Government. Alexander now died in a mysterious silence.[3] The next heir, Constantine, had resigned his claim to the Russian throne in order to marry a Polish countess; but his younger brother Nicholas knew nothing of this, and proclaimed him Emperor in St. Petersburg. Constantine meanwhile proclaimed Nicholas in Poland. The two brothers were absolutely loyal to each other, but the temporary confusion gave occasion for a revolutionary movement. When Constantine's resignation was at last made public, some Liberals in St. Petersburg declared that it had been forced from him, and induced some of the troops to rise for "Constantine and Constitution": the soldiers appear to have thought that Constitution was the Polish wife of Constantine. The revolt was stamped out; but it left its mark on the reign of Nicholas I.

The English Government of that time seemed to Englishmen of the time very reactionary, but it never identified its interests with the police-ring of European sovereigns under the leadership

---

[1] *I.e.*, one of timorous piety.

[2] For instance, the surrender of Lithuania and White Russia, where only the gentry were Polish.

[3] The cause of his death is not definitely known.

of Russia. Since Paul planned with Napoleon the invasion of India, Englishmen had grown more jealous of every advance of Russian power. England and Russia had played the greatest parts in the overthrow of Napoleon, and were now left facing each other. Canning not only refused to enter the Holy Alliance, he opposed to the policed Continent a world of Western seas[1] in which Russia had no power. In 1830, a Government after the English model was adopted by France; and the two constitutional powers began to form a rival camp to that of despotism.[2] The autocratic States—Russia, Austria, and Prussia—still stood more or less closely together. Thus we find that the Western group had its way in Belgium (1831), but the Eastern group still controlled the affairs of Poland.

The Poles had seized the occasion of the split between East and West to rise against Russia. Warsaw drove out the Russian Viceroy and troops; and the Polish national army, which had survived the union with Russia, now fought with a great measure of success. But the Poles wanted everything, even to the limits of their old empire at its widest extent, including the Russian provinces of Lithuania. Compromise, then, was impossible; and Poland was not strong enough to get her way by force. She now lost most of her liberties, and, after another protracted but always abortive rising in 1863, she lost the official remains of national existence and the ordinary rights of language and property.

Amongst the Russians themselves this was a period of great progress, even if that progress was limited to an elect circle, and was chiefly intellectual rather than moral. Modern Russian literature may be said to date from the reigns of Elizabeth and Catherine. The year 1812, and the questions which it raised, had called into existence a galaxy of great writers. Pushkin is one of the world's great poets; Lérmontoff, but for his untimely death, might have been as great, or even more so; Griboyédoff wrote one of the very cleverest of social satires. I do not know any modern comedy which in simplicity and force is equal to Gogol's "Revisor"; and the first part of his "Dead Souls,"

---

[1] Including the new South American republics.
[2] " Form, O. ye peoples, your holy alliance ;
    Join hands, join hands, all round."—Béranger.

which is a picture of the Russia of his time, is a work of the first order. This is the time of the greatest poet of Poland, Mickiewicz. Turghényeff, Dostoyévsky, and Tolstoy are still to come.

The split between the Western and the Eastern camps, between the Liberals and the Absolutists, was further widened by the revolutions of 1848. The struggle was like a conflict between two faiths. The gospel of Mazzini touched Germany and Poland; and revolutionary leaders from Italy, Poland, and Hungary were to be found fighting together in many causes. Nicholas I. held with absolute firmness to the principles of autocracy; the bureaucratic control over the Intelligents in Russia was further and further exaggerated, and the Government gradually became more and more isolated from thinking people.

In his double task of repression at home and abroad **1849.** Nicholas won a last triumph by his reduction of revolutionary Hungary for the profit of the Austrian autocracy. But he was now to see his own country invaded, first by the arms and then by the ideas of the Liberal West.

We have seen how dangerous Russia became to Turkey in the reign of Catherine II. She gained a vague claim of protectorate over the Christian subjects of the Sultan. For the extension of this claim only force seemed to be required. Most of these Christians were Slavs. When the Greeks rose for an independence of their own, Alexander and Nicholas had been sorely puzzled. Did the " Holy Alliance " in favour of authority cover the mis-government of the non-Christian Sultan? Would the success of the Greeks react on the revolutionaries of Europe? For once religion seemed to be fighting in alliance with Liberalism. Russia had the final solution of the question, and settled it in favour of the Greeks. The West feared more than ever the extension of Russian influence at the expense of Turkey; and England abandoned, here at least, her Liberal convictions, through an unnecessary fear for the security of her Indian Empire.

The Crimean War was the outcome of the conditions which I have described. Nicholas fought for his hold over Turkey, England for her naval power and trade, and Napoleon III., nominally, for the championship of the Latin Church. Yet, for all that, the war was also a direct encounter on Russian soil between the camp of the constitutional West and the camp of the autocratic East of Europe; and the West won, this time not by genius, but on its merits—that is, because, even when pitted against very moderate generals, the Russian autocracy was altogether too inferior in preparing and employing the machinery of modern war. The war gave the occasion for a great movement of reform in Russia. Reforms, which would not have been accepted at the price of independence, might seem natural enough when suggested to an awakened nation by its own consciousness of failure.

CHAPTER II.

REFORM AND REACTION.

(1854—1904.)

DURING the reign of Nicholas I., though the Government was always reactionary it was not at all times equally severe. Its action now depended, more than ever before, on what happened to be going on in Europe. If Europe was quiet, the tightness of despotism was relaxed; and indeed after each special effort of despotism in Russia there is always a psychological moment when the immediate task of repression seems to be accomplished, when the Governor reports that all is quiet, and when rewards are distributed to the officials. If Europe was troublesome, then the work of repression was resumed in Russia. Few phrases are more illuminating than a remark made at this time by a Liberal censor, Nikityenko. " If they play tricks in Europe, the Russian gets a hit on the back." The Empire was ruled not so much by regular laws as by special ordinances; and sometimes the relaxation of these ordinances points to some kind of hesitation, or even to the prevalence of some softer mood at the court itself. During the forties the earlier aristocrats of literature, such as Pushkin, were succeeded by a new race of literary workers—men more widely national, more laborious, and more earnest,—Liberals of that great breed which at this time produced notable men in almost every country of Europe. The direction of their efforts was not to be mistaken; and the darkest period of the reaction was the so-called " plague streak " which preceded the Crimean War. Nicholas himself, who was personally a generous patron of literature, had done his best to make the conscientious industry of the sovereign a substitute for public opinion, and even he was forced by the evidence of hard facts to consider far-reaching plans of reform; but he felt that he could not change, and he tottered to the end of his period like a great honest giant, who felt the future coming on him and wished to get to the end of his time first. "My successor," he said, "may do as he likes." As we have seen, his policy naturally culminated in the Crimean War.

During this war, Nicholas, who had been considered and respected as one of the arbiters of Europe, saw his own territory invaded by those two Powers which represented constitutional government. The war, which only made one military reputation, that of Todleben, could not fail to bring into the light of a glaring publicity a whole host of abuses in the Russian system of government; for instance, if our English contractors sent out a number of boots which all proved to be left-footed, many of the Russian boots, being made of brown paper, came to pieces before they reached the scene of war, and the peasant cobblers of Kimry, when reproached with their bad work, boldly answered that the value of the boots corresponded to the price paid for them—which was their way of putting the blame on those Government officials who had filched half the contract money. In the absence of railways, Russian reinforcements took longer in marching from Moscow to Sebastopol than our soldiers took over the sea voyage from England; in a word, though opposed by divided forces and by mediocre generals, autocracy proved to be a very poor machine for making war. Nicholas, who, following the tradition of 1812, had put his chief confidence in "General February"—that is to say, in the Russian climate—was himself the chief victim of his defender. There is little doubt that he wished to die. Seized by a strong chill, he threw away all precautions and exposed himself freely to the frost. He himself drew up the official notice which announced the imminence of his own death.

Already a storm of indignation had been rising all over Russia. Denunciations addressed to the Emperor had reached their destination; higher officials themselves reported that the continuance of the old order of administration was impossible. The Emperor Alexander, who had learnt his ideas of humanity from his tutor, the kindly poet Zhukóvsky, was by nature a man of generous heart and vague but noble aspirations. Devoted to the memory of his father, he was yet open to the impressions which might reach him from all sides; and even his lack of **1856,** strong personality made him all the more able to reflect the mood of the nation. He continued the war until peace could

be made with honour, and then had the moral courage to put himself at the head of his people as he found it ; in one of his first
official pronouncements he definitely proclaimed a period of
reform. The war resulted in an outburst of literature of
March, every kind, of which the most prominent feature was
1856. invective against the evils of bureaucracy. The great
writers of the forties had done much to create a
literary public, but the mass of the nation was still illiterate ;
and the reforms which followed were therefore due to the pressure
of a small and enlightened minority, which, as it could plead an
almost overwhelming case, was able to force the majority to be
silent.

We may pause to note the approximate coincidence in date
between the Russian reforms and those of the great Ministry of
Mr. Gladstone, and may recall the witty phrase in which Mr.
Disraeli compared the front Ministerial bench to a row of extinct
volcanoes. As reform after reform was pushed through in Russia,
the motive force lost more of its energy, and the reformers became
more divided amongst themselves and less convinced of the
absolute rightness of their formula. The Emperor, perhaps more
than anyone else, shared in this change of mood ; and indeed
he was especially accessible to the arguments of the defeated
bureaucracy. Thus each reform was less complete than the
last.

The effects of the reforms of Alexander II. are the chief subject
of this book. The first reform and the most far-reaching was the
emancipation of the serfs. The serfs, who numbered some fifty
millions, were more or less equally divided into those who belonged
to the Crown and those who belonged to private owners. Of
these last a small minority served in the houses of their masters ;
it was these house servants whose conditions of life were the
nearest to slavery. The ordinary serf was more or less left to
himself, as long as he produced a given profit for his master out
of the soil which he harassed. Land tenure amongst the
peasants was communal, and, according to the principles of the
government, almost socialistic—as land was presumed to be held
from the Emperor in return for the performance of obligations
to the State. It was very difficult to decide between the gentry
who claimed to be masters of the serfs and the serfs who claimed

to be occupiers of the land. But, with a generosity which has not found many parallels in Europe, both the writers, who led the thought of the nation, and the Government and gentry, who followed their lead, at least became quite clear that it was useless to emancipate the serf without giving him land. A landless emancipation had at the beginning of the century been initiated in the Baltic provinces, where the landowners were Germans; the present movement originated in the borderland between Poland and Little Russia. In Poland the squires had had to free their serfs at the time of Napoleon. Further to east, where the Polish noble lived amongst Russian peasants, the landowner was anxious to take the initiative of emancipation, which, if conducted by the Government, might have results even more unfavourable to him. It was for Alexander to decide whether this step of the Polish nobles should be countenanced and imitated; the Emperor sent out a circular in which he commended the step and invited the Russian gentry to do likewise. The final law, which was not elaborated for some years, was the result of a series of local commissions in which the gentry said how much they would do, and of central commissions in which the local results were summarised and co-ordinated. The Emperor himself took a leading part in this work, and set an admirable example by freeing those serfs who belonged to the Crown. The final application of the general law to local conditions was carried out by arbitrators appointed for each district. The work of these men was at the time considered to be very devoted and very impartial. Roughly speaking, the peasants received half of the land in perpetuity, but were to pay for it a moderate price in instalments extending over some fifty years. In the meantime, the Government advanced the whole of this amount to the gentry, who in many cases proceeded to spend it, and, selling what remained of their estates, came to swell the ranks of the Intelligents of the towns. Those who prophesied that the peasants would prove incapable of using their liberty have been entirely falsified by the results; but this first real attempt at a land settlement in Russia, coming as late as it did, failed to destroy in the peasant the idea that he had all along been the real master of the land, and that in principle he still ought to be so.

1816— 9.

1861.

The second great reform of Alexander II. was the establishment of County and Town Councils all over Russia **1865,** proper. It was natural that a reforming autocrat should **1870.** try to find a basis for local government rather in the country than in the towns, and rather in the class of landed gentry than anywhere else. The County Councils (or Zemstva) were established five years before the Town Councils, and, owing to the narrow-spiritedness and backwardness of the merchants, who were taken as the unit on which the latter were based, it was the County Councils who from this time onward represented the cause of constructive reform in Russia. All these Councils were elected on a high franchise, and in many cases the elections were indirect. However, this new national institution was of enormous importance; and there is reason to think that the Emperor, when he created it, realised that the local bodies could not exist by the side of the bureaucracy without sooner or later taking over much of its power.

Thirdly, Alexander introduced into Russia for the first time the principle of trial by jury. So far the law courts had **1862,** been entirely governmental; and in the recent period, **1865.** when the Government had thought it necessary to take up a position of hostility to the Intelligents, the judges could only too easily become the representatives of sheer power. Now, with the introduction of debates and lawyers, the admission of a certain measure of publicity, and above all the introduction of a popular element in the shape of the jury, it was certain that sooner or later the ancient habit of administrative arrest without any kind of trial would come into general disrepute.

It was at this time that the principle of conscription was introduced into Russia in its modern form. Opponents **1873.** of militarism are inclined to look upon it as a kind of disease, which is sure to swallow up all the vital energies of the nation; but we must remember that there is a reverse side to the picture. In order to turn a whole nation into an army, it is necessary to put arms into its hands; and as authority is diffused it tends to become weaker, so that at some time or other the Government may find that it has to deal with an armed nation. The old system, which made a small mercenary force the one prop of authority, was probably far less dangerous to autocracy.

There was one other reform which was demanded with especial vehemence, but which the autocracy was especially unwilling to concede. Freedom was claimed for literature; yet even a Government which invites the country gentry to take a share of responsibility, is not necessarily ready to give the right of whole-sale criticism to an irresponsible Press. Obviously the old system of examining every article before it could be printed had to be modified. If Russia had already possessed a vigorous tradition of free trial, perhaps it would have been enough to define by law what was not permissible, and to have allowed each editor to run his own risk. Such law courts, however, did not yet exist; also it was exceedingly difficult to say in advance what kind of utterances the Government might from time to time consider to be dangerous to itself. Anyhow, the great subject of Press reform, after being given enough publicity to arouse the highest expectations, passed into the hands of the Minister Valúyeff, a man of selfish ambitions and equivocal opinions. The punitive censorship did, indeed, in part replace the preliminary; but the power of punishing remained in the hands of the Minister of the Interior—that is, of Valúyeff himself. It was the Intelligence that had brought about the whole period of reform, and the prize which it especially coveted for itself proved to be a blank.

The reforms, though their importance was never adequately realised outside Russia, were a great achievement, and had the most far-reaching results; but their first effect was to produce widespread dissatisfaction. Some of the newly-freed peasants plunged into drunkenness, and for a long time there was a decline in peasant morality. The old checks had been removed, and the new responsibilities had not yet been learned. Some of the peasants alleged that there existed a Golden Letter from the Emperor which granted to them, not half the land, but all of it, and some even rose in arms to make good this claim. The Intelligence, which had shown so much public spirit, found itself pushed back into silence. Under Nicholas I. the Slavophils, or National Conservatives, had suffered as much from the censorship as anyone else; the Government continued to resent any attempts at public criticism, and the censorship even forbade one of this school, Mr. Katkoff, to discuss the immense question of emancipa-tion which it had itself brought forward. It is a dangerous thing to dangle the promise of freedom before people's eyes and then to take it away. The Russian public, formed by the writers of the forties, by the Crimean War, and by the spectacle of great changes in the State, had now far more volume, and was much more in earnest than ever before. The sudden extension of public interest had admitted into the ranks of the Intelligence a great host of new men, who had educated themselves as best they could in holes and corners during the intellectual stagnation of the reign of Nicholas. These new invaders of civilisation brought an element of savagery into the Intelligence itself. As yet utterly untrained in all political responsibility, they were full of undigested fragments of modern German philosophy; and, taking themselves seriously as the future regenerators of Russia, they set about their self-imposed task with an entire absence of scruple and with a certain savage ability, which counted for nothing their country, their teachers, and their personal careers. Some of them were ready to use any means to impose by force their vague and novel theories. They condemned not only the traditions of the Government, but also Shakespeare, Raphael, Beethoven, Goethe, Pushkin, Turghényeff, and even that special champion of the down-trodden, Dostoyévsky. Unconsciously true to the Slavonic creed, many of them condemned wholesale the West and Western civilisation ; for several of their socialistic ideals seemed to have as good a chance of realisation in Russia as in the West. Most of their " short formulæ " were either stale commonplaces or sheer negations, such as Turghényeff has so brilliantly described as " commonplaces by opposition." It is hard to say that they added anything to the thought of the world ; they can rather be explained as a race of disinherited upstarts, who grudged the superiority of their literary predecessors and sought before all things to invent something new. They were directly anti-social; for the methods which they employed or approved were as tyrannical as those of any despotism. It was only very few persons who adopted the full Nihilist programme, but these reposed on the indifference, or even approval, of a discontented population. A generous instinct induced many students to go down to the people, and to try to mix themselves with it. With Russian simplicity, these men thought it necessary to get away from their own identity ; and, though they never succeeded in making themselves into peasants, they from that time represented a further leaven of discontent, or at least a nucleus around which other malcontents could group themselves. Their very devotion made them convincing; and if the peasant has come to entertain wider interests and higher aspirations, if he sets more value upon education and progress, this is very largely due to them. Meanwhile, the local councils brought to their work a very similar spirit of devotion and principles which, if not revolutionary, at least bore the stamp of novelty. In the Zemstvo, or County Council, public-spirited men of good family, who might scorn to enter the official ranks, now found a worthy field of public work. As the system of local government was at the bottom incompatible with a continuance of an absolute autocracy, the Zemstva were always stimulated by the hope that their sphere of activity would sooner or later be extended. The Church, which in Russia is ordinarily in very close touch with the people, could not fail to be influenced by the prevailing spirit of change; when old traditions were at a discount, there were even priests who freely admitted that some of the ceremonies of their religion were obsolete, and defended them only on the plea that they were suitable to the peasant intelligence. On the other hand, the wounding of old instincts was rapidly bringing about a reaction in favour of all that was old-fashioned. The bureaucrats had found themselves in complete discredit after the exposures of the Crimean War, and they too for some time had to yield to the fashion of Liberalism, and to acknowledge many of the faults of the system ; but, as the reforms came to be carried out, there were more and more bureaucrats who shook their heads and asked how the Emperor was going to rule the country if he kicked away all his old supports. These men, who felt themselves abandoned, were naturally in touch with those less enlightened country gentry who were still smarting under the effects of the emancipation. To all of them alike society seemed to be breaking up, and the Emperor seemed to be wilfully going to his ruin. Feeling that they had been disowned by him, they yielded to the apathy so common in Russia and left him to face his own fate alone. The Emperor himself was no Peter the Great; while the reforms were still in progress, he several times asked himself whether his nearest advisers were not right and whether he had not, like Frankenstein, raised a monster which he could not control.　Until the wall of autocracy could be still further broken down, it was impossible for him to form an accurate estimate of the various moods of different sections of his people.　Several times he passed into a mood of reaction, which was at once reflected upon the life of the people, and further embittered all the champions of change.　The prolonged but abortive rising in Poland did not tend to confirm him in his Liberalism; and now into the confusion which surrounded the Throne came a still more disturbing factor.

Russia was always peculiarly dependent upon education from the West.　Since the French Revolution, the ties which bound her to Europe had become far more close.　If any European country were to approve of the work of Alexander II. it ought to have been England and France, those two Liberal and constitutional countries which had in the Crimean War proved the superiority of their principles, and from which Alexander II. had been man enough to learn.　A war had started the reform movement; a war was to bring it to an end.　The English mind, which had been only mildly interested in the reforms and only very moderately informed about them, still identified the Russian Government and the Russian people, and regarded both as one vast threatening force of despotism; while they respected us, we still feared them, and still held to the formula that any advance of Russia was selfish and dangerous, and that any issue by Russia from her hopelessly land-locked position threatened our naval empire. This was not patriotism; it was an unworthy distrust of ourselves, and it caused us to misinterpret one of the most generous outbursts of Russian national feeling.　Reaction had come in England as it had come in Russia, and, in the words of Disraeli, British interests were become our standard for judging the affairs of the world.

We are not able to estimate the influence of the reforms in Russia upon the misgoverned peoples of Turkey.　But the Christian subjects of the Sultan live under conditions **1874.** which make economic progress impossible.　Periodically some section of this population finds its conditions of life so intolerable that it dares all dangers to change them.　The people of Bosnia and Herzegovina rose against the Sultan.　The war was with them a defensive one, and they were able to hold in check

considerable military forces. Their prolonged struggle was bound
to awaken the keenest sympathy amongst their kinsmen and
co-religionists of Servia and Montenegro, who knew what
the Turkish yoke was, and had with difficulty freed them- **June,**
selves from it. These joined in the war; the disturb- **1876.**
ance in the Balkhans assumed proportions which claimed
the interference of Europe. The Emperor Alexander was by
nature peace-loving, and, as we have seen, he had special reasons
for not wishing for a war at this time; but by now Russian
volunteers were pouring into Servia. Russia also was Slav and
of the Greek Church; and the national feeling was such that
no peddling solution of the Balkhan question could be
accepted. The Emperor was content to act frankly **Dec. 24.**
in concert with the other Powers. Common remonstrances were indeed drawn up, but the Porte treated them with
polite contempt, and it transpired that the British Government,
being far more full of the fear of Russia than of indignation
against the Turks, was taking a line which tended to strengthen
the resistance of the Sultan. The Porte went through
the farce of calling a National Parliament as a bid for **Nov. 23.**
the support of the constitutional Powers, and this Parliament rejected with special contempt those proposals which had
been separately put forward by Russia. Russian blood
had already flowed in the cause of Servia; and, as the **April 1,**
so-called Concert had achieved nothing, Alexander was **1877.**
compelled by the public feeling to carry through the
matter alone. The war which followed gave many more proofs
that the Russian autocracy was still a quite inefficient
military instrument. The notes of Count Loris **April 24.**
Melikoff, who commanded in Armenia, show that
court intrigues were still more powerful than the interests of
the nation. For a long time the main Russian army was baffled
by the splendid determination of Osman Pasha, and kept waiting
outside the fortress of Plevna; but when once the Russians passed
the Balkhans the Turkish resistance seemed to break up, and
the road to Constantinople lay open. Alexander had promised
Europe that he would not annex the city: he did not even
attempt to enter it; but a British fleet was despatched to the
Bosphorus. The Turks at San Stefano treated for peace; Russia

claimed but little territory for herself, but she created a strong
Bulgaria, and practically settled in advance the questions
March 3, which have latterly been agitating Macedonia. Alexander
1878. was, however, persuaded to submit the treaty to the
revision of all the Powers in Congress at Berlin. The
decisions of the Congress were practically arranged in advance,
and were all hostile to Russia. The claims of the Christian
Slavs of the Balkhans suffered from this hostility. Macedonia
was thrust back into Turkey, and Bulgaria was thus
July 13, brought back to narrower limits. Russia was further
1878. embroiled with her ally Roumania by her acceptance of
a district of that country, for which the Roumanians
received inadequate compensation. Meanwhile Austria, who had
this time done nothing to free the Slavs, was authorised to occupy
the large province of Bosnia; and England, the chief champion of
the integrity of Turkey, in return for a guarantee of Turkey's
Asiatic dominions against Russia, obtained the island of Cyprus.
Certainly the English policy was clever, but both its soundness
and its honesty were more than doubtful. The Russian Plenipotentiary spoke of the signing of the Treaty as the worst day's
work in his life. Bismarck, who had claimed to be the honest
broker, was execrated all over Russia. After winning the war,
Russia had been humbled in the Treaty; and she was not even
able to reap the moral reward of her interference on behalf of the
Balkhan States, which were now put under the guarantee of the
whole Concert of Powers. "I see here," said a Bulgarian,
"many Russian graves, but no French or English graves."

Such was the recognition meted out by Europe to the Emperor
who had carried through the reforms. It discredited him with
his own people, and it discredited Europe with them too. Any
irritation from the side of Europe leads in Russia to a revival of
the old Slavophil suspicions. The reaction rapidly gained in
strength and volume, the hopes of the Liberals grew faint, and
the Emperor was left to deal as best he could with the war
between the Nihilists and the bureaucrats, to both of which
parties he was equally distasteful. The Nihilist temperament is
typical of a whole generation of the Russian Intelligence; but the
actual Terrorists who waged war against Alexander II. were
a very small body of men—perhaps not more than three or four

hundred. A much larger section of the Radicals did not believe
in terrorism. It would be ridiculous to think that if a man
murders someone else for political reasons he necessarily represents a well-founded political grievance: murder is not a sane
way of conducting a political campaign; but the attempts on
the lives of officials which now took place were so numerous as
to prove that the moral sense of the public, whether rightly or
wrongly, did not vigorously condemn them. After one
of the first of them, that of Karakózoff, the great **1866.**
Liberal Hertzen wrote an article condemning all such
methods as proper only to barbarous peoples; but from that
moment his famous newspaper, *The Bell*, which had long been
a better mirror of Russian opinion than any other, ceased to
have influence. The very mystery with which the attempts were
enveloped testified at least to the neutrality of the public.

As official after official was attacked, the Emperor found himself
more and more involved in his fatal waverings. Murder is not
an argument except to a coward, and Alexander was a brave man;
but it is one thing to see yourself in danger, and another to see
your officials struck down all round you. What was the way out?
Under the pressure of events the Emperor returned to the idea
of further reform. It was the Liberals who were the middle
term between the Emperor and his people, and it was precisely
because Liberal opinion in Russia was so weak that the civil war
between the extremes was possible. At this time a
notable member of the County Council of Chernígoff, Mr. **1878.**
Petrunkyévich, managed to arrange with the revolu-
tionists a short truce, during which he was to try the effect of
more moderate claims; but the address in favour of a constitution
which he proposed to his local Zemstvo was suppressed, and he
himself was exiled to another part of Russia. At last
the Nihilists published a sentence of death against the **Dec. 4.**
Emperor; there had already been several attempts on his
life; on February 17, 1880, sixty soldiers of the Guard were killed
by an explosion at the Winter Palace. He naturally could
not concede even the minimum of their revolutionary **Jan. 26,**
demands; the programme which they put forward would **1880.**
not have been approved by one hundredth part of the
Russian peoples; but in making Loris Melikoff practically

dictator of St. Petersburg, he at least tried the effect of a vigorous repression of disorder accompanied by, an attempt to improve the system of Government administration.   At this time several suggestions of reform were considered by the Government, and at last the Emperor so far yielded to the advice of his counsellors as to summon elected representatives from the County and Town Councils, and even from those provinces where such Councils did not exist, to form with members nominated by the Crown a consultative national Commission.[1]   After all, when once County Councils existed all over Russia, it was only consequent to summon their representatives to St. Petersburg, and this alone would be an immense step towards the triumph of the principle of representation.   The summons was decided upon, then postponed, and finally sent to the Government Press.   While it had had not as yet been made public, the Emperor went for his customary drive through the streets of St. Peters- **Mar. 13,** burg.   He avoided the Nevsky Prospekt, which, as it **1881.** happened, was undermined at more than one point, and turned down the road which led along the Catherine Canal. Here a man threw a bomb at the carriage.   The Emperor, who had escaped injury, got out to look after the wounded.   It was while he was thus engaged that a second bomb was thrown at him; he was torn to pieces, and only survived to be carried to the palace.   The murderers had put back the clock in Russia for twenty-four years.

The new Emperor Alexander III., as has been said, "mounted to the throne as a soldier mounts the breach."   For Russian sovereigns the moment of accession has often been critical. Nicholas I. became Emperor in the midst of the Decembrist rising, and remained reactionary to the end of his days. Alexander III. was a rough, honest man of narrow intelligence, immensely laborious, and devoted to his duty.   He could not consider that the murder of his father, the Tsar Liberator, was a proof that Russia had now become ripe for constitutional government.   He was advised to issue a summons for an assembly, and to make this his father's legacy to the nation ; but while terror induces some men to make concessions and others to stiffen

[1] " The Constitution of Count Loris-Melikoff and his private letters " (Berlin) ; pp. 82–8

themselves, it is only a rare man who can go on as if nothing had happened. The summons was recalled, and Russia was plunged into a reaction which was to last almost to the present day. The public opinion of Russia was as yet so imperfectly developed that it is hard to say how far the country welcomed this reaction. Certainly there still remained a mass of arrears for reformers to deal with; but also there had latterly come to be more and more volume in the voice that suggested that the reformers were going too fast. Anyhow, the Government proceeded without regard for the nation; but the Liberals at this time were almost paralysed by the murderous blow which the Emperor's death had dealt to them, and they submitted to their fate without any show of general resistance. For the present, Russia was to hope everything, not from the influence of public opinion, but from the personal honesty of her Emperor. Alexander, indeed, worked very hard in order to correct the abuses of officialdom, but he was engaged in a struggle with the impossible, and it became more and more obvious that for an empire as large as Russia to depend upon the knowledge and judgment of a single man was nothing less than disastrous. If proofs of this are needed, we find them in the increase of abuses during this period and in the early end of Alexander, who succumbed to his impossible task.

Even in the most reactionary policy one can often discover some positive and constructive principle. Certainly, when Alexander initiated a period which was to correspond in date and character with that of our own Imperial reaction, there was real work for him to do. He had to re-establish order, not only in public life, but in men's minds. There were many questions of practical administration which had to be dealt with. The peasants needed a period of quiet progress in order to get used to their new-found liberty; the Church was partially disorganised, and needed to quietly assimilate some of the lessons of the great reforms. Russia, who had been gorging herself upon ideas suggested by the West, wanted time to recover her own self-consciousness. She was politically isolated by the effects of the Crimean War, and she needed to re-establish her influence in the Councils of Europe. This she could only hope to do by a policy of peace; and peace with the West would give her an opportunity of gradually developing her movement of national expansion eastwards. But all this might have been done without the prohibition of all private initiative, and without the aggressive attitude which the Government thought it necessary to take up against all that suggested Western civilisation. It is unreasonable to excuse the reactionary policy on the plea that Russia had a mission to teach the East; it is only her own education from the West that can ever enable her to do so. But this second reaction, like second reactions in several other countries, was hopelessly doctrinaire. It was when the Italian army was marching on Rome, and when the Papal State was soon to become a thing of the past, that a peculiarly vacillating Pope declared himself to be infallible. In the same way, the men now in power in Russia tried to turn reaction into a formulated political creed. They even wrote books on it; and that no upholder of autocracy would ever do till he felt that the ground was disappearing beneath his feet. The natural instincts have a right to rise and protest against the deductions of modern reasoning; but that man who tries to borrow the weapon of reason from the armoury of his enemies in order to prove that reason itself is to be suspected, though he may interest us by his ingenuity, is only proving to us his own want of conviction. Such is the effect produced by the notable book of Mr. Pobyedonóstseff, which I have analysed in another place. Mr. Pobyedonóstseff saw that the Russian Intelligence had issued a challenge to the religious instincts of Russia. He took up this challenge, and boldly suggested that religion should be used as a weapon to combat intelligence. It would have been nothing if a professor in his study had put forward so curious a programme; but Mr. Pobyedonóstseff was early able to secure the ear of the new Emperor, and continued his hold on the Throne far into the next reign. As a kind of political confessor, he was able to see that his programme was carried out; and he himself, as Lay Procurator of the Holy Synod, established such a tyranny over the whole Church system as to make it one of the most powerful engines for the realisation of his central idea.

This, then, was a period of doctrinaire negation. To be quit of the inconvenience caused by the invasion of Western ideas, a kind of wall was built along the Russian frontier, and the system of passports was now so exacting as to make it difficult for the Russian subject to travel even from one part of the Empire to another. It would not be reasonable to imagine that it was ever really possible to break that connection between Russia and the West, which had been created by Nature itself; it will be remembered that at many points of the frontier the population is Polish on both sides. Inside the Empire, the passport restrictions fall heaviest of all on the peasants; and if, at every change of sleeping-place, it is necessary to depend upon the goodwill of the police, clearly there is no resource for the humbler and poorer of the population against an aggravating series of petty vexations. It has even been said that anyone who is caught in Russia without a passport is sure to be an honest man, because the manufacture of forged documents is so extensive as to provide for anyone who wishes to be on the safe side. But it was not only in ordinances that the new principle of suspicion found expression. Both the Government and its officials made unconvincing efforts to show their sense of contempt for the West, and, with the help of the censorship, a vogue was given to the creed that Russia is quite different from the rest of the world, and that if certain ideas apply to other countries they for that reason probably do not apply to Russia.

It was not enough to close the door to Europe; there were Europeans inside Russia who were equally dangerous. If Russia was once more to learn that she was Russian, perhaps these aliens could be convinced that they were Russian too; at least, the Government possessed one weapon of persuasion—force. Thus the period of doctrinaire reaction is marked by unprovoked attacks on alien races and on alien confessions of faith. Since the abortive rising of 1863, Poland had ceased to be governmentally a separate unit in the Empire; the old geographical divisions of the kingdom had been broken down, and the Polish language was forbidden in the schools, in the railway stations, and in public offices. It was also made very difficult for the Poles to retain their landed property in what had once been Lithuania. It would have been dangerous to attack so strong a **1887.** corporation as the Roman Catholic Church; but there was in White Russia an undefended sect which, though much less offensive to the Orthodox mind, lay far more at the mercy of the Government. The Uniats were those who had agreed to acknowledge the nominal supremacy of the Pope while retaining the right

to believe and worship in their own way. They were an
Orthodox peasant race, who by their tenacity had been able to
impose this one-sided bargain on their Polish persecutors. When
Poland was swept from the map, it might have been
1595. anticipated that the Uniats would sooner or later return
of themselves to the Orthodox Church; but though
Polish persecution had failed to drive them into the Roman
Catholic communion, the Russian Government succeeded in doing
this. In 1839 a petition was presented to Nicholas I. from a
certain number of Uniats; they asked re-admission into the
Orthodox Church. The Emperor, yielding to their request, by
a stroke of the pen made all the Uniats Orthodox. Russian
priests were now sent down to the Uniat churches; they found
the doors closed against them and the local population collected
outside. Now was the time for police and Cossacks. The persecution of the Uniats has continued off and on almost to the
present time. While Mr. Pobyedonóstseff has been in power it
has been regular and vigorous. In the first Duma there was one
Polish peasant whose family had suffered for its faith for three
generations.

Poland had for a long time contained an enormous proportion
of the Jews of the whole world. It was not likely that this race
of wanderers, oppressed by all and armed only with its cunning,
1881— should escape persecution at such a time as this. Taxes
8. were imposed upon the Jewish dress, candles, and meat;
it was made very difficult for Jews to travel into the
interior of the Empire, even for the collection of their just debts;
Jews were forbidden to own land ; Jews were herded together in
the towns of certain areas ; they were forbidden to live within a
certain distance of the frontier. As it was they who made the
best use of educational opportunities, the percentage of Jewish
scholars was cut down, even in the schools which were built inside
the pale of Jewish settlement and chiefly out of Jewish money.
Naturally enough, many Jews saw their only safety in leaving the
country; and the Government, which at one time was ready to
get rid of them on any terms, encouraged the Zionist movement aiming at the establishment of a Jewish colony somewhere
outside Europe.

Almost equally hard was the lot of the Baltic Germans, who

had been even subserviently loyal to the Empire from the time
of their first annexation, and had taken a disproportionately large
share in its administrative and military work. They had supplied
an endless number of officials and generals to Russia. As servants
they had been only too exact; they are to be found in every Russian
chancellery, in which it is said that one German can do the work
of three Russians. And heaven preserve us from Russian law as
interpreted by Germans! The Russian official may not take a
Russian law very seriously, but one can be sure that the German
official will. The one offence of the Germans was that they had
a culture of their own, far superior to anything that had been
developed by Russia. They never claimed general political
rights; they only asked to continue to administer their own
part of Russia by their own bye-laws. But German culture
was dangerous, and Protestantism was dangerous. The
Lettish and Esthonian peasants of the Baltic provinces **1882.**
had always very naturally hated their German masters,
and they were now encouraged to rise against them. When
German estates were sacked, Count Ignatieff is said to have
declared that " it was not the business " of the Government to
interfere. The German language was excluded from schools in
towns where the population was chiefly German. The University
of Dorpat, a little oasis of German culture, was entirely
Russianised. The professors were ordered within a **1887.**
given period to read their lectures in Russian; half of
them resigned, and were replaced by men who were practically
Russian officials; and to Dorpat, as to Warsaw, were sent those
Russian students who were considered not trustworthy, and were
therefore thought to need a closer system of supervision. Priests
were sent down to conduct an Orthodox campaign in these
provinces, and one of them who was able to secure a large
number of nominal converts was rewarded with a civil decoration, the only fitting recompense for such services. Those of
the "converts" who wished to return to their own Church
found the way barred by the Russian law which makes it
a penal offence to leave the Orthodox confession. Pastors,
who received back their erring parishioners or consented to
marry a couple of whom one might be Orthodox, were sentenced to imprisonment; one such pastor, a man of seventy

years, universally respected, died before the sentence could be
carried out.

It was only in the next reign that similar measures were
applied to the Finns. Here they were even less justifiable.
The Finns are one of the oldest constitutional monarchies in
Europe ; when they were annexed to Russia, their old rights
were guaranteed to them. They are a people of higher culture
than the Russians, and their one offence was that the Russians
might learn from them to ask for a constitution too. To a
Government so autocratic as the Russian, the possibility
of free speech so near to St. Petersburg might indeed seem
to be a danger. Yet in this case it was the Finns who
were conservative and the Emperor who was revolutionary.
Encroachments were made on all their national rights,
the Finnish army was dispersed all over Russia, and Finland was filled with Russian soldiers. Their Customs system
and even their constitutional system were attacked, and yet it
was only after long provocation and by the isolated murder
of General Bobrikoff that they gave Russia any excuse
1904. for employing violence against them. As the Finns
were the last to lose their liberties, so they were
destined to be the first to recover them ; and Finland, which
might have remained out of touch with Russian politics, has
become a kind of barometer of freedom for the whole Empire.

What is true of Finland is also true of the Poles and the
Jews. All being alike aggravated by the weight of a common
oppression, have in the last two years united to seek a common
salvation. If the Russian reactionaries of 1905–1906 point
derisively at the union of Russian Liberals with all the Western
aliens, they are only confessing how completely the system for
which they stand has failed.

The same policy which penalised the aliens for being aliens
also penalised the Russian Intelligents for being intelligent. The
Russian Universities had been founded with the object of producing well-informed officials. During the first reaction of
Nicholas I. they had been kept under the closest supervision ;
but the students of all Russia were like a kind of republican
corporation which stood solid for the principles of liberty ; and,
with the rare generosity of Russian character, instead of using

their special opportunities exclusively for their personal advantage, they devoted themselves to sowing the seed of intelligence all over the country. During this period they were more suspect than ever to the Government. The Rectors named by the Minister were expected to be instruments of repression; the inspectors, whose only duty was to forbid and to punish, became more important than the professors themselves; police agents assumed the dress of students and sat with them in their classes; all association and intercommunication of the students was carefully watched; clubs and societies could only exist by defying the police. The students, infected with Nihilism, were certainly revolutionary in spirit, and needed watching; but this régime taught each successive generation to take up an attitude hostile to the Government, and to government in general. As yet most of the professors confined themselves to teaching their subjects and obeying regulations; and many of the students, when they had to set about making a livelihood, were ready to give up their young ideals; but the Universities as a whole were already fortresses of the spirit of opposition. It was the same even with the Secondary schools, the Gymnasia, and the Real schools. The Government did not found any more Universities during this period, with the significant exception of that of Tomsk, in Siberia.[1] It preferred to found technical institutes, as being more practically useful and not so likely to foster abstract thought; but all these new Higher-Schools became as revolutionary as the Universities. In no profession is the proportion of Radicals higher than amongst engineers; and indeed, to deal with economic questions was the soundest way of learning the inadequacy of the system of administration.

Whereas the country and the country instincts were always being extolled as supports of the Government, the towns lay under a kind of ban. In the towns where supervision was much closer the police were not only proportionately far more numerous but they confined themselves more exclusively to the work of prohibition; yet all the while a stream of peasants was pouring into the towns and later returned to carry the town intelligence into the country.[1] As the country had been taken as the main unit for local government, the town councils held a position subordinate to that of the

[1] Significant as typical of the idea of Eastern expansion.

Zemstva. Inhabitants of the towns had to contribute both to the one and to the other. Yet the Zemstva themselves came to be suspect to the Government, and during the Second Reaction they, as the champions of economic progress, had to struggle hard for their very existence. Thus the country itself, which had been looked upon as the natural support of autocracy, took the initiative in the demand for constructive reform. The Government narrowed the franchise of election for the Zemstva and cut down their powers. As it had now come to suspect every non-Russian nationality and nearly every class in Russia itself, it placed its hopes on the willing obedience of the most ignorant of the population, that is, the peasants.

Reverting to the old Slavophil formula of Tsar, Church, and people, the Government counted the peasants as being almost the only trustworthy representatives of the popular tradition. Alexander III. was at least a peasant Tsar. Amongst the Cantonal Elders assembled from all Russia he felt that he and his family could walk without a guard. Several times the Government, which at the emancipation had made all the peasants its debtors, remitted large amounts of dues. A Peasants' Bank was founded to enable the small holder to borrow money at low interest in order to increase his holding, but in the very same building there was established a twin Bank which existed for the purpose of selling the land of the gentry to peasants. This Bank was paid in paper, and, in spite of the difference of value, demanded cash from the peasant buyer, and the whole operation tended to become a means of enabling highly connected gentry to sell their land to advantage ; anyhow the price of land went up. Meanwhile there were instituted Land Captains, or official squires, who had a right to interfere in all the peasants' concerns, and seemed to the peasant mind like a partial revival of serfdom. No officials ever came into so close a contact with the peasants, and none were ever so unpopular with them.

Following out the Slavophil programme, Mr. Pobyedonóstseff tried to magnify religion as a bulwark against modern ideas. Undoubtedly there was room for a Church revival in Russia, and to a certain extent a real revival took place, but Mr. Pobyedonóstseff by preference appointed to high posts in the Church those persons who would be docile instruments of his policy. He surrounded himself with a number of place-hunters, and through them intimidated the local clergy into being the instruments of a political reaction. Priests were instructed to preach according to the ideas of the Government, and to the Government religion meant something hostile to intellect. Thus to set religion and intelligence at each other's throats was to do an amount of mischief which only religious men can adequately estimate and deplore. The triumph of this system was crowned by the canonisation of an honest but ignorant peasant, Seraphim, and by the excommunication of the greatest of the Russian Intelligents, Leo Tolstoy, for his endeavour to renovate the religious sense as he understood it.

It remained to magnify the Tsar. The Government had entered upon a policy of friendship with France, which, different as were the instincts of the two countries, at least enabled both of them to recover their rightful influence in Europe. This policy implied a truce with the West; and indeed the Russian Government wished to have as little to do with the West as possible. Russia thus succeeded in recovering her credit in Europe; and perhaps the chief importance of the Peace Congress of the Hague is that it crowned the legitimate efforts of Russia to repair the breaches made by the Congress of Berlin. It also enabled the young Tsar Nicholas to figure in the eyes of his peasants as the man who had enforced peace on all Europe; and this assumption has been developed in some of the reactionary "appeals" of 1905–1906.

The reactionary policy could hardly have been carried out without at least the concurrence of some section of the nation. The Press, it is true, had to work at this time under restrictions which made all genuine expression of thought practically impossible, and condemned the journalist to be what Shchedrin calls a "froth skimmer." The great Slavophil Katkoff was dead, and had been succeeded by men who were willing to exploit, or at least avail themselves of, the favour of the Government. In St. Petersburg Mr. A. S. Suvórin, editor of the *Novoe Vremya*, a journalist who in ordinary times might have been an able champion of moderate Liberal opinion, set himself to study how much could be said at a given moment without offending either the Government or his increasingly democratic readers. Mr. Suvórin's work will prove to have had its value in Russian history. Pliable and even changeable, he at least showed from day to day that Russian public opinion had refused to die, and the " Little Letters " which he wrote under his own name bear the stamp of a sufficiently convincing personality. Very different is the case of the *Moscow Gazette*, once the organ of Katkoff. This paper passed into the hands of Mr. Gringmut, who, hedged round by the protection of the Government and speaking boldly as if in the name of all Russia, condemned all nations but the Russian, and all religions but the Orthodox, appealed to racial and religious spites, and urged Russia upon the path of Eastern conquest. There were always a certain number of country gentlemen who held official posts, and took their views from the *Moscow Gazette*. Even newspapers and men of much more ordinary views shared in the propaganda of advance eastwards.

Meanwhile the bureaucracy, now that rigid restrictions made the expression of public opinion impossible, was becoming more and more demoralised. Nicholas II., who acceded to the throne in 1894, was in no way the equal either of his grandfather or of his father. It was already clear that the reaction had exceeded normal limits; and the natural work of this reign would have been to co-ordinate the liberal aspirations of Alexander II. with the restoration of authority which was the desire of Alexander III. Much had been done by the Russian people itself to prepare the way for such a policy. The Zemstva, after they had got over the novelty of their new responsibilities, and had abandoned as impracticable some of their earlier claims, had settled down to constructive economical work. By the opening of schools and hospitals, and by ministering to the agricultural needs of the peasants, they were helping to change the whole face of the country. The landowners, whose high birth and instinct of authority qualified them to be the leaders of country life, had thrown themselves with a remarkable devotion and breadth of purpose into this national work ; and at last the existence of this new middle term between despotism and revolution was creating the nucleus of a great Liberal party, which would offer far more hope of a satisfactory solution than either of the extremes could do. On the one side this practical spirit was being gradually extended to the mass of the Russian Intelligents. A large number of professional men found in the Zemstvo system a sphere of practical work which put them in close touch with the labouring classes, and educated in them the sense of responsibility. Even the revolutionary bodies felt this influence. The terrorists had practically disappeared; and even the most important section of the Social Democrats set itself to study more exclusively economic questions. On the other side this general study of economics was bound to lead to a more constructive political programme. Some members of the Zemstva had met as occasion offered to discuss their common work, and some few Zemstva had kept alive the claim for political reform. The Zemstvo of Tver, in congratulating the young Emperor on his accession, dared to ask that he should listen to the voice of the population as well as to that of officialdom, and that officials, like other people, should be kept to the observance of the law; but these very moderate requests were characterised by the Emperor as senseless dreams: surely he can hardly have meant to say that the population must not expect to be listened to, and that the officials need not keep the law. Nicholas was no strong hard-hearted man; his nature was gentle and sentimental; and in his answer to the Tver address we see a petulance prompted by the sense of weakness, an attempt to resent the suggestion that he himself was insufficient for all the needs of Russia. We are reminded of Louis XVI., who when threatening to dissolve his first parliament had the want of humour to say, "Seul je ferai le bien de mes peuples." We must remember that Nicholas II. was brought up in a very atmosphere of reaction, whose impossible assumptions had almost become a second nature to him. It would have been easier to have discussed the ideas of Pobyedonóstseff with Pobyedonóstseff himself than to have tried to uproot them from the mind of his pupil; such is the evil that can be done by a doctrinaire in power. Historically it has been the misfortune of Nicholas II. that he succeeded at a moment when Russia had naturally come to the end of a period, and that he himself, with whom lay at that time the initiative of starting a new period, had not enough vigour to do so. As Pobyedonóstseff had condemned the human race and remained in power to rule it, so the men who had risen in his time and who had nothing like his honesty of conviction, now fell away from their faith in his or in any other dogma, and were content simply to exploit an accidental state of things in which they happened to find themselves at the top of society. The Court itself, while being always further and further isolated from all knowledge of the nation, began to split up into a number of warring cliques and tendencies, and there was no supreme will to give any unity of direction. "In the time of Alexander III.," says one who knew both him and his successor, "at least there was a man: the Grand-Dukes had to keep their places; there were intrigues, but at least the game was tolerably open; now the atmosphere has become ignorant and narrow, and each courtier makes his own bid for power." In fact, the autocracy had reached that moment when it of itself cancelled out for sheer want of will in the nominal ruler, and degenerated into a selfish and unrepresentative oligarchy. The Grand Dukes, then, were important factors at Court; and there were men of old family who were equally convinced that the world had been made for them and for their class. In such an atmosphere morality, whether public or private, had but little force; for instance, sailors were seen in the streets beating the carpets of a lady who happened to be mistress of a high-born official at the head of the navy. When during the Japanese war Madame Balletta appeared in magnificent jewellery, one critic whispered, "There goes a good warship," and another suggested, "C'est une toilette à bas l'Etat" ("à Balletta"). Even the more honest of these high-born courtiers were become almost incapable of sustained effort, though they held posts of great honour, and often of great responsibility. The real work was done and the State was governed by men of very different origins; these were in no sense representatives of the old nobility, but new men who had risen to the top of the bureaucratic service, whether by docility or by will-power or by a judicious mixture of the two. Mr. Goremýkin, it is true, represented the Conservative[1] landed gentry. Mr. Witte, who ousted him from office, rose from humble beginnings. He was far superior in ability to the mediocre bureaucrats around him, and never took the trouble to school himself to win the good-will of his competitors. His great experience in the administration of railways helped to raise

[1] *I.e.*, as opposed to Reactionary.

him to the post of Minister of Finance; and in this position
he was all-important to a system which forgot the business
principles that are indispensable to a large concern, and yet
needed great supplies of money. At the same time the Court
took as little pains as Mr. Witte to disguise its antipathy. Mr.
Plehwe, who, in the absence of Witte, succeeded in ousting him in
his turn, was a typical servant of autocracy, who was faithful to
it because he had not the breadth to see anything outside it, and
whose narrow ambition made him scheme for an authority for
which he was quite unqualified. The officials of such a time,
not knowing what Court breeze would prevail at a given moment,
naturally confined themselves to not disobeying orders. It was
safest not to indulge in an initiative of any kind, unless one felt
sure that one was anticipating the desires of somebody who
to-morrow would be supreme; and even then one might be disowned by him. Thus morality was dissociated still further from
official work. Some officials had committed generous indiscre-
tions in their youth, and were now before all things anxious to
retain their posts. Again, the absence of public morality
naturally prejudiced private morality; and men, who spent their
office hours marking time, might reward themselves by a
prodigal use of their private freedom. While the Government
was almost monopolised by a new self-made aristocracy, the democratic instinct gained ground everywhere. Very few Russians
are snobs; and it now came to be a point of honour to scorn the
opportunities for personal aggrandisement which officialdom
could offer. The anti-governmental sense grew fast, and the
ordinary Russian took pleasure in sneering at all that was official;
but this exclusion from public responsibilities naturally ended by
accentuating the laziness to which Russians are so prone; the
unofficial Russian was content with being a lazy critic. At this
time the decadence, which everywhere in Europe is following on
the great political convulsions of the nineteenth century, had in
Russia so wide a vogue as to seem almost the most prominent
feature of the life of the time. Pushed back into private life,
men philosophised on their sensations and analysed their nerves;
and many with absolute cynicism set themselves to secure at
least a short-sighted gratification of sensual instincts. From
this state of things society was awakened by what has been called

the "shuffling of the nerves,"—the tremendous sensation of the Japanese war.

The Eastern policy was complementary of the anti-Western policy. The Westernising school had long since been described as the " Western light," and the Slavophil school as the " Eastern light." Sometimes the Government had put out all the lights together, as when the Slavophil Aksakoff fell under the heavy displeasure of the censorship; but the degenerate Slavophils of the period of reaction could hardly be accused of trying to kindle any light at all; in fact, any illumination of public opinion would be likely to show up their own isolation. Yet, as enemies of the West, they naturally preached expansion eastwards. Apart from this, it seems impossible for a whole generation to be fed on simple negations; if the West was barred off, the East had to be opened, if only as an outlet for superfluous energy, which might otherwise become dangerous. The programme of Eastern advance pleased many classes of Russian society. To the Emperor it not only promised an extension of dominions on apparently easy terms; it even tended to Orientalise the conception of the monarch in Russia itself, and thus to make him more despotic than ever. The Church might naturally accept the mission of extending Christendom, and the weapons by which this would be done had been sufficiently acceptable to devoted Christians in other countries. The peasants, who, in consequence of the increase of population, already began to feel their lack of land, at one time emigrated to Siberia in such numbers that it was necessary for the Government to regulate the operation. Even the Russian Intelligent, seeing no hope of political rights, might throw himself into the task of developing the economy of the new settlements; in the late nineties, many young professional men looked forward with enthusiasm to the hope of interesting work in Siberia. But those who had most to gain from eastward expansion were those who would have the direction of it, that is, the Court favourites. To these was opened up a vast prospect of unlimited speculation. Even the conflicting cliques might find a meeting point in this programme; for to Mr. Witte, the champion of peace and prosperity, fell the initiative of the great scheme of the Trans-Siberian Railway.

The Government decided, then, to give prominence to the

Eastern idea. Possibly the journey of Nicholas II., while he was still Crown Prince, through Japan, China, and his own future dominions was little more than a general tour of education ; but at least he signalised his passage through Vladivostók by cutting the first sod of the great railway at its farthest end, and Prince Úkhtomsky, who was the annalist of his travels, made a very definite appeal to the energies of Young Russia, inviting men of enterprise to come out to the East, where there was plenty of elbow room, and where every man who wielded authority could be almost as free as a little Tsar. The railway, though it cannot be said to have finally accomplished its object, was at least a very great achievement, and developed immense possibilities for the future. It helped to identify public opinion with the Eastern policy in general ; for, after Russia had laid down so many thousand versts of railway in order to get an Eastern outlet to the sea, even the average Russian would certainly make sacrifices for the preservation of this outlet, and would naturally look with suspicion on any Power that might threaten it. The Eastern idea helped, by implication, to aggravate the Russian mind against England. During the interval of peace with Europe after the Crimean war, Russia had pushed forward her line of advance through Central Asia, in the direction of India ; her battles were chiefly against the deserts ; the peoples of Turkestan did not possess any compactness or unity which could be formidable to the invader. So far as India was concerned, this advance was but an attempt to go forward in some direction in order to give a chance of hitting back at England, whose fears prompted her persistently to block every outlet to Russia. This idea was acceptable to the mass of the nation ; but there were probably only a very few Russians who really hoped for a conquest of India. Kryloff had long since, in an admirable fable, mocked at this dream.[1]

The Russian line of advance through Siberia was far more like a road than like an empire. Western Siberia, it is true, was being gradually filled with emigrants from Russia, and here her

[1]   " Of things in no way us concerning
    There's many a one of us that gladly prophesies ;
    The fate of India, with all its whens and whys,
        So clearly he descries ;
    Yet see, before his very eyes
    His house has nearly finished burning."

policy of expansion was indeed national; but in Eastern Siberia
the government is military, and the Russians are settled only
along the main road, branching off in some cases to follow
the valley of some river.   So far from Russia being concentrated in her might in this far corner of the world, her
difficulty was to resist the real invasion of Chinese labour.
Having traversed great empty distances, she had reached a point
where a huge mass of population, stubborn in adherence to the
oldest traditional instincts, blocked her further passage.   It was
not entirely without reason that Russian politicians talked of
the Yellow Danger.   Morally, as geographically, Russian expansion in Siberia was a long thin line stretched to the point of
bursting.   National aspirations associated themselves with the
possession of Port Arthur; but in pushing forward their specula-
tions into Corea the Eastern group lost all touch with the vital
interests of the nation.

Meanwhile the sudden transformation of Japan had raised up
against Russia an enemy far more formidable at this point than
England.   How deep this transformation goes we cannot yet say;
but at least Japan owed her new strength to her willingness to
learn from the West.   We cannot picture a Japanese army
equipped with bows and arrows attacking Port Arthur.   And it
was not only a question of arms : the renovated Japanese army
was filled with that instinct of personal patriotism which implies
that the individual plays a responsible part in the affairs of the
State.

It is not every generation that has the privilege of witnessing
with its own eyes one of the most momentous changes in the
history of civilisation ; yet we stand at the crisis of a whole era.
The Russian Government had run away from Europe ; it had
plunged itself into the heart of Asia, and its advocates even maintained that Russia's mission in the East was justified precisely
by the fact that Russia was morally, as geographically, a semi-
Asiatic power.   In this flight from the West she found even her
Asiatic outlet blocked ; the ambitions which stood in her way
were those not merely of a Government, but of a whole nation ;
and this was precisely the one Asiatic nation which had taken its
models of government from the West, and had proved capable of
producing as good results.   The triumph of Japan over Russia

was not really a triumph of the yellow race, but a triumph of the West; and in the struggle the Russian Government, by the very formula of the reaction, was deprived of the effective support of the Russian people itself. Here, at this far corner of Asia, the Russian Government and the Japanese people fought out the battle between reaction and progress. The Russian Government was defeated by the West, which again confronted it in the Far East. It was inevitable that the triumph of the Japanese people should facilitate the triumph of the Russian people too; the Japanese would not enter the Kremlin, but the Russian people at last would do so. Forced back into the den with its own malcontent subjects,[1] the Russian Government had to face a vast movement of protest in Russia; the great spirit of transformation, which had passed from England into America and France, and from France into nearly every country in Europe, had at last rounded the circle, and coming back through Russia, brought a fresh breath of reform even into Europe itself.

Events marched fast. The Boxer movement in China was a protest against the spoliation of the East by foreign empires. When a number of Chinese crossed the river Amur to Blagovestchensk, it was realised, at least in St. Petersburg, that a disorderly mob had been sufficient to cut the thin line of advance, that Vladivostók was isolated from Russia, and that for the moment the only remaining connection lay by the interminable sea road. Russia, like other powers, was threatened by the danger to the legations of Pekin, and had to make common cause with her neighbours. She was able for a time to exploit the disorders of China to her own advantage; Manchuria became practically her own. But Japan had still to demand a reckoning for the coalition between Russia, Germany, and France which had robbed her of her gains after her war with China. The concessions which Russia had obtained in Corea led to a diplomatic war, in which at one time Japan tried to secure nothing more than a division of areas. At this moment it seemed as if dreams which were far dearer to the Russian people might be realised in the Balkhan peninsula. Again the Christian subjects of the Sultan had risen against oppression; again a kindred people already emancipated —this time the Bulgarians—was ready to join in the fray; again

[1] Compare the connection between the battle of Bouvines and Magna Charta.

the concert of Europe had failed; and on this occasion Russia and Austria, Russia being clearly the dominant partner, seemed to have secured a mandate for settling the question. It can hardly have been a coincidence that the Japanese chose this moment for pressing their own claims on Russia; but the Russian Government quite failed to realise that Japan was in earnest, and after protracted negotiations the Japanese cut the knot by declaring war. The Japanese at once assumed the command of the sea, which they retained to the end of the war. Corea was won by them almost without a blow; from the Yalu the Russians were pushed back to the Liao river; they were defeated at Liao-yang, definitely cut off from Port Arthur, and driven back to Mukden. The one brilliant commander in the Russian navy, Admiral Makároff, fell in what was probably an attempt to restore the *morale* of his men. Port Arthur, in spite of the most dogged pluck of the Russian soldiers and the heroism of Kondrashchénko, gradually succumbed to its fate without any apparent plan of resistance.

The general demoralisation of the bureaucracy was likely to be felt at the extremities of the Empire more than anywhere else. Here, even in normal times, the official was almost independent of his chiefs. Here inertia, laziness, and incapacity in the presence of danger, might best hope to escape the eye of the sovereign. The system which claimed a monopoly of will-power for the Emperor made a war in Manchuria almost an absurdity. The agents of the Eastern group often did not wait for any permission, and set themselves to create accomplished facts. Admiral Alexéyeff, a typical Court favourite, was the kind of commander who would be chosen by the champions of the Second Reaction. It has been stated without contradiction that, disliking all disturbance, he would go to sleep in his Pullman car on the single railway-line which connected the army with Russia, and that by his orders all traffic would be stopped for the night. The Russian army as a whole showed the greatest bravery, but for some of the higher officers the war was almost a picnic; soldiers tell unpleasant tales of how some of their officers hid from the firing, and at any rate discipline was notoriously slack. Surrounded by nominees of Court favour, General Kuropatkin, the able and energetic Commander-in-Chief, must have found himself hopelessly overweighted in his struggle against the Japanese intelligence in arms.

In Russia the war did not at first awaken much interest. Even Prince Úkhtomsky, who was a strong upholder of the Eastern idea, considered that no credit could be got from defeating the Japanese, that " the troops ought not to return with empty hands " after so long a journey, and that the question of India had better be settled at the same time.[1] Russians cared for Port Arthur, and cared still more that their army should not be defeated; and a mobilisation of reserves which I witnessed in July, 1904, showed quite as much serious patriotism as the departure of our own troops for South Africa. But if the Russian peasant felt that he had " got to win," if even Liberals hurried off to the front to save the honour of Russia, the general interest in Manchuria continued to be small, and St. Petersburg did not seem like the capital of a country which was at war. There were, however, certain sides of the war which appealed to everybody : the medical students volunteered in large numbers; the Red Cross Society would naturally have commanded the sympathy of the people; but even here the Government allowed itself to be isolated from its subjects : the gifts which Russia sent to her wounded too often failed to reach their destination. When to all these irritations was added the bitterness of defeat, when it was only too evident that the Government did not dare to allow the publication of genuine news, there rose slowly and surely a great tide of indignation all over the Empire. This was inevitably accompanied by a demand for further reform. Important as were other elements of public opinion, the Zemstva and some of the Town Councils still monopolised the experience of responsible administration. It was natural that the movement should be resumed at the point at which the death of Alexander II. had interrupted it. It was not for nothing that the Zemstva had for forty years fought as best they could in the cause of reform. Thus all eyes were fixed upon the Zemstva.

Originally the Zemstva had been instituted only in Russia proper. Often there had been talk of creating Zemstva in other parts of the Empire. In White Russia they were indeed introduced, but in such a form as to be of no value; there was no

---

[1] A conversation of Prince Úkhtomsky with the author in June, 1904.

Zemstvo assembly, and the Zemstvo board was nominated by the Government; the Poles, who still composed the mass of the gentry in this district, were excluded. In Russia proper, during the reaction, the franchise for the election of the Zemstva was narrowed down, and the peasant members were nominated out of a number of elected candidates by the Government. The Justices of the Peace, who had served as a link between the Zemstva and the peasants, had been abolished, and had been replaced by the Land Captains, who were nominated by, and responsible to, the Government. The Zemstvo's powers of levying a rate had been restricted; the control of the prevention of cholera and of the relief of famine had practically been taken out of its hands. During the ministerial struggle between Mr. Goremýkin and Mr. Witte, the latter sent in to the Emperor a confi-

1899. dential memorandum, in which he pointed out in the clearest terms that the order of local government was practically incompatible with the principle of bureaucratic control; sooner or later, he said, the one order would necessarily swallow up the other; but though he exactly hit off the truth of the situation, and though he was an opponent of continuous efforts at repression which would reduce society to "human dust," he left it very doubtful what course he himself would recommend. If anything, he almost seemed to suggest that it would be best to crush the Zemstva altogether. During this period, Ministers who had lost for the moment the ear of the sovereign sometimes tried to obtain a mild degree of popularity by whispering a hint of reform; and, towards the end of his ministry, Mr. Witte summoned

1901— local commissions to inquire into the needs of the
2. peasants. To these commissions representatives of the Zemstva were invited, and some of them, such as Mr. Mukhánoff, of Chernígoff, explained in bold language that drastic reform was required. But the commissions were brought to an end by Witte's rival, Mr. Plehwe, the Minister of the Interior; rebukes were administered to the champions of reform, and Witte himself confessed to Mukhánoff that the deliberations had never been more than illusory. It was not long afterwards that Witte was ousted from his ministry by Plehwe. In 1904, the *Moscow Gazette* was advocating that the powers of the Zemstva should be still further diminished. During the reaction,

some individual Zemstva were brought into conflict with the Government by their economic programmes ; thus the Zemstvo of Novotorzhok was dismissed and was replaced by nominees of the Ministry. Prince Peter Dolgorúkoff was punished for his action on the Zemstvo of Sudzhan, and many isolated champions of reform in other Zemstva suffered a like fate. Mr. Ródicheff was disfranchised of his Zemstvo rights for presenting the notable address of Tver to the Emperor.[1] Throughout the darkest period a number of prominent workers, including those whom I have named, held together under the able direction of Mr. Petrunk-yévich. The older economic group of fellow-workers had almost died out, and the vanguard was now led by a number of younger men whose aims were more directly political. They came to be known later as the Zemstvo Constitutionalists. With them were in close touch prominent representatives of the Russian Intelligents, professors, writers, and even students. From these two elements, the more progressive of the Zemstvo men and the better balanced of the Intelligents, there began to be formed something like a Liberal party. To this party the Zemstvo men contributed the political experience ; in fact, they were the teachers of the others, and later supplied the most able men in the Imperial Duma ; but they needed to create the rank and file of a party, and to do this they would have to broaden their basis. Some of them desired to establish a Liberal newspaper ; they failed to get leave to do so in Russia, and the paper, which was known as *Liberation,* was published in Munich. The **1902.** editor finally selected was Mr. Struve, who had earlier been known as a brilliant champion of Social Democracy ; his political development into Liberalism was only typical of what was taking place with many others. To *Liberation* articles were contributed by such men as Professor **1898—** Milyukóff, Professor Vinográdoff, the eminent writer **1902.** Korolyénko, and the Zemstvo leaders already named. In close touch with the newspaper was established the " League of Liberation," which held conferences, at first in South Germany and later in Finland and Russia.

The Liberators were but few in number, though they were remarkable for their intelligence and devotion. Meanwhile there

[1] See p. 71.

was in progress another movement of a more general character. There were on the Zemstva many men who thought that the time had come for reviving the claim for economic reform. These men, using the narrow powers which the Zemstva already possessed, set about dealing more effectively with the economic needs of the population. The most notable of their leaders was Mr. Shipóff, the President of the Zemstvo Board of Moscow. To Englishmen he can best be described as a man of true and enlightened Conservatism who, without ever changing his fundamental principles, gradually convinced himself that reform offered the only hope of averting a national catastrophe. He had of course the hearty assistance of the Zemstvo Constitutionalists, who, fully realising the value of his great moral influence, were ready to unite in an attempt to secure even a minimum of improvement. Shipóff called a conference, which, in spite of the extreme moderation of its requests, brought down upon him the rebuke of Plehwe. When he was re-elected as President of the Moscow Zemstvo, his election was cancelled by the Government. This was all the more absurd because his successor, Mr. Golovín, whose election was allowed, was one of the most able and decided of Zemstvo Constitutionalists. Shipóff, without in the least degree straying from his Slavophil basis, had organised a common committee through which the local Zemstva could exchange useful information on economic questions, and statistics as to how they were dealing with them. At this early period he was recognised as the natural leader of the cause of reform.

We have seen how the Russian Intelligents began to contribute to the formation of a Liberal party, and how revolutionaries themselves became Liberals. During this same period of reaction, revolutionary thought in Russia underwent other not wholly dissimilar modifications. One of the most prominent features of the period had been the wide spread of socialistic principles amongst the Russian Intelligents. In one way or another the vast majority of educated non-official Russians came to be tinged with socialistic ideas. Socialism naturally appeals to the family instinct of the Russian people, and indeed the autocracy itself had produced results which were curiously suggestive of State Socialism. The very chief of all differences between England and Russia is that in the first country the

instinct of individualism is still overwhelmingly strong, and
in the second it is almost altogether lacking.   The Russian,
with his reverence for ideals, turns Socialism into far more
of a creed than it ever was in Germany.   Naturally the
reaction which denied all share in responsibility to the nation
tended to give to Socialism a generally anti-governmental bias.
The Socialists did indeed become more practical and constructive during this period, though never constructive enough ; but
they could not have shown their contempt for the Government
more completely than by disregarding for a time the whole question of political reform.   The Social Democrats, considering that
a change of political conditions would be quite inadequate unless
there was also a complete remodelling of the social structure,
devoted themselves almost entirely to the study of economic
questions.   In the country districts their propaganda practically
met with no success at all, but in the towns or in factory districts
they were able to gain a powerful influence over the working
men.   Naturally enough, they met with most success in those
provinces which were most discontented, for instance amongst
the quick-witted Little Russians of the south, amongst the Poles
and the Jews of Poland, amongst the disinherited Letts and
Lithuanians, and in the Caucasus and Siberia.   They
held a congress at Byelostok, which was followed by   **1898.**
wholesale repression ; their second congress was held in
London.   The Government employed different weapons to
counteract their propaganda.   The most ordinary weapon was
repression ; but Mr. Witte, who as Minister of Finance
had to depend largely upon the prosperity of industry,   **1895.**
introduced a series of factory laws which were meant
to convince the working classes that the Government was their
best friend.   Certainly these laws were in many respects only
too generous to the workmen, though always at the cost of
the employer.   Workmen enjoyed a degree of protection such
as they would not find in other countries ; only one thing was
denied to them,—initiative.   They were to entrust their cause to
a special representative of the Government, the Factory Inspector,
who, without necessarily having any knowledge of industrial concerns, had a right to interfere between masters and men.   But
the workmen were not conciliated by these means ; and, when in

1905 Mr. Witte became Prime Minister of Russia, his appeal to the memory of the factory laws was only met with derision.   In fact, the success of Witte's attempt was prejudiced by other Ministers and officials, who tried to apply his idea with far less intelligence and with far cruder methods.   A Mr. Zubátoff suggested the idea of public lectures, to advance the education of working men and to dispose them to look to the Government for support against their employers.   He secured the protection of Mr. Plehwe, Mr. Pobyedonóstseff, the Grand Duke Sergius, General Trepoff (then Head of the Moscow Police), and others of the more extreme reactionaries ; but, though his organisation assumed large proportions, he did not really capture the working men themselves.   Some of them came and listened to the lectures and asked unpleasant questions without committing themselves. In Moscow and in several other towns attempts to organise large demonstrations ended in a fiasco.   Zubátoff and his colleagues were, indeed, successful in promoting important strikes in some towns, notably in Odessa ; but these strikes only led to such disorders that, in spite of the protection of the police, some of the chief leaders had to be arrested.   The Minister of Finance tried to explain to the Emperor that the movement, so far from stopping revolution, was promoting it; and it was one of Zubátoff's adherents, the priest Gapon, who was later to lead the great crowd of petitioners to the Winter Palace in January, 1905.

The men who had fought the Government of Alexander II. had split up into different sections.   The experiment of terrorism had not proved successful; and the Terrorists as a party were almost annihilated.   However, there remained individual workers of that original group which had preached that the Intelligents must " go to the people."   From this group it is easy to trace the descent of the Socialist Revolutionaries, who in the last years preceding the war tried to develope a political interest amongst the peasants.   Working almost exclusively in the country districts, they were more individualistic than the Social Democrats of the towns; their work depended more on the ability and the conviction of individual propagandists. Their close touch with the peasant life made them also much more practical, and they tried to link on their Socialist schemes to the instincts already created by the ancient communal system.   They hoped, not for State Socialism, but for a division of the whole country into local self-supporting societies. Up to the war their work was all uphill. Their only chance of moving the peasants was to capture large masses of them at a time; but when the news of the war began to be read with avidity all over Russia they got an exceptional chance, which they utilised with great ability. They were wise enough to see that the question of Tsar or no Tsar had better not be raised; but of course they joined in the demand for a national assembly, and of course they demanded the independence and extension of local government. For the rest, they were content to wait for the duly elected representatives of Russia to decide all details of administration. This circumspection removed many obstacles which stood in their path; and later, in the autumn and winter of 1905, they were able to capture the votes of whole peasant villages at a time by their simple formula of " All the land for those that labour."

Such were the developments of public opinion which were taking place in the last years of the reaction. Most of them were still incomplete; no body except the Zemstva was as yet prepared to take the lead of the nation in the cry for reform. The reaction had at least been able to make it impossible for the different leaders to gauge the strength of their respective followings; and naturally the repression had weighed heaviest of all upon the revolutionaries. In the autumn of 1904 it could not yet be said that the nation as a whole was in favour of drastic changes; but such had been the mistakes of the Government, that, except for an almost inconsiderable fraction, the whole country was united in support of the minimum programme identified with the name of Shipóff. In fact, Shipóff himself, while appealing to the traditions of the past, could have reasonably denounced the period of reaction as quite abnormal in Russian history; it was the Government itself which, by its unreasoning fear of progress and its resistance to all Western ideas, had created the great gap which now lay between itself and the peoples of Russia. Nothing makes this more clear than the attitude of Poland during the beginning of the war. The Poles made no hasty attempt to snatch at the chance of liberation; the cry of separation was not raised at all; on the contrary, as time went on, the Poles came into close touch with the

Russian Liberals, who found it easy to include the Polish claims in their own programme. In fact, all sections of the population of the Empire had been oppressed by the same persons and were claiming the same minimum. Mr. Shipóff, as has been seen, had endeavoured to unite the Zemstva; during the first months of the war the Zemstva attempted to establish a common organisation of a broader kind. They chose their ground admirably. The Government was despatching to the far East a remarkably large proportion of reservists, presumably because it wished to keep the bulk of the regular army in Russia. The departure of the reservists meant the absence of the bread-winners from many homes all over Russia. The distress thus created was not special to any given district, and with the common question of relief the Zemstva proposed to deal in common. If the Government wished to satisfy the very moderate desires of the Zemstva, it would sanction this common organisation; if it could see the wisdom of reconciling to itself the mass of its subjects, it would give to this organisation a yet broader character by renewing the summons of Alexander II. for a meeting in the capital. Plehwe looked at things otherwise; there is good authority for saying that he tried to frighten the Emperor by suggesting that if concessions were made he could not answer for his Majesty's life. Obstacles were therefore put in the way of the common Zemstvo organisation; but though Plehwe got his way, the event proved that he could not answer for his own life. A young revolutionary named Sazónoff threw a bomb by which the all-powerful Minister was blown **July 28,** into fragments. The violent death of Plehwe was **1904.** but one link in a long chain of developments. He had acted with the utmost brutality to the students, and the average Intelligent, demoralised by years of repression, looked at Sazónoff as the "avenger of the national grief." It is more important to note that the Government listened to such arguments as bombs, while turning a deaf ear to the most modest claims of reason. Plehwe was succeeded by Prince Svyatopolk-Mirsky, a gentleman of ancient family and broad and liberal sympathies, who was best known for the wise use which he had made of his power as Governor-General in Vilna. Prince Mirsky was no seeker for office, and before accepting the post he laid his ideas before the Emperor. He issued to the public what seemed an astonishing appeal as coming from a Minister: he asked for its confidence. His appeal produced a glow of enthusiasm all over Russia; the Press at last felt free to give voice to its real aspirations, and the disappearance of unnatural restrictions was hailed with a deep-drawn sigh as of escape from some monstrous nightmare.

The new Minister authorised the holding of a general Zemstvo Congress in St. Petersburg itself. At last the plan of Alexander II. was on the eve of realisation; but Mirsky had to fight with other influences far stronger than his own at the Court, and, if the people had issued from the atmosphere of suspicion which enveloped Russia, the Emperor had not. After some consultations it was decided that the Congress must be held in a private house, and its resolutions were communicated to Prince Mirsky, not officially, but as a piece of news to a personal friend; in this way they came to the ears of the Emperor.

This first Zemstvo Congress was held under the presidency of Mr. Shipóff. It was clear that the great majority of the deputies from the various Zemstva, who came **Nov. 16–19,** rather by invitation than by any direct election, **1904.** were ready to go farther than the minimum of Shipóff: in fact, but for his own great moral influence, the president might have found himself almost entirely isolated; but here, as so often afterwards, the difficulty of the whole task acted as a restraining influence, and the majority was wise enough to content itself with a unanimous vote in favour of the minimum. These so-called requests expressed before all things a desire for order, and for the corporate development of the whole country. The Congress states that Government has been separated from Society, and that this gap must be bridged at all costs. In the tenth out of the eleven articles it puts forward two resolutions, one representing the majority and the other the minority; both alike request that a national assembly should be summoned without delay, but the majority claim for the assembly definite legislative functions. Though the peasants were only indirectly represented on the Congress, a special article, which was accepted unanimously, emphasises the need of improving the conditions of peasant life. The eleven points may be summed up in the following requests :—No one without the sentence of an independent court of law ought to be subjected to punishment or limited in his rights. There must be means for bringing officials to account in the civil or criminal courts. There must be guarantees of freedom of conscience and religion, freedom of speech and press, and also freedom of meeting and association. The personal rights of citizens of the Russian Empire, both civil and political, ought to be equal. The peasants must be made equal in personal rights with the members of other classes. The country population must be freed from the wardenship of administrative authorities in all manifestations of its personal and social life. To peasants must be guaranteed a regular form of trial. Representation in the Zemstva must not be organised on class principles, and must include as far as possible all the actual forces of the local population. Small country units (Parish Councils) ought to be created. The sphere of local government should be extended to the whole province of local needs. Local self-government must be extended over all parts of the Russian Empire. The Conference expresses a hope "that the supreme power will summon freely elected representatives of the people in order, with their co-operation, to bring our country out on to a new path of Imperial development in the spirit of the principles of justice and of harmony between the Imperial power and the people." This great document, so vastly superior in spirit and substance to any proposals that had issued from the Government of the Reaction, marks the beginning of the reform movement. It bears at almost every point the personal impress of the mind of Shipóff. The nobility with which he pleads for reform, as essentially necessary to the cause of order and as the natural request of loyal subjects, continues to stamp the movement at many of its further crises. The minimum programme of Shipóff was accepted with enthusiasm by the whole country, and one public body after another ratified it; the volume of the national demand became so great that Russia could be said to possess a real public opinion which was practically unanimous.

CHAPTER III.

RUSSIAN society is organised on the basis of the class system.

The three chief classes were the gentry, the merchants, and the peasants. Each was organised separately, and carefully kept in its own special compartment of the governmental system. Each class had, at least, some measure of control over its own affairs.

Of the three classes the merchants were and are by a long way the least important. The general foundation of the life of the country was before all things agricultural. The towns themselves were very largely concentrations of the country essence, nearly all of them being much more like our county towns than our great manufacturing centres. Each of them has, if one can only see it, a special character of its own. Thus in Novgorod we find the tradition of native vigour embarked in great enterprises of trade ; Kieff reminds us of the great loose brotherhood of the early Princes and stands for Christianity and Constantinople ; Vladímir is the monument of the first attempt to found an imperial dynasty and of the crushing catastrophe of the Tartar invasion ; Ryazán represents the sturdy resistance of Russia to the foreign dominator ; Tver recalls the first generous attempt at liberation ; Moscow incorporates the whole story of the rise of the national dictatorship—of its dangers, of its patient hope, of its recurring catastrophes, of its undreamed-of triumph ; Nizhny is the first foothold against the invading East ; Kazán is the beginning of Eastern empire ; Kostromá is the cradle of loyalty which sheltered and saved the infant dynasty of Románoff ; Smolensk, as " the precious necklace of Russia," [1] is the evidence of her final triumph over the Pole ; St. Petersburg, a great governmental barracks on the shore of the European seas, is the incarnation of the purpose of Peter the Great, which violently displaced the centre of

---

[1] Words of Tsar Borís Godunóff.

Russia's consciousness in order that she might learn her Western lesson at a breakneck speed. Thus every town means something, but rather as a phase of the story of vast agricultural Russia than as a type of individual achievement. The merchants, then, were a kind of necessary adjunct to the other two classes. They have had, it is true, their own separate tradition in ancient Russian history, notably in the story of the republics of Novgorod and Pskoff; but these republics were annihilated and their very tradition itself was swamped in the overwhelming mass of country life. Russian trade was never wholly managed by an alien people such as the Jews were in Poland; but trade is still more or less despised not only by the country gentry, but also by the peasants. In Russia, trade was but poorly developed, and, in comparatively early times, a great part of it fell largely into the hands of foreigners. The Government was glad to use their services, but kept them under a suspicious control. It never had a real trade policy of its own; when John the Great won Novgorod the measures which he took to control the city very quickly "killed the goose that lay the golden egg," and a similar disregard of some of the first principles of trade has been characteristic even of the Second Reaction.

The country gentry, when they came to their town houses, brought the country atmosphere with them. In the town they expected to find a centre of supplies of provisions, and the town merchants were fully as servile as those of the country. Trade was rather a peddling barter than a bold enterprise. A large understanding of public interests might have been expected even of the peasants with more justice than of the traders, who, in a narrower spirit, simply followed at a distance the traditions of rural Russia. The Russian merchants were as patriotic as other people; when Napoleon broke into Russia and Alexander went to Moscow to ask for patriotic offerings, the traders, with clenched teeth and tears in their eyes, subscribed far more than they could afford, to repel the common enemy; but no champion of the old system could tell you with conviction that he hoped to find a powerful support in the merchant class.[1] A considerable amount

---

[1] Count Paul Sheremétyeff, a strong advocate of the old system of compartments, confessed to me that his chief hopes lay in the peasants and certain fragments of the gentry.

of the smaller trade is in the hands of Old Believers, whose spirit is narrower still. The merchants are generally considered as small-minded and pig-headed ; for this reason most of the Town Councils for a long time lagged in enterprise far behind the County Councils, and it is only the recent rapid extension of trade in the larger towns, and still more the chance which educated persons now have of sitting as representatives of corporate bodies, that have lately pushed the Moscow Town Council so much to the front in the championship of reform.

The merchants have their own elected chief and assembly in each considerable town, and in the largest towns many class institutions such as hospitals and schools, and also special law courts of a commercial kind. By belonging to the greater or to the lesser guild, whose subscription varies in different places, a merchant gets facilities for travel and for opening branches of his business in other provinces.

Beneath the merchants are the " Townsmen " or smaller town-folk. These are by no means a distinctive class ; there is not much difference between them and the peasants who have come to live in the towns, though the physique of the latter is by all accounts distinctly better. A successful Townsman can easily pass into the class of the merchants. In fact, this is an arbitrary classification made to keep up the appearance of completeness in the class system, and to label those who have no other place in it elsewhere. The Townsmen choose their own elders, who are confirmed by the Governor. There are a Townsmen's office and a Townsmen's Board. The elder is expected to know all about the members of his class, to certify cases of distress, and to serve as an intermediary in the distribution of passports. The Townsmen of the capitals have established some fine charitable institutions for the use of their own class.

It is to the country, then, that we must turn if we wish to understand the old life of Russia. The most, and in my opinion far the best, of Russian travelling consists not of railway journeys and sight-seeing, but of expeditions in carts over country roads. So great are the distances, so complete is the isolation, and so powerful and absorbing is the feel of the country, that, as Russians would say, " when one has reached the railway one's journey seems to be over." The " country " is practically supreme in its own vast dominions. The man whose nature will have none of it will find nothing to stay his eye; enveloped by a monotonous alien atmosphere, he will sink into self-absorption; robbed of the check that is elsewhere imposed by the company of his fellows, he will magnify to exaggeration his own moods, fads, and theories. Meanwhile, behind the constant sense of great distances being traversed, there will always be ringing, like a little bell at the back of his mind, the syllables that spell out the place of his destination—for the lover, the country home of his sweetheart; for the young boy, the town of his future; for Napoleon, Moscow.[1] Will this insistent longing for a distant goal allow him to contemplate one by one the single steps that lead him towards his prize? Rather he will rush over them as if they were all one great vague dream. The sense of detail is gone; it is all illimitable veldt.

"Is it not thus that thou too, O Russia, movest forward, just like some flying troika that none can keep up with? The road smokes beneath thee; the bridges groan; everything falls away and is left behind. The astonished wayfarer stops to gaze at this wonder of heaven; surely it is some child of thunder that has leapt straight from the firmament. What means this awe-stirring, rushing portent, and what invisible strength lives in these horses, so strange to eye of man? Eh! horses! horses! what horses are ye? Is it whirlwinds that sit in your manes? Is there some subtle instinct that burns in your every vein? They have heard from the heights the song that they know; with a pull, with a will, they have pressed their iron breasts to the yoke, and, scarce touching earth with their feet, they seem changed to one strained outline of movement that flies through the air and streams forward, all instinct with the breath of heaven. Say, Russia, whither art thou pressing? Give answer. But answer gives she none. The bells peal out their strange music; the air groans and parts into whirlwind around her; everything flies past, all that this earth contains; and other peoples and

---

[1] No more typical picture of this state of mind can be found than Ségur's description of the moods of Napoleon during the Moscow campaign, notably the scenes at Vitebsk and Smolensk, at which places Napoleon tried to stop but simply could not.

Governments look askance at her, stand aside, and give her passage."[1]

Let us go slower. We shall be more likely to arrive somewhere. It is an old Russian failing to think that, because one has been behind time at the last station, one must necessarily be before time at the next.

Russia proper is a vast, low, undulating plateau with many and great rivers, which generally cut their way through at a somewhat lower level between red-brown banks.[2] Some think that "Russia" means the red land. Often there are wide views, which, as in Yorkshire, make one realise that one is in a great country. Wide stretches of plain, of marsh, or of plateau have inspired that poet of space, the artist Shishkin. Sometimes, near the railway, one may see half-hearted, broken-down fences, or, for the matter of that, old railway lines used up to fence in a high-road; but as a rule one will not notice any division between field and field until one looks more closely. Then are seen the long, narrow ditches which separate one peasant's strip of land from another. As many of the crops do not grow high, the first look may not tell one that what seems like a great bare, greeny upland is really a vast field of flax, which, as the Russian peasant says, "smells of riches." Flax is said to be a risky crop, and one that exhausts the land very soon: one will not see it everywhere in Great Russia; the staple crops are rye and oats. A piece of village land is really a picture of all the families of the village. A normal strip is, say, two yards broad and eighty long. Thus, a motley look is given to the whole. Here is a grey strip of oats, next a brown strip of rye, much of a door-mat colour about harvest-time; then, perhaps, a silky yellow line of flax, and last the deep dark green of a strip of potatoes. The strips vary in width; some families possess, let us say, two portions and a half, and others only one. Measure each strip with the eye, and you will know how many peasant portions belong to the family which cultivates it. Here, then, are a people who evidently live off the land, and when one gets used to the sight of this rough and ready map, one wonders rather what feeds the people who live in the towns, where the

---

[1] Gogol, end of the First Part of "Dead Souls."

[2] The following description applies mainly to the Central Provinces of Great Russia.

ground is covered with houses and paving stones; and one thinks of their fortune as something dangerous and adventitious. Every now and then, even in well-tilled districts, there are patches of waste land, abandoned to reeds; this is sometimes due to sheer want of enterprise, sometimes to the fact that there are many acres and few hands to work them, and that, perhaps, this land is far from the village: in many cases, however, it simply means that the soil is bad. The marshes cover a very considerable part of the surface of Russia; and twice a year, in autumn and spring, a much larger part is under water, so that most roads become almost impracticable, and, whether one is patient or impatient, it is best to stay where one may happen to be till they mend. These waste patches are in spring-time covered with a very carpet of wild flowers, of which the most remarkable is the "John-and-Mary," a purple flower and a yellow one growing on the same stalk. In watery parts there grow bushes which bear "wolf-berries," so called by the peasant because they are not of use to him, and possibly may be to the wolves. The waste patches, even in Central Russia, sometimes extend for miles, and are covered with copse. There are apparently endless forests, a ceaseless alternation of pines, firs, and silver birches,[1] varying in height and in closeness to each other, but all generally thin and tall: these trees are all remarkable for the height of their lowest branches from the ground, the comparative absence of foliage, and the strikingly bright colours of their bark; glistening white alternates with a bright red; they are taller and more stately than elsewhere in the Baltic provinces (where forestry seems to have been studied), and as one approaches Moscow from the north. Under these trees grow many kinds of mushrooms, which seem to appear in almost every Russian dish. When one reaches a Russian country house, the hostess very probably proposes that the whole party shall set out "to pick mushrooms"; this is the usual excuse for a sort of everyday informal picnic. A Russian forest may be so full of undergrowth that the vastness of the country becomes further complicated by its dense and various detail; in a square mile of such country it is easier to lose oneself than in a much larger area of our little England; the passer-by

[1] Small oaks begin somewhat north of Moscow.

will now and then twist and turn some sprig in a given direction as a guide for any who may follow him. Thus a forest
will often serve as a boundary between two different worlds,
that is between one village and another. As you glance at the
edge of a thickly wooded line of heights, it may seem to you
to be the beginning of a great enveloping wilderness; and, at
evening, the peasant on his bare fields will sing, in awe of the
unknown,—

> "Now the sun is sinking
> Far, far behind the dark woods ;
> See yon heavy cloud that rises there
> And covers all the skies :
> Hushed is now the little bird's singing,
> No sound or voice is heard." [1]

The broad rivers sometimes wind so much that you will need
as many as nine bridges over a single stream in the course of a
few miles. The town to which you journey will perhaps be hidden
in some hollow almost invisible until you are just above it, as if it
were drowned in an ocean of country.

In dry weather the best roads are the side ones ; they are
simply tracks through the fields, but are fairly level : after rain
they are rather alarming, with their sudden dives over shelves and
gullies and through swamps. The main road often looks like a
river separating into two channels to circumvent some island of
difficulty. Least of all did I like the causeway; the part which
has been specially cobbled by the Government or by the Zemstvo
is just the part which one carefully avoids. I can remember an
autumn journey in early frost, when the rough fields were infinitely
preferable to the frozen ups and downs which went by the name
of road. From the Volga to Kashin I hardly used the road at
all ; it was like the waves of the sea, and we preferred the fields,
with their innumerable little trenches, at each of which we stopped
to encourage our three horses to a special effort. The same
pause is advisable before each of the little bridges of logs
loosely strewn over the many small marshy streams. These bridges
are always bad ; a gentleman sitting in a cart approaches one of
them ; the driver makes a dash on to it, and it immediately
collapses beneath them ; the gentleman just shrugs his shoulders

---

[1] Peasant's song, Government of Simbirsk, village of Pramzino. The tune,
which is quite irregular in time, is a very atmosphere of desolation.

and grumbles to himself : "Fool !" he says; " he sees it is a bridge,
and yet he tries to cross it." Most roads depend for repairs on
the care of the local gentry. This duty is supposed to be compulsory, but certainly no one compels ; how can the average landowner repair a road ? Some of the roads in peasant districts
show haphazard relics of conscience, in the shape of rustic sign-
boards erected by order of the village authorities.

There are no inns in our sense of the word, only the posting
stations. These are like the waiting rooms at our stations. One
carries with one everything but hot water, and brings one's own
bed. I remember asking an old postmaster for a bucket of cold
water "to throw over my head " ; he asked if it would not do as
well for me to go and stand, presumably stark naked, on the muddy
road under the rain. Later a Russian of my acquaintance passed
his house. " Oh ! " he asked, " do you know that man who poured
cold water over his head ? Who is he ? " " Well," said my friend,
" he is an Englishman ; they all do that." The postmaster
thought for a moment ; "Is he dead ?" he asked. In such a
place I heard the village policeman explaining to the postmaster
that I was an English spy, who was going to guide our invading
army when the time should come.

Wallace,[1] with that nonchalance which makes him so excellent
a critic of things Russian, advises one to expect no pretty scenery
in Russia. This is one of the few general statements in his great
book which I cannot bear out. There are gullies and scarps very
pleasant, and the low hills and white churches which peer up from
time to time often give one the feel of home. The grey villages
are more dreary ; they may even wear a forbidding look, perched
on little hills as if in distrust of the main road and often surrounded
by fences and gates. The low, long, weather-worn houses lie along
either side of the broad, grassy village street. The projecting
beams are often carved to curious patterns. The houses vary
very much in size, shape, and degree of decoration, and these are
the surest tests of prosperity or its opposite. Some have a
spacious stable and cow-shed under the same roof, so that the
whole colony of men and beasts may meet the cold of winter
together as best they can. In the Ryazán Government, where

---

[1] " Russia " : Sir D. Mackenzie Wallace. It is admitted by all Russians to be
much the best book written by an Englishman on their country.

wood is scarce and houses are small, the peasant will often sleep
in the same room with a little pig or a young calf. A typical hut
in this district is a low building of rude clay and wood ; there is
a little room which is almost a passage where roams, possibly, a
stray chicken ; a small inner room contains benches for sleep ;
the peasant prefers to lie on the top of the stove. In summer
the whole family sleep outside. The courtyard contains a line
of buildings of loose thatch, partitioned off into small spaces for
the horse, the two cows, and the pig. Beyond lies a little garden
planted with trees. The hostess is a pleasant wise-looking old
lady, who does the honours with quite a grace of her own. In
a suburban hut (Smolensk Government), I find a big living-room
with many ikons, and a bedroom with a big bed for the whole
family, standing close to the stove and covered with a rough heap
of bedclothes. In another very small hut of similar arrangement
to the first (Ryazán Government) I meet a little pig ; but I am
also surprised to find a hand-loom for making rough transparent
cloth of a large check pattern, some of which is worn by the maker
and some sold to other peasants.

The peasants in ancient times were called " the smellers."
By nature they were made for harrying the soil, and have a
pride of their own as the natural champions of Russia in
this toilsome combat. They have not the minute conscience
and cleanliness of the Germans, but they are especially adapted
for making something out of nothing with hardly any tools,
and for that reason they are born colonists ; in fact, movement
may be said to run in their very blood. They are a people
of the high-roads ; but they are a great family : they have always
carried with them everywhere their Church and their country.
It was this spirit of movement that induced the Government to
fasten them to the soil, in order that the smaller gentry should
not be deprived of all their workers by the richer landowners.
Serfdom, so far from diminishing the evils of migration, tended
for a time at least to aggravate them, and runaways of every
kind scoured all Russia in the search for fortune during the
" Time of Troubles." Peter and Catherine, instead of relaxing
the chains of serfdom, drew them tighter and applied them to new
sections of the agricultural population. The serf who laboured
on the land was at least in a great measure free of interference

from his master, and, as the life of the capitals began to develope, these masters, if only they could, began to leave their estates regularly for some part of the year, often confiding their serfs to the not very tender mercies of a German steward, who, with his peculiar conception of loyalty, was an excellent instrument for squeezing from them as much money as possible. However, if they satisfied certain requisitions, they might in general expect to be left to earn some kind of a competence for themselves, and, by means of their village societies, they continued to enjoy the relics of an ancient and democratic independence. Very different was the life of those serfs who served in the master's house. These were liable to be "favoured up" or "favoured down" ("raz-zhálovanny") by sheer caprice; and there was no court of appeal whatsoever. The master might order a boy of nineteen to marry a woman of eighty-nine, and the command had to be obeyed without delay. Yet a man who owns horses does not go to their stables and cut their throats for the fun of it; and there were between many serfs and their lords relations more affectionate than those which bind together a horse and its master. Nekrásoff tells a pathetic story of a landowner near the banks of the Volga; this old gentleman, accustomed to implicit obedience, had a paralytic stroke when he heard the news of the emancipation; his peasants therefore agreed to declare the rumour false and to continue to serve him till his death, which mutual engagement they carried out to the end, even flogging within an inch of his life one of their members, who, in the frankness of his cups, had denounced the pious fraud.[1]

The peasant always believed that the land was really his own, and that the gentry had been simply placed on the estates as so many sentinels in the Government service, to enforce the corporate obligations of the whole nation. "Our backs," he would say, "belong to our master, but the land belongs to us." He was, at least, very nearly right. For a long time grants of land were issued revocably as a reward for Government service. Peter the Great forced the gentry to serve the State in a far more rigid manner than before; but when Peter III., in 1762, freed the gentry from their obligations to the State, the peasant began to shrewdly guess that the time would come when he too would be freed from his obligations to the gentry; he had to wait almost exactly

---

[1] Nekrásoff : "Who can live happy in Russia?"

one hundred years, and the emancipation, when it did come, was due much more to the work of the "Intelligents" than to the generosity of the landowners. When he was emancipated, the peasant received something like half of the land, to be held as property of the Village Society; for this land he had to pay a reasonably low price in instalments, which were spread over some fifty years; but the whole sum due from him was paid down without delay by the Government to the gentry, who, in many cases, proceeded to sell their estates and migrate to the towns. The gentry might have been able, in the past, to exercise the strongest pressure over the Village Society, but it appears that they practically took no direct part in its deliberations. Now they were, so to speak, struck out of the life of the peasant; their place was taken, at first, by the Justices of the Peace, who exercised, in a very liberal spirit, the authority entrusted to them; but these officials have now been replaced by the Land Captains, who are appointed by the Government and may be described as official squires of something like the old type.

However, the Village Society acquired an altogether new importance from the fact of the emancipation. It was a primitive Russian institution, and those who saw in it a germ of home-born civilisation, secured its preservation at a time when Western influences were everywhere rampant. But the fact that it was at this point preserved is almost as important as its original development. Russia has always been like a great family; "father," "uncle," "brother," or "son" are the natural terms by which one may address one's fellows. "Father" is used of the Emperor, of the priest, and in addressing almost anyone of mature age. "Mother" is used in a similar way. Mary is never "the Virgin"; she is always the "Mother of God." A peasant calls his fellow-peasants brothers. A general addressing his soldiers or an official addressing the peasants will probably call them children. One of my peasant drivers shouts out to a quite unknown peasant-woman, "Auntie, do get out of the way somewhere." Common ownership, especially of pasture-land, has been a stage in the history of land tenure in many countries, as is still testified by our own use of the word "common." Serfdom is in itself a leveller, as making every man equal in the absoluteness of his subjection. Now the system of common ownership received a further sanction;

but the Village Society as an institution was far more on trial from
the day that the peasants were declared free.

The village, then, is, in principle, an independent and self-
governing community.   The heads of houses meet in free council
on the basis of "one man one vote," as no more complicated plan
would be practicable.   They have the general management of the
property of the whole village.   This is no illusory phantom of
responsibility; for the matters with which they have to deal are
those which most nearly concern the life of each individual
peasant and are, therefore, the best qualified to teach him the practice of democratic administration.   And, as no regular interference
in such affairs can be effectively organised by the Government,
the peasants have had to learn how to go their own way.   The
village assembly has the right of dividing the village property
amongst its members, of admitting new members, and of instructing
a father to divide his own share with his son.   It can discipline
its refractory members.   It controls all leases of its land to
outsiders, and can, if it chooses, embark in corporate enterprises,
such as the buying of a fire-engine or other machinery; and, lastly,
it can expend money on the relief of its own poor.   The votes
are not necessarily counted; many questions are settled by a
kind of acclamation.   When a question has been proposed, it
is the custom to allow the meeting to, so to speak, go into
committee, that is, it breaks up into many little groups; all
seem to be talking at once in loud voices with emphatic gestures.
Certainly it cannot be said that there is any lack of interest.
But these noisy discussions are by no means disorderly; on the
contrary, the peasant has his own very definite tradition as to the
authority of the society as a whole, and, when the general discussion is resumed, there is immediate silence and attention.
The meeting elects the village elder (" Stárosta "), who, during his
term of office, has the duty of calling meetings when necessary
and of presiding over their discussions.   In some smaller villages
there is no elder, but a kind of deputy called "the elected one."
The elder or the elected, being dependent on the village council,
cannot of course rule without it; he will have a constitutional
sense of his own, and, when any major question is raised, he will
say, " This means a meeting."   He is assisted by a village Tenth
man (not to be confused with that other Tenth man who is the

lowest official of the country system of police).   Each full
peasant's portion of so many acres must supply a village Tenth
man for one month in its turn; thus, the board which sometimes
marks his house has to be moved about.   This Tenth man is a
kind of informal secretary, and goes round with a long pole, tapping
the window of each head of a house, when a meeting is to be
called.   As the Village Society pays its taxes in a lump sum from
the village, the elder and an appointed tax-gatherer have to see
to the proportioning and collecting of each man's share.   I have
heard of the elder of a poor village who was chosen simply because
he used to drink, and because the peasants thought that he would
be the right man to have for a buffer between themselves and
the Government; as they put it, "the Government could beat
him for not collecting the taxes, and they could beat him for
collecting them."   Some of them said, " He will do ; he is not the
kind of man for us to pity."

I told a Land Captain who was a strong Liberal that I should
like to attend a village meeting (July, 1904).   " Well," he said,
" then, of course you must go without me, or they would not be
quite themselves.   You might say that you want to rent a little
of the village land ; there would have to be a meeting, and, if you
use your wits, you will see a good deal."   This plan, however,
depended in a measure on his co-operation ; I might, for instance,
find that I was really thought to have rented the land ; and, as
he was called away on a long journey, I went about the matter
more simply.   As I drive through a little village of the Rostóff
district, a horn is sounding to call a meeting ; I dismount and
seek out the Police Tenth man, a dreamy old man with pink eyes
and long grey beard ; he is the only illiterate whom I have met in
this district.   We walk to the village green, where benches are
placed and the men are gathering.   The women stand together
within earshot ; they are now entitled to hold land independently.
The elected, a hearty, capable, brown-faced man, welcomes me
with evident interest ; we sit down on a bench and talk and
smoke ; when all the men are assembled the elected stands up.
" God has sent us a good time," he says ; " shall we all go haymaking to-morrow ? "   As the pasture land is common and
undivided, this question requires a meeting, and during haymaking time there may be as many as three meetings a week.

It must now be decided whether to-morrow is a suitable day, and if so at what time the start should be made, and who should be set to work on each part of the land.   There is no vote-taking, only a general expression of opinion on each point.   The meeting wavers for a while in deciding between 4 and 4.30 a.m.   When everything is settled there is a kind of unanimous " Hurrah ! " and the decision is ratified by general cries of " Good luck ! " (literally, " at a good time ").   All face towards Rostóff, whose domes shine up in the setting sun, and the elected says a word of prayer.   This is the only time when I have seen the conventional village chorus off the stage.

Geographically, Russia is a land of individualism ; but the genius of her people has made her the strongest home of the social instinct.   If the magnetic spark of a single idea can easily run through the vast barracks of a Russian factory, we can also easily understand how it may, under given circumstances, carry with it wholesale all the members of the Village Society.   A village meeting will sometimes be induced to resolve on measures which none of its individual members would have separately contemplated ; this, it may be urged, may be a public danger as facilitating the propagation of ill-digested ideas ; but if we think twice, we shall see that it is this very education in corporate instincts that has held Russia together in the past and will serve as the very best basis for a more free future.

Each village sends one man from every ten houses to the Cantonal meeting, which will represent say some thirty villages. Even the Canton is not under the strict police control that prevails in the towns.   The Police Corporal, who is the lowest real administrative official, has to control two cantons, and the Police Captain perhaps nine.   The cantonal assembly elects two or more candidates for the post of Cantonal Elder, but the Land Captain has a right to confirm either or any of the candidates in the appointment.   He will, however, probably be present at the meeting, and will try to direct it.   This meeting also chooses some five judges from the peasants to serve on the Cantonal Law-court, whose work will be described in another chapter.   It also has to vote the salaries and incidental expenses of the administration of the canton.   As in the village assembly, so here, a resolution which secures a majority of two-thirds is a legal decree of the meeting, subject to the ratification of the administrative officials. One can imagine that in critical times the official may interfere with even the most ordinary resolutions, and also that on occasion a meeting may dare to concern itself with political questions which relate to the general welfare of the peasant class. In these respects the limits between the rights of an elective assembly and those of the administrative power have remained unfixed, but at least public opinion has a chance of hearing itself expressed and, by means of the written " decree," of finding an audience outside the district concerned.

The elections are held at the Cantonal Court-house, which is permanently occupied by a Cantonal Clerk, an official named from amongst the peasants by the Government and receiving £35 to £50 a year. In the Court-house sits the peasants' law-court; it is also the centre of the Cantonal Elder, who receives a salary of £60 to £100, and has to leave his own affairs during his three years of office to travel round his district and attend to its needs. He is endowed with a discretionary authority to arrest for administrative purposes for a term of a few days. He is under the pretty close control of the officials; as a cantonal clerk says to me, " he can follow the way that is marked out for him; there is his power! " In a district such as Rostóff, where economical enterprise is great but political ambition not so dangerous, a Cantonal Elder, being more or less left to himself, can be a worthy representative of peasant civilisation and peasant interests; and in general, if the Government did less to control the elections and to guide the other deliberations of the meeting, the system might claim admiration even outside Russia. But the Land Captain has often, especially in recent years, tried to dictate to the meeting a formulated expression of satisfaction and abject submission, and it is only lately that bogus resolutions of this kind, designed for the further deception of the Emperor, have in several cases been flatly rejected by the peasants. The peasant has made a shrewd estimate of the potentialities of the existing system, and that is why he demands almost before everything else the abolition of the Land Captain, an official who has no long tradition, who specially represents the Second Re-action, and who is near enough to the peasant life to bring home to it most convincingly the dictatorial character of that period.

I will describe a cantonal meeting which I attended in the Ryazán government (July 16, 1905). A large open space lies in front of the neatly built Court-house. The horses of the Land Captain stand outside. In the outer room there is a crush of dirty feet, and a crowd of petitioners of all ages. The Land Captain sits at his table in the inner room. He has had to wait from 10.0 to 1.0 for the legal quorum of two-thirds to come in from the surrounding villages. Sometimes the meeting lasts a whole day. Here every eight houses choose an elector, and the village elders and tax-collectors come *ex officio*. The list of all the members contains 116 names. On every question, the meeting has to vote "yes" or "no" by ballot, which takes a very long time ; and, as each name on the list has to be read out for each vote, the piece of paper is very dirty and torn by the end of it. The first business is the election of the Cantonal Elder. By law a list of the candidates should be drawn up, but the Land Captain, on the excuse that many illiterates are present, has a rough and ready plan of his own. He recommends the nomination of a single candidate first, and even directly suggests who he should be. He takes a vote on that name. Of course, even if the candidate gets a majority of the votes, the peasants are entitled to propose another; and perhaps in this next case even more will say "yes " and even fewer "no." It is not that this meeting is any more directed than an ordinary committee meeting in England ; but the difference is that the direction is official, and the Land Captain talks so often that the appearance of free choice is lost in an atmosphere of patronage and submission. The retiring elder, a simple capable man with a quiet voice and a responsible manner, evidently enjoys a considerable influence. There is a great deal of talking in groups, which is suddenly hushed when the election begins. A rough ballot-box is put up outside the courthouse ; the Land Captain reverently covers it with a towel, but by watching the hands one can quite easily see which way a man is voting. The towel often falls off, but less frequently than one might expect.

The Land Captain, in a high thin voice which does not reach the outside of the meeting, makes a short speech explaining the duties of self-government; it is the sort of thing which in England the not very intelligent rich sometimes allow themselves to say to the intelligent poor; underneath it runs the suggestion, "See how lucid I am; this is the only way in which you dull people can understand it." It recalls books specially written for the poor.

He now invites the naming of a candidate; there is a unanimous chorus of discordant voices crying, "The old one! the old one!" The name of the retiring elder is balloted. The Land Captain deals out a number of little balls, which are put into a dish and handed out by the assistant clerk. Village by village, each voter is called up; they are a motley train; orderly but deeply interested, they crowd about the ballot-box; there is a rugged obstinacy about some of the faces, while others look smooth and cunning. One old peasant makes a bow to the Land Captain and passes on, quite forgetting to vote; there is an outburst of rough laughter: "He forgot." Another crosses himself to the ballot-box as if it were an ikon, and then passes on. When the box is opened, it is found that all said "yes." It is pretty clear why. The peasants want to re-elect their old favourite, and they give him a unanimous vote in order that the Land Captain may have less excuse for finally naming the second candidate. A great cheer goes up, as if the election were already decided.

When the Land Captain begins asking for other names, the interest in the meeting disappears. One Ivánoff is suggested by a large group; a smaller number, standing close together, reply by shouting for Alexéyeff. The Land Captain selects Alexéyeff to be balloted for, but he only gets three or four votes. Several have dropped their turn; and two or three have even, by mistake, dropped their balls, apparently from listlessness. Lusty cries again demand Ivánoff; "I have nothing against Ivánoff," says the Land Captain, "but he is a member of the law-court, and it would be clumsy if he were also chosen as elder." This is special pleading; for unless the Land Captain means to frankly withstand the will of the meeting, the elder has already been chosen, and it is very unlikely that the second man would be called upon to serve. The Land Captain now leaves the ballot-box and reasons with different groups; his place is taken by the retiring elder, who has no business to be conducting the election at all; however, there is no reason why anyone should

object, and no one does.　When the election is over, there are
brought up some petitions from peasants, drawn up with a
windiness that is more than official, and suggesting someone who
was trying to think and could not manage it.　This canton has
a peasant member on the Zemstvo, and he asks for £1 as
travelling expenses; the request is refused.　As they pass, the
voters often express their opinions.　" All right," says one ;
" Don't like it," says another, who almost guides the hand of
the first towards the ballot-box.　The cantonal driver ("yamshchík") has had to make many journeys in connection with
the relief of distress, and asks for £4 10s. extra ; meeting with
general opposition, he stumbles in speech, as not knowing how
to put his very reasonable case.　The Land Captain declares
that this expense is a public duty, and talks of the Red Cross
Society ; but it is quite clear, long before the declaration of the
voting, that the driver has not a chance ; he stands there in
his coarse fur coat good-naturedly resigned to the inevitable
refusal.

In a neighbouring canton another elder has been chosen ; he
and his new colleague now go together to the church, where there
is no one but the priest, an able and rather stately-looking person,
who recites the formula of the Cantonal Elder's oath.　The two
peasants, with their hands raised, repeat the oath after him
word by word ; it is mostly about fidelity to the Emperor.　At
the end the priest blesses them with a copy of the Gospels
and with the cross, and then gives an excellent explanation of
their moral responsibilities, especially counselling them to work
for the diminishing of drunkenness as the root of all sorts of
trouble.　The two elders listen earnestly, cross themselves, and
quietly go off to their work.　The Land Captain drives off in
his troika, but the electors still wait about in front of the
Court-house conversing with each other.　Later I pass several
of them, returning at sunset in separate groups to their respective villages.　They seem to be gravely discussing the events of
the day.

The cantonal meeting also names peasant candidates for the
Zemstva, and from these the Governor in a very haphazard way
selects as many as are required for membership.

The land of each village has a distinct boundary.　It may be

let on lease, but may not be permanently alienated, so long as the communal system exists. Peasants are, however, free to buy land, for instance from the gentry; and they can do this in their corporate capacity as a Village Society. A village which prospers will probably possess a greater number of " hands," and can to a certain extent redress inequalities by leasing land from a less prosperous village. Inside its own boundaries it can redress them far more effectively. Imagine that there are two families each consisting of ten members; cholera attacks the village and takes nine from one family and none from the other; a majority of two-thirds of the tax-paying heads of houses declares for a re-division, and each of the eleven survivors whom we are considering receives an equal share. But a re-division cannot take place more often than every twelve years, and I have seen villages which have never decided to re-divide at all since the emancipation; one village, for instance, felt a difficulty in doing so the first time (when the division would mean far more than it had meant in times of serfdom) and has never divided at all, thus passing naturally into the conditions of personal ownership. The poorer members went so far as to set fire to ricks and houses in order to compel the richer to divide, but the community was prosperous enough for the richer to possess a stable majority. Garden property cannot be divided at all.[1] In many cases, therefore, the peasant has lived for some time half-way between two systems of ownership, and the manner in which the question of re-division is settled is at least thoroughly democratic. Divisions ordinarily take place in the spring, and no allowance can be made for those who have taken more trouble in sowing their land with good seed. It is quite impossible to retain the same portion which one has held during the preceding period, for all the land devoted to crops may become pasture land; and the pasture land is always the common property of the whole village.

The peasants are scrupulously fair about the division of land. At the time of the Emancipation many of the gentry secured the best land and thus interposed their estates between the holdings of the Village Society. In some cases they were even able to establish a kind of economic tyranny, making the peasants pay for the right of passage to the water. Parts of the village

[1] It can be inherited by sons or daughters, but not by the children of daughters.

holding were therefore far from the village. These parts were equally divided, and then perhaps the whole of the distant land was left without cultivation. The village divides the land into three categories—good, moderate and bad. Each portion has a share in each category of land. This again puts a distance between the different parts of a man's holding. The system of "strips" is in many ways most inconvenient; but a long strip is perhaps easier to plough than a square patch.

There are also the special divisions between father and son, which may take place at any time. Russian peasant custom has attempted to deal with questions whose solution we in England have left more or less to hazard. An English landowner holds his land till he dies; an English wage-earner can claim no part of his son's wages. In Russia, the family system is so developed, that a peasant who goes to work in the town cannot resign membership of the Village Society without buying himself out, and ordinarily continues to send home a considerable part of his wages to assist in the payment of the village taxes and dues. The grown-up son who stays at home will probably continue to live in his father's house and to work for the family until he marries. The marriage of course introduces a new element, that is the daughter-in-law.

After the harvest the more steady young men pass in review the eligible girls; even in Moscow it is still the custom for the marriageable young women to be paraded about the streets for inspection. Marriages are by tradition very largely a matter of arrangement between the parents. Leaving aside the old régime of force at the time of the Tartar yoke and the arbitrary power of the serf-owner, who might match his peasants as he might match his horses, even the peasants themselves have taken this view of marriage. In several parts still lingers the old plan of betrothal by match-makers, and the two families concerned will still visit each other's houses in family deputation "to see the riches." In the old days, when large peasant families lived in large houses, what was wanted before all things was a good strong servant to take her share of house-work, and the worship of physical lustiness survives more in Russia than elsewhere. For such reasons as this, weddings were more often than not sad affairs. The bride would complain "that her brother had sold her to a Tartar."

The wedding songs are some of them very beautiful, but most of them very sad :—

> " Not a breath of air : sudden rose the wind ;
> Not for guests I looked : suddenly they came ;
> Full was all the court, full of chestnut steeds,
> Full the chambers all, full of maidens sweet ;
> Várushka, my heart, wept and cried aloud,
> ' Come, O mother mine, come and comfort me.' " [1]

In former times one of the first signs of a wife's allegiance was that she knelt down and took off her husband's boots.

The bride in a large peasant household was practically a servant to her mother-in-law, and the traditional relations between the two were never more vigorously expressed in the literature of any country. Nekrásoff gives us the picture of the mother-in-law standing in the small hours at the bedside of her daughter-in-law and droning :—

> " Get up, get up, get up, you lazy one ;
> Get up, you lazy one, you drowsy one, you frowsy one." [2]

The relations between mother-in-law and son-in-law appear to be no better ; and we can well imagine that the former is often somewhat insistent in the claims that she makes for her daughter. Here is a peasant song in which the singer begins with his deepest national aspirations, and breaks off sharply into the simplest domestic interests :—

> " I'm going, I'm going,
> Down to Byzant [3] I'm going ;
> I'll break there, I'll break there,
> Wall with hatchet I'll break there ;
> I'll find there, I'll find there,
> Crown all golden I'll find there ;
> I'll beat her, I'll beat her,
> My wife's mother I'll beat her ;
> Then she'll be, then she'll be,
> Nice and gentle then she'll be ;
> I'll beat him, I'll beat him,
> My wife's father I'll beat him ;
> Then he'll be," etc.,[4]

all this to a most musical melody ; and so we go on through the whole of his wife's family.

---

[1] Song of the government of Nizhny-Novgorod, district of Knyaghínino.
[2] Nekrásoff, " Who can live happy in Russia ? "
[3] Literally Tsargrad, the Emperor's town, which means, of course, Constantinople.
[4] Song of the government of Samára, district of Stavropol.

It will, then, easily be understood that the son's wife soon stirs him up to claim his independence.   By all accounts, it is generally soon after marriage that he demands from his father a division of property.   Let us say that he has worked for hire and has been able to build his own house.   He will now be an acceptable candidate for membership of the Village Society; he has shown that he is capable of paying his share of the taxes, and the more taxpayers there are, the better it will be for everybody.   If he is accepted as a member by the village meeting, the elder will send an order to his father to divide.   These divisions cause no end of trouble.   After many hard words on both sides, the father may tell his son to be content with a ridiculously small share.   In principle, he has to provide him with enough to live upon, and with implements for work; but if he has very little for himself, how can he give?   If he yields the cow and keeps the horse, dividing the land into equal portions, neither of them will be able to keep his beast properly; for this very reason cattle are in some districts becoming scarce, and therefore there is little manure for the land.   More probably reference has to be made to the peasants' law-court, which, however, has no final power to enforce a fair division.   As a rule, the father gets the better of it; often he will even complain to the village meeting that an absent son is not sending him a due share of his town wages, and will get the Society to support him.   While rowing me across Lake Nero, a young peasant told me the simple story of his quarrel with his father.   There was hardly anything to divide, and the affair ended in a violent scene, at the end of which his father turned him and his wife out of doors.   His " document " from the Village Society had done nothing for him, and now his brothers would legally inherit all his father's small property.   He had persuaded his aunt, who held land, to migrate with him, but she still refused to will away her " portion."   His father and he, though living in the same village, had not spoken to each other for three months.

The Village Society, by all accounts, acts well as a substitute for poor law relief; the peasant continues to his death to be a part owner in the village land, and can retain his share as long as he can induce someone to cultivate it for him.   But, on the other hand, the pace of development is that of the whole body, that is, the pace of the slowest.   Agriculture is made difficult by quite

unnecessary portioning up of the soil. The allotting, to be equit-
able, must sometimes be unbusinesslike; for instance, each must
have some of the good land, so that a man's holdings are often far
apart; and it is impossible to introduce any improvements unless
you can persuade the Village Society to do so as a whole. Last,
and most important, it is of no use to spend much labour and money
on the land if you are aware that you have no sure tenure of it, and
that in any case a competence[1] is assured to you. The communal
system therefore in some ways puts a premium on laziness.[2]

The peasants are stoutly built, as if for slow and persistent
labour.[3] The men are full-faced, with snub noses, little twinkling
eyes, and rough beards; the complexion and the hang of the
limbs usually suggest a low standard of diet. The younger
women are robust, vigorous, and often comely; the old ones, with
angular features and with sunken eyes and cheeks, suggest the
impenetrable shrewdness of an old witch. The northern type of
Central Russia is a tall, strong-looking man, with flaxen hair and
blue eyes. In Tver the outlines of the features are sharp. In
Yaroslavl the men are particularly well-looking, but not the
women. In Nizhny there is a businesslike suppleness of the
figure. The women of Vladímir and Novgorod struck me as
particularly vigorous and full of mother-wit. In Moscow and
southwards there is a darker type, less tall but sometimes stouter,
with dark eyes set in a full face. The Ryazán peasants look
weak, and the Smolensk peasants look bedraggled. Bare feet are
common; so are putties, and also great top-boots of grey felt,
worn through at the critical points. The men wear caps or go
bareheaded. On feast days they favour shirts of bright colours,
especially lilac, with very often a pattern worked down the front;
such work is noticeably good in the Smolensk government.
The breeks are of thin stuff, highly coloured; the peasant makes
his own long sheepskin coat, and often wears it throughout the
sultry Russian summer. The peasant women wear kerchiefs over
their heads, of cream, dull red, or black, according to age, with
curious patterns in these often-recurring colours. I have one
such head-dress which is a map of Russia, surrounded with

---

[1] The Russian phrase is "a bite of bread."
[2] Serious modifications have been introduced into the communal system in 1906.
[3] The following description applies to the peasants of Great Russia.

pictures. They, too, favour lilac for feast-day skirts or blouses; the skirts are short and businesslike; they seldom match the blouse. Red is of all the most favoured colour. Peculiarly bright are the costumes of the government of Ryazán; I saw one old lady with a beautiful apron of sage green. Children are often dressed in pink. Town dress is gradually coming in amongst the peasants. Several already wear hats. In the district of Rostóff I met a curious mixture of town and country, a bare-footed woman in an excellent mackintosh. Peasant girls, I am told, will sometimes prefer dress even to food. A peasant servant-maid of the Ryazán government, when asked by her mistress what she would like for a wedding present, declared for a silk shawl and some curtains.

The peasants often carry themselves very well. It is not that they ordinarily would think of challenging comparison with other classes or other peoples; on the contrary, they are something distinctive, which knows what it is and does not try to be any-thing different; they are very proud of their class name, which really means " Christian " or "man of the cross." Their loose-limbed easiness looks natural and has a grace of its own; their gestures, though often almost barbarously violent, are a very good expression of their thoughts and feelings. Sometimes, even in friendly discussion, their voices and gestures seem almost like blows. On a dirty patch of ground in Ryazhsk I saw several peasants rallying a stout middle-aged woman; she suddenly turned on them with a loud "Boo!" and walked away amidst general laughter. At Novgorod, I saw a young woman keep a whole roomful of peasants spell-bound by a flow of vigorous clever talk, full of inflections, which sometimes suggested the old Saxon "Out on you!" It was the first time that I had seen a peasant woman "hold a *salon*." The peasants are, before all things, kind-hearted, friendly, and sociable; and their simple, homely natures have many curious shadings and quaint fancies which make them very interesting. The heart is the best part of them, and it is sound; it informs the mind. The peasant mind moves freely enough in its simple circle, and is full of kindly shrewdness and wit. Their talk is excellent; it is unconsciously artistic, full of natural poetry, yet never strained. They show their kinship with the classic literature of Russia, by generally saying in terse and suggestive language just what they can bring to the occasion of conversation, and nothing more. They will often make no effort to put their thoughts into shape, but will let them speak for themselves. They can, however, when they choose, make quite a pretty picture of any event or fact to please the companion of the moment; and this power, though they are half unconscious of exercising it, enables them to deceive one very effectively. They have, moreover, like most Russians, an excellent sense of humour; and a smile from the listener will provoke a smile from the speaker which breaks through the deception. I remember walking under the wall of the China Town at Moscow, and seeing a witty, bearded man selling a book; he was reading from it Russian popular poetry, which some illiterate might buy for a friend or even for a chimney-piece decoration. By looking over his shoulder, I saw that the book was, as a matter of fact, Otto's " German Conversation Grammar," yet he was in no way discomfited by my discovery, and smiled pleasantly for my approval of his wit. I daresay that many small thefts (the prevailing crime of the peasants) are perpetrated in the same spirit; cunning is here a word of praise.

The peasants are lazy; for this reason they are little able to depend upon themselves. And so, of course, their employers cannot entirely depend upon them either. The fact is, that they really do not much care what happens to them. This spirit is a product of history; as an able Liberal said to me, " if you never see your pay coming, you lose interest in your work."

There was always a certain obstinacy about the Russian peasant. He had his own atmosphere, which he knew through and through, and of what was outside it he knew but little, except that there was a great governing force based on himself and the mass of his fellows.[1] In his eyes this force represented both his nation and his religion; what was alien to it, whether inside or outside of Russia, was still more alien to him. A settled order of things, with all its familiar by-ways, he accepted, but made little or no attempt to understand anything outside it. For this reason, he is more or less unintelligible both to the officials and

---

[1] See Kryloff's admirable fable, "The Leaves and the Roots." The roots, which are the peasants, remind the leaves, which are the Intelligents, that they are the bottom foundation of all.

to the Intelligents, who are, we must remember, members of one and the same theorising class. They will describe him, for instance, as a man who simply knows how to drink himself silly on feast days and thus spoil the morrow's work; or, again, as "a purely material animal, who works and drinks and lies about like a dog"; as "absolutely indifferent to government and laws and only knowing that he has got to obey, and that the authorities can do what they like"; as "not bothering about politics even when he is a man of substance"; and as "hanging like a dead weight on any national movement, being quite indifferent as to who sits there in St. Petersburg." Another Intelligent, while in some ways greatly admiring the peasants, looks upon their progress as purely economical; this gentleman, when in the government of Perm, "felt as if he were at the bottom of the sea, living under a huge pressure of water amongst strange fishes, who could not live if brought to the surface." The peasant has in general refused to be drawn into the dreams of the student, and has clung to those simple instincts and traditions which have so far made life tolerably intelligible to him; and in doing so he is a true representative of his country, which has, over and over again, refused to accept either Asia or Europe at their own price; for that price is the sacrifice of the individuality of Russia. He is, therefore, stubborn to a degree, and no less so when he appears to be yielding. Some things may be done without him, or in spite of him; but to anyone who tries to force him to act against his instincts, he will oppose an utterly indifferent and regardless inertia, or a calculating shrewdness which knows how to seem the same thing. Yet this very faithfulness to instinct is a guarantee of his soundness, and acts as an invaluable counterpoise to the Slav wit and fancy. It keeps the gaze of the peasant on to the ground; it ties him to his own world, which has indeed been filled by him with a whole wealth of variety and detail.

Peasant life and peasant work are, as we have seen, corporate. Great herds of cattle and horses, interspersed with ducks and geese, wander about the common land of the village. The cutting of hay suggests a great army at work. During the summer the peasants use all the good light of the year. You will see masses of them concentrated on one part of the village land, or you may meet them returning in a great band from their haymaking, carrying their scythes shouldered like spears or banners. They work slowly but with resource, much as nature bids them, gradually harassing into kindness the soil which is at once their enemy and their mother. Many of them still continue to use an old-fashioned apology for a plough, the sokhá made of wood and shod with a point of steel. In the fields, the women seem as busy as the men, but they probably get through much less work; for instance, in a backward province, the women may get sixpence, boys fourpence, and girls threepence or twopence, while a man may earn a shilling.[1] The peasant pays three taxes, none of which seem overwhelming. First there is the Government tax of, say, a few pence on two and three-quarter acres. This of course excludes special gifts, and corporate subscriptions in war-time, which are extra burdens. Secondly, he pays the country impost, which is much heavier than the Government tax, but is levied by the Zemstvo, and in great part returns to him in the shape of improvements. Lastly, he is still paying instalments for the redemption of his land from the ownership of his former lords; this payment is to cease in 1907. It is hardly possible that famine should extend over the whole country; but the arrangements of the Government have been very inadequate. Corn has been exported when it has been wanted at home, and there may often be scarcity in a given part. Though warehouses are established to store corn, I am told that often, when the corn is wanted, it has been found that it has all disappeared through the dishonesty or gross negligence of the caretakers. The peasants cannot take their corn from the store without the leave of the Land Captain. The conditions of country life are hardy but healthy. The peasant is used to privations, and would be astounded at the amount of meat consumed in England.

The feast days take up nearly as much as half of the year. In December comes the feast of Nicholas the Wonder-worker, when priests go visiting their parishioners for about two weeks, and no work is done. Soon afterwards come the feast days of Christmas. A recent law enacted that men should not be punished for working on feast days; but the Synod, in its interpretation of the law, made this concession almost nugatory, and public opinion among the peasants is still in some parts a very strong deterrent. Religion,

[1] *I.e.*, for hired labour in the service of a neighbouring landowner.

as we shall see, is one of the chief recreations of the peasant, and plays a very real and important part, at least in his outward life. It is in many cases closely allied to gross superstition. The peasant has peopled the woods and rivers with fairy spirits, usually of a malignant character. The belief in the evil eye still lingers on. A priest told me of a woman who went to a doctor for a certificate to the effect that she was built like other women and did not have a tail. One of my country friends had a sorcerer living on his estate (1905). This man believed that he could exercise a special power, for instance, through the eye. My friend, a very acute person, asked the sorcerer to give him lessons, but the man had a superstitious scruple against instructing one who was older than himself. He professed to be able to whisper, that is, use spells, which, in his case, were always of a beneficent kind. He had certain traditional blisters and tricks, some of which have been adopted by the medical profession. He thought that he could, if he wished, communicate infectious disease without having it. Such men used to live apart in lonely places; now they will live in the villages. The peasants believed in this sorcerer, but thought it safer to have nothing to do with him. "And does he call himself an orthodox Christian?" I asked. "Oh yes! that doesn't hinder."

Another common relaxation is music. The peasant songs are countless; they have grown up out of the soil, and in many cases have never been committed to paper. They are sometimes legends and sometimes romances of ordinary peasant life. They are not rhymed, and go on, verse after verse, in the most irregular scansion, leaving very much to the fancy of the singer. But the melodies, which lend themselves to this variety, are sometimes even beautiful, and their simplicity and their fancy will appeal to one who knows them at all well in such a way as to put him out of conceit with the more regular and less ambitious folk-songs of other countries. It must be remembered that one of the chief subjects of school-teaching is Church singing without an accompaniment; but the peasants, whose voices are harsh and weird, have a natural tendency to flatness. I can remember a night entry into one of the most miserable towns[1] in Russia to this dismal

---

[1] Novorzheff. Pushkin, who lived near here, says, "Luga would be the worst town in the world if there were not my Novorzheff too."

accompaniment, and, indeed, these songs are used less as a means of entertaining others than as a lightening of the spirit. There are songs of the pilgrims, and there are an especially large number of songs of the Volga bargees, which may sound very musical if heard over a wide expanse of river.

Sometimes the workers who are rolling a barrel on to the ship will divide into two parties, the optimists and the pessimists :—

> " He won't go through."   " He shall go through."
> " He won't go through."   " He shall go through."
> " He goes, he goes, he goes, he goes ;
>   He's gone, he's gone, he's gone."

Many of the songs are designed for impromptu dances ; and the peasants often dance, though they are sometimes very clumsy and do not like to display themselves before persons of other classes.

Perhaps the most common of all diversions is drinking. Vodka, I think, cannot have been invented to give pleasure ; its mission must be to produce forgetfulness, especially of its own exceedingly nasty taste, and that as soon as possible. It is, in fact, not the taste of vodka that is relished, but the feeling inside which it produces. The fancies to which it can quicken the peasant are, of course, many and various. I am stranded in a dirty little village ; a slack-looking man in a blue blouse engages to drive me on. Unfortunately, while I am paying a visit at the next village, he gets drunk. " Yes," he says, when we have resumed our journey, " it is written in our law " (the Scriptures): " ' Kingdom shall rise against kingdom, and people against people ' ; this proves that there must be war between England and Russia." " But," I ask, " does it say when ? Perhaps it has come true already." " God grant that we may not live to that day," he continues ; "but have you got a God ? We Russians fear nothing except a universal war : we shall all go ; I'll go. We're all brothers ; you're a good fellow. It's a terrible thing to answer before God. We shall take them all alive ; God grant we may not live to see that day." He is almost the only man whom I met who talked like the *Moscow Gazette.*

The Russian peasants are exceptionally sociable. Great waste spaces seem to suddenly fill with men and women all going in one direction. The rough-bearded man walks in front, and his

wife follows, carrying his top-boots and her own ; they will put on
the boots when they approach the village, and so will make a
clean show at the feast.   At last we reach the heart of all this
interest, a dirty village street with grey weather-beaten houses,
and a white church with a green roof.   There are booths with
diverse wares of curious fancy, but all bearing the stamp of a
common taste.   The carts are all put up in a common shed.
There is a throng of men of different ages, talking in voices
of different pitch, like a great family of fathers and brothers,
often quarrelling, but always a family.   The stranger who tries
to enter the group will see the same look of mutual understanding
and reticence on all faces.   The crowd stands patient and reverent,
waiting for hours till the priest has carried the ikons past in
procession.   The church is thronged with men standing silent
and awestruck, or kneeling before an ikon and beating their
heads against the stone floor.   When the sacred hour is past,
the peasants sit down together, by families, on the grass, and
eat.   As the afternoon wears on a cry of " Thief ! " may be raised,
and you will see a whole mass of movement stream in one direction.   Later the less steady (the peasant word is the "weaker")
will be seen lying anyhow on the ground ; and the Russian
peasant has a weak head, lives on poor diet, and means business
when he starts drinking.   In the darkness one may run upon a
group of men and women, dancing hand in hand and singing
their hoarse weird songs.

The earliest nobility consisted of the bands of "companions"
("druzhiny") who accompanied the Varanger chiefs into Russia.
These men, who soon became Russianised, were rather servants
of the State than hereditary nobles.   The different sovereign
princes were all of one family, and the "Boyars," as they came
to be called, had the right of migrating from one prince to another.
It will be remembered that a prince would often move on to a new
principality, in which case his band of companions would accompany him thither or else be disbanded.   The grant of land which
the Boyar received was very definitely a pledge of State service.
As Moscow became supreme, the descendants of other princely
families became ordinary nobles ; their importance in the State
depended, like that of their fellows, on Government service,

and, as the autocracy became stronger, this dependence became more absolute. There were, of course, many different grades of nobles, and constant quarrels went on as to questions of precedence. A noble, tracing back the rank and service of his ancestors, would refuse to take a post under another whose family was less illustrious. These squabbles intruded even **1682.** into the palace and to the table of the Tsar, and became such a nuisance that the records of precedence were destroyed.

Grants of land continued to carry the obligation of State service, and the Russian word for a landowner means more or less " the man on the spot." Serfdom was established precisely in order to enable the smaller gentry to execute their State functions. Peter the Great, while making serfdom more general and more rigid, also made the consideration of all the gentry to depend more strictly upon service to the State. A man's rank was to go not by his birth, but by his office. Peter III. declared the gentry free of the obligations imposed by his grandfather, but under Catherine the Great the gentry became perhaps more servile in their relations to the throne than they had ever been before. Suvóroff himself showed his genius by finding out new ways of grovelling. Paul declared that there was no one of consequence in Russia except him to whom he himself spoke, and that only while he was speaking. His son Alexander I. introduced a more liberal atmosphere; and from that time onward, though Nicholas I. and later Alexander III. have tried to draw the bonds of authority tighter, there has gradually been coming over the whole class a change which tends to identify it more and more with that section of Russian society known under the name of the Intelligents. The noble, then, was a State servant, but though his authority was, in principle, delegated, at a distance from the capital he would be as supreme as a little Tsar. Some families, like the Stroganoffs, owed their importance to great enterprises of commerce and colonisation. The estates which they built up were almost like separate principalities. In some districts, such as Perm, there are hardly any gentry, only considerable peasant farmers. Serfdom was worst nearest to Moscow, which shows to what extent the system was governmental. The absolute rule of the master and the patriarchal character of his relations with his peasants have already been indicated.   Much of this atmosphere still remains ; but the emancipation, so to speak, struck the gentry out of the peasant life.   The landowner, instead of being charged with the interests of the peasants, was now an alien or almost hostile power established at their side.   He lost his serfs; he lost half of what he considered as his land.   From the time that the life of the capitals began to develope the gentry had flocked thither for at least a part of the year.   Born travellers, like the rest of the nation, they were the very moths of civilisation, and desired before all things to go and burn their wings at Paris.   Their clever minds developed fast under such influences ; but autocracy never taught character, and the emancipation in many ways absolved the gentry from responsibility.   Many of them, on receiving the compensation payment from the Government, did not know what to do with so large a sum of money and spent it.   Many sold the remaining parts of their estates, whether to peasants or to parvenu merchants, and went away to live in the towns, thus identifying themselves even more closely with the Intelligents.   The Government of the Reaction meanwhile has tried to restore something of the old authority of the landowner by instituting the post of Land Captain.   This man is far more of an official than the old master of serfs, and is much more closely under the control of the Government.   The Land Captain is supposed to be chosen from amongst the gentry of the district, but in some cases there is only one gentleman in two cantons who can suitably be nominated to the post.   Sometimes the place will be filled by a landowner who is not a member of the gentry at all, and sometimes it is hard to find a suitable candidate even of this kind.   A Marshal of the gentry of a District described the exodus to me as a " sauve qui peut " ; he has to find five Land Captains, and ten years ago he could easily enough name two for each post; now he has with difficulty filled up four of the posts, and one remains vacant, as there is no one suitable ; he has had to write to the Governor of the province and ask him to send a simple official to discharge the duties.   This arrangement is most unsatisfactory.

The gentry of the District meet to elect their Marshal ; the Marshals of the District meet to elect the Marshal of the gentry of the whole province ; the election is almost invariably confirmed by the Emperor. The gentry discuss in common their own institutions. They have clubs in most District towns, and some large charitable institutions for their own class in the capitals. They relieve the distress of their own poor; they give scholarships to the sons of poor gentry. They can appoint wardens to look after the interest of minors, and these wardens are subject to the control of a kind of class law-court, consisting of all the local gentry. They can admit or refuse candidates who are qualified by law to rank as gentry and ask to be admitted to membership in a particular District; thus a Jew who was legally qualified was refused by the local gentry. They may levy a very small tax upon themselves for common objects. They can discuss in common the needs of their Districts, and, in 1905, the Marshals of the gentry of several Governments joined together to make a moderately worded claim for the most necessary reforms. The Marshal of the gentry has a great deal of business in connection with the government ; but all real power is in the hands of the Police Colonel. The Marshal is consulted on the appointment of Land Captains, but his advice is not necessarily taken. He presides over them when they meet at the District Sessions ; he regulates their leave of absence. Officially he takes precedence of the Police Colonel, and presides on all local committees, such as those which deal with recruiting, the maintenance of prisons, the upkeep of schools, and public temperance ; but he is always over-weighted by official votes. His chief real responsibility is the presidency of the local Zemstvo assembly, in which the atmosphere is far more free. He has the entry of the Court; but it is of little use to him as a representative of his class or of the population. He can only be dismissed by the Senate and after an investigation. If he satisfies the Ministers, he may be appointed to some high governmental post ; and that is the real importance of his office. The nobles have been described as " a corporation from which officialdom recruits its forces."

The country house will probably lie on a private road, where the little bridges may be even more rudely extemporised than on the high-roads. On the better estates there will be something park-like about the approach. One comes to a wooden barrier, and passing through a gate, enters a grassy and neglected court-yard, around which stand detached buildings of many kinds and uses,—barns, stables, kitchen, and dining-room. The house will be low, spacious, and attractive. The amount of paint on it may give an index of the character and self-respect of the owner. The porch is in the middle of a verandah. The rooms open out one from another; they are spacious, but not too closely adapted to any one use. The drawing-room may be a room of special sacredness and elegance, with mirrors and carefully covered-up sofas, yet I have often slept in it. Each room will, of course, have its ikon, usually in that corner which first catches the eye as one enters. There will be a kitchen garden, tended or weedy, as the case may be.

1. At the distant station a trap is waiting for me in charge of a business-like young driver. Through high and graceful fir trees, we drive over loose sand to the broad desolate Dnyépr. Here, almost exactly at the spot where Ney escaped in 1812, the banks shelve steeply down some twenty-five feet. A rustic rope ferry carries us across. The Zemstvo is, as usual, still busy at road repairs, so we strike out boldly on to a low heath, where a thick mist rises to a height of some ten feet and makes luminous circles round the harvest moon; through well-tilled fields and up a graceful slope we pass to the great courtyard, and an ancient servant in a blue shirt comes out to support my arm as I mount the steps of the porch. I sleep on a sofa in the spacious "study," which is evidently the library of a genuine student. I have no looking-glass with me, but I find that a picture held in a certain way will serve nearly as well. The house, which is of two storeys, is like a white castle with a red roof; its tower dominates a sweep of open country up to the high birch trees which stand sentinels over Napoleon's road. There are an outer and an inner courtyard, surrounded by detached buildings of brick, plaster, or wood. The rooms have but little furniture, and that quite plain. The library contains all the Russian classics, in the edition of the newspaper *Niva*. There were many special books on peasant customs and husbandry, but nearly all, in the course of several years, have gone out on loan and have never been returned. The garden is full of good fruit, and contains beds of curious grasses in brilliant shades of red and yellow. In a far corner is a chapel built in memory of a lady of the family. On the big prosperous estate are rye, oats, and potatoes, some spring wheat, and much wood. Next day two

carriages with plumed coachmen drive up into the courtyard; my host and his two children have returned from a distant journey. He is one of those who make one feel perfectly at home at once. There is the same easy air about the whole family. Visitors go in and out of the house, and are pressed to stay as long as possible. Informal meals seem to be going on at all hours; there is a great table in the garden, on which stand an ever-boiling samovar and dishes with light cakes, rusks, and cheese biscuits. A peasant child comes up to the house every day to play with the youngest son; the homely old peasant nurse seems like a member of the family. The little boy of three brings me flowers from the garden. Another, who is thirteen, takes me to a wood where there is an ancient encampment, which he explains with excellent intelligence.

2. The master's house lies by the side of a small river in a pleasant plantation. I decide to dismount and get some information; nothing simpler. The front-door bell will not ring, but when I try at the kitchen door, the prince comes through in a rustic peaked cap, a peasant shirt and girdle, and long top-boots. My letter for the peasant elders is no introduction, but at least explains my purpose. He reads it through casually. "Will you come in for a little day?" he asks. I slept last night in a peasant court-house, and would like first of all to have a shave; for this purpose I am taken into the best room, a very tasteful drawing-room in blue and white, with a good sofa, mirrors, a little furniture, and a bare brown floor. The rest of the low house is very simple and primitive, and entirely lacking in at least one thing which is considered a necessary. We sit down to a long talk. The whole day is one continuous conversation, and always about interesting subjects. We talk of the war, of the relations between England and Russia, of the degree in which reform is desirable and probable, of the neighbouring gentry, and finally of sport. "You need a rest," he suddenly says, and I go to sleep on the sofa in the drawing-room, which room he locks me into.

3. Two magnificent troikas meet us at the station. After a ten-mile drive we enter a broad enclosure. On the verandah stand our hosts with their family; the welcome which they all give us suggests a lifelong acquaintance; we are all going to enjoy

ourselves. Within a few minutes we are swinging round a
"giant's stride," or playing our host and his cousin at lawn-tennis,
as "England against Russia." " How badly they play!" says
the lady with refreshing frankness. " Yes," says he, " I never
expected it." The next day we take our plunge in Volga waters,
and then go off with our host to question some of the neighbouring villagers. On rainy days we teach indoor athletics to willing
learners. When we go, we feel that the first impression was
correct; clearly we must have made friends with them all, without
knowing it, years ago.

Life, in a country house, moves slowly and easily: a walk in
the woods, a shooting expedition, and probably endless games of
cards, which the Russians play with peculiarly quick intuition.
The country houses are far apart, and one may have to travel
some five or six miles to spend an evening with one's nearest
neighbour. Such a visit is an expedition, an event. One may
find quite a number of other guests who have come a like
distance, and the entertainment will be a long one, with many
intervals for refreshment. Or, again, there may be a meeting
for hunting purposes; a bear may leave some bones about, and
the whole district will turn out with guns or beaters. The
beaters will form a wide semicircle, gather in round the bear, and
drive him in on to the guns. Some bears are sensible enough
to run in the direction of the cries, that is, of the beaters. In
this case they will get through, leave the neighbourhood, and
give similar notice of their presence in some other part. The
Russian gentry are almost as accustomed to hardships as the
peasants. While out shooting, they will sleep a whole night in
a marsh, as best they can. At times the court of a country house
will fill with peasants, who have come in to settle for their hired
labour; but, generally speaking, the house will be left to its
solitude. I have been astonished at the indifference which some
gentry have shown for their neighbours, living near each other
for years without caring to visit or to be visited. At a dance in
a country house at which I was present many of the guests did not
seem to know, or to care to know, each other; two in particular,
who had arrived together, walked up and down the middle of the
room amongst the dancers, almost as if they were in the general
waiting-room at a station. Some of the country gentry can talk

of nothing except women, horses, and dogs; and a family will often prefer to live by itself, perhaps with a large stock of Russian, and even of foreign novels. Suddenly the jingling bells of post-horses announce the visit of some possibly unexpected friend. No one is surprised; all are interested; and what would be in an English house a revolution of arrangement for the lodging of the new guests is carried through quite simply in a few minutes. The guests disappear at their own time and at a few hours' notice, and the house settles down at once to its old life. There is little fighting with circumstances; folks submit easily to the isolation from this friend, to the intimacy with that stranger. Little household politics spring up, grow by the absence of competing interests, absorb the whole life, and are either welcomed or tolerated. Little quarrels become feuds; likings become passions; there is the most intimate and frank talk on all subjects, especially on the larger and more universal questions of life, yet each individual remains in his own corner, and an English novelist in search of copy can hardly believe that there are so many variations of actual first-hand experience. Almost everyone has his own romance, and everyone's romance is exceptional, because so many have transgressed all the known rules of the game and, in nine cases out of ten, have paid for it. Meanwhile the obsession of the country surroundings is so real that one may very soon forget that there is any other life than one's own.

I have suggested that there is variety in country life, and the variety is endless. Hardly any two houses have the same atmosphere. In England public opinion reigns in every drawing-room. In Russia for centuries there has been no recognised public opinion at all, at least in the definite sense in which we use the term in England. Every corner has its own perspective, its own fads; the Russian, if asked why he does something unreasonable, may answer, "I am like that," or "Do not hinder my mood." Where moods rule, a reasoned agreement between two persons is almost impossible, nor is compromise any easier, for a Russian often thinks it ignoble to say anything at all which he does not feel, or to make any effort whatever in order to agree with some-one else. He has so keen a critical sense that with him such a compromise can never last for long. Then, too, the great distances, the silence imposed by the Government, and the docile misrepresentations of the Press, have often made it extremely difficult for the Russian to know how many people think one thing and how many another. And without this sense of general perspective the average man cannot be expected to square his convictions with those of others. In consequence, each little circle may be a law unto itself. In one family, the most hopelessly impossible theories will be advocated and received without any likelihood of contradiction ; in another, the opposite extreme of view is equally triumphant. In one house, a consistent family training has been given to each son and daughter; there is a single master of opinions, and amongst the rest one sees an even tedious sameness. In another—and this is more common—we stumble on to a republic where different influences are trying to command the dunghill, but as yet the conflicting forces remain in balance. In such a house, there is almost the keenness of war; there will be alliances and counter-alliances, and each combatant, with a peculiar want of reticence, may try to bring in a passing stranger on his own side. Some of the family will not be combatants at all, but will simply go their own way, as if the persons with whom they live were quite indifferent to them. In general, it is the atmosphere of a novel of the Brontës. Yet even these factions are, in a sense, signs of life. They do not necessarily belie the family instinct, which indeed, under the conditions which I have described, is almost compulsory. At least, if you stay, you will probably have to take your part in this small world.

CHAPTER IV.

RUSSIAN Conservatives have summed up the tradition of their country in the three words "Tsar, Church, and People." The Church was, for a long time, the link which united the other two. Though the present sketch must be limited to a few main facts and some personal impressions and views, the influence of the Church in Russia is a subject which claims serious study. The vast majority of the Russian people is, at least by instinct, "Orthodox."

The Orthodox tradition is specially represented by the "black clergy," or monks, who supply all the higher Church officials.

A clergy-training school, or "seminary," will not admit pupils above the age of sixteen; some enter at fourteen. The younger may finish at nineteen; others stay till twenty-three. The more talented will pass on to a Religious Academy for four years, and can obtain the grade of Student (a simple certificate of residence and study), Candidate, or Magistrant. The Candidate who would become a magistrant must send in a thesis, which will be tested in a debate between him and his examiners. Candidates for the priesthood sometimes serve an apprenticeship. A term of two or three years may be served as a "psalm-singer" (parish clerk) or as teacher in a parish school. Vacant benefices are advertised; anyone who has the degree of Candidate may apply. The parish is allowed to petition in favour of one who has been clerk or teacher in it. The deacon, who may not celebrate the Eucharist, is administratively under his priest, the priest under his bishop or archbishop. "Archbishop" is a personal title without reference to a local jurisdiction, so that a bishop may become an Archbishop without leaving his see. Bishops and Archbishops are under their Metropolitan. All alike are subject to the Synod.

A boy or a man may attach himself to a monastery and become

a "servant." At thirty, not before, he will perhaps become a monk, whether on the official list of the establishment or as a supernumerary. He may also become a deacon, then a priest, and later an arch-priest. Bishops, Archbishops, and Metropolitans are all arch-priests, and as such are equal : it is a kind of "army rank," and has nothing to do with administration. Amongst the monks, the Archimandrite is also an arch-priest ; he wears a mitre, and can be selected as the head of one of the greater monasteries. The lesser monasteries are ruled by "igúmens" or priors. The heads of the three historic Lavry (or greater monasteries) are the three Metropolitans. The three Lavry are the Cave Monastery at Kieff, the Trinity Monastery near Moscow, and that of St. Alexander Nevsky in St. Petersburg. The Metropolitan rules his monastery through a "namyestnik" (or lieutenant)

A parish priest can win by service certain Government decorations ; he can thus become a " personal gentleman," and his sons will then be "hereditary citizens." A clerk is an "honourable citizen," his sons having no special rank. A parish priest must be married ; if he cannot find a bride, one can be found for him, almost always from the family of another priest. There thus tends to be a priestly caste, often recognisable by the family names. These marriages, official as they may be, are said to be amongst the happiest in Russia. The children, too, often have a better chance of a good home training in character than others. But the atmosphere of the seminary has latterly been more demoralising than that of lay-schools, and the seminarists sometimes become the most unscrupulous of place-hunters or the most violent of revolutionaries.

Laymen, except the Tsar, may marry twice ; the priest may only marry once. If the priest's wife dies, he may continue to work in his parish as a widower, or he may become a monk ; and, as all bishops are monks, it is only now that he becomes eligible for a bishopric. If his wife lives, he can rise no higher than rural dean. Thus the closest connection is maintained between the bishops and the monasteries, and the power is in the hands of the black clergy, or monks.

The Church is governed by a Synod, to which is attached a layman, the Tsar's Procurator. This Synod replaced the

Patriarchs, who had seen Russia through some of her hardest days and had rendered great national services, but whose authority was judged by Peter the Great to be a rival to his own in the eyes of the peasants. From that time to this the taint of politics has penetrated into the Church. The Tsar's Procurator is the real director of Church policy; during the Second Reaction the post has been filled by Mr. Pobyedonóstseff, who has raised it to the first importance by his sinister policy of using the authority of the Church as an instrument of governmental repression.

The government of a diocese is exercised by the bishop in conjunction with the Diocesan Consistory, which is an administrative body corresponding to the secular Government Administration. It consists of black clergy, white clergy, and laymen. Attached to it are a secretary and clerks. It controls, amongst other things, the Church schools and seminaries, the relief of poor priests, and the pensioning of those who have retired; and it holds a court of law for religious offences—a court which is generally considered by laymen to be peculiarly corrupt. It is in close relations with the rural deans, who are responsible for the control of the other parish priests. Its real master in latter days has been its secretary, the nominee of Mr. Pobyedonóstseff; the Procurator has prejudiced all the spiritual interests of the Church by his appointments and promotions, and by the political discipline which he has tried to establish. It will, however, be clear from the notes which follow, that a general condemnation must not be extended from Mr. Pobyedonóstseff to all the men who have been under his supervision. On the contrary, the growth of public opinion, which dates from the reforms of Alexander II. and the competition into which it has forced the Church authorities, have had admirable results in reviving the creative instincts of the Church, and in encouraging the country clergy to a deeper and wider sense of their responsibilities. The better of these men are in much closer touch than they could have been twenty years ago with the spiritual and secular interests of their flocks. They are as deeply wounded as any of the laity by the political imposition which has recently been practised upon them, and for which, as they well know, the Church, and religion too, may have to pay dearly when the inevitable reforms have been accomplished in the State. This applies far less to the monks, who remain very much as they were—except that they show less faith and less self-denial than they used to. But of the many country priests whom I have met, all except the most ignorant have utterly refused to bear out Mr. Pobyedonóstseff in his doctrinaire denunciation of schools, initiative, and progress. On the contrary, I know but few of them who have not at least one worthy interest in the affairs of their parish. Sometimes they are trying to teach the peasants to cultivate their fields better; often by means of public readings they are taking their part in helping forward the general movement of progress; often, again, they are energetically fighting that great enemy both of progress and of religion—drunkenness. Altogether, too many writers have dismissed the priests with a word of all-round condemnation. So far the close compartment system has succeeded in keeping almost every class in Russia ignorant of every other class. Yet there is evidence that the merits of good priests are not unrecognised even amongst the Intelligents. One priest has collected the different portraits of clergymen which have found their way into secular literature,[1] and from his very interesting analysis it is easy to see that the scorn with which it is fashionable for some critics to regard the whole order is forgotten even by the Intelligent, when he wishes to give a true picture of village life.

All this only makes it the more necessary for us to emphasise the mischief which has been done to the Church by the policy of Pobyedonóstseff. When Peter the Great abolished the Patriarchate the higher ecclesiastics, capable as they might be, came to be rather statesmen than ministers of the Gospel. Even from that time the Chief Procurator of the Synod, who in principle was to act as the Tsar's eye, began to usurp an undue authority over the Church. When Pobyedonóstseff came to occupy this post, Russia had just entered upon the Second Reaction, a period when the old vague traditions of autocracy were formulated into a hard and fast dogma. Pobyedonóstseff himself wrote a remarkable book[2] in which he used his acute intelligence to prove that all intelligence is suspect. It begins with a chapter called

---

[1] N. A. Kolósoff, "Types of the Orthodox Clergy in Russian Secular Literature."

[2] Published in English under the title : "Reflections of a Russian Statesman."

" Church and State," which words suggest indeed the motto of
his policy. He next proceeds to pulverise " The New
Democracy." "What is this freedom," he writes, " by which
so many minds are agitated, which inspires so many insensate
actions, so many wild speeches, which leads the people so often
to misfortune ? In the democratic sense of the word freedom is
the right of political power, or, to express it otherwise, the right
to participate in the government of the State. This universal
aspiration for a share in government has no constant limitations,
and seeks no definite issue, but incessantly extends, so that we
might apply to it the words of the ancient poet about dropsy :
' Crescit indulgens sibi. . . . The history of mankind bears
witness that the most necessary and fruitful reforms, the most
durable measures, emanated from the supreme will of statesmen
or from a minority enlightened by lofty ideas and deep knowledge." The next chapter is on " The Great Falsehood of Our
Time." "Amongst the falsest of political principles is the
principle of the sovereignty of the people. . . . Thence proceeds
the theory of parliamentarism, which up to the present day has
deluded much of the so-called Intelligence and unhappily
infatuated certain foolish Russians. It continues to maintain its
hold on many minds with the obstinacy of a narrow fanaticism,
although every day its falsehood is exposed more clearly to the
world." The next deals with the Press. " From the day that
man first fell falsehood has ruled the world, . . . but never did
the father of lies spin such webs of falsehood of every kind as in
this restless age. . . . Thus we are bidden to believe that· the
judgment of newspapers and periodicals, the judgment of the
so-called Press, is the expression of public opinion. This too is
a falsehood. The Press is one of the falsest institutions of our
time." The chapter on " Public Instruction " opens with the
words, " When reason is severed from life it becomes at once
artificial, formal, and in consequence sterile." From this truism
Mr. Pobyedonóstseff has deduced a policy which is not only
suspicious of all instruction, but even definitely hostile to it.
" Humanity," he writes, " is endowed with another very effective
force : inertia. As the ballast in a ship, inertia sustains
humanity in the crises of its history, and so indispensable has
it become that without it all measured progress would be

impossible. This force, which the superficial thinkers of the
new school confuse with ignorance and stupidity, is absolutely
essential to the prosperity of society." In a brilliant chapter on
" The Malady of Our Time," the author deals with the general
discontent, neurotic disease, abstract science, the search for
happiness, hasty reform, the power of wealth, rival schools of
thought, and universal vanity. To all these evils he opposes the
precept, " That ye love one another." Knowledge he contrasts with work. After stating his conception of "Faith," he
makes some very clever criticisms on Darwinism, the new
religion, and the new marriage. Considerable space is devoted to
" The Spiritual Life " and " The Church." In the course of this
study, he says : " How many men, how many institutions, have
been perverted in the course of a false development! For these
rooted principles in our religious institutions are, of all things,
the most precious. May God prevent them from ever being
destroyed by the untimely reformation of our Church." There
follow some clever but most pessimistic sketches of characters
in higher Russian society, and the following apophthegm on
power and authority : " Whilst humanity exists it will not cease
to suffer, sometimes from power, sometimes from impotence.
The violence, the abuse, the folly, the selfishness, of power raise
rebellion. Deceived in their ideals of power, men seek to dispense with it and to replace it by the authority of law. This is
a vain fancy. In the name of the law arise a multitude of
unauthorised factions which struggle for power, and the distribution of power leads to violence worse than that which went
before."

This clever and interesting book suggests criticisms at every
step. For instance, was Mr. Pobyedonóstseff a member of an
enlightened minority? Did stable reforms come from the Throne
during the period of his power? Did inertia carry Russia
through the crisis of the Japanese war ? Were the "feeble deeds "
of which he speaks those of the soldiers who defended Port
Arthur, or those of the generals whom the oligarchy set over
them ? But, without here entering into a discussion of the
familiar principles of reaction, we may simply assert that they are
in the highest degree doctrinaire and one-sided, and we can then
pass on to the final defect of this line of argument. Mr.

Pobyedonóstseff is a confessed pessimist. In a conversation with one of the most honest and religious of his opponents, he admitted that he was surrounded by men of poor ability and feeble morals. These were the men whom he had chosen; yet he never submitted to the obvious inference from this test of his own party, and continued to distrust and exclude from all responsibility the vast majority both of the Church and of the nation. Such a man could be excused if he retired to a monastery on the White Sea; but when he has condemned the world in general, and movement in general, he never offers to explain why he himself should remain in power. Apparently it is because he happens to be there, and because inertia is opposed to change. What is the result for the rest of Russia, on whose faith and energy Mr. Pobyedonóstseff thus imposes his unnatural restrictions? It is by no means clear that he has a faith of his own, yet he cancels all the aspirations of others. Byron, speaking of a far greater man, the first Napoleon, says: " For sceptred cynics earth were far too wide a den."

The book of Pobyedonóstseff becomes important by the fact that he was in power, and therefore was able to impose its principles on others. Certainly, true religion is at all times needed in Russia; but Pobyedonóstseff saw a chance of putting religion into conflict with modern ideals, using it as a political asset, and supporting his conception of it with the full force of the police. People were to be religious in his sense, instead of being intelligent. He himself was a layman; and though he has been wittily described as " a man in a ' schema,' [1] " he had no real right to control even the Russian Church. The violence done by his policy to Russian subjects of other confessions has already been noticed. Within the Russian Church, he was able as Procurator to establish a positive dictatorship. Though in principle he possessed no right of speech in the Synod, it was he who reported all its debates to the Emperor. For every post the Synod sent in three names, and the Emperor, that is, Mr. Pobyedonóstseff, would make the final choice. In fact, no ecclesiastic could be a member of the Synod except by his consent. As there is the greatest inequality in Russia between the values of different livings, the priests, who are married, think

[1] A last and exceptional monastic vow taken before death.

more of promotion there than elsewhere; and all local appointments come from the Synod. The Procurator established his secretaries in every diocesan consistory; so that the whole organisation of the Church was a vast machine dependent upon him, and holders of authority had to cower before him. It might be said that two-fifths of the clergy held aloof, and went their own way without hope of place or power; but the majority, though by no means content with the system, were made to accept it. We can imagine how it would break the backbone of the priest's morality, and would cut him off from his proper influence over those of his flock who were able to think. The one hope for the future lay in the admirable instinct by which the peasants distinguished between their priest and the religion which he professed: "All that," they would say, "is only the priests." How very different from the undiscriminating Frenchman of the Revolution, who concludes that, if his own priests are bad, all priests and all religions are worth nothing.

There were, of course, able men amongst the higher clergy; but as time went on nearly all of them succumbed, at least in part, to the general fashion of obedience. The young Arch-priest Nicholas dared to report that the priests, being very ignorant and very busy, should not be entrusted with the control of all village schools; at the next meeting of the Synod, the Procurator's coadjutor suggested that he should be made Bishop of Kamchatka. The priest Petroff, who was once tutor to some of the children of the Grand Dukes, had to send in all his sermons to the religious censor, and after years of persecution found himself practically excluded from religious work; yet this is one of the men who best represent Russian loyalty to religion. Count Leo Tolstoy was, as we know, excommunicated altogether, and the holy man of the Reaction, John of Kronstadt, attacked him in a pamphlet of which I can give the best idea by quoting some of the phrases underlined in the original: "A godless man; . . . he spitefully and unjustly defames; . . . his awful blasphemy; . . . he perverted his moral character to monstrosity and abomination; . . . a second traitor Judas; . . . his self-love as a Count and as a writer; . . . like the dragon of the Apocalypse; . . . his real father is the devil; . . . Leo Tolstoy, child of the viper, calumniates the Church more than Satan himself; . . . like the well-known madman Nietzsche (will this name now pass into the peasants' vocabulary of bogey-men?) . . . he laughs at sanctity and saints; . . . this is the roaring lion seeking whom he may devour; . . . beware of him." . . . "You may know the lion from his claw," adds John of Kronstadt. Is it possible to recognise the spirit of Jesus Christ in John?

The influence of Pobyedonóstseff on the schools was particularly mischievous. The children of the more well-to-do priests who hold town livings usually enter the secular schools; the Church schools are filled with the sons of the more humble clergy, and they are brought up in a very atmosphere of cowardice. Those who break away from this system usually go into the opposite extreme. Seminarists who stop short of ordination may only enter alien universities, such as those of Warsaw and Dorpat, where they can be policed by the same machinery which punishes the aliens for being alien. The masters in the Church secondary schools are now almost exclusively monks. These men have not got the family instinct so necessary for their work, but Pobyedonóstseff was more successful in imposing his policy on the monks than on the secular clergy; indeed, that is one reason why nearly all monks have to deplore a spiritual decline in the monastic life. In the country several of the lower Church schools for some time had little more than a paper existence; Pobyedonóstseff desired to show that the establishment of lay schools was unnecessary; and this could be done by writing down statistics which proved that the local needs had been adequately met.

Nothing more annoyed the educated public in Russia than the canonisation of the new saint, Seraphim. This poor peasant was a good man; but Pobyedonóstseff selected him for the honours of sanctity because he especially represented peasant ignorance, and even peasant superstition. The Emperor was induced to go down to the country and pray at his tomb. A year after his return an heir to the throne was born; and the *Moscow Gazette* solemnly explained that this was the work of Seraphim; in other words, the Emperor promotes Seraphim to sanctity, and Seraphim uses his new influence on the Almighty with the result described. Dogma as proclaimed by the Synod is compulsory for all Orthodox Christians, and objections can be silenced by civil penalties. The Russian Intelligence saw in this affair an intentional slight designed for itself. Kryloff tells us of the cuckoo whom the eagle appointed to be nightingale. The cuckoo complained that no one would listen to his singing. The eagle replied :—

> "I may compel the birds to call you Nightingale ;
> But make you nightingale is more than I can do."

I have dwelt at this length on the work of Pobyedonóstseff for two reasons : I would wish to clear the Russian Church from the taint put upon it by a doctrinaire layman and a group of place-hunters, and I must also point out that if the cause of religion is to suffer grievously in Russia the responsibility lies with them. If I have spoken strongly of these men, it is because they have parodied what is dear to very many of us both in England and Russia.

To confirm the main outlines of this general sketch of the Russian Church, I will now give a few typical examples.

The Trinity Monastery.

This is, in a peculiar sense, the very heart of the Russian Church. The hermit Sergius built his cell on a slight eminence in a dip between some hills. The monastery, protected on three sides by a natural gully and by a ditch, slopes downhill from the north. It is four-square, surrounded with high white walls eighteen feet broad. These walls are crowned with battlements and many towers, red or white, square, octagonal, or round. A gallery runs round the walls inside, and here passes a 1608— procession on the anniversaries of the great siege. 10. Inside are broad spaces and variegated groups of churches and buildings. The small Byzantine cathedral of the Trinity is painted a light pink and crowned with one gilt dome. The entrance looks like a low side door, and brings one straight on to the "ikonostase." Godunóff and Michael Románoff gave jewels for the ikons ; the gorgeous canopy of the tomb of Sergius was given by Anne ; John the Terrible, who was christened here, offered the pearls. It was hence that Basil the Sightless was dragged by his enemies to be blinded. A faint ikon, executed on a part of Sergius' first wooden coffin, was carried by Peter the Great during his campaigns. Dimly visible is a great dark wall-picture of the Last Judgment with a huge snake winding through it ; a brown bullet-headed devil bites into a man's bare shoulder; the adulteresses have serpents at their breasts ; the slanderers have their tongues on fire ; the misers are covered with streams of silver flame ; the drunkards stand in a huge drinking-bowl over a furnace ; on a great ribbon, which winds through the picture, are the words, "there shall be weeping and gnashing of teeth." The singing is, of course, as always in Russia, unaccompanied ; a few monks repeat over and over again the mechanical but tuneful refrain, "Reverend Father Sergius, be gracious." A priest in black robes with red stole bows to the tomb, to the altar, and to the congregation. Peasants, especially women, stand bowing themselves, not regularly, but with sudden devotion, as if a thought came home to them. A child in arms crosses himself, and the father kisses the little hand. Suddenly all the singing monks mass in a body before the screen and chant a wonderful full-voiced prayer in harmony. The peasants reverently approach the shrine in turn ; the mechanical refrain begins again ; in the porch a priest is monotonously reading a special family mass for the dead. The high Renaissance belfry in four stages, by Rastrelli, is in the hands of blind monks, who have a particularly clear sense of tune. Outside, under a canopy, is a fountain which is said to be miraculous. Close by stands an obelisk recalling on its four sides the chief services of the monastery to Russia : St. Sergius blessing Demetrius of the Don for his great battle against the Tartars, the Polish siege, the letters which went out hence and stirred Minin and Pozharsky to march to the relief of Moscow, and the shelter given to Peter the Great, when his life was threatened by a plot of Sophia.

The sacristy is full of riches : vestments sewn with pearls, mitres of different patterns, sacred vessels, and pastoral staffs. Kuropatkin came here before starting for the East, received a blessing, and was entrusted with an ikon, on the back of which are recorded the names of the campaigns through which it has passed.

Not very far from the monastery is a hermitage where more special austerities are practised ; men would even live in isolated holes underground, receiving their food at fixed times. The old wooden church rests on wooden piers like a lake dwelling.

In another church four hundred special prayers are in course of reading. The monks bow deep at some twenty or thirty in each hundred; to the rest "they bow in their minds." There must always be one monk in the church reading the Psalter to himself; each takes a spell of some two hours. Some still wear chains, but secretly. "We don't see it," says my guide, and in general "each saves himself as God helps him to."

An Archimandrite.

Great Russia.—The Archimandrite is a big powerful man with small eyes and a look of narrow common sense; age is making him grow pale-faced and sleepy. His reception-room is spacious but bare; there are portraits of the royal family and Church pictures, especially of the new saint, Seraphim : Seraphim visited by the Mother of God, Seraphim accomplishing an exploit of nightly prayer in the forest, Seraphim feeding a bear. "The people went out to him in crowds; all got well : the lame walked, the blind saw." The Archimandrite implicitly believes it all and relates it in a quiet, interested, but rather monotonous voice, quite in the style of the "Lives of the Saints"; for him there is no difference of era, and the new spirit of reason does not trouble him. His "cell" is a bright, comfortable room with a bare floor, looking out on trees. Here too are many ikons ; over the oratory hangs one of Seraphim, who, he tells me, died praying. There are services here at 4, 6, and 8 a.m. In the refectory a very simple meal is laid, a piece of black bread on each plate.

The Archimandrite once wore chains (" sinful that I am," he says) for a year; but the Head of the House made him leave them off, because, as he tells me very simply, they cut into his shoulders, and he fainted in church. His talk is largely of recent miracles. A sick boy in St. Petersburg went to kiss an image ; " I am sound," he cried, and it was true. So too a daughter of Alexander II., on seeing the same image, fell into "an unusual perspiration " and cried out that she was healed. A hostel entertains the poor here free of charge for two or three days. Pilgrims come, and also habitual " wanderers," who spend their whole lives going bare-footed from one sacred place to another. There are,

however, fewer "exploits" of devotion than there used to be;
monks, too, do not pray as much, or fast as strictly and as often
as their predecessors ; "they live an easy life."

A MONK.

The monk is a sedate black-bearded man, singularly gentle
and simple, sufficient to himself, and with a quiet natural dignity.
He wears a long black robe and a high black hat without a brim,
from which a black veil descends over his back. He was born
at Moscow and educated "out there, in the world." At sixteen
he came to the monastery as a "servant." Some of the monks
have been here since childhood ; some have come here at a later
age, to get out of the world. It is much better to have been
here from the start. "As for me, I don't know how they live,
out there in the world ; God knows." Life here has a great
sameness about it. Of course he reads a great deal, mostly the
lives of the saints ; "else what to do with one's spare time ?"
But there is plenty of work. There are sixteen services to be
held in the monastery every day; the many churches have to be
cleaned. There are the service of the refectory, the carpenter's
work, and a school for the copying and printing of ikons.
Excellent little copies of all the best known ikons are sold here
for one penny or less, and mounted on squares of white wood
which one could put into one's pocket.

All are expected to attend the "Brothers' Prayer" at 2.30 a.m.
daily, but this rule is very loosely observed. A monk is
expected to attend three services a day : matins, one liturgy, and
vespers. He goes to bed when he likes ; earlier, of course, if he
is to be up early. He eats fish or lighter food. There is but
little travelling, and little communication with other monasteries,
for the Head of this House says that monks should sit in their
cells and not go out into the world. My friend has relations in
Moscow, but he does not care about going to see them, nor about
their coming to see him. When last they came, they said,
"Well, why don't you talk ?" and he asked, "What can we talk
about when we have not an interest in common ?" He is quite
happy : "now in church, now doing something, now in church
again, and so the time passes." The chief task is "to have no

will," to "follow those who lead." "Servants" can always
leave the monastery if they dislike the life. So can monks, only
it is more difficult for them. For five or six years they forfeit
their civil rights and cannot hold posts. Besides, they are
suspected in the world as "bad birds, not trustworthy, not up to
the height of their engagement."

The "schema" is a specially strict vow which is generally
taken shortly before death. The vow of silence means even
more; in this House, it is almost impossible.

A "HERETIC" MONK.

There are many "heresies" in Russia, and the "heretics"
take themselves very seriously. I remember a visit to a monk
of the "Old Believers." This snuffy little man in an untidy
cell was very friendly. His whole interest lay in the discussion
of ceremonies. It was absurd to cross oneself with three fingers:
three represents the Trinity, and the Holy Ghost was never on the
cross; but two means the dual nature of God and man, and both
of these natures were crucified.

Anton Yegórovich has written a book called "The Sword of
the Spirit." Will I accept the rejoinder written by himself,
Yegor Antónovich, called "Sixty-three Remarks on the Sword
of the Spirit"? Will I write to the *Times*? He hears that
Gosudár (the Sovereign) reads the *Times*. I might plead for
better treatment of the Old Believers. And, by the way, Anton
Yegórovich wrote a pamphlet called "Seventeen Questions for
Yegor Antónovich." Will I accept his reply, "Twenty-one
Answers to Anton Yegórovich"? I did not delay my leave-taking.

THE MILK-DRINKERS.

The Government distinguishes between sects that are harmless
and sects that are noxious. In the latter class it places both
those that are hysterical or immoral, such as the "Dancers"
and the "Self-mutilators," and those which, like the Stundists
or Dukhobors, make it part of their creed to refuse the Government service and taxes. These were excluded from the religious
toleration promised by the manifesto of 1905. The Milk-
drinkers, however, are considered harmless.

In a house which is neater than its neighbours, I find the Elder of the sect, a simple, brown-faced peasant, with a few of his friends. Most of the Milk-drinkers, he tells me, live away in the Caucasus, where they are a strong and prosperous body. In this village of six hundred souls there is an isolated little community of some two hundred. The teaching descends from father to son. They call themselves the people of Christ, but usually talk of themselves by their popular name of "Milk-drinkers." Their creed allows no ceremonies; there is no Eucharist; the feast days which they observe are the Sundays, and the days peculiarly associated with our Lord's name, such as the Nativity, the Passion, and the Ascension. They look upon all saints, including the Apostles, as simply good men; they are, in fact, Bible Christians, taking all their dogma from the New Testament. They have a service on Sunday at 7 a.m. The Elder reads a passage from the New Testament; he expounds it and then prays. The service used to be congregational, all joining in where they thought proper; now, if one is speaking, the others must wait till he has done. "There must be no interruptions," as the Elder explains to me, "because we believe the speaker to have the Spirit; but everything must be done in good order." Even more importance is attached to the private prayers of each member at morning and at evening. Their Bible is the New Testament in Russian and also in Church Slavonic; it is the same as that used in the Orthodox Church. In fact, these peasants know nothing of textual criticism, and take the Bible as they find it; but they make far more use of it than the ordinary Orthodox. Of the many who went to the war, we may be sure that none was without his own copy. Their principles forbid the eating of meat, the drinking of alcohol, and smoking; however, they admit that these rules are not strictly observed by all. Each chooses his own season for fasting according to his own religious mood. At these periods, which will last for one or two days, they will abstain from all food. The children are sent to the schools of the Zemstvo, as the Milk-drinkers have none of their own, but their religious teaching is given to them by their fathers at home. They are a simple and friendly folk, patient and contented. They get on very well with the other peasants, and enjoy a good name for honesty and sound work. As one neighbouring landowner told me, Orthodox peasants will leave their work if you pay them in advance, but the Milk-drinkers, while asking less pay, are far more trustworthy and make it a point of honour to do a job well. They are only tillers of the soil, but they have close relations with their more prosperous brothers in larger communities elsewhere; and, when one of them travels, he knows who will befriend him in any part of Russia. In some ways they reminded me of the Society of Friends, of which they were anxious to hear all that I could tell them.

A Rural Dean.

Government of Yaroslavl, 1904.—We pass to the parish clergy of the Orthodox Church. This is a quiet able man, who answers all my questions easily and thoroughly. The priests' position, he says, is certainly much better since the emancipation of the serfs. The priests themselves were peasants; many of them were drunkards; they could do no good unless the landowners allowed it. Now they are more educated; they are also in a position to educate others; they are the most enlightened of the small farmers, and are naturally the first to improve their land and to use the special advantages offered by the Zemstva. He would like to see plenty of country factories to keep the peasants from the towns, and still more country schools. The monopoly has done good; but education has done far more. So have the Temperance societies. There is far less drunkenness now. A pledge may be taken for three months, for six months, or for a year. He is quite glad to accept a pledge for life; but the peasants prefer to " try their patience." He has consented to administer the life pledge to one peasant as many as three times; to one he refused it the third time because it was clear that the man was " exploiting his profession." Often the reason for taking the pledge is one of practical common sense: one man came back to take it again because he had been robbed of £2 while drunk. He has seen several instances of a complete change of life: one man, whom he formerly would not have trusted with three shillings, had since borrowed from him quite a large sum and had repaid it. The taking of the pledge is accompanied by a short religious service (probably in the church and without spectators); the peasant makes a promise before the cross, which he then kisses. The fear of this oath makes a great difference. The priest gives the peasant the little book of membership of the Society of Temperance; and the peasant when invited to drink (as he is sure to be at the next feast), instead of going into explanations, just shows the book "to be free of importunity." His fellows then respect his oath, and would not like to make him break it; they would even be afraid to sit down to drink with him, as he would be a perjurer. There is, in short, ten times less drunkenness now. The peasant used to drink through the whole of the feast day; but the new Crown depôts close early. Some will still go many miles for drink when they have none at home.

COUNTRY PRIESTS.

1. Kashin District, 1904.—A man like a great bear,—big, kind, and awkward. He has two parishes and five hundred parishioners. His two churches are two miles apart. He fully believes that literateness has done good; so has the emancipation. The peasants, though at first they were not ready for it, have come to quite understand and use their freedom; but there is still much laziness and drunkenness. His peasants are not more indifferent to religion than they were.

2. Kashin District, 1905.—This is another kind of bear, a good type of the more ignorant priests. He wants to see my passport, and ventures pig-headed corrections as to Lord Lansdowne's titles, which, he seems to think, vaguely refer to me. I show him a letter from the Police Colonel, which, he says, might have been taken by me from someone else. "Do you know," he says, "what the Japanese are doing?" "No, I have no idea." "Well, they are sending spies all over Russia." "Indeed?" "Perhaps you are one of those spies?" "Perhaps not; do I look very like a Japanese?" "I don't know."

He directs my attention to the neatness of the peasants' houses, which is very noticeable. "They are progressing fast," he says. "Of course, literateness greatly improves them. They are very pious, as there are no heretics." This priest was just the man whom I might have expected to agree with Mr. Pobyedonóstseff; he did not.

3. Kashin District, 1904.—A supple man with black beard

and long curly hair. He has quick brown eyes and a rugged
face that is now lively, now long and solemn. It is almost
impossible to get him to talk slowly. In his enthusiasm,
he often rises from his seat with a kind of triumphant " There
you are ! " to point the success of his keen argument.

He examines my passport (" to convince himself as to my
personality "). The position of a priest, he says, is a much
higher one than it used to be. For one thing, none of the gentry
used to take orders ; now some of them do. The landowner has
now dropped out of the peasant life, and the priest has far more
to do with the peasants than before. He acts as a counsellor,
especially now that they are literate and come with questions for
him to answer.

Those who stay in the country are more healthy than the " go-
aways," and literateness is a sheer gain to them ; progress is the
great need of the country. But the earnings from the land
must be eked out in some way or other. He especially desires
that there should be more industrial villages and more country
factories, and also more lower technical schools all over the country.

His peasants are all God-fearing ; there is no difference in this
respect between those who live here throughout the year and
those who spend half of it in the capital. In twenty-five
years, he has only met with one case of anti-Orthodox propaganda ; the man claimed to be an adherent of Tolstoy. Of
political propaganda he has not seen a single instance ; in fact,
the success of such propaganda with the peasants is, in his
opinion, not to be thought of. Morality has got worse since the
emancipation ; there is more licence. But even here, he says,
one must be careful to qualify.

" To sum up, a great change has taken place since Wallace
wrote. It has been progress all along the line, only one partial
regress, and that is in morality."

He discusses the possibility of an understanding with the
English Church. In dogma there is hardly any difference, except
the *Filioque.* Ceremonies are not considered in Russia to be
the essence of religion. Confession (which is much more strict
and effective here than in Roman Catholic countries[1]) is a

---

[1] Absolution is only given after the candidate has gone through a severe discipline. The seal of the confessional is peculiarly sacred. A priest, to whom a

Russian instinct. Of course, all questions of ceremony must always be settled separately by each branch of the universal Church.

4. Rostóff District, 1904.—An old, bowed man, homely and benevolent. His hobby is gardening, which is the chief industry of his parishioners. He is constantly giving them grafts from his pear trees, which are of forty-one different kinds.

In winter he reads to his flock in the church or elsewhere, most often the Gospel, "because that is the foundation of everything," sometimes the lives of the saints and moral tales; sometimes he takes a secular subject. He uses a magic lantern. His peasants get books from the town, mostly tales; they read the newspapers straight through, but especially the crime and the war news. However, there is great progress in literateness, in intelligence, and in enterprise.

5. Rostóff District, 1904.—The village lies by the side of a great high-road. The priest is a jolly man with twinkling eyes, who talks very freely. Loafers of all sorts pass through—decayed officers, gipsies, anyone—say seven hundred a year, and, in the spring-time, twenty-five a day. There are more pilgrims than there used to be. The parish is very God-fearing; almost all have been to see the Life-giving Cross (which is not far off), and many have made the long march to the great Trinity Monastery. He is peculiarly enthusiastic about the growth of enterprise and self-respect amongst the peasants of the district. Some, perhaps, are become less moral.

6. Ranenburg District, July, 1905.—The priest is a smooth-haired man with a peasant face and a peasant mind. He insists on seeing my letters, and twice asks if I have a secret mission. He has five hundred parishioners, all peasants. He started public readings last year, only getting permission after long delays. Sometimes it is he who reads: sometimes it is the school teacher; between them they went through the whole of Gogol's "Revising Inspector."[1] The room was so crowded that they had to give it three times in the week. The peasants' keenness for instruction is very noticeable. He and the schoolmaster read out anything

murderer had confessed his crime, was arrested as guilty of the murder: he went to Siberia for life sooner than break the pledge of secrecy; later the murderer, while on his death-bed, made a public confession; and the priest, who all this time had not spoken, was restored to liberty and honour.

[1] The greatest Russian satire on officialdom. See p. 243.

that they can get from the Zemstvo, including a little Pushkin and some of Tolstoy.

7. **Ranenburg District, 1905.**—An intelligent but ambiguous man. He conducts missions amongst the heretics; he tells them that a Church which has no material forms and does nothing must be dead. In his own parish he has Temperance members; they cannot meet because they are too scattered, but he visits them personally, and they often come to him. He sometimes refuses to give the pledge because he knows that the candidates cannot last out; he invites them "to try their strength first." The school children are tolerably keen to learn. They may be divided into two classes; those who really learn something gain very much by it, but there are others who only think that they know, and that does them harm. The peasants are very fond of buying books, and will read just anything that they can get hold of. Piety is still strong, but seems to be decreasing.

TOWN PRIESTS.

1. **Moscow, 1905.**—A grave, simple man. Though his parish is in Moscow, he has to deal more exclusively with peasants than many a country priest, who at least may have one or two Intelligents amongst his parishioners. His only Intelligent is a retired colonel who is over eighty. The vodka monopoly of the Government has in some parts made things better and in others made them worse. All that one can say definitely is that drinking has been driven out of the vodka shops on to the streets. The peasant may not drink his liquor in the Crown depôt; but he is very quick at getting at it as soon as he is outside; he has a peculiarly clever knack of driving out the sealed cork by hitting the bottom of the bottle. It is true that the depôts are closed for half the day on feast days; but the peasant, when he gets to work, drinks his liquor all at once until he is drunk. It cannot be said that there is less drunkenness. In Moscow there are plenty of illicit drink shops; in some cases some kind of a relish is offered as a cover for the drink that is sold; the peasant takes the drink and not the relish. In this parish there are Temperance members, who often fail to keep their pledge. When they go to him and tell him so, he reminds them that at

least they have lasted out for a certain time, and considers that their regret and confession are not without value.

Morality is, he thinks, certainly declining. Peasants who come here usually marry in the country, and often send wife and children thither from the town. It cannot be said that all the girls in factories lead bad lives, but natural births are exceedingly common. One may divide the immigrant peasants into two classes : some are firm and solid ; others, and more, go from bad to worse. These become loafers, or " bare-legs " ; occasionally the worst are sent away to their villages, but somehow or other they manage to get back to Moscow. In piety, the town peasants have undoubtedly deteriorated ; the town life makes them indifferent to religion. Rich men, who go to church themselves, will not allow their servants to do so. It is the same in shops ; and peasant employers are in this respect the least considerate of all. The peasant who is in town service is at first sorry for this deprivation ; then his religious feelings become dulled, and finally he is indifferent or even hostile to religion.

2. Moscow, July, 1905.—A man of very considerable intelligence. In the town, he says, there is such a difference of income between different parishes, that priests unfortunately move very frequently from one to another. In the country they remain longer in one post. A country priest in a backward government, such as Smolensk, will receive £40 a year ; his deacon will have £20, and his clerk £10. In the rich southern governments the land is better, and the parishes are richer. A priest will there receive £100 to £200 or even more. A town priest will receive from £150 to £400, but the average payment is between £200 and £250. Priests are far more dependent than they ought to be on the alms of parishioners ; this encourages servility, of which there have been very bad instances, and the relations of the poorer priests to their flocks should be put on a regular and sound basis. The fourth child of every priest, the third of every deacon, and the second of every clerk can claim free education in the Church schools.

No help is given by one parish to another. There are far too few parish institutions. There is often a so-called " parish wardenship," which, according to its statutes, should collect money for the decoration of the churches, for the bettering of the priest's house, and for helping the poor. It does not collect much, and very properly devotes it all to the poor. It administers relief to the destitute, secures light paid work for the disabled, and sometimes keeps up a parish almshouse. There are also Church almshouses which are not on the parochial basis.

He has many " go-away " peasants to deal with ; one-third of them go home for every summer. Town life exercises upon them a thoroughly bad influence. Almost 40 per cent. of the children in the parish are illegitimate, and they are often abandoned by their parents.

Drunkenness is worse than it was. The monopoly has simply driven it on to the streets, and made the peasant drink more at a given time. Brawling is as frequent as it was, but thefts are more confined to professional criminals ; in factories, in spite of the frequent opportunities, they are exceedingly rare.

Superficial " religiousness " has not decreased, but real faith is very much at a discount. In the town the peasant begins to conceive doubts, and he has no friend to consult. If he does indeed go to the priest (as he might naturally have done in the country), the priest cannot talk straight to him, because his instructions so tie him that he may say nothing out of the way. No doubt peasants are still assiduous in their attendance at religious processions. A man may discuss what is the right method of genuflexion, or how you are to cross yourself with three fingers when an accident has deprived you of two. But it does not follow that his religion goes very much further.

The peasant calls the priest "father," but he also calls the priest's wife " mother." These good ladies, of whom I have met several, are generally capable, shrewd, and homely. They keep their houses notably cleaner than other people. They have the fear of God, and they are old-fashioned and anti-Liberal ; but their sons go off to the universities or academies, and they have to interest themselves in the new culture. They continue to share in some of the milder superstitions of the peasants. One tells me, for instance, of a local " sorcerer " who said to a peasant, " You shall be in hospital for seven years " ; " And he was," she adds, evidently with a vague idea that this is evidence.

The deacon, as compared with the priest, is more humble, more ignorant, and less intelligent. One old deacon whom I met had an admirable little garden, which he kept in perfect order by his own labour. He was particularly proud of the village church, which he described as " finer than most cathedrals," and again as containing "many hundredweights of ikons."

The Church, for a long time, had charge of most of the schoolteaching in Russia; but it did the work very badly, and many of the schools only existed on paper. The marked improvement in the general standard of clerical life and work and the strong competition of the Zemstva schools have forced the schools of the Church up to a much higher level of efficiency. They are called " shkoly " ("places of education"), while the Zemstva schools are called "places of instruction." The Church schools are of two kinds: simple schools of literateness and parish schools; the pupil will attend the first from eleven to fourteen, and the second from fourteen to seventeen. In the parish schools the programme includes religious teaching, Church Slavonic (the language of the Church service), the first four rules of arithmetic, Russian history, geography, and a very little physics; also, for some pupils, certain more advanced teaching in Church history, the Old Testament, and the New Testament. As has been mentioned, the schoolmaster is generally not a trained man, being simply a candidate for the priesthood. I met one such in the District of Rostóff. He was a fat, untidy, blank-looking man, with something of the air of an official. He said that his pupils were easy to teach, being quick-witted and interested; but his work seemed to be rather a *corvée* to him.

The instinct of religious reverence is strong in all classes. On feast days the churches, in town and country, are full of men and women. The services never seem to lose their atmosphere of pious awe. The genuflexions of the congregation, vigorous and even violent as they sometimes are, at least do not shock the sense as being mechanical or insincere. A peasant woman, to whom I acted as guide in the Cathedral of the Assumption in Moscow (August, 1904), threw herself on her knees before " The Mother of the Don," which commemorates the victory of Demetrius over the Tartars, and said quite simply, " Lord, help our father the Tsar against his un-friends." As a tram passes a chapel many of the passengers bow deep and cross themselves. A

bicyclist passing through a sacred gateway will cross himself
without dismounting. The little street chapels are always full of
patient orderly worshippers. Everyone is a traveller here, and
travellers are under the peculiar protection of St. Nicholas the
Wonder-worker. A Volga boat stops at a little country quay,
close to a quiet monastery; on the quay an old priest, with
two singers, reads a service and sways a cross towards the
boat as it goes off. The steamship company pays by the year
for this blessing. In Mozhaisk I see a rough-looking peasant
having a little service to himself; he prostrates himself; the priest
sways over him the Gospel and the cross, which he kisses. A
mistress and her servants stand together in the church, listening
to the high, weird tones of the mass for the dead. Each room in a
house has its ikon ; perhaps a priest is invited from time to time
to cense the house all through. As I am about to leave some
friends, we all sit silent for a minute; it is a prayer for my safety.

With the peasants belief has, of course, a strong admixture
of superstition. At Mozhaisk an intelligent Church servant, who
knows far more detail about our Church than most of us
know about his, shows me an ikon five hundred years old " drawn
without hands." I ask him how this was done; and he says
that he supposes that there was a vision, and that the colours
remained. The Church in no way inculcates the worshipping of
ikons; in more than one instruction which I possess, it fully
explains that what is reverenced is the dear friend whose
picture is there. The saints are, of course, only intermediaries.
" They were our helpers while they lived," said an Archimandrite
to me, " and so they must be now." But the beliefs of the lower
monks are formal and unintelligent, and the peasant is even
more ignorant. His mind is often full of a whole host of non-
Christian superstitions, of native poetic traditions, glen and wood
and water fairies, and curious prejudices as to " luck." " Luck " is
more often than not " bad luck." Religion is much too seldom
applied to life. A great awe seizes the worshipper in the church,
but it is no guarantee even against crime. It is not that he is
insincere; it is because his worship is an emotion. It was put
to me that with us reason stands in the foreground, but with them
feeling; and this generalisation, which applies to all classes,
helps to explain much that is Russian besides the religion.

Feast of a Patron Saint (1904).

It is the feast day of Michael of Good Faith, Prince of Tver and Grand Prince of Russia. He was guilty of the crime of fighting and beating a Tartar garrison. When summoned to the Khan under pain of invasion of his State, he decided to be a peace-offering for his people. " Some time," he said, "I shall have to die ; better that I lay down my life now for many lives." He made his will and went with presents to the Khan. For more than a month he was left at liberty. At last the influence of his accuser and successor, Youry of Moscow, triumphed. He was chained, and a heavy yoke was put upon his neck. Thus he would sit reading, while his page turned over his Psalter for him. " If I save myself and leave my people in trouble," he said, " what kind of glory is that to me ?" A Tartar chief came to revile him in the market-place, and ended with the words, " To-morrow or the day after they will free you from all this trouble, and you will be in great honour." The next day his Russian enemies entered his tent. They dashed him against the wall, clubbed him to death, stabbed him, and plundered his body; it was a Tartar who ordered a cloak to be thrown over it. It was brought to Tver, and buried in a silver ark.

The long straight Milliónnaya is lined with a great expectant crowd—peasants from all round, ladies, and officials. It is a mass of colour : red, black, cream, yellow, blue, and lilac. All the men are bareheaded ; there is plenty of interest, but no pushing. Soldiers and police keep open a passage, along which pass little bands of priests in full vestments, and Church officials, carrying the ikons, banners, and crosses of their parishes. Suddenly from the high belfry there rings out first one little bell, then the great ones ; the quick peal of all the little bells joins in. An awe comes over the multitude ; all cross themselves devoutly. " Vexilla Regis prodeunt." The slow procession sways forward, first sixty Church banners, with tassels yellow, orange, or red, then on one side fifty priests bearing crosses, and on the other the Church officials carrying the dark ikons in their gorgeous frames. And now passes the silver ark, borne on high ; all along the road the peasants throw on to the bier little squares of coarse cloth, which they have worked as offerings, and which are later sold for the profit of the Cathedral; a halt is made after every few steps to arrange them on the bier. The procession traverses the town, and comes back to the cathedral. On the steps stand the Government officials, from the Governor down-wards. Priests and ikon-bearers halt and form a circle in the square in front. The Archbishop comes down from the west door in heavy mitre-crown and vestments glittering with gold. The ark passes into the nave, men bowing straight with their whole bodies as it passes. Several follow in and stand praying before the different ikons.

The peasants sit down anywhere on the grass in family groups, all simple and good-humoured. The procession has broken up, and each little group of priests and ikons makes its way back to its own parish. As long as their direction permits, groups still march together. Many stay the evening on the great waste patch by the river, where stalls have been set up. There one can buy very sugary biscuits, simple quaint toys, or clothes. A peasant runs along holding out his jacket. "Who'll buy this? I must have money for beer."

It is in Moscow that one can best appreciate how strong the religious instinct still is in Russia. The Emperor on his arrival always pays his first visit to the ikon of the Iversky Virgin, on whose face there is a mark said to have been inflicted by a Tartar's hand. This ikon goes through the streets of Moscow, in a carriage with six horses, to visit the homes of the poor or of the rich, and every man takes off his hat as it passes. Outside some of the chapels, one will find in the small hours of the night a throng of invalid peasants, waiting for the gates to be opened and for the angel to descend to work his miracles. Through the Saviour's Gate of the Kremlin no one, not even a foreigner, may pass without taking off his hat. The three cathedrals of the Kremlin commemorate the joys and sorrows of the anointed Tsars[1]; and between them rises the belfry of John the Great, from which on Easter Day rings out the promise of a new life to all the faithful people. The streets are thronged with an

---

[1] In the Cathedral of the Good Tidings they were baptised and married, in the Cathedral of the Assumption they were crowned, and in the Cathedral of the Archangel all up to Peter the Great lie buried.

expectant crowd, and at the thrill of the first note from the belfry the silence is broken, and each salutes his neighbour with the words, " Christ is risen." And to Russians resurrection still means more than it does to us Westerners. The winter is long and hopeless, and the return of spring, when one has almost despaired of it, comes each year with a sudden beneficence which gives it the aspect of a miracle. So too throughout its clouded history, the patient Russian race has lived through long and hopeless winters simply by that instinct which ordered it at all times to stand together and persevere, and sometimes the solution of difficulties has at last come, and the reward has seemed even greater than the promise.

This is no chance ; it is the natural result of something which lies in the very spirit of the people. I have described it as solidarity, but the Russians use a word which means far more : " sobornost." This word covers not only the corporate sense of any great gathering, but also the awe inspired in each individual by the sense of that great national unity of which he is part. No matter in what field, the Russian is essentially a believer ; when he adopts a foreign philosophy or a foreign political formula he applies to it his own native sense of reverence, and he is able to draw from it something spiritual and inspiring. This tendency may be half unconscious; but the real corporate force which underlies it can claim, as no isolated individual can, the right to live and to succeed ; and history has given abundant proofs that it is not in vain that Russia has lived and still lives by that most primitive and fundamental instinct which we call faith.

CHAPTER V.

THE modern Ministries are more or less the direct descendants of the old Prikazy, or Crown departments of the times of Moscow. Everything is centred round the Tsar; St. Petersburg is not, of course, the heart of Russia, but it is the fountain of instructions. Till October, 1905, the Ministers were appointed quite independently of each other ; the Emperor chose each as a suitable instrument for a special task. They were in no sense responsible to each other; Mr. A., appointed as Minister of the Interior, might complain that the Foreign Minister, Mr. B., was courting a war which would ruin the country; Mr. C., Minister of War, might complain that Mr. D., Minister of Finance, was unwilling to supply him with the sinews of war. Each Minister was anxious to put in the place of his colleagues a set of men of his own choosing. A recommendation from one Minister would not necessarily carry weight with another.

Each Minister is represented all over the country by a series of officials and institutions subject only to himself; thus, in the capital of a province, the military Commander-in-Chief is under the War Office; the Treasury Chamber is under the Minister of Finance; the Chamber of Financial Control is under a special Office in St. Petersburg, the head of which, though not a Minister, is directly responsible to the Emperor; judges are named by the Minister of Justice; the local bishop or arch-bishop of course depends upon the Synod. There is overlapping of every kind. For instance, the Minister of Public Instruction is in competition with other school authorities, such as the Synod and the County and Town Councils ; and he is not even allowed to control all the schools which depend directly upon the Government, some of which are under the jurisdiction of the Minister of Finance, the War Office, the Admiralty, or the administrator of the institutions of the Empress Maria Feódorovna. Quarrels between provincial officials who represent different jurisdictions have to be referred to their respective chiefs, and tend to become quarrels between the different Ministers. In 1904, however, a plan was devised for making all the local officials, with the exception of Church authorities, more subject to the local Governor.

Overlapping and dualism of control are especially noticeable in the police service. The local police, who are also administrative officials, are under the control of the Governor, and the Governor is subject to the Minister of the Interior. The political police, who are better paid, are quite separate, and receive all their orders direct from St. Petersburg. Over and over again the Governor has had to complain that he did not know what they were doing, or at least that he had no control over their actions ; yet at the same time the political police have the right of ordering the local police to help them without necessarily giving any reasons. Their work is exceedingly unpopular, dealing as it does with administrative arrest—that is to say, arrest without any legal warrant and not followed by any trial at law. There is, therefore, a great deal of friction between the two kinds of police, and often the local police are held responsible by the public for what is really the work of their colleagues.

The political police are themselves of two kinds, the so-called Defence Section and the Gendarmes. The Defence Section, which exists only in large towns, was originally attached to the secret chancelleries of the City Prefects of St. Petersburg and Moscow, but in many places it is not a section of anything in particular. Its mission is to defend the life of the sovereign and, by inference, to maintain public order in general. Not only the public, but also many officials, think that Russia would lose nothing by its abolition. The Gendarmes are divided into two sections. One deals specially with all the railways of the Empire. A gendarme is quartered at every important railway station. During 1905 the local police maintained that this service was often quite inefficient. The other section of the Gendarmes has a small force in every government town. Both sections are controlled from St. Petersburg, but even the control of the Gendarmes is dual: the Commander of the Corps makes all appointments, and has the right of punishing, but he does not issue the instructions. The Department of Police in the capital sends out the instructions, but can neither appoint nor punish.

In 1905, under General Trepoff, there was another dualism inside the department itself. Mr. Garyn directed the ordinary work, and Mr. Rachkovsky had a special commission to control the political work. The dualism even went higher. At this time, General Trepoff, the Assistant Minister of the Interior, was made quite independent of his chief, the Minister of the Interior. There had been something of the same kind in the time of Count Dmitry Tolstoy, but his assistant, though partially independent, could not report separately to the Emperor. Trepoff, on the other hand, could, and he made frequent use of his privilege. We can foresee what would be the results upon the unity of authority in the Empire.[1]

In the huge, barrack-like buildings where the central officials of St. Petersburg work, the atmosphere is indolent and doctrinaire. Report writing becomes a fine art. The mental oppression produced by masses of unconsidered papers is relieved by interminable cigarettes and ever-recurrent cups of tea. There are plenty of people about; to the bureaucratic office more than to any other place in Russia we may apply the maxim that it takes three men to do the work of one. The resigned but comfortable official talks to his friends in his cabinet; the resigned but unsatisfied suitor chafes in the anteroom. "Be of good hope," says one of the officials as I invade the Ministry of Public Instruction. I find myself among many suitors. We all rise as the Minister passes through; for some two hours he receives his Heads of Departments; these generally shake hands with their friends before entering the Presence; very diverse are their expressions of face as they come out again. Meanwhile we wait; the first animation of the ladies soon subsides into boredom; an elderly gentleman, broken in to the habit, sits easy and listless and counsels patience; at last we all form a file, each with his written petition in his hand. The Minister enters; he is a General—a big, rugged-looking man, with small twinkling eyes,

---

[1] All the above statements have been verified by one who has held one of the highest posts in the Police system.

ruddy complexion, and bristling beard. He takes the ladies first. The function is little more than a piece of "representation," for he cannot possibly deal with a tenth of the business in the .time. But his manner, military and kindly, is very suitable to the task. He seldom says more than "H'm! h'm! We'll see." Particularly effective is his fatherly and decisive way of passing on from one lady to another. It does not, however, follow that applications to the Government take more time in Russia than in England ; and, once obtained, the ministerial permission will carry one through a world of persons and institutions which is more or less complete in itself.

In Russia, titles are less permanently attached to a given post than in England. The autocracy has kept itself free to vary the nature of the local authority according to the local conditions. A "Governor-General" is appointed to rule over a given area in which fuller powers are thought for the time to be necessary ; he has the right of amnestying prisoners, a right which was liberally used by Prince Svyatopolk-Mirsky as Governor-General at Vilna. The Governor is the chief civil authority of what is called a "Government," that is a province ; he is the head of the local police, but he is also far more than that. It would be a bad mistake to imagine that, in normal times, the police have only been entrusted with restrictive or preventive powers. The Governor is the representative of his sovereign in a province which may be as small as Wales or as large as England. Of this province he is the administrative head, and the residence in which he lives often recalls the traditions of some independent prince. Thus, though his hands are pretty closely tied by his instructions from St. Petersburg, distance and the largeness of his sphere of work tend to give to his office at least some measure of greatness, and he is free enough to do an immense amount of good. Public spirit and intelligence, which may be very small in the lower official, broaden out into something nobler as one ascends the scale. The term of office varies very much according to the degree of influence possessed in St. Petersburg. The position of the Governor and the local officials will be much better understood, if it is remembered that the main responsibility for action against political offenders lies with the Gendarmes, or political police. "They can whisk you off by the administrative

system," said a Police Captain, "so that you are never heard of
again."

The Government buildings stand close together round the
residence of the Governor. He has his own Chancellery, his
personal office, so to speak, for affairs which require his signature.
Here there are secretaries, attachés, and clerks; the attachés,
who may be civilians or soldiers, are young men of good family
who are learning the routine work of administration, and serve
on special missions for the investigation of local questions. Looking through the day-book of a Governor (August, 1904) I find the
business to be very various; it includes the selection and control
of the ordinary police, the examination of complaints against
officials, the following up of criminals who have fled to other
governments, and administrative expulsion of persons whose
residence is considered undesirable. These last will be removed,
say, to the Government of Archangel; they may lose some of
their civil rights, but they are allowed to live in their own houses;
if they run away they are brought back and punished with, say, a
week's imprisonment. The day-book is full of petitions which
are being attended to. A landowner askes that peasants be
prevented from trespassing on certain ground; a priest complains
that a certain bridge is out of repair (and presumably the Governor
will ask the Zemstvo to attend to it); a peasant desires that
an official postman should be appointed to take the place of
the nominee of the peasants; one Jew asks that his term of
residence should be extended; another asks for leave to change
the place of the synagogue, another that Jewish meat shall only
be cut up in the town slaughter-house, where a Jewish official
can see that it is done properly. Often these petitions are
backed by "intercession," for instance, of the local Land
Captain.

The Government Administration ("Upravlénie") is a separate
institution. In principle, it controls the action of the Governor,
having a right to criticise anything which he does, if he seems to
exceed the limits of the law. It is, in fact, described to me as a
kind of "depôt of the law," which it is supposed to interpret,
referring for necessary explanations to the Senate of the Empire;
but in practice no close line of definition separates it from the
Governor's Chancellery, and one of the officials looks puzzled

when asked to give a summary of his duties.   Here are received
claims for naturalisation, and applications from Jews who wish
to be baptised; here lies the control of certain of the larger
prisons; there are also sections which deal with sanitation,
surveying, and building.   In a word, almost any business may
come to the Government Administration.   Associated with it, or
with the Governor, are all sorts of Commissions.   The so-called
"Governor's Presences," administrative or juridical, deal with
such questions as conscription, factories, the control of the
peasants' law-courts, and the trying of complaints made against
officials.   Officials cannot be accused in the ordinary law-courts
until a Governor's Presence has submitted that there is a true
bill.   This means that the preliminary trial of officials is administrative, that it is conducted by persons of the same class interests
as the accused, that the calling of evidence is not properly
guaranteed, and that no further action can be taken if the
authorities choose to hush matters up.   The Vice-Governor, who
is always in residence when the Governor is absent, presides over
some of these Presences; he is assisted by two councillors,
either of whom may, if he wishes, present a minority report.   This
report will be sent to the Minister of the Interior, who is able to
confirm it, but probably will not.

In every Government town there is a Treasury Chamber
under the Minister of Finance; in every District town there is
a local treasurer.   The Government town has also a Chamber
of Control, which was once under the same jurisdiction, but has
now been turned into a separate audit office.   Here are verified
the accounts of the Treasury Chamber, of the post and telegraph,
of the Imperial domains, of the army, of the excise, and of the
secondary schools, in a word of all jurisdictions except the
Church.   The books of the District treasurers are sent here for
examination, and once or twice a year a commissioner goes to
look through the accounts in each District town, to see whether
the money in hand corresponds to the balance in the books.
There is also a conscription office, under the jurisdiction of the
War Office.   It has a sub-office in each considerable town of
the government.   All men of twenty-one years of age are, in
principle, liable for service.   The War Office states how many are
wanted; those who desire to serve send in their names first.   A

lottery decides who else is to go ; those who escape the lottery are considered to be free from any obligation for the future. An only son is not taken, and, in a family of two sons who are divided by a considerable interval of years, both are held to be free. The service is for four years. For those who have passed through half of the course in a Gymnasium (or Secondary Classical School) it is reduced to two ; for those who have passed through the University or some other Higher School it is reduced to one year. A medical examination rejects the unsuitable, and the vacancies are filled up from those who drew the next numbers in the lottery. After finishing his service, every soldier passes into the reserve. When the reservists are mobilised, widowers with more than five children are exempted ; I know of a father of a family who was excused because his wife had run away. Service in the reserve lasts to the age of forty-three ; up to forty-eight some remain enrolled as "Warriors of the Reserve " ; these, with some others who have escaped previous service, compose the national militia ("Opolchénie"). The pay of a private consists of a few shillings of "pocket-money," and often the soldiers are not even tolerably supplied with the necessaries of life ; since the beginning of the movement for liberation these conditions of life have been improved. Russia is supposed to be able to bring into the field for purposes of home defence, about four millions of men who have received some kind of training.

Governments are of various sizes ; it depends upon population. The Government is divided into Districts. A District which is, say, of the size of Sussex, is divided into Cantons. The Governor has to spend a great deal of his time in travelling " on revision " through his Government and meeting the village elders and tax-collectors, canton by canton, in their Court-houses. In every District there is a Police Colonel ; his Russian title means "the Corrector." Over an area of the size of an English county he exercises a paternal authority. It would be a great mistake to think that his time is entirely taken up with the prevention and punishment of crime, and in Great Russia, in normal times, it is not often that he has to deal with questions of political or religious propaganda ; as compared with the Governor, he is more of a police official. Yet he has, at least, some experience in what I may call "government proper"; he is an *ex officio* member of every committee in his district. He receives a salary of £120, with an allowance of £75 for travelling expenses. He is almost absolute in his little realm; and this very probably makes him arrogant. If he is an energetic administrator, it is generally because he chooses to be, and not because he must be.

The towns are under a much more strict surveillance than the country. Whereas a country crowd, in ordinary times, will at the worst be indifferent to authority, a town crowd will often be directly hostile. Administration is much more complex in the towns, where there are more distinctions of class and even of race and religion, and where there are many special dues to be collected. The Government has long been suspicious of the towns. To the country Police Colonel corresponds the town Police-Master, but the latter has less to do with administration, and is really a kind of superior constable. Since 1905 the nerves of these men have been constantly on the stretch; but even in ordinary times their chief function is to restrict and to punish.

The Districts are subdivided into " Stations," each of which is under the control of a Police Captain ("Pristav.") Town posts of this kind lead more quickly to promotion, but the country officers are much more at home in their work, which is more varied and less negative of human sympathy. The country work is laborious but healthy. In addition to the salary of £60, a sum of £50 is allowed for travelling expenses. There may be three Police Captains in a District. Their work is chiefly amongst the peasants, of whom they can generally give as accurate information as any-one else. They have in some cases served through the lower grades of service (police corporal, registrar, and secretary), or they may be ex-officers of the army. Most of those whom I know are men of simple instincts, narrow education, and quiet observant minds, rather suggestive of the intelligent farmer. They are generally unambitious and domestic—not very energetic, but almost always at their work. The Police Captains of the town are far more at issue with the population amongst which they live. In 1905 the better and the worse of them have been alike exposed as marks for revolvers, and in many of them we must admire the simple honesty which alone has kept them at their unenviable work. Their ideals are, however, anything but high; and they generally recruit their small incomes by perquisites and "tips" of various kinds. In many cases they are local tyrants; and latterly some of them have been involved in the organisation of the infamous Jewish massacres.

From this point downwards the country administration is different from that of the towns. In the towns there is a rank and file of policemen, engaged by the Government largely on private recommendation. The candidates are not tested by any particular standard of height and strength, except in the most important towns. They receive a very small wage (£14 10s. a year), and the Town Council has the responsibility of providing them with quarters. When on duty, each is usually within easy hail of a comrade, and all of them carry swords. The service is highly unpopular, so that the men obtained are usually those who have failed at something else.

In the country, up to the Japanese war, there was no such complete service of police. The Police Captain of a country station as large as Rutland had under him some three or four Police Corporals and no governmental rank and file at all. The Police Corporal is by birth and education something like a superior non-commissioned officer; often he is a capable ex-soldier. He has great distances to travel, and receives but little help from the elected village police. It is a post which demands and trains common sense and quick judgment; the Russian name for it is the "Arranger." He has the charge of prisoners on their way to the nearest town, and unnecessary arrests are not to his advantage.

In most parts of Russia, the number of Police Corporals has recently been increased, and there has also been created a rank and file of policemen, appointed and maintained by the Government. Till this was done the Police Corporal had to content himself with the help of Hundredth men and Tenth men elected by the peasants. The Hundredth man served for one year; he received £3 from the Government and as much as £12 from fees in connection with cases. He had to report once a week to the Police Captain. To help him there were two or three Tenth men, who were also chosen by the peasants, but were not paid at all. They served for one year each, and wore a badge of office, but neither they nor the Hundredth man had any other uniform. They were not bound, as he was, to travel over their district. The

Tenth men were some of the most incapable of the peasants. In one district, Rostóff, the only illiterate whom I met held this post. The peasant wishes to be a peasant and to look after his land, and the Tenth men were those who had not wit enough to escape selection. They continued to potter at their peasant's work while pottering at their official duties; they would even contrive not to see crimes committed under their eyes. With the Police Corporal the official system really ended; and all that the peasant police did was to link that system on to the very different order of peasant local government, which has already been described. On the other hand, the policing of the peasants could, under ordinary circumstances, be left to the peasants themselves. In many cases, they have themselves seized propagandists and handed them over to the police. In 1904, I was walking over the battle-field of Maloyaroslávets, when a peasant, who took me for a Japanese spy, asked me what business I had there ; he pointed to some others who were working in a neighbouring field and told me to go with him thither in order to be arrested: " I'll cry out to them," he said, "and we'll go into this." One part of the preliminary examination would probably have been that my clothes would have been stripped off my back. When I told him that I had in my pocket letters to the police, he fell away into a request for a few coppers.

It was a part of the policy of the Reaction to guard the peasants against all educating influences, and to keep them isolated from other classes and from each other. With this object was insti-tuted the new post of Land Captain. At the time of the emancipa-tion, the landowners were, by a stroke of the pen, struck out from all participation in peasant interests. There were instituted judicial authorities under the name of "Justices of the Peace" to form a link between the country gentry and the peasants. These Justices of the Peace have almost everywhere been abolished. The Land Captain who takes their place is, before all things, an administrative official, and is subject to the Minister of the Interior. He is considered to be a kind of controller and advocate of the peasants committed to his charge, and he has manifold duties. Plehwe sent out a general circular to the Land Captains asking them if they could undertake larger districts ; one humorous Land Captain of my acquaintance replied that "he thought he could not, as he found that the time claimed by his present duties amounted to 540 days in the year." He was told that such an answer might be considered to be impertinent. "But I," he said with a smile, "thought that I had put it very moderately." The Land Captain has an administrative power over the peasants, against which there is apparently no appeal; his judicial decisions are, however, subject to revision elsewhere. He is usually a local landowner of some importance, and receives a salary of £180 a year. He can imprison for a few days without giving a reason. He may, for instance, allow himself to give orders that the road which leads past his house is not to be used. In many cases, he may even seem to be a revival of the old serf owner without the serf owner's natural care for his own human property. Land Captains, like pretty well everyone else in Russia, whether officials or Intelligents, seem to find it difficult to speak to the peasants without indulging in long-winded doctrinaire assertions; they will even try to dictate to the peasants, when the latter are called upon to express their grievances in writing. The peasants, who have known through long centuries of subjection how to keep themselves alive as a self-sufficing and morally independent class, resent as much as anything that spirit of interference which established the post of Land Captain, and desire as much as anything else its abolition. That does not, however, mean that the Land Captains are all of them depraved scoundrels. Of those whom I have met, most seemed to be trying, according to their lights, to do something for the peasants, but they suffer from the fault of dogmatism which is common to nearly all members of the educated classes, and the peasant does not want them.

There are, of course, many more officials in Russia than in England, for all public institutions are much more closely tied to the Government. In the educated class nearly everyone is, in a broad sense of the term, an "official." It must not be forgotten that the bureaucrats are to a large extent the ex-students of the universities. In Russia, then, the difference is not so much between the official class and the rest of the nation, as the difference between a man in his official capacity and the same man as a private person. When he has put on his long blue-grey overcoat, he is often a machine, assiduously and painfully obeying instructions of which he may not be able to see the bearing ; when he has taken it off, he is possibly a kind, hearty gentleman with a natural leaning for Liberal ideas. The official of lower class is even more fearful and unintelligent in the execution of orders, and even more "bonhomme" when left to himself. I give some types of administrative officials from my own experience.

A Town Policeman.

A stoutly built, bearded man, much like a kind bear, in manner quite simple, but with a childlike instinct for the theatrical.

He has served sixteen years ; many serve even longer. Some like the work ; some only care about the wages. He notes that street brawling has increased here (Smolensk, August, 1904), and that there is less respect for the police ; but resistance is very seldom offered because of the policeman's sword, and because his mate is probably not more than three hundred yards away. To use bad language to the police is an offence ; to resist them is a still greater offence.

The most common crimes are small thefts ; the growth of literateness does not seem to diminish them in number. Drink is the chief source of crime, but he cannot see that the Government monopoly has had any good effect in this respect. He proceeds to a curious explanation of how customers used to be able to drink themselves drunk inside the tavern. The publican would take their purses, and would next day give them half their money back, saying, " Think yourselves lucky to get that." Now no one may stay on drinking in the Crown depôt. The customer goes out to be robbed in the street, for which curious reason this policeman considers that the monopoly has done harm.

A Police Corporal.

A tall, thin, bronzed man, with keen eyes, long moustache, and a military carriage. His superior describes him as a man of great discretion : " ' the chief thing,' I say ; ' the very chief thing,' says he." He is very much at home when we visit the priest, much less so when we visit the doctor.

He points to a village, past which we drive. " Quite a nice part of the country," he says, " the people well off, and a church near. In Siberia, towns grow up as soon as a church is built,—without that life would be uncomfortable. We all know that Russia has not lived as long as England. Russia only began to live with Peter the Great, and then again with Alexander II. Before the reforms the landowner could do as he liked ; he ruled with the stick, but the stick is a poor anchor. The peasant would say in the evening, ' Thanks be to Thee, O Lord; the day has passed, and master has not hit us.' " With a hoarse military laugh he alludes to the "droit du seigneur." The peasants were married off anyhow : if a man chose such or such a one, " it did not please Him " ; in fact, all was feudal, as in Germany or France. The peasants had to work all day without pay ; the land was not their own. Then came the liberation, carried through by Alexander II. "to his eternal memory." He remembers how the decree was read out in the churches. Now the peasants could marry whom they liked. They at once adapted themselves to the new order (" made it their own"). Landowners are now only "ordinary people." If the landowner takes off his hat to the peasants, they will do the same to him ; if not, not. Practically all peasants have land.

As a boy, he lived for several years in St. Petersburg ; he served there as staff clerk in the army for four years. He has also been in Finland. He knows a little German, and is anxious to talk it ; the Germans he likes, but not the French, " our allies, of course, but only good for pomade and dress,—too light of thought." He has been here for twenty-four years; he knows the district in and out, and points to a high-lying village where he was born. He seems to have the right word for everyone whom we pass ; all exchange with him an easy salute.

There is far less drunkenness now in this district (near Rostóff), and therefore much less crime. He thinks poorly of the small towns, as they are full of loafers ; the country-folk are much better. The police Tenth man is of no use at all ; a capable peasant will pay to escape election. Tenth men and Hundredth men are peasants, and will go to look at their fields while the criminal escapes. One prisoner sent out for vodka, made his captor drunk and escaped. For himself, he neither drinks nor smokes, so he is not caught napping. He has two whole cantons under his charge, and may be summoned to a distance of twenty miles. In future there is to be for each canton a Police Corporal with three assistants, and the salary is to be raised from £41 to £50. The peasants will help the police to catch a criminal, if the offence is a public danger, such as arson, or a great sin, such as sacrilege or murder; otherwise they wish before all things to avoid being summoned to the town to give evidence. When sent for by the Tenth man, he goes to the spot, examines the case, and, if necessary, sends for the Police Captain. Little use can be made of the telegraph. The escort of the prisoner to the town varies according to the character of his offence, but peasants never resist.

A town mob is hostile to the police. Often it is best for the police to give the crowd its head. A man knows what he thinks; a crowd doesn't: if you can leave it alone, it will soon separate. Even a country crowd is far more indifferent than a German, a Finnish, or, as he understands, an English one. He has never had to deal with an actual riot, nor has he come upon traces of propaganda work of students, labour leaders, or Jews (July, 1904).

Through the war the peasant is learning geography in the widest sense; he used to think that the Japanese were savages. In 1876, when men were sent to the war, they cried, cried like sheep; now there is no crying. The war is teaching them politics; they make it their own business. They always knew that they had got to win; now they are really interested in the details of the fighting. That Russia should lay down 10,000 versts of railway, and that her outlet to the warm seas should then be blocked? Absurd!

Why do the English help the Japanese? Are they not helping? Well, then, why the alliance? It is like touching an unclean thing. An Englishman wouldn't marry a Japanese, nor would a Japanese father give his daughter to an Englishman; it is like putting one's hand into dirt. Theirs is a surface civilisation. We know that a Japanese landowner will allow himself to do anything with his labourers. England is embarked on a bad speculation, for Russia is certain to win in the end. So are the Americans; but then they will try anything for money.

POLICE CAPTAINS.

1. Rostóff District.—A rough but kindly man with full beard, rather like a superior English farmer. He is always

travelling, and has some sixty miles to cover. He enjoys his work, "has got used to it"; he likes the local society, especially several well-educated and well-to-do-peasants. Crime is diminishing fast as a result of the increase of education ; in the amount of drunkenness he sees but little change.

2. District of Krasny, August, 1904.—A ruddy-faced ex-officer, hearty and natural, the kind of man with whom one is intimate from the start.

He says that crime is less than it was, and drunkenness rather less. He likes the peasants, and always has a talk with them when possible, but he thinks those of this part backward and wanting in initiative. " On business," he says, "their talks with me are short." He commends the work of the Zemstvo, which, he says, should not be restricted, but developed further. He has nothing but contempt for the *Moscow Gazette ;* "a low paper must needs try to stir up excitement."

3. Smolensk, August, 1904.—An ex-officer of Lithuanian birth, a pleasant companion, who delivers lucid little lectures on everything that we see together.

The police are unpopular, and the inhabitants will not give them any assistance. Persons must not be touched now, even when they insult the officials. The official must draw up a charge of offensive language, " and that affair lasts long." Everyone, judges included, must say to the prisoners "you" instead of "thou"—" What will you be so good as to eat ? " etc. The prisoners alter their behaviour in consequence. " The so-called humane system has spoilt everything."

4. Borísoff, August, 1904.—At 3.30 a.m. I reach a little station in the Jewish pale; the station officials seem to be mostly Jews. I have no letters for this place. Through a delay of the railway my luggage is limited to a knapsack, a mackintosh bath, and three Napoleonic cannon-balls from Krasny, which are wrapped up in a newspaper. I sleep in a neat Jewish hotel. After breakfast I am studying a military map of 1812, when I feel that there is something behind me: the little shifty hotel servant is looking over my shoulder. " What do you want ? " I say sharply. " Oh, nothing," but a few minutes later he comes to tell me that I am requested to step over to the police station.

The Police Captain is a small man, with a thin beard and rather a rough skin; he has the quiet spiritless manner common to many of the officials. I thought that he might have taken my cannon balls for bombs, but he does not know of them. He wishes to ask why I have taken horses to drive out to S. I explain that I must see the battle-field. "Why is it interesting to you? Anyhow have you any special permission?" I produce the cards of officials of other Governments. "Well, I cannot doubt your identity, but to go to S. you must have the leave of the Police Colonel." "But surely S. is only a village like any other?" "You must get leave from the Police Colonel." At this point I am called aside by the clerk, who asks questions as to my passport, Lord Lansdowne's titles again requiring explanation. He asks for the cards again, and "doesn't see that my credentials prove my case." Perhaps I may see schools and institutions, but I have no leave to see a "fortress" (so he describes a half-ruined wooden village); "and how is he to know that these cards really belong to me?" Here I put in a protest to the Police Captain: he has at least been civil, but his clerk has not; and I have been asked to report to St. Petersburg any incivility with which I may meet. There is a doubtful silence, and I go off to the Police Colonel. With this gentleman I begin at the right end of the stick: I explain my object, my introductions, and why I have no letters to him, just showing some of the cards as casual evidence; no doubt he will give me the same assistance as I have had elsewhere. "Of course," he says; "what can I do for you?" "Well, I want to go to S., and your Police Captain says that I must have your permission." "Why to S.? To see the monument?" "No, to see the battle-field." "Why should you see it in detail? There is nothing left of it. There is a gentleman here who knows all about it. Why don't you go to him instead?" "I should like to do both, but I must go to S. first." He goes to the telephone and rings up the Police Captain. The latter appears and is told off to escort me. "How long do you want to be there?" "A few hours."

We seat ourselves in the hooded carriage which I have hired. It is a seven-mile drive, and there is a cold thin rain nearly all day. The Police Captain is not inclined to interest himself in battle-fields. He seems half to wish to set up a separate conversation with the Jewish driver, but gradually becomes more sociable.

As we near S., I get out, and telling the driver to wait, strike out over the fields and walk along the Russian and French positions. When I return, after five hours, my companion says: "Well, you've tortured me pretty thoroughly." I explain that I had to see the field, and that, as he was evidently not interested in it, I had supposed that he would like to wait in the carriage. "But why is it necessary for history to go into such detail?" "Well, that's just what history is." If he made any further comment on history he made it to himself.

On the way back he became much more talkative. What was the capital of England? He had thought that London was in some loose connection with Great Britain, as Finland with Russia. His chief talk was of restaurants, and he accepted the olive-branch of an invitation to dinner and dined very heartily.

5. Ranenburg District, July, 1905.—A thin, bearded man, with a body something like that of a very lengthy ant; he carries everywhere gloves and sword. To a peasant woman who gets in the way of our cart he shouts, "Devil take you!" His imperious voice calls the Hundredth man from his house at a quick trot to show us the way. A Tenth man is sent to fetch some villagers; he comes back, half timorous, half surly, to say they won't come. "Won't come?" says the Police Captain in a tremendous voice, and the Tenth man shuffles off again with better results.

His father lives quite near, but the strain of work is so great that they have not met for eighteen months. There are no substitutes, and, when one Police Captain is on leave, the work of his nearest colleague is doubled. The country stations, however, are far preferable to the town sections. One is one's own master, and can get to know the peasants who are most interesting. He gives me little lectures on their lives in front of them, and explains to them and to me that they are very ignorant. I ask if there are any illicit stills in the village; a peasant says, "One or two"; the Police Captain cries, "One or two? Come, twenty"; and they all laugh together. Sometimes he walks about the road while I go in and talk to the peasants alone. His conversation is simple and interesting, and he does everything that he can to make my journey agreeable.

A Police Colonel (July, 1904).

A powerful, well-made man, conscious of his responsibility and his power; he is well read and full of intelligence. Certainly it seems to be his chief anxiety to be always doing good. He is almost too ready to conduct a whole conversation for me. We visit a tea-room together. Suddenly he says to a ragged peasant, " You're a tippler." "Yes," says the peasant, with the look of a dare-devil successfully shamed. " This gentleman comes from England," says my companion, "and we can't tell him that people in Russia dress like that." He points out a fishy-eyed man to me as a specimen of the average toper; the man protests, and there follows a quick scene, which ends with the Police Colonel saying, " Show that gentleman out: he doesn't know how to behave." The fishy one gazes for a moment and then goes. On the road we pass a caravan of Jews or gipsies. " Who are you ? " says my companion." " We are organ-grinders." " You drink!" to which they reply with a furtive, negative smile. " They are no use," he says to me; " they won't work; they are too lazy," to all of which they give a kind of official consent. " Where is your passport ? " They produce it with a petitioning attitude. " Go to my assistant; I can't sanction it." Later on we pass some peasants at work. " Where's Basil ? " "Not at work to-day." " He's lazy." Basil came to the Police Colonel to ask for money; the Police Colonel, instead of giving money, bought him some of the good seed which the Zemstva sell at a very low price : Basil's land now gives better crops than that of his neighbours, and others, who were formerly careless, are now buying the Zemstvo seed. When we pass a peasant, my companion remains at the salute till the peasant's hat comes off. With the Police Captain his manner, though not obtrusive, is that of " him who commands." We meet a wandering monk, who does not give us any good reason for having left his monastery. "Eh! You're one who lives strong in winter," says the Police Colonel; the man says "yes," as if he had to, and at once becomes the text for another discourse to me. This system is in fact only adapted for the government of children; if the children will not remain children, the official will be at a loss.

We visit a factory together. The manager has been in

England; he thinks that the English respect a man only according to his balance at the bank, at which the Police Colonel appositely quotes the proverb, "Moscow won't even believe tears." He has had to mediate here between manager and employed, and his decision, which seems to have been a sensible and moderate one, was given in favour of the workmen. He keeps his business manner for certain classes, persons, and occasions. The kindliness of the man does not cease to be apparent. He shows me a beautiful copy of Shakespeare, of which he is very proud.

For internal order, he says, the crisis will be the moment of junction between the student propagandists and the working men. But that moment is really very far off. The Nihilists now say that they wish well to their country, but they want a "jerk" instead of quiet advance. They attempt to spread their propaganda, but rarely outside the great towns, and no case has come within his experience. When one of them goes to a factory, the men laugh at him and say, "He's not one of us," or even push him out, for the labour questions are narrow and separate; the men only care about getting shorter hours and more kopeks, and take no interest in politics. As for the Jews, Russia is too young and untrained to admit them to full freedom everywhere. What is wanted is a period of total exclusion, such as there was in English history. Then they might come back without being dangerous. The French, by their revolution, broke with all their traditions and thus set themselves back for years. He hopes and believes that his own country will never do that.

In St. Petersburg, Moscow, and some other large towns, the City Prefect has the authority of a Governor, though his position and work are far more those of a chief officer of police.

The Governors to whom I was directed were not only courteous, but really kind. One, for instance, discussed with me what different aspects of Russian life would be most interesting to me, and took considerable pains to think out which people, from various standpoints, could best enlighten me upon each. "But," he said to me with a quick smile, "of course, you won't believe anything I say, because I'm a Governor." He made an excellent choice, directing me to one convinced Conservative and one advanced Liberal; I found them lunching together. This

Governor was exactly the opposite of that melodramatic picture of a Russian official which is so common in England: he was a small-built man of quick witty speech, absolutely without self-consciousness, and with a peculiarly easy and attractive manner. When we travelled down the Volga together, his progress was a kind of triumphal procession; children waved handkerchiefs to him from distant houses, and on every pier where we stopped there were people who wished to exchange a word of friendship with him. I noticed the pretty tact with which he always bowed lower to those who saluted him than they did to him.

A Governor on Revision.

On a bare rise we see a big peasant Court-house, and a number of men drawn up in an open square. The village elders and tax-collectors, who are White Russians, look much less able and intelligent than those of Great Russia. Their clothes are of rough brown cloth; some of them do not wear boots. Many are illiterate; some are born talkers. The Governor passes down the line, followed by the Land Captain, the Police Colonel, the Police Captain, and the aged cantonal elder.

The Governor asks each elder whether he is literate, what disorders there have been in the village, and so on. Both he and they are "thou," not "you"; the conversation is simple and easy. The peasant tax-collectors, many of whom are illiterates, have to be ready with their books. He looks at some of these books, and makes pithy remarks; it is more or less a lesson, to show what is expected of them.

We next enter the Court-house, and the peasant judges stand in line before him. One is a clever-looking man with a permanent grin; he does not take the lead in the talking, but sometimes confirms the speaker with a drastic comment. The next is a bearded old man with the look of a dreamy seer; he too says but little. Most of the talking is done by a bearded peasant in the prime of life. The fourth man, who has a coarse face, smiles to himself and sometimes murmurs a smothered criticism. All of them stand throughout, and stand very straight. Many books are called for, but all seem to be in order. The Land Captain sits by the Governor, and often helps the peasants out with short explanations, which the Governor at once accepts.

One of the peasants argues hurriedly, but persistently, in favour of a common reserve of grain. The Governor, who goes fully and simply into each question raised, explains that with railways so near there is no necessity for it; he contrasts the colder and the warmer governments, and tells his own experience of the corn-supplying region of the south. The peasant is not for letting the reserve go without its being registered; this the Governor readily accepts. "Then I'm agreed," says the peasant, and he supports the plan against the objections of others. The judges greatly desire to have a local school, and give good reasons, such as the distance from the town, etc.; they are ready to do their part, if some benefactor will come forward to help them: the cost should in part go to the town. The Governor, according to the current official predilection of the period, suggests a technical school to teach the peasants trades; all welcome this idea.

The cantonal elder has given his frequent explanations simply and satisfactorily. The Governor inquires, closely but kindly, how he can learn in good time of any troubles that arise; it is clearly impossible for him to travel everywhere himself; at last the Governor satisfies himself that the village elders really report as they should. The peasants have no fear of a famine; "Things always grow here," they say. "Then I'm glad for your sakes," says the Governor, but he warns them not to be too confident. He thanks the judges, the clerk, and the Land Captain. "For you, old man, who have served so long," he says to the cantonal elder, "no thanks of mine are required."

During the period of reaction, for reasons which were quite abnormal and have been explained elsewhere, it has been the fashion in governmental circles to assume that there were two truths, one for Western Europe and one for Russia. The autocrat was identified on the one side with God, and on the other identified with the lowest of his police corporals. This involved a double responsibility, which no system in the world could adequately discharge. In 1905 the pet words of abuse in Russia were the words "bureaucrat" and "official"; the outcry has been so loud that even most of the officials have been forced to be ashamed of being officials. I see then two extremes of mood, peculiar to two exceptional periods, and would wish to be more discriminating in the record of my own opinion. I first protest against the lazy mistake of both sides in lumping together a certain whole category of human beings and declaring that they are all naturally vicious. Even if it were so with the officials, " no single man can betray a whole people."[1] If a small ruling caste did actually impose its despotism on the Russian people, then the Russian people must be blamed for gross apathy and laziness ; and, as a matter of fact, history makes it abundantly clear that the Russian autocracy was a product of the Russian people, and that when the people could have simply allowed the autocracy to die in the Time of Troubles, it preferred to re-establish it. But if Russians at one time voluntarily renounced their political individualism in order to face, under one national dictator, a series of great national trials, it does not follow that autocracy always was, and will be, the only possible mode of political development for Russia. And the system exaggerated itself. Even the first reformers, Peter and Catharine, were reformers on the throne, and worked even more for the profit of autocracy than for the profit of the Russian people. It was only after the French Revolution that a few sporadic efforts began to show that there was growing up in the nation itself a small band of individuals who were anxious to claim a share in the government of the country. Of these men, and of their fellows in Western Europe, the Government suddenly became afraid ; it lost its initiative as the enlightened leader of the people, and with its initiative it lost the chief reason for its existence ; and meanwhile the system, like many other systems in other countries, had developed itself into almost a " *reductio ad absurdum.*" Dogs had been placed to guard the sheep, but in the end there were so many dogs that the sheep had to be sacrificed to support them,[2] and many of the dogs entirely forgot why they were there at all. Later on the mischief became only too evident, and many honest attempts have been made to give credit and effectiveness to the old system ; but, for the most part, its defenders have limited themselves to asserting its principles in an always more and more exaggerated and even absolute form. Yet " autocracy " is a word

---

[1] Oriani, an exceedingly democratic writer on the " Conditions of the Present Strife in Italy."

[2] Kryloff's fable, " The Sheep and the Dogs."

like any other, and the repetition of this single word will not
finally satisfy any people in the whole world. Even to the will of
a Napoleon there are natural limits : the limits of the sight, of
the hearing, and, above all, of the will. Not even a Napoleon or
a Peter the Great can control the whole thought of a nation which
is beginning to think, the whole enterprise of a nation which is
learning to exert itself; and where the powers of the autocrat
stop, there begin the powers of the oligarchs, of the men who
have been able to capture the prestige of the autocrat and to use
it in such ways as they may think necessary or desirable. In
Russia the Emperor is often officially described as the " Supreme
Will," but what is to happen if the Supreme Will ceases to will,
that is, disappears? No heredity of succession will ever guarantee
that it will not; and, at that moment, autocracy, without any
revolution, disappears too and gives place to wholesale oligarchy.

Why did republican Rome not earlier change into an empire ?
Was it because there was no man strong enough to be emperor ?
No ; it was because there were too many, and they held each other
in check. Autocracy, then, implies not so much the supremacy of
one will as the cancelling out of other wills, and according to the
measure of the autocrat will be the measure of his servants.
Even a Napoleon I. must be afraid of a Moreau or a St. Cyr
whose ability might compete, in one field at least, with his own ;
a Napoleon III. must choose inferior instruments. As to the
servant, his ideal tends to become that of blind obedience and
ignorance ; and ignorance, in the long run, leads to stupidity.
Further, it is almost inevitable that where there is no initiative,
no responsibility, there, in the long run, we shall find no conscience. This result can hardly be evaded. How can there be
conscience where consciousness is itself repressed ? Of course
the Russian officials have not, by any means, touched the
lowest potentialities of their system ; what is bad is not so much
the officials as the extreme exaggeration and one-sidedness of
the system itself. If they are not worse than they are, it is
because they are still men, that is, because the system could
not be realised in its full absurdity. But they are generally
waiting for orders from above ; if orders do not come, it will
be safest for them to do nothing at all and simply draw their
salary. Initiative or the permission of initiative will very possibly

be punished; laziness and the prohibition of all enterprise will very possibly satisfy the superior officer. The world may sleep for your lifetime or for mine.

The official then is a product of two different factors, the system and the country, and the country comes first. As a Russian, he is pretty sure to be very good-hearted, and at least fairly quick of wit. Of the system he may have in him either the best or the worst: he may have the instincts of a loyal and patriotic servant, or he may be simply lazy and unintelligent. With him, as with other Russians who are not officials, the chief lack may well be a lack of character. He, like many other Russians, may separate his career from his private enjoyments, and may even be at once shameless and self-seeking in the first, and shameless and self-indulgent in the second. More commonly he is as inquisitive as an untrained child; and this is one of the reasons why so many Englishmen have come home with the report that they have been continually under official inspection during the whole of a visit to Russia. I remember a Police Colonel who, on my first landing in Russia, asked me every imaginable question as to the details of my previous life. I found afterwards that this was a characteristic common to the non-official classes. They simply wanted to interest themselves; "What is your religion, and do you really believe in it?" was quite an ordinary question of the Russian Intelligent; and intellectually at least he would not be put off with any conventional commonplace for answer.

The officials then, are usually pleasant gentlemen, like other Russians, probably more disciplined, probably rather more self-seeking. What is specially wrong with them is simply this, that when they don their official uniform they are obliged for the time to enter an atmosphere in which denseness and stolidity are at a premium. Sometimes, when one is dealing with the lower officials, their stupidity is very troublesome. A post-office official detains many of my letters, which are of no value to him, because the words "poste restante" have not been written on them and, as he truly says, I am not an employé living in the post-office. Another makes me write a telegram over again because, on the only form which has been put out for public use, someone else has written a word and scratched it out; he gives me a fresh form, but expects me to write my message without ink.   Several custom-house officials spend a whole afternoon in delivering to me my portmanteau, which is the only box that they have on the premises ; they take an hour to write on a ticket a number which is supposed to be the duplicate of that on my box, and then they write the wrong one.

These are perhaps insignificant details, but they suggest the benumbing effect of all-round bureaucracy.   The worst results of the system are far more serious.   There exists a certain kind of official who has definitely set himself to make his fortune through officialdom.   He has perhaps had to silence secret scruples and to give up former ideals.   He may have had great difficulty in obtaining his post ; for promotion he depends upon the goodwill of his superiors ; correct in dress and manner, obsequious where it is necessary to curry favour, he lets off his feelings in bullying his inferiors, and gets his reward by making money out of the opportunities of his office.   So common are such officials that the habit of browbeating seems almost to be a feature of the whole class, and that wholesale perquisites of a certain kind are generally looked upon as "sinless takings."   If such a man is astute, he will always be trying to follow the changes of wind in that quarter from which all breezes of promotion come.   Picture such a man in a great national crisis, where authority is divided, where the prestige of officialdom is itself in danger, and guess whether he will stand for the letter of the law or for any means which may help to re-establish the old absolutism, by which he has profited so much.   We can already understand the reasons which made certain local officials the ready tools of the policy of provocation, of the policy of the "pogrom."

PART II.—THE "INTELLIGENCE."

CHAPTER VI.

ORIGINS OF THE "INTELLIGENCE."

PUBLIC INSTRUCTION.

WE have now to see how those elements which the autocracy had failed to create were supplied very largely from outside Russia ; and how what is called the Russian " Intelligence " grew up under the most unfavourable conditions and almost as a foreign plant.

Why should a certain class in Russia be called the "Intelligents"? Does this imply that the rest of the nation is devoid of, or even adverse to, intelligence ? Does it mean that this particular class is deficient in other sides of human nature, say, the moral ? And if, then, the claims of the Intelligents are so far-reaching, by what functions of the mind was Russian history directed when this class did not exist ? We shall, of course, assume that to none of these questions could a precise answer be given. But, at least, the distinction between the Intelligents and the rest of Russia has been so abruptly marked, that urgency has been claimed for all sorts of fundamental questions which are more or less dormant in our own country.

We may, for the purposes of this study, divide the actions of any person into two classes: those which are the result of an instinct of which he is unconscious, and those which are the deliberate applications of a thought-out plan. Clearly this line between the unconscious instinct and the conscious intelligence cannot be a hard and fast one. Instinct has only to become gradually conscious in order to pass into intelligence, of which indeed it is the root. Intelligence, as one gets older, and has a greater mass of experience behind one, tends to breed instincts. To glorify the conscious use of the intelligence as alone useful to man would be to imitate the boaster who tells you that he never does anything without having thought the matter out. Did he begin breathing in this way? Did he settle that it was, on the whole, a desirable thing to sometimes sleep? At least more than half of the things that he does, and that the most important half, are the result of a process which was dictated to him, not by conscious thought, but by instinct. If he had refused to obey this dictation, he would not now be alive. To take the question back to the beginning of all things, he never settled that he would be born or arranged the details; in other words, his centre of gravity is somewhere outside him. "Man is born free," we are told, "yet everywhere he is in chains." Nonsense; man is born a baby, and the first thing that is necessary to him is not freedom but dependence on those who were here before him. To say that man is born with a heritage is quite another thing. However, it would be equally ridiculous to maintain that because we breathe without knowing why, we ought never to understand why we breathe, and that breathing in general is not a fit subject for the study even of medical men. Amongst the other functions with which we are endowed, at least one of the highest is the sense of reason, which, though walled within a human head, can extend its regulating and illuminating influence over every sense. The man who, so to speak, excludes the head from the body, who refuses to use this best gift of nature, is as wanting in religion as any other blasphemer.

The creed of mind alone, or rather, of only certain functions of the mind, has in it fallacies which have been allowed to play havoc with much of the story of the nineteenth century in Europe. The mischief of it is that it preaches half-truths as if they were whole truths. It claims to be a new and final dispensation, and its evils are to be found, not so much in what it states, as in what it omits. By the very finality with which it imposes on all time the dogmas of a certain generation in a certain country—the France of the Revolution—it is essentially parvenu and makes a break with the past. The chief thing that it leaves out is the duty of building our civilisation on foundations laid by others. The past is assumed to have been practically all wrong; and that, to all intents and purposes, means that, so far, no God has been guiding history. And if we square everything by the standard that the intelligence of a single generation or, as must logically follow, of a single individual is the only test of truth, the new creed leaves no room for God at all.   He represents something outside of us, and that is exactly what we do not admit.   We acknowledge nothing that is not within the scope of our own understandings. So no generation must count for anything except my own, and in logical development, no individuality must count for anything except myself.   We are not the products of a great external force which made us without our co-operation; we are all types of that supreme intelligence which pertains to mankind as a whole. We are the final arbiters of truth.   This might be all very well if your sense of logic, or my sense of logic, could be absolutely identified with logic in the ideal.   No one ought to be such a fool as to think that God has so bungled His creation that it can only work out in defiance of truth.   No doubt if we knew everything and could see the whole of the great framework, all would be absolutely of a piece.   But to expect to see that framework all at once is to claim, as the French of the Revolution claimed, that the human race is finally grown up.   Why grown up? when did that happen ?   Was it on the birthday when one was twenty-one years old, and does it happen for everyone at exactly the same distance from one's birth ?   Why not seventeen, or even nine, or even nought?   But the principle of us Christians, and of all others who have a religion, is that a man is not fully grown up even at a hundred; that something is still to be looked for and waited for.   And this is not only the principle written all over history, but,—more than that,—it is the only bond which ties man to the future of his race, that is, which gives him a prospect of a real immortality.

Then, too, this creed claims that all men arrive at the same point at the same time.   But this claim the practical experience of France during the Reign of Terror was quite enough to prove to be utter nonsense.   You and I are each of us grown up; therefore the mind of each of us offers an absolute and all-sufficing criterion of truth ; but somehow or other my truth turns out to be quite a different thing from your truth.   We have each in the seclusion of our cabinets, in conference with those minds which Heaven gave to each of us as final judges, written out constitutions for the whole human race ; but your constitution and

mine do not agree.   This we find out, as we each rush on to the
stage with the all-important documents in our hands, and jostle
together in the middle.   Is my final statement right or is yours?
Well, I can get more people to agree with me than you, and you
are a traitor to my ideas ; and so I must guillotine you.   So, from
our failure to use our new-found minds and our new-found
liberty, we come back to those old rules which we had both been
laughing at together ; to " reason of state," that is, to the
necessity of a government of some kind, which is never more
absolute than at a time of social dissolution, to the supremacy of
a moral as well as a political dictator far more absolute than the
king whom we have destroyed.[1]   In fact, the practical settlement
of all questions is left to force ; and the Maratist or the Nihilist will
take a pride in methods of which a Louis XIV., or a Catherine II.,
might have at least been ashamed.

The next generation will claim the same prerogative of formu-
lating truth ; and, if it be concluded that the existing definition is
inaccurate—why, then, truth is absolute, and there is nothing left
but to cancel the definition altogether.   Hence the series of Constitutions which has followed the French Revolution.   Almost
any one of them was good, but, as everyone should have known in
advance, not one of them was perfect ; therefore, away with them.
Talleyrand, when taking the oath to Louis Philippe, is said to
have exclaimed, " It is the thirteenth, and, pray God, it may be
the last."   Under such pressure, the moral sense withers ; in
fact, it never has time to root itself in the new formula.

The assertion has been made that all men are equal.   It has
hardly ever been definitely asserted that they are all equal in
knowledge, yet it is a principle of modern institutions that one
man's vote on a given subject should have exactly the same value
as anyone else's.   Again, why put an arbitrary limit of twenty-one
years of age, or why exclude women ?   And, if all men are equal,
why bother about the acquirement of that most precious of all
exclusive possessions—character ?   We are all sheer mind now,
and are simply thinking of how, in principle, the world should be
ordered.   Moral education is unnecessary ; for the man is grown

---

[1] The most intelligent view of Robespierre is that he was the first of the new
dictators, the predecessor of Napoleon, who has himself been called " Robespierre à
cheval " (Robespierre on horseback).

up. The connection with the past is gone. Each man is a law
unto himself. Sin, the potentiality of which is really the noblest
thing about him, has lost his attention. The body, emancipated
from tutelage, claims more and more for itself. Rights supersede
duties. The world exists for man ; and, as the individual interprets its construction only by the narrow code of his own personal
insight, death is become a blot, and, as licensing death, God has
become a sinner. Meanwhile, man must seek pleasure where he
can find it. The religious principle once struck out, the worship
of mind tends rapidly to become a worship of the body, and of
this sinister phenomenon we shall see instances enough when we
study the lives of the Russian Intelligents.

Those who know Russia well will probably not think that too
much has here been said of this side of the subject. For good or
for evil, perhaps no country in Europe, not even France herself,
can show the effects of the French Revolution developed in so
extreme and logical a form as Russia. It is largely the fault of
the Intelligents that the methods of autocracy have been able to
exaggerate themselves so long. If Russia had learnt " character "
as soon as she had learnt intelligence, she would have been
practically free long before this. Probably the greatest obstacle
to reform at the present day is what is called in Russia " unýnye "
or despondency, an aspect of pessimism which is far more
characteristic of the Intelligents than of any other class. The
obscurantist Pobyedonóstseff, when he wished to deny the right
of any initiative to the Russian people, could, at least, find a
foundation for his Jeremiads in the corruption of Russian society.
But he himself had nothing more to offer than the flimsy Nihilist
who will dynamite away the whole existing system of government
without knowing what he wants to put in its place. He and his
opponents lived on each other's negativeness, and it was only thus
that he could remain in power long after he was really dead.[1]

But if I have dwelt on this negative side it is because we can
more easily understand how much is to be said on the other.
The Intelligence was necessary to Russia ; in fact, it was Russia's
greatest need. Despite its foreign models, it was still essentially
Russian. There was never, at any time, anything like as much

---

[1] I allude to Count Paul Sherémetyeff's admirable description of Pobyedonóstseff
as a "man in a schema," p. 133.

reason as the Russian Government pretended, to suspect it of wholesale disloyalty to the traditions of the country, and even if it had
been otherwise, the only rational cure for the evils of the Intelligence was always as it is now, responsibility.   Even under the
immense disadvantages under which it developed, it has been able
to render the most signal services to the country.   It made the
reforms of Alexander II. inevitable ; it gave to them a generosity
of scope which will some day be the envy of other countries ; it
regulated the working of the reforms ; it has prepared the country
for another great step forward which can hardly be long delayed.
Considered in its intellectual influence on the people, the Russian
Intelligence has been a light shining in a dark place.

The first great interruption in the story of the Russian consciousness came, of course, with the Tartar invasion.   Its effect
was to isolate Russia from Western Europe, and thus to later
give a more revolutionary character to Russia's attempts to
re-educate herself in European civilisation.   Of these attempts
the first comes with Peter the Great.   It cannot, of course, be
said that, but for Peter, Russia would never have sought an
education from the West ; on the contrary, she had already begun
to do so.   But, as an eminent Russian writer puts it,[1] " Peter
found things ripening extremely slowly ; he found an evolution
which was advancing as quietly as possible and suddenly turned
it into a stormy enterprise, into a revolution."   The historian
Shcherbátoff estimates that Peter crushed into some thirty years
a movement which should have taken two centuries.   Solovyéff,
the author of the standard history of Russia, writes, " The absolute
necessity of suddenly satisfying all needs at once was inevitably
bound to give to our so-called 'transformation' the character of
a revolution.   Our revolution of the beginning of the eighteenth
century can be explained by comparing it with the political
revolution which followed in France at the end of that century.
As here, so too there, diseases had accumulated in consequence
of stagnation.   In Russia a single man gifted with unprecedented
strength took into his own hands the guidance of the movement
of revolution, and this man was born chief of the State.   The
change was accompanied by a fearful struggle.   The transformer

---

[1] N. Engelhardt, " Sketch of the Story of the Russian Censorship," p. 5.

met with strong resistance in his people; consequently the act of transformation was an act of violence from the side of the Supreme Power."[1]

From Peter's time onward, the educator of Russia was Germany. The new organs of the Government, "little Governments," as they have been called in the Imperial Instruction of 1767, were rapidly filled with Germans. For a time (1730—1740) Russia might almost be said to be under German rule. But Germans easily become loyal servants of a new master; they are the quickest of Europeans to lose what is politically distinctive in their nationality. They had, at this time, no German patriotism to carry abroad with them, but only a culture of a more or less cosmopolitan character, which was exceedingly useful to those at whose service it was placed.

With Elizabeth, the ally of Louis XV., begins the period of French influence. The tutorship of France was altogether a different thing from that of Germany. Firstly, France was a nation, whereas Germany was not. In at least one great crisis of her history—the wars of the Reformation—she had preferred her national unity to the settlement of the gravest questions which could trouble the conscience of the individual. In this national solidarity she had resembled Russia; and in spite of their different ways of showing it, the two peoples shared a certain wonderful vitality which enabled them to tide over crises which would hardly come at all in the lives of some of their duller neighbours.

Germany was neuter ("es"), but France and Russia were ladies and mothers. France was a person, and, moreover, one with a very specialised individuality. She had her own moods and fancies and her own conventions for compromising with great questions, conventions which were personal and presumably did not apply to anyone else. Thus, religion must be accepted as "a part of that sacred whole which we call country"[2]; but the mind and the conduct remain free. Again, you may not marry without practically the consent of your whole family; and therefore you may remain as free as you like after marriage. Again, an insult must be wiped out in blood,

[1] Solovyéff, "History of Russia," Book III. pp. 1055, 1056. Solovyéff throughout does full justice to the governmental side of Russian history.

[2] Words of Napoleon. Thiers, "Consulat et Empire," Vol. IV., p. 680.

but a scratch on the wrist is enough to satisfy honour. But France, who is truly "a fountain of genius and light,"[1] has such a strong personal charm that natives of less happy countries may easily wish to be second-hand Frenchmen.

Though the ideas of France may change, her whole weight will, as a rule, go to the propagation of the idea of the moment, and that idea will assume a very different importance in the world from the time that France begins to preach it. And, in spite of her saving instinct of solidarity and her saving grace of humour, France has been peculiarly logical in the ideas which she has preached. The reason why she has so often abandoned one idea for another is simply because she has got to the end of it; she has turned it into a kind of "reductio ad absurdum." Her mistake was in ever seeking a final definition in the formula of any single idea. She did not invent what we call feudalism, but she developed it more logically than anyone else. Her Protestantism was peculiarly daring and constructive. When she found salvation in the principle of a centralised monarchy, she carried that principle almost to the denial of the existence of the French people, except as "the sponge to be squeezed," and, of course, she was singularly sincere in the wholesale changes which she made at the time of the Revolution.

France is second-hand Rome; she makes the same claims of world leadership, but interprets them to the special profit and glory of France. Unlike Rome, she is a bad learner; the French school-book of history is " une histoire de France et du monde ; " but the part about " le monde " is a kind of necessary appendix to the story of France. Thus, what France has presented to the world is, in the main, the pleasant picture of her own personality. If we are to deal in monarchs, then France has the Grand Monarque; if it is a question of peoples, then France is the Grand Nation—the standing outrage on the principle of equality. Thus she tends to claim a kind of Roman dignity for each of her own varying phases as it passes. If the French have a republic, the Swiss, the Dutch, and the Italians must have republics too; if France accepts a Napoleon, there must be Bonapartes on every throne of Western Europe. And the wonder, of course, is that

---

[1] A common French catch-word; it occurs in the famous "convivial" speech of M. Pelletan.

she is able to do it, and this would not be possible unless she had such a charm as could make us all take her at her own price.

So much has had to be said because if the Russian peasant is the father of the Russian Intelligence, France is undoubtedly its mother. At the present day one can mark down a thousand traits of the Russian Intelligence as simply second-hand French. The best of the Russian writers have cried out against the slavish imitation of everything French. Here is an example from Griboyédoff:—

" Sophy (to Chatsky) : ' Say, what makes you so angry ? '

" Chatsky : In that room, just a trifling encounter. A Frenchman from Bordeaux, with chest puffed out, had gathered round him a kind of parliament, and was telling how he prepared for the journey to Russia, to the barbarians, with terror and with tears. He came and found that there are unending caresses for him; he never met with a sound of Russian or a Russian person ; he might have been in his own province with friends. Why, look ! at such a soirée as this, he feels that he is a little Tsar. Just the same talk about ladies, just the same fashions. He is delighted, yet we are not delighted. . . . I, standing apart, uttered my humble wish that the Lord would destroy this unclean spirit of empty slavish blind imitation. . . . Let them call me an Old Believer if they will, but for me, our North is worse a hundred times since it gave up all that it had, to be exchanged into the new pattern. . . . As in the clothes and hair, there is a shortage in the minds too. Oh ! if we were born to imitate everything, why should we not have borrowed from the Chinese a little of their very sensible ignorance as to foreigners ? Shall we ever have a resurrection from this foreign despotism of fashions, so that our clever good-hearted Russian people may, if only by the language, know us apart from Germans ? "[1]

We have nothing like it in England ; but all through Russia's long communication with the West, there has run just this strain of irritation,—the acknowledgment of superiority blended with the resentment of patronage ; in fact it is one of the chief characteristics of Russian history.

The France with which Russia became acquainted under Catherine II., was the France of Louis XV. ; which was itself a

---

[1] The peasant calls all foreigners Germans.

parody of the France of Louis XIV. French exteriors were rigged out for use at the cringing Court of Catherine. French phrases of Montesquieu were on the lips of the Empress and the other proprietors of serfs; any French barber was good enough to be tutor to the heir of one of the noblest families ; but it was to this spirit of imitation that Russia also owed the foundation of some of her most valuable institutions, those connected with public instruction.

Peter and his second wife, Catherine I., had founded in St. Petersburg an Academy of Science, when there was, as yet, hardly any regular teaching in the country. Under Elizabeth, as under Peter, young men had been sent from Russia to study abroad, but their chief study was trade and book-keeping. In the same reign, however, Count Ivan Shuváloff founded the University of Moscow, of which N. Turghényeff wrote in 1844, " Never in any country has any institution been comparatively more useful and more fertile of results. To-day it is rare that a man who writes his own language correctly, an honest and enlightened official, or an upright and firm magistrate, has not at some time been a student in the University of Moscow." The University was founded by the Government, and definitely with the object of training capable officials. It had thus, from the first, an official character. The student carried a sword and was of the tenth rank of officials. There were ten professors and three faculties—Law, Medicine, and Philosophy. Shuváloff established some schools on the southern frontier, and others for the children of those living in exile ; he also sent young men abroad to study medicine. Lastly, he created the Academy of Fine Arts at St. Petersburg, where the teachers were mostly Frenchmen. The Russian theatre received its first serious development from Volkoff and Sumarókoff; these men were protégés of Elizabeth, who also kept up a French theatre.

Catherine II. went further. In 1766 deputies from all Russia met to discuss a new code of law for the Empire. Each received a medal with the motto " For the happiness of all and each." The instruction from the Empress to the Commission contained the words, " The nation is not made for the sovereign, but the sovereign for the nation ; for citizens equality consists in only having to obey the law; liberty is the right of doing everything that is not forbidden by law; it is better to spare ten criminals than to ruin one innocent man." Other maxims condemn intolerance, religious persecution, and cruel punishments.[1] She wrote to Voltaire, "I think you would be pleased at this assembly, where the Orthodox is seated between the heretic and the Mussulman, listening to the voice of an idolater, and all four are doing their best to make their opinions tolerable to the others." She established a College of Pharmacy at Moscow, and introduced vaccination; she wrote to Voltaire, "We have inoculated more people here in a month than they have at Vienna in a whole year." She founded boarding-schools under a French directress for 480 daughters of the nobility and bourgeoisie. But Catherine was a born autocrat, and no more absolute sovereign has ever sat upon the throne of Russia.

Catherine reigned till 1796, and the year 1789 is the turning-point in the destinies of the Russian Intelligence. France, the model of Russia, dared to demand rights for herself, instead of waiting obediently for favours from her sovereign. Catherine was taken ill in 1793; the Government fell into a panic, excluded French books, and expelled Frenchmen who acknowledged the Republic. Her son Paul was a thorough-going autocrat, but after sending Suvóroff to fight for throne and altar in the West, he recognised Napoleon as the re-establisher of order. Alexander's French alliance was never popular,[2] and even Rambaud records the strong anti-French bias of the writers of this reign. Rostopchin published his satire "Oh, the French!" and in another work[3] wrote thus: "Are we to imitate the monkeys for ever? . . . If a Frenchman escapes the gallows and reaches Russia, at once everyone scrambles for him. . . . What do we now teach our children? To speak French well, to turn their toes out, and to curl their hair. The only man whom we call witty is he whom a Frenchman will take for a compatriot. . . . In all countries people teach their children French; but simply for them to know it, and not that it may replace their mother tongue."[2] Alexander at the beginning of his reign chose liberal

---

[1] Rambaud, "History of Russia," pp. 476, 477. I am indebted to this admirable work over and over again.

[2] "Tilsit! at that ill-omened name,
    How blushes still the patriot's pride!"
                    —Pushkin, "Ode on Napoleon."

[3] "Thoughts aloud on the Red Staircase" (1807).

Ministers, and contemplated great reforms. The ban which Paul had placed on foreign travel was removed. Ministries on the foreign model replaced the old "Colleges" of Peter the Great. The Empire was divided into six educational circles, of which each was put under the charge of a capable and liberal administrator. The universities of Moscow, Vilna, and Dorpat were reorganised; those of Kazán and Kharkoff, and later that of St. Petersburg were founded. An Institute of Oriental Languages was created, and a great Commercial College was established at Odessa. Fifteen Military Schools and two important Lycées, or public schools, were established, and also a number of Gymnasia (or secondary classical schools), District schools for the less well-to-do, and, finally, parish schools for the country villages. The system of Church schools, seminaries, and religious academies now received, on paper at least, a large measure of development. Speránsky, the chief minister of these liberal times, had strong French sympathies, and enlarged the Council of the Empire in such a way as to make it almost a kind of national representation. He even wished to introduce some such law code as that of Napoleon. He gave to members of the University a degree of precedence over other candidates for Government rank. But in 1812, when war with France was on the point of resumption, he was suddenly banished to Nizhny-Novgorod and then sent to Siberia.

The new European situation created by Napoleon's failure in Russia has already been discussed. The Grand Army had visited Russia at home. It was the ideas of the Revolution that had given the initial push to this vast force, and, even before the eyes of the Russian peasant, it had been demonstrated that the force was great enough to compel one to take the ideas seriously. On the other hand, the Russian Government, which had really been saved by the Russian people, had an interest in putting the whole triumph to the credit of throne and altar. The impressionable Alexander read one thought into every detail of the story—the triumph of authority over lawlessness. He sank into religious mysticism, and there followed a long period of sheer reaction. This reaction had started from Russia itself in 1812; but as Alexander crossed the frontier, was joined by ally after ally, and pushed home his counter-stroke to Paris itself, it was carried all over Europe. Thus, the very reaction brought Russia into far closer touch with the Western States than ever before; and in its foreign relations, as in its home policy, the Russian Government definitely stood for the ideas of the " Holy Alliance," that is, for the policing of all peoples.   Thus home and foreign policy were one, and the Russian Intelligence, quickened to new political interests in 1812, but pushed back into the darkness immediately afterwards, tended to find its natural friends in all the Western champions of the rights of peoples, and more particularly in the great French people.   France, who was to finally expel the Bourbons in 1830, was still the most powerful opponent of despotism; and from that time to the present, there has been conducted a war of a new kind between the Russian Government on one side and the French ideas on the other.   We must understand that the French ideas became the creed of the Russian Intelligence.   Now, more than ever, it could be said of the latter that its centre of gravity was outside Russia.

The favourite of Alexander's later years was a kind of police corporal, Count Arakchéyeff, who seems to have been disinterested, and was certainly a hard worker, but who cringed to the Emperor and bullied those under him.   The law code sketched by Speransky was not worked out.   French theatres were closed.   The revolt of a regiment of the Guard, and the murder of his protégé, Kotzebue, were represented to Alexander by the friends of despotism in such a light that he abandoned his last relics of liberalism.   Even the British and Foreign Bible Society was found to preach too much liberty.   The universities were subjected to a special supervision, and the Curators of the various educational districts, such as the notorious Magnitsky pushed repression of thought beyond all limits.   Magnitsky, wishing to organise instruction "on the principles of the Holy Alliance," expelled eleven professors from the University of Kazán, excluded from its library books of the most reasonable content, forbade the teaching of the theories of Buffon and the systems of Copernicus and Newton as contrary to the Scriptures, and ordered the Professor of History to take as his model the work of Bossuet.   Dissection was forbidden as disrespectful to the dead.   Economics were to be a " politico-moral " study, showing how material good can be transformed into spiritual. Nikólsky, the Professor of Geometry, represented the triangle as the emblem of the Trinity.   At Kharkoff and St. Petersburg, other professors were expelled, one being accused of impiety for teaching the philosophy of Schelling, and another of " Robespierrism," for having criticised serfdom and the excessive issue of paper money. Russian students were forbidden to study beyond the frontier. Professors who had studied abroad were made ineligible for posts in Russia.

Yet this was the time of Zhukóvsky, Kryloff, Griboyédoff, and Pushkin. Clearly the Russian Intelligence was quickened in its development by the very excesses of the reaction. Literary and scientific societies were established in the chief towns [1]: in 1814 the Imperial Library of St. Petersburg was opened to the public. The Press developed apace.

"From the return of the Russian armies to their country," writes N. Turghényeff, " we must date the beginning of the propagation in Russia of what were then called liberal ideas. Apart from the regulars, great masses of the militia had also been abroad; these militiamen of all ranks, as they in turn passed the frontier again, went home to tell of what they had seen in Europe. But events themselves spoke louder than any human voice; that was the real propaganda." Colonel Pestel, who names the Restoration of 1814 as the turning point in his political convictions, writes : "I then saw that most of the essential institutions founded by the Revolution had been preserved at the re-establishment of the Monarchy as beneficent. . . . I was confirmed in my idea when I noticed that the States in which there had been no revolution continued to be deprived of many rights and liberties." Such men would find much to criticise, on their return to Russia, in serfdom, in the Church and administration, and notably in the discipline of the army. French books of political content were far more widely read. Freemasonry, which had been proscribed under Catherine and Paul, now spread all over Russia. Secret societies were formed : in 1816 the " League of Safety " ; in 1818 the "League of the Common Weal," an imitation of the German Tugendbund. Such societies were recruited chiefly from the highest families. Liberalism sprang not from the people, but

---

[1] Such as the Arzamass, the Besyeda, the Friends of Science, Literature and Art (St. Petersburg), the Friends of Russian Literature, the History of Russian Antiquities (Moscow), the Archæological Society (Odessa), the Society of Patriotic Literature (Kazán), and the Friends of Science (Kharkoff).

from the gentry; with many it was little more than an engaging and dangerous fashion, as with the Repetíloff of Griboyédoff's play. Out of the "League of the Common Weal" grew after 1822 two societies, that of the North, which aimed at a constitutional monarchy, and that of the South, which, under Pestel, advocated a republic, and whose inner circle even contemplated the murder of the sovereign. An active propaganda was carried on in the army; the soldiers were to be won by the promise of lighter discipline and of peasant freedom. These societies were in touch with the Patriotic Society of Poland.

Alexander I., soured and moody, anticipated death; he had the mass for the dead performed when he passed the Trinity Monastery on his last journey to the south; there he died a mysterious death, murmuring the futile apology, "And yet they can say what they please of me; I have lived and I shall die a republican."[1] His successor, Nicholas, was prejudiced, at the outset of his reign, by an attempt of Pestel and his fellow-workers to overthrow the autocracy by means of the troops. This attempt, though it had the great advantage of being made at a time when the succession was being debated, ended in a tragic fiasco. The soldiers who rose in St. Petersburg did not understand for what purpose they were rising, and they were, at most, but a tiny fraction of the army. After they had been shot down, and after a similar rising in the south had succumbed to the immense difficulties of distance and apathy, the chiefs of the conspirators were hanged; and Pestel, while fully adhering to his political creed, acknowledged before his death, "My greatest fault was that I wished to reap before sowing." The social, and in some cases literary, distinction of many of the conspirators, helped to strongly attract the public interest to the story of this abortive movement, and it is important in Russian history as a phenomenon typical of a growing volume of instincts and aspirations.

Nicholas, who was by no means lacking in information or in common sense, was by nature and training fitted to be a benevolent despot. In him, at least, the "Supreme Will" was no fiction. Stamped at his accession as the enemy of revolution, he continued to combat it all his life, both in Russia and in

[1] Rambaud, p. 634.

Europe. He aimed, as Lamartine put it, "at stopping the movement of the world"; but he could do no more than delay the efflorescence of the new life that was growing up underneath him. He was a generous and distinguishing enemy, and thus he was himself the chief patron of the best writers. He established commercial law courts. He created a class of honour amongst the traders, for which one of the qualifications was a certificate of education. He encouraged the private liberation of serfs, and though he never actually attacked the main question, he seriously considered the issues of a general emancipation. The first railways grew up under him, but slowly. He established two corps of teachers for higher and secondary instruction. But even private tutors were required to have a certificate of their character and political "trustworthiness" from one of the universities. Special permission was necessary for study abroad; the passport system was made more rigid, and foreign languages and literature were less taught. A new University was founded at Kieff; but that of Vilna was suppressed. Very typical of the reaction was the treatment of the teaching of philosophy. There were no longer to be separate chairs of philosophy, and the teaching of the subject was handed over to the Church. The military schools were more thoroughly organised, and a law school and a technological institute were founded. In all this, we can see a single idea: the raising of a wall along the frontier, and the direction of study to those subjects which were less likely to make men think, and would train them in the shortest time to be subservient and effective agents of the official system. There was no longer the vague mixture of principles which was to be found in the pronouncements of Catherine and in the mind of Alexander; the issue was frank. The Emperor had the sense to see that he required intelligent officials, and that a great literature would contribute to his own glory; but thought and writings could find favour from him only if they as frankly accepted this position. And indeed, in this reign, the innate patriotism even of the Russian Intelligents made the compromise a far more possible one than we might have imagined. We can quite understand how Glinka came to write his opera, "My Life for the Tsar," under Nicholas I. The relations of Nicholas to his protégés were sometimes more

honourable to him than to them. Witness the following anecdotes: Zhukóvsky, we are told, sent the first volume of one of
his books to the Emperor; Nicholas replied, "I send you some
of my own productions," enclosing a draft for so many roubles;
later Zhukóvsky sent the second volume with the words, "I
am anxiously awaiting your second," and the Emperor replied
with another draft, adding the words, "Volume second and last."
It is reported that the clever mimic Gorbunóff, after one of his
performances, was called to the Emperor's box. "Gorbunóff,"
said the Emperor, "mimic me"; and the actor, assuming just
the manner and voice of Nicholas, turned to the Court treasurer
with the words, "Sheremétyeff, give Gorbunóff a thousand roubles
at once." There were then, and still are, relics of the old servitude; but though the public interest in literature was never in
this reign anything like as great as we should gather from the
character of the writings, the Intelligence was steadily gaining
in volume, and was gradually becoming at least more representative of the nation, and less a creature of the Court.

Nicholas wished for friendly relations with England, which had
been a great ally of his country against Napoleon. Perhaps he did
not appreciate the vast transformation which, on the basis of old
English traditions but under the special influence of the French
Revolution, was in course of progress in England. His special
hostility was directed against France, where "Paris, periodically
by a day's work, shook the soil all over Europe."[1] In 1830
France had expelled the ally of Nicholas, Charles X., and had
given the signal for the rising of Poland. The Russian Emperor
had barely recognised the accession of Louis Philippe, and had
even tried to form a coalition against him. But England was at
this time becoming the centre of gravity in Europe. Her influence
over Russia was never in volume a quarter of that of France; but
though Russians did not love England, many of them respected
her and wished to emulate her. The best club of the Russian
nobility in Moscow bore the name English. England had made
her own revolution for herself long before 1789, and her writers
had exercised the greatest influence over the French philosophers
of the eighteenth century. No French Revolution could ever be
complete until it had penetrated into every corner of Europe;

[1] Rambaud, p. 658.

the French were, in a way, the exaggerators and the martyrs of their own ideas. But England, like Russia, had never been willing to sacrifice her moral consciousness to foreign ideals, however excellent, and, like Russia, she had met the French Revolution with arms in her hands. The lessons which she was to learn from France were, as in Russia, to come later. But from 1832, the year of the great Reform Bill, these lessons were beginning to be learned. The first French Revolution had forced Pitt and England into an unnatural reaction, and now we began to take our place again amongst the leaders of the thought of Europe. England never joined the "Holy Alliance"; and Canning set up his own corner against it when he took an independent line in Portugal and in South America, and claimed "to have called into existence the New World in order to redress the balance of the Old." From 1832 onwards, France and England stood together as the champions of constitutional rule.

They were an unequal pair. France, during this period, twice altered her manner of government. She was the incarnation of the restless spirit of change. England, on the other hand, was now slowly working out her transformation in detail, and, as Mazzini has said of her, " every idea accepted by the intellect was certain to soon pass into the sphere of action, and every improvement once made was secured for ever." In 1848—1850, while Nicholas was the patron of all thrones (for instance of the Austrian domination in Hungary), Palmerston was, at least, the friend and abettor of all peoples; and from 1850 we may date the comparative eclipsing of the French influence all over Europe by the English. Manin, Cavour, Garibaldi, and Victor Emmanuel were practically Italian Englishmen.[1] Even Bismarck, pessimist and absolutist though he was, represents an innovation carried through by common sense. From 1850 the great achievements of reform in Europe were such as to give to the whole period rather the character of composition (not to say compromise) than that of revolution.

The revolutionary period of 1848 and 1849 was signalised in Russia by a special awakening of public interest, by the appearance of a breed of reformers who are one in spirit and in nature all over Europe, and who did not care against what odds

---

[1] This statement is based on the criticisms of several Italian writers.

they might be working, and, lastly, by the extreme exaggeration of restrictions on the Press. Nicholas had the last of his successes when his general Paskyévich restored the Austrian domination over Hungary in 1849. But five years later he found himself facing the united forces of France and England on Russian soil. The Crimean war is an epoch in the history of the Russian Intelligence. A vast underground literature circulated all over Russia. "Awake, Russia," said one of these pamphlets, ". . . awake from this long sleep of ignorance and apathy. . . . Get up and stand, calm and firm, before the throne of the despot. . . . Tell him boldly that his throne is not the altar of God, and that God has not eternally condemned us to be slaves. . . . Tsar, you have forgotten Russia! . . . You have created the contemptible race of censors in order to sleep in peace, in order not to know the needs or listen to the murmurs of your people. . . . Throw yourself into the arms of your people; there is no other safety for you." Nicholas, who could not change, went down in this storm of indignation, apparently by his own deliberate purpose. He died of an illness which he refused to combat; and his successor, Alexander II., gave to Russia her first education in responsible freedom.

The reforms themselves and the influence which they have exercised are considered in detail in other parts of this book—in general, they were grounded not so much on French ideals as on the English tradition of practical work of detail. At least a section of the Russian Intelligence became more practical in its aims through obtaining some measure of responsibility. If the Revolutionaries are strong to-day, it is not because of the reforms, but because of the Second Reaction, which followed the reforms. But when this has been said, two most important qualifications must be made. In the first place, Russia was not yet used to responsibility, and the early end of the reform period was, therefore, premature. In the second place, the scope of the reforms was in every way restricted in the period which followed them, and only a certain part of the Intelligence was able to acquire the training of responsibility.

Russia came wonderfully well out of this first trial of liberty. She had a far greater reserve of loyalty than some foreigners had imagined. "The ancient harmony and unity of sentiment," wrote one newspaper, "which, except for abnormal periods, has always existed between the Government and the people is quite re-established. The absence of all feeling of caste, the instinct of a common origin and of a brotherhood which unites all classes in Russia into a single homogeneous people, will allow her to accomplish peaceably, and without effort, not only those great reforms which have cost Europe centuries of bloody strife, but also other reforms which the nations of the West, enchained by feudal traditions and their caste prejudices, are still incapable of achieving." And large as this claim is, the emancipation at least was a great-hearted settlement, only possible because of the generosity of those who made it.

But too many vested interests had been disturbed for the new Russia to be at once contented. Some grudged what had been given ; others claimed more. The newly emancipated were, naturally, at first unused to their liberty, and even mistook it for licence. The Polish rising of 1863 frightened some minds and excited others. At this time the students of St. Petersburg demonstrated their sympathy with the Polish insurgents, and those of Kazán with the peasant Petróff, who raised a revolution on the plea that the emancipation was incomplete. The Government by raising the cost of university study, and forbidding demonstrations and even private meetings, raised a storm which resulted in the closing of the universities of St. Petersburg and Moscow.

There were now eight universities in the Empire, that of Odessa having been founded in 1864, and that of Warsaw having been Russified in 1869. Amongst some 6,000 students two-fifths received Government scholarships. There were nearly 200 girl students of medicine and surgery at St. Petersburg. The 198 classical secondary schools contained 50,000 pupils. There were 246 schools of the same type for girls. Modern schools had recently been founded to train boys for the less liberal professions. The number of primary schools in Russia had, at least, been greatly increased.[1] We notice, however, that, as in other countries, higher education preceded primary, and instruction in general remained more or less the monopoly of the upper and middle classes. Of these, the middle class now

---

[1] Rambaud, "History of Russia," pp. 697, 698.

supplied the greater number of scholars and students, and this was precisely the class which was most cut off from all responsibilities. Schools and universities were chiefly recruited from that suspected population of the towns which had developed late in Russian history, and for which no regular place had been found by the Government. The students would in many cases be the sons of poor officials; but that would not necessarily give them any greater respect for the system of bureaucracy. Further, if Russia had already produced her greatest writers, the volume of literature was now indefinitely increased. Every subject of political, literary, or scientific interest was now being dealt with by capable critics, and for the first time in the history of Russia there was a really considerable reading public. Attention must also be called to the comparatively rapid development of instruction for women in Russia. This has united, with other circumstances already mentioned, to give a special tinge to the political aspirations of the irresponsible Russian Intelligence.

The exaggeration of Western ideas by many of the Intelligents naturally led to a counter-stroke. The theory of the Slavophils was that Russia could work out a civilisation of her own, independently of the West. They have always stood for preserving the moral conscience of Russia intact at all costs. After the flood of Westernising talk which characterised the beginning of the reign of Alexander II. there was a revulsion, and Katkoff, perhaps the most notable of the Slavophils, replaced Hertzen in the journalistic direction of public opinion. One of the oldest instincts of the Slavophil was a desire to liberate the Christian subjects of the Sultan. In fact, this course was almost forced upon Russia by the risings in the Balkhans and the utter futility of the concert of Europe. Unfortunately, however, for the cause of reform, the war, which was in the end successful, was followed by a treaty which turned success into fiasco.

Many circumstances had now contributed to endanger the position of Alexander II. in Russia. General dissatisfaction was followed by general apathy, and this gave an opportunity to men of extreme views. The universities, long the fortresses of criticism, had united within their walls a number of young men who were never again in all their lives to meet so many of their fellows under the inspiration of a common ideal. Here they were still young in heart and brain, and as yet unhampered by the practical concerns of life. They did not represent any ruling class; naturally, their interests were quite as much social as political; and students or ex-students, especially those who had crossed the frontier, might be expected to carry on a scheme of social propagandism as whole-hearted and as all-embracing as any other of the enthusiasms of the Russian nature. The universities were by their merits, as by their defects, a very focus of revolution.

The origins of what is called Nihilism are still obscure. Some say that its ideas are first to be found in Buchner's book, " Force and Matter." The Nihilists are not men of great political content. All sorts of ideas jostle together in their minds; they have no really constructive plan to offer in the place of that which they propose to destroy. They were never a considerable section of the nation, and, personally, I should deny to them the importance which is claimed for them on the strength of so many acts of violence. Certainly they were never likely to do anything but harm to Russia, but they are interesting as a mixture of many psychological elements. Here we find the simple want of discipline of the lawless savage, and there the most absolute abnegation of self in the presence of an impossible task. Here we find great undigested fragments of the views of French or German Socialist writers, there the old Russian pride showing itself not by praise of Russia but by a cynical contempt of everything Western. What can be said definitely is that the Nihilists were intellectually a product of hysteria. The melodramatic fears of the autocracy have successfully called forth a spirit of melodrama in its enemies. A man of surprising mental power and possibly of surprising devotion and perseverance may be found preaching a creed which can only be explained by pathology. The listener will have his choice of either disregarding such talk as meaningless, or of deserting all his own standards to sink himself in a new world where everything will always remain inexplicable; this is precisely what his teacher has done before him. Pathologically, the Nihilist is a product of the mistakes of the autocracy; he could so easily have been made impossible. We can, however, well understand how in a time of general apathy he might be allowed to conduct a single-handed duel with officialdom, or even how in a time of great agitation his violence might represent the discontent of many others who in no way shared his views.

Chernishévsky helped to found this creed of " Young Russia." In this bureaucratic country the traditional method of appealing to the public is by paper; any other method is almost impossible. The Nihilists scattered broadsheets amongst the people. For one of his manifestos, Chernishévsky was arrested in 1862 and sent to Siberia. In 1866 Karakózoff made an attempt on the life of the Emperor. His trial and that of Necháyeff in 1873 further acquainted the Government with the views and organisations of the conspirators. Other trials followed, such as those of Alexéyeff, Mýshkin, and Vera Zasúlich. There sprang up secret presses, from which issued the organs *The National Will* and *Land and Liberty*. On April 17, 1878, the Rector of Kieff University was attacked and badly handled. On August 15 General Mezentseff, chief of the special police, was stabbed in open daylight on a square in St. Petersburg. On August 2, political offences were referred to the jurisdiction of courts-martial. On February 21, 1879, the Governor of Kharkoff was mortally wounded. On March 7, at Odessa, Police-Colonel Knoop was murdered. On April 10, at Archangel, Police-Master Petrovsky was stabbed in his house.

The nation looked on while some few hundreds of persons employed against the autocracy an exaggeration of its own worst methods, and claimed, with even less justice than those whom they wished to replace, to represent the will of the nation. The many causes of this apathy have already been mentioned ; but none of the evils which were complained of were likely to be cured by the dagger or by the pistol. The fact is, that the peasants were still not awake enough to intervene on one side or the other, and that the Russian Intelligence, thanks very largely to the previous policy of the Government, was still deficient in the means of forming a sound political judgment. Meanwhile the Nihilists gloried in their successes. "Assassination," wrote the newspaper *Land and Liberty*, "which whole army corps cannot prevent, which cannot be anticipated by legions of spies, however clever, subtle, and tricky they may be—that is the great weapon of the friends of liberty." It is simply the guillotine over again ; and if it succeeds, it must as inevitably lead back to despotism.

On April 17, dictatorial powers were confided to six Governors-General. At St. Petersburg the house-porters became simply agents of the police. On December 1, 1879, the Imperial train was thrown off the rails by the explosion of a mine. On December 4, the executive committee of the Nihilists published the death sentence of the Emperor. It also published an ultimatum, in which it demanded the satisfaction at once of the most reasonable claims and of the most ignorant theories. On February 17, 1880, the dining-room of the Winter Palace was blown up just as the Imperial family was about to enter it. Loris Melikoff was now practically made dictator of Russia. On March 3, an attempt was made to murder him. He restored to freedom some two thousand students who had been expelled from the universities, but this only increased the active army of his enemies. He endeavoured to persuade the Emperor to grant some kind of a national representation, and on March 13, 1881, Alexander actually sent to the *Official Messenger* the announcement that the elective bodies of the Empire would be asked to send deputies to the Council of State in St. Petersburg. But on the same day, as he drove along the Catherine Canal, a bomb was thrown at his carriage and wounded some of his escort. He jumped out with the words, " Let me see the wounded," and a second bomb, thrown at his legs, exploded beneath him. Hopelessly mutilated, he was carried back to the palace, where he died without being able to utter a word.

The Emperor Alexander III., not being a coward, refused to concede the demands which, amidst the general apathy, the Nihilists still urged upon him; he also withdrew the summons to elect representatives which his father had been on the eve of publishing. Loris Melikoff retired, and Russia plunged into a period of reaction, which lasted till 1904. Like Nicholas, destined at his accession to struggle with revolution, Alexander attempted to replace the voice of his people by his own assiduous attention to its needs; this effort, the story of which has been told elsewhere, could not be finally successful, and Russia is again face to face with the questions which were adjourned in 1881. Meanwhile, many inevitable changes have taken place in the data for their settlement. Here I will only mention those general modifications which have passed into the

views of what I will call the "irresponsible Intelligence." On
the one hand, the excesses of the Second Reaction in the use
of the censorship, and again in the supervision of schools and
universities, have more than anything else tended to keep the
views of this section of the nation Radical rather than Liberal.
On the other hand, it was a wholesome lesson for the nation to
learn that if an Alexander II. were murdered, he might be followed
by an Alexander III. In general the Intelligents have gained
from that practical responsibility into which a number of them
have been called by the work and aspirations of the new County
and Town Councils established by Alexander II.

The reader has then to choose between the amount of importance
which he attaches to the education which Russia has in the last
forty years received in the study of questions of local government on
the one side, and, on the other, to the pernicious results of the
recent exaggeration of the old system. In any case it is despotism
alone that has perpetuated revolution. These two are twins.
This should be sufficiently clear from a simple record of the
common disasters which have befallen both since the time
when they first came into conflict. Both for the Government
and for the Intelligence, there is, in any case, no final safety
except in reform.

These main issues we will consider in detail later. I will conclude this chapter by following the fortunes of Public Instruction
up to the present time. The Minister of this department—the
post has more than once been filled by a general—has far too
often acted as a kind of police officer. It is not without reason
that he has been styled "the Minister for the prevention of public
instruction." This one might gather from the obstacles which
have been put in the way of all external teaching similar to our
own University Extension work. Two gentlemen engaged in this
work have told me that so many subjects were struck out of
their programme that teaching became almost an impossibility.
Encouragement was given to a public benefactor to erect a large
building in St. Petersburg for the work of a People's University,
and, when the building had been completed, it was announced that
permission to hold courses could not be granted. In spite of this,
teaching of this kind has sprung up all over Russia. As to regular

scholastic work, the boy, while still almost a child, has had to learn that he is under special police supervision precisely because he is a scholar ; and, in the universities, repression has been so rigorous that all the best professors have had to protest against its methods. In 1882 there were students' troubles in the universities of Kazán and St. Petersburg, and in 1887 in the same universities, and also in those of Moscow, Odessa, and Kharkoff. There followed the use of the troops, expulsions, arrests, and punishments, all of which made so many more enemies of the Government.

In 1887 inspectors, who were practically police officials, were attached to each university. Entrance to schools and universities was more strictly limited to certain classes. On the other hand, the programme was made more practical, and a number of industrial schools were created ; there were also established manual schools for young girls. One new university was established at Tomsk ; in the course of its short life it has been as energetic as many of the others. The Government was always more willing to do something for technical studies ; and a Technological Institute was established at Kharkoff, and an Institute of Experimental Medicine at St. Petersburg ; a Women's Institute of Medicine was founded in St. Petersburg in 1895, the first Electro-technical School in St. Petersburg in 1896, the Polytechnic of Kieff in 1898, the Higher School of Mines of Ekaterinoslav in 1899, the new Commercial Schools in 1900, the Technological Institute of Tomsk in 1900, and courses for Technicians and Handicraftsmen in 1902. At least education continued to increase in volume. In 1886 there were 35,500 registered schools in the Empire, excluding those set apart for persons of alien religions or for special studies.

The Minister of Public Instruction has not a jurisdiction over all the schools in Russia.[1] The Minister of Finance has technical schools of his own. Some schools of engineers and of railway employés are under the Minister of Ways and Communications. The Departments of War and Marine have the control of military and naval schools. Many girls' schools, both for the rich and for the poor, are still under the jurisdiction of the administrator of the institutions of the Empress Maria

[1] For the details of the present system which follow, I am indebted to an official of this Ministry.

Fedorovna. In fact, there is a similar confusion of functions to that which obtained in France before the French Revolution. For this and other reasons, there have never been any really accurate statistics of school-teaching in Russia. When Mr. Falbork and Mr. Charnolúsky undertook the great enterprise of supplying this want, they discovered that even the statistics of the respective jurisdictions could not be trusted. Some schools, especially amongst those of the Synod, were found to have little more than a paper existence. To offer to the public the first accurate information on the subject, they had to send all over the country lists of questions to be filled in by trustworthy persons on the spot. This work, which was initiated from outside the Government circles, is solid and comprehensive, but is not yet completed. The initiative of the Ministry of Public Instruction, which controls the major part of higher and secondary education, stops short after only touching the fringe of primary school-teaching. Primary education is almost entirely supplied by the Church schools and by the schools of the Zemstva and Town Councils. However, the energy of the local councils has acted as a spur to the Ministry, and there are a certain number of ministerial schools for peasants, which, as the local councils are limited in their expenditure, are better financed and can offer better salaries. The Ministry of Public Instruction has also founded some training colleges for primary teachers.

Its yearly budget amounts to some £4,000,000, that is, say, less than 2½ per cent. of the expenditure, or one-tenth of the sum allotted to the Ministry of War. The only Ministry which receives less is that of Justice. The Minister has a council of some thirty members, composed of ex-lecturers and ex-professors of the universities, former heads of departments, and a small number of other men selected for their learning. In the Department of Common Affairs there are five sections, dealing respectively with—(a) the pensions of primary school-teachers, (b) questions of law, (c) credit, (d) the control of the inspectors, and (e) statistics (since August, 1904). The next Department deals with the teaching and includes five sections :—(a) for the higher schools; (b) for the secondary schools; (c) for the primary schools; (d) for questions which concern the above three sections in common; (e) for the control of what are called learned institutions, such as the Academy of Science and the learned societies, which are composed of teachers and outsiders and have been founded in connection with the universities and secondary schools. The third Department deals with technical schools, but is not so clearly marked out into sections. A Learned Committee revises the school-books of the secondary and lower schools. It settles what libraries and maps are requisite, and can suggest the establishment of laboratories and other improvements; it is composed chiefly of specialists.

The Church schools are, in the main, supported by their respective parishes, but also receive help from the Synod. The Zemstvo entirely supports its own schools. The schools of the Town Councils must be opened by permission of the Minister; they are, in the main, supported by the Town Councils, but the Minister sometimes grants a subsidy. The ministerial country schools are almost entirely supported by the Ministry; but some contributions are received from peasants and from Village Societies. The secondary schools may be founded on the initiative of the Zemstvo or Town Council, which, after securing a donation or a bequest from private charity, can ask the Minister to establish the school. Statutes regulating the finance, and even, perhaps, defining the application of a school to a given class will be sent by the original proposers to the Minister, who may confirm them or modify them. The school when once founded is supported in equal proportions by the Ministry and the local councils. Something like the same process obtains in the foundation of Higher Schools and Universities. A private committee will collect money, a building will be erected by the local council, but the Minister has the responsibility of establishing the school and of contributing the chief funds for its permanent support. On these lines, the foundation of a Higher School for women at Kieff was in progress in the autumn of 1905.

Each Educational Circuit of Russia (and each Circuit includes several provinces) is ruled by a Curator, whose duty it is to convey the orders of the Minister and to report to him. He appoints all teachers of secondary schools in his district. He seldom visits and examines a school, but delegates this work to his two Inspectors of the Circuit. Attached to him is an architect who has the inspection of all school-buildings.

The discipline of a secondary school is left in the hands of the Director, who has an Inspector as his assistant. In a Town School (which is a higher primary school) the two authorities are united, and the director is called "Teacher-Inspector." The head of a ministerial country school similarly combines the two attributes. In fact, the principle of Government discipline runs throughout. A teacher may complain against his director to the Curator, or even to the Minister, who can, after sending a special investigator, remove the Director or the assistant and make a new appointment.

Up to September, 1905, the regulation of the universities was as follows :—

The Rector was named by the Emperor on the recommendation of the Minister. He had the right of appealing directly to the Minister in important matters, or the Minister could himself ask for a direct report. But, undefined as his relations were to the Curator, he was, in the main, dependent upon this official. He was assisted by a University Council consisting of all the professors. Lecturers ("private docents") had no votes on the Council, but might bring proposals before it. This Council chose candidates for professorships subject to the confirmation of the Minister, who could, however, make the choice himself. It could fix the programme of studies, but the Minister could modify it. It could raise other questions for his decision. The Council was directly subject to the Curator and to the Minister, but the Rector had the control of individual professors, and could administer reprimands to the students and send them to the University prisons.

The Council, besides the right of finally judging the dissertations of the students, had a certain control over discipline. It could arrest a student, deprive him of his scholarship, or exclude him from the University. But the chief authority of this kind was in the hands of the Inspector specially attached to the University, who was in much closer touch with the Curator and with the Minister. The duties of this official were those of police. By examination of the "custodes," or sentries, or even of the students, he would decide whether this student or that was "of good hope," that is, politically a safe man. On his report students would be expelled from the university, in some cases being deprived of civil rights and sent into the army. The Minister of the Interior, on his own administrative authority, can inflict a three years' sentence of this kind. The local Governor can declare a state of siege and, without trial, inflict arrest of three months or a heavy fine. To the Minister of Public Instruction belongs the right of punishing or expelling professors.

On June 19, 1905, when Prince Sergius Trubetskóy, as spokesman for the representatives of the local councils, was urging the Emperor to again pledge himself to reform, he was invited to draw up a report on the grievances of the Universities. Largely as a result of this report, the University Councils were authorised to freely elect their own Rectors, and this carried into the system which I have described a wholesale modification, whose effects will have to be developed in the future.

Let us imagine a boy passing through the school system. At seven he may go to a village ministerial school, which may contain one class or two. A class is supposed to represent a year's teaching. If well off and proficient, he may enter a Town School of four classes. Hence he may in principle pass on to a secondary school; but in practice this was in 1905 impossible, because at the entrance examinations subjects were required in which he had received no teaching; in very few cases has this obstacle been surmounted by the exceptional enterprise of the scholar. The scholar of the secondary school is then of a different class from that of the primary. He can enter at the age of ten either a Real School (modern), or a Gymnasium (classical); the examination of the Gymnasium is the more severe for those who have not had special preparation; if Latin and Greek were not compulsory, this difference would disappear. In the Real School there are seven classes, and in the Gymnasium eight. The teaching is such that the boys who leave these institutions are generally far better informed than the average English public school boy or grammar school boy. There is no corporal punishment (a concession to the " dignity of the human person "); but extra work can be set for one hour, two hours, or even three hours on end. If one boy is being punished alone, he will be locked into a schoolroom by the caretaker; if several are punished together, a master will be present.

A pupil can be detained at the school instead of going home to dinner. There is detention on Sundays and Feast Days for more serious offences; and, lastly, there is expulsion, temporary or permanent. For the ordinary effectiveness of authority as sheer authority, corporal punishment is not missed; for the Government has a complete hold over the future career of each scholar. Balls are the system of marks, both for good conduct and for good work. Five is the maximum. A boy who has lost only one conduct mark will often find that there is no room for him in the next educational institution into which he wishes to pass. To have lost two marks means that one's case is hopeless. The upper system of public instruction is closely knit together; learning means a career, and probably a Government post; the openings of other kinds are comparatively few in Russia. If the boy cannot pass from the Gymnasium to the University, all the higher posts become inaccessible to him. It is, then, all the more mischievous that school conduct should be judged largely by the political views of the scholar. All social intercourse is from the first considered suspicious. Under Plehwe, all association for common amusement or for common study was forbidden; as my official informant said, "it was sure to be political." From 1896 to 1904, not more than two or three boys were allowed to walk together in the street; this was a direct instruction from the Minister. Certain diversions are, however, officially provided for the boys. In almost every school there is a place for gymnastic exercises; in many a string orchestra is organised by some of the teachers; concerts and entertainments are given in the large hall, and sometimes the boys will themselves act in Greek, French, or Russian plays. In vindication of the natural friendliness of the Russian character, I may mention that all over Russia it is the fashion for great bands of teachers and pupils to travel together during the holidays; for instance, an excursion from Kovno, on the western frontier, passed down the Volga to the Caucasus, and completed a circuit embracing almost the whole of Russia in Europe.

The scholar, if he wishes to go on to a higher institution, must pass a severe examination on leaving school. To boys from Real Schools the University was for a long time debarred.

They had entry to such special schools as the Institute of Civil Engineers, the Electro-Technical Institute, the Technological Institute, the Mining Institute, or the Academy of Military Medicine. The boy from a Gymnasium will spend four years in the University (more in the case of medicine); he will be examined once a year. Five is full marks; he will pass if he obtains three in every subject; in case of failure in one subject, all the subjects must be taken again. If he fails for two years running, he has to go; for there are always fewer places in the Universities than there are candidates to fill them. He may spend six years in all at the course. In his last year, he will enter for the Imperial university diploma. At this examination he may have three attempts. This diploma is necessary for any important post in the civil service; those who have not got it cannot rise higher than assistant secretaries in Government offices; all lawyers of the higher class require it; it qualifies for posts of teachers in secondary schools; it is also essential for those who wish to be doctors.

A Training College for Primary Teachers.

There is an air of formality both about the building and about the Director. The class-rooms are high, and the three dormitories are spacious. The pupil-teachers are admitted between the ages of fifteen and twenty-two, and leave between the ages of nineteen and twenty-two. They number ninety in all. If there are few vacancies, the younger candidates are preferred. The programme includes those studies which will have to be taught by the pupils later on, and also a wider general education in history, geometry, arithmetic, algebra, Russian literature, natural history and physics, but not in any foreign language. Each teacher has a special subject; but each is also responsible for a particular class, acting as a kind of tutor, giving advice, and taking care of the pupils' money. Each teacher is on duty in turn, to look after the behaviour of the whole school in play-time.

There is special instruction in teaching, which is in the hands of the Director, and is, in fact, his only class work. It begins at the third class, where the pupils have to write essays on subjects connected with teaching for his correction. In the fourth or top class the pupils are sent together, without a master, to teach in a model primary school which stands in the same enclosure, under the supervision of the schoolmistress. While one teaches the others look on. In the evening a debate is held; the pupil who gave the lesson explains what he was aiming at, and where he failed to satisfy his idea of the lesson; then come criticisms from the others, and finally the Director sums up. There are no examinations; when a pupil leaves, the Director asks him where he would like to serve, and then writes to the Curator giving his own opinion of the pupil's capacities.

A REAL SCHOOL.

The very big building contains good class-rooms, especially that of natural history. There is a large hall for entertainments; musical or literary meetings are held here. The provision of maps and other material is not satisfactory.

There are five hundred boys and twenty teachers. Pupils enter between the ages of ten and thirteen, and leave between those of sixteen and twenty. There are seven classes, the smallest containing twenty-eight and the largest forty-eight boys. The highest class qualifies for entrance to the Higher Technical Schools; the next highest qualifies for some ranks of the Government Service.

Mathematics is the most important subject; the programme includes physics, chemistry, and natural history. German is begun in the lowest and ended in the highest class; French is begun in the second class and ended in the sixth. History is taught in the two lowest classes by way of narratives given by the teacher. The whole course begins with Russian history, passes on to ancient history and then to general European history, and concludes in the top class with a more special study of Russian history and modern history.

The most usual punishment is to stop a boy's feast-day outings. The Director is very dissatisfied with this plan. He regrets the abolition of corporal punishment, and blames the "liberal tendencies" of the time and the interference of newspapers. Boys read and talk so much now about the dignity of man that they think that they ought not to be touched. Parents complain if a hand is raised against their son.

Some games are played, such as a sort of "skittles," and also a kind of "rounders" with a straight run instead of a circular one; a catch, as with us, dismisses the whole side. There is but little space to play in; boys do not play after the age of sixteen.

The school, though not a boarding establishment, has its own teaching priest; he teaches religious knowledge in different classes for five hours of every day; on Sunday he officiates in the school chapel, which has its own trained choir, chosen from amongst the pupils. Attendance at chapel is not compulsory, but is encouraged; not many come.

The boarding-house established for the sons of gentry of the district admits some outsiders who are attending the Gymnasium or the Real School. The Director is in touch with the Warden of this house and also with the Director of the Gymnasium, with whom he serves on the Local Council of School-Teaching.

The boys wear uniform and are easily recognised in the streets; their behaviour there is strictly regulated; as the police help in seeing the regulations observed, the boy very early gets a taste of their influence. For drunkenness or immorality long terms of detention are generally imposed. For political offences the punishment is expulsion. Clubs are not allowed at all; no definite number is fixed as constituting a club, which is taken to simply mean habitual and regular meetings. Supposing that certain students wished to meet to study Pushkin or Shakespeare, the Director would gladly welcome them to the school and lend them a room, but they would not care to come to this house of supervision, and all their clubs end in political discussion. It is only recently that pupils of the Real Schools have been allowed to enter the Universities.

A GYMNASIUM.

There are three hundred boys in the school. The number of classes was four, but is being increased to eight; and the ages range from ten to twenty. In a lower class there will be some sixty pupils, in a higher one some twenty-four. The class-rooms are tolerably large, but the play-room is absurdly low and stuffy. New and spacious buildings are being added, one of whose windows is so large that, as the Director says, "you could drive a troika through it." The walls are hung with excellent school pictures, peculiarly like the best of our own. Formerly, the masters were appointed by the Director; but he had difficulty in finding the men that he wanted. Now the Curator appoints. The modern languages are taught by natives of the respective countries. The teachers are not all specialists, but most of them concentrate their attention on one or more subjects. Thus there are specialists in divinity, physics, mathematics, history, and natural history. In the lower classes the system of class-masters, each of whom has a responsibility for the general work of his class, is thought more appropriate. The programme of Gymnasia has become easier in recent years. Greek is taught only in the top class; there is less Latin translation and no Latin composition. The Director believes in making boys work, whether they happen to find the subject interesting or not. His boys will not work unless they are compelled, and now, as everything is made too easy for them, they do nothing. This reacts upon discipline, which has undoubtedly declined since the days of Count Dmitry Tolstoy, "who forced them to work." In girls' schools of the same type, there is no Latin, but more French and German in the higher classes. The favourite subjects are, for the ablest boys mathematics, and for the average boy Russian. Each lesson lasts fifty minutes; after each there is a break of ten minutes. There used to be examinations for leaving the fourth and the sixth classes, now there is only the ordinary leaving examination. Every three months a mark for work is given by the teacher; these marks are collected, and promotions are made accordingly. The maximum is five; three is enough to secure promotion, and a scholar who has only two marks may be promoted if the Council of the school gives a special sanction.

The boys are of all classes; most of them are sons of officials; but there are also sons of shopmen and even of peasants, of whom the Director seems to have a poor opinion. All get on very well together, and one would not notice any marked distinction between them. All are day boarders here; but a neighbouring Gymnasium boards one hundred. In the big classes at the bottom of the school order is very hard to keep. There are official helpers of the class-teachers, who keep order during the intervals and also on the streets and in the Town Garden. Through some streets the boys are not to walk. They are supposed to be indoors by nine in summer, and by five or six in the winter. No smoking is allowed, and a careless way of wearing the school uniform is considered as an offence; thus, for instance, parts of the summer uniform may not be combined with parts of the winter one; long hair, moustaches and beards, rings, high collars, demonstrative watch-chains and sticks are all forbidden. The school rules, which open with an appeal to the boy's respect for his own honour, go on to explain that he must be prepared to stop and salute any high official, and more particularly those of educational institutions, all of whom, whether connected with his school or not, are put in authority over him.[1] Detention is the ordinary punishment, but the Director tells me that it does not work well; yet three hours' detention on Sunday or on a feast-day he finds very effective. He is in favour of corporal punishment for certain offences, but not as it was practised.[2] "They used," he says "to whack them all round." The police sometimes complain against a scholar to the Director, who, with his Council of masters, goes into the case. I have known a boy who was punished for speaking to another boy who was under police supervision. For thieving or immorality a boy is dismissed on the spot, for constant opposition to the rules of the school he will be sent away; and on the statement which is issued by the Director will depend his chance of ever entering another school. Most of the boys find their own amusements for themselves. Groups for ,joint study are allowed, but only under inspection.

HIGHER TECHNICAL SCHOOLS.

Under the Emperor Nicholas no more Universities have been founded, but many technical institutes have been established. A Polytechnicum may have about 1,000 students. A professor's salary is about £400 a year. Students who have succeeded in

---

[1] The last two sentences are a summary of the copy of the rules which every boy has to carry on him.

[2] This is the whole point. We are told that English schoolboys have, before now, rebelled against the abolition of the birch, but at least they recognised in it a moral weapon, not a political one, and at least there was a measure of responsibility for the use which was made of it.

getting a diploma pass into the employment either of the Government or, more often, of private businesses.

Moscow University.

Lectures may be attended by students and by "free listeners." It was in the latter capacity that I made my acquaintance with the University in 1898–1899. The standard of scholarship amongst the professors seemed quite as high as in an English university, and the standard of lecturing considerably higher than here. I met with doctrinaires, but not with pedants. The students whom I got to know struck me very much by their mental ability, but still more by the wide scope of their interests. As a chance example I mention a student who, in addition to his ordinary studies, was teaching himself Welsh. Intelligence in Russia is keen and aims straight. It has a freshness and an easiness which suggests, at one and the same time, laziness and a reserve of force. The use of the intelligence is a natural delight to most Russians.

The Russian Government hampers the intellectual development of the student in the name of morality, but it does not provide for him any moral training at all. In England the education of character is considered to be more important than the informing of the mind. In Russia it is the moral control that is absent. I will mention the most extreme instance of which I happen to know. A young engineer visited Moscow for the day and missed his last train; as he had not his passport with him, it was impossible for him to sleep in any hotel; but a police officer who met him explained that he could conform to the law by sleeping in a brothel. Nowhere is the incompleteness of Russia's moral education more clear than in the life of the students. They are drawn from all classes, but mostly from the middle class. Learning comes easy to them; but most of them have a tendency to be lazy, flighty, and superficial. They are born theorists, and can usually put a case simply and well. The life which they live is often frankly animal, only without the open-air exercise. If it were suggested that this so-called "natural life" of self-indulgence is one of low ideal, most Russian students would conclude that the speaker was a hypocrite. For all that, in this country of contrasts, one may meet many who are more absolutely faithful to their ideals than even a superior Englishman. These will usually have discovered for themselves some special reason for dissenting from the ordinary view ; it may be a fad, it is likely to be something different from what we call common-sense. The students are very heady and very serious in their love affairs; they push things to their logical conclusion, and often compromise themselves finally by their imprudent matches. They are children, but they have the passions of men ; and so their mistakes are far more determined and far more fatal. It is Adam in the garden of Eden picking at the tree of knowledge. There is no cultivation of discipline, no conscious control ; they go on eating of both trees, the tree of knowledge and the tree of life, up to the moment of indigestion, which varies according to the vitality of the eater. After that comes bitterness or scepticism, or frenzied angry work for what is left of one's ideals, or more often the pursuit of sheer worldly interests, or the apathy of a Government post. And the Government system which fails to direct their ideals provides plenty of posts for apathy.

The students are specially under Government supervision. The fear of everything Western has tried to surround them with a kind of palisade. Spies dressed in their uniform sit with them at their lectures ; attempts have even been made to use the professors for the purposes of police work, or at least as lures in moments of crisis, that the police may be able to ascertain which students have refused to attend lectures. Every effort is made to dissolve any grouping of the students, to morally confine them in separate cells.

" Woe to the land where the king is a child," and woe to the land where the chief champion of reform is a child. The political importance of the Russian student has been exaggerated in Russia, and still further exaggerated in England. The prominence of the student carries with it one sinister inference which we cannot escape. What has become of the ex-student? In fact, he very often ceases to be a reformer when he ceases to be a student, that is, when he becomes a man. He begins to get experience of life, and he leaves his ideals behind him. This is a condemnation of the Government system ; but it also discounts the political value of the student's ideals. At the time of the strikes of 1899 one student said to me, "You must take our side, because we sacrifice everything." There is certainly something pleasing in the feeling that one has the world and nature and Providence itself against one—that the rights of man have been wronged by the universe. But, if I want you to become a Buddhist, it is no argument that I should cut off my hand. And what the student sacrifices is often either something which is not his, or something of which he does not yet understand the value. When he has his own bread to earn, he in most cases sets himself to earn it, or at least to get it. But if the students were put in their place as the rank and file of an army instead of its leaders, the generosity which prompts them to be ready for all sacrifices would be a very valuable asset to the nation. Friends of reason and of liberty must be grateful to the universities for offering at least the nucleus of a protest of principle. In a word, one has much less reason to quarrel with the spirit of self-sacrifice amongst the students than with the instinct of self-interest which so many of them have shown when they have passed into the ranks of officialdom.

In 1899 the Rector of St. Petersburg University, at a public function, warned the students to abstain from unruly behaviour. They considered themselves insulted and hissed him. Punishment followed, and they marched in a body towards the Winter Palace. The Cossacks drove them off, not with their swords, but with their heavy leaded whips. The students struck work; letters, travellers, rumours brought the news to Moscow. A number of the Moscow students met and declared for a strike; but the hall was full of disguised policemen, who suddenly closed the doors and took the names of all present. That night the student leaders were expelled from Moscow. Next day the great staircase of the University was thronged with angry groups of talkers. Hardly any professors got an audience for their lectures. As my professor entered his class-room, the men stood up and refused him a hearing. He was far more likely than most of them to make real sacrifices when the right time came, as was abundantly proved afterwards, but cries of " place-hunter " were hurled at him. Not in the least disturbed by the constant interruptions, he made them an admirable little speech. He would not enter into political questions; they well

knew that there would be no result of their action except broken
careers; he was here to read his lecture; politics had nothing to
do with the continuance of their studies; those who wished to
go out might do so.   One bearded student, with a strong Irish
brogue, called out, " Thoroughly right, Professor."   A heated
discussion was held by the men, of whom about one-half left the
room, the " Irishman" (a Little Russian) launching after them
the cry, "You noble fellows ! "   Some of these returned quietly
during the lecture.   On the next day, during the interval, a poll
was taken in each class-room on the question of the strike.
This was done with remarkable boldness and celerity : a student
rushed in, stated the question and the figures already registered
for and against, took the votes, and disappeared in a twinkling.
There followed further arrests, and finally the University was
closed for the term.

Yes, it has been a vicious circle.   Because the peoples dared
to ask for rights, the Russian Government became afraid ;
because the Russian Government is afraid, political education
has been denied to Russia.   The evils of ignorance are to be
averted by keeping people ignorant.   But the student is at least
not ignorant, and therefore he must be specially policed.
Because responsibility has been refused, apathy was till lately
very general.   Because apathy was general, the student might
himself seem to be the leader in the popular cause.   Because he
did not acknowledge any responsible leaders, he did not get any
real political education.   The only way to get out of a vicious
circle is for everyone to push at every point of it with all the
strength that he has.   But the thing has been done before and
must be done again, whenever the consequences of an initial
mistake have to be averted.

CHAPTER VII.

THE LITERATURE.

For building up a genuine literature the Russian mind was from early times excellent material. Its quickness and fancy, however, which offer so strong a contrast with the more solid and less soaring German, were peculiarly out of harmony with the normal conditions of Russian history. This poetic and striving people, yearning for the unknown, straining after distant ideals, revelling, before all things, in the sheer delight of wandering, found itself confronted with constant dangers, which imposed upon it the severest discipline and restricted for centuries the free flight of thought. Yet it is precisely that severe discipline which has given the peculiarly keen and concentrated flavour to Russian literature—a flavour so keen that it makes itself felt even in the very worst translation.

Through the early literature of Russia run the three great strands of Russian life—the People, the Church, and the State. The better Russian writers have all been in a peculiar degree writers of the people, that is, of the nation. The peasants were themselves an admirable literary foundation. Throughout Russian history we meet a never-ending series of legends (" byliny "); the word means "things that were"; and with a simple frankness the title may sometimes be extended to "things that were and things that were not." These legends are notable, not only for their free fancy, but also in many cases for their deep moral significance. The moral must be gathered from the story itself, but the story is sure to leave the reader thinking, and sometimes its content is as profound as the account of the sacrifice of Isaac, or that of the contrast between Esau and Jacob. Elia of Murom, for instance, starts life as the strongest man in the world; half his strength is suddenly taken from him, but he is encouraged by a voice that says to him, "This much shall be enough for you "; it is the angel wrestling with Jacob. The heroes of these legends are sometimes simple folk of the people, not attached to the " druzhina "

of any prince, but coming into the political arena as representatives
of the great reserve force of the nation, to save the rulers when their
inadequacy has been proved. It is the whole allegory of 1812.
We find legends that date from before Vladímir, the "beauteous
sun" of Russian story and the establisher of Christianity. There
are others that tell of Russian life under the Tartar yoke. Others
again tell how the championship of national interests was
surrendered to the powerful and triumphant dictator Peter the
Great. There are even "byliny" on episodes of the Japanese war.
But not by any means all the legends are loyal. The turbulent
brigands, such as Stephan Rázin, have a cycle of their own. In
recent times a man of great means, Mr. Beláyeff, with the aid of
many helpers, collected from all over the country the traditional
songs of the peasantry, and handed over the melodies, many of
which are very beautiful, to be set to accompaniments by some of
the best Russian composers. Here is one song from the
collection:—

> " In the city stood our princess,
> In the city stood our young one,
> In the midst of all her maidens,
> Her precious keys all jingling,
> Her golden ring all shining.
>
> " To the city came the king's son,
> To the city walls came roaming ;
> Cut through, my lord, the first gates,
> Cut through, my lord, the next gates,
> Cut through, my lord, the third ones.
>
> " To the city streets come up, sir,
> Draw near, sir, to our princess,
> Bow low, sir, to our princess,
> Bow low, my lord, and lower,
> Yet again, to bow still lower.
>
> " Now take, my lord, our princess,
> By her fair white hand now take her ;
> Now kiss, my lord, our princess,
> Now kiss her yet more fondly,
> Yet again, to kiss more fondly.
>
> " What think you of our princess ?
> What think you of our young one ?
> Her fair white face so peerless,
> Her eyebrows dark and comely." [1]

In the earliest times the separate principalities had their several
annals; they were often the work of ecclesiastics, who then

Government of Tambóff, district of Spásskoe. Accompaniment by Balákireff.

represented the learning of their country. They give a very convincing picture of the political life of Russia, and are remarkably simple, direct, and pointed. Each sentence stops short at the right moment, and leaves the reader thinking over an accomplished fact. The annals of Novgorod the Great are the most pithy and concise, the annals of Súzdal are more arid, and those of Little Russia are almost florid. When the people of Novgorod expelled their prince, the annalist tells us that "they saluted him and showed him the way." "We can see," says Solovyéff,[1] "that the men of Novgorod did not care for a great deal of talk; they did not even care to go to the end of what they had got to say, and yet they understood each other very well. One may say that, with them, action served as the end of a sentence." Yet the point lost nothing by this conciseness. An early Russian bishop, in one of his charges, tells his flock that "by drunkenness they drive away their guardian angel"; and there is surely nothing to add to this, as there is nothing to take away.

It will be remembered that the Russians, to save themselves from the Tartars, sacrificed what may be called their political individualism, and this could not fail to stunt the free expression of thought. When the old easy life of the principalities disappeared, when Moscow established a centralised authority, and when the trading republics succumbed to it, Russia had, so to speak, to adjourn further progress in literature. The records were no longer the expression of the free views of different sections of a great nation, but the simple register of the decrees of the Grand Prince. Yet there was one power which stood even as high as he—the Church. Christianity had given the alphabet to Russia. The Russian Church was in close touch with that of Constantinople; and from Greece were introduced into Russia not only ikons and saints, but also books. Every monastery still had its own tradition of some great wonder-worker, and the "Lives" of these free spirits have long been the staple reading of the Russian peasant.

One example of such "Lives" will serve for many. Irenarch, of the monastery of Borís-and-Glyéb near Rostóff, was a third son. As a boy "he would not even look at games" and "limited

1 "History of Russia," Vol. III., end of Chapter I.

himself in everything." At the sight of a monk he said, " And I,
too, will be a monk like that." In the monastery he lived "suffering ridicule from some ignorant evil-wishers, and not thinking
of anything material or that concerned the body." One day, while
escorting a friend on his way, he was overcome, as was natural
for one who rarely passed the monastery wall, by all the little-
nesses of the place, and longed to go to one of the larger and
more austere houses. But a voice said to him, "Don't go to
Kirílloff or Solóvki; you shall save yourself even here." He wept
sorely, and counted over all the difficulties of his present position.
He even looked to see if the voice came from a passer-by; but he
could see no one, and the voice said the same words three times;
so he resigned himself to obedience.

"For sleep he would lie simply on the earth, and that not for
long." The new duties of bell-ringer he accepted "not only with
obedience but with joy." He gave his boots to a beggar, praying,
" Give me, Lord, warmth for my feet," and henceforth went bare-
foot. The prior, a lax man who hated his austerity, would keep
him in his cell for two hours at a time, or needlessly send him to
ring the bells in the hardest frost, or force him to wear a coloured
robe, or keep him foodless for days. "But you can humble a
beast; a man you cannot humble."

He now felt called to confine himself in his cell, where he lived
for three and a half years on end. "The sufferings of the
crucified Saviour became more and more the object of his love."
He was "ridiculed and dishonoured by the brotherhood," but a
young novice came to share his seclusion. He made and wore
heavy chains.

Another ascetic with whom he talked prophesied to him that
" for their lawless drunkenness the Lord God will bring into the
country strangers, but the Most Holy Trinity will, by its strength,
drive all of them out." Irenarch became more constant in labour
and in prayer. A large bronze cross was given to him, and from
it he made one hundred small ones. The monk Leontii wore
chains with thirty crosses; he was killed by robbers and left his
crosses to Irenarch. Others sent to him presents of crosses. At
this time he seldom slept for more than two hours, and grew so ill
that he could not recognise people. On his recovery the hostility
against him revived, and he was turned out of the monastery.

He had the gift of second sight, and once in a light sleep " he saw the Tsar's city of Moscow ravaged by the Lithuanians, all the kingdom of Russia seized and endangered by them, and houses and churches everywhere burnt down "; he " sobbed and wept without comfort." He went to Moscow and kissed the relics there. Thence he returned to his monastery.

The Time of Troubles had begun; Dmítroff and Rostóff were taken and sacked by the Lithuanians (1609); church relics and treasures were everywhere despoiled. Mikulinsky appeared before the gates of Borís-and-Glyéb. Irenarch, when sent for by him, and accused of praying for a Russian Tsar, said boldly, "I live in Russia and serve a Russian Tsar, not the Lithuanian king, nor the Khan of Krimea, nor the seducer of the world. Your corruptible sword I fear not one whit; our faith and our Russian Tsar we will not give up. If you will cut me down for that, I will suffer it, even with joy. You will not find much blood in me, but my King, the living God, has a sword of that kind that He will cut you down without your seeing it, not wounding your body nor shedding your blood; for He will destroy your soul for ever in torment." Mikulinsky spared the monastery and retired.

The Russian prince Skopin now beat the Poles at Tver and at Kolyázin; and the famous Sapiéha, still fresh from the bitterness of defeat, appeared before the monastery. Irenarch comforted the brethren: "If they kill us, we shall be new martyrs, like the holy fathers, and shall be for ever crowned by Christ our God with heavenly crowns." But such was his countenance before Sapiéha that the Pole gave presents to the House, and went away saying, "I never saw such a Father, neither here nor in other lands ; he is not afraid of our sword." Skopin received a cross from Irenarch, was by him inspirited to fight again, and sent a special message to announce his victory. Sapiéha was driven from the walls of the great Trinity Monastery to die, as Irenarch had predicted to him, in Kaluga. What the Trinity Monastery now did for Russia we already know. Other Poles appeared before Borís-and-Glyéb, but, warned by Irenarch, returned quickly to their own country. Next came Pozharsky and Minin with their great relieving army, on their way to Moscow. Irenarch blessed them for their enterprise and gave them crosses. Moscow was won back, the first of the Románoffs was elected Tsar, and Irenarch died, having seen the deliverance.

After the Tartars and under Moscow, Russian literature in general had to grow up under new conditions. It had lost its popular origin, and tended more and more to become one of the instruments of the authority and the glory of the prince. " The Order in the House," edited by the priest Sylvester, is one of the few notable works of this dark time. Sylvester, who had been the guide of the youth of John the Terrible, was the chief of his Ministers during the happy part of his reign. It may be assumed that Sylvester wrote the last chapter of " The Order in the House," which recalls the will of Vladímir Monomach, and is a practical summary of moral duties. The book is a picture of the manners of the time, put into the form of a precept. John himself was far above the level of his subjects in reading, information, and literary ability. His letters to the rebel prince Kurbsky are long polemical statements full of curious and ingenious detail. John was also a clever and interesting speaker. In a word, he deeply cared for learning and was a typical forerunner of that training of the intellect which the Tsars were to invite into their country from Europe. After the Time of Troubles, Russia's desire to learn gathered increasing volume in the reign of the mild and liberal-minded Alexis, the father of Peter the Great.

And here the development quickens to such a pace as warrants our regarding this period as a fresh start. To Peter is ascribed the creation of the modern Russian alphabet, as distinguished from the old alphabet of ecclesiastical origin. The Russian characters were simplified; they still look very alarming to the stranger, but they are nothing if not practical. Phonetically, this alphabet is probably the most complete in Europe; and it is, therefore, a peculiarly well-constituted instrument for the transcribing of foreign sounds. It was to such a use that Peter now put it; and the quick intelligence of the Russians made the introduction of Western learning, if anything, too easy. Peter wished to introduce a host of ready-formed Western ideas, and he therefore forced on the Russian language a plethora of strange words which gave it a lasting indigestion. Any Western word was given a Russian tail, and counted for good Russian, though possibly no Russian could understand it. For a country in Russia's position, translation would always be an important section of literature. The fact that there was as yet no modern Russian literature made it all the more desirable that the use of translation should be moderated. But Peter borrowed a whole literature from abroad, and the reader found himself in a new and strange world. Thus, a reconciliation between his intellectual interests and his practical experience being comparatively hopeless, he might easily tend to leave the two, so to speak, in separate compartments of his consciousness.

For these reasons, learning came into Russia, not as a product of the life of the fundamental classes of the country, but as a definite "inspiration" from an official dictator. And Peter was not able, during his lifetime, to witness any literary accomplishment on the new lines dictated by him. Printing had been introduced into the country not very long before, but had remained a kind of monopoly of the Church. Now the Conservative school was more or less driven to the use of underground literature, to utter its very genuine protest against the innovations. On Peter's side there were only a few official satires from supporters of the innovations, and for the beginnings of modern Russian literature we have to wait till the reign of his daughter Elizabeth.

Lomonósoff (1712–1765) was the son of a well-to-do fisherman in the Government of Archangel. Peter had been the first to develope the prosperity of this part of Russia, and his gigantic personality mingled, in the imagination of the sturdy and adventurous boy, with the storms, the snows, and the strange lights of the north. Having learnt by heart a grammar and an arithmetic which fell into his possession, he set out, with three borrowed roubles and a load of fish, for Moscow. It was by the protection of a monk that he entered a school, and he later had to pose as a priest's son in order to join the Academy of the Image of the Saviour, then the only higher school in the city. Privations and ridicule could not deter him from his self-imposed task. Dissatisfied with the class programme, he spent hours on end reading mathematics and physics in the library of the monastery, but neither here nor in the Academy of Kieff could he satisfy his intellectual appetite. Narrowly escaping ordination, he

became a student in the new Academy of Science at St. Petersburg, and, at the age of twenty-four, was sent as the best of
Russian students to the University of Marburg.   Like Peter, he
had at last crossed the frontier.   During his five years in
Germany he gave himself such an education as no Russian had
ever had before, and his abilities were such as to make his
professors say that the most civilised country in the world might
be proud of him.   In 1739 was printed his first ode "on the
taking of Khotin"; it was on the model of the pseudo-classical
French and German verses of the time.   But supplies from
Russia were scarce and, after marrying the daughter of a
German tailor, he attempted to escape to Holland.   On the way,
he was enlisted by a Prussian press-gang.   He eluded his
captors and reached The Hague; but the Russian Ambassador
would not help him, and he returned to Marburg, whence a draft
from Russia enabled him to come back to the Academy of St.
Petersburg.   There he taught for the rest of his life.   He
enjoyed the favour of the Empress Elizabeth, but was often at
variance with his fellow workers.   Some words which he spoke
shortly before his death may be quoted as especially typical of
the story of the Russian Intelligence: " For the common profit,
and especially for the establishment of learning in my country, I
will not count it a sin even to stand up against my father.   To
this I dedicated myself, that to my grave I should struggle with
the enemies of Russian learning."   Lomonósoff, as the first
Russian man of letters, had to make a beginning everywhere at
once.   Besides his odes on Imperial subjects, there are others on
Scriptural themes; he wrote the first Russian Grammar, and the
first Russian hand-book of Style.   He helped to found Moscow
University, and, believing in the potentialities of the vast resources
of Russia, worked hard for the intelligent development of the
trade of the North.

Von Wisin (1744–1792) was the first notable satirist, and he
was a German.   As a child he was a voracious reader, but
showed remarkable ignorance when passing the leaving examination from the Moscow University Gymnasium.[1]   After a very
haphazard education, he entered the Government service, but he
was too flighty to make a good official.   When little over twenty

---

[1] He did not know into what sea the Volga flows.

years old he brought out his comedy " The Brigadier," a satire on official corruption and ignorance, and also on the apish imitation of French manners which then prevailed. He was invited to read it aloud to the Empress Catherine. Count Panin said to him, " Your Brigadier is related to all of us." It was only in 1782 that he published his second great comedy "The Minor." Von Wisin never completed any other great work, and his pleasant and comely life ended at the age of forty-eight.

Derzhávin (1743–1816), the court poet of Catherine, came of the smaller gentry. He had some Tartar blood, and his childhood was passed in Orenburg and Kazán. His first school-master was a priest, his second a drunken German, who made his scholars repeat German sentences without understanding them. His next teachers were military, and they were no more intelligent. " At that time," he writes, "they taught us religion without explanations, languages without grammar, geometry without proofs, music without notes, and as to books, except for religious ones, they hardly gave us any." From the Kazán Gymnasium he was summoned to service in the army. In the barracks he read books at night and wrote odes on the model of Lomonósoff; but for ten years he had to spend his days amongst ignorant and dissolute companions. He then became an officer and fought against Pugachéff. Receiving a small estate from the Government, he passed into the civil service. From this point he lived in St. Petersburg amongst the more educated men of his time. An ode in praise of Catherine, 1782, won her lasting favour. An honest, but by no means a capable official, he served as Governor in two provinces and later became Secretary of State. He was far more of a poet than Lomonósoff; but he wrote without discipline and without forethought ; and his style was often long-drawn and florid. Poetry he practised as a means of pleasing, especially of pleasing his kindly superiors,[1] but his religious poems are more genuine and of much higher merit. He is best remembered by the lofty thought and language of his ode entitled " God."

Karamzín (1766-1826) grew to manhood under Catherine, but lived on into the reign of her grandson Nicholas. He, too,

---

[1] His description of his own work runs thus :—" Nice amiable poetry, pleasant sweet, and useful, like tasty lemonade in summer."

came of the smaller gentry, had traces of Tartar blood, and passed
his boyhood on the Volga (near Simbírsk).   The sentimental and
idealising boy was sent to school in Moscow, but at sixteen he was
called to serve in the Regiment of the Guard in St. Petersburg.
Leaving the service on the death of his father, he ultimately
moved to Moscow, where he fell under the influence of the notable
littérateur Nóvikoff, who did so much for the cause of popular
instruction.   With him Karamzín worked for four years, and, on
his return from a trip of eighteen months abroad, he devoted himself exclusively to literature.   In 1791 he founded the *Moscow
Magazine*, and in 1801 the *Messenger of Europe*. His
"Letters of a Russian Traveller" helped to put Russian readers
in touch with the Europe of the time.   His very popular romance
"Poor Lisa," which brought tears to everyone's eyes, suggests a
comparison with "Paul et Virginie" or the writings of Rousseau,
and may be considered as the first Russian novel.   On the other
hand, the great work to which Karamzín devoted the last years
of his life, "A History of the Russian Empire," is much more
governmental in character.   The author, while writing it, received
a yearly pension of £200 from Alexander I.   Instalments of the
work were read aloud to different members of the Imperial family.
Alexander contributed a large sum towards the printing, gave
Karamzín a Chinese cottage in the park of his palace at Tsárskoë
Seló, and often paid him informal visits.   During his last
illness, an Imperial yacht was prepared to carry him abroad;
he died in the Tauris Palace, and was laid to rest with all
honours in the Monastery of Alexander of the Neva, not far
from Suvóroff.

Karamzín's History, as we should expect, pays but little attention to the development of the Russian people; it is the story of
the Russian autocracy.   The work has been described as rather
an artistic production than a history.   The language is stately
and sometimes stilted.   Possessed with his one idea, the author
often seems curiously deficient in humour, as when he tells us
that St. Stephen was able to make great progress with the conversion of Perm, "thanks to the letters of the Grand Prince, the
favour of God, and his own piety."   His chief maxim is that " only
under autocracy was Russia ever strong and glorious, and that
whenever the autocratic power became weak, the country had to

live through misfortunes of various kinds."[1]   Karamzín, then, was
at once the Intelligent and the apologist of the Government, and
it is not without justice that Pushkin has written of him :

> " With elegance and with simplicity
> The quite impartial Karamzín points out
> How needful is autocracy
> How charming is the knout."

Zhukóvsky (1783–1852) serves as a link between Karamzín
and what is to come.   His father was a landowner of rank and substance in Central Russia ; his mother a Turkish prisoner of war.
He early acquired a great facility in European languages.   Brought
up almost entirely among women, he was of a dreamy and artistic
disposition, and lived in an atmosphere of literature, guarded from
all the harder rubs of life.   At eighteen he became an official,
but, within a year, returned to his feminine country circle.   In
the next year (1802) his translation of Gray's " Elegy " in the
Messenger of Europe won general approval.   An infatuation
for his niece, whom he wished to marry, was interrupted by the
campaign of 1812, in which he served as a volunteer ; he attracted
the favour of the Court by his patriotic verses, " A Singer in the
Camp of the Russian Warriors " and "A Message to the Emperor
Alexander " (1814).   His niece had married a German professor
of Dorpat ; and Zhukóvsky must needs go and live there too.
This mild-hearted man was now more or less broken in spirit, and
became indifferent to public interests.   But being named by
the Emperor Nicholas I. as tutor to his son Alexander, he lived for
twenty-five years at the Court, and served his country to the very
best purpose by giving to his pupil a liberal education in the
widest sense of the term.   When this task was finished he went
to spend the rest of his life in Germany, where he married a girl
of nineteen.   He died two years before the Crimean war, and was
buried close to his friend Karamzín.

The importance of his services to Russian literature is far
greater than the measure of his own individual achievement.   He
set all his peasants free, as not having the right to be an owner
of souls ; and he carried into the high places, of which he had the
entry, a generous championship of literature and of literary men.

---

[1] This and some other criticisms are drawn from Ostrogorsky's little school hand-
book on the lives of Russian writers.

But his own personal kindness to young men of promise was less important than his services in opening up a new world to the whole literary public of his country. And let us remember on what critical times his life fell. Like Karamzín, he was one of the earliest Russian pupils of that school of romanticism which the breath of French liberty kindled to life all over Europe. It was with this new world of sentiment that Zhukóvsky made Russia more familiar. He himself translated Schiller's "Maid of Orleans" and Byron's "Prisoner of Chillon." Besides this he translated Indian and Persian legends, parts of the "Æneid" and of the "Iliad," and the whole of the "Odyssey."

Born two years later than Karamzín and fifteen years earlier than Zhukóvsky, Ivan Kryloff (1768–1844) passed his earliest childhood on the border of Asia, and, losing his father at the age of eleven, lived in the greatest straits with his mother at Tver. This very capable lady had the greatest difficulty in providing any education at all for her son, and at fourteen he had to take service as a clerk in a provincial law court. A year later he made his way to St. Petersburg. Here he had trouble in even earning a living. His early essays in play-writing led to no success, and it was not before his thirty-eighth year that he found his *métier* as a writer of fables. Four years later (1809) his first twenty-three fables were on everyone's lips. In 1812 he obtained an appointment in the Public Library, which he retained till his death. In 1812 his fables on the Moscow campaign brought him to the knowledge of the Emperor, and from that time he was one of the chief figures amongst the men of letters at the Court. He lived to be the father, or, as he was called, the grandfather,[1] of Russian Literature, died in ripe old age, and was buried in the Monastery of Alexander Nevsky. Kryloff, who did not begin his public career until he was of mature age, was by no means merely the Court *littérateur*. On the banks of the Volga, he had acquainted himself with the pithy language of the peasants and boatmen. He had in him all the instincts of Great Russia, and he entered his weighty protest against the prevailing imitation of the West. One of the most remarkable of his fables describes how, in the lower world, an author and a robber were each punished by being

---

[1] This was originally a pet name given to him by a young girl belonging to a family with which he was very intimate.

suspended in a huge cauldron over a fire. The robber's flame
burnt fiercely for a time, but soon died out; the author's grew
stronger with every year. The author protests to Megæra that
his punishment is excessive; she replies:

> " His life was violence and wrong ;
>   His race is run,
>   His sins are done.
> But thou,—thy bones, indeed, have mouldered now full long ;
>   Yet not one day the sun can rise
> But that he brings to light thy new-wrought infamies.

> *   *   *   *   *

> Look ! " and the map of life before his eyes unrolled,
>   " The million evil deeds behold.
> The million miseries which in thy count we see.

> *   *   *   *   *

> Didst thou not glorify unfaith and call it knowledge ?
> With fair alluring word seductively entice
>   To passion and to vice,
>   Till see, as scholars in thy cursèd college,
>   Yon whole disordered nation
>   Runs rife
>   With murder and with devastation
>   With mutiny and civil strife."

This was, not unreasonably, taken to be directed against France
and Voltaire, but Kryloff seldom condescended to explain his
fables.

In another fable, " The Liar," a Westerniser walks across the
fields complaining that there is nothing to see in Russia, and
describing a Roman cucumber which was of the size of a mountain.
His friend replies :

> " Why we ourselves are now approaching something strange.

> *   *   *   *   *

> You see out there a bridge across the stream,
> Which we have got to cross ; though simple it may seem,
>   It's quite of a peculiar class.
> There's not a liar here who'll dare that bridge to pass.
>   Perhaps half-way across he'll stumble,
>   Then, sure as ever, off he'll tumble.
>   Who tells no lie,
>   May drive a coach and four quite safely by."
>   " Oh, really, what's the depth below ? "
>   " Eight feet or so."

He plays his bridge against the other's cucumber with such success that, in the end, the boaster cries out,

> " What need to cross the bridge, why can't we find a ferry ?"

It must not be supposed that Kryloff has no strictures left for the methods and working of the autocracy. Even Kryloff had a good deal of trouble with the censorship. One of his fables which had been forbidden he printed by the device of reading it first to the Emperor, who was delighted with it and gave him a free mandate to publish it. The Emperor he describes as " the sun which lights up all parts on which it happens to be shining "; but this compliment implies that there is always half a world in darkness. In another fable, written while the Emperor was on a tour of inspection, there is a fox who has been appointed to govern the fish, but cooks them on a gridiron instead ; the lion bursts in upon this entertainment and is told that " the fishes are dancing for pleasure at the arrival of their tsar."

The promotion of stupid officials is taken off in more than one fable. A man sees his friend trying to shave himself with a blunt razor, because he imagines that it will not cut. There is also the fable of the squirrel who served as the lion's page and was promised a pension of a load of walnuts. The service lasted long and the pension came late :

> " These nuts were splendid, none could beat them,
> All choice ones, nut for nut as good as could be,
> And only one thing not quite as it should be :
> The squirrel had no teeth to eat them."

Kryloff is quite as severe against the laziness of the peasants. Two " unlucky ones " meet each other : one has burnt down his house because he took a light to fetch some vodka on Christmas day. The other is crippled because he did not take a light and so fell down the stairs. The wise old man of the village, to whom they both complain, sums up as follows :—

> " A drunkard with a light may blunder,
> And in the dark may blunder worse."

Kryloff baldly raises the question : Is instruction a good thing or a bad thing? He at once finds for the first alternative, but he gives more detailed judgment by the allegory of three pearl fishers. One sat on the shore and expected the pearls to be washed up to him; the second explored the waters close in to the shore, taking all due precautions; the third imagined that the pearls must have all rolled together at the very bottom of the sea, so he chose the deepest water that he could find, dived into it and never came up again.

Griboyédoff (1795–1829) was a young man of distinguished family, who, after a not very happy youth, entered the army in 1812. As a hussar, and later as a Foreign Office clerk, he spent enough time in St. Petersburg to make himself thoroughly acquainted with all the weak spots of Russian Society. After a visit to Persia, he returned to the capital to see to the publication of his brilliant comedy, " The Mischief of being Clever." But this was the time of the First Reaction, and, though the play circulated in manuscript all over Russia, the censorship forbade it to be printed. In 1825, Griboyédoff returned to the Caucasus, where he married ; but in 1828, at the early age of thirty-seven, he was murdered by a Persian mob while serving as plenipotentiary of his country at the Court of Teheran.

" The Mischief of being Clever " may, without fear of exaggeration, be described as one of the wittiest comedies ever written. Though the treatment and the language are direct to a degree, it cannot be well appreciated without some knowledge of the times to which it refers. But almost every one of its caustic phrases has, like the fables of Kryloff, passed into the vocabulary of the Russian Intelligence. The plot of the play matters little. The hero, Chatsky, is a brilliantly clever man who returns from abroad to Moscow to find that the atmosphere is impossible to him and that he is impossible to the atmosphere. After a series of bitter disillusions, he seeks the ordinary refuge of the Intelligent, quick travelling without a thought of a destination, and the play ends with the words " a carriage, Ho ! a carriage." Nowhere is the conciseness of Russian classics more notable than in this play. Often the point is contained in a line of two syllables. Take a chance instance : a servant girl plagued with the attentions of her master :

" Excuse me, sir, your hair is white."

The master answers,

" Not quite."

When Chatsky has been inveighing against the aping of French

manners and the worship of underbred Frenchmen, he points
his meaning in a line of a single syllable :

" Look ! "

and the eye travels to the apers of apes moving in couples round
the room to a trivial French jig, in a half-barbarous imitation of a
Paris drawing-room.

Alexander Pushkin (1799–1837) was born in Moscow on
Ascension Day in 1799, the year in which Napoleon made himself
master of France.   His father came of an ancient family of Boyars
who played their part in Russian history.   His mother was a
granddaughter of the well-known coloured attendant of Peter the
Great, from whom the poet inherited his dark complexion, his
curly hair, his thick lips and, possibly, his extreme sensitiveness.
Both his father and his uncle were known in Moscow as society
wits ; the latter wrote light verse.   The hospitable house was
frequented by Karamzín, Zhukóvsky, and other well-known
writers.   French was more in vogue there than Russian.   The
parents paid little attention to the boy, and left him to the charge
of his excellent grandmother, and of his clever nurse, who taught
him peasant songs and peasant legends and continued to be one
of his favourite companions even after he was grown up.   Very
early he acquired a thorough knowledge of French.   He threw
himself with appetite on books French and Russian, and by the
age of nine had already written many French verses.   Perhaps
the most striking of his characteristics was his intellectual vitality,
but he never had any thorough teaching, and literature itself was,
in his family, looked upon as a pastime.

At the age of twelve Pushkin was sent to the Lycée of the
Imperial Palace at Tsárskoë Seló.   This school was almost a
kind of Eton : it was in the very nest of the Imperial tradition,
and had access to a richly stored library ; but the scholars, all
of them members of illustrious families, were left to complete
their education very much in their own way.   They were always
invited to the great festivals of the court ; they could wander
at will through the great gardens full of memories of the past ;
they would naturally stand closer than any other boys in Russia
to the great European events which were happening at this
time (1811–1817), and they had a special tradition of honour
and nobility ; but they acquired only scraps of knowledge at their

own choice and a general lofty disregard of the more serious business and more solid rules of life. They learnt to despise money while spending it far beyond their means, and Pushkin, after his six years here, found, like many an English public school boy, that he had to begin his own self-instruction for himself afterwards.

His next two years were passed in St. Petersburg society, in wild pleasures and noisy revels which left a permanent mark on his health. A set of daring verses against a person in high office resulted in his banishment to South Russia. After a roving life of four years in this part, he visited the Caucasus, (which was by nature a training ground for Russian poetry), served for a time in Kishineff and Odessa, and, in consequence of a bold letter, was ordered to live on an estate belonging to his family in the Government of Pskoff. To the next few years of relegation and recuperation we owe the man. He renewed his close acquaintance with the fundamental instincts of Russia, and for the first time seriously set himself to literary work (1824). So far he had written much excellent verse, the legend of " Ruslan and Lyudmila " and the first section of the remarkable society poem, " Eugene Onyéghin." He now set himself to master English, and to acquaint himself thoroughly with the works of Byron. Here he made a special study of the Bible, the old Russian annals, Shakespeare, and others of the best foreign writers. Here he completed " Onyéghin " and wrote his admirable tragedy " Borís Godunóff," and others of his greatest works. He lived alone with his old nurse, and was constantly wandering amongst the peasants, joining in their talk and recording their legends and songs. His only neighbours were the kindly family of Osipoff, with two daughters, who, apparently, supplied the heroines of " Onyéghin," but he was visited from time to time by many literary friends.

In 1826 he was allowed to return to St. Petersburg, and he thenceforward enjoyed the special favour of the Emperor Nicholas. He was now recognised as Russia's greatest poet. But his abrupt and ardent character and his caustic witticisms made him many enemies. He quarrelled with his relations, squandered his money, and became touchy and pessimistic. He seemed unable to satisfy himself, whether in the capitals, in the heart of the country, or on distant travels. In 1831 he married a society beauty; but his trivial and spendthrift wife completed the ruin of his fortune. He now found it necessary to engage in journalistic enterprises which were not in the *métier* of the reckless and lofty-minded noble, and, from the time of his marriage, he was not able to plan any serious composition. A rumour against the good name of his wife was industriously circulated by his enemies; he received several anonymous letters on the subject, and at last challenged to a duel the man indicated as his rival; in this duel (February, 1837) Pushkin was mortally wounded. Some affectionate messages passed between him and the Emperor Nicholas, but he finally turned his face towards the shelves of his library, and expired with the words, "Goodbye, my friends." He was only thirty-eight years old.

Pushkin is one of the great poets of the world : I would try to describe him as Byron and more than Byron. The foundation of his work is the extraordinary vigour and vitality of his imagination. But it was directed by an equally extraordinary sureness of instinct, which made him at once fasten, Napoleon-like, on the one thing that before all wanted saying, and then choose his manner of expression with an easy facility that left nothing to be added. Often the printed work would be the result of hours of careful thought and selection, always illumined by the most ardent imagination. But so potent is the simplicity and naturalness of it that the reader will hardly think of how or why Pushkin came to say this or that, and will be entirely absorbed in the contemplation of what he describes. Yet the content of a sentence of Pushkin's is generally so great, that the further one is removed from the time of reading it the higher will be one's estimate of the imagination which prompted it. To me none of his work seems greater than his fairy tales in verse, such as the legend of King Saltan, and the legend of the Dead Princess and the Seven Heroes. Nothing in the order of the words suggests that the exigencies of verse composition are any greater than those of prose; not a word has been misplaced, not a word has been inserted. In fact, these legends are sometimes printed for children as if they were prose; yet the simplest child, if reading each word as he came upon it, could hardly mar the natural beauty of the rhythm. There is never a sentence

of explanation, and the writer passes, with an admirable directness, from one picture to another. I may take as an instance
the beginning of the "Dead Princess." In sixteen short lines,
some of which contain no more than three or four words, we are
told of a king who starts on a journey leaving his wife gazing
all day at the fields of snow in which he has disappeared. For
nine months she gazes and then gives birth to a daughter. The
eight next lines tell us how the king returns, how she looks at
him, sighs, cannot bear the rapture, and dies at the time of
vespers: we go on,

> "Long the King was inconsolable;
> But how to be? And he was sinful,"

which tells us in a word that he will marry again; and then the
plan of the story begins.

The tragedy "Borís Godunóff" has a solemn and simple
stateliness; one feels all through that what is said is less than
half of what is thought. The atmosphere of the unknown is
around one from the start. The old monk, completing his last
chapter of the chronicles of Russia in the peace of the monastery,
looks back on the finished record of peaceful times. Opposite
him stands the young novice, who already meditates flight from
the monastery, and is later to sit on the throne of Moscow as the
false Demetrius. The intrigues which surround the throne of
Borís are never openly displayed to the spectator, but every word
that is spoken makes one guess and wonder. Throughout there
is the suggestion of something not final. When Borís dies
and his young son is massacred, the dull crowd outside the
palace is invited to acclaim the usurper Demetrius, and the play
ends with the stage direction, "the people are silent," or, as the
Russian words say, "the people have no voice."

"Eugene Onyéghin," a story in the easiest of verse, is a picture
of Pushkin himself and of the society in which he moved.
Onyéghin, bored with the life of St. Petersburg, goes to his
country estate. His neighbours are a young poet, Lensky, and a
family named Lárin, with two daughters. One of these daughters
is engaged to Lensky; the other, Tatyána, falls in love with
Eugene, and, with characteristic simplicity, writes him a letter to
tell him so. When he meets her, he gives her a little lecture,
explaining that he is too *blasé* to be a good husband, and that it

will be wiser for her not to throw herself in the same way
at anyone else's feet.   This is gall and wormwood to the
innocent little girl.   Eugene, to complete her cure, flirts out-
rageously with her engaged sister.   This leads to a duel with
Lensky, whom Eugene, without the least ill-will, kills at first
shot ; he does not mean it, but he does it.   Eugene now travels
over Russia to forget his grief, and meanwhile the Lárin family
goes to Moscow.

Eugene returns to Moscow, to find Tatyána the belle of
Moscow society, but married to an old general.   It is his turn
to fall in love with her.   He writes her very much such a letter
as she wrote to him, and, though she tries to avoid his attentions,
he at last succeeds in forcing his way into her house.   In answer
to his ardent professions, she goes over the story of the past :
" Yet happiness was so possible, so near, but my destiny is
already fixed.   May be, I behaved thoughtlessly, my mother
begged me, conjured me with tears ; for poor Tánya all lots
were alike ; I married.   You must—I beg you — leave me.   I
know in your heart there are both pride and rigid honour.   I
love you, why make a mystery of it ? but I am given to another,
and I shall always be faithful to him."   She goes out, leaving
Eugene dumbfounded.   A bell rings, the husband enters, " and
here, reader, in this moment so malicious for my hero, we will
leave him for a long time, for ever.   Long enough we have been
following his track all over the world.   We will say good-bye to
each other from the bank.   Hurrah !   And we might have done it
long ago, might we not ? "

Of Pushkin's odes, I will take as an example the one written
on the death of Napoleon.   Manzoni, Béranger, and Byron all
tried their hands at this subject ; Pushkin's attempt was the
most daring of all.   In fifteen verses, of eight lines each, he
covers the whole of Napoleon's career.   It is a triumph of the art
of selection.   The picture is full of variegated life, but one
strong and definite judgment pervades the whole.   The most
accurate, and what is more the most intelligent historian could
hardly wish a single word to be more true or more enlightening ;
yet the whole is a simple piece of narrative, running through the
channel of an admirable rhythm as simple as if it were prose.
Here is some kind of a translation of the verses which deal with

the Moscow campaign; to adequately translate Pushkin we shall
need another Pushkin :—

> " Foolhardy, who thy mind did ply
>   And goad to doom with fatal art ?
> Throned in thy wondrous thoughts so high,
>   Couldst thou not gauge a Russian's heart ?
> Not prescient of the great-souled fire,
>   Thou deemest in thy high estate
> That peace we wait at thy desire,
>   And readest Russia all too late.
>
> Russia, our queen of war, take heart,
>   Thine ancient glorious rights reclaim ;
> Bright sun of Austerlitz, depart,
>   Rise our great Moscow, rise in flame.
> Gone are the times of bitterness ;
>   Our late-soiled honour still we save,
> Russia, thy glorious Moscow bless ;
>   War ! war ! our treaty is the grave.
>
> With hands benumbed that grasp the prize,
>   Still clutching fast his iron crown,
> He sees the gulf before his eyes,
>   He reels and reels and so goes down.
> Now run, ye hosts of Europe all ;
>   Around, the cruel blood-stained snows
> Shall publish to the world your fall ;
>   And thaws with them all trace of foes."

Pushkin's lighter work, such as his epigrams and his verses
for albums, has similar merits, but here the art seems more
conscious and we shall be more often inclined to exclaim " how
well that is done ! "   I take eight lines addressed to a former love :

> " I loved you once ; perhaps not all extinguished
>   Within my heart the flame that burns in vain ;
> But let my love no longer still disturb you,
>   I could not wish in aught to give you pain.
> I loved you once : now jealous and now fearful,
>   My heart nor hoped nor asked for love from you.
> I loved you once, as tenderly, as truly
>   As he you'll love,—God grant,—shall love you too."

When Pushkin died, a young man of twenty-three, named
Lérmontoff, wrote a set of stinging verses showing the magnitude
of Russia's calamity and the rottenness of a society which could
let its greatest poet die in such a way.   Public opinion at once
accepted him as Pushkin's successor in the laureateship, and the
Government ratified the decision by exiling him to the Caucasus.
Lérmontoff, who came of Scotch ancestry, was born in Moscow

and was brought up by his grandmother, an ambitious and harsh-minded woman of the world, who despised her daughter for having made so poor a match. Lérmontoff's father seldom visited him, and that only with difficulty. Early orphaned and under no illusion as to the character of his grandmother, the boy grew up amidst luxuries which should not have been his, to be an extreme type of a certain kind of Russian Intelligent, both in his altogether remarkable ability and in his utter absence of moral scruple. He tortured animals, and allowed himself the utmost licence in his behaviour to his grandmother's servants. At twelve he entered a school for young nobles. His early heroes were Pushkin and Byron, and everything that was best in him united to prompt him to put into verse the picture of his own miserable youth. At sixteen he entered the University of Moscow, where he was feared and respected as a maker of bitter witticisms. At eighteen he was expelled for indiscipline; he now passed two years in a cavalry school, where he learnt little else than how to wreck his fortune and his health, becoming the leader in the most desperate excesses and riots, which he celebrated in sardonic verse. As a hussar he was stationed at Tsárskoë Seló, until the sentence which sent him to the Caucasus, whose wonderful scenery supplied more than one of his poems with a background of glorious imagery. He was soon back in St. Petersburg, where he remained only because he could not face the deprivation of luxuries which a quarrel with his grandmother would have entailed. Though his cynicism made intimacy with him almost impossible, he had a few friends who valued his heart no lower than his talents. But his general isolation, and the consciousness of his own failure to act up to his ideals, brought him down into an early pessimism. In 1840 he was again expelled to the Caucasus because of a duel. His novel, "A Hero of our Time," was issued in his absence. The hero, Pechórin, is a man of charming manners, who easily wins the affection of others; he is utterly selfish and heartless and absolutely self-contained, and he manages to get anything that he wants. Practically Lérmontoff is satirising himself. In 1841 Lérmontoff fell, at the age of twenty-seven, in a duel deliberately provoked by his wantonly insulting behaviour. He had always courted danger, and here, too, seems to have gone in search of it.

Lérmontoff had a wonderful power of imagination, and an admirable simplicity and conciseness of expression. A deep undercurrent of cynicism runs through most of his poetry, as, for instance, when he makes the old soldier who tells the tale of Borodinó revert more than once, in his description of the army of 1812, to the refrain "Heroes, not You;" or again when he excuses himself for keeping the portrait of a lady whom he once loved, by saying to her—

"The temple deserted is always a temple,
The idol o'erthrown is always a god."

But there is so much more in his poetry besides sheer cynicism that it only serves to give a relish to the whole. "The Demon," which has supplied the text of a remarkable opera by Rubinstein, is a poem of the imagination, very suggestive of Byron, though for the matter of that, Lérmontoff, in a few fugitive lines, says:

"No, I am not Byron . . . .
I am either God or nothing."

It is the story of how the banished angels come down to woo the daughters of men; and the power of the presentation is such as to leave an overwhelming sense of awe at the problems which the poet raises. Had he lived, he might have left to us work of the same scope, and perhaps even of the same value, as Pushkin, but this typical representative of the Russian Intelligence had the most miserable life of all and died the youngest.

Not much longer and not much happier was the span of Koltsoff, a young man of humble birth, who had a natural but untrained talent for picturing in easy verse the most homely aspects of peasant life.

Nicholas Gógol (1809–52) was a southerner, being the son of a country gentleman of Little Russia. His grandfather had served with a Cossack regiment, and Gógol retained all his life the instinct of the steppe, the craving for space. In his later years, he would come back hither from time to time, as if driven by the simple need to breathe; and, in one of his works, he exclaims in genuine rapture, "Damn you, steppe, how beautiful you are!" His kindly open-handed parents did a great deal of entertaining. His father wrote amusing plays for home performance, and the boy, who was soon a remarkably clever mimic, had an early yearning for theatre life. He received but a poor education, and, when only twelve years old, lost his father. Religious and sensitive, he felt the loss terribly, but early set himself to be the support of his mother. At school he was chiefly notable for making clever sketches and organising theatricals. He collected, with his fellows, a little library of literature and edited a school newspaper in manuscript. He never had a small opinion of his own ability, and believed that he was marked out to do great things. Side by side with his humour were many of the features of the ascetic and of the preacher.

At nineteen he came to St. Petersburg, but could not find work, even as an actor. He wrote stories, but burnt them. After two years, however, he obtained a small official post, which made him acquainted with that world which he was afterwards to satirise. His first successful work was on the home-life of his dearly loved Little Russia. He now had the friendly offices of Zhukóvsky and Pushkin, and secured a post, first as teacher and then as professor, at St. Petersburg University, but he was poorly qualified for this work and devoted himself entirely to literature. He now produced some excellent stories and, by Pushkin's suggestion, wrote his great comedy "The Revising Inspector" (Revizór). The strange discords of his personality are perhaps nowhere better illustrated than by his account of the reception of his play. He amuses himself by writing a confused scene, representing the babel of superficial criticisms which he overheard as the audience left the theatre. This scene is certainly comedy, but of a very tragic kind, for Gógol cannot conceal how deeply each wound goes home.

His admirable story of Cossack life "Tarass Bulba" won general approval, but the "Revizór" was treated as almost a piece of disloyalty to Russia by the servile Press of the day. Pushkin, however, stood by him, and so did the Emperor Nicholas. Pushkin suggested to him the subject of "Dead Souls," and, with a subsidy from the Emperor, Gógol left Russia and set to work. He returned only for short visits, and even then his caprices made him almost unapproachable. During his stay at Rome, his proclivities towards asceticism came so strong upon him, that he doubted whether the life of a writer of novels was not altogether displeasing to God. After the publication of the first part of "Dead Souls," which met with enormous success, he fell into a kind of religious remorse. He tried in vain to find rest in excesses of self-mortification and in a pilgrimage to Jerusalem. During the intervals between these fits of depression he made spasmodic efforts to continue the second part of "Dead Souls." On his last visit to Moscow, in 1851, he burned the greater part of it in an access of remorse, and after a self-imposed fast, during which he refused all medicine, he died at the age of forty-three in the following year. On his grave are carved the words of Jeremiah—

"With the bitterness of my word I will laugh."

The "Revizór" is a most daring attack on official corruption. The public expected a farce, and realised with sudden confusion that it was listening to a great comedy. The Revising Inspector is likely to arrive *incognito* in a small provincial town. The mayor and the officials are gathered together, planning how to put the best face upon their lazy and corrupt administration; they suddenly hear from two gossips of the town that a young man is staying at the hotel and has said that his bill will be settled later. This young man, Khlestyakóff, is by nature neither an honest man nor a rogue. Flighty and pleasure-seeking, he simply uttered the first excuse which came into his mind, but the result is that he receives a visit from the mayor, who begs him to " come to another place." Khlestyakóff thinks that he knows what that other place is likely to be, and at first refuses; but in the end he finds himself a more than honoured guest in the mayor's house, and uses his opportunities by making love almost simultaneously to the mayoress and her daughter. He is entertained with a sumptuous dinner and comes back distinctly the worse for drink, murmuring the word "salmon-trout." There follows a series of amusing scenes, in which only sheer chance saves him from showing that he is the wrong man. Being a friendly creature and ready to borrow money from anyone, he explains to the mayor that he is short of cash for his journey; and his host, taking this to be a polite way of asking for the regular bribe, gives him anything that he asks for and begs him not to think of repayment. It is not suggested that Khlestyakóff ever really knows why he is being treated with such exceptional kindness; but he is glad to use his opportunities, and when the officials come to call on him one after the other, he extracts from them all the bribes which they have prepared for the Inspector. He began by asking too little, he ends by asking a great deal too much ; he began with the mayor, he ends with the peasants who come in with their petitions. Gógol has so far utilised to the full the possibilities of each situation. The play, which is full of good dialogue, never lags, and, many as are the developments, they are all perfectly natural and are naturally treated. And now Khlestyakóff goes off with the best horses in the town, to ask the blessing of a country uncle for his union with the mayor's daughter. The mayoress holds a great reception, and she and her husband discuss, before their very envious guests, the style on which they will now live in St. Petersburg, and the honours to which the road now seems open. They are interrupted by the postmaster ; he has intercepted a humorous letter, in which Khlestyakóff describes to a St. Petersburg friend as poor as himself the various foibles of all these good provincial people. At this point a gendarme enters at the back of the stage and announces, " The Revising Inspector has come, and wishes to see you." The whole party petrifies into a *tableau vivant*, for which Gógol made the original sketch. They remain in various positions of consternation or exultant jealousy for a minute and a half ; the curtain drops, and the play is over. We are not interested to know how they all got out of their difficulties.

" Dead Souls " is an unusual title. Property in Russia was measured by the number of hands or " souls," and not by the number of acres. The census came seldom, and it was difficult to make it complete. The serf, until he was struck off the list remained a soul, and, if he died, he was a dead soul.

The adventurer, Chíchikoff, conceives the idea of buying up the title-rolls of as many dead souls as possible. This certificate of property can be turned to financial account later. Armed with good introductions, he goes down to a provincial town, and forages for " souls " amongst the country gentry of the neighbour-hood. As his mission is an unusual one, his hosts show far more of their character to him than they would to an ordinary visitor. Some pleasant and obliging creatures, who imagine that he may be a useful friend to make, surrender their dead souls for next to nothing. One bearish farmer, Sobakyévich ("son of a dog"), puzzles out in his slow way that if someone wants to buy dead souls, dead souls must have their price, and drives a very hard bargain indeed. Chíchikoff is at last exposed, and seeks the usual refuge of a long aimless journey; this gives Gógol the chance of introducing a remarkable poetic outburst, which has already been quoted. Gógol is, in fact, a poet, although he writes in prose. He characterises every scene and every person with a keen distinctness which suggests something more than the ordinary light of day. Even in the first part of "Dead Souls" there are at least glimpses of the morbidness that was coming over him.

Goncharóff, the son of a well-to-do merchant, was educated by his capable mother and later by a literary priest with a French wife. He served as an interpreter in the Ministry of Finance. At his chief work, "Oblómoff," he was at work for ten years. His record of a voyage on the frigate *Pallada* was a model for books of travel. Later he published his other great novel, "Obryv." Born three years later than Gógol, he lived nearly forty years longer. He is less fond than Gógol of picking out the worst points in human nature, and his work is rather delineation than caricature. Very able are his sketches of the helpless Intelligent who has a Government post, a man of the most attractive nature, but quite deficient in what we call character. Here is a picture with which he begins his chief work. To those intimate with Russian life, every word will count :—

"In the Gorókhovaya street, in one of those big houses whose population would be enough to fill a whole District Town, lay one morning in bed in his own quarters one Elia Oblómoff. He was a man of thirty-two or thirty-three, of average height and pleasant exterior; his dark grey eyes wandered carelessly about the walls or the ceiling, with that indefinite pensiveness which shows that one is not thinking about or bothering about anything. From his face, carelessness passed into the pose of his whole body, even into the folds of his dressing-gown. Sometimes his eye clouded with an expression of something like fatigue or boredom ; but neither fatigue nor boredom could for a minute drive from his face that gentleness which was the dominating and fundamental expression not only of the face but of his whole nature. This nature shone so openly and clearly in his eyes, in his smile, in each movement of his head or of his hands. And a superficial observer, glancing at Oblómoff, would have said, 'Good soul, no doubt; simpleton.' One whose sympathies went deeper would look at his face for a long while, and then go away in pleasant meditation, with a smile. . . . He wore a dressing-gown of Persian material, a real Oriental dressing-gown, without the slightest hint of Europe, exceedingly spacious, so that Oblómoff could have wrapped himself up twice in it. Oblómoff always went about his rooms without any necktie or waistcoat; somehow he loved elbow-room and free movement. His slippers were long, soft, and broad; if he put his legs on the floor without looking, he was, all the same, sure to fall into them at once. With Oblómoff, lying down was neither a necessity, as it is with the sick or with one who wants to sleep, nor an accident, as it is with one who is tired, nor a recreation, as it is with a born sluggard; it was simply his normal condition."

A literary tradition had now been established in Russia and a new era was opened by the labours of a band of men of genius. Within six years were born a number of men destined for distinction in the story of Russian literature: Turghényeff, in 1818, Dostoyévsky and Nekrásoff, in 1821, Grigoróvich, in 1822, and Ostróvsky, in 1823.

Grigoróvich, the son of a country gentleman of Tula and of a well-born French lady, passed into the Academy of Arts, but his intimacy with Dostoyévsky and Nekrásoff led him to devote himself to literature. He, for the first time, put before the Russian public pictures of peasant life, which he rather tended to idealise. He thus called attention to the evils of serfdom.

Ostróvsky served in a commercial court, which dealt with cases between merchants. The merchants were the least important of the three old classes, and probably the least known; and Ostróvsky, in his numerous comedies, acquainted the intelligent public with them practically for the first time. His scope can be gathered from the titles of some of his plays, " The Bankrupt," " We can settle amongst ourselves," "Poverty is no Vice," " Sit in your own Sledge." The pig-headedness and brutality of this class, especially in relation to its women-folk, is one of his most common themes.

Ivan Turghényeff (1818—1883) came of a wealthy family of

country gentry. Both his parents had some of the worst defects of the old aristocracy, and were hard taskmasters. The boy was early instructed by foreign tutors, but found more pleasure in the company of a kindly and lettered servant. At eleven, he was taken to school in Moscow, and to his French and German he now added English. At the University of St. Petersburg he was befriended by a friend of Pushkin, Professor Pletneff, and was by him introduced to Gógol, Koltsoff, and other well-known writers. At twenty, he entered the University of Berlin, and coming to the conclusion that serfdom was the chief enemy of education in Russia, he devoted himself to the cause of emancipation. At twenty-two, he returned to St. Petersburg with such a store of knowledge and judgment as perhaps no Russian had ever had before him. He quarrelled with his mother because of her cruelty to the peasants, and, making the sacrifice of which Lérmontoff had been incapable, became independent of home support and took service as an official in St. Petersburg, where he sometimes even had to go without his dinner. He was already attracting attention as a writer, and in 1847 he published the first of his "Notes of a Sportsman," which are the best picture of Russian peasant life yet offered to the world. Meanwhile he had inherited the family estate, and at once proceeded to free all his serfs ; he lived for four years amongst them, doing everything that he could to lighten their dues and to improve their conditions of life.

Here he wrote "Rudin" in 1855. In the next year he went abroad, and except for a few visits, lived out of Russia until his death. Like all Russian writers, he carried his country with him, and he became the friend and helper of his compatriots in all the places where he settled. In 1858 he published "A Nest of Gentlefolk," and soon afterwards "Fathers and Children." He was himself the chief of Westernisers, the most definite but the most reasoned and moderate, and he could all the better bridge the gap between his country and the West if he had one leg over the frontier. He lived in Paris, London, and Baden, which is the scene of one of the best of his works, the novel "Smoke." But he would sometimes visit Moscow and spend a whole summer on his country estate. He also carried on a vast correspondence with his Russian friends, and kept in touch with Russian literature and with foreign publications on Russia. He spoke Russian by

preference to the end, and his last words in that language were
"Live, and love your fellows." His funeral at St. Petersburg,
in 1883, was one of the most signal demonstrations of affection
and reverence which had ever taken place in the country.

Turghényeff is, to my mind, much the greatest master of
Russian prose. The pleasantness of his personality pervades
everything that he wrote. His style has the merit of perfect
simplicity and proportion to the occasion. Most of his stories
are comparatively short; the writer maintains his complete mastery
in every sentence. When one looks back over a tale which
seemed at the first reading to occupy but a few pages, one is
surprised at its wealth of content. "A Nest of Gentlefolk" is a
charmingly genuine picture of country life. "On the Eve" is
another charming story with a sad ending. In "Rudin," we
have a picture of the idealist who has no firm roots. Rudin
is a brilliant conversationalist; what he says seems at once
original and incontrovertible; further, he is always on the side
of the good. In a country house he reduces to silence the cocks
of the local dunghill, who are easy cynics; and friends and
enemies almost all anticipate for him a notable future. At this
point he breaks down. He has proposed to a daughter of the house,
and her mother has refused her consent. The girl meets him in
the fields, waiting for his decision as to what they are to do. Rudin
simply accepts the mother's refusal as final; and, though the girl
would have gone to the end of the world with him, he departs
alone. It is not a question of morality. The fact is that his
kaleidoscopic mind was capable of grouping together at a given
moment all the combined knowledge of a roomful of people into
a united and pleasant picture; but it is all words, not deeds, and
Rudin cannot be responsible for any one of his eloquently spoken
opinions. He returns later a broken man, because he has ceased
to believe in himself, and now, for the first time, he becomes
tolerable to his critics. He redeems himself by dying in a
hopelessly forlorn cause on a street barricade in Paris.

Nezhdánoff, in "Virgin Soil," is a poor creature; his ideals
are far too big for his nature and his physique. Without any
preparation except an untrained enthusiasm, he "goes to the
people." As tutor in a country house he forms an attachment
with a young girl of embittered life who has somewhat similar

ideals; and the two set out together on their strange mission. Apparently "going to the people" means for them, first, the abandonment of all that is individual in themselves, and secondly, the turning of themselves into imitation peasants. Nezhdánoff's first attempt to provoke a demonstration against officialdom ends in a public-house, where he is persuaded to drink far too much vodka in order to show his complete brotherhood with those whom he has set out to free. He returns in shame to his companion, loses all his bearings, and after gazing aimlessly at a barren tree in the courtyard which has a strange fascination for him, he eludes his friends and goes thither to commit suicide. How shall the blind lead the blind? The path of the future is suggested by the student-girl's second attachment for a young factory manager, who has set himself quietly and practically to educate all those who are naturally within reach of his influence.

Bazároff, in "Fathers and Children," is a man of common family and breeding, but of strong purpose and ability. All his ideas and all his plans are virile. All the force of his nature goes into a desperate love for a widowed lady, whose sympathies and ideals are not nearly deep enough to answer to his own. He gets a refusal, with some difficulty pulls himself together, and goes to work amongst the peasants with his old father, a doctor. The radical difference of instincts and views in the two men is bridged over by the deepest natural affection. He applies his great strength to just a little corner of the vast problem, and very soon contracts blood-poisoning from an operation which he has had to conduct in a cottage without any of the necessary appliances. The death scene lasts long, and is a wonderful piece of writing; it brings into strong relief the relations between the two so different generations, and the apparent hopelessness of the task which the young Bazároff has attempted.

In "Smoke," a young engineer, Litvínoff, arrives at Baden on his way back to Russia after years of ardent and capable study in Western Europe. His is a simple strong nature; he aims at the practicable, and his life seems certain to be a valuable one for his country. At Baden he has to wait for the arrival of his *fiancée*, a good girl with a straightforward nature, who fits into all his plans for the future. He meanwhile becomes acquainted with the Russian colony, and finds himself drawn into a chaos of embryonic ambitions and projects, social and political. With firm but gentle hand, Turghényeff sketches for us a circle of propagandists, who are far too vain and feeble for the work to which they have set themselves. Amidst this confusion, Litvínoff stumbles upon a kind of recluse, Potúghin, who may almost be taken to be Turghényeff himself. This man has, before all things, judgment; and seeing through all the frothiness of the propagandists, he yet understands how progress is possible, and what are its data. First of all, he would wish to get rid of melodrama.

"They all despond; they all go about hanging their heads, and at the same time they are all filled with hope—almost as if they would climb up a wall before your eyes. . . . 'But wait a bit,' they say; 'have a bit of patience; it's all going to come. And how is it going to come? You may care to be curious about that. Why, because we, you see, the educated people, are rubbish; but the people, oh, that's a great people! You see that sheepskin coat? Well, that's where it's all to come from.' Really, if I were a painter, here's the kind of picture I would paint: an educated man stands in front of a peasant, and bows low to him: 'Cure me, father peasant,' he says; 'I'm dying of degeneration.' And the peasant, in his turn, bows low to the educated man: 'Teach me, father gentleman,' he says; 'I'm dying of darkness.' Well, and, of course, neither moves a yard from the spot."

Litvínoff admits that Russia has to learn from her elder sisters; but he suggests that she cannot take over all improvements at sight, and instances a foreign winnowing machine, excellent in itself, but smashed by the thoughtlessness of the peasants. "And who compels you," says Potúghin, "to take over at sight? Why, surely you borrow something from someone else, not because it belongs to someone else, but because it is of use to you; that is, you use your own judgment, you choose. . . . Just you offer good food, and the stomach of the people will digest it in its own fashion; and with time, as the organism gets stronger, it will bring its own sap to work. . . . The whole question is simply this: is your constitution strong enough? And as to ours, don't you bother. It will stand it.

We're not so shaky as all that. . . . Come, it's well known, from the bad to the good you will never pass through the better, but always through the worse ; and in medicine even poison is often useful. Leave it to fools and knaves to point triumphantly to the poverty of the peasants after emancipation, to the increase of drunkenness after the abolition of leases. Through the worse to the good!" "But Russia," asks Litvínoff, "your country, do you not love her?" "I passionately love her, and I passionately hate her." "Oh, that's all Byron!" interrupts Litvínoff. "Yes, sir," Potúghin goes on, "I both love and hate my Russia, my strange, pleasant, dirty, dear country."

Amidst the babel, Litvínoff is suddenly confronted by an old love, Irene. He had been passionately devoted to her, and had with difficulty and against all obstacles, won a promise of her hand; she had abandoned him without a word after her first ball to marry for wealth and position. He now tries to avoid her, but she is disgusted with her military husband, a well-bred but empty man, and with a revulsion to her old feelings, she persistently puts herself in Litvínoff's way until he is on the point of running away with her. The story of the crisis is a great piece of work. At one moment, as he passes in a storm of conscience and passion along the street, one of the propagandists says, "There goes a man of iron." He is just saved, but only just. The admirable girl to whom he is engaged arrives, and though the story does not end here, the battle is won, and he finally makes his peace with her after a frank explanation. He has been rescued for the future.

Nekrásoff was the son of a Police-Colonel of Yaroslavl. His father ran away with a Polish lady of good family, and took little pains to lighten for her the hardships of his wanderings. The boy, whom he often took with him on his journeys of investigation, was early acquainted with the sadder aspects of peasant life. He failed to pass the entrance examination of St. Petersburg University, but he attended the courses as a free listener. His father, who had destined him for Government service, cut off all supplies, and Nekrásoff often wandered half famished about the streets of St. Petersburg, and even accepted shelter from the poorest. He took any work, private lessons, correcting of proofs, hack journalism, but he managed to make useful friendships, and became acquainted with prominent writers and editors. In 1846 he published a magazine, and its success enabled him to take over the editorship of the *Contemporary*. It is his large sympathies that give distinction to his writings. He is the poet of the women and of the poor. Dostoyévsky called him "a wounded heart."

Theodore Dostoyévsky (1821–81) was the son of a Moscow doctor. In the family circle, religion and affection were strong; the sensitive and nervous boy was described by his parents as "all fire." At ten he moved with his parents to a small country estate, and formed friendships amongst the peasants and with the local deacon, a man of great eloquence and of burning faith. He had a French tutor; his favourite authors were Pushkin and Walter Scott. His parents carefully kept from him all disturbing influences; but, at sixteen, he lost his mother, and soon afterwards entered the School of Engineers at Revel. He would hide in corners of the building to read his favourite books, especially Gógol. Here he began his first work, "Poor Folk." In 1843, he entered the Government service, but without any kind of inclination for it. His father now died; and spending his money on theatres and concerts, he was constantly in need; he would always be giving his last penny to help his married brother. He continued to write about the poor, and took his "Poor Folk" to Nekrásoff, who, with Grigoróvich, read it through in a night and roused him from bed to cover him with praises; it is quite usual for his readers to find themselves unable to drop a book of his before it is finished. He was already prematurely old and infirm, but his favourite subjects, religion and the people, were a part of his very being and could always light him up into a glowing and enlightening enthusiasm. In 1849 he was arrested for belonging to a circle which gathered to read forbidden books and to discuss forbidden subjects. After eight months in the fortress of Peter and Paul, he was sent as a convict in company with common criminals to Siberia. This blow he faced like a man. Unlike many others of more sturdy physique, who have succumbed to exile in Siberia, he saw in it an opportunity for learning at first hand about another class of unfortunates, and brought back the material for his "Notes out of a Dead House." At the expiry of his sentence, he had to serve for some years as a private soldier.

He married, but without happiness; and the epilepsy which he had contracted as a convict, became more frequent in its attacks. In 1859 he was released from the army and received, with an Imperial pardon, the "privilege" of living where he liked and of writing. With shattered health, he returned to St. Petersburg. Here he founded his own magazine *The Times*, in which he printed "The Dead House" and "The Humbled and Slighted." His next novel, "Crime and Punishment," was printed in the *Russian Messenger*. Having fallen into financial straits, he went abroad with his second wife, and, after four years of distress and of arduous work, often paid for in advance to clear him from his debts, he returned to lead this same life of constant stress in the government of Novgorod. In his journalistic work he had no collaborators; he answered his huge correspondence himself, and was constantly in request for public readings and other similar engagements. He died completely worn out at the age of sixty. The scene at his funeral proved how deeply he was loved; he was buried in the monastery of Alexander Nevsky.

Dostoyévsky has been called the poet of the poor, or, with better insight, the doctor of diseased souls. His work is all of a piece. Like another great writer who is full of pity, Mazzini, he appears to leave questions of style more or less to take care of themselves under the dictation of that ruling instinct which alone prompts him to write. The life of his books seems to be the life of that great army of the afflicted which he studies, and the life of Dostoyévsky is the life of his books. The reader sinks easily into this living world and himself lives in it without interruption as long as he may. Dostoyévsky might be described as an artist, not so much of expression as of his great special subject, the disease of the mind. This is what seems to attract him in any surroundings, and with the surest instinct he brings into prominence and analyses each symptom of the ailment. In " Crime and Punishment," a murderer, who is almost half an idiot, is examined by a lawyer of profound ability. The lawyer brings forward proof after proof which the criminal succeeds in refuting. In one case the criminal stumbles; the lawyer himself supplies him with the right answer, and, in the end, obtains such a hold over the murderer's confidence, and so acts upon his conscience, that after successfully refuting all evidence, the prisoner confesses of himself. It is all a lesson in the psychology of the guilty man's mind. The reader almost feels that there is something in himself which is under the knife of the dissector. Another novel, "The Brothers Karamázoff," analyses the minds of rogues who are practically kleptomaniacs; their characters are complicated; but, if there is in them much of evil, there is also much of honour. Crime, in fact, is for Dostoyévsky a disease to which the least fortunate are naturally the most liable ; and no phrase has been more often quoted or misquoted in Russia than his maxim, "To know all would be to pardon all." This whole-hearted man, full of sympathy and full of attraction, has exercised an enormous influence over his fellow-countrymen; and what he sought to teach has become a vital part of the creed of the Russian Intelligence.

Leo Tolstoy, who was born in 1828 at Yásnaya Polyána, in the government of Tula, came of one of the noblest families in Russia. At the age of two he lost his mother; he was educated at first at home and from 1837 in Moscow. In this year his father died. Of his home training in the hands of foreign governesses and tutors, he gives a picture in his "Childhood" and "Boyhood." At fifteen he entered the university of Kazán. His unfinished sketch "Youth" tells us that this part of his education was most superficial. He next established himself in his country house, paying occasional visits to Moscow and St. Petersburg, and later, visited the Caucasus, and published sketches of the life which he saw there. He entered the army, and fought on the Black River against the French and Piedmontese, and in the repulse of a general attack on Sevastópol. His "Tales of Sevastópol" were the record of these experiences. In 1855 he left the army, and in 1861, always continuing to write, settled himself in the country, where he himself taught in a national school which he had founded. In 1862 he married the daughter of a Moscow doctor. The first period of his life, marked in its earlier years by restlessness and even by dissipation, was now over; and in the next period he published his two great books, "War and Peace" and "Anna Karyénina," which, with "The Death of Ivan Ilyích," won for him a leading position amongst Russian writers. But even in these works, the instincts of the preacher show signs of later prevailing over those of the artist. He set himself to write little books for popular reading, and Turghényeff, in his last letter, which he sent from his death-bed, wrote, " My friend, return to literary activity. All this gift of yours comes from that source whence comes everything else. Ah, how happy should I be, if I might think that my request will weigh with you. My friend, great writer of Russia, hear my request." But Tolstoy went farther and farther upon his new path. A man with so many of the instincts of the great artist could hardly have sunk them entirely in the preacher; but Tolstoy was more and more dominated by the desire to propagate a particular creed. This creed, which some trace in part to a peasant sect known as the Sytáyevtsy, was found by Tolstoy only late in life, and suggests more than anything else an extreme revulsion from a flighty and unsatisfactory youth. In his mode of life he is singularly sincere to his later ideals, dressing and eating as a peasant. There can be no question that Tolstoy has been a great benefactor of his peasants; but it cannot for a moment be admitted that he has made himself one of them, even though he puts in the forefront of the national needs those claims which are most commonly on their lips. Such evidence as one can obtain suggests that to the peasants Tolstoy is unintelligible. If he has not succeeded in making himself a peasant, he has at any rate dropped out of all harmony with the Intelligence of Russia. In the last twenty years, the Intelligence has tended to substitute reform for revolution, and practical compromise for the realisation of ill-digested ideals. With such a movement Tolstoy would not be likely to have any sympathy. Russians nearly always distinguish between the works of his prime and those of his old age; in the latter they take but little pleasure. " The Kreutzer Sonata " seemed to most of them simply unpleasant. " Resurrection " certainly attracted far more than a passing interest, and round the hoary head of this great champion of idealism hangs a double halo, the memory of the great artist of his prime and the dignity of a man who lives as he writes. Further, Tolstoy has a political importance as the one man whom the Government has never dared to touch, that is, the one man who could speak freely. When he was excommunicated by the Synod of his Church, such a sympathy was aroused as made the blow recoil upon the attacker. But, while the great wave of liberation has been rising all over Russia, Tolstoy has stood apart muttering formulæ of an out-of-season creed, which represents hardly anyone except Tolstoy and not the best of him.

If we examine more nearly the strangely mixed impression which Tolstoy leaves on most of his readers, we shall probably blame him not for being a preacher as well as an artist, but for quite failing to control and master the combination of the two instincts. He seems, in fact, to be run away with by himself, and it is precisely in this want of mastery that he is also as a writer inferior to Turghényeff. Not possessing that sure touch which will tell him at once what he wants to mention, he will go wandering around the furniture of a whole room, in a way that is German rather than Russian, calling the reader's attention to detail after detail that has no importance in his story. Perhaps this may be meant for a scientific study, but it comes out as bad art.[1] There is a question of method, upon which one may surely make bold to pronounce an absolute preference. "Ha! snows a little," writes Jane Austin when she wishes to tell us how comfortable the sleek Mr. Elton felt in Mr. Woodhouse's carriage, with the prospect of a good dinner in the company of the lady whom he intended to marry. But Tolstoy's method will be rather "No! he said, thinking that it would be very pleasant if," etc., etc. The unexplained picture is however far the more convincing. Then, too, in Tolstoy one seldom gets away from the undercurrent of the sneer. Horace can write of the most unpleasant subjects, and yet his presentation will be pleasing; but when Tolstoy makes a man come into a room and notice a " strong smell of woman," one thinks of him as exactly the reverse. Besides this, even in the works of his prime, there are sentences on sentences which are either superfluous or at least out of season. Why spend pages to prove that there were no dominating causes of the war of 1812, except that every French soldier wanted war, when we know from the best historians that France, and even the army, were sick to death of war? Or why demonstrate at length that there is no such

---

[1] I may, perhaps, justify myself for making this criticism by explaining that I learnt Russian very largely from the writings of Turghényeff and Tolstoy, and had to go at such a slow pace as to spend far more time than the average reader in puzzling out the possible inferences of each sentence.

thing as military genius, in a book in which you have described the battle of Austerlitz—the best modern example of the way in which one man's genius can make up for a deficiency of forces? Why argue at length that Moscow was burnt by chance and not by design, when we know that Count Rostopchin, the Governor, took all the fire-pumps away with him? This ardour for levelling down all that seems too noble is a kind of moral Nihilism. I should not stop to make these criticisms but that we all have to recognise that Tolstoy is a writer of genius. The canvas of "War and Peace" is one that no lesser man could have dared to paint on. In this great book there is as much of history as in Zola's "Débâcle," but incomparably more art. Tolstoy could put the great main issues before us. Take, for instance, the broad intuition shown in these sentences:—"The Englishman is self-confident because he is well aware that he is a member of the best-ordered State in the world, and that whatsoever he does as an Englishman will be well done. . . . The Russian is self-confident because he knows nothing whatsoever about the matter in hand and does not want to." I take an instance at hazard, but there we have nearly all the psychology of the great struggle which these two nations waged in their different ways against Napoleon.

"Anna Karyénina" is, I think, an even greater work. Not only Anna, but even the most subordinate persons of the story are real to the life. So broad and full a sketch of a whole society is in itself a wonder. The same directness and simplicity run through "Resurrection." To an Englishman perhaps more than to anyone else the story will be astounding, but for all that it never fails to be convincing. If Russia was to be morally divided by so great a distance from the west of Europe, she at least had the greatest of good fortune in finding such an interpreter.

Chekhoff, who has been called "the poet of the twilight," was the best literary representative of the present-day Russian Intelligence. He has the general characteristics which I have claimed for Russian literature, and he is undoubtedly a great artist. Each of his short stories works out a single idea which is well worth working out. I take, for instance, the story of an old doctor with literary tastes who, although he is quite free from self-consciousness, cannot help feeling his isolation and superiority in the stunted society of a provincial town. He finds one man worthy of his friendship, a poor monomaniac in a hospital. Those who grudge him his superiority use this fact to gradually edge him out of his post, and the narrative of the process is in the highest degree natural. In the end he is sent to join his friend in the hospital, and the two die together.

Gorky, not merely a champion but almost a member of the class which he pourtrays, has rendered a great service in making real to us that floating population which has sprung out of the emancipation and the development of industry, and for which the Government has as yet found no place in its system. As a record, his work is likely to stand; but it has its own kind of exaggeration, which consists in the idealising of the "disinherited." He wrote at the top of a European wave of more or less unintelligent pity; and the interest which will be felt in his works later on is likely, I think, to be more special than some at present suppose.

We may here venture on an analysis of the lives of the writers whom I have mentioned as representative of Russian literature. Most of them have in them an instinct of religion; in Derzhávin, Gógol, and Dostoyévsky this instinct is unusually strong. Practically all are, in the larger sense, deeply patriotic, and indeed this patriotic tinge separates even the Russian revolutionaries from their fellow-thinkers in other countries. Far the greater part of them come from Great Russia. The north is represented by Lomonósoff; the north centre by Kryloff and Nekrásoff; Moscow by Griboyédoff, Pushkin, Lérmontoff, and Dostoyévsky; the south centre by Zhukóvsky, Grigoróvich, Turghényeff and Tolstoy; the Volga by Derzhávin, Karamzín, and Goncharóff. None of them were born in St. Petersburg. The one notable representative of Little Russia is Gógol. In the matter of class there is a tolerably distinct line between the aristocrats, such as Tolstoy, Griboyédoff, Pushkin, Lérmontoff, and Turghényeff, and the middle class, such as Kryloff, Nekrásoff, Dostoyévsky, and Koltsoff. More than we should expect were partly of foreign parentage, such as Von Wisin (German), Zhukóvsky (Turkish), Pushkin (Negro), Grigoróvich (French), and Nekrásoff (Polish). Most were originally educated by travelling French tutors; few had the advantage of any good schooling; many were members of Moscow University. Several, such as Zhukóvsky, Gógol, and Turghényeff, spent a considerable part of their lives abroad. Most, at one time or another, held some official post—Nekrásoff being the most notable exception. Most of them grew up in unhappy homes, such as Lérmontoff, Koltsoff, Turghényeff, and Nekrásoff. Some lived in great luxury, some lived in great straits; two, at least, Turghényeff and Dostoyévsky, deliberately chose the latter. Most of them were persecuted. Pushkin cursed himself for being born with wit in Russia; Griboyédoff's great work is called "The Mischief of being Clever"; Lérmontoff was exiled; Turghényeff, though he lived mostly abroad, was arrested and subjected to many vexations; Dostoyévsky was a convict; Tolstoy was excommunicated. Several, on the other hand, and notably the earlier writers, owed all their worldly fortune to the patronage of the Court, which was often called in to save them from the irritations of the officials. Lastly, whereas most of them were strong Westernisers, practically all were profoundly Slavophil.

I must add that literary taste in Russia is of a very high standard, that one will find Shakespeare, and also Herbert Spencer, in almost as many houses in Russia as in England, that the best of current foreign literature is promptly translated and made accessible almost everywhere, that a Russian guide-book to Russia is a more serious undertaking than what would suffice in our country, and that many Russians, thank Heaven! have practically no small talk.

CHAPTER VIII.

THE PRESS AND THE CENSORSHIP.

PETER the Great, who found one printing press in Moscow at his accession, established a second there, four in St. Petersburg, and others in the provinces. He founded the first Russian newspaper, the *St. Petersburg Gazette*, himself at first correcting many of the articles. Catherine the Great, who was herself an authoress, was the patron of Nóvikoff. This remarkable man, who was an indefatigable worker, raised the *Moscow Gazette* to a circulation of 4,000, which was altogether exceptional for this time. He also made improvements in printing, and published a whole series of reviews and magazines, not only for the best reading public, which was exceedingly small, but for the home-side, for the young, and for the almost illiterate. He also founded literary societies and established book-shops.

It is from the French Revolution that we must date the organisation of the Russian Censorship. In the seventeenth century, it is true, the Patriarchs anathematised several books which were published by erudite Little Russians in Kieff. Elizabeth ordered the correction of all books printed under the Empress Anne, and excluded from sale those which mentioned the names of high officials. Books imported from abroad were submitted to the judgment of the Synod, which decided whether they contained anything contrary to the faith. No regular censorship was as yet required, because the reading public was limited to the higher class, and there was as yet hardly any literature but that of panegyrics. After the French Constitution of 1791 things were very different. Catherine suddenly arrested Nóvikoff, imprisoned him in the fortress of Schlüsselburg, and put an end to all his enterprises.[1]

---

[1] For most of the details of the story of the Press and of the censorship I am indebted to N. Engelhardt's " Sketch of the History of the Russian Censorship in connection with the Development of the Press, 1703—1903 " (St. Petersburg, 1904).

In May, 1792, Prince Prozórovsky had written to ask the Empress "to take measures to prevent the delivery of books, especially from disturbed France, which serve only to lead astray and pervert people who have no foundation in the principles of honour." A decree of 1796 founded censorships in St. Petersburg, Moscow, Riga, and Odessa, and on the Austrian frontier. Each was to consist of one ecclesiastic and two laymen. Every book printed in Russia was to be submitted to one of the censorships of the capitals. The censor of Riga, Tumánsky,[1] saw danger in Swift, Goethe, Schiller, Kant, and Klopstock, and confiscated 552 out of 639 books between 1797 and 1799. In 1798 the censorship was further extended; the decree announces that "the Government now existing in France, wishing to spread its godless principles to all well-ordered States, seeks to pervert their orderly inhabitants by compositions full of pernicious ingenuities. . . . Many journalists depart from the straight line of their duty and, under French inspiration or from their own evil disposition, seek to imitate these writings." But this decree was not fully carried out, because it was difficult to find enough censors. In 1800, all foreign books were excluded from Russia. Tumánsky sent to the Emperor a long list of the "Jacobins of Riga," headed by the name of the worthy Governor-General. Alexander I. simply remarked that Tumánsky must have "gone off his head," and pensioned him off. In 1804, an Imperial decree established a more regular censorship. However, this statute, which is short, shows traces of the liberalism of the early years of Alexander I. The censor is to mark any passages which run counter to religion, the Government, morality, or the personal honour of private individuals, and to return these passages to the author himself for correction. When a censor has a doubt as to the meaning of a passage, he is to give the benefit of the doubt to the author; writings once passed by the censorship need not again be submitted to it at the time of reprinting; the censorship is not to detain articles till they lose the value of novelty; if a writer sends to the censorship a writing which plainly denies the existence of God, insults the Imperial power, etc., he can be prosecuted at law. This statute was retained till 1826, but it would be a great mistake to regard it as practically the law of the land.

---

[1] His name means in Russian "The Foggy One."

Though the censors of 1804 would have been far from making any such admission, they found that in practice the only effective censorship was that which adapted itself to the times, day by day, and dealt with questions as they came up, without tying itself to hard and fast rules. The force to be combated—what I have described as the "Intelligence"—had its strongest foothold in the higher or governmental class, and sometimes the Government itself might be swayed by liberalism. At such a moment the rules might be relaxed. At the same time the censorship was the watchdog of authority; if an emperor could allow himself to be liberal it did not follow that an official could do the same.

Thus the censorship, as specially entrusted with a repressive authority, would meet those dangers which it saw or imagined, not by reference to any statute, but by a series of special regulations, which in Russia have the name of circulars. In 1802, for instance, a panegyric of Napoleon was sanctioned and printed; in 1807 (the year of the battle of Friedland) the censorship condemned the writer as a "base worshipper of usurpers." In the same year Russia made an alliance with France at Tilsit, and those who publicly blamed Napoleon were persecuted. In 1812 Napoleon was again officially declared the usurper and the Antichrist. The main enemy was, of course, revolution, and in 1818 the censors were ordered to "look more closely into it that passages in books already printed, which contain thoughts and tendencies contrary to the Christian religion, manifesting free-thought, godlessness, infidelity, impiety, or the self-will of revolutionary licence or dreamy philosophising, or, again, the besmirching of the dogmas of our Orthodox Church, should be strictly forbidden to be reprinted." Thus practically all existing literature was again referred to the censorship, because of the special fears of the particular time. I may notice as curiosities a circular forbidding to print anything against the Old Believers, "because the Government has already taken suitable measures for putting them on the right path," and an instruction that books omitting the useless final letter (the hard mark) which concludes so many Russian words "should not be allowed to depart in this way from the general rules of the language."

During the reign of Alexander I. the Russian Press attained a more considerable measure of development. Amongst the current literature of St. Petersburg were the *Northern Post*, the *St. Petersburg Messenger*, and the *Northern Messenger*. Amongst that of Moscow were the *Messenger of Europe*, edited by Karamzín, and the *Russian Messenger* of S. Glinka, who "did everything to over-excite the national sentiment . . . . by making it distrust every intellectual or moral influence which came from outside, and above all, the imitation of French manners."[1] This publication ceased at the end of the struggle with Napoleon; but its work was continued by the *Son of the Fatherland*, whose editor was Grech. It must be understood that the vast distances and the thinness of population in Russia practically confined journalistic enterprise to St. Petersburg and Moscow. Even the Moscow journalists were hampered, in comparison with those of St. Petersburg, because it took them longer to guess in which direction the wind of the moment was blowing. Thus in 1834 Polevóy, who had séverely reviewed a patriotic play, found, on his arrival in St. Petersburg, that it had pleased the upper society. "What are you doing?" said his protector, the Administrator of Police; " you see how they take the play here ; you will have to agree with this opinion, or else you will get yourself into terrible trouble." A special feature of early Russian journalism was the predominance of the magazine or review as opposed to the newspaper. News, as one may imagine, was at a discount with the Government; and it was far easier to supply one's country subscribers, once a month or once a fortnight, with a thick volume containing readable articles on every interest of the family circle.

Such was the character of the long journalistic activity of the Pole, Bulgárin. He was dismissed from the army in 1811, reached the rank of captain in the service of Napoleon, and served in Spain. "In excuse," he says, "I have nothing to offer except my Polish birth and my inexperience ; however, I always retained my brotherly love for Russia and did not take part in the war of 1812." After the break-up of Napoleon's empire he returned to Warsaw, and later settled in St. Petersburg. In 1819 this plausible person asked leave to establish a paper for Polish ladies ; "if one wishes to spread the principles of morality and religion, one must begin with the training of women; only by a pleasant path, strewed with flowers, can we lead the fair sex, who

[1] Rambaud, p. 631.

are always so sensitive and so quick-witted, to the temple of virtue." The request was refused because none of the censors knew Polish. In 1822 he was allowed to establish the *Northern Archives*; in 1824 he joined hands with Grech, and in 1825 founded the *Northern Bee*. For thirty years Bulgárin with his *Bee* and Grech with his *Son* were the principal purveyors of light literature in Russia. Bulgárin, who was an intimate friend of Griboyédoff, was able to keep in close touch with many of the best Russian writers. From the Emperor Nicholas he secured a special testimonial: "His Majesty the Emperor," writes Count Benckendorff, "condescended to say that your labours and zeal for the public good are exceedingly pleasing to His Majesty, and that His Majesty, being convinced of your loyalty to his person, is always disposed to extend to you his gracious protection." But Bulgárin's chief asset was his remarkable ability in gauging his public. In a memorandum on the censorship in Russia which he sends to an official friend, he writes: "The majority of voices or of judgments makes up public opinion. . . . Most people, through mental laziness, their engagements, lack of information, weakness of character, innate pliability of mind, or irritability of feelings, are far more fitted to accept and assimilate someone else's opinion than to form their own. . . . As public opinion cannot be annihilated, it is far better that the Government should take upon itself the duty of directing it by means of the Press. . . . To rule public opinion we must know its elements. . . . The first element consists of persons of rank and wealth; most of these, say nineteen-twentieths, have had the most superficial education, and have not that knowledge which can be got even in the ordinary preparatory schools of Germany. They have been brought up by French tutors, and enter the world with no idea of men or things and with absolutely no knowledge of Russia; they look at everything with French eyes and judge everything in the French manner. They take for the height of learning the principles of the French encyclopædists, which they call philosophy." Next comes the middle class, consisting, according to Bulgárin, of well-to-do gentry in the Government service or on country estates, of poorer gentry who have passed through Crown institutions, of officials, rich merchants, and even tradesmen. This is the so-called Russian public. It reads a great deal, and mostly in Russian. The Throne might win not merely its love but its adoration, by offering the shadow of freedom of thought. " Complete silence," he writes, " produces distrust and compels people to think that you are weak. Unlimited publicity produces self-will. . . . But when you have made a public opinion, you can easily direct it as your own property." " The lower class has not yet attracted attention, but it reads very much. Several times peasants and street pedlars have come to me to ask that I should sell them or give them a number of our magazine ; the magic rod by which you can guide at will the lower class is 'Mother Russia.'" In 1831 he writes: "Whenever His Majesty the Emperor may be pleased to use my pen for political articles, I will try accurately and zealously to execute His Majesty's will."

We can imagine how Bulgárin would deal with each question of the day. When Gógol's comedy "The Revising Inspector" seriously attacked the evils of officialdom, Bulgárin wrote : " Such cynicism we never saw on the Russian stage or in Russian literature. . . . A decent lackey of to-day will not say, ' The soup stinks,' but ' The soup smells nasty ' ; not a single writer with taste will say, 'He picked his teeth with his finger.'" As Engelhardt observes, " Bulgárin does not notice that he here couples a writer of taste and a decent lackey." Bulgárin was undoubtedly both. But even he had sometimes to be reminded of his servitude. In 1848 a writer in the *Northern Bee*, having attended a concert at Pavlosk, writes that the cabmen, though their fare had been regulated, refused to drive women and children in pouring rain, until they had extorted more. The censorship complains that the question has been " handed over for the common judgment of the public " and, whilst acknowledging that " the paper concerned is generally conspicuous by the goodness of its intentions, and by a tendency which completely answers to the aims and views of the Government," makes it clear that " in future there must not be allowed even the most indirect animadversion on the acts and dispositions of the Government or of the established powers, to whatever rank these last belong."

In 1830, Bulgárin, Grech, and their opponent Voyéikoff were arrested for continuing a controversy on a historical novel after the Emperor had told them to stop. It was in this year that there appeared in St. Petersburg the *Literary Gazette*. It enjoyed the co-operation of Pushkin, Zhukóvsky, and Prince Vyázemsky, who represented the aristocratic school of literature as opposed to the plebeian. The paper, according to Pogódin, had hardly one hundred subscribers, and in 1830 it was stopped for printing a translation of four lines of Casimir Delavigne, inscribed on the monument raised in Paris to those who fell for the revolution of July in that year. The year 1830 is known in Russian literature as "the year of cholera": it was fatal to some of the most important of Moscow papers, including the *Messenger of Europe* and the *Moscow Messenger* of Pogódin; this last died for lack of subscribers. Polevóy's *Moscow Telegraph* was forbidden in 1834 for the reason already given. Polevóy had irritated the aristocrats by an attack on the History of Karamzín; and Zhukóvsky wrote: "I am glad that the *Telegraph* is stopped, though I am sorry that they stopped it; the *Telegraph* was worthy of its fate. . . . Polevóy was the pet of the police." This only means that Polevóy was protected by the Chief of the Police, Count Benckendorff, against the extreme hostility·of the Minister of Public Instruction, Uvároff. "The Police," he wrote, "behaves to me as if it were the Minister of Public Instruction, and the Minister of Public Instruction as if he were the Police." Uvároff actually sent to the censorship an order to forbid the printing of anything whatsoever which was written by Polevóy, and for some years this brilliant and capable editor was cut off from his livelihood without hope of redress. No better fate attended the *Moscow Telescope,* founded by Professor Nadyézhdin, one of the best known critics of the old *Messenger of Europe*. He associated with him the young Byélinsky, who was reported to have been expelled from Moscow University, and who was destined to be one of the greatest figures in Russian journalism. In 1835, Nadyézhdin went abroad and Byélinsky turned the paper into a critical review of very high merit; but in 1836 Nadyézhdin, who had returned, finding it impossible to keep up the circulation, tried a desperate remedy: he printed a "philosophic letter" from the pen of Chayadáyeff, which would be sure either to attract the attention of the public or to end in the closure of the paper. It did both. This is accounted to be the first instance of " heroic suicide " in Russian journalism.

In 1832, Kireyevsky persuaded the best writers of the day to help him with his new paper the *European*. Pogódin had soon to write : " The *European* . . . has only fifty subscribers ; there is a new strange proof for you. What will happen next ? " The leading article of the first number was written by the editor and entitled " The Nineteenth Century." Benckendorff writes to the Minister of Public Instruction that this article is " nothing else than a discussion of higher politics," though at the outset the writer declares that he is talking not about politics, but about literature. " But we have only to be attentive to see that the writer when he pretends to be reasoning about ' literature ' means something altogether different, that by the word ' instruction ' he understands ' freedom,' that ' activity of the reason ' with him means ' revolution,' and that an ' artificially elaborated middle term ' is nothing else than a ' Constitution.' The editor, Ivan Kireyevsky, has proved himself to be a man of evil intentions and of evil character." The *European* was forbidden, and Russian society felt itself offended ; but the only man who dared to express himself was Zhukóvsky ; and when he told the Emperor Nicholas that he would go bail for Kireyevsky, the Emperor's answer was, " And who will go bail for you ? "

A well-known bookseller of St. Petersburg, Smirdin, who seems to have lent or given money to different literary men, gathered a great house-warming party at which most of the best known men of letters were present. Each guest, on the proposal of Zhukóvsky, gave one of his own productions to be published in an almanack called *The House-warming*. Very soon (January 1st, 1834) there was issued instead the magazine called *The Reading Library*. This was to be the only serious competitor to Bulgárin and Grech ; but though the best writers had all been induced to give their names, they very soon found themselves dissatisfied with the enterprise. Their articles were corrected at will by the able editor, the Pole Senkovsky (Baron Brambeus). This man had a wonderful capacity for work, a mass of all-round information, and the talent of easy and clever expression ; he could expound such subjects as Semitic Philology or Greek dialects in such a way that " the reader would swallow without a frown an article of the most scientific kind."

Smirdin conceived another enterprise. Such a pen as Polevóy's might surely be put to some use, but it was before all things necessary that his name should not be bruited about. Smirdin therefore persuaded Bulgárin and Grech to accept Polevóy as a fellow-worker and, in fact, to leave to him the bulk of their work. Bulgárin, it will be remembered, enjoyed the special confidence of the Government, and, of course, the censors were well aware of the arrangement. Polevóy writes in 1837 : "I understood that I was not to show myself more than was necessary, not to strike the eye. My living, breathing, and working they do not hinder; what else do you expect?" But Uvároff, according to Bulgárin, said : "You don't know Polevóy; if he writes the Lord's Prayer there is sure to be something troublesome in it." Polevóy very soon discovered that though the papers entrusted to him still kept up a magnificent outlay, their circulation had fallen in the case of the *Bee* to 2,500 copies, and in that of the *Son of the Fatherland* to 279. There follow some nine years of furious work. In 1839 he writes : "I have been sitting up till two or three every night, though I always get up at six. . . . ; my head's going round "; in 1840 : "In all, I've written and corrected in this month more than seventy-five printer's sheets "; in 1841 : "I have been compelled to pawn my bear-skin coat for food ; what am I to do? Endure, pray, and work. There is only one way for me to stifle the oppression of my present almost intolerrable position, and that is work." Smirdin, who was in turn heavily in debt to Polevóy, was on the brink of ruin : "He has lost even the list of his debts." Polevóy describes how he could not go out because he had split his last pair of trousers. "Next year I shall be forty-six, and it is twenty-five years that I have been writing. . . . If I had sat for twenty-five years in a tobacconist's shop, perhaps I should not have had to die of hunger." In desperation he revived the *Russian Messenger* of Glinka ; this meant redoubled work, but brought no salvation. "Sometimes," he writes, "I am like a kind of writing machine, which is, so to speak, wound up by someone, and writes anything that you like, drama, novels, history, criticism. How my

health lasts I don't understand; how I filled six numbers
of the *Russian Messenger* for this year I don't know.   Not a
farthing for expenses."   The publication of the *Messenger*
aroused all animosities against the man who had been killed
once and still dared to wriggle.   The editor of two of the
best magazines in Russia, though he was working himself to
death, owed it to his play " Helen Glinsky " that he could buy
something to eat.   In 1844 the debtors' prison seemed to be
opening for him.   In February, 1846, he writes : " I fell down
on the sofa as if struck by lightning, and have since then been
without sleep and food, and have fallen into a kind of moral
and physical torpor.   My life, one might say, has become something between life and death."   On receiving this letter, his
brother hurried to St. Petersburg, but before he could arrive
Polevóy was dead.

The *Moscow Observer* was issued by Andrósoff in 1835.
It passed into the hands of Shevyreff and Pogódin, but not
succeeding under their editorship, it became the property of
Byélinsky.   Ardent and sincere, "capable of loving and hating
disinterestedly,"[1] Byélinsky was at the same time possessed of
the surest critical instinct.   Many of his contemporaries feared
him as a kind of "bull-dog," under which pseudonym, indeed,
he sometimes wrote.   But he was the first real interpreter
of the great Russian writers, and his brilliant essays on them
were for a long time the most serious study of their kind.   He
despised the work of Bulgárin, and considered that Russian
literature, as an organ of the national consciousness, did not yet
exist.   He himself would in no way truckle to the tastes of his
time, and that is why he was able to do more than anyone else
to create a real reading public.   With him and the group of
able men that he gathered round him, the favourite interests
were the art of the great modern classics, such as Shakespeare
and Goethe, and the German philosophy of Hegel.   Byélinsky,
according to Hertzen, was a kind of new Peter the Great.
" The young philosophers," says the latter, " had a conventional
tongue of their own; they did not translate into Russian, but
transposed wholesale, even, to save trouble, leaving all Latin
words as they were and giving them Russian terminations and

---

[1] Turghényeff : Literary Reminiscences, p. 23.

the seven Russian cases." He adds that "the Russian scholars of Hegel, strong, sanguine youths like their master, entered a kind of monastery of metaphysics, . . . though they were always talking of 'reality.'" Financially Byélinsky's Moscow paper met with little success, and in 1839 he agreed to help Krayévsky in the *Notes of the Fatherland,* and left Moscow for St. Petersburg. Here he modified many of his earlier views and his German enthusiasms made way for French influences; he now took his political models not from Prussia, but from America, England and France. His brilliant critical articles helped to bring *Notes of the Fatherland* into competition with the *Reading Library* and the *Northern Bee,* but he credited his colleague "with neither mind, nor talent, nor conviction, nor knowledge, nor education." In 1846, to the surprise of everyone, he became the collaborator of a far less experienced journalist, the comparatively unknown Nekrásoff. But Byélinsky, who had suffered as many disappointments as other Russian writers, was already fast sinking into consumption. He died in 1848.

In Moscow, meanwhile, Pogódin and Shevyreff, with the help of Zhukóvsky, started the *Muscovite* (or *Moskvityánin*) (1841). This paper ought to have satisfied the Government; it opposed Byélinsky and his Westernisers and was strongly Slavophil. "The West and Russia," said the first leading article, "stand face to face; will the West carry us away in its universal aspirations, or shall we stand firm in our moral independence? Shall we form a world of our own, on our own principles and not on those of Europe? . . . In our sincere, friendly, and close relations with the West we fail to see that we have to do, as it were, with a human being who carries in him an active and infectious disease. . . . We do not feel, in the pleasure of the feast, the mortality of which he already reeks." There follows the exposition of the creed of the Slavophil: "On the other hand, we have kept pure in ourselves three fundamental instincts, in which is the seed and pledge of our future development. We have preserved our ancient instinct of religion. . . . The second instinct which makes the strength of Russia . . . is the native sense of her moral unity. . . . Our third fundamental instinct is the consciousness of our nationality; . . . against this instinct dash themselves in vain all the efforts of our fellow-countrymen to graft on us that which will not suit the Russian mind and the Russian heart." Prince Vyázemsky wrote to Shevyreff: "Go on, and we (the Slavophils) shall at last have a paper; only, for God's sake, be careful, diligent, acute, and intuitive. . . . A journalist must have unusually fine tact. In this respect, it is very hard to edit a newspaper in Moscow ; you, over there, guide yourselves by good sense and conscience, and think that that is enough. Not a bit of it ; there are a thousand other indispensable conditions." Pogódin, to cater for all tastes, printed amusing anecdotes, and, in view of the number of officials in Russia, it was not surprising that sooner or later two of the anecdotes had reference to this class. At once Benckendorff writes to Uvároff: "Articles of this kind show a want of respect for the educated public on the part of the editor, and a desire to please the most corrupt class of people. Besides this, such anecdotes show in the editor not only bad taste, but also misuse of the confidence with which the Government has invested him as a journalist. . . . These, in my opinion, are more than reasons enough that Mr. Pogódin should be forbidden to edit the *Moskvityánin.*" Uvároff wrote to Pogódin : " This time I can stop all this noise ; for the future I do not answer." In 1850 a number of gifted writers became collaborators of Pogódin. He paid ridiculously little, sometimes nothing ; they lived " on locusts and wild honey." One of them wrote : " A copy of your paper will serve me as fee, because I need no pay in money." For all that, this Slavophil paper which suffered special persecution from the censorship, also quite failed to secure the support of the public. " You see yourself," wrote Pogódin in 1851, " that it improves as a paper; everyone praises it, but that means nothing," The circulation went down until the editor had to write in his note-book : " A message from the office that there are only seven subscribers ; I have lost heart."

Pushkin in 1836, a year before his death, received permission to bring out the *Contemporary ;* afterwards it was continued by Zhukóvsky, Pletneff, and other friends for the profit of Pushkin's family. It had no more than five hundred subscribers. The young Nekrásoff, largely by the art of making friends and conducting business, made himself in 1847 the editor of the *Contemporary.* Amongst his contributors were Byélinsky, Hertzen, Goncharóff, Turghényeff, Grigoróvich, and Dostoyévsky.

The times had changed: the labours of Polevóy, Vyázemsky, and, above all, Byélinsky, had at last created a serious reading public; and Nekrásoff's *Contemporary* enjoyed a great success.

Looking back over the pre-reform period, we must acknowledge the general correctness of Bulgárin's estimate of the reading public. There were but few magazines; most of them had short lives and a very meagre circulation. Engelhardt gives the following figures for the year 1843: the *Reading Library* of Senkovsky, some 3,000 subscribers; the *Northern Bee* of Bulgárin, some 3,000; the *Notes of the Fatherland* of Krayévsky, and, what is more to the point, of Byélinsky, some 3,000; the *Son of the Fatherland* and the *Russian Messenger* (of Polevóy), the *Moskvity-ánin* (of Pogódin), the *Contemporary* (of Pletneff), the *St. Petersburg Gazette* and the *Moscow Gazette* some 500 subscribers each and altogether 13,000. This gives us 12,000 subscribers for all the chief magazines in Russia. The three greatest of the nine named above, and three of the others, belonged to St. Petersburg, the rest to Moscow. Journalistic failures were due quite as much to the indifference of the public as to the persecutions of the censorship; in fact, it was precisely because the public was indifferent that the censorship was free to do as it pleased. Naturally the censorship felt more free to prohibit those magazines which had hardly any subscribers, while the reader, on the other hand, liked Bulgárin's *Bee* just because it was never prohibited and arrived regularly. From this we pass to another obvious conclusion. The censorship was in this period altogether premature in its apprehensions. One cannot help feeling throughout the whole story that it was a steam-hammer employed to crush a fly.

Magnítsky, one of the most ridiculous of the censors, has already come before us. Bulgárin describes his successors as worse; and, as time goes on, the oppression becomes even more intolerable. In 1815, old Admiral Shishkoff, a relic of the days of the great Catherine, presented a memorandum in which he described the censorship as " utterly insufficient." " The language in the books that are published," he says, " becomes more improper and more impudent from hour to hour. . . . The word, adorned in motley by the cunning of the mind, is more poisonous and dangerous than the snake which seduced our first parents. Under different aspects, now entertaining with sweet sentiments, now with the wit of jests, now with the assumed importance of wisdom, now with secrecy of thought, and sometimes by its very obscurity and senselessness, it fascinates and blinds inexperienced minds." When the memorandum was read to the Imperial Council, some members were dumbfounded and others laughed. In 1822, Shishkoff came forward with a second memorandum. "Infidelity of thought and freedom of mind have infected all our schools; there, under the pretext of a new manner of thinking, has been preached contempt of all that is holy, of the language, of the Government, of the laws, of morality, and even of the faith itself. . . . We have known for a long time that German professors try to obscure the clearness of science, mixing up with it unintelligible principles expounded in incomprehensible words and thoughts, in order that, under the guise of deep and secret wisdom, they may inspire in their scholars a high opinion of the value of their teaching, and may continue a little longer to receive the payment for their lessons. . . . The surest preventive is a censorship intelligently and studiously observant of its duties." In 1824, Shishkoff was named Minister of Public Instruction, and asked leave to send in a sketch of the best means of "quietly and decently stifling that evil which, though it is not called Carbonarism with us, is the same thing." He stopped the work of the Bible societies and the translation of the Scriptures into the vulgar tongue; the Hebrews seem to have been as bad as the Germans. It is of little consolation to us to know that Shishkoff was honest; if he had not been so, he would have been far less dangerous. In 1826 his new statute of the Censorship was confirmed by the Emperor.

This statute contains two hundred and thirty clauses, as against the forty-seven of that of 1804. The authors (for Prince Shirínsky-Shikhmátoff was associated with Shishkoff in the work) claim that there are too few censors to cope with the mass of published books. Their object is "to make printing harmless," and also to direct public opinion "conformably with the existing political views and circumstances of the Government." "The right of publishing a newspaper can be entrusted only to a man of good character, well known in the field of national literature, who has shown by his writings that his way of thinking and his intentions are good. . . . But the Minister may prohibit any current publication; and the editor or editors, who have once been subjected to prohibition, are for all time deprived of the right of editing, whether alone or in company with others" (sections 129, 137 and 138). "Articles which concern a Government institution may not be printed without the agreement of that Ministry under whose jurisdiction are the matters therein discussed" (section 141). It will be seen that by this article a whole number of censorships were established; and, indeed, a censor, Nikityenko, declares that at one time there were more censorships than books published in the year. "Passages in compositions and translations which have a double sense must not be sanctioned, if one of these meanings is contrary to the rules of the censorship." "Writers and translators[1] are forbidden in their productions to mark whole spaces with dots or other marks, put there, as it were, for the purpose of making the reader guess for himself the content of the omitted statement" (sections 150, 151). ". . . History may not include arbitrary fancies which do not belong to the story. . . . Except the handbooks of logic and philosophy necessary for the young, all other compositions of this kind, filled with the unprofitable and ruinous inferences of modern times, must not be printed at all." The most extraordinary article is perhaps the 213th. "As the statute of the Censorship must not be unknown to any of the writers or artists who issue their productions," the responsibility for the content of their printed works is not ended by the fact that they have been printed with the consent of the Censor, for "far more guilty is he who, free to attend only to his own composition, thinks out in the stillness of his study something harmful to the safety and morals of society, and afterwards publishes it, than the censor who has looked through the composition, amongst several others, in the course of his work." Thus the rise of any favourite to power might make a book of ten years back become guilty.

This statute was found, like that of 1804, to be no permanent bulwark. In 1828 it was completely remodelled, and Shishkoff resigned his post. The Government returned to the old system of circulars.

Here is a typical circular of November 3rd, 1852. Writers are

---

[1] We notice that foreign books are constantly in the minds of the authors.

told "(1) to narrate events simply, avoiding, as far as possible, drawing any conclusions ; (2) sometimes to accompany the news with expressions of approval, sympathy, indignation or mockery, in the way in which this is sometimes done by the *Northern Bee ;* a single suitable word at once imparts a special meaning and significance to the news which has been given ; (3) to make only the slightest allusion, if any, to the representative assemblies of second-class European States, or to their Constitutions, elections, projects of law, and deputies ; (4) to avoid speaking of the will of the nation, or the demands and needs of the working classes." Now that every Government institution had its own censorship, it was necessary for an encyclopædia to be sent for examination to some twenty or thirty different jurisdictions ; and the claims of any jurisdiction might lead to a circular. Thus " all journalistic articles which in any way touch on the theatres must before printing be communicated to the Director of Theatres for pre-liminary examination " (1845). " All articles on the building of St. Isaac's Cathedral . . . must be first handed in for examina-tion to the Commission for the building of this cathedral " (1847). Other circulars run thus : " Opinions of the Committee of Foreign Censorship on whether the translation of novels and tales into the Russian tongue may be allowed are only an auxiliary sugges-tion, and cannot be a decisive and obligatory instruction to the Internal Censorship, which must not feel in the least bound by these opinions. . . . It is itself in a better position to judge by its own experience what kind of impression can be produced on Russian readers by the perusal of foreign novels " (1851). " Requests for leave to found new periodicals are for a time forbidden " (1836). " All articles for or against universities are absolutely forbidden " (1848-1849). " Most strictly are forbidden, in whatever language they appear, criticisms, however well intended they may be, on foreign books and compositions which have been forbidden and therefore ought not to be known." In 1850 metaphysics and moral philosophy were withdrawn from the programme of the universities, the latter " because it was practically useless to young people acquainted with the principles of Christianity." The chairs of philosophy and divinity were united. In 1853 the Slavophils came in for punishment because, " being clearly ill disposed to the present order of things, in the error of their thoughts they unceasingly wish to throw back our country to the times of the apostolic Prince Vladímir." And though, to some of them, "suggestions have already been made, this has had no effect on them; even since these suggestions, they impudently bring forward for printing articles which reveal their open opposition to the Government. . . ." It is decided "to submit all these persons, as openly ill disposed, not to secret but to public police inspection." And these were the opponents of the Westernisers, the only men who could see any reason for the repressive measures of the Government. Really it seems that these censors definitely wished to have the nation against them, and we cannot help recalling the fable of Kryloff called "Parnassus." The asses finding themselves allowed to graze on Parnassus, conclude that they are the legitimate successors of the Muses:

> "'They want no Muses now, it's clear;
>   It's us they chose to sing up here:
> Why then, come on' says one, 'my brothers, don't lose heart;
> 'I'll strike you up a tune, and each shall take his part.
>   Now, don't be shy, 'twould be absurd;
>   We'll chant the glories of our herd;
>   Louder, ay louder, than the sisters nine
> We'll form the asses' choir and raise our hymn divine.
> And if some headstrong ass the bounds of asshood passes,
> We'll keep this golden rule, which ass-like I may
> Whoever has a voice that fails to please us asses,
>   We won't allow him here at all.'"

Thus the Western light and the Eastern light, as they were called in Russia, were extinguished almost together, which means that Russia was left in darkness.

In 1840, anatomical and physiological books were forbidden to include anything "which might hurt the instinct of decency."

In 1848, newspapers were forbidden to publicly commend inventions until they had been investigated according to the rules of science (we are not told by whom), and pronounced to be thoroughly sound.

In 1857 were forbidden "repetitions of those utopias which have been preached at the Peace Congresses of Paris, in 1849, and of Frankfort, in 1850." The Censors feared that minds might be perverted by "the harmful and false teaching of the so-called peace conferences."[1]

---

[1] Officials seem fond of this lazy way of questioning accepted terms; we are reminded of Pobyedonóstseff's phrase "the so-called Press."

In 1851 the Censorship imagined that musical notes might be written in a kind of cipher, to conceal ill-intentioned compositions; a committee of musical experts was formed to investigate, but we are not told that it made any discoveries.

1848–1855 has been called the "plague streak" in the story of Russian literature. We have only to remember what the years 1848–49 were to Europe, and we shall see that the rigours of the Government were aimed as much against Europe as against Russia. As Nikityenko, the liberal censor, writes in his notes on March 28th, 1850, "if they play tricks in Europe, the Russian gets a hit on the back." "Our position," writes Granóvsky, "becomes worse from day to day; every movement in the West is reflected here by some measure of repression. Delations come in in thousands." Papers came out without leading articles or political correspondence, simply giving the Government news and adding a colourless novel. Magazines were full of long, dry scientific treatises. As the literary public became stronger and as reform became more inevitable, "more and more prohibitions were heaped upon literature, that it might not point a finger at the guest who was standing at the door."[1] At this time was specially developed the so-called "language of Æsop," which, of course, consisted in saying a thing without saying it. As Aksákoff writes in 1865, "the old system of censorship brought a crook even into the province of the printed word. . . . The writer, as if he were a thief, used every art to carry his thought through to the public between the lines. Between reader and author there was a conventional language of circumlocutions and hints. . . . When the author sat down to his work he thought not of how he could best explain his genuine conviction, . . . but only whether he could somehow drag his thought, like contraband, through the guard-room of the Censorship. The higher the value which he set on the truth which he served, the more intolerable for him was this humiliating path. . . . After long and stubborn wrestling between the author and the Censor, the written word tore itself away from the Censor's hands and entered God's world, ruffled, crumpled, and mutilated, and was welcomed by the public as a token of victory, was keenly relished as a forbidden, secret and seductive fruit." In

[1] Engelhardt, p. 174.

1848, the Emperor ordered "that those of the forbidden compositions which show in the writer an especially harmful tendency, political or moral, should be handed over by the censors without publicity to the Third Section (the police)." A Secret Committee was formed under Búturlin to watch and supervise even the Censorship itself. Another Committee was established to supervise the recommendations of the first. Everywhere there was distrust. Korff told his brother that he was disgusted by all that was done in the Secret Committee and would have escaped from it long since, if he had not still the hope of sometimes doing something to help those who were being persecuted. Even Count Uvároff, late Minister of Public Instruction, had the greatest difficulty in getting a censor to pass the word "demos" in his book on the Greek antiquities discovered in Russia. The censor would not allow him to say that certain Roman emperors were killed, but only that "they perished." Nikityenko, himself a censor, was called upon to explain what he meant by using the term "the movement of minds." The censor Yelághin removed from a scientific book the phrase "forces of nature." The censor Freigang told Nikityenko that the officials spied on each other; "They have no kind of system," writes Nikityenko, "and only follow the inspiration of panic. Out of a thousand facts here are some of the latest: the censor Akhmatoff stopped a book on arithmetic because, between the figures of some problem, was put a row of dots. The censor Yelághin would not pass a statement in a geographical article to the effect that in Siberia dogs draw sledges ; the reason which he gave was the absolute necessity that this statement should first receive confirmation from the Minister of the Interior."[1]

All through our story have run the two constant refrains of the literary man, the theme of the indifference of the public and the theme of the stupidity of the Censorship. But it is significant that the first complaint gives way more and more to the second. In other words, literary interest is going forward, and the Censorship is going backward. Even the respectable Bulgárin is forced to complain bitterly in his letters to Nikityenko : " To strike one character out of a novel is to tear up the novel and compel the author to write another. . . . I swear to you by the

[1] Diary of Nikityenko, February 25th, 1853.

happiness of my children that I have only a moral aim, and have no person in view; I live far from men and society, and don't want to vex anyone. . . . We had a hard time of it in the days of Magnítsky and Arakchéyeff, but not a single article of mine was forbidden at that time, even by Krasóvsky, and all my novels went through without excisions and without persecutions. . . . Respected gentlemen of the Censorship, be just; for you too there is a posterity" (1835).   "I beg you most humbly, when you next see Freigang, to tell your colleague that I and Grech are not the slaves of Mr. Freigang, that we are not given over into his service, and that we are not defenceless orphans whom he can bully to please anyone. . . . Patience is running out" (1839). "I don't blame yourself! it's the time! But we, fools and cattle, wept in the days of Magnítsky and Rúnich. Why, that was the golden age of literature in comparison with the present. . . . How write a novel from life without touching on anything that concerns life ? Is that really harmful to the Church and the altar, to the morality and the peace of citizens? Really I want to cry." Yet in 1852, as we already know,[1] Bulgárin's *Northern Bee* is held up by the Censorship as a model for the correct telling of a story. The fault was not necessarily with the censors. Some of them were, like Shishkoff, utterly unsuited for their work; but, as Freigang has explained to us, almost all of them were oppressed by a stupid fear imposed from outside. It would be even less intelligent to heap the blame upon the Emperor. The causes of this utterly abnormal state of things must be found far back in the story of the intellectual relations of Russia with Europe, in the gulf which opened between the old and the new in Russia, and in the panic which reigned in the reactionary camp. But at least one can understand how the struggling Intelligence of Russia might find its ideals of freedom in the proscribed West; one only wonders that it was never more untrue to its old deep-rooted instincts of nationality. If morality was presented to him by the Government as synonymous with subservience, and if intelligence was denounced to him as treason, surely the Intelligent might be excused for considering that nobility of heart and conduct, as opposed to servility, was the highest of all virtues, and for rapturously embracing the creed of the dignity of humanity. Did

[1] See p. 275.

that creed ever mean as much to anyone in France as it meant to him? Was it ever more necessary? Yet if the Westerniser has the more urgent claims on our sympathies, it is a Slavophil who best analyses the mischievousness of this régime. I. S. Aksákoff, who had himself suffered from the Censorship, writes thus: " If a State wishes to live, then it must observe the unalterable conditions of life, outside which are death and destruction. The chief condition of the life of a State is the life of a society; the chief condition of the life of a society is freedom of speech as the instrument of social consciousness. Which are more desirable for a Government, transparency and publicity, with all their temporarily inevitable inconveniences, or complete darkness, dulness, and silence? We must have freedom of intellectual life, else we shall never get to know ourselves, and shall never fully develope the soul of our nation, that is, we shall not do our duty.[1] Yes, and the Government needs for its work not intellectual children, but citizens grown-up and fully developed."

> " Thou marvel of heavenly birth,
>   The lamp and the flame of the mind,
> Thou ray from the sun to the earth,
>   The standard and sign of mankind,—
> Thou art young with perpetual youth,
>   At thy voice all the shadows must flee ;
> Thou leadest to light and to truth,
>   The Word that goes Free." [2]

The Crimean war began a new epoch in the history of the Press. On December 6th, 1854, the Secret Committee of Búturlin was dissolved by the Emperor ; in a report of its president, Baron Korff, it was confessed that the system had led " to the spread of manuscript literature, which is far more dangerous—for it is read with avidity, and all police measures are powerless against it."

There was at once an extraordinary outburst of journalistic activity. In 1856 the *Russian Causeries* (*Besyéda*) of Koshelyeff and Philipoff and the *Russian Messenger* of Katkoff were started in Moscow. In 1857 were founded Governmental organs in four towns of Siberia, and eleven Russian magazines for special interests, such as the *Engineer's Magazine*, the *Library of Medical Science*, the *Shareholder's Magazine*, the *Economic*

---

[1] Compare Mr. D. I. Shipóff's claim for responsibility rather than for rights.
[2] Aksákoff : " The Word that goes Free " (Svobódnoë Slovo).

Indicator, and the *Educational Messenger*. There were also many new street newspapers.[1] The public interest in journalism was not sustained, and many of these papers very soon failed for want of subscribers. The most important of the new magazines was the Slavophil *Russian Messenger*, which was moderately Liberal and at once won favour by the capability with which it was edited. In St. Petersburg the chief publications were the *Contemporary*, the *Notes of the Fatherland*, and the *Reading Library*. To these were added the *Economic Indicator*, preaching free trade, the *Spark*, soon to be an important Radical organ, and the *Russian Word*. Kireyevsky founded the *Voice* in St. Petersburg, and Katkoff took up the *Moscow Gazette*. Leading articles now came more into fashion and tended to raise the level of journalism. But it must not be imagined that the Press enjoyed anything more than what Aksákoff calls "a glimmer of freedom." It was a period of jolts ; and, during the years while the new Press law was in process of elaboration, the Censorship, which had fallen almost into final chaos, acted spasmodically and irregularly. Even Katkoff had to abstain from treatment of the chief political questions throughout nearly all the year 1861. On March 5th, when the Emancipation was promulgated, not a paper in Moscow or St. Petersburg had a word on the subject. Only on March 7th could the *Moscow Gazette* insert a few sympathetic lines in an obscure corner of the paper. Yet surely the Government had required the support of enlightened opinion, if only to strengthen it in its struggle with the enormous mass of vested interests which it was attacking. The fact is that progress and reaction were still fighting within the Government itself; and an article which was sanctioned to-day might be prohibited to-morrow.

This is why the chief Russian journalist of this time edited his paper in London. Hertzen is to the history of modern Russia something of what Mazzini was to the history of modern Italy. He had in him the faith, the courage, and the good sense which characterise so many of the great Liberals of the forties. His paper was the *Bell*. Its motto was, "I call the living ; I mourn the dead ; I break the thunder bolts."[2] The *Bell* was full of

---

[1] *I.e.*, newspapers sold on the streets and not only sent out to the subscribers.

[2] "Vivos voco, mortuos plango, fulgura frango," the inscription on a mediæval bell which is prefixed to the opening lines of Longfellow's "Golden Legend."

" articles of exposure " ; but it had too much conscience and political insight to ever become an organ of terrorism. Hertzen was for a few years the real director of public opinion in Russia. He was free from all the vexations of the Censorship; and that very state of chaos which made it impossible for editors in Russia to know how much liberty would be allowed from day to day, prevented the Censorship from ever dealing effectively with a newspaper which had openly defied it and was introduced into the country from abroad. In fact, no serious attempt was made to keep it out, and, as the most interesting paper and the best guide to public opinion, it found its way into the cabinets of every official and of the Emperor himself.

In February, 1856, Count Sollogub's play, " The Official," was given at the house of a Grand Duchess. The Emperor said to Pletneff, " The piece is very good, isn't it ? " Pletneff answered, " It is not only good, your Majesty ; it makes an era in our litera-ture. It says that about the state of our morality which earlier it was impossible even to think." " It was time to say it," said the Emperor. In February, 1857, Prince Vyázemsky, the friend of Pushkin, was made the chief of the Censorship. He drew up a report advising that the regulations should be relaxed ; but the Emperor only half approved of it, and Vyázemsky resigned. " We want improvements," wrote Nikityenko in 1858, " and think that we can get them without the help of public opinion, by means of that bureaucracy which is so besmirched with peculation." Thus when Kavyélin wrote, in 1858, advocating that the emancipated peasants should receive land, he was censured even for advocating exactly the course which the Government was going to take. In the same year the street newspapers were abolished, and the word " progress" was prohibited. In 1859, the Secret Committee was re-established " to direct the Press in harmony with the views of the Government." In January the Committee practically advised its own dissolution. In 1859 the Censorship was made indepen-dent of the Ministry of Public Instruction. " I am sure," said Isákoff to the Emperor, " that publicity is indispensable." " And so am I," said the Emperor, " only with us it takes a bad direction." In 1859, Nikityenko was put at the head of the Committee of the Censorship. But in 1860 he has to write: " For literature there has come a very unfavourable epoch ; the chief thing is that the

Emperor is strongly set against it." In 1862 the Censorship was divided into two parts: the preventive section, under the Minister of Public Instruction, and the punitive section, under the Minister of the Interior. In 1862, Nikityenko writes: "Now we have reaction of the genuine kind."

The punitive power was now in the hands of the chief administrative official, the Minister of the Interior. This satisfied the real aims of those two-faced people who controlled the reorganisation of the Censorship, though they chose to pretend that the administrative punishment of editors was only a temporary expedient. Of these persons the most important was Valúyeff. The Commission of 1863, of which Nikityenko was a member, collected all possible information from the histories of Germany, France, England, and Belgium. The preamble of the statute which it recommended acknowledged that "arbitrariness and violence were inevitable characteristics of regulations of censorship." It declared for an "institution which should administer Press affairs by its own power, independent of the chance interference of higher Imperial regulations." It added that, now that public interest was taken in political questions, "every inevitable mistake of the Censor gives an enormous advantage to one opinion or theory as against another." The statute tried to make a transition from the system of preliminary censorship to that of legal punishment of offending journalists. But it admitted that "this transition is conditional on the existence of regularly constituted law-courts and organs of prosecution." "This first and most essential condition," it added, "at the present time we do not yet possess" (section 6). Therefore it did not claim to be a permanent measure (section 7). It proceeds to ordain that "all works concerned with the province of science, literature, and art, and containing twenty or more 'printer's sheets' can be printed and published without preliminary censorship" (section 1). We must not, however, forget that in Russia all the great novels first had to appear as serials in magazines. Next, all periodicals, of whatever size, must pass through the Censorship before they are printed and issued (section 4). "Newspapers, magazines, and other periodicals may at the request of the publishers, be freed from the preliminary censorship by special permission of the Minister of the Interior."

By an ordinance of 1862, the Ministers of the Interior and of Public Instruction had received the right of jointly prohibiting any periodical for eight months ; the statute now gave to the Censorship the power of subjecting any such publication to administrative punishment : that is, the paper might be stopped, either after three warnings or by a single prohibition (sections 143,144). It, however, altogether failed to define what constituted an offence ; " by the words ' a harmful tendency,' " it stated, " is expressed a general idea," in fact, the Press would still depend upon the caprices of the party in power. Meanwhile the circulars of the Censorship still continued.

Valúyeff introduced important alterations into the statute. Baron Korff maintained that " the system of administrative punishment is still more infected with arbitrariness and injustice than that of preliminary censorship, for it punishes for a fault not anticipated by any definite law." Valúyeff, however, won his point. On April 18th, 1865, the statute became law, and Nikityenko had to write : " Valúyeff has got what he wanted ; he has taken literature into his hands and has become its complete master. The statute . . . gives over to his absolute control every printed expression of thought." By Imperial decree of the same year were freed from preliminary censorship all existing periodicals whose editors asked for this indulgence (it might be refused to the founders of new publications), and also all original works of ten printer's sheets or over, and all translations of twenty printer's sheets or over. By the statutes of 1864 which regulated the law-courts, prosecutions of editors were, in ordinary cases, to be referred to the Circuit Courts. But the St. Petersburg Circuit Court only had time to judge two Press cases before the new law of December, 1866, deprived such courts of the right of prosecuting ; and such cases as were referred to them were often delayed even for years, during which, very probably, the temporary prohibition of the incriminated writings inflicted a severe loss upon the publishers.[1]

Thus in the lottery of the great reforms the Press had drawn a blank. We can quite understand that liberty of the Press, that is, the right of irresponsible criticism, would be more distasteful to any autocrat than the concession of local government, or even the

---

[1] As in the case of a translation of Herbert Spencer.

acknowledgment of the principle of law.   But this reform was
hardly a reform at all.   The censor Fuchs observed that "to the
preliminary system was adapted all the force of the punitive."[1]
The *Messenger of Europe* admitted that political criticism no
longer had to stop short at the reign of Catherine II., and that the
work of the journalist, though "not easy and not without danger,"
was "such as the Press could not dream of some years ago."
But the fundamental guarantees were all lacking.   The punitive
power belonged not to the law-courts, but to the Ministers ; the
accused had no right to be heard ; the punishment was not confined to the offender; the offence was not defined by any law ;
the accuser was the judge.   The new law did not remain a dead
letter ; it could point, indeed, to the special conditions of
the time as excusing its severities.   On April 4, 1866,
Karakózoff fired his shot.   The *Contemporary* and the *Russian
Word* were at once suppressed for eight months, and the
reaction grew stronger and stronger till 1868.   Already, for
three years, Valúyeff's power over the Press had been almost
absolute ; and now there was rising a new generation of journalists,
who were clean out of harmony with the ideals and the moderation of the men of the forties.   In a word, terrorism and hysteria
were on both sides gaining ground fast.   Hertzen's *Bell*,
founded in 1857, had in four years won a circulation of 2,500
copies.   But in 1863 Hertzen wrote sympathetically of the
insurgent Poles, and by this he so alienated the ordinary Russian
reader that the circulation fell to 500.   In 1866, in his article on
Karakózoff's crime, entitled " Irkutsk and St. Petersburg," he
said : "We are astounded at the thought of the responsibility
which this fanatic took upon himself.   Only in barbarous peoples,
or in those that stand on the down grade of civilisation, exists the
desire to resort to murders."   This article alienated from him the
goodwill of the Radicals.

Katkoff, on the other hand, seized the occasion of the Polish
rising to make himself for a time almost the dictator of the greater
section of public opinion.   His articles were inspired by a genuine
patriotism.   The *Moscow Gazette* in his first year of editorship,
1862, had a circulation of 6,000.   It attracted the attention
of Europe, and in 1865 was described by the correspondent

---

[1] Fuchs wrote in 1862, before the statute was issued.

of the *Times* as the foremost journal in Russia. By the next year the circulation had risen to 12,000. Katkoff, as the enlightened and able leader of the Slavophils, was able to withstand even the enmity of Valúyeff, who oppressed this party as much as any other. The high and dignified position which the editor was able to take up proved, at least, that there were now the beginnings of a public opinion in Russia. Ninety-five pounds were paid in fines to the Government in one month, and Katkoff published the figure in his journal. When ordered to print a first warning which had been administered to him, he flatly refused and said that he would prefer to resign his editorship. On the next day took place the crime of Karakózoff, which naturally brought back the Government towards Katkoff and resulted in the appointing of his patron, Count D. Tolstoy as Minister of Public Instruction. A crowd of students collected outside his house to sing the national hymn, and shouted, " Continue your work." A month later Valúyeff administered the second and the third warnings, and stopped the paper for two months. Before this term was up the Emperor visited Moscow, received Katkoff, and encouraged him to resume publication. His triumph was celebrated by a dinner in the hall of the University (1866). When Count Muravyéff, who had been charged with the investigation of Karakózoff's crime, prematurely announced at a dinner that " it was the result of lying teachings," Katkoff wrote : " All these lying teachings and evil tendencies against which we now hear complaints are the fruit of thought crushed and undeveloped, slavish in all its instincts, which has gone wild in its obscure caverns." And again : " They were born and acquired strength amongst a society which knew neither free learning, respected and powerful, nor publicity in all acts which concern our dearest interests, a society which found itself under the censorship and the inspection of the police in every sphere of its life." In 1868, Valúyeff resigned, but was succeeded by a new Minister, Timasheff, who declared his intention of following the same system.

Katkoff was the exception. In St. Petersburg, from 1862 to 1868, the Press deteriorated fast. Uspyénsky writes: "There was absolute desolation. With the great writers of the school of the forties I had no relations, but my colleagues, men who were ten years older than myself, almost all without exception went to ruin under my eyes, as drunkenness seemed almost inevitable for the talented men of those times." "They had no readers," we are told; "they did not know for whom they were writing, and simply praised each other. Their isolation attracted them to the excitement and noise of the restaurants." Already in 1862 the *Contemporary* and the *Russian Word* had been closed for eight months. The two papers belonged to two different generations, and their animosity was expressed in ridiculous torrents of personal abuse, suggestive of a street brawl. Dostoyévsky founded an excellent paper, *The Times;* but it only lived for two years. We are, in fact, on the threshold of a development of the most pernicious kind.

In 1868 appeared in the *Contemporary Review* of Tiblen an article on "Poor Old Men." Turghényeff was represented as " crossing his useless hands on his useless breast."[1] It was a contemptuous attack on the men of the forties by the men of the sixties. Turghényeff's popularity culminated with " On the Eve," in 1860, and began to fall very rapidly with " Fathers and Sons," in 1862. The cause had nothing to do with the talent of the author ; " Smoke " and " Virgin Soil " were still to follow. Písemsky, Goncharóff, Dostoyévsky, and Hertzen were also at this time condemned as obsolete, and their names were uttered with a sneer. They had no cause to be ashamed of that, for the same condemnation included Pushkin, Raphael, Beethoven, and Shakespeare; and Goethe was dismissed as a " secret councillor of state." Písareff, one of the leaders of the new school, writes on the subject of lyric poetry : " Why do lyrics grow up with us like mushrooms after the rain ? Why, simply because journalists are accustomed to fill clean sheets with verses, . . . and to this day these respected journalists cannot understand that a clean sheet is far better than a lyric composition—firstly, because the reader does not waste over it a single minute ; secondly, because the editor has not to pay a farthing for it ; thirdly, because the existence of clean sheets does not encourage any branch of reprehensible parasitism. . . . The reader will think, perhaps, that my *bête noire* is æstheticism, and the reader, in this case, will not be wrong. Æstheticism and realism are, in fact, irreconcilable enemies, and realism must utterly destroy æstheticism,

---

[1] A quotation from Turghényeff's " Enough, a Fragment of the Notes of a Dead Artist."

which at the present time is poisoning and stultifying all branches of our activity, from the highest spheres of scientific work down to the most ordinary relations between man and woman. . . . Æstheticism is the most solid element of intellectual stagnation and the most effective enemy of the progress of reason. . . . Human tastes are endlessly various : one man may like to drink before dinner a glass of strained vodka ; another likes to smoke after dinner a pipe of bad tobacco ; a third likes to amuse himself in the evening with a violin or a flute. . . . Well, there is nothing like it. Let them amuse themselves, the Society of Sportsmen and the Society of Theatre-goers, the Society of Lovers of Jam-puffs and the Society of Lovers of Music. . . . Great Beethoven ! Great Raphael ! Great Canova ! Great chess-player Brown ! Great confectioner Jones ! Great billiard-player Robinson ! We can only rejoice at this fertility of genius, and walk circumspectly past all these ' Societies of Lovers,' carefully concealing a smile. . . ."

Why should all this rubbish be quoted ? Is it meant for a joke ? Is it just the overflow of the writer's exuberance ? No, it is quite serious, or at least the writer takes it as such. Here is his ideal of the poet : " When the poet has grasped with his powerful mind all the great idea of human life, of human struggles, and of human grief ; when he has thought himself into their causes, when he has seized the strong connection between separate phenomena, when he has understood what he must do and what he can do, in what direction and by what springs he must act on the minds of reading people, then thoughtless and aimless composition will be for him simply impossible. The general object of his life and work gives him not a moment's rest. This object beckons and draws him to itself. He is happy when he sees it in front of him, clearer and, as it were, nearer ; . . . he suffers and is angry when it vanishes in the fog of human stupidity and when the people around him wander about groping and pushing each other from the straight road." Písareff, destined for an early death by drowning, was one of the foremost journalists of his time, and the creed which he preaches is that which has frightened all the world under the name of Nihilism. The "new men," as they called themselves, were anxious to supersede the old ; but it is usual to proceed with more decency. What then were the new formulæ, whose utterance was to make Raphael, Shakespeare, Beethoven, and Goethe obsolete, not to speak of Pushkin, Turghényeff, and Dostoyévsky? Short formulæ were indeed specially the weapons of the new school, and here are some of the most favourite of them : " Love is a sexual attraction and nothing more "; " Photography is higher than art "; " All that is natural is moral "; " Man is an animal "; " The belly is the centre of the world "; " The end justifies the means "; " Ten thousand heads for the good of mankind." Turghényeff, then, or that most genuine and devoted of workers, Dostoyévsky, was condemned not for anything in himself, but on purely general grounds, especially as he was undoubtedly one of the ten thousand heads. So far we see only the indecent haste of the young aspirants for notoriety, and nothing more. We must not then be surprised if the best works of Russian literature, which, of course, continued to come from the men of the forties,[1] are from this time deeply permeated with opposition to the new school (" Fathers and Children," 1862 ; " Smoke," 1867 ; Goncharóff's " Obryv," 1868 ; Dostoyévsky's " Goblins," 1871). The criticisms were far more kindly than the attacks, because the critics were far stronger than the attackers. They were stronger by right of the aristocracy of the great breed to which they belonged, and their initial cause of offence was precisely that their superior genius and vitality were considered to encroach on the future by the narrow, nervous, scrambling generation that came after them. They had another title and a greater one : they were born not from nowhere, but out of the past. They will continue to live by the strength of that main tradition of the world's progress with which they have identified themselves, whereas their accusers have already met the fate of all those who, like the French philosophers, attempt to make a gap in the world's history. The ideals of the forties, peasant freedom, peasant proprietorship, freedom of conscience and of speech, publicity of law, self-government, responsibility, humanity in the home, in the school, in the barracks, the principle that women should be treated as

[1] Amongst the men of the forties we may count, amongst many others, Mazzini, Garibaldi, Kossuth, Petöfy, Cobden, Bright, and even Gladstone and Cavour. As a rule the stamp is unmistakable. Those of this great army who are still alive can easily be distinguished even to-day by the abundance of their vitality and the abundance of their faith.

men are treated—these great ideals have constituted the programme of the national movement for liberation during 1905.

What then are the " new ideas " ?   So far we see nothing but a
simple grudge. After many hours of reading and listening I have
little more to do than to register Turghényeff's verdict on the
positive content of this creed—"smoke," "nihil." Where one
does seem to see something positive, it is only by lurid glimpses.
Half an hour's conversation with a Nihilist will convince one
that it is exactly the same with him. He, too, is unable to disen-
tangle even the clearest and most illuminating of his aspirations
from the initial mood of the grudge.

I assume then that Nihilism, generally speaking, is a form of
hysteria, and it remains that we should again notice its causes
and its effects. Engelhardt is, of course, right when he represents it as a special and sudden break in the traditions of the
Russian Intelligence itself. We have only to look back to the
time of the great reforms to see that Russians were quite capable of
moderation, sound sense, and generosity. The harm done by the
censorship of Valúyeff was incomparably greater than any harm
which could have been done by the censorship of Nicholas I.,
when the nation was not yet awake. But we must also recall the
long habit of servility in Russia, the early character of the Intelligence as fixed by Peter the Great, and the gulf opened between
the old and the new by the French Revolution. The maxims
preached by the men of the forties stood in sharp enough contrast
with the Government's achievements in the direction of reform.
The impatience of the "new men" is very intelligible. The
comparative passivity of their predecessors vexed them, and
seemed to be treason. Their mood was disappointment and
vexation, and their cry was, before all things, "action." They
did not recognise that much of what they had said had been said
far better before by the very men whom they scorned.[1] Anyhow
they pushed past with the most unbecoming haste. Peculiarly
poverty-stricken in constructive ideas, they found a certain self-
satisfaction in sneering at all that had been done without themselves. The censorship had driven thought into obscure corners
all over Russia ; in these obscure caverns the untrained thinker

---

[1] Surely Dostoyévsky made a sufficient sacrifice of his whole being to his
purpose.

THE PRESS AND THE CENSORSHIP. 291

had lived, feeding upon himself. He had been driven, according to the prophecy of Nikityenko, and the fear of Hertzen,[1] back to a state bordering on barbarism; only it was the barbarism of the man who is intellectually awake, the man who can form his desires, and cannot satisfy them. This generation has left on Russian thought and life a blight of cynicism which has not yet vanished.

Nihilism was the most potent friend of reaction long before the monstrous murder of Alexander II., which pushed Russia back from the path of progress into the stupid cycle of revolution and repression. "From 1855 to 1862," writes Engelhardt, "reaction and repression of the Press were only based on the party of the serf-owners, the obscurantists. From 1862 to 1868 a dark underground activity unfortunately gave infinitely more reason for reaction and for the terror of the Censorship. . . . This split" (between the two generations) "went deep into Russian society. All its sensible moderate elements were compromised, and were reckoned as behind the times. The extremists, utterly unscrupulous, deprived of all 'centres of restraint,' prevailed and stood at the helm of public opinion. . . . The equilibrium was broken; the extremes triumphed, and, of course, if, amongst the young generation, the extreme Nihilists were the leaders, in governmental circles it was the extreme reactionaries who prevailed." These were as hysterical in their repression as the others in their attack.

Repressive laws were applied to the Press in 1866, in 1867, in 1872, and in 1873. The year 1872 was one of especial reaction. The Press found no salvation except in marking time. Saltykoff-Shchedrin gives us an amusing contemporary picture in his "Statute of the Great League of Froth-skimmers," established "in the absence of regular work and with the purpose of spending time harmlessly." He explains that the only other alternative for the Press was to commit suicide. "Membership of the League of Froth-skimmers is open to anyone who can in a harmless way expound the confused sensations which he from time to time experiences. Neither knowledge nor ideas are demanded of him. If he sees a driver ill-treating his horse," and can recall instances from antiquity to prove the evil of this

[1] See p. 285.

custom, "this will not merely escape the censure; it is even the very highest form of froth-skimming." Persons may join the League "although they do not possess quite a clear understanding of grammar." The first duty of a member "is not to let pass any contemporary question, and to write on everything in such a way that nothing whatsoever will come of it." On some trifling question of the uniform of policemen it is his duty "to take as strong a line as if he intended to get the third warning." He must continue to write on Russian thought and learning, "often expressing the hope that a new word will some day be spoken." According to Shchedrin, "all the important organs have joined the League."

Since 1861 there has been a very marked change in the character of the Press. The Bulgárins and Senkovskys could no longer stand at the head of journalism, and were superseded by really literary men, such as Valentine Korsh, of the *St. Petersburg Gazette*. The "fat magazine" was also being superseded by the daily newspaper, which clearly could do much more to keep up the everyday interest of the public in politics. But the daily newspaper, as especially the object of suspicion to the Censorship, was kept under far more close control than the magazine. Thus it could not say what it wanted to say; it would begin sentences without finishing them; it would continually try to balance the danger of saying this against the danger of saying that. Many of the articles would simply mark time. Perhaps, amidst a flow of talk which meant nothing, there would come a single word or phrase which, passing the sleepy censor's notice, would show the public that the writer was still thinking. The reader had to live on such scraps, and to develope the surest instinct for picking them out at sight from a mass of rubbish. Certainly this so-called "method of Æsop" involved a study in the art of expression; but the censorship had succeeded in giving a revolutionary character to the printed word itself; and even the Russian language has suffered thereby. Yet the men who conducted this dangerous profession were no longer simply, to adopt the comparison of Bulgárin, "decent lackeys."

"Servi siam, si, ma servi ogni or frementi."[1] Shchedrin, the

---

[1] "Slaves we are, yes, but slaves each hour rebelling" (Alfieri).

author of the skit on the "Froth-skimmers," found the task very difficult. "Apart from our almost living in an ambuscade," he says, "we do not know even why and for whom we are writing. Who hears us, and what does this hearer get out of the word which we address to him? Who distinguishes a passionate worker for literature from the lightly balanced literary mandoline (balaléika), which, according to the chance of its mobile temperament, is ready to court any haphazard passer? To whom would it occur that somewhere in some literary burrow, deprived of light and air, at every moment is being accomplished a sacrifice in which the heart bleeds and the long-suffering soul of the writer inflames under the burden of pains beyond its strength? . . . He wraps up and wraps up his thought, deceives by all possible circumlocutions and allegories, and only when he has fulfilled, so to speak, all the complicated ceremony of a masquerade, will he give a sigh of freedom and say, ' Thank God! Now, it seems, no one will notice.' No one will notice? And the public, will it, too, not notice? Can there be in the world any deeper taint than this interminable ' Æsopism,' which has passed into such an everyday habit that not seldom the very man who uses it ceases to recognise himself as an 'Æsop'?" For how many others is Shchedrin speaking? The Press has been separated from the public; and this revolutionary achievement of the Censorship must inevitably propagate revolution in others. What wonder if the "new men" of the sixties should have for their creed the doctrine that the mere recognition of the existing system, the mere recognition of the traditions of the past, is treason, and that the highest of all virtues is not morality, but nobility of protest in the time of servitude?

The *Messenger of Europe*, which maintained its dignity and moderation in this period, thus sums up, in 1880, the condition of the Press:—"The provincial Press is, as before, without rights. The special censorships—religious, theatrical, and foreign—are, as before, absolute. . . . The rôle of the law-court in affairs of the Press has been reduced to a minimum. In its jurisdiction have been left, *de facto*, only trials for defamation and calumny against private persons or the lower officials. . . . From 1865 to January 1st, 1880, there have been 167 warnings; fifty-two publications have been stopped."

In St. Petersburg the chief papers were the *St. Petersburg Gazette* of Korsh and the *Voice* of Krayévsky, and, from 1877, the *New Times* (*Nóvoë Vrémya*), of Suvórin. The *Voice* and the monthly *Messenger of Europe* (of Stasyulévich) kept flying the flag of a strong but moderate Liberalism. The *Messenger*, assisted by some writers of great ability, among whom were Annenkoff and Arsényeff, tried to secure and define the working of the recent reforms, and, with a respect for the past, to continue the tradition of progress. It did much to restore the balance of Russian society. To the right were the organs of Aksákoff and Katkoff, to the left the *Notes of the Fatherland*, the magazine of Nekrásoff and Shchedrin and their able colleagues. The more Radical *Dyélo* (*Affair*) of Blagosvyétloff had more of the tone of Písareff, and was the organ of his school. The *Voice*, whose views may be taken as tolerably representative of the whole Press, stood for " active reform "; it claimed to have been founded by Reform and to have always served Reform. Revolution, it maintained, could never develope on Russian soil or take proportions which would threaten the calm of the State and of society. The first Nihilist attempts it explained as showing how few the revolutionaries were, and how little chance there was of their becoming really dangerous. " All this talk of 'revolutionary forces' in Russia is pure nonsense; we should not believe such talk; it is simply a case of madness and moral corruption in a few isolated persons." It claimed freedom for the Press, because " the Press throughout the whole of this period has been standing firm for the interests of Government and of society." It took its part in the new movement of Imperialism, claiming that the Russian Party was the mass of Russian society. It considered the Church to have the same claim on a Russian's respect as any other aspect of the national and Imperial life. It was a strong supporter of Russification, though it showed no bitterness against the Poles. It constantly supported the claim of the Zemstva and Town Councils for further decentralisation. From 1865 to 1877 its circulation rose from 5,000 to nearly 23,000, but it was practically ruined by the general hysteria that followed the murder of Alexander II. in 1881.

This event was itself the product of hysteria; it plunged Russia into twenty-four years of reaction, and again handed over the predominance to the twin conflicting camps of absolutism and revolution. The *Voice* was soon reduced to silence, and with it the Liberal *Notes of the Fatherland* and the Radical *Dyélo*. The great Slavophils, Katkoff and Aksákoff, died in the eighties and were succeeded by men of little ability and little authority, who seemed to desert all the principles of the Slavophils in order to cringe to the Reaction, and to make their own capital out of its protection. Engelhardt compares the death of Alexander to an obstacle put in the way of a train :—" Many carriages are smashed ; there are many wounded, and whoever survives has the mark left on him. Society asked for quiet ; journalists became indifferent commentators on the various tendencies of public life." The *Messenger of Europe*, the new *Russian Thought*, the *Wealth of Russia*, and *God's World*, seemed to live wholly on the past. The Press, as a whole, was monotonous and colourless. Not that there was no talent or no development : the provincial Press, especially that of South Russia, assumed much more important proportions. Small penny papers, such as the *World* (*Svyet*) and the *Exchange Gazette*, were issued in the capitals, and, with some of them, the circulation exceeded 100,000. An enterprising magazine the *Field* (*Niva*), which issued practically the whole of the Russian classics in the form of free supplements, had a circulation of over 200,000. Somewhat similar was the *Magazine of Foreign Literature*, which acquainted the Russian public with the current writings of Western novelists. Excellent as are some of these publications, it is most mischievous that, in the ordinary periodical, literature should have to limit itself to novels ; this particular result of the abnormal condition of the Press in Russia has had the worst effect on Russian life. The most serious and expensive daily of this last period has been the *Nóvoë Vrémya*, whose circulation in 1900 was more than 60,000.

We see that, whereas there were now far more readers than formerly, the subjects of their reading were more strictly limited than ever. Thus the incitement to revolution became more acute. Daily newspapers began to find subscribers in the distant country districts ; but the formation of a strong public opinion was made impossible. In other words, the Second Reaction (1881–1904), was much more abnormal than the First (1812–1855), and a further gap was made in the public consciousness, which rendered it hard for the traditions of the great reforms to exercise their due influence over the public of the future. From 1890 onwards the two strongest tendencies of Russian literature have been decadence and Marxism. Neither of them can be described as an ordinary or normal development. The tendency to decadence found expression in the *Northern Messenger* of Volynsky, which had but a short life, and in the *Moscow Scorpion ;* it is, however, visible all over the modern literature and life of Russia. The tendency to Marxism was far stronger. Its organs, the *New World*, the *Beginning*, and *Life*, were extremely popular, but were all closured ; it is often stated that nearly all the young Intelligence of Russia is Marxist. One of its most gifted leaders was Peter Struve, who later became a Liberal. Amongst the prominent writers of the school is Maxim Gorky. We shall remember that the peasants were long cut off from all participation in the life of the Russian Intelligence ; but since the emancipation they have themselves been going half-way to meet it by their wholesale migration into the factory life of the towns. Clearly a thorough study of economic questions would bring nearer that moment when the Intelligence could join hands with the working classes, and could therefore find a really effective support for the realisation of its social and political ideals. But it was a characteristic of this movement that social ideals preceded the political ; and one of its results is that the settlement of political questions has been complicated by the claim that advanced social theories should be realised all at once. In 1905 the Liberal leader, Professor Milyukóff, confirmed my fears on the subject ; and in 1906, owing to what seemed to me the mistaken tactics of his Party, this claim did much to wreck the first Russian Parliament.

Before 1900 there was a serious diminution in the number of important publications. The *Russian Review*, the *Russian Messenger*, the *Northern Messenger*, the *New Word*, and the *Week* all disappeared, and with them also the *Son of the Fatherland* and its accompanying monthly the *Cheap Library*. A number of new enterprises came to nothing, such as the *Beginning*, *Life*, *Echoes of the World*, the *People*, *Rus*, the *Northern Courier*, and *Russia*, though the last three enjoyed for a time great popularity.

The machinery of the Censorship, elaborate as it is, is not

nearly elaborate enough for the work which it has to do. Provincial papers still have to submit their copy in advance; and, though this successfully prevents them from becoming interesting, the provincial work of the Censorship falls on officials who have never been trained for it and sometimes have other more important duties to perform. In 1905 the reactionary *Moscow Gazette* advertised, as one of the most pressing requirements of the time, the need for more censors. Most newspapers of the capitals print what they like at their own risk; but the third warning is followed by suspension. Later on the same group of collaborators may appear again under another title. The quick changes of *personnel* in the Ministries, especially in 1905, and the halting of the supreme power between totally antagonistic counsels, made it more necessary than ever for the journalist to know exactly how much he could say at a given moment. Journalism was more than ever a game of hide-and-seek. The threatened ship had to steer, with the help of St. Nicholas the Wonder-worker[1], through countless shoals. The fitful changes of Court favour had to be closely followed. The chance of a moment had to be boldly seized, and the writer had to know by instinct and without delay when it was again necessary to bow with submission beneath the rod. Impossible things became possible under Prince Mirsky in 1904, and after the battle of Tsushima in 1905. The policy of the Censorship cannot be ascribed to the Emperor, nor to the Ministers as a whole. It may be a weapon used by one Minister against others. In 1905, copies of the Emperor's speech to the delegates of the Zemstva were confiscated all over the country. Again, it must not be assumed that all censors are tyrants. Of Nikityenko and Fuchs I have already made mention. Tyútcheff, another censor of the same sort, wrote in the album of a colleague an agreeable impromptu describing his very liberal understanding of his duties.[2] The system of special circulars has been

---

[1] His ikon hung in the office of the *Rus* of 1904.

[2] " While standing sentry o'er the mind,
    Obedient to supreme command,
We really were not so unkind,
    Despite the musket in the hand ;
We held a power by us unsought,
    And, seldom frowning and severe,
Preferred to make our watch on thought
    A guard of honour, not of fear."

continued.   When the news of the mutiny on the *Prince Potyemkin*
reached Moscow, a circular from the censorship immediately forbade its publication.   A correspondent of *Rus* at Nizhny Novgorod carefully investigated the attack made by hooligans on
the reformers; he was at once stopped by a circular: "Nothing on Nizhny Novgorod."   From 1904 onward, foreign
correspondents have been free to send practically any messages
that they like, and a detailed account of each day's sitting of the
Moscow Congress of July 19th to 21st was allowed to enter Russia
freely in the *Standard*, while at the same time the *Slovo*,
a paper of the most moderate views, was stopped for making
mention of the Congress.   The work of blacking out an article
used to be done in a very crude way.   A Russian newspaper was subjected to the process so soon after printing that the censor's ink
blended with the printer's; but English papers only reach the
frontier some days after the ink on them has dried, and with a
little turpentine it used to be easy to remove the censor's blacking and read that passage first.   In this way I have discovered
that the censor had suppressed a harmless remark of *Punch* at
the time of the Peace Congress: " The Tsar's tip for the
Lincolnshire : General Peace,—and it came off."   Some sympathetic verses on Nicholas II. and Tolstoy suffered the same fate,
but a somewhat impertinent paragraph in another paper, describing
the Palace wrangles " over the body of the Emperor" was allowed
to go through.   Perhaps this particular censor only looked out
for the word Tsar.   The censorship has its own finesses ; thus
a book of a certain size and price is allowed to speak more freely
than a pamphlet, because few will be able to buy it.   Those who
have special leave to receive unexpurgated publications are by no
means few.

Russian newspapers, up to 1905, were much more colourless and,
generally, less hysterical than our own.   The private life of the
Emperor had to be absolutely respected ; and one would read no
snobbish comments on the personal appearance of celebrities,
written from over the corner of a crowd by the man in the street.
Foreign telegrams were printed in any order, under the names of
the towns from which they had been sent.   This meant that news
was hardly arranged at all; but it also made it easy for the
editor to thrust into the background anything which might

challenge the attention of the Censorship. The diseased exuberance of detail as to crime was altogether absent. Practically no
news of home politics was allowed to come through, so that the
Press could not be called, in any sense, a reflection of the national
life. Wherever, as in the *feuilletons,* literary expression was
left free, it reached a higher standard than that of the average
English newspaper ; but sometimes one would read surprisingly
weak articles, in which the writer would try to give an analysis
of his own sentiments after the manner suggested by Shchedrin
to the " froth-skimmers," or, again, long dreamy fantasies on the
slightest of political themes, which must have been inserted either
to please the Government or simply to mark time.

The Daily of the longest standing in St. Petersburg is the
moderately Liberal *Nóvoë Vrémya* (*New Times*) of A. S. Suvórin.
The editor, who is one of the chief figures in contemporary
journalism, is a man of strong individuality, and the part which
he has played under the Second Reaction, probably the most
difficult of all periods in the story of the Press, will undoubtedly
claim recognition later. But the study of how to say as much as
was possible under the régime of repression was not the best
qualification for leading the thought of a nation during a great
movement. The paper is inspired by a quite remarkable acuteness in gauging changes of the political barometer ; but it has so
often altered its tone during 1904 and 1905 that it no longer
commands any confidence. In May, 1904, it set about reporting
in detail all that concerned the Zemstva ; after Tsushima it spoke
with such boldness as hardly to be recognisable as the *Nóvoë
Vrémya* which we knew, and to attract the indignation of some of
the most reasonable of the Slavophils, who accused it of playing
to the gallery. But it has since then bowed to the rod more than
once. It has tried to hound on opinion against Finland and
against England. Many men have found it difficult to work
with A. S. Suvórin.

Rus was founded in December, 1903, by his son, A. A. Suvórin,
who had for some years played a prominent part in the management of the *Nóvoë Vrémya* and desired to take a bolder line. We
should not be far off the mark if we said that *Rus* was started to
lead the reform movement ; its views were strongly Liberal, and
it was edited so cleverly and so boldly, that it from the first

carried with it the warm approval of the majority of the Russian Intelligence. In June, 1905, it was stopped for a month, partly for its comments on the Emperor's speech of June 19th, partly, it would seem, in order that it might be prevented from influencing public opinion against the bureaucracy, during the period which was to precede the election of a national assembly. Since then the editor has been condemned to a year's imprisonment, and *Rus* has been extinguished. However, *Molva* and the *Twentieth Century* have practically been the same newspaper as *Rus*, only under different names.

Our Life and the *Son of the Fatherland* are more Radical in tendency, and have suffered many interruptions during 1905. Both have been placed under the preliminary Censorship; and the *Son of the Fatherland* has sometimes refused to appear at all, because nearly everything in it has been struck out. It has been especially active in exposing the weaknesses of the bureaucracy, and copies of it which bear this character have penetrated into the very depths of the country districts.

Perhaps the best newspaper of 1905 in St. Petersburg was the *Slovo*, or *Word*, founded during the reform movement and representing the common-sense and liberal patriotism of Slavophils who strongly desired reform. It was punished by the Censorship; and, at the same time, its moderation deprived it of the support of the public. By 1906 it was practically dead. It would have been sought as an ally by almost any Government which was not determined to rule Russia in direct opposition to the aspirations of the whole nation.

The *Exchange Gazette* certainly gives a great deal of news, but is neither daring nor steadfast. *Novosti* (the *News*), is supposed to be an organ of Jewish opinion, and does not carry much weight. The *St. Petersburg Gazette*, which has no great literary pretensions, has had a good deal of support amongst the humbler classes. The *Petersburg Sheet* (*Listók*) is little more than a reprint of telegrams for the man in the street. The *Village Messenger*, published in St. Petersburg, told the peasant that which the official class thought it desirable for him to know, and was widely read in the country districts. A number of fugitive papers of extreme tendencies have appeared and vanished; one, indeed, instead of giving fixed dates of publication, announced that it would issue " according to the disposition of the Censorship." Particularly was this the case during 1906; but the description of *Rech, Strand*, and many others of the more recent papers must be left to the historians of the Liberation Movement.

The *Svyét*, or *World*, was in 1905 the only reactionary paper which commanded extensive support; it had a strong national tinge, and penetrated into many country districts. It did not pretend that there was no need for reform. Much more extreme is the *Citizen* of Prince Meshchérsky, a man who has played a long and important part in Russian journalism, and who now boldly champions the most reactionary ideas. Outside its subscribers it has but small support, and the editor, clever as he is, enjoys but little credit.

The *St. Petersburg Gazette* (*Vyédomosti*) of Prince Úkhtomsky has naturally suffered from the collapse of the Eastern policy, of which its editor was one of the chief exponents. This paper has a special character of its own. It has been peculiarly violent in its attacks upon England, but they were never so base and unscrupulous as those which were a staple article of supply in the *Moscow Gazette*. Prince Úkhtomsky, Imperialist as he was, always had leanings towards Liberalism, and even towards Radicalism. A second newspaper, the *Break of Day* (*Razsvyét*), was started by him in 1905.

All the newspapers which I have mentioned are, or were, published in St. Petersburg. In Moscow the *Russian Word* (*Russkoë Slovo*) was in 1905 a paper of moderate views, and at least of respectable merit. The *Nóvoë Vrémya* daily sends by telephone, for publication in Moscow, some of the more important parts of its morning edition; but the best evening paper in Moscow was the *Evening Post*, strongly Liberal in its views and eminently business-like both in style and in arrangement. It was perhaps the first Russian newspaper to give anything like an adequate conspectus of the contents of each number. It suffered much from the Censorship.

No paper in Russia has a higher standard of character and of literary ability than the *Russian Gazette* (*Russkiya Vyédomosti*). It is pronouncedly Liberal; in a special sense it issues from Moscow University, as several of the professors are amongst its collaborators. Its studies of the chief questions of the time are detailed and serious, and its critical articles are written by men who have the weight of experts. It is only in volume that it is inferior to any English paper of the present day. It has often been threatened by the censorship, and was stopped for a time in January, 1906. *Put* (the *Way*) is more Radical.

The champion of reaction in Moscow is the *Moscow Gazette*. The old organ of Katkoff has certainly degenerated; the present editor has apparently no more to do with Katkoff than Torquemada has to do with St. Paul. The *Moscow Gazette* is still printed in the best type and on the best paper; even its enemies must own that in style it stands much higher than most of its contemporaries; it can also still claim that it strives to support the Government. But there its connection with Katkoff stops. It seldom dictates to the bureaucracy; rather it acts the part of jackal. It has recommended an increase in the number of Land Captains (1904) and an increase in the number of "trained censors" (1905); it has attacked the "weakness" of the police, and proposed that Russia should be placed under a military dictator (1905-6). During the war, a leading article compared Russia to ancient Rome, and explained the bloodshed in Manchuria by saying that it was the purpose of Providence that Russia, the only country that held the true faith, should some day conquer the world. This article was written in the style of a mystic; it had the character of a prophetic pronouncement; but even the most superficial observer could not think that the writer really believed what he was saying. In 1905 a reporter of the *Gazette* interviewed Father Barnabas, presumably because he felt the need of consolation; the holy man, when asked what would happen in the war, said that Russia was sure to win. "But," said the reporter, "our armies have been beaten, and our fleet has been destroyed." "We shall have a fleet," replied the Father, "and we shall have victory." And the *Moscow Gazette* assured its readers that there was now no further reason to be anxious. The *Gazette* shows no kind of scruple in its attacks on the Jews. During the war it insinuated that those who were killed outright were more fortunate than those who were trusted to the mercy of a Jewish surgeon; there was not a shadow of evidence for this charge. It was very largely responsible for the murder of the Liberal expert in land values, the converted Jew Mr. Herzenstein; for, shortly before the crime, it printed in heavily leaded type on its front page an indictment accusing Mr. Herzenstein by name of swindling certain peasants.   Before the elections it printed a map showing how Russia was to be dismembered by the Liberal party. It always assures the Emperor that the reformers are revolutionaries, and explains the Russian defeats by saying that they are a punishment for the nation's sins.   It is especially spiteful against England.   It suggested that our evacuation of Wei-hai-wei was intended to conceal secret designs of ours upon Port Arthur. Such reports as that which hounded on the hooligans of Moscow against the English colony as the fomenters of revolution always have the support of the *Moscow Gazette*, and as often as not are invented by it.

Amongst the more able provincial papers I may mention the *Region of the South* (*Yúzhny Kray*) of Kharkoff, a very important Conservative organ ; the *Kieff Citizen* (*Kievlyánin*) ; and the *Odessa News*.   In Sarátoff there are two good newspapers, in Yároslavl two that are moderately good, in Siberia one that has merit.   There are, of course, hundreds of provincial newspapers all over Russia.   In Warsaw all the best papers are Polish ; and in the Baltic provinces most are German.

During the summer of 1905, when officialdom was completely disorganised and discredited, the Press seized on its opportunity, and seemed, for the time being, to have completely changed its character.   One Slavophil described certain newspapers to me as " half newspaper, half *café chantant*."   No doubt the cry against bureaucrats was altogether exaggerated, and the Intelligence seemed to forget that the bureaucrats were its own product and even flesh of its flesh.   But for myself I was surprised that the Russian Press should as a whole have remained so loyal and so moderate.   The underground literature, which has so long existed in Russia and has been specially developed during the Second Reaction, might ordinarily draw off into secret channels some of the more violent attacks.   Yet in this year, when so many men came forward for the first time with their real opinions in the authorised Press, one had ample evidence for concluding that the champions of the throne had all along been frightened by a spectre.

Právo (*Right*) is a Review which, under the editorship of the two Hessens, has powerfully contributed to the formation of a Liberal party. The official Review of this party is the *Messenger of the Party of National Freedom.* The *Weekly,* founded by Prince Sergius Trubetskoy in Moscow, represents more moderate reformers but has few readers. The leading Reviews, the *Messenger of Europe* (Arsényeff) and the *Historical Review,* have rendered signal services, the latter by publishing documents of what may perhaps now be called the old régime.

A PRESS DINNER (June, 1904).

A large roomy summer restaurant almost outside the city. There is a busy hum of clever lively conversation ; all the doors are open ; other parties are dining in other rooms ; a throng of waiters hurries to and fro. We take the " foretaste " of *hors d'œuvres* and vodka standing at a very lavish kind of private buffet. The editor is a clever, humorous, hearty man in the prime of life ; I find myself seated opposite to him.

It might have been a Christmas party in a large united family, outspoken, hearty, and at times boisterous. Yet there was a great diversity of types : a thin bearded man like a French student, wearing no collar ; a keen, furious, and witty " Irishman " ; a big humorous man suggesting Corney Grain ; a professor with shrunken erudite face, who wrote *feuilletons.* One whose ability impressed me as much as anyone's was a solid-looking man with strange block-like face, quaint and shrewd, speaking seldom and in a high weak voice. The others felt a deep respect for him, and when his health was drunk all thronged round H.H. to kiss him.

The dinner was a hearty one : birds came round, and each man took one and ate it ; beer and champagne flowed freely. The first toast was the newspaper : " young it might be ; but childhood is eternal : Ἕλληνες ἀεὶ παῖδες : so that does not count," an excellent speech, of which the most applauded parts were short sentences uttered in a lowered voice. Next, the health of the English guest is proposed, " Many lessons have been learnt from England, as, for instance, in the freeing of the serfs." After this the fiery " Irishman " rises and pours forth a brilliant improvisation on English literature : " Byron wrote, and then Pushkin ; Byron was one of the few glorious men who could sing and speak together : speaking is only the half of utterance."

When this fiery frenzy is over, the editor, in carefully chosen language, lays down the policy of the newspaper : " There is a crisis ; there exists the strength which lifts, and makes new life possible." A hot-headed man proposes the toast, " May we have a Government which really represents us, as England has." He is interrupted by the capable H. H. : " We have heard of how our ironclads failed of effectiveness, because they consumed their coal too fast. Our editor is our ironclad. Let him keep in store a good stock of coal." So the professor gets up and talks with cool acumen of the literary work of England.

There are other speeches, and then we keep up a more or less general conversation :—Russia will be quite different in ten years, but the task of the reformers is immense. Russians are in a way vexed with England, because England is the lucky one ; she has passed the crisis of Reform and now uses her advantage to secure national successes. Russia cannot yet bring her full strength to bear on foreign questions. We talk over different disputes between England and Russia, and the antecedents of both English and Russian patriotism. I mention the great deliverances of the early years of each century : in the seventeenth the Poles could not keep the Kremlin ; in the eighteenth the Swedes could not reach it ; in the nineteenth Napoleon had to march out of it ; in the twentieth the Japanese will never get near to it. A quick-witted neighbour interrupts, " In the twentieth the Russians will be masters of it." I am asked to suggest the English canons for a reform movement. I sum up : the first word is faith, and next come insistency and moderation. " But Tolstoy," I am told, " says nothing of insistency and moderation." And this is indeed the difficulty ; to succeed, to have a right to succeed, these men must contain themselves ; and some said things at this dinner which they never contemplated saying when they entered the room. But there are many in Russia who are, with all their powers of mind and heart, working quietly for the sorely needed regeneration of their country. These are looking for the last key of the last door.

CHAPTER IX.

LIVES OF THE INTELLIGENTS.—THE REVOLUTIONARIES.

In this chapter I cannot pretend to make any adequate or all-round study of the present-day life of the Russian Intelligents. I cannot here do anything like justice to those general features of Russian life, which throw the charm of a genuine homeliness over every day that is passed by a foreigner in this country. I have a special purpose which is essential to the present study. I have to follow into its recesses that pessimism which has wrought such havoc in Russia, and has made revolution almost the normal attitude of many minds; and with this object in view I have often, so to speak, to pick out the worst. But it would be most unfair, if I were to let it be thought that my picture represents in proper perspective the whole life of the class with which it deals.

It is always interesting to hear an Englishman's account of his Russian acquaintances, because he nearly always fixes on the same words to describe them. Nearly all are hearty and pleasant, attractive and interesting, with the intellectual keenness of quick-witted children. Practically all the Englishmen who have lived long in Russia, especially those engaged in trade, will tell us that the Russian Intelligent is lazy, variable, and surprisingly easy-going. Yet the longer they stay in Russia the more they come to look upon it as home, and the more kindly they speak of the Russians. As one of them put it to me, "It is hard luck leaving England, but at least I'm going back to Moscow."

We enter a railway carriage, and it seems as if we had had a lifelong acquaintance with everyone in it. If a group of people are already talking they break off their conversation to ask us where we come from; the more distant our home, the greater is their interest. Somehow their questions are hardly ever impertinent. A Russian family in a railway compartment seems to have taken possession of it. They bring, perhaps, their own teapot, and ask you to join them. The children, without any *gêne*, go on with their own little jokes and stories and rhymes; the elders freely discuss their most private affairs. At night the passengers whom chance has thrown together compose themselves for rest with the easy comradeship of a group of schoolboys, and, at the same time, with a real regard for their neighbours' comfort. At the "dacha" or country villa, the day soon passes in clever talk and leisurely amusements. The whole party seems to do most things together. Perhaps it is an expedition to see the new boat-house, or to look on while the younger people play tennis; many Russians, especially ladies, are keen and skilful players. Croquet is also a favourite game. At St. Petersburg there are several yacht clubs; the members need not be at all wealthy, as most of the yachts are little sailing boats of the smallest size. There are frequent horse-races. The Russian boy is, by nature, a sportsman. I remember a keen cricketer who, for want of something better, spent an afternoon with me catching a croquet ball at long range and saving boundaries. He would not own that it "stung up" until I did. There are plenty of magazines and novels lying about. Perhaps someone gives a musical skit on the piano. The conversation is often of a very intimate kind. A Russian never spares himself, whatever subject he is discussing; if his own experiences bear on the question, they are at your disposal. In all this there is no over-assertion of the personality; on the contrary, it seems to be entirely forgotten, or rather treated as purely objective. After all, what does he matter to you or to the world in general?

Russian boys of this class I have always found peculiarly attractive. They seem to have the breeding, the intelligence, and often the information of a grown-up man, but without the passions, the selfishness, and the cynicism. Such was a boy of sixteen with whom I travelled for some days on the Volga. He might have been taken for the best kind of Eton boy of eighteen. I was making some criticisms on the Poles to him, when he interrupted me: "Yes, that's very interesting; I think I ought to tell you that my father was a Pole; but it's all right: go on about the Poles." His father, it seemed, had lost his estate and his rights of nobility, and had settled on the lower Volga. He wanted to know what class he belonged to; they said, "You can be a tradesman or a peasant"; "Oh, I'll be a peasant," he answered. The boy was therefore practically a Russian. He was a keen athlete, and slept lightly covered with the window open. Even when there was nothing in it, his conversation was always interesting. For instance, he told me a long story, full of imagination and detail, of how his mother was run away with and "came dashing past with dishevelled hair," and of all the strange things that happened to her when she lost her way in the streets of Berlin. I told him that a byelaw of an English railway forbade one to travel on the roof of a carriage. This idea he embellished with quite a pretty fancy. He goes up to an imaginary ticket collector. "What class, sir?" "Oh! well, I'm no class really; I'm simply going on the roof." When he received his money from home for the journey,—he was still at the Gymnasium,—he started in a very lordly style and soon had very little left. Twice running he unaccountably declined to dine on the boat, casually saying that he "did not care about dining to-night." When I found out the real reason, I had the greatest difficulty in getting him to be my guest; he only consented when I told him that I was very much hurt at his refusing my invitation. As we loafed through the streets of Nizhny, he slipped away from me to a shop and returned with a clumsy-looking parcel. When we got back to the boat, I found him in the cabin eating large chunks of cold sausage, bread, and cheese. We had it out, and at last he consented to borrow a small sum, which he returned by money order as soon as he reached his home.

The Russian Intelligent is before all things a creature of mind; mind in fact is what he idolises. A sure instinct tells him what is intellectually bad; and criticism is of a high order in this country, because people never scruple to say what they think. The cheap rubbish which is used in conversation by the unintellectual in England in order to mark time, would be utterly ineffective in Russia, because no one would pretend to enjoy it. A Russian is not very likely to offer to sing before company unless he really knows how to sing. Intellectual vigour is strong enough and general enough to prevent any one man from ever having a monopoly of a conversation, unless his superiority is exceptional. One of the highest compliments which can be paid to anyone is conveyed in the words "an educated man." A good saying, a quick thought, runs like a spark through this sympathetic audience. The great Russian writers enjoy a consideration which makes them almost the gods of the Intelligents. We all have our consciences of different kinds; in Russia a pointless criticism of Pushkin or Lérmontoff would give something like a shock to all who heard it. A clever and good lady, with whom I used to discuss many subjects, once said to me : "What a terrible thing it would be if a girl married a man who couldn't answer questions!" I assumed that she was thinking of questions as to his past life, but no, she meant purely general questions such as "What is the composition of coal?" or "Who was Attila?" I suggested that it would be more serious if she married a man who deserted her, as is constantly happening in Russia; she owned that she had not thought of it in quite that way. In a word, the intellect altogether takes precedence of the character.

The old instincts are so deep that few even of the Intelligents stand aloof from the corporate religious festivals of the great Russian family. Men whose lives in no way suggest religion will turn into a wayside chapel, to pay their due to what is after all the religion of the heart. Such a man will stand in a great dimly lighted church, awestruck at the thought of the majesty of God and of the littleness of himself. His emotion is undoubtedly sincere, but he may come out and resume his worldly life as if he had never had any thoughts of the kind. I heard of one woman of the class called "unfortunates" who insisted upon crossing herself in front of her ikon, before resuming her ordinary life of sin, "because to-morrow she would not be in a position to." Often it would almost seem as if religion were in one compartment of the mind and morality in another. Russians have more than once said to me, "With you in the forefront of religion stands reason ; with us it is feeling." A lady once threatened to invite a gentleman to meet me, because he was the only man whom she knew beside myself who ventured to give reasons for his belief. Apparently we were to have a trial of strength in the presence of outsiders. Religion is indeed one of the favourite subjects for midnight conversation. If you say you have got any, they want to understand all about it. "Now what is your dogma? And do you really believe it? No, surely that won't work out?" We can imagine a Jesuit priest spending much labour on such promising material, but at the end of it all he would probably find that his pupil took a simply objective interest, and just wanted to hear about something interesting. The subtle pleadings of casuistry generally fail completely against the critical ability of the Russian mind. A priest, however, who knew what he was talking about, told me that, indifferent as the Intelligents appear to religion, possibly some 40 per cent. say their morning and evening prayers to themselves. "The most serious," he said, "will be very reticent on the subject of religion, but it enters more into the practice of their lives than the casual observer would suppose."

In general, however, it is tolerably clear that whereas Orthodoxy is still the creed of the heart, the creed of the mind is very different. The mind worships intelligence, mind in general. This creed has already been described, and I have expressed my opinion that it often degenerates into a worship of the moods, or even a worship of the human body. My studies of it in Russia suggest that it engenders a great deal of sheer intolerance. A keen sense for the false note may, indeed, excuse the true musician for hearing discord everywhere; but it is less easy to justify the doctrinaire who throws dirt at the personality of anyone who simply does not happen to share his opinion. This is that worst side of femininity which is so strongly developed amongst all who have taken their creed from the French Revolution. The Intelligent is very fond of quoting such generalisations as "the dignity of man." I have heard a weedy little man, who had apparently failed to give up his ticket in a railway carriage, protest, "I too am a man." It is the old assumption that when once we are men we are all equal, all above the line, without any further need of discipline. It has led, not unnaturally, to that deification of everything human, even of the coarser instincts, which we saw in the short formulæ of the Nihilists. The human race has not spent century after century in the effort to eliminate its less honourable tendencies in order to take this sheer plunge back into what it calls nature. It is just like the rich heir who goes to gamble his all at Monte Carlo. Pleasure is the ιim of man, and God, if He exists at all, exists to supply man with pleasure; when God fails to do this, He must be cursed or denied. Those who ordinarily deny Him will even, in their vexation, invent Him again in order to curse Him. It is, again, the neurotic who throws himself from the top of a house because he is dazzled by the height to which the labours of his forefathers have raised him. And the nature to which he claims to return is not the true nature; it is rather what I will call a "black-coated" nature, full of all the assumptions and conventions of a highly specialised civilisation. A savage may feel free to go after anyone else's wife if she happens to be attractive; but the savage has to live a hearty open-air life in order to supply himself and his family with food, and must even be able to knock on the head, if need be, the man who wants to take his own wife from him; and the instinct of leaving another man's home alone was one which grew up very early, even amongst the most primitive peoples. In the same way, it was early discovered, by the majority of mankind, that the plan of general free love simply did not work out. What was to happen to the children, if they practically could not identify their parents? The jealousies of the harem may produce romance, but not what can really be called history. On this scheme, too, death is the one great blot; and the natural law which makes a man grow old condemns him from the first to a final despondency. Let him seize the moment of pleasure while it comes; there is no larger hope, and he must always be fearfully looking for the time when even his powers of enjoyment will fail of themselves. It is, in fact, a creed that has no roots in human nature or in the history of man. Cut off from their parentage, the "superfluous men" (as they call themselves in Russia) are condemned to a morbid self-examination, a sort of continual photography of oneself without one's clothes; and a single century or even a single generation has been enough to reduce the adherents of the new creed to an atmosphere of pessimism, in which the sensations are either stamped out or only survive to accentuate despair.

Into this pessimism and into the exposition of it has been poured, we must remember, the best work of some exceptionally good minds. The average Englishman, if he is sufficiently modest, may easily find himself at a loss when debating the question. None of his happy-go-lucky conventions, which simply tell him that he is " all right," will help him in the matter ; and he can only appeal to the broad fact that, at all events, the best ages of the world's history thought as he does.

Indeed, this is a wave which, like many others that issue from the great convulsions of the eighteenth century, has been felt strongly all over Europe, and perhaps nowhere so strongly as in Russia. We make a great mistake if we assume that it is entirely Russian in origin and peculiarly characteristic of Russia. We can further limit down the origin of distinctly decadent ideas to the new men of the sixties. If we may trust the maxim of the barometer, " Short notice, soon past," we have no reason to fear that this period will be eternal. But cynicism received a great deal of encouragement from certain conditions which are specially Russian. The nation was predisposed towards cynicism because it was one of the most backward in European civilisation. Clearly if civilisation could be proved to be a bad thing, then Russia had a very good chance of pre-eminence. It is thus that we must explain the imposing attitude assumed by the Russian Government after the fall of Napoleon, and the hysterical awe with which other peoples regarded it.[1] Besides this, the Russian Government was itself very cynical towards its subjects ; it claimed that it did not give them responsibilities because they were not worthy of them. And the Russian Intelligent has always been cynical towards his Government : " Crown stuff can't spoil," he says when a little vodka is spilt. A great " not " goes through everything in the country ; it is everywhere in the language. A pretty woman is described as " not ugly," an ugly woman as " not pretty " ; bad as " not good " ; clever as " not stupid." How many Russian names, in history and in fiction, begin with

Compare " The Cossack to his Courser " (" Chant du Cosaque "), Béranger :—

" All the bright lore of which Europe is proud,
    All the great dreams of an age that is gone,
  Sink in the dust that goes up like a cloud
      Round me and o'er, as thou bearest me on ;
  Temples and palaces fall 'neath thy stride,
      Laws, manners, memories, take themselves wings ;
  Neigh, my proud courser, ay, neigh in thy pride,
      Trample to ruin all peoples and kings."

" not," such as Nekrásoff, Nelidoff, Nezhdánoff, and Nekhlyúdoff.
It was " not " that conquered Napoleon.

> " No, no ! my Moscow never went
> To him in lowly homage bent ;
> No gift, no feast of welcome, no ! " [1]

One meets with several Russians, who seem to make it a point
of conscience to praise no one, to believe in no one. If any man
seems to believe or do anything that is good, he must be either
a fool or a hypocrite. One Emperor, who lived a very moral life,
was considered for that reason to be "not clever." In England
the cocksure guard, as the train starts, announces to the cocksure
passengers, "All right."   In Russia the corresponding expression,
almost the most common word in the language, is "nichevó,"
"nothing wrong—that is, as far as I know." It is always nothing
until it is something, and the something, when it comes, is nearly
always something bad.

There is, then, a strong prejudice in favour of the negative ; let
us see how it overpowers the struggling personality as it emerges
into life.   Here each fresh individual has to start out of nothing,
and the little life of a single man is generally not strong enough to
cope with the immense difficulties that hinder the development of
character. In 1898 a Russian friend wrote an article in the
Nóvoë Vrémya on some talks which he had had with me about my
first impressions of Russia. He expressed surprise that I should
have dared to say that 80 per cent. of Englishmen have a certain
amount of initiative and are tolerably contented with their lot;
to him, as a Russian, this seemed impossible. Later he told me
of two books on the subject of morality which had recently
appeared ; the one championed domestic fidelity, the other free
love. Both writers, he told me, acted up to their opinions, and
most people had not yet decided for themselves which was right.
In England the average man may be a poor creature, but he
is supported by a whole mass of traditions and conventions.
He finds, in every drawing-room, a narrow but fixed code,
to which he is likely to conform unless he is either possessed
of a strong will or liable to momentary hysteria. Not only what
he is to do, but what he is to think and believe, has been settled
in advance for him, and that not merely by a living autocrat, but

---

[1] Pushkin's " Eugene Onyéghin."

by all his own antecedents. A Russian has to fight his way to his own beliefs. Clearly, if he succeeds, they are likely to be very genuine, but what of the man who has not strength enough to succeed by himself? And even he who does succeed finds no machinery of public opinion which can put his experience at the disposal of others. In education proper as distinguished from instruction, that is, in the training of the will and of the character, the Russians are still novices. They are often talking about it because they know what is their lack. "Training, training, training—from our earliest childhood that is what we want"; so spoke a Russian lady in 1905 to the author of "Russia: Travels and Studies," Miss Annette Meakin. People who cannot discipline their own homes have told me how much they wished to set up a school, how charming it would be to train little boys. "A Russian," said Miss Meakin's informant, "hardly comprehends the meaning of the words 'sustained effort.'" If one man has this power, others look upon it as one of his personal attributes, and, though they admire, escape the need of imitation by the easy phrase "I am like this" ("ya tak"). Character is assumed to be due not to discipline, but to natural strength of will. Few phrases are more often used in Russia. At a dinner of the higher Intelligence, everyone around me seemed to be talking of "strength of will, strength of will." I thought it a curious subject for small talk; so I asked my neighbour, "Why are they all talking of strength of will?" She answered: "Because they haven't got any." It is, then, in a lack of moral traditions that the young Russian grows up. In no country is home feeling likely to be stronger; but control is rare. Indeed, one meets with many fathers from whom it would be unreasonable to expect control; they are too unrestrainedly pleasant. "What is 'Navy Cut'?" said a bearded man of forty to me, reading from a tin of my tobacco. "It's a way of trimming a beard," I said. "What is it like?" "Why, if you cut off that tuft of yours, your beard would be 'navy cut.'" He took a pair of scissors and cut it off. "Now," he said, "I'm 'navy cut.'" Such impulses are too quick for us Englishmen; another friend, with the excuse that he saw in my face a resemblance to the portrait of Sir H. M. Stanley, threw his arms round me and kissed me before I could get my guard up. Even men of importance are sometimes almost like big children in their lack of reticence and self-control. A leader in the first Duma would claim twice his real number of adherents. A member of a party would claim to be the chief leader; even one of the foremost men talked much too often of what he would do when he was Minister. One can, then, easily imagine that the rare boy, who takes the trouble to discipline himself, has very independent opinions as to his teachers.

The ordinary child grows up in an atmosphere of feeling; and it is feeling that he is encouraged to glorify. "Nobility" is his ideal, but his interpretation of it is likely to be a haphazard one. Thus, most Russians are peculiarly generous about money. If you want some, you ask your friend; and if he has any, he gives it you as if it were a matter of course; if he does not, it is "ignoble." You ask me for the £10 on which my family is to live for the next fortnight; it will be noble for me to hand it to you without a thought. "Reckoning" is in Russia a word of sinister taste. The Englishman's generosity, which acts after reflection, is too complicated a thing for the Russian to understand. He recognises, with pleasure, that the effect seems to be the same; but he is a little suspicious of a balancing of motives which his mind does not follow. Nobility consists in absolute fidelity to the instincts, not in the control of them. A genuine man should say what he thinks, and, as his moods and consequently his thoughts will change from day to day, his nobility may make him an interesting, but a rather surprising companion. For instance, he may suddenly become very disagreeable; do not interfere with him; perhaps it has nothing to do with you; perhaps all that he wants of you is that you should not "hinder his mood." Subjective words are much more commonly used in Russia than in England. "Nice," they will say, where we say "good." "So-and-so," I said to a friend, "is a good man." "How do you know that he is a good man?" I was asked. "You can only say that you like him." To-day a plan or a person may seem nice; to-morrow moods may change. Wallace tells of a foreigner who was invited to see over a large Russian business. When he arrived his host said: "Otkhotyél (I have stopped wanting it)," and the next train was not too early. If I fall in love, it is my duty to obey the holy instinct. Love should leap all barriers, including that of a previous marriage;

hesitation would be ignoble; in fact, it would prove that there was no love. To-day's love is of course the only real love; but next time will be the same when it comes. "I," said a friend, "shall toss up when I want to marry"; and, to illustrate his view, he told me of the following experience. He fell in love with a charming lady and asked her to marry him. After a year, she said that she liked him well enough to consent. He obtained a post, went down to the country, and worked hard to make an early marriage possible. One day two letters reached him by the same post, one from his lady and one from his best college friend. Both letters said the same thing: "they were very sorry, he was the last person in the world to whom they would have wished it to happen, but they had fallen in love with each other, and love cannot be resisted; would he be best man?" He agreed, and took his mother with him to support him through the ceremony. To her the bride's mother frankly remarked: "Your son is the only lucky one of the three." Just before the ceremony, both the bride and the bridegroom drew him aside, each separately, and said: "I am not so sure now whether this was the right thing. Supposing it all turns out wrong, will you stand by me and be my friend?" Though he in each case refused, he did indeed later receive a letter from the lady begging for his advice and help. I remember another Russian acquaintance who for a few days looked very sad. I asked if he had heard some bad news, and was told, "Oh, no; his brother's being married." The bride had been engaged to my acquaintance, but the brother had, to use the Russian phrase, "fought her out from him." And this, I was told, was not so unusual a matter as to warrant special pity; on the contrary, the failure was supposed to put a kind of slur upon him.

In the life of the young Russian one sometimes sees an analogy with the Russian seasons of the year. Russia has a quick and extraordinarily vigorous spring, a sultry and tempestuous summer, a dreary, miserable, and piercing autumn, and then the long, cold winter. The young man is full of hope and aspiration. He believes in the good, and is going to work for it; yet what he dreams of is a human paradise, in which the glory of his achievements will be, after all, personal.

It is not that he seeks the praise of his fellows; it is that he
wants to taste to the full what he calls the joy of life. It is
an exuberance of vitality proper to a certain age, and as such
his elders regard it; they look on with encouragement, but
also with a smile. The boy becomes a man; his work, his
passions, and their consequences become serious. The warmth
of his vitality is concentrated, but there is no strong society with
wise rules to tide him over the transition which comes with the
first consciousness of manhood. On the contrary, even at school
he has bruised himself on the barrier which has been set up against
all initiative; and the system which refuses him responsibility
leaves him perfectly free as to the choice and manner of his
pleasures. The boy of common stuff or weak nature will be
debauched before he knows what dissipation is; friends will take
him to evil places, and by the time he is conscious of what has
happened the mischief will have been done. The best kind of
Russian has much of the nature of the poet; with him it will be
different. In spite of the pessimism that is whispered all round
him, he may hold to the ideal that the world is good; but it will
be largely an ideal of emotion, and probably an important part of
it will be the belief that a twin soul is waiting for him somewhere.
One of the "rights of man" is to have a perfect wife; if this is
not supplied, Providence has cheated us. The perfect wife is a
product not in any way of training, but entirely of nature. The
success of a man's marriage in no way needs to be prepared
by his discipline of himself; it is to come as a gift of God.
Thus the young idealist, quite forgetting his own imperfections,
expects an angel to tumble out of the skies into his arms; and
indeed, sooner or later, something very agreeable, quite like an
angel, does fall somewhere near him. He need not hesitate;
he clasps her to his heart. But the women of Russia are
pretty well as intelligent as the men, and even more exacting.
After a time it transpires that they are both human. The undis-
ciplined idealism on both sides makes the disillusionment more
abrupt. In many cases there comes a sudden repulsion which
is purely physical. Physical perfection has been asked for, and
that is a very hard claim to satisfy. Thus Anna Karyénina has
something like a shock whenever she catches sight of her
husband's big ears. "What a shame to give me a man who has

big ears!" The proverb says that "birds of a feather flock together"; very often it is just the opposite. Reason certainly unites, but moods separate. If two persons are both unreasonable, it does not follow that they will therefore get on well together. The man who worships his own moods cannot reasonably expect an equally moody woman to follow him dutifully through all the changes of his temperament; and Russians, as I have said, make no difficulty about following the instinct of the moment, or about telling other people what they think of them. Possibly the young affection collapses once for all in a single violent scene; and from that time both parties are disillusioned. Very possibly there will be no attempt to resist the new mood of cynicism. I used to discuss with an intimate friend what a Russian and what an Englishman would do under given circumstances. We once imagined a young engaged man, sitting at breakfast with a brother who is his nearest friend. He opens a letter from his sweetheart and finds that she has suddenly jilted him. My Englishman handed the letter across to his brother, who, after a minute's silence, said: "Hard lines, old chap!" His Russian also handed over the letter to his brother, who, after a short pause, said: "Let us go to the Gipsies." The Gipsies are a kind of *café chantant* entertainment, described to me by a witty Russian as "Green grow the rashes, oh!" There the two brothers would eat, drink, sing, laugh, and weep; "and then," my friend added very impressively, "there would be a rift in his heart for ever,"—quod erat faciendum. Very often such a crisis may be accompanied by strong physical sensations. As the novelist tells us, "a light went out of his eyes, the white world became grey to him," and so on. I have chosen a love affair as my instance, because in nine cases out of ten the first great disillusionment is of this kind; but it is quite as easy for the young political idealist to break away in keen disgust at a piece of treachery or even at a manifestation of pettiness in one of his colleagues. In this case, too, the real has proved to be different from the perfect; therefore he has been wronged. Some get to this state simply by the contemplation of how much they have sacrificed, and how little material good it has brought to them. But, whatever be its cause, a sudden break of some kind seems one of the most common phenomena in the life of the ordinary Intelligent. After it is over, he knows something, he is wise; he has an advantage over the youthful dreamer. Men who are ten years younger than yourself may say to you: "You are young; when you are older, you will understand." And indeed the fruits on the lower branches of the tree of knowledge may easily produce both this sourness and this pride.

After the break anything may be expected. With some there is a long apathy, varied by a calculating pursuit of creature comforts. With others there is the habit of a constant snarl, with others, again, a wonderful self-renunciation and a long life spent for the good of others, without the hope or desire of any reward. More commonly there is a haphazard, disjointed, nervous existence without any purpose at all. Often, however, the cynic will take another innings of aspiration. " There she is again," says the widowed Prince Andréy in "War and Peace," when he hears a young girl singing in the room above him. He looks at the old oak; it has broken forth into leaf—oh, wonderful! —and his heart is full of gladness. When next he passes the oak, its leaves have withered away. Oh, fate and destiny ! For these revivals there is a conventional name in Russia, "second youth," which is supposed to come almost in the ordinary course of nature ; it is even given as a reason against early marriages, or marriages between two persons of the same age. There is a great deal of theorising on youth in general. "He," says a Russian, "has a mass of youth." It is like having a balance at one's bankers against future excesses, whether noble or ignoble.

We have tried to account for the wave of pessimism, and to follow its action on a chance individual. There was a little English boy of seven who, as his elder brother was a musical genius, used to say : " And I will be a joiner ; I will do something useful." Sour grapes are equally sour in Russia. If I meet a man who says that he has got something that I have not got, either he must be lying, or it must be not worth having. No one, of course, really leads a moral life ; but I, at least, am better than some others because I make myself out to be worse than I really am. In fact, many Russians wonder that anyone should embark in an independent enterprise of his own at all, unless it is for the intelligible purpose of making his fortune. The Russian martyr suffers more devotedly for his ideals than martyrs in other countries ; but we are now discussing the ordinary man, without backbone or purpose. This man is in the hands of what he calls " destiny." If something goes wrong the fault is always with destiny.[1] I do not suggest that there is no destiny, but I never could understand from my Russian friends how they came to know what was destined, why destiny was always against them, why it was always to be recognised in anything that hindered activity, and why its judgment had to be at once accepted as final. I would almost feel inclined to translate the word " destiny " into English as " laziness." To Russians I am saying nothing new ; laziness is recognised as a Russian characteristic, whether it is treated as a pleasing weakness or as a besetting sin. It was so at the time of the Will of Vladímir Monomach ; and in 1904 the Metropolitan Antonius chose this term to illustrate to me Russia's present-day progress : " You will find less laziness."

Another very favourite word with the Russian Intelligence is " despondency." Nervousness is rampant all over Russia ; nerves are a subject of common talk. A doctor, who is called in to see you, asks if you have "nerves." A schoolboy who had received a bad mark shot his teacher on the spot ; another hanged himself by his belt to save his honour. The Russian Intelligence cannot be called superstitious in the usual sense, yet it believes in bogies as much as the Russian peasant. It willingly dwells upon gloomy thoughts and allows them to take colossal proportions. In 1905, while Russia was filled with the echoes of a thousand conflicts, the despondency of the Intelligence was more noticeable than ever. Twice in ten weeks (June to August, 1905) I could feel it come over the whole country,—a kind of mental paralysis, an overpowering mood which said to the zealous reformer : " No, the task is too big for you ; you cannot go through with it." It was just the same after the

---

[1] See the two fables of Kryloff, "The Two Countrymen " ("Dvá Muzhiká ") and "The Calumny " ("Napráslina "). In the latter a Brahmin who has been cooking eggs over a candle on a fast-day is surprised by his superior, and puts all the blame on "some cursed fiend " :—

" But here from out the stove a voice cried out for shame :
' Yes,' says the little fiend, ' it's always us you blame ;
Why, I myself from you
Have just learnt something new ;
And till to-day I never knew
How eggs are cooked by candle flame.' "

dissolution of the first Duma. Naturally enough, the mere strain of doing two days' work in every day, that is, of attending to one's ordinary duties and also appearing at the reform meetings, told very heavily even on the most vigorous. Beyond that, Russia holds so closely together, that her salvation must needs be a corporate one or nothing at all; and to watch all at once the thousand warring interests mapped out on that huge canvas would surely be enough to distract the most confirmed optimist. But these sudden fits of despair have not always so good an excuse. In 1898 a friend who was engaged on some admirable work was staying in a Moscow hotel; when I visited him there he said to me: "I mean to give it all up, and go back and live at home." The reason was that he had overheard a party of girls laughing and singing in the next room; this had reminded him of home, and he could no longer bear to be alone. Other instances are to be found in any present-day Russian novel. The Russian nature, like the Russian language, is in many respects soft and pliable. If one pampers one's feelings, it is easy to make something out of nothing. Training is the only cure for this evil.

The irregularity of life of the Russian Intelligents is a commonplace all over Russia, and is frankly admitted by the Intelligents themselves. They would probably claim, and perhaps with justice, that immorality in their case means not bad morality, but no morality. It is as if they believed that morality is simply superfluous. In default of the newspaper, the Russian novel has been the mirror of Russian life; and its clear and convincing picture shows us that scruples of morality have been the exception. The most common kind of immorality is that which comes from sheer want of backbone. A friend once showed me a picture of an extremely smug-looking family of all sizes and ages, such a family as one of our own poor would describe by the words "little steps upstairs." I confessed that I found the picture simply plain and commonplace. "Oh, no," said my friend, "it is not commonplace at all. You see that old man of about seventy: he was long ago married to this middle-aged lady of fifty; these were their children;" and he picked out the larger-sized figures in the photograph. "Well, one day this man said to his wife: 'It is not fair that you should always be tied to me; I am getting old and cannot be the right sort of husband for you. Now, I have thought of a plan which I think should make you happy: I shall divorce you, and I have found an excellent fellow to take my place ; I have noticed that you seem quite to like him already." The wife answered : " You are my best friend, my constant benefactor ; that is just what I should like, but I hope you will go on living with us ; I look upon you as a father." To this he consented. The second husband was now introduced ; the second family began to appear. But the whole family—or, shall I say, colony? —remained so harmonious that they were able to produce long afterwards this smug and respectable photograph. I take this story on trust, and tell it because it is one of the least unpleasant that I can find to illustrate my subject ; but I do not know how these good people settled the divorce question. Probably, as in so many other cases, the sanction of the Church was not asked for.

Englishmen who have found themselves condemned to town life have set about finding a substitute for the hard exercise of the country ; and hence comes much of the popularity of our games. In Russia the Intelligents are often cut off from the sports of the field ; and the enterprising man is, perhaps, best able to show his prowess in the field of love-making. Anyone's wife will do, and, in fact, as Tolstoy explains in " Anna Karyénina," the sporting suitor feels a special relish in the conquest of a married woman. There are in Russia many Don Juans, impervious to rebuffs and able to count on the general approval. In one of his short stories in verse, Pushkin relates how Count Null (Núlin) arrives at a country house in the absence of its owner, spends an enjoyable evening with his hostess, and tries to push his success to the furthest point in a single day ; he gets no more than a slap on the face, and none of the characters seem to think the adventure at all out of the way. Chekhoff is the accepted exponent of the present-day Intelligent. In his "Duel," the heroine, who is in the best society of a provincial town, practically goes the round of all the good-looking men in the place before she settles down to a steady life. In another of his tales, which, as a piece of narrative, is of a very high order, he gives a simple convincing account of a young man's adventure in the country. The young man is made to tell his own story. He goes to stay with his oldest friend, who has a beautiful wife. He has often casually thought of his friend's wife, and imagined for his own amusement conditions under which he might fall in love with her. One day, as he and his friend are returning from a visit to the nearest town, the husband, in an access of unnecessary frankness, says to him: "You think I am happy: I have a beautiful wife and beautiful children; but, at the bottom of it all, I know that my wife does not love me." The wife, so far, has always adopted a peculiar manner towards her guest. Whenever they are alone, she will say: "It is dull for you here without your friend." Our hero now thinks that he sees daylight through the riddle. To say that he is in love with the lady would be ridiculous; he simply thinks her very agreeable, and it appeals to him that she should not love her husband. On his return, he is left alone with her; and when she again talks about his being dull without his friend, he draws her into a very intimate conversation. When she says "Good-night," or rather, as it is in Russian, "Quiet night," he answers, "Damn this night if it's quiet!" He then practically walks into her arms. Next day he leaves the house for good, and ends his account by saying that he believes the husband and wife are still living together. It would be impossible to be more cynical. The Russian's view is that what is natural cannot be wrong,[1] and he will state it over and over again in connection with this subject. Dissipation of the most common and methodical kind is not concealed from a man's sisters; I have even heard them joke him about it. It is assumed as a matter of course, even by the best kind of lady, that if a man becomes engaged, and goes away for a year, he is almost certain to be unequal to the ordeal of waiting. By some, early marriages are advocated as the only possible chance for conjugal fidelity. A student of twenty often marries a girl student of the same age, at the shortest notice and with the least possible amount of ceremony; I know of one girl who only interrupted her work for the wedding day and returned to it next morning. The question of means is hardly considered at all; the young couple will live in a single room at a students' hotel. I am told of cases in which two couples have shared one room. "Short notice, soon past." The wife may naturally fear her husband's attraction for other women; she may easily begin to fear, before there is any actual reason to fear. Often there will be no ceremony at all; love and nature can, of course, dispense with it. Some

---

[1] This axiom was one of the "short formulæ" of the Nihilists.

marriages are purely quixotic. It is impossible to tell how affairs of the heart will end ; a sudden access of generous impulse will settle a question which has been dragging on for months, in just the opposite way to that which one would have expected. Sometimes such a sudden impulse will become to the man who feels it a permanent asset of self-respect, and he will remain extraordinarily constant to it. A man of my acquaintance, who married a woman with a natural daughter, brought up the daughter as his own child, making, it seemed, no manner of difference between her and the children of his own marriage. Some students, I am told, gathered from Dostoyévsky's writings that it would be noble for them to redeem someone, and, not stopping to study their own qualifications as redeemers, they married women off the streets. To those who know anything of Russia, there is nothing untrue to life in the plot of Tolstoy's "Resurrection." Nekhlyúdoff's long effort to rehabilitate the woman whom he has ruined will commend itself as noble to the young man who still has his ideals, and will be condemned as folly by the cynic; but it is equally intelligible to both. Friendship is, of course, much less exacting than love, and much less selfish ; and, as a choice of the heart rather than of the mind, it can at least be quite as deep and as constant in Russia as in England.

There is ground for thinking that the official system, while refusing to its subjects what was most necessary to them, has made altogether unnecessary concessions to their sentimental ideals. If there is any love element in an atrocious murder, even though that love element be of the most disreputable kind, the criminal may get off very lightly. The Intelligent is so impregnated with the "dignity of the human person," that one can see a shock go through him when he hears that we still retain corporal punishment. Of course for him flogging is simply one of the worst weapons of the absolutist system, employed without any discrimination or justice. For him the dignity of the person is one of the noblest causes, whose victory has not, by any means, been adequately secured. Historically he is right, but it seems a pity that two boys cannot fight out their own quarrel without both becoming criminal before the authority which claims the sole right to punish. It seems a pity, too, that any bold action of an offended man, unless it invests itself with the pseudo-nobility of the duel, should be looked upon as an insult to authority, and all the more so in a country where public opinion is so weak and law so ineffective. There are many Intelligents who would have been kicked at one of our public schools, and to whom a kicking would have done a great deal of good. A country gentleman of my acquaintance asked the priest's son to come and join him and the village schoolboys in a game of football. "I," replied the young Intelligent, "occupy myself with mental exercises." My comment was that the boy wanted kicking. "That's just it," said my friend : "no one is ever kicked in this country." There are other far more deserving cases. Many a boy grows into manhood without respect for anything except cleverness in looking after one's own interests, because he has never been chastised by a crude but just public opinion. The lack of initiative in this respect is as regrettable as in any other. Strange as it may seem, kicking, as we understand it, is indeed non-existent in Russia ; or, if we must regard official control as its substitute, it is too often the wrong people who get "kicked."

In Russia the real substitute for public opinion is a spirit of kindly toleration. The Russian, who has but little self-consciousness and does not worry himself, is, in general, very charitable towards the failures of others. It is not that he is necessarily prepared to right their wrongs : it is not that he approves of their conduct ; what he feels is pity. All victims of destiny or of the Government are to him "unfortunates"; of course he can distinguish the generous soul who has given his career for the public good from the ordinary criminal ; but he extends a common pity to all who have fallen under the displeasure of authority. Thus the prisoner who comes out of gaol is not precluded from finding employment; society bears him no grudge. In fact, if one raised this question, a Russian would probably tell one, in his easy pleasant manner, of whole villages where all the inhabitants are thieves. If a servant-girl loses her character, it is a matter of indifference. As a lady once said to me, "Well, they have pretty well all gone through that." The merchant who has embezzled on a large scale can return to society after the expiry of his term ; there will be comments, but there will be no general ostracism. The difference is, of course, that we in England are trying hard to defend ourselves as a society, and are sometimes very prudish and very merciless in doing so, whereas in Russia

it is not a society that is defending itself, but a Government as
the warden of society.   A Russian friend expressed great surprise
that I should expect to find a public opinion in the country.
Russians often complain that, as the Press is never able to summarise and compare the tendencies of thought all over Russia, it
is impossible to know whether the extremist views of this
drawing-room are more representative than the equally one-sided
but opposite views of that one.   Of course the Russian Intelligents,
as followers of nature, have their own moral sense; but the
exaggerated worship of the mind, of "humanity," and of the
dignity of man, accords very ill with the reckless and selfish
dissipation of some of these modern pessimists, and their disregard of the chief attributes which differentiate men from other
animals.   "They are *baboos*," said a brilliant Russian critic; "they
have a coat and no trousers."

On no account should it be forgotten that the bureaucrat
is very often an ex-student.   In Russia nearly everyone is
directly or indirectly an official.   Work which in England would
be free of all Government interference is there under very
direct control.   But it is easy for there to be a conflict between
Government employment and personal ideals in a country which
has had the history of Russia, and in a class which has suffered
as the Russian Intelligents.   To accept a frankly official post
may seem to some almost like a recantation.   On the one side
are the generous and happy-go-lucky instincts of an untrained
individualism; on the other the calculating pursuit of what is
expedient.   The man who settles down into official life may in
some measure have to break his connection with the past.   But
unfortunately, this sudden sacrifice of what a man counts to be
best in himself is often demanded at the moment when the
student finds it necessary to earn a living; he has hardly any
choice except either to take a great many things as he finds them
or to set himself against the whole system of society.   Naturally
it is very few who have the moral courage to choose this second
lot; and even they will hardly find in their ideals or in their
training sufficient strength to guarantee them a safe conduct
through so great a struggle.   The evidence of all my informants goes to show that those students who have shouted
loudest against the Government become the most submissive

and self-seeking officials. I remember, in particular, an official
who told me his own story. The students of Kharkoff rose
to remedy several very real grievances; they demanded that
spies should be excluded from the University, and that the
rigorous control of the police should be replaced by a university
court of honour. As one of the ringleaders, he was sent to
serve as a private soldier in the army; later he was restored
to his rank by special grace of the Emperor, partly in consequence of the intercession of powerful friends. Of his former
ideals no trace was to be seen except the bitterness which they
had left behind them. "Once," he said, "I had to touch my
hat to them," pointing to the railway conductor who passed
through the compartment; "now they must touch their hats to
me : my shoulders are too broad" (which means, "My protectors
are too powerful"). He seemed to find pleasure only in his
personal escape from tribulation.

The man who has become a bureaucrat is aware that promotion comes by favour or as the prize of obedience. In so
far as he takes an interest in his work, he perhaps becomes a
simple *carriériste*, an opportunist who is trying to look after himself. It would be ridiculous to say that there is no sense of
duty or responsibility amongst Russian officials; the material is
too good for that to be possible. But what right has one to
expect this sense as a matter of course from a man to whom duty
means following the various whims of various Ministers, and for
whom there is little responsibility except that of obedience?
It has been said, "In Russia don't be born clever, but be born a
cringer" ("podléts"). Such men may easily come to the top.
The honest man may think the whole game not worth playing at
all; and he will, perhaps, sit despairing amongst reams of official
reports, drinking endless cups of tea, smoking endless cigarettes,
and generally doing his duty in that state of life to which he has
limited himself. We can quite understand that the nation, as a
whole, might refuse its confidence to any Minister who has
been trained in this close atmosphere. In Russia there are also,
unfortunately, a large number of parasites who sponge on the
opportunities of the official system. The censor Freigang has told
us that the censors were practically all spying upon each other,[1]

[1] See p. 278.

and there has never been a lack of "informants," who would try to pull a man down for the sake of winning favour for themselves or place for their friends. I have seen instances of the way in which a number of clerks will set themselves to hunt a senior out of his post.

The official is more often than not two persons wrapped up in one; as a Government employé he may even be lazy and resourceless, constantly waiting for orders, and too often rough and brutal in the tone which he adopts to those under his charge. Let him take off his official coat, and he can almost as easily shuffle off the official manner; he is now an ordinary member of the Russian Intelligence, and is probably exceedingly proud that he belongs to Europe rather than to Asia. The private morals of the officials, over which the Government assumes no control, are the same as the morality of the Intelligents; the only difference is that, as the official may possibly have made a sacrifice of his best ideals, he is perhaps less scrupulous and a little more cautious than others in his pursuit of pleasure. Officialdom is seen at its worst where it is farthest from headquarters. Some tales of life in Siberia or Central Asia offer a picture which it would be hard to match for thriftlessness, laziness, corruption, and sheer demoralisation. According to one of my informants, who had served as an official, nearly all his colleagues were rogues[1] ; they were men who had failed in European Russia. All the real work which he had to get through in his two years of Government service could have been done in one week. Men would go on shooting expeditions, and put down the expenses to the Government. The natives all deteriorated in proportion as they got to know the Russians better.

The *insouciance* and recklessness of Russians is nowhere better illustrated than by Russian revolutionaries. These people are certainly very forgetful of themselves and their own interests in their devotion to the corporate task which they are attempting. Things which we should expect to be told only to a chosen few are communicated even to children. A boy of sixteen comes to me with the smile of a sly child saying, "Ha, ha! I know

---

[1] An English friend told me that on entering a saloon in Canada he found the company, which consisted entirely of old public school boys, discussing for what offence each had been expelled from his school in England.

who killed Ivanoff; it is my friend Kok," and he shows me a postcard with the words " Takok Ivanova," which he interprets : " Terrorist Anarchist Kok killed Ivanoff." The boy addressed me simply as one interested in Russian politics ; he knew that I did not share his opinions and detested these methods. Was it needful to send him all announcements in the manner of a German "Bierverein"? In the course of my investigations I have met persons responsible for the conduct of revolutionary organisations, and have been struck by the freedom which they allowed to themselves when questioned by foreigners. While taking many somewhat demonstrative precautions to insure secrecy,—which, indeed, is very natural,—some of them would neglect other safeguards which seemed far more obvious. I entered a shop in one of the chief streets of a large town. " Is George here ? " I asked. " No." " Well, then, is Basil ? " " Yes, but who sent you ? " " Why, Jane." " Oh, then come and have a talk." " But," I suggested, "let us come to my hotel." " Oh, no ; these people are all ours "; and that though customers were coming in by the open door from the street. More than this, some of them were ready, without any prompting, to commit themselves to statements, which, one would think, should have been withheld from all outsiders, and that apparently for no other reason than that they were led away by their enthusiasm for their subject. If they had limited these confidences to those who shared their views, it would have been more intelligible ; but it almost seemed that they sought any opportunity of posting foreign correspondents in their doings. One of my acquaintances received a quite unnecessary letter : " Citizen, this is to tell you that the general strike has begun." Certainly a strike had been decided upon, but it never had any real existence, except on paper. Sometimes, when the revolutionaries have been asked why they did not keep more secret the plans of their demonstrations, they have answered: "That is impossible, so we tell everyone, in the hope that as many will come as possible." I have known them sell tickets for a meeting in advance. All this would seem to suggest that they are aiming rather at publicity than at success ; it is as if they knew what the Foreign Press expects of them and were willing to use to the full the opportunities which it offers. Thus life is made more interesting for us by the frequent announcement of " Revolutions ". which, in the end, prove abortive.

I have had to emphasise certain common aspects of the average Intelligent; but of course I do not assume that we can judge a whole class of people together, or that the average individual is only this or only that. Idealism is nowhere more triumphant than in Russia; sacrifice is nowhere more devoted, or more complete. Russians themselves often divide people into those with character and those without, and they include the vast majority under the second head. Where one does meet character— and one meets it more and more often in every succeeding year— there is a perseverance and an independence which the average Englishman will sometimes feel to be above his limited understanding. I have met not a few of such men; they are not merely the salt of Russia, they are the salt of the whole earth, and one longs for the time when they may be able to fulfil their perfect work in it. Such, to take one of the rarest examples, was Prince Sergius Trubetskóy, who, though allied by birth and position to many other interests, was specially a champion of the Russian Intelligence, and was capable of seeing far enough into its aspirations and its failures to be able to approve or to pardon where the less wise could only smile or condemn. And even in its present untrained state, the Intelligence as a whole, taken at its worst, is never lacking in the extraordinary charm of a strong personal attractiveness, which remains in the memory long after unpleasant details have passed out of it. The keen intellectual atmosphere, the simple good breeding, the genuine good nature, the broad and generous hospitality, the easy intimacy and the long earnest conversations, that power of extracting pleasure from haphazard interests which one associates with the ideal travelling companion, all these make Russia, to the intelligent Englishman, nothing short of a second home.

It is said that one friendship teaches more than very many acquaintances. " The Russ," when I first met him in St. Petersburg, was just leaving the University. He was a quick and clever youth, somewhat Byronic, with his mind rather in his heart than in his head. He had powerful friends, and was starting work as a journalist. He had schemes for telegraphing pictures, and, if a whole page of a newspaper could thus be telegraphed at a low cost, one of the journalistic problems of Russia would be solved.

His patriotism had nothing Chauvinistic about it. It was a natural instinct which only made him the more intelligible to an Englishman. His religion was deep and native; he never felt called upon either to apologise for it or to force it on others. He would step in to the Iversky Gates to worship, or would in all seriousness discuss doctrine for hours with Old Believers. A rush of sympathy came over him when he saw the altar of the Priest-less People sealed up. Of his many gifts to me those which meant most were two ikons.

His interests were wide, and he started on a journalistic tour through Russia. In winter he would jolt with peasants in the midst of a waggon-train, or march with pilgrims; in summer he would float down the Dnyépr on a peasant's raft, taking his morning header each day in his chain and cross. For the peasants he conceived a great love, and he was certainly the right person to talk with them, for a more simple natural man I have never known. He also got to know some of the best of Russian thinkers, many of whom then lived isolated in their country homes.

He came as a correspondent to England, and spent some months travelling about with me. He never learnt the language well, and depended upon my interpreting; but he so thoroughly fitted into our home life that everyone seemed to forget that he was a foreigner, and looked upon him rather as an Englishman who happened to be a Russian. He talked over the Boer war with complete intelligence and sympathy, though I traced in his first article thereon all my own opinions, allotted now to a comely lady who crossed her legs, now to an elderly Englishman with whiskers. Being refused leave to see Portsmouth Harbour, he gazed steadily out to sea while we were passing the mouth of it, murmuring, "I may not look: I am a Russian spy." When we bicycled past an ugly cemetery, he said, " I would rather not die than lie in that cemetery," as if renouncing his most treasured privilege. The view which most appealed to him was that from the Wear Bridge in Sunderland; he said that it "meant life." This English world was strange to him; the great shipyards gave him the impression of moving through a pomp of stage scenery. At the farthest point of a mine which runs far under the sea, we talked with a naked man who was working there alone; this man knew that every item of his work was registered for payment above. My friend was amazed at his initiative. "A Russian," he said, "would under such circumstances just sit down or go away." Together we visited many people who were worth listening to. By his simplicity and by his quickness he seemed always to get the right information on the main points; but he was at his best when talking straight away out of his own consciousness, and it was always a pleasure to notice the interest starting up in his hearers as I turned his words into English. At public institutions I usually invited the inmates to put him some question to be answered in Russian; no question ever took him aback. Certain children chose for their question "What would you do if you were out in a boat?" and quite a fairy tale was at once constructed on this idea. One of his most interesting conversations was with an able dockyard man; "the Russ" asked about sharks, and the old sailor about Siberia; "the Russ" was as simple as a child, but the old sailor ended with the words, "Thank you, sir: you have considerably increased my knowledge of Siberia."

In the country a foreigner is more easily identified than in the town, but hardly this one. We bicycled through Hants and Surrey, lay for some time at the top of Hindhead, and had a long talk with some gipsies on the way down. In a village public-house, he gathered a throng of open-mouthed yokels round him by playing "Mother Volga" on the crazy piano. He spent an easy afternoon watching cricket as an Englishman should. I had already taken him to a League football match, and his criticism at the end was rather amusing: "You English unite the Greek ideal of the joy in life with the Christian ideal of self-sacrifice." He picked up quaint refrains from all quarters. One day he descended to the kitchen, and was greatly delighted to see all the servants sentimentally waltzing to the tune of "Just one Girl." He had a real respect for England as a land of character, and felt himself thoroughly at home here. Perhaps he would have found "just one girl," only that there was difficulty in making a choice. To a lady with whom he was never acquainted

I was to say that "he had suffered much for her." I used to
remind him that a Russian girl (unknown) was waiting for him.
He returned to Russia and planned to edit a magazine, which
was to be both patriotic and intelligent. But Amphiteátroff's
audacious skit on the Imperial family had just appeared, and
the Russian Censorship did not want any new magazines for the
present. My friend, therefore, went to serve his country on the
Afghan frontier, where he made several journeys on horseback,
picking up valuable knowledge, and returning with a selection of
Afghan songs, presents from native rulers, and a face black with
the heat. After the failure of a plan for a tramp through the
Balkhan peninsula, he took service as a correspondent in the
Japanese war. Thence he despatched to me a long telegram,
announcing that he was married and had found a suitable place
for the honeymoon " on the Amur River."

The autocracy has always looked more or less askance at professional work. Professional men were there simply to be useful.
A doctor, for instance, was simply an instrument for healing;
it was not desired that he should think. This same suspicion
and fear, as we already know, runs through all the relations of the
Government to public instruction. It was only in recent generations that the professional bodies came to be important, for the
Government had always failed to satisfy the professional needs of
the nation. The old system of class compartments was applied
to the new professions; and, in some cases, even a certain measure
of class self-government was given, as in the case of non-official
lawyers; doctors, too, might meet each other as doctors to discuss
medical questions. In 1905, the professions were able to turn
the close-compartment system into an instrument for fighting the
Government which created it. If doctors could only meet as
doctors, then clearly it was at medical congresses that they would
express their sympathy with the cause of reform; and this
sympathy came with infinitely greater force when it became
clear that all the representatives of a given profession had almost
identical political opinions. When lawyers, doctors, schoolmasters, engineers, professors, and other professional units, each
in turn put forward the same moderate political demands, it was
evident that these demands were the minimum programme of the

whole professional class. These demands were for freedom of
conscience, freedom of meeting, freedom of association, freedom
of the Press, and freedom of person and property, and also for a
national representative assembly. Some Russians have asked,
What are the grievances of the Intelligents ? These demands
supply the answer. The intelligent man must needs protest
against a system which puts him under the tutorship of the most
ignorant street policeman.

The very defects of the Intelligents, so far from being a proof
that the nation is incapable of responsibility, are so many signs
that responsibility should be conceded as soon as possible. It is
the natural cure. Yet those who have dared to claim initiative
have been looked upon as traitors for that very reason. What
political sense was to be expected from the young theorists who
had grown up under the conditions which I have described ?
But it mattered little whether their demands were extreme or
moderate ; the Government, lumping together reformers and
revolutionaries, drove out of society all those who would not
accept the doctrine of infallibility above and submissiveness below.
Occasionally one may meet some student who has returned after
years in Siberia to live as a peasant or as a working man in Russia,
permanently declassed. Was this the way to isolate the working
classes from all contact with the Intelligents ? Was it a good
substitute for that natural influence which a wise Intelligence
under a wise Government might have exercised to the profit of
the whole nation ? The number of lives which have been broken
in this way, the bitternesses which have been spread broadcast
throughout the nation, certainly pass our powers of estimation ;
and the remedy for which the intelligence of the whole nation
has asked is precisely responsibility—"training, training, training ! " Mr. Pobyedonóstseff's remedy was to write a book
emphasising the immorality of the whole nation, and more
especially of the society in which he himself lived. But the
best of the reformers have asked for responsibility not because
it is a pleasure, an indulgence, but because it is a duty, a
natural function, and because without it Russia is deprived
of her normal education, of the means of advancing peaceably
along the path of progress in loyalty to the best traditions of
the past.

THE REVOLUTIONARIES.

It is only as a claim for initiative that we can understand and do justice to the development of the revolutionary movement in Russia. This movement of course came out of the Intelligents, and bears the marks of their failings; but, as will be seen from the following chapters, it has steadily progressed towards a better and more practical conception of the object to be aimed at and of the steps by which it can be attained. It is for that reason that the present sketch of the revolutionary activities occupies this place in our study.

The ideas of Western Socialism were introduced into Russia by several fearless men, of whom the most notable was Michael Bakunin. At first it was chiefly young students and schoolboys whom they captivated. From 1865, when the Government seemed to be falling into another reaction, groups were formed in several towns to propagate such ideas amongst the labouring classes, and more particularly amongst the peasants. All the groups were agreed that, if a social revolution were to be carried through, it was necessary " to go to the people." Many of the propagandists learned trades in order to be independent, or became teachers in primary schools. They aimed at carrying through a social revolution without any bloodshed, and by sheer teaching; they circulated secret literature. They enjoyed but little success in the villages. The Government was very quick to seize them, and several hundreds of them were put in prison : some remained there for three years before they were tried ; many of those who escaped spent the rest of their lives abroad. At this point a change in the character of the movement took place. The propagandists were forced to be political; they saw that they would have to secure freedom of the Press and the right of meeting; they already aimed at some kind of a Constitution. A party was formed under the name of " Land and Liberty," which was also the title of a secret newspaper; it was revolutionary, but not Terrorist. It was now that Terrorism began. There were two tendencies : some continued the former propaganda; others definitely waged war upon the Government. At a congress at Lipetsk the party split up into the Terrorists of the "National Will " and the propagandists of the "Black Partition."

The latter section existed only for three years, and later joined hands with the remnants of the "National Will." The "National Will" had an executive committee for conducting the political struggle ; it made the attempts on the life of Alexander II.; but, as we have seen, the success of the final attempt only put the clock back in Russia, and the chief members of this organisation were arrested in 1881 and sent to the fortresses of Peter and Paul and of Schlüsselburg, or to Siberia. The section of the "Black Partition," after some kind of fusion with the "National Will," continued its work beyond the frontier, and thence tried to establish in Russia groups of propagandists for the "freedom of labour." This section, which had always been Socialist, had now adopted the ideas of Karl Marx. It recognised that to realise these ideas it must embark in a political struggle with the autocracy, and joining hands with the European "Internationale," it attempted to influence the Russian working men. In 1884 it issued a programme drawn up by one of its most capable members, Mr. Plekhánoff, who had been one of the earliest revolutionaries. This programme was at first published secretly, and was but little known ; but this was the beginning of Social Democracy in Russia. In the eighties there began to appear in Russia groups of Social Democrats, of whom some were allied with the programme of Plekhánoff and others were independent. They soon established a very strong vogue, and their propaganda amongst the working men appeared to meet with some success.

Since the seventies, there had been formed through the agency of those pioneers who had first " gone to the people " little groups of working-men propagandists ; at the end of that decade an important organisation of this kind was started in St. Petersburg. Its chief leader joined the Terrorists at that time, and was executed for taking part in the murder of a gendarme. These groups continued to exist, and in the eighties became Social-Democratic. From 1883 to 1890, when the reaction seemed to be at its height, their proceedings had to be very secret; they concerned themselves with public instruction and circulated literature on social questions. They were ultimately broken up by the Government, and their chief members were exiled. Groups of the original " National Will " still existed.

The development of social interests received a great stimulus from the famine of 1892. A keen controversy arose between those Socialists who still adhered to the "National Will" and the "Marxists." The most prominent of the latter was Peter Struve, who put forward his views in a brilliant and lively work entitled "A Glance at the Economic Future in Russia." The discussion, which became very acute, aroused general interest. The Nationals tried to draw the peasants into local unions of a Socialist character; whereas the Marxists marched straight to the conquest of capital in general. The controversy lasted from 1892 till close on 1900; it may be said to have called the attention of the Government to the need of economic reform, and thus to have led to those Commissions on the needs of the peasants which played such a large part in the story of the Zemstva. Struve himself was never fully identified with the Socialists, though he still had connections with them in 1899; within three years from that time he was the editor of the first definitely Liberal organ, "*Liberation*."

There now appeared, for the first time, in St. Petersburg, a really strong group of Social Democrats. It was soon arrested, but it had already created many smaller groups, especially amongst the Jews of the North-west Provinces; in St. Petersburg there were constant arrests. Socialism was rapidly developing itself in Germany, and most of the works of Marx were translated into Russian. The methods of Terrorism fell further into disrepute, and more and more was done to propagate the ideas of Social Democracy amongst working men. This work proceeded very rapidly; the first of May was celebrated in St. Petersburg as a feast of labour; books, pamphlets and leaflets were circulated. Some of the more responsive working men were formed into groups by the Intelligents; they were arrested, but new groups sprang up. The students became increasingly socialistic, and thus the numbers of the Social Democrats went up. In 1892 was formed the St. Petersburg group of the League for the Liberation of the Working Classes, which united several groups together; this body had more peaceable tendencies than some of the others. Some very vigorous workers joined the movement, such as Lenin (Ulyánoff) and Martoff (Sederbaum). Propaganda was energetically conducted in the suburbs of St. Petersburg, in order to remedy special grievances in certain factories. Special

demands were made to the employers and to the Government;
the organisation of workmen on the basis of their respective
trades enjoyed evident success; the intellectual horizon of
the working class was widened ; it was not only autocracy
that was attacked, but also the stifling influences of the
middle class or bourgeoisie. From 1895 the development
became broader still; the leaders in St. Petersburg gave a
common tone to the provincial movement, especially to the Jews
of the North-west Provinces. In 1896 took place the first big
strike ; 30,000 workmen protested against the food regulations in
their factories. They obtained a legal limitation of the daily
work to eleven and a half hours ; the Government was much
frightened by the energy and the solidarity of the workmen ;
there were also several strikes in the North-west Provinces ; the
Social Democrats now had a wide hold over whole masses of
workmen. Meanwhile, the remaining adherents of the "National
Will," who were still independent, joined with a new generation
of students to produce the modern Socialist Revolutionaries ; but
these could not yet be described as a party. The Government
often tried to crush the Social Democrats by exiling members of
the League for the Liberation of the Working Classes, but the
organisation was always reconstructed, and some of those who
returned from Siberia were amongst its most energetic agents.
In St. Petersburg, the movement now directed itself more
exclusively towards economic reform ; the Social Democrats,
though in principle they were pledged to destroy autocracy, began
to think that they could carry out their objects, without openly
raising this question, by uniting the men of each trade in a
struggle for their special interests. But these tactics led to a
split in the Social Democratic party and thus indirectly strengthened the Socialist Revolutionaries, who, being openly hostile to
the system of Government, were for reviving the methods of
Terrorism. In 1898 the first congress of the Social Democrats
was held in Byelostok; deputies came from many towns, a
central committee was formed, and the party was definitely
constituted ; but the congress was followed by numerous arrests.
As a matter of fact, it seems to have been the arrests alone
which preserved the external unity of the party. A controversy
was waged between the economist leaders in St. Petersburg

and the exiled champions of the Liberation of Labour, who had the support of many of the Social Democrats in Russia. However, groups and committees continued to be formed, for instance in Moscow, Kieff, Kharkoff, and the Caucasus, and especially the North-west Provinces. The propagandist labours of students and ex-students gave a further large development to the work in St. Petersburg. The Social Democrats had but little success with the peasants except in a few districts of northern Russia, where most of the peasants had at some time lived in towns, and more notably in the Caucasus. There continued to be a split in their ranks; whereas the minority wished that the workmen should regularly elect their own representatives to the Central Committee, the majority, fearing the surveillance of the Government, wished the leaders to be appointed once for all. The second congress was held in London in 1905. The Social Democrats took only a secondary part in the great national movement of that year, usually coming in after the event and claiming more of the credit than they deserved. Unlike the Socialist Revolutionaries, they definitely objected to the use of bombs, and in the main wished to confine themselves to simple propaganda; but they had a section called the Fighting Organisation, and they were at one time ready to join in an armed rising. The majority practically boycotted the first Duma; the minority were represented in it by a few working men of no particular eminence.

The Socialist Revolutionary party was reorganised in 1901; it contained certain veterans of "Land and Liberty" and "The National Will." In 1900 a literary campaign was initiated amongst the peasants; some of the pamphlets were circulated in hundreds of thousands; the murders of the Ministers, Sipyághin and Plehwe, were the work of this body. The Intelligents in general despaired of any success for propaganda amongst the peasants; but after the agrarian riots in the Governments of Kharkoff and Poltáva some thought that there was a chance, and the Japanese war opened far wider prospects, which the Socialist Revolutionaries were quick to cultivate. They have a Fighting Organisation, but the number and names of its members are unknown to the main body; one representative of this section sits on the Central Committee. The party does not scruple to assasinate officials; but the victims are first "tried" by the

Central Committee, or by the local committees. The Fighting Organisation undertakes the execution of the sentence. In answer to the punitive columns of the autumn of 1905, the party organised flying columns, to one of which belonged Spiridónova, who killed Luzhanóvsky. Very often volunteers who are not attached to the party come forward to execute the sentences ; the local committees have power to accept such help. The programme of the Socialist Revolutionaries is far more intelligible to the peasants than that of the Social Democrats ; it tries to graft itself on to the traditions of the old communal system. Till quite lately, the Socialist Revolutionaries, though convinced Republicans, did not dare to raise the question of monarchy ; in fact, it was impossible to do so till after the Duma had met, and it was by deferring this question that they were able to obtain wide support from the peasants by the foundation of the Peasants' Union in the summer and autumn of 1905. The party is not for State Socialism ; it is not for the division of Russia into so many racial areas ; it would accept the principle of autonomy for Poland and the Caucasus, but fears that such a division will only lead to racial antipathies and thus indirectly confirm the predominance of the bourgeoisie in each area. It would prefer much smaller units such as Parish Councils, which should be as independent as possible in local affairs. Whereas the Social Democrats would municipalise factories and capitalise all the means of production, the Socialist Revolutionaries would only nationalise land. The Social Democrats had not, till lately, any definite land programme, and they have been content to borrow one in part from the Socialist Revolutionaries. But if the Socialist Revolutionaries were successful in carrying through the main articles of their scheme, it is probable that there would be a split within their own ranks, and that the more important section of them would draw closer to the Social Democrats. The successes of the party have been greatest south of Moscow and more particularly on the lower Volga. Since the organisation of the Peasants' Union, the peasant element has become more important in the councils of the party, and has clearly exercised a moderating influence ; but the dissolution of the Duma for a time put an end to this most significant development.

The Terrorist Anarchists, who are very few in number, and the not very dissimilar Anarchist Communists, are strong only in Little Russia and in a few other places such as Byelostok; it was their activity which led up to the "pogrom" in the last-named town. In Odessa bands of such men established a kind of tyranny in the earlier months of 1906; they would enter restaurants and "hold up" all who were present. They are almost more bitter against the middle class than they are against the Government; their violence knows no scruple, and there is little to distinguish them from organised brigands.

In connection with the revolutionary bodies, it is interesting to notice the rapid development of strikes. The first really organised strike took place in 1870 at the Narva factory. In 1895-7, in fourteen provinces more than 20,000 persons struck work. In 1901 alone, there were 22,000 strikers. It was from 1896 that the question of shortening the working day became acute. So far strikes had usually been isolated, but in this year nineteen factories of the same trade struck work simultaneously in St. Petersburg. Fifteen thousand workmen joined in the strike, but at the end of a fortnight nearly all had returned to work. In March, 1898, there was another great but unsuccessful strike at the factories of Necháyeff-Maltseff. So far the strikes had not led to any violence, but from 1897 to 1899 such movements were often accompanied by pillage and sometimes by murder. Large manufacturing areas such as those of Riga and Ekaterínoslav rose with more appearance of a common purpose. In 1900, the Government tried to counteract the propaganda of the Revolutionaries by the equivocal scheme of Zubátoff.[1] In November, 1902, the Social Democrats of Rostóff-on-the-Don organised a strike which, though of the largest dimensions, was conducted with full publicity and without any disorder. However, whilst the claims of the workmen were still exclusively economic, the party professed to be initiating a revolution. In July, 1903, there was a great strike at the Naphtha works in the Caucasus; the masters called in the troops, and some of the men later set fire to the works. During this strike the factory inspectors, who had formerly been looked upon by the workmen as protectors, were condemned by them as being "a bureaucratic chancellery." In the middle of 1904, there was organised in these parts a most

[1] See p. 477.

powerful body of working men which openly associated political needs with economic; by the end of the year, it started a great strike which led to the use of troops, the death of some workmen, and the firing of the works. "There," said the workmen, "you see the candles for our dead." This brings us to the great strike in St. Petersburg, which began under the guidance of Gapón and on the initiative of the Putíloff factory, and led to the notable events of January 22nd, 1905.

PART III.—BRIDGING THE GAP.

CHAPTER X.

LAW AND THE ADMINISTRATION.

THE Intelligents were the prophets of a cosmopolitan creed; they set out in search of a single and all-embracing truth, which was to dominate the whole world, not by the adaptation of existing conditions, but by the constant assertion of its own absoluteness. Brotherhood, the love for humanity, was one of its great doctrines; and, in principle at least, this doctrine was incontrovertible. Another was the setting up everywhere of a moral standard of law, not, of course, finally embodied in any single written code of laws, but conveying the very spirit and essence of law itself, being, in fact, a general principle, which should in the end be realised in the practice and detail of the life of every state. "The Spirit of Law" was the title of the great book in which Montesquieu tried to lay a foundation for the legislation of the future. Law meant the moral standard of right and wrong. So far the laws had too often been the safeguards established by the conquering caste, the possessors of the good things of this world, who desired to secure their own possessions. If a man might be punished because he had done something wrong, he might also, with much more likelihood, be punished because he had offended "the Government." It was natural that the Government should take even greater pains to defend itself than to defend the abstract principle of right. But the new creed demanded that all men in general, and responsible persons in particular, should, so to speak, efface their own self-consciousness, and objectively consider themselves as only members of the great world of brothers. Altruism—the giving to one's neighbour of just the same consideration that one bestows upon oneself—was put forward as an invariable rule, which must never be broken, and as one of the chief tests by which a responsible Government should be judged. As a man remains a man and can never finally detach himself from the personal basis on which he lives, pure altruism is impossible; but that does not mean that it is not worth trying for. We have to believe in the oneness of truth, and to try to approximate our institutions to this belief. Where the Intelligence has done wrongly, it has erred because it has forgotten that it is the Intelligence of a certain land, and of a certain time. But the excesses of Intelligents are not only much more attractive but much more excusable than the sleep of sheer negation or self-interest.

The early preachers of the creed of the French Revolution in Russia were one-sided men, who forgot their limitations and failed precisely because they left out cardinal truths, as true as any of those which they saw. They had one kind of belief and could not understand another; they claimed to establish one kind of authority, and could not see any soundness in those reasons which had established another. It was required not only that they should educate their country, but also that their country should educate them. This bridging of the gap between the old and the new was not undertaken till the 'forties. The first triumph of Reform, during the reign of Alexander II., began an education which could never be finally arrested. Russia's best instinct, that of the family, had carried her through this first great crisis without such convulsions as were the price of reform in many other countries; and that, alone, is a good reason for thinking that Russia is not likely to collapse whilst she is taking her second great step forward. The first period of reform secured to her some forty years of gradual and practical education such as Turgot in vain desired to give to France before the French Revolution.

The greatest of the reforms were the emancipation of the serfs, the institution of local government in all Central Russia, and the establishment of a standard of law. We will consider the last of these reforms first. The best of its influence still lies in the future; but it illustrates in the broadest possible way what is at issue between the old world and the new, and what are the conditions of their gradual reconciliation.

Of course, there were judges and law courts before Alexander II.;

but they were practically a part of the administrative system. The police had the preparation of all cases. The judge was a kind of clerk, who, like any other bureaucrat, proceeded by means of long-winded reports written amongst masses of paper. Of oral examination there was little, and of oral pleading nothing at all. There was no jury. The judge, being dependent on the administrative system, had about the same measure of intelligence and morality as other bureaucrats. By the decrees of 1862 and 1865, there was introduced into Russia a whole system formed on the Western model; it handed over the preliminary investigations to judges of instruction specially appointed for the purpose; it established oral pleading of a public character; it introduced a jury. Justices of the Peace, with much of the character of English magistrates, were appointed to deal with minor cases, especially such as concerned the peasants; their sentences could be sent for revision to Sessions of the Peace, which were something like our quarter sessions; for all the more important cases was introduced a complete system of law courts, which I will describe later.

The judge, so far from being subordinate to the police system, became, in many respects, its chief rival. More than any other part of the system of reforms, the law courts might be said to specially represent the best ideals of the irresponsible Intelligence. It was from the Intelligence that the lawyers and judges were drawn. They might, naturally, partake of the faults of their class. Many of the men who were first set to fill these posts were more than ordinarily sensible of the loftiness of the ideal which they represented; but it could hardly be expected that the fine instincts and the intelligent traditions of law, which are in England the product of centuries of training, should be developed in Russia all at once.

The old system of administration had not been abolished; it continued to exist side by side with the new system of law. It was obvious that under normal circumstances the system of law must finally control, and in great measure replace, the system of administration. If equity were to be done between the two conflicting principles, there is no question as to which would receive in the future the greater degree of development. But the period of reaction which set in after the reforms made it hard for the law courts to do their work, or even to exist at all. Even the local Councils, which were more limited in their functions and in their sphere of work, had a hard time of it; and the law courts were, so to speak, more of a bid for doing everything at once by the application of a single principle. Of course, the formation of a great professional tradition was bound to proceed slowly; and meanwhile, the new institutions were several times tinkered in a reactionary sense. The Justices of the Peace, who had been appointed by the Zemstva and Town Councils, were practically abolished altogether, and their place was taken in 1889 by the Land Captains, that is, by frankly administrative officials. As one peasant remarked, "We have no more judges; we have commanding officers." As the Government continued to be suspicious of the law courts, the jealousies and antipathies between the Government and the Intelligence now reappeared inside the established order of things in the relations between the law courts and the police. The judges, not being encouraged to make themselves responsible exponents of the true governmental instinct of the people, partook of the defects of irresponsibility, and seized occasions to give little slaps in the face to the very officials with whom they were supposed to work. They made themselves, in fact, the spokesmen of a kind of public opinion critical of, and hostile to, the administration. I give a somewhat trivial example which came within my own experience.

A Police Captain offered to show me a Town Law Court. A young man was being charged with riding a bicycle in a street where cycling is forbidden; the Judge turned politely to the Police Captain, and asked if he were come to conduct the prosecution which, in any case, stood in his name. The Police Captain explained that he was not there for that special purpose. Evidence was given which proved that the bye-law, forbidding cycling in that particular street, had been duly published in the newspapers, that the cyclist had been warned to that effect by a passing civilian, and that he had ridden on. An English magistrate would probably have said at once, "a shilling fine and a shilling costs." The Judge begins a long formula, "in the name of His Majesty, etc.," at which the general public rises and the Police Captain, as a simple member of it, rises too; the Judge, after restating the evidence which has proved the offence, adds: " And the sentence of the court is that the accused be—acquitted." A titter goes round the crowd, and all eyes are directed on the Police Captain, who leaves the court with me in some confusion. Outside, we meet the cyclist and walk home with him in friendly discussion of his case.

Such little protests of an adverse public opinion are provoked by a much greater licence on the part of the administrative authorities.   By special laws and circulars, these have over and over again set up limitations which have prevented the principle of law from taking anything like general effect.   The more the administration has been proved to be inefficient, the oftener has it taken refuge in these special exclusions ; and of late years, especially in 1905, the exceptions became so general that it was impossible to recognise any definite principle at all, whether of law or even of administration.   In fact, everything has depended upon the pressure of public opinion and the degree to which the Government might think it necessary to yield to it.   In one case a right decision will be arrived at, and in another exactly similar case the decision will be precisely the opposite.   As opposed to the principle of law, further and further development has been given to the practice of administrative, or arbitrary, arrest.

Corporal punishments were abolished in principle in 1863, but some years later a man named Bogolyúboff, accused of conspiracy, had a dispute in his prison with the elder General Trepoff, the Governor of St. Petersburg, and was flogged. A young lady named Vera Zasúlich sought an audience of General Trepoff and shot at him. During her trial it was made clear that the police had on several occasions proceeded in the most arbitrary way. She was acquitted. The police tried in vain to re-arrest her administratively outside the court; it was precisely against administrative arrest that the verdict was a protest.

These instances may serve as examples of the conflict between the two authorities. Yet it may be said that the spirit of the Intelligence has for a long time been passing more and more not only into the officials themselves, but even into the system which they are called upon to administer. Thus, in many cases, the Government has even unduly deferred to a morbid and introspective standard of the preciousness of the human person, and of the passions which are considered natural to it. A man guilty of embezzlement on a huge scale may later be appointed to a most important post in the administration of a Siberian province. The Government has indeed made concessions, but in the wrong way and to the wrong people. Its enemies are not so much the criminal as the enterprising; not so much the weak-kneed as the men of character. Clearly a complaisance of quite a different kind is required, and if responsibility were given to the Intelligents, we should soon see in process the formation of a genuine public opinion, which would be hostile to those personal failings to which the Government has sometimes been too merciful.

The existing legal system in Russia is a product of old and new institutions which are not satisfactorily harmonised. At many points, especially at the bottom of the system, we find Law jostled by Administration. At the bottom, there still exists a series of institutions founded on the old class basis; and in law as in the administration itself, we must not look for any unity until we are half-way up to the top.

Some one hundred and fifty peasants, chosen from each village, elect at the cantonal assembly some five peasant judges, who sit in the cantonal Court-house to try minor cases concerning peasants only. Their competence includes civil cases, such as questions as to the possession and division of land, which do not involve a money value of more than £3. They may also deal with the more ordinary offences of peasant life, such as brawls and small thefts, and can sentence to seven days' imprisonment in the little prison-room at the Court-house. This prison is usually just an ordinary compartment of the building, only closer and with a smaller window: there is a division between the parts allotted to the two sexes; escape from these buildings, which are made of wood, must be exceedingly easy. There is a president of the court, but the sentence is settled by the majority. Each case is registered with a considerable amount of formality. First there is the summons; then come the documents which have been put in, and, on separate sheets, an account of the sitting, a copy of the resolution of the judges, consisting of a statement and a sentence, an order to execute the sentence, a note that the culprit has been imprisoned, a note that he has been let out, and a final registration of the whole case; all these sheets are enclosed in a "dossier," and are later submitted for the approval of the Land

Captain. I have seen several of these judges; they are simple peasants, and quite unlearned except in their peasant customs, which compose a whole mass of tradition, varying in different parts of the country. They usually have the look of shrewd rustics and may be capable of giving very sensible reasons for their decisions; but this Court represents a legal distinction between the peasants and the other classes, which most of the peasants would like to see abolished. The Cantonal Elder is elected by the same assembly; it is seldom that he will be a member of the court. The most permanent occupant of the Court-house is the cantonal clerk, who is a somewhat more educated peasant, appointed by the Government and receiving a small salary.

The cantonal court can only try cases concerning peasants, and its decisions are subject to the revision of the Land Captain. In principle he has simply to decide whether there is ground for an appeal to a court of higher instance, namely, the District Sessions. Cases between a peasant and a member of another class can be tried by the Land Captain himself in the first instance. When these are civil cases they must not involve a money value exceeding £30. His Court then, which exists only in country districts, is somewhat like the petty sessions of our own county magistrates; but he is himself an administrative official, subject to the Minister of the Interior. In principle, according to one authority whom I consulted, he can only imprison in execution of the law, that is to say, not administratively; but there seems to be plenty of evidence that he has often used his administrative power in this way too. Amongst the Land Captains whom I have known, none seemed to me to entirely justify the bitter outcry which has been raised against them. One was even a pronounced Liberal, not merely in opinions but in instincts; his chief fault was that he seemed to know almost less about his peasants than a traveller might find out in a day or two. Another was an amiable young man, in every way a type of the Intelligence—quick-witted, fussy, academic and talkative; he had the common Russian fault of always saying " listen " (poslúshay) to everyone else and, apparently, never listening himself, but he had almost an exaggerated respect for what the French would call " legality." Others are lazy and thriftless, and, while all have the temptation to exaggerate their own authority and their own caprices, there are some who have shown themselves, under what cannot be considered as exceptional conditions, to be capable of downright brutality. In 1905 one Land Captain had to be removed and punished for killing an unoffending peasant in cold blood. In general, the mischief is not so much in the men as in the position and work which have been assigned to them. In the system of peasant law flogging has been preserved.

Land Captains have themselves complained to me that their work was neither desirable nor efficient. "I have too much to do," says one. "I have to cover six cantons and attend to 30,000 people : the function of relieving distress has been taken away from the Zemstvo and given to us ; we can't do it. I have constantly to be writing to the Government town to get something done which I may not do myself : the Zemstvo could do this work much better ; you see all these peasant law-suits that I have to look through ; it is too much." It is likely that the whole system of peasant law courts will soon be abolished ; that is very desirable ; and, in 1905, a plan was already being drafted in the Ministry of Justice for the institution of some other system. The cantonal eldership, too, may be greatly modified ; there will probably be an elder, but he will probably not be a peasant.

The whole system of peasant law is kept distinct, and the appeals within this system go, in the last instance, to the Governor, that is, to the chief administrative authority of the province. But in the towns, the law court which corresponds to that of the Land Captain is already a part of the other system, that is, it is subject to the Minister of Justice, who names its judges. Its competence is the same as that of the Land Captain, and, within these limits, it can try members of any class, except that the gentry, if charged with theft or fraud, are sent straight to a court of higher instance. It corresponds to our borough petty sessions.

Mention must here be made of some other courts which owe their origin to the system of class compartments. The Orphan's Court names guardians and controls their action. The Gentry's Wardenship, a class institution, controls the guardians of children of the gentry. The Commercial Courts concern themselves with civil cases between members of the trading class, or with any pecuniary case where the money value involved exceeds £50. They deal with bankruptcies of persons who live on commercial credit. Of bankruptcies there are three kinds : firstly, " chance bankruptcy," which is not punished; secondly, "unlucky bankruptcy," for which there may be a comparatively small fine with arrest until the fine is paid; thirdly, "malicious bankruptcy," which is considered as, in a sense, breaking the peace, and can be punished with imprisonment. Commercial Courts exist only in a few of the largest towns; elsewhere similar cases are decided by the Circuit Court.

Courts-martial are, of course, separate from all other systems; they are conducted by nominees of the local staff, and in more important cases appeal can be made to St. Petersburg. The Church, again, has a separate jurisdiction. The Consistory is an administrative body which is, to the bishop of a diocese, that which the "Government Administration" is to the Governor. According to opinions which I have heard, not excluding those of priests, the Ecclesiastical Courts in connection with the Consistory are peculiarly venal. One priest never went thither without small presents of money for all the chief officials. An earnest supporter of the Church told me that when he visited such a court everyone stared at his pocket, and one member ostentatiously jingled money. These courts have jurisdiction over divorce, and are exceedingly hard to satisfy. Divorce can be allowed for insanity, if it began before marriage and was concealed; for an incurable disease, contracted under such conditions as to make it a new factor of which the other party could not be cognisant; and for adultery. In this last case most exact and circumstantial evidence is required. Other reasons allowed are: the degradation of one party from his or her class by sentence of a law court, or absence of five years without any news, or of ten years, if the person concerned is known to be outside Russia; if a husband returns after this period he has legally ceased to be a husband, but, in case his wife has not married in his absence, he has no need to go through the marriage service again.

We now follow out the main system of law courts. We must remember that for every case, there are three "instances" of jurisdiction. The court of the first instance tries the cases; the court of the second instance hears appeals; the court of the third instance can quash any previous decision on a point of law.

After the Town Court and the Land Captain, we come to the "District Member of the Circuit Court." This trained law officer

is detached from the Circuit Court to sit alone in judgment on cases
of the same kind as those judged by the Town Court and Land
Captains, but which are just outside their competence. The
money value involved in cases which he tries may range from
£30 to £50 ; and he has a corresponding extension of criminal
jurisdiction. This is a court of the first instance.

We next come to the District Sessions, consisting of the
Marshal of the District gentry (who is *ex officio* president of this
court) ; the District Member (who is *ex officio* vice-president), and
any Land Captains or Town Judges of the district who are able to
attend. This court, whose jurisdiction is both civil and criminal,
is a court of the second instance for appeals from the Land
Captains and the Town Judges and also for those appeals
against decisions of the peasants' cantonal law court which
have received endorsement from the Land Captain. Of course,
no Town Judge or Land Captain can sit as assessor on a case
which he has himself tried in the first instance. A member
of this court told me that its business was altogether too much
for it. He himself was appointed as an honorary Justice of
the Peace, and as soon as he entered, one of the Land Captains
(who are overwhelmed with work), seeing that there was a quorum
without him, would leave his seat. In one year, he calculated
that the average time allotted to each case was seven minutes and
one second ; generally, no witnesses were called.

The court of final resort for all peasant cases is the special
"Presence " of the Governor. This court is really a department of
the "Government Administration." All appeals made by peasants
against decisions of the Land Captains go direct to this "Presence,"
which decides them finally, there being no court of the third
instance in this case. It will be remembered that a Governor's
" Presence " also deals in the first instance with any complaints
made against officials, and decides whether there is a case to be
submitted to the higher law courts. An official cannot, then, be
prosecuted without the permission of his superior.

From this point the system of law is much more uniform. In
every Government town there is a Circuit Court (Okruzhny Sud).
We are now in the midst of the new atmosphere created by
Alexander II. To this court go nearly all the graver criminal
cases, and most of those civil cases which involve a money value

of more than £50. Those who are not peasants or "townsmen" are subject to the jurisdiction of the Circuit Court. The president of the court and the two other judges are all trained lawyers, and are appointed by the Minister of Justice. Attached to the Circuit Court are jurists, who, though not members of the court, possess the rights of judges and receive even a higher salary. They cannot be removed except by the Emperor, or by the sentence of a law court. These can order the arrest of a murderer and report on the case to a Crown Prosecutor; the Prosecutor writes his act of accusation and sends it to the Law Chamber, which will be described later. The Law Chamber, with closed doors, decides whether there is a true bill. The Crown Prosecutor then hands over the case to the President of the Circuit Court. The chancellery of the Circuit Court must counter-sign all acts of the court; if it refuses its signature, that alone is ground enough for the case to be taken higher. This chancellery, which has a great deal of work to do, is composed of candidates for judgeships; but it is not necessary that all its members should be trained lawyers. It may be one of the objects of the barrister to get the chancellery to declare itself against the decision of the court.

In all cases which involve Crown interests or those of minors, wards, or imbeciles, a Crown Lawyer will be present indepen-dently of the rival barristers, and will give his opinion in writing to the judge; this opinion the judge is not bound to confirm.

For criminal cases, a jury is employed. Those who are called serve in turn, as selected by lot. There is no pay; and busy people greatly object to the service. A juryman must not be deaf, dumb, imbecile or over sixty years of age. For each case fourteen are chosen, including two extra jurymen who can be empanelled in the middle of a case. Both the Crown Prosecutor and the defending counsel have the right to object to individual jurymen. In cases where the accused will not in any case be deprived of civil rights there need not be a jury; for instance, if his offence is striking policemen in the execution of their duty, he can be sent to prison, but no deprivation of rights need follow. The court is a large, airy building. The Crown Prosecutor sits on a higher seat than the counsel for the defence. The accused is guarded by a sentinel. The witnesses are confined together in a single room, from which each one is admitted in turn to the court. The oath is taken on the Holy Gospels, or, by Jews and Mahometans, in other ways. There is a place for the public, and the doors are open. In the civil Circuit Court the same judges sit as in the criminal, only without any jury. The advocates are here called " men entrusted under oath."

Next above the Circuit Court comes the Law Chamber (Sudyéb-naya Paláta). In the Law Chambers, of which there are some six in Russia, three judges sit on each case without any jury. They hear appeals from the Circuit Court. They can also judge, in the first instance, offences against the service of the Empire, of which the most part are, of course, offences committed by officials. In some minor cases of this kind, such as small embezzlements, there may be adjoined to the Law Chamber certain representatives of different classes, such as a cantonal peasant elder, the mayor of a town, or a marshal of the gentry. These play something like the part of a jury; but they are, after all, officials, and their votes, I am told, are sometimes prompted from above.

At the top of the judicial structure is the Senate of the Empire, which quashes decisions on points of law. Its jurisdiction in some ways corresponds to that of our own House of Lords. Cases may be brought before it from the few Justices of the Peace who still hold office in the larger towns, from the ordinary Court of the Land Captain, from the Circuit Court, or from the Law Chamber. That department of the Senate which exercises its judicial powers consists of what may be called the " veterans " of the legal profession, that is, some two or three professors and the Chief Crown Lawyer, with his secretary. As a court of first instance, it deals only with the gravest offences against the Empire. For such cases there is created a special " Presence " of the Senate. Though in principle the death penalty does not exist in Russian law, this special court can, for the worst kind of political offences, sentence a man to be hanged. It can also act as a court of appeal for grave offences referred to it from the Law Chamber, or from the ordinary court of the Senate; for instance, it might try, on appeal, a Governor who had been convicted of stealing. The Senate can also perform the functions of our grand jury; certifying whether or not there is a true bill for a case which is to be tried in the Law Chamber.

The Senate has, of course, many other functions which are not of a judicial kind. It should here be mentioned that laws of the Empire are enacted by the Emperor through his Imperial Councils, which now include the Imperial Duma, and that the Senate has the responsibility of publishing these laws and seeing that they are executed.

In training and status there is a distinction between judges and Crown lawyers on the one side, and advocates (private lawyers) on the other.

A student who has completed the course of law in a University or in a Higher School, can become a "junior candidate," being attached to a Circuit Court or a Law Chamber for eighteen months without salary. He will be examined by the judges of the court. He will then become a senior candidate for eighteen months. He is next eligible to be appointed an Investigator (Juge d'Instruction) or an assistant Crown Lawyer. After two years more, that is after five years in all, he can be appointed Judge or Crown Lawyer, and is eligible for all higher posts. The Justices of the Peace are also, in principle, appointed in this way, but the law is often broken. A Crown Lawyer can be appointed Judge, and a Judge can be appointed Crown Lawyer. The age at which all these appointments become possible is twenty-five years. To be a simple Member of a law court, it is enough that the candidate should have had five years' legal training, even if only as a private lawyer or advocate. Those who wish to be private lawyers will, after the completion of the course in a university or law school, apply for appointment as "Assistant Advocates"; they are named by the Circuit Court, but each candidate must find a Senior Advocate who is willing to be responsible for him. The Assistant Advocate must be twenty-one years of age. He will apply for a licence from each court under whose jurisdiction he proposes to work; for instance, he will pay £7 10s. to the District Sessions and £7 10s. to the Circuit Court; some have as many as four licences; if the court concerned refuses the licence, there is no right of appeal. After five years' training, if there is a vacancy in a given town amongst the Senior Advocates, he can be chosen to fill it. There is amongst private lawyers a professional organisation called the Council of Advocates; it has the right of advising the Minister of Justice as to how many advocates are required in a given town; it may naturally wish to restrict the number, but the Minister can, if he likes, disregard its recommendation. It has its own library and also its own room in the law court, which no one may enter without the introduction of a member. It also acts as a disciplinary court in cases where an advocate, without breaking the law, has violated the traditions of the profession. Advocates are also under the control of the president of the court in which they serve, who can administer rebukes to them.

Solicitors are divided into Crown Notaries and Commercial Notaries. All candidates, though they do not need to complete a university course, must pass a special law examination in the Circuit Court. The Government settles how many are required in each district; in principle it is supposed to make appointments to vacancies on the results of the examination, but in practice there is a great deal of what is called "protection." A certificate of character is required, but I am told that there are many rogues in the profession. A Crown Notary is really an official; he receives a small salary, and is supposed not to engage in private practice. His sphere of work includes questions of real property, debts, mortgages, and arrears of taxes. He receives, let us say, £240 as salary and £60 for chancellery expenses, which are far more than covered by this allowance. A Commercial Notary may work up small cases for the Crown Notary of a given Circuit Court, but will also have a private practice which may bring in very large earnings. Some private notaries make as much as £1,000 a year.

In the country, a peasant prisoner may be arrested by the local Tenth man or Hundredth man and taken to the peasants' Court-house. Prisoners who must be tried in higher courts are escorted by the police corporal or his deputies to the District town, and for graver offences will be sent straight on to the Government town. Arrest is distinct from imprisonment. A person may be confined to his house, or placed in a special house of arrest which is under the control of the District Member.

While under trial, an ordinary prisoner may be allowed bail; if convicted, he will, except in the case of the very gravest offences, be imprisoned for the whole of his term in the prison of the Government town. This prison contains what is called a "corrective section." Prisoners who are certified to be "under correction" are sometimes allowed a diminution of the term of punishment; this right is conceded to those who have conducted themselves well in prison.

Two such prisons I visited in July, 1904. The Inspector of Prisons I found engaged in devising a new and more sanitary kind of building. He sent an official with me to show and explain everything.

There is no "imprisonment for life." In theory the first six months (here, in practice the first two) are spent in solitary confinement. For the rest of the term the prisoner lives in a common dormitory (kámera). These rooms are large and airy, with plenty of windows; by day they are a series of open compartments like those of a railway carriage in a corridor train, furnished with stools and tables, on to which the bed descends from the side of the partition at night. There is a special building for those described as "formerly of the privileged class"; where this plan is followed, there can hardly be any complaint that men of different degrees of refinement are herded together anyhow. The system of "living in common" is in harmony with the most pleasing instinct of the country, that of sociability; and it seems far more merciful than the puritanical plan of seclusion.

To every convict in these prisons is supplied a little book of rules. It first states the term of the sentence, the date of entry into the prison, any remission of a part of the term, and any trade in which the convict is already experienced. This book he keeps in a locker in his ward, and, with it, a receipt for his property, receipts for any money taken from him on the day of entry or sent to him during his term, and a record of work done and wages earned during imprisonment. If he loses these records, they are replaced from the corresponding record kept at the prison office.

He is obliged to "speak politely to the officials, never allowing himself to raise his voice, much less to use abusive language." He must take off his hat to the governor of the prison. He may not lie on his bed in day-time except after dinner, and then only after taking off his coat and boots; he may not smoke, play games, quarrel or brawl, talk loud or laugh loud, hang up clothes to dry in the ward, talk with men in other wards, sell clothes or food, or hand over money to other prisoners. When his turn of service comes, he is responsible for the cleanliness and good order of the ward. A man who tries to escape is put into fetters. The prisoners are examined when they leave the wards and when they return, or at any other time of the day or night. There must be no mutilation of Crown property. The Church festivals and the Church fasts must be rigorously observed. The prisoner may, subject to the permission of the prison governor, keep the following articles in his cell: small ikons, the cross worn by all Orthodox next to the skin, tea-pot, cup (or glass) and dish, tea-caddy, comb (or brush) and mirror, a white handkerchief, books from the prison library, and provisions as allowed by the regulations.

In summer the prisoners rise at 5 a.m., in winter half an hour later. They wear rather thick holland suits of a dull light-brown. Samovars (tea-urns) are brought round to the wards for meals. There is half an hour for the first meal; then the men are marshalled and go off to work. At 12 o'clock there is a break of an hour and a half,—for dinner, a nap, and a walk in the yard. The work ends at 7 p.m. in summer, and at 6.30 in winter. Ten minutes are then allowed for tea; at 8.0 there is supper, and 9.0 is bed-time. There are eighteen holidays, exclusive of the feast day of the prison chapel. Those who are not Christians keep holiday on the chief feast days of their religions, up to the same number of days as is allowed to the Christians. On holidays the prisoners rise an hour later, are in church from 8.0 to 10.0, and clean up the wards or read books till dinner-time, after which they may be allowed to see their relations. From 2.30 two hours and a half are allotted to "reading, religious and moral conversations, writing letters and petitions."

All are obliged to work unless exempted by the prison doctor. There is no pay for what is called the household work, that is, cutting wood, carrying water, trimming the prison gardens, cleaning up the wards and corridors, lighting stoves, looking after the court-yards, cutting cabbages, peeling potatoes, carrying dinners to the other workmen, and so on. Porters get $7\frac{1}{2}d$. a month, those who look after the lamps or clean up the office

1s. 10½d.; 3s. are the wages for cooks, bakers, washermen, carpenters, trained gardeners, tailors, shoemakers, locksmiths, whitewashers and plasterers.   Mattress-makers, stove-makers, coopers and wheelwrights are paid by the job,—the bargain being made between the prison governor and the customer.

Prisoners, if their behaviour satisfies the governor of the prison, may spend half their earnings on small luxuries; those exempted from work may spend a corresponding sum of their own money.   The extras thus purchased (only once a fortnight) are restricted to: ¼ lb. tea, 1½ lb. of sugar, 2 lb. of bread or rolls, 2 lemons, milk, 1½ lb. of sausages, 1 lb. of meat, 10 eggs, 3 herrings, and 1 tin of sardines.   Other supplies of food or of money, if passed into the prison, are confiscated.

After two years a prisoner may be passed on to the list of " those who are correcting themselves."   He may then count ten months of imprisonment as equivalent to one year.   For any offence he can be put back on to the first list.   If he tries to escape, his sentence is re-dated from the time of his attempt.

The various punishments are carefully numbered; and in the prisoner's little book is entered a note of each punishment, stating when it was inflicted and what for.   The punishments rise in severity as follows:—Private rebuke, public rebuke; a month's deprival of reading, of correspondence, of visits, of the right of buying extras, or of the right of spending half of one's wage; one (or two) month's confiscation of back wages; less food, down to bread and water for three days; a week in the light cell; three days in the dark and four in the light cell, (with strait-waistcoat and hand-cuffs in case of violence)   a month in the light cell; a month in the light and dark cells   fifty strokes of the rod.   More than one punishment may be inflicted for the same offence, but all must be noted down.   Crown property, if mutilated, must be replaced out of the prisoner's wages or private money.

The little book concludes with a warning to the prisoner " not to put the prison authorities under the necessity of applying to the culprit the punishment which answers to his offence, beginning with a rebuke and ending with the birch-rod"; he is to understand that " it is not the authorities who are punishing him ; rather he himself, by breaking the general rules, compels them to do so, in order to force him to fulfil exactly the claim which the law makes for the discipline and good order necessary in places of confinement." He is given the choice of "availing himself of all lawful rights and privileges," or of being punished "with every possible privation which the law admits."

Those who wish may learn in the prison-school religion, reading, writing, reckoning, and the Russian language.

It is clear that exceptionally wise officials, in Russia as elsewhere, are required for administering the prison regulations; but here there is an air of more than military fear. The salute of the lesser official is sheepish, cowed and bending: a throng of officials, arranged in exact order of procedure, followed me through the prisons ; men who were called came running up, a good deal quicker than a Russian would ordinarily run. I was usually ushered into each ward at the head of the procession ; as the heavy padlocked doors swung open, the inmates would rise all together and, in a loud hard voice, shout to me, "We wish you health, sir!" The wards were high, spacious and clean ; some were almost empty, very few were full (say fifteen as a maximum in one large room). The men did not look uncomfortable ; sometimes we found them drinking tea off their little tables much as if they were in a peasants' restaurant ; they were a very ordinary looking lot, most of them seeming appropriate to their surroundings,—in fact they were rather genial specimens of the ordinary criminal class. One complaint was made, and got a kindly hearing. The sanitary arrangements are, of course, altogether better than anything which the peasant has been accustomed to outside. The hospital is visited weekly, or more often if necessary, by a doctor attached to the prison but living outside ; it was here that I saw the most hopeless faces. The steam-bath was full of prisoners, one of whom had ominously tattooed a double-headed eagle on his arm. In the chapel, on the wall of the chancel, a painter was busy painting a dove, from which rays melted away into the dark air on every side. I was told that most of the prisoners have a sense of religion—"in fact, a man will pray on his way to a murder."

In the workshops it seemed to me that the moral atmosphere associated with prisons was hardly perceptible. The workers were busy, but seemed quite at their ease. Some men were spinning brown holland cloth. There was a painters' department. The smiths were at work on machines, for instance, bicycles: most of this work consists of repairs ; but a pleasant, intelligent prisoner, who seemed in no way to bother himself about the conditions under which I saw him, showed me a prison-made bicycle and explained the superiority of the Dunlop tyres over the Russian, which last one year to the others' five. It is definitely desired that a prisoner should show that at least there is some good point about him : to be able to do artistic work is better than nothing at all; I saw one very prettily worked easel.

We cannot take for granted the wickedness of all Governments and the viciousness of all officials. If prisons must exist, they are sure to be difficult to manage. This people, in character and in habits of life, is behind us. The officials whom I met were kindly men, if too much afraid of superior orders from men who were probably as kindly as themselves. The immense majority of the prisoners were apparently members of the casual criminal class; most of them are constantly coming back, and look at the prison as " home." Except in a few cases, they are, for their own sakes, forbidden to live in the town in which they have been imprisoned; but there is no general ostracism of prisoners by masters of trades, and there is therefore no great difficulty in getting work later.

In Russia there is, in principle, no death penalty except for extraordinary offences. Transportation was very early practised by the Government. There were in Siberia vast empty spaces. The distance alone was enough to make escape improbable. For murderers, it was made more difficult by shaving the hair close on one side of the pate, so that they could easily be identified. The climate of Siberia, if not of the most desirable kind, was at least not insupportable. Russia is not a country favoured by Nature ; and it could hardly be expected that a little Garden of Eden would be found for the use of criminals or of political prisoners. The Government itself may be said to have gone into exile from Russia when it planted itself in St. Petersburg, a spot where Nature, by those warnings which are at her disposal, had banned the residence of man. For the earliest political prisoners, a very large part of the punishment involved in transportation was the distance which separated them from the centre of the autocracy, that is, from the source of all favour. Transportation was in principle not unmerciful; instead of being killed off, the prisoner was put in a place where he could do but little harm to his fellows and had the chance of making a fresh start. But in countries which are ruled by favour the wounded wolf is an easy mark for the attacks of the whole pack; and the very distance from the centre of government, and the necessary delegation of great authority to the local official, made appeal almost impossible. A good system of transportation involves a far closer system of inspection and a far stronger control of public opinion than the Russian Government would ever have been willing to admit. In practice, therefore, the prisoner might be subject to the full weight of uncontrolled petty tyranny. I have elsewhere suggested that a vast extension of Empire, so far from being a substitute for home reform, becomes absolutely mischievous in the absence of reform. Nowhere in the Russian Empire was the control of the central authority weaker than in Siberia. A large number even of the free inhabitants of Siberia were fortune-seekers; and the fortune-seeking official is a very noxious person indeed.

As peasants and adventurers of other classes began to take up more and more land in Western Siberia, and even, to a lesser degree, in Eastern Siberia, public opinion, in spite of the system of government, began to approach this realm of isolation. On the one hand Siberia, instead of being looked at as a kind of Botany Bay, came to be regarded almost as a new Eldorado. The Government itself, so to speak, advertised the country as playing a prominent part in the idea of Eastern expansion. The present Emperor, while still Crown Prince, travelled through the country and cut the first sod of the Trans-Siberian Railway at Vladivostók. To Western Siberia was in part extended the normal system of administration which was in use in European Russia. On the other side, the wrongs practised on the prisoners, so far from remaining hidden, became one of the favourite objects of the sympathy of Western Europe. Escape became comparatively easy; and I have it on the authority of one engaged in this work, that to rescue a political prisoner came to cost no more than an average of £12. If the Russian Government did not admit the control of the public opinion of its own subjects, it was subjected to the fiercest lights of criticism from outside; and to this criticism it could not be indifferent at a time when it was anxious to restore its influence in Europe by eliminating misunderstandings with other nations, and in particular by allying itself with republican France. The good opinion of Europe was necessary to the financial credit of Russia. Further, the Russian in general, being fully conscious of the disadvantages which penalised him in the competition with other more civilised countries, has, from the very origin of his history, been peculiarly sensitive to outside opinion. We can therefore understand why the present Emperor, in principle, abolished transportation to Siberia altogether; and, if the principle has not been carried out, it still remains as a condemnation of the practice by the very power which is supposed to license it.

The Emperor's manifesto abolishing transportation was vague in expression; and the Senate and the Governors of provinces have interpreted it in their own ways. There are, therefore, all sorts of exceptions, and we may almost say that, owing to the troubles of recent years and the consequent increase of political prisoners, no fewer have been transported yearly than was the case before the manifesto. This punishment is also applied to violent robberies, to aggravated thefts and burglaries, and to "habitual offenders"—that is, to men who have been convicted four or five times, or have been convicted for the third time for a theft of more than £3. In the case of the privileged classes,—that is, the gentry, the priests, and the higher merchants,—rape, sacrilege, and murder receive this punishment. But the great majority of those transported consist of "politicals." Some of these last are confined in the fortresses of European Russia, others are sent first to a fortress and then to Siberia. These may later be let out of prison and may live in banishment as "colonists," and finally may be brought back to Russia to live anywhere except in St. Petersburg or Moscow,—unless a special pronouncement of the Emperor authorises them to reside in the capitals. Those exiled to Siberia may easily experience bad treatment on the road, because the soldiers behave roughly and there is no appeal; but on their arrival they, in most cases, find that they are now very well treated by the officials and police;—such, at least, is the report which I have obtained from persons who have undergone this form of

punishment. They will probably be set at liberty immediately on
their arrival, and, even if they have been sentenced to four years
labour as convicts, they may perhaps never enter a prison at all
from the time when they reach Siberia. Illiterates who are incapable of supporting themselves, will more probably be imprisoned
and have to do a certain amount of spade work; the others
may live by themselves under inspection, not being treated any
differently than the other inhabitants of the district in which
they reside. Houses and money are usually given to them.
They are allowed to engage in paid work, as soon as the Government recognises them as " colonists." They cannot hold any
Government rank,[1] and are deprived of the rights of Government
service, such as pensions; but an exile of this kind may rise to be
a Councillor of the Government Administration of the province,
or even Secretary of the same.

Apart from transportation, there exists also the malicious
practice of administrative arrest. The victim may be removed to
a distant government, such as that of Archangel, to a fortress, or
to Siberia. No term is prescribed, and he cannot see to the end
of his sentence. I am told on reputable authority, that as many
persons are subjected to this form of punishment as are suffering
by reason of sentences inflicted by the law courts; but it would
be a mistake to think that all of them are political prisoners in
the narrower sense of the words; for instance, a person who is
considered to be troublesome and inconvenient for social reasons
may be removed in this way. It is the exercise of a paternal
authority without form of trial, such as existed in France before
the Revolution or in Piedmont later.

In the past, the religious authorities had power to banish
persons for religious reasons to the Tundras, or marshy plains of
the north, or to confine them to monasteries. This punishment, in principle, was applicable only to members of the Orthodox
Church; but it could be inflicted for the simple offence of passing
from that Church into some other. This kind of punishment has,
in principle, been abolished.

To sum up:—The Government is anything but merciless in
its dealings with ordinary criminals. The mischief is that it

---

[1] Rank is a different thing from posts, though it is often a necessary qualification
for them.

reserves its enmity for those who show initiative, and that such men are lumped together with the lowest of the people in a crude and common punishment.   The Government has, in principle, capitulated to the principle of law, but has, in practice, so multiplied the exceptions that they altogether swamp the principle. Thus it has not yet been possible for the ordinary Russian to have any confidence in the principle of law as protecting him from arbitrary and exceptional chastisement.   But the very fact that the legal *régime* stands in such open contrast with the administrative has led, almost as much as anything else, to the development of a public conscience, a force whose influence is already very perceptible, and in the end is practically certain to prevail everywhere in Russia.   This conquest may come, as in other countries, first in theory and later in practice too.

CHAPTER XI.

THE erection of the standard of law in Russia was a vast change of principle, but, as we have seen, practice followed on principle very slowly. It was very different with another of the great reforms of Alexander II., the institution of local government throughout Central Russia; here was a practical change of the very first importance, whose principles passed at once into action. To give over certain definite responsibilities of local government to a body elected by the nation was to create the necessary middle term which should serve as a link between the Sovereign and his people. Such a representative institution would, by its work and methods, throw into deeper relief the neglect or violation of national interests by the underpaid or overfed official; at the same time it would reduce the students and other inexperienced claimants for revolutionary change to their natural position of comparative insignificance.

When Alexander II. instituted the Zemstva in 1865, he was establishing a new principle of government by the side of the old; it was from that time certain that, sooner or later, one must succumb to the other. Some think that the Emperor intended gradually to increase the powers of the Zemstva until they became the foundation of a new and reformed Imperial Government. The Zemstva were from the first peculiarly a Russian institution, established (not merely accepted) by the head of the Empire; they were at first instituted only in the purely Russian provinces; further, the Emperor, when he made the division of functions between the Zemstva and the central administration, gave over to them all the more beneficent functions of government, reserving for the bureaucracy the work of police in its more extended sense; thus to the Zemstva was secured popularity and to the bureaucracy unpopularity. The Zemstvo was not a town unit but a country unit; it was therefore representative of the distinctive characteristic of Russian life, and in it was embodied those very country instincts to which the bureaucracy was to turn for its support during the next period of reaction. All this implies in the governing power a policy of trust and of hope; and, indeed, the men who had, from the first, the direction of the Zemstva were the representatives of the oldest families in Russia, those to whom, if the nation were not to be distrusted wholesale, the confidence of the Government would naturally first be extended.

The Zemstva were based on the principle of a special representation of each class; the gentry sent so many, and the peasants sent so many ; the number was fixed by law ; the peasant representatives had to be peasants. So long as there remained in Russia so clearly marked a dividing-line between the classes as that which still separated the country gentry from the peasants, the system had very much to be said for it ; when a peasant question was brought up, the peasants had their own representatives, who would, of course, be able to speak with the greatest authority. It was in fact a continuation of the Russian principle of "government by experts"; instead of asking a kind of general elective committee of "omniscients" to decide all questions, those were consulted and those carried the day who had the best right to speak on the matter in question.

The Zemstva had the right to levy, at their own discretion, a rate for the purposes of local government; and, though they had not yet any control over the bureaucratic officials in their district, that was, sooner or later, bound to come. One link between them and the people was created by the institution of Justices of the Peace, who replaced the old absolutist squires as the arbiters of questions between peasant and peasant. By all accounts, these Justices carried out their work very conscientiously.

Adhering to the old units of administration, Alexander II. established a Zemstvo Assembly for each District and a higher Zemstvo Assembly for each Government or province. It was not yet thought necessary to recognise the existence of any middle class between the gentry and the peasants. In the country districts, the rating which qualified for franchise amongst the gentry was a high one. Each Assembly of the District or of the

Government had to be summoned at least once a year. A meeting would last for several days; during the intervals between the meetings a standing committee or Board acted as the executive of the Assembly. The District Assembly chose its delegates for the Government Assembly; peasants who might be willing to attend the District Assembly would not be likely to wish to serve at the more distant Government towns; but they had, at least, a degree of influence which corresponded to their degree of public interest, and when they wished to extend this interest no regulations would prevent them from doing so.

In 1870 was established the similar institution of Town Councils. Here the problem of the Government was more difficult, for there already existed a rapidly developing middle class which defied the old classifications. The regulations were similar to those which governed the Zemstva; but the merchants (Kuptsý), who are recognised in Russia as the intervening class between the country gentry and the peasants, were taken as the chief unit for the basis of the Town Councils. The merchants are but poorly developed in political interest, and the work of these Councils was carried on in an altogether narrower spirit than that of the Zemstva. The professional man, as such, had and has practically no representation on the Town Councils at all; and it is only of late that the most important of the Town Councils have availed themselves of their advantage of dealing with a more compact area, and have taken anything like the broad initiative which has throughout characterised the Zemstva.

During the period of reaction which followed the brutal murder of Alexander II. the Zemstva and, to a less degree, the Town Councils have had to fight hard even for their very existence. It is clear that, as they politically educated themselves further and further by the practice and development of responsible work, they differentiated themselves more and more from that simple, crude protest against bureaucracy in general which they originally shared with the Radicals; and there is no doubt that, as they became more and more representative of public opinion, they exercised upon it a moderating influence, thus showing the possibility of the creation of a middle term between "bureaucracy" and "revolution." The flighty theories which the Zemstva at first shared with others, and which some of them even desired to put into application in their new work, tended to change into a simple and modest assertion of the more self-evident principles of true Liberalism. Yet the Government which persisted in identifying Reform with Revolution, which even looked upon Reform as a most insidious form of Revolution, and which regarded any criticism of itself as impiety, was not likely to be pleased with this change. Continuing on those demoralising lines along which its predecessors had travelled since the great fright of the French Revolution, it developed further and further the policy of sheer negation and persecution. The composition of the Local Councils was altered by the Government in 1892; the franchise was restricted in 1890, and a proportionately overwhelming representation was given to the gentry as against the peasants. In 1866 the presidents were given the right of coercing the Councils. In 1866 the Zemstva were forbidden to tax industrial concerns. In 1874 the direction of schools built by the Zemstva was in principle taken out of their hands, but the laziness of the officials practically allowed them to retain the real management. In June, 1900, Zemstva were forbidden to raise their rates by more than 3 per cent. of the budget of the previous year; by this enactment all new developments were prejudiced. At the same time the Zemstva were deprived of the function of relieving distress.

To the Zemstvo, as a country unit, had been given, from the first, a predominance and even an authority over the Town Council as a town unit. But this only helped the Zemstva to develope the principles of free government much faster than the Town Councils. Russia is an agricultural country, and the Zemstva rested directly on the people; they became full of vigour and of plans and programmes. Thus the very elements out of which the bureaucracy hoped to make its own fortress passed into the hands of its antagonists, and, in the end, we find the *Moscow Gazette* urgently pleading that the Town Councils should be made more independent of the Zemstva (1904). It was, indeed, a part of the Government's policy of " divide et impera " to keep Zemstva and Town Councils perpetually at loggerheads with each other. Communication between them was made so difficult that they hardly even knew each other's *personnel* and were always hostile to each other. But one effect of the great national wave of feeling that has passed over Russia since the beginning of the war has been to break down this wall of partition; and Zemstva and Town Councils have now heartily joined hand in hand in a common campaign for reform and a common programme of liberty.

Bearing in mind these main features of the Zemstva, we will now briefly trace their relations to the central Government.

As early as 1867 the Zemstvo of St. Petersburg was suspended for petitioning that delegates from the various Zemstva should be allowed to discuss economic questions in common. In 1878 Mr. Petrunkyévich, of the Zemstvo of Chernígoff, was able after some difficulty to arrange a meeting for himself and a colleague with some forty revolutionaries. These men represented the so-called "people's men" (Naródniki), of the Terrorist party of the "National Will." Petrunkyévich was surprised to see amongst them several men of standing whom he did not know to be revolutionaries. At first they showed some animosity; they clung to the idea of acting by means of terror. Some seemed to think that they could get what they wanted by killing the Emperor (Alexander II.), but they were as yet in no way tinged with Socialism, and their final objects, apart from method, were not unlike those of the Zemstvo Liberals. Petrunkyévich managed to induce them to postpone their attempts, to give the Liberals a chance. Taking as his excuse the disordered state of the country, he suggested to his Zemstvo friends that they should address the Emperor, practically asking for constitutional government. At the next meeting of the Zemstvo the building was crowded. The president knew the contents of the address of Petrunkyévich, and would not let him speak, but Petrunkyévich stood up and began reading at the top of his voice. Soldiers came in and cleared the hall; Petrunkyévich was arrested and sent to Kostromá.

Other Zemstva, such as those of Tver and Ryazán, were at this time Liberal. They at first claimed further independence for the Zemstva and freedom for the work of public instruction, on which they were very busy. This of course suggested the need for a constitutional order of things. While Loris Melikoff was in power, several Zemstva pronounced themselves in favour of a constitution. In 1878 there was even a Congress of some sixty persons in Moscow. The claim for a constitution was coldly received, but nevertheless the Congress decided to move forward. An attempt on the life of the Emperor caused the Zemstva to hasten their declarations. Alexander II. had, indeed, decided to summon the presidents and representatives of the Zemstva for common deliberation, but the revolutionaries had by this time resumed their operations, and in 1881 the Emperor was brutally murdered. The revolutionaries gained nothing; their organisations were completely crushed; half of the men who had met Petrunkyévich and for the time deferred to his arguments were now hanged or shot. Society as well as the Government was seized with a panic; even the more moderate men were driven into reaction. Alexander III. did indeed occasionally summon experts on special subjects, for instance on the emigration of the peasants and on the redemption dues, but this was little more than a demonstration. When Count Ignátyeff sent in a report on some of his semi-liberal projects, the Emperor himself wrote in the margin, " Why do we still need them ? " Members of the Zemstva had no other means of propaganda than pamphlets, private conferences, and the foreign Press. Some continued to meet in the south under the name of the Zemstvo Union; the conferences in the north bore no name. These meetings were now concerned only with economic questions, and for some years were practically interrupted altogether. In the early nineties the panic was disappearing, and the private conferences were resumed, but they still only dealt with economic questions such as statistics and peasant needs. The accession of Nicholas II. was the signal for several Liberal addresses from local Zemstva, such as those of Tambóff, Kharkhoff, Kursk, and Chernígoff; the best known was that of Tver. The story of the Emperor's indignation and of Mr. Ródicheff's exclusion from all Zemstvo rights has already been told. In the nineties a Committee of Literateness was started in connection with the Free Economic Society; it aimed purely at founding libraries and spreading culture. Mr. Falbork and Mr. Charnolúsky, who are now known as the chief experts in Russia on the system of public instruction, were foremost in this work. The Committee after a time began to co-operate with the Zemstva, and extended its operations to South Russia; but all its relations with the Zemstva were stopped, and its funds were by an administrative order transferred to a new official society which made a show of doing the same work. Mr. Petrunkyévich, Prince Shakhovskóy, and others still formed a little nucleus of Zemstvo Liberals. Meanwhile Mr. Shipóff, who worked purely on economic questions, organised conferences of members of different Zemstva at the Zemstvo Board of Moscow. Solely on economic grounds he was forced into the consideration of the relations between the Zemstva and the provincial Governors. The first conference under Shipóff's presidency met in 1897 without permission, but the first Congress which had any political significance was that of 1902.

In February, 1892, Mr. Witte became Minister of Ways and Communications, and shortly afterwards he was promoted to the post of Minister of Finance. In his construction of railways he appeared to consult other considerations than the need of exploiting the agricultural resources of the country; but some attention was paid to the emigration of the peasants to Siberia, and in 1893 some Commissions, armed with very insufficient powers, were appointed to deal with the needs of the peasants. The Council of State passed a resolution on the necessity of taking some measures; but Mr. Pobyedonóstseff appears to have thought this movement very dangerous, and it came to an end in 1894. Mr. Sipyághin, who took part in this work, invited the local peasant assemblies to give expression to their needs, but though four volumes of reports were printed by the Government in 1895, nothing was done. Mr. Goremýkin, who was considered to have special knowledge of the peasants, had now become Minister of the Interior; he was in constant collision with Mr. Witte on questions concerning agriculture and the Zemstva. At this time it was suggested that Zemstva should be established outside Russia proper. Witte was against this, as he regarded the Zemstva as competing with the central Government. Goremýkin, though wishing to exclude the Poles and the Jews, maintained that Russia had in many cases recognised the principle of local government, and that without it there could be no local life. He would, however, have kept the Zemstva under police control, and have left to them only the financing of schools and hospitals, depriving them of the actual management of these institutions. But he was replaced by Mr. Sipyághin, who was considered to be more of an absolutist and was in friendly relations with Mr. Witte. In the autumn of 1901 there were new Commissions for examining the needs of the peasants; but in April, 1902, Sipyághin was assassinated, and his successor, Mr. Plehwe, was not at all likely to work on friendly terms with Mr. Witte. He seemed to think that Witte was threatening the foundations of the Empire and encouraging the revolutionaries, and even accused him of provoking disorders. Witte, on the other hand, now wished to bid more definitely for the support of the Zemstva. By his invitation local Commissions were again summoned to discuss the peasants' needs; and members of the Zemstva were invited to attend.

It was now that Mr. Shipóff, on his own private initiative, summoned the presidents of Zemstvo Boards and a few others, such as Petrunkyévich, Count Heyden, and Novosíltseff, to a Congress in Moscow. The Congress carefully drew up an answer to the Government, suggesting that the welfare of the peasants demanded important changes in the administrative system; a few persons agreed to serve informally as a kind of committee of the Congress. The answer of Shipóff's Congress to the questions of Mr. Witte was heliographed and distributed to all the local committees which Mr. Witte had summoned; most of them adopted it as their own. In the Vorónezh Zemstvo one of the members pointed out the need of fundamental changes, and Mr. Martýnoff advocated a conjunction of the two principles of freedom and order, and the summoning of a representative assembly. Both men were punished, Martýnoff being sent to Archangel. Prince Peter Dolgorúkoff, President of the district Zemstvo of Sudzhán, was dismissed from his post by Mr. Plehwe for the opinion which he expressed on the local committee. Mr. Mukhánoff had told Mr. Witte that he considered the committees to be only a demonstration; Witte, who seemed to agree with him, suggested that he should say so publicly in Chernígoff; this he did without receiving any support from the Minister. At this time the influence of Plehwe was prevailing. All members of Shipóff's Congress were censured, and his re-election as President of the Moscow Zemstvo was cancelled. The opinions put forward on the district Zemstva were forbidden expression on the provincial assemblies. War was declared on the Zemstva practically all over Russia; a senator was sent down to report on that of Moscow, and the Government took steps to limit the competence of all these bodies. The repression continued up to the murder of Plehwe in 1904. After the failure of the Commissions Mr. Witte went to the far East; while he was gone Plehwe succeeded in ousting him from the Ministry of Finance.

Throughout the Second Reaction, and especially while repression was at its height, the different local Zemstva were kept aloof from each other in so many close compartments. Amongst the foremost District Zemstva in the country was that of Novotorzhók. It had built schools all over its district; it had founded a quite admirable hospital; its development of household industries had been a real blessing to the district; and it put on its staff agricultural experts, or " agronoms," of whose advice the peasants learned to make the greatest use. Enough money was secured for these objects without raising the taxes; but the Governor of Tver, after allowing the legal time limit for protest to elapse, lowered all the items of the Zemstvo budget. The Zemstvo Board refused to obey him, and was put on its trial. The president of the law-court resigned his post, giving it to be understood that he knew that the case had been decided upon in advance. He was, however, replaced by a less scrupulous judge, and the Zemstvo Board was convicted. Amongst its members was Mr. Románoff, who has helped to found sixty schools in the District. The Senate of the Empire vindicated the Zemstvo on appeal, but the Board was replaced by nominees of the Minister of the Interior, two of whom were too busy in other districts to attend to the needs of their office. Many school teachers and practically all the doctors resigned their posts, and were replaced by inefficient substitutes, "for who," as one local doctor said to me, "will go and serve under a nominated Zemstvo ? " The Governor of Tver received instructions to deport any dangerous persons; he expelled Mr. Petrunkyévich, who on his return from Kostromá had bought an estate in this District. General Stürmer, who had in 1895 been nominated President of the Tver Zemstvo Board, was sent down to report on all cases of insubordination.

The provincial Zemstvo of Tver was also in disgrace for refusing to vote subsidies to the District Zemstva if the schools were transferred to the control of priests. A new Zemstvo Board was nominated in Tver, and some persons were deported; one of these could only be described as a moderate Conservative. Professor Kuzmín-Karaváyeff, another moderate who spoke against the transfer of the schools, was made to resign both his professorship and his seat on the Zemstvo, and was sent out to Manchuria. It was not until the Ministry of Prince Mirsky that Tver was allowed to elect its own Zemstvo.

Outside Tver, on land given by a local landowner, had been established a lunatic asylum of a new and admirable kind. The patients lived in a big colony, on the so-called "open door" system, which has proved very successful. The lunatic asylums provided by the Government before the creation of the Zemstva had been few, inefficient, and often intolerant; their principle of authority had been that of undiluted fear. The Government could have nothing to say against the management of the asylum in Tver; but the head doctor, a man of moderately Liberal opinions, was expelled as a "revolutionary." All his assistants accompanied him, and the whole work of the institution was utterly thrown out of gear. Neither this asylum nor the hospital of Novotorzhók, though their respective Zemstva are now able to act freely, has yet recovered from the mischief which was thus done.

Repression, as we have seen, was not confined to the Liberals. Count Heyden, one of the leaders of the Conservative reformers, who under Alexander II. had held the important post of Reader of Petitions, was long under the displeasure of the Ministry for his action on the Free Economic Society. Mr. Michael Stakhóvich, who is the best type of an old Russian Boyar, and whose deep religious instincts urged him to play an active part in the foundation of schools, was rebuked for making a speech in which he attacked religious persecution. He stood to his guns, maintaining that his very respect for good order made him speak out, and that it would be the worst possible thing for Russia if opinion were silenced on this point. He was a Marshal of the Gentry, and had powerful friends at court, so that, despite his open defiance of Plehwe, the matter was dropped. To a certain circular sent out to him as Marshal by the Minister he replied that such instructions were lacking in respect to himself, and again he escaped unpunished. An attack was later made upon him by the reactionary Prince Meshchérsky, but he referred the matter to the law-courts. The number of instances might be multiplied indefinitely; hardly a member of the Imperial Duma, of whatever shade of opinion, but had directly or indirectly suffered persecution from the Government.

The Zemstva in general had to suffer many limitations during the period of reaction. The franchise is so restricted that the average member of the Intelligence is excluded from it, under the plea that he is neither a country gentleman nor a peasant. The substitution of the administrative Land Captains for the Justices of the Peace was a serious blow to the Zemstva. The power of levying rates has been restricted, and the supporters of the Government—for instance, the *Moscow Gazette*—are allowed to assert with impunity that the leaders of the Zemstva have enriched themselves out of the public purse.[1] Lastly, the duty of relieving distress has been taken away from the Zemstva, on the plea that they did not deal efficiently with the cholera of 1891. The real reason for this change was the fear of the Government lest the Zemstva should by this precedent be enabled to deal in common and on a large scale with great national questions.

In 1891 the ideas of Marx had a strong following amongst the students. Most of the Liberals, for instance, even Mr. Ródicheff, were too individualist and had too much sense of responsibility to succumb to this vogue. In 1891 there was great agitation amongst the students; in 1898–9 they made a whole series of protests, culminating in the great demonstration in front of the Kazán Cathedral in St. Petersburg. The Zemstvo Liberals felt the need of counteracting this movement by a more orderly appeal for reform. Thus were started the newspaper *Liberation* and the League of Liberators. Amongst the most prominent of the Liberators were Petrunkyévich, Ródicheff, Shakhovskóy, the Dolgorúkoffs, and later Nabókoff. Other members, such as Professor Milyukóff and the writer Korolyénko, represented the leaders of the Intelligents rather than the Zemstva. This little band, as the reader already knows, was to form the nucleus of that constitutional Liberal party which later on, under the name of " the Cadets," was destined to predominate in the first Imperial Duma. To sum up, the Zemstva fulfilled their mission of creating a middle term in Russia. They supplied the programmes and the leaders of both those parties which now divide between them the support of the majority of intelligent Russians.

---

[1] I have not met with any evidence of the truth of this charge; but even if true it would not be an argument against the control of public opinion over elective bodies, nor for refusing all publicity to charges against the peculations of administrative officials.

From a member of the Moscow Town Council I received some interesting information as to the attitude of the Government. "You understand," he said, "that you are studying the last days of the present régime, and also that the rights of Town Councils on paper are quite a different thing from the exercise of them as permitted by the Government." The Zemstva and Town Councils are subject to the authority of the Governor, or, in the case of Moscow, of the City Prefect. The Governor has a special "Presence" or court for the decision of questions of local government; this Presence contains a majority of officials, who care nothing for local government, veto the resolutions of the Town Council wherever possible, and often decide that it has no competence to deal with this or that question. Their point of view is purely bureaucratic, and the representatives of the Town Council are constantly outvoted. Often the proposals of the Town Council are sent back to be corrected, and it will have to ask leave over and over again before it gets permission to deal with the most simple and practical questions; it can, however, appeal from the Governor's Presence to the Senate. At St. Petersburg two candidates must be chosen for the post of mayor, and the Government will often choose the candidate of the minority. The Town Councillors are supposed to enjoy some kind of immunity, but they may be hurried off to Siberia all the same. Two councillors were once ordered by the Government to resign and go away. One of them stayed on, and of course none of his colleagues objected. It all depended upon the mood of the Government whether he would be further troubled, but he was not.

The towns have to find quarters for the troops, and must make room for as many as the Governor chooses to send. Repairs, heating, etc., in the barracks are all a part of their charge. Moscow has to pay an enormous proportion of its city rate for the support of its police; this sum must cover the cost of quarters, heating, uniforms, arms, and a part of the expenses of living; but the Council has no control whatsoever over its expenditure. The same must be done for the Gendarmes, or political police, but both these bodies receive their salaries from the Government. At St. Petersburg the Government returns a part of the sum demanded for the Gendarmes, but it is not so at Moscow. The Town Councils may choose sanitary officers to carry out their byelaws, but hardly any town can make a real use of this right. Its agents will neither have the support of the police nor any independent authority. In one year all the sanitary officials resigned for this and similar reasons. Such control over the police as was once possessed by the Justices of the Peace was in 1898 transferred to the Governor-General, that is, of course, to the police themselves. The Town Councils, like the Zemstva, were deprived of the right of taking precautions against cholera; this right was transferred to the Governors, who were to act in conjunction with special committees appointed for the purpose from the officials and from the Town Councillors. These last all refused to join, and asked for the restoration of the old order of things. In March, 1905, doctors from all Russia, assembled in council, condemned the new order as inefficient.

When the Town Council buys land for public purposes it has to petition the Emperor. A commission is then appointed to settle the price, and the matter is afterwards referred to the Governor and to the Minister of the Interior. Dealing with the Village Societies is a very tedious affair. The commission will include the Marshal of the District Gentry, the Police Colonel, the Inspector of Taxes, the President of the District Zemstvo Board, and a member of the Town Council Board. Such a commission has been known to fix the price of land at a far higher sum than the peasants could ever have dreamed of asking. It is impossible to count up all the disputes between a Town Council and the Government, or the cases in which the Government has treated the Town Council with negligence or even contempt. An engineer tried to secure from the Government a contract for making underground railways at St. Petersburg and Moscow. When at last the two Town Councils could make themselves heard, they were able easily to prove that the speculator was no more than a simple adventurer (1902). Though the streets are under the control of the town, the telephone is part of the regalia of the Government. In 1904 there was reason to fear that all the town schools would be taken from the hands of the Town Councils, and handed over to the Ministry of Public Instruction and to the Church. In the matter of hospitals the Government has done hardly any work at all, and there is therefore less interference. Every difficulty was put in the way of the Town

Council when it wished to acquire the private monopoly of tramways and to establish an electric service. How many petitions have been left without an answer! It is not merely that there is no support, but that no attention is paid at all.

We must continue to bear in mind the constant indifference, suspicion, and open opposition which have characterised the relations of the Government to the Local Councils; and we must also remember that the administrative power was entirely in the hands of the Government. It is only in this way that we shall be able to appreciate the work which they have been able to accomplish in spite of these drawbacks. To this subject we now address ourselves.

The country gentry choose their own representatives on the Zemstvo by direct election. Landowners who do not satisfy the very high gentry franchise meet together to choose their representatives in a more indirect way. These may be poor gentry or retired tradesmen, and between the tradesmen class and the so-called townsmen there is indeed very little difference in provincial districts; the townsman who has become rich will easily become a tradesman. The peasants choose representatives from their peasant societies, their franchise being in no way specially limited; these representatives of the Village Societies will choose cantonal representatives. I am told that some peasants will give vodka all round in order to escape election, but if they are chosen they cannot refuse to serve. From the twenty-five or so who have been chosen from the different cantons the Governor will, after confidential advice from the Marshal of the Gentry, choose ten. These will be members of the Zemstvo, and the other fifteen may be used, on a similar plan of nomination, to fill up vacancies. The elections do not need to take place in any particular building.

The District Zemstvo will comprise some thirty to forty members. The Marshal of Nobility is its *ex officio* president. Its annual sessions will last from seven to ten days, and if an extra sitting is licensed by the administrative authority its duration will be one or two days. The Zemstvo can levy a rate on land and houses. The peasant houses are of so small a value as to be hardly worth rating; perhaps a single room in the house of one of the gentry would be worth several peasants' cottages, and on these latter it is therefore impossible to lay a heavy tax.   The tax on a factory can only be imposed on the buildings, not on the goods.

The ordinary sessions of the Government Zemstvo will last for three weeks, and the extra sessions from two to seven days. All District Marshals of the Gentry sit *ex officio*.   The Marshal of the Gentry of the Government is *ex officio* president.   The Zemstvo elects a Government Board of four or five members, who do not divide their work by districts, but rather by special functions.   Any decision of the Government Zemstvo can be cancelled within a certain time by the Governor.   This power he uses far more than he formerly did.   An appeal may, however, be made to the Senate.

In the offices of the Zemstva and Town Councils there prevails a spirit which is quite different from that of the chancelleries of the bureaucracy ; this is clear to the most casual onlooker.   The hand-shake which is customary between Government officials at any chance meeting is here far less a matter of form.   In Zemstva offices, as elsewhere in Russia, the number of officials seems to an Englishman superfluously large.   Much of the work of a Government Zemstvo is concentrated within the walls of the office, for it is the chief task of the Government Zemstvo to co-ordinate the work of the different District Zemstva of the province.   For instance, it will look after the asylum ; it will also see that certain areas which lie on the frontiers of different Districts are not neglected ; it will help to found hospitals and schools.   There will be separate sections of the office to deal with accounts, roads, sanitation, improvements of agriculture, insurance, hospitals, schools, and charitable institutions.   But these divisions will vary according to the activity of the Zemstvo concerned.

In the foundation of schools the Zemstva have obtained most important results.   Before their time, nearly every District town possessed a school ; but it was probably a very poor one. Many of the Church schools only existed on paper.   Now it is altogether different : the Zemstva have covered the country districts with schools, and the Church schools have, by this competition, been compelled to become far more efficient.   The general result can be tested very easily ; every year the number of literates amongst the recruits increases fast.   The Zemstvo schoolmasters are very poorly paid, as their work covers little more than half the year (of course, the winter half). There is therefore far too much inducement for them to seek better-paid work by changes from post to post. Their relations with their employers are in general most cordial. The Zemstvo Board often asks their advice on new appointments, and is willing to submit any protest from them to the local Zemstvo Assembly.

The other chief item of the Zemstvo budget is the work of hospitals. Formerly, under the bureaucratic institution called "the Common Solicitude," there were hardly any hospitals at all; and these were so bad that the peasants were afraid to go to them: to send a friend thither was thought to be like sending him to his grave. Now there are very many rural hospitals. In each Government town the Government Zemstvo maintains a hospital, and the Town Council contributes to its support; but in the capitals this work is in the hands of the Town Council.

With the roads less trouble has been taken, but a general improvement is visible. The Zemstva sell good seed to the peasants at very little more than cost price, acting, so to speak, as practically unpaid middle-men. They also have their own depôts for the sale of very good ploughs (to replace the antiquated "sokha"), winnowing-fans, and other machines. An excellent system of insurance has been developed; this is a peculiarly important work, because the thatched roofs of the peasants' cottages are constantly catching fire. Iron roofs are sold at a low price, which is paid in instalments.

Novotorzhók spends about half of its local rate on schools, and a third on hospitals. The chief hospital is well planned, but veterinary work has so far been only feebly developed. The agronomical department has only a small share in the budget. The depôt of school-books and pictures and that of agricultural instruments are so well equipped, that the Zemstvo may here be regarded rather as fostering the enterprise of the population than as simply administering to it. An attempt is being made to establish a society of small credit for the peasants. The Banks are too slow and clumsy for small operations, and are not ready to lend money except for the acquiring of new land. Such a new society could lend capital for improvements in the present holdings, and it would enter into competition only with the existing private companies, which are certainly less disinterested.

The story of the development of household industries in Novotorzhók is typical of the enterprise of the Zemstva and what it means to Russia. There were in this district ancient industries: lacemaking, gold-stitch work, and leather work in three colours with patterns; this last existed only here and in Kazán, where it was in the hands of Tartars. An active and clever member of the Zemstvo Board was once talking with the mayor of the town. The mayor urged the necessity of money relief for the poor, and the Zemstvo member maintained that such a measure could be no more than a palliative. The women, he said, or more probably their husbands, would spend the money and come again; surely it would be better to revive the household industries of the district, which were so decayed that wretched work was being turned out. The mayor replied with a friendly challenge defying him to show that this could be done. About that time a German trader came to the district; he was applying for a contract with the Ministry of Marine to make all the badges for the different ranks of the navy. He proposed to get the work done in Novotorzhók. The Zemstvo member wrote to the Minister explaining that the Zemstvo was itself in a position to take over the contract. After a delay of three months, an official from the Ministry arrived in the town; he first went and acquainted himself with the state of this household industry, and, when he met the Zemstvo member, he had already seen many women at their work, and was well posted up in all its details. The two men, by a simple calculation, soon discovered that it was possible to greatly raise the wages of the workers and at the same time to make for the Zemstvo a profit of 40 per cent. This was a far more moderate tender than that of the German, who seemed to expect to make a profit of nine roubles on every rouble. Also the Zemstvo proposed to devote the main part of its profit to the developing of the work and the further raising of wages. After another delay the Ministry announced that it would make a contract with the Zemstvo, on condition that the latter would pay a large premium. The Zemstvo member replied that, so far from being able to pay a premium, the Zemstvo itself asked for a single subsidy of £100. After two months this claim was confirmed by a special order from the Emperor, which is not subject to any alteration by the Ministers, "a very pleasant order," said my informant.

The Zemstvo began by the making of badges, and gradually extended its enterprise to all the three industries which existed in the district. There are now 150 lace-workers and 400 gold-stitchers. The lace work is always sold at once. As the public demand is now adequately supplied, it would be difficult to extend this trade; but the prices have been raised, and the profit has been put to the increasing of the wages of the workers, who now earn from 5d. to 2s. a day, with an average of 9d. instead of 2½d. The workers can leave their wages with the Zemstvo, receiving them with interest at Christmas-time. The Zemstvo takes 10 per cent. profit on this work, in order to pay the expenses of the central depôt and of the six attendants who serve in it. On the badges the Zemstvo still has a profit of 40 per cent., which not only clears all expenses of the enterprise, but makes it possible to develope it. The Zemstvo member possesses a coverlet stitched out of the various badges, as a little memento both of this contract and of the fact that he was for several years under the displeasure of the Government.

The Zemstvo keeps an artist who supplies to the workers old patterns, for instance from ancient Church books, and modern patterns of his own drawing. Some peasants make their own patterns from memory, and these are very quaint, such as fanciful pictures of leaves, frogs, or geese. During the winter the work is taught at the depôt to some fifty girls; and the number of workers is fast increasing. In summer, colonies of workers are quartered in the country, one being at the house of my informant at the time of my visit. The Zemstvo employs an agent in America, but so far has sold few of its goods in England. As this enterprise has supplied it with a capital of £400, it has attempted to import new household industries, such as net-making. Here, however, it has not succeeded. The work has been bad, as it did not lie in the spirit of the people; and it is found to be far more easy to develope an existing industry than to introduce a new one. As to the workers, who, in many cases, used to be idle for five to seven months of the year, they have now an admirable safeguard against sheer starvation.

Few Englishmen are likely to go to Novotorzhók, but visitors to Moscow will make a mistake if they leave the city without examining the admirable depôt of household industries (Kustárny Sklad) which has been founded by the Moscow Zemstvo. This is the biggest institution of the kind in the country; it has been copied in several other provinces, and it has found an extensive market for its goods in Paris and in America. It has done very much indeed to revive the almost lost arts of ancient Russia; and this work, as essentially Slavophil rather than Westernising, has given to it a strong claim on the affection of those who love Russia best.

All this work of the Zemstva is, from one point of view, propaganda, and that of the most legitimate kind. The Zemstva have attended to the best interests of the districts which they administer, and have thereby made evident both the previous negligence of the bureaucracy and their own claim to be set to work on the political interests of the Empire. For this and similar reasons, just as the Zemstva have been forbidden to unite for any purposes whatsoever, they have not been able to publish any record of their work which deals with the whole country. Each Zemstvo issues its statistics separately; and some pamphlets, issued quite recently, deal with certain general aspects of the work. Amongst these may be mentioned two entitled " Country Medicine " and " Town Medicine." They have been published both in Russian and in French.

We turn to the organisation of the Town Councils.

The Town Council of Moscow is chosen for four years. The following are the electors: all Russian subjects of twenty-five years of age who have lived for one year in Moscow and possess real property to the nominal value of £300; tradesmen who possess a certain yearly revenue (the three highest of the seven so-called " categories ") ; all learned or trading societies, which have a right to choose special representatives. Women who own property may be represented by their nearest relatives. All who have votes are eligible for election. In St. Petersburg in 1902 there was established a lodgers' franchise, which includes those who pay a lodgers' rate of £3 (equivalent to a rent of £180). In Moscow the electors are chiefly local merchants. Several

professors do not enjoy the franchise; in general, the ordinary
Intelligent can only be elected as representing some learned body,
such as the University.   All women are excluded from the direct
exercise of the franchise.   The others specially excluded are—the
Governor and all members of the Governor's "Presence for the
control of town affairs"; priests; Crown lawyers; the police;
persons deprived of or limited in their civil rights; men excluded
from Government service; those who have been convicted of
offences against property; those who are accused of offences for
which they might be deprived of their civil rights; fraudulent
bankrupts; unfrocked clergy; persons excluded from the class to
which they formerly belonged; men who have not paid their town
rates; persons under police supervision.   By this last provision
the Government can exclude anyone whom it pleases.   Nobody
has more than one vote for his own property, but he may vote a
second time as representing the property of someone else.   The
elections are held on the ballot system in the town hall; the
mayor is the returning officer.   There are, however, other polling
booths; the different wards do not all necessarily vote on
the same day.   These arrangements may be slightly different in
different towns.

The elected candidates, on taking their seats, take an oath of
allegiance.   In St. Petersburg or Moscow they number about
160 members; in towns of 100,000 inhabitants, about eighty
members; in other Government towns and big District towns,
about sixty members; in the smallest towns a £10 rate qualifies
for the franchise, and the Council consists of some twelve
"plenipotentiaries."   Vacancies are filled up from the first names
amongst the unsuccessful candidates.

One-third of the full number constitutes a quorum.   The first
act of the Council is to choose a Mayor; candidates are proposed,
and are asked whether they will serve if elected.   The Council
Board, which is the executive of the Council, is similarly elected
by ballot; the Council may choose not only from its own members
but from all who were qualified for election to itself.   Besides the
members of the Board, the Council elects certain persons for the
performing of special functions.   In Moscow these functions are
not of great importance, but in St. Petersburg they include such
work as the making of bridges and the administration of hospitals

and schools. By law, the members of the Council Board may not number more than six persons; on special petition the Council is sometimes allowed to elect three more. A town of 100,000 inhabitants has a Board of four members; a Government town or a big District town has a Board of three. The duration of office is four years. All members of the Board have votes on the Council, whether elected to it or not. The Board itself arranges the division of its functions, but this division must be confirmed by the Council. The Board acts as a kind of Cabinet Ministry, deciding in common all questions which affect particular departments, and reporting in common to the Council. It meets almost every day. The Mayor of Moscow has a salary of £3,000 a year, which is generally considered to be far too much. Members of the Board have £500 a year each, and are not allowed to take other paid work.

Members of the Council enjoy no inviolability; they can be arrested at the Town Council as legally as anywhere else; but that is hardly likely to happen. In practice they can be arrested the day after they have been sentenced by a law-court, or even by administrative order without trial if the Government so desires. If a state of siege is declared by the Governor, they can be expelled by the police.

Twenty-four sittings of the Council are licensed for every year. For extra sittings the Mayor must make a requisition, on the ground of public necessity or arrears of business, and must obtain the consent of the Governor or, in the case of the capitals, of the City Prefect. At such a sitting, only that business which has been sanctioned by the authority can be discussed by the Council; and the goodwill of the authorities is very variable. From June 15 to August 15 only specially licensed sittings can take place. Before a sitting the mayor sends out notice of the agenda; interpellation of the Board is allowed if notice has been given three days in advance. The Mayor opens the meeting by submitting a report of the Board, which has already been sent out in advance to the members of the Council; it is usually in criticism of this report that new suggestions are made at the Council, and such suggestions will be referred to the next sitting. Current business, however, can, under certain circumstances, be added to the agenda of the meeting. All resolutions are referred to the Board for execution within the limits of the instructions of the Council. The Board, however, can make a request for further funds, or for the foundation of some new institution. The public is allowed to attend the meetings of the Council. Very few avail themselves of this privilege; but there are some persons in Russia, as elsewhere, who seem almost to be professional listeners, especially at times when the Council has to appoint an official. At ordinary business meetings there will not be more than twenty or thirty listeners, who are very possibly visitors from the provinces; but in 1905-6 this privilege has been used to the full.

The Council makes such proposals as it desires; but all business is referred to the Governor or City Prefect, who can stop progress at once and transfer the whole matter to his own " Presence." On this court sit the Mayor and one Member of the Council, and also the President of the Government Zemstvo Board. But these will probably be outvoted by the Governor (or City Prefect), the Vice-Governor (or deputy Prefect), the Administrator of the Treasury Chamber, and the Special Member appointed by the Minister; there is also the Procurator of the Court of Assizes.

I add a few notes on the organisation of a Town Council in an average Government town (Smolensk). The smaller a town, the less independent it is of the local Zemstvo. The Town Council is chosen from the enfranchised householders, in the proportion of one member for 500. There are forty-seven members; these fill up their vacancies by co-optation, and choose a Board of three Members and a Mayor. They have twelve regular sittings in the year. The Council, as in the capitals, can pass byelaws, which, if sanctioned by the Governor, have the force of law; it can levy a rate on real property up to 10 per cent.; it leases out town land, and also derives dues from shops and stalls; it makes contracts, for instance, for tramways, reserving to itself so much of the profit; it collects all taxes, and it hands on what is due to the Zemstvo and to the Government. Inhabitants of towns must pay dues both to the Town Council and to the Zemstvo. Each member of the Board has his separate department,—finance, building and repairs, or sanitation. The Council possesses its own schools; it sees to the paving of the streets and the upkeep of the public monuments and the town gardens ; it has its slaughterhouse ; it inspects buildings, and can, for instance, veto the construction of a factory on the ground that the health of the surrounding district would be prejudiced. It possesses a small hospital of its own, with two beds and a large practice amongst out-patients. In this town the Zemstvo has a large hospital, and there is another which is managed by the Doctors' Association. The Town Council employs a medical officer, with twenty assistant sanitary inspectors. There are no drains here; rubbish is simply carried out of doors; but chimneys must be kept clean, and unsound buildings can be condemned. The Town Council must supply quarters for the police, firemen, and troops.

The Town Council collect not only its own rate of 10 per cent., but also collects the rates and taxes for the local Zemstvo and for the Government ; it revises all budgets of its own Board, which must be approved by the City Prefect, the Treasury Chamber, and the Chamber of Control. These budgets have often been attacked in the Press, but chiefly for the reason that criticism on the budgets of the bureaucracy was not allowed at all. In 1905 the Press could speak more freely, and the Government is now the object of financial attack.

The spirit of fear still regulates the bureaucrat's relations to his superior. The old official word " nachalstvo," which means at once authority and initiative, implies, in bureaucratic circles, absence of all initiative in those who have to obey. There is none of this in the relations between the Town Council and its employés, and when I have seen the heads of departments doing business with their assistants, I have thought that their simple, intimate manner, free from any trace of snobbery, would be a good model for officials in other countries. Both the official and his employés are equally responsible to the public for effective work.

There are in all some 19,000 employés of the Moscow Town Council. They receive better salaries than the employés of the Zemstva. They are entitled, for certain terms of service, to pensions out of the town chest. On thirty years' service there follows a pension, regulated on the average of yearly pay which the employé has received during the whole of that period and amounting possibly to £200 a year. If an employé has to retire through some illness which incapacitates him for work, he receives after ten years' service one-third of the full pension, after fifteen years two-thirds, and after twenty-five years the whole pension. If he has come to need constant medical attention, he receives after five years one-third, after ten years two-thirds, and after twenty years the whole sum. For special cases of temporary disablement he receives special subsidies in proportion to his salary. The Town Council is now guaranteeing the funds for these pensions under a new scheme of insurance ; in some other places, the funds for pensions are still derived from the contributions of the employés themselves.[1]

A very large number of schools are under the jurisdiction of the Town Council ; and there is a common programme for all of them. The educational activity of the Council is subject to the Minister of the Interior, who is supposed to send an official to inspect the schools ; but practically all real inspection is done by the member of the Council Board responsible for this section of its work. There are two institutions for the training of teachers in Moscow, one secular and one religious, but both of them send most of their pupils to work in country schools. The town takes its teachers from the Government Gymnasia, or in some cases, where a knowledge of modern subjects is required, from the Government Real Schools. A class teacher starts at £38 a year, and rises by an increase of £4 every four years to £60. A head master starts at £60, and receives six subsequent increases of £5 each. The pension for a class teacher is £30 and for a head master £40.

The town has a more complete jurisdiction over hospitals than over schools. There are, indeed, hospitals which have been founded by the Government,—for instance, amongst the so-called " institutions of the Empress Maria Fédorovna,"—and others which owe their creation to the initiative of certain classes : the nobles of Moscow, the traders of Moscow, or the " townsmen "

---

[1] For these and many other details of the work of the Town Council of Moscow I am indebted to the detailed explanations of Mr. Nicholas Astroff, secretary to the Town Council, Mr. Dmitry Matvéyeff, the member of the Board responsible for hospitals, and Mr. Puzyrévsky, the member responsible for schools.

of Moscow; but far the greater part of this work has been done by the Town Council. By law it is under the obligation of putting the sick into hospitals,—hardly anything else is defined,—and the work of the Council is therefore practically free from control. The Minister of the Interior nominally sees to the inspection of the schools, but only to ascertain whether anything is being done contrary to law, and whether the hospitals are conducted in an orderly way; he takes no real initiative in the matter. Experts are constantly being sent westwards to study medical work and organisation in other countries, for the Town Council realises that Russia has more need to learn in this matter than the older countries of the West. For the organisation of hospitals England is taken to be the best model; but we are severely criticised in Russia for abandoning our hospitals to the support of charity, for trusting to the honorary services of physicians who have private practices, and for leaving the larger part of the work to young house surgeons and physicians, paid at a very low rate and sure to give up their work when they have secured the testimonial of having held a hospital post : this to the Russian seems like exploiting both charity and professional ability. The best steel instruments are imported from England and from Switzerland.

All the town hospitals are large. The Council often buys up old schools or big houses with large rooms, but usually builds its hospitals for itself, which takes some two or three years in each case. In Moscow the Zemstvo does not build hospitals, but contributes to those of the town ; in return the Moscow hospitals serve many provinces besides that of Moscow. Thirty-three per cent. of the patients come from outside the town, but no questions are asked ; the attitude of the Council is rather, " Well, let us do what we can"; and it is only in a big hospital that the most serious operations can be performed.

For the post of doctor a university degree is demanded. The salary starts at £100 ; it averages £200 and rises to £350. Most of the doctors spend all their life in this service. There is no long furlough, as is the case with the doctors of the Zemstva ; but in Moscow there is not the same need to get away from the narrow routine of work and to refresh one's studies. In the ordinary six weeks of yearly holiday, the absentee's work is

taken by a substitute instead of being divided, as in the case of the
Zemstva, amongst his colleagues.   The salaries of the Zemstva
doctors are lower, and they often enter the service of the town.
Ladies of good family are beginning to take up nursing work
instead of entering monasteries.

The town gave a subsidy of £100,000 for the war; a very large
part of this was expended in medical aid, and several doctors and
100 beds were sent out to the far East.   In 1906 the Town Council
equipped an ambulance which went under fire during the Moscow
rising to help the wounded.   Mr. Matvéyeff saw a man shot
down beside him.   The Town Council invited subscriptions for
the relief of all who had suffered in the Japanese war, the Moscow
rising, or the agrarian riots.

The Council has built a large home of the nature of our poor
law unions, in which the aged and the young are housed and
the unemployed can find housing, work, and pay.

The town possesses much property in different districts.   It
has assigned huge open spaces to the erection of town buildings,
for instance, for electric lighting, and a number of architects are
maintained.   The head of each department sends in an account
of the repairs or new building work which he claims, and these
accounts will be passed through the building section of the Board.
In each ward an engineer, with a few assistants, inspects and
reports on pavements, bridges, and chimneys.   The town is
constructing a large building to house a People's University,
after the model of our own University Extension ; the lectures,
as elsewhere in Russia, will be given gratis, and not necessarily
by the present staff of the University.   The Council exercises
the functions of trade police over markets, bazaars, and the booths
which are erected on large open squares.   It possesses a Town
Savings Bank, conducted partly as a business concern and partly as
a charity, and never paying its own expenses.   It has bought up
one of the two great tramway monopolies, but is not allowed to
secure the second before 1922; thus half of Moscow is likely to
remain without an adequate electric service for the present.   The
Council has for five years been engaged on the difficult and expensive work of draining Moscow for the first time. So far it has drained
only the central part of the town ; but certain other sections,
notably those in which there are large manufacturing colonies,

have adhered to the scheme on their own initiative. The war has deferred the completion of this work, which has already involved a heavy deficit. No man can be compelled to have his house drained. Several of the houses are wooden and not worth rebuilding; to drain them would be to destroy them, and so there has been much opposition. The rubbish of the town is carried away to a distance of ten miles, and is utilised on sewage farms, which have so far been very successful. The slaughterhouses, which are under the administration of the Council, are satisfactory; but more are required.

The water supply of Moscow has for a long time been excellent. The springs near the Trinity Monastery were even supposed to be miraculous. The main sources are at a distance of twenty miles; and these, if worked too hard, might give a less good quality. A new supply was therefore necessary, and was found by filtering the water of the Moscow river ten miles above the town. In this way all requirements of the near future have been amply guaranteed, and an English engineer, who visited the new waterworks, said that they were the best example of the kind that he had ever seen.

To complete our picture of the activity of the Local Councils we will now see some of their institutions at work.

In the neighbourhood of Moscow the country depends upon the hospitals of the town ; but the Zemstvo has established small hospitals in the environs. At Rastópino there is a broad, white, countrified building which attends to the needs of the northern outskirts of Moscow ; the approach is rutty and miserable ; the courtyard is desolate and dirty. In the neighbourhood there is a large population of "go-aways," and the hospital is, therefore, as full in the summer as in the winter. Additions are constantly being made to the buildings, but how the needs are going to be met no one seems to know (August 4, 1905). In the crowded department for out-patients we find a doctor, full of work, but apparently never in a hurry, and with time to be hearty to everyone. The nurse who shows me round seems ignorant, but not incapable. There are, in some wards, three times as many patients as there ought to be. In the untidy passages, parts have been screened off to make room for extra beds. Some of the patients do not look very ill, but I am told that in this neighbourhood the conditions of home life are such that anyone who feels the approach of any illness thinks it better to go to the hospital at once. The wards for infectious diseases are as crowded as any others. The midwifery department is tolerably full. There are two doctors and three "felshers"; the felsher corresponds to a trained "dresser" in our army : he may be an old soldier who has passed one and a half years in the ranks, one and a half years as a pupil, and two years as a regimental felsher; or he may have received an elementary medical instruction in a special civil school established for the purpose.

The Zemstvo of Kashin (Government of Tver) founded a small hospital, and in the eighties put up the present structure. It is a pleasant, low, rambling building. There are rooms for one, three, five, or more patients. The beds are white and clean ; the windows have no curtains. The hospital has three doctors, one medical student, and some female assistants attired in white smocks or dresses (July, 1904). There is little room to distinguish between different diseases. I see a case of typhus among the ordinary cases, but this case is declared to be not infectious. There is a department for infectious diseases, and there is a separate hut for complete isolation. The very small library contains only the most necessary books. There is a very meagre stock of small instruments. The operating room is miserably small and inconvenient, without space enough to work in ; there is another larger one, but here too there is not adequate room for six workers. There are much better arrangements for operating in the midwifery department. This is, in many ways, the best-organised and most encouraging part of the whole work. I see four cases ; about 120 come in during the year. It is a work of sheer education ; the peasants have the vaguest idea of what is necessary, and in their houses the accommodation and the nursing are utterly inadequate. The hope is that some of the lessons learned in the hospital will later be remembered at home. Thus the peasants are not expected to pay, though the towns-people do. The doctor or female attendant may have to travel ten miles by road to see or bring in a case. One patient, with a most difficult complication, has been brought in from the next Government; she had to travel over twenty miles of wretched road, and the journey lasted from 7 p.m. to 7 a.m. All the babies here are doing well. The mothers are always wanting to get out to their work. To this place, as a first point, lunatics are brought in from the district, but they are soon moved on to the provincial town. There are many more such cases than there used to be; the doctors put this down to alcohol and the spread of town conditions of life. The little room set apart for them is therefore often in use. It was once on the first floor, but a madman broke off the window grating and, crying that "it was better to die than live," jumped down to the ground. He only broke his leg. Now there is a little separate hut with only one window, which has a strong grating, giving very little light. The small waiting-room for out-patients is hopelessly overcrowded; three corners have been screened off from it to enable the three doctors to all work at once. The kitchen is spacious and very well kept. Every day a list is posted naming the diseases, and the doctor's prescriptions of food: he often prescribes beef tea, but the peasants do not like it; the usual food is cabbage soup, meat, jelly, and milk. Clearly the resources of the hospital hardly admit of much more than an attempt to deal with natural ailments by means of bettering for a time the ordinary conditions of life. The great enemies are poverty and ignorance. The hospital must take what workers it can get. An excellent new machine for heating, which cost £30, was very quickly spoilt by the clumsiness of the servants. The Zemstvo, always starved of funds, "will have to think and think before it can replace it." So it is with questions of building: "there comes a point when the improvement cannot be avoided." And other Zemstva are not as liberal as this one. The staff are sometimes kept very busy; but the work is not too hard. At least there are three educated men living together, which is better than being alone in the "solitude" (the country proper). There are three doctors of the Zemstvo in the rest of the district, and each is relieved by a doctor from this hospital for one month in the year. Also, after three years' service there is a three months' holiday. This term may be used for the continuance of one's studies. It is not of any use to go to the hospital in the provincial town; as it is far off and not well enough developed to be a good school, it is better to go straight to St. Petersburg or Moscow. "What," I ask, "do the doctors of Siberia do with their holidays?" "Well,

Tomsk ought to be developed as a school, but it is not; and these men get tired of the solitude, and spend their holidays in the big towns of Europe looking at people and life."

At Kesova Hill (Government of Tver) there are four beds for ordinary cases, only one of which is occupied. For one particular bed no charge is made to the patient. The ten beds for infectious cases are all empty. There are some good instruments, especially for midwifery and dental cases. There is a room for bandaging, but no serious operations are performed here.

Distance is the great enemy. The whole work is primarily educational. Peasants learn to observe a few simple rules, such as not to go out straight into the cold, (for their houses have no passages), after drinking anything hot. Their physique is weaker than it was. The causes of this are :—(1) that too much tea is drunk, (formerly the quantity was more rational) ; (2) alcohol, but the temperance societies have already shown very good results ; (3) poor food. The health of the peasants must, however, have improved, for the population is increasing.

At Koy (Government of Tver) there are seventeen beds. The ailments are mostly of the lungs or of the stomach, the latter being a consequence of the poorness of the food ; there are two casualties. All the wards are clean. There are a doctor, two felshers, and a female attendant ; the doctor and one of the felshers do the travelling work. The felsher left in charge is a military one; he is described to me as not an educated man, but able and skilful. He has been for two and a half years in Krásnoë Seló, near St. Petersburg; he has an honest face and a military manner, has served long, and is very keen about his work. The furthest journey is ten miles. The peasants rarely make unreasonable calls ; on the contrary, " they drag out their illnesses " as long as possible.

The country hospital of Voshcházhnikovo (Government of Yaroslavl) is a small building; there are six patients, but there is room for ten or more. The plan of the building is such as to waste much space. The Zemstvo is poor, but does what it can in the way of equipment. There is a dispensary, but no operations are done here. I see a woman with an injured leg who proposes to walk home at once to join in the haymaking. All the patients are always asking to be let out. The doctor, a dreamy man with a full face and a beard, does not seem to belong to this country atmosphere. He has long journeys to make, but is assisted by two capable military felshers, one of whom lives at the farthest end of his large district. During his holiday, a doctor comes on market days, (twice a week), from the District town. He seems less hopeful than some others; the peasants do not observe the ordinary rules of health; they dislike this side of his work, but in illness they will make use of the hospital. He was trained at Moscow University, and finds life very dull here. He is glad to use all his yearly holiday for "seeing people." Some Zemstva demand an account of work done during the triennial leave of three months. He is cut off from any chance of further study. The school is empty just now, and during haymaking time there is a crèche in one of its big rooms. Some of the children are in "lyúlki" (a kind of hammock); some are left alone playing on the floor. Close by is an almshouse, kept up by private charity; it has two big rooms, one for old men and one for old women, who look fairly comfortable.

At Ranenburg (Government of Ryazán) I enter the hospital by passing through the Zemstvo building and a particularly dirty courtyard. The capable doctor is a typical Intelligent. He has one colleague who is specially responsible for the health of the whole town. There are a felsher and a felsheritsa, and also an unqualified medical student. There is no other hospital in the District, (which is of the size of an average English county), and the four First Points send in from the country all cases with which they are not able to deal; all serious operations are performed here. He may be called out as far as twenty-five miles, but at least the hospital does not have to send men to work at the First Points when the doctors in charge of these are taking their holiday; such temporary work is done by doctors from a reserve list. In Siberia, he tells me, doctors have to cover districts of "legendary size." He is himself a surgeon; but here it is impossible to have any speciality.

There are sixty beds, with some eight patients to a ward. Sometimes the patients number as many as seventy, but at present (July 15, 1905) many beds are not occupied. The most common cases are of women's ailments and of inflammation of the lungs. Eruptive typhus, which is a rarity in Western

Europe, is here not uncommon. I have seldom seen disease so impressive as in this hospital; it was a very gallery of miseries. A woman had had both legs amputated for gangrene; an epileptic had twice fallen under a railway train, and had lost an arm and a leg. The doctor had an easy manner, and seemed to consider as quite tolerable such cases as we might have described in a whisper. Of a very bad case of meningitis he said comfortably, " Oh, he may get well." In a desolate-looking room lay a little boy, half imbecile, with a peasant girl of seven or eight, who sat with him to look after him. There was a small section for infectious diseases. The out-patients' department was quite full, though the peasants do not come in so often while work is going on in the fields. The doctor moved about, complaisant but busy, usually ending each hasty survey with the words, " We'll manage it." There was a bandaging room, which, though in very fair order, he described as " not clean." The operating room was good and well lighted. The Zemstvo grudges no outlay on instruments, and the doctor took especial pride in the steriliser. Though much restricted in means, the Zemstvo does what it can to feed the patients well. Four different diets are prescribed; the first of cabbage soup and gruel; the second of broth and other luxuries ; the third of chicken, white bread, etc.; the fourth of special nutriments for special ailments.

I visit (July 16, 1905) one of the First Points at Dubróv-shchina, which is within tolerable communication with Ranenburg by road and by rail. I pass out of the rain into a small building which smells strongly of drugs. The lady doctor in charge has gone away to a village where there are three cases of eruptive typhus. I am entertained by the two felshers, one of whom has passed through both the military and civil schools, serving in hospital and passing an examination ; the other has had only the military train-ing. The Zemstvo has been liberal in supplying all the necessaries: the instruments, which include dental ones, have been kept very clean ; the drugs have been stored in a cellar here and at the doctor's house. Each of the staff has one free day in the week, and spends two others on country journeys. Whatever the outside calls may be, one is always left on duty, and serious cases can be admitted at any time. The area covered consists of six cantons.

Women's ailments and inflammation of the lungs are the most common cases. Medical help is given at the first accouchement in each family; the doctor herself attends in all serious cases; the mothers usually get up some three days after the birth and walk in as out-patients. The peasants make but little difference in their food in such cases; perhaps one little cake will be cooked as a delicacy. Sometimes they say, " Everything would have gone right if the docter had not been here"; but the chief value of the work is educational, and far more faith is now placed in the doctors. The peasants will now consult them even if they are not sure that they are really ill; and the out-patients' department is far more used than formerly.

There are some wounded from the war; their chief desire seems to be to get well as soon as possible and to go at it again.

A "felsheritsa" is a female assistant, the counterpart of a "felsher." I visit one who is on outpost duty at a little village in the Government of Smolensk (Khóklovo). She is a vivacious little Polish woman, and is well capable of managing by herself.

She has a moderate supply of instruments, chiefly for dental and midwifery work. She finds it difficult to keep them quite clean. Her store of drugs is more complete. There is a little room for examination, but none for bandaging.

Distance is the great enemy. The doctor comes here to inspect at rare intervals; he cannot do more. She herself is constantly called out. The distances are great, and she has to take the patient in to the nearest hospital. When the passage of the Dnyépr is not interrupted, for instance by floods or floating ice, she will take them to Katan (eight miles), else they must go to Smolensk (eleven miles); there is no railway.

Most of her cases are midwifery ones. The peasants' cottages are deficient in everything that is necessary, and they do not like to go into hospital. A typhus case was taken in there; the patient did not at first know how ill he was; he got worse, put it down to the hospital, and insisted on coming out. The authorities "had no right to detain him" (would not a little autocracy be in place here?); when he got home he recovered, so he went round proving to everyone that hospitals were bad. Still the peasants are perhaps learning to take reasonable precautions in cases of birth.

The Town Councils have to deal with conditions much more similar to our own. With them distance is not so formidable an enemy; there is no need for "felsheritsy" on outpost duty. But here, as elsewhere, the foremost aspect of the work is educational, and it bears something of the same missionary character as in the country. In private practice, the average income will be £300, and some may make even £2,000 or £3,000, but the hospital work is, of course, far less lucrative.

Mr. Matvéyeff, chief of the medical section, and his professional coadjutor, Dr. Petróvsky, were so good as to show me over the chief hospitals in the town. Moscow is not remarkable for any particular diseases. The Council has made ample provision for epidemics, and keeps up a great midwifery section, of which far more use is made than formerly, and especially by persons of a higher class. One cannot yet say that there has been any noticeable effect in the rise of the population; but the work of draining, which has been carried out in the last five years, has already diminished the frequency of epidemics. Doctors as yet have no ground for saying that drunkenness is decreasing; but of late years there has been the most marked general progress in literateness, intelligence, and general initiative, which has led the working classes to pay far more attention to the ordinary rules of health. The war and the internal troubles have delayed this progress by throwing everything out of gear and upsetting the public mind. A notable feature is the increasing commonness of "nerves" during recent years, but this has had one good side: Russians have learnt to ask themselves more often whether they are ill or not; they no longer say, "It's nothing," until the doctor has told them that it "really is nothing."

There are two chief colonies in which the town hospitals are situated. Both lie on higher ground outside the town, the one on the north, near the admirable park of Sokólniki, the other on the south side, in the direction of the Sparrow hills. The soil is in each case sandy, and the sky unclouded by smoke, and there are pine woods in each neighbourhood. The Council possesses in these parts such large tracts of land that considerations of space are unnecessary. In the south of Moscow there are also several hospitals which are not under the jurisdiction of the Council, such as the old hospital of Nicholas I., a large stately white building with colonnade and spacious wards; a huge institution of the "townsmen" class, containing a hospital, a school, an almshouse, and a large playground for children; another large hospital maintained by the gentry and used exclusively by them; another that owes its origin to private charity; and one more which is under the special jurisdiction of the Empress, and is very capably worked. It will then be understood that the Council has not a complete monopoly of hospital work, but it has infinitely increased that work in volume, and the spur which its energy has given has reacted upon the older institutions. If Moscow is not behind other great cities of the world in this respect, the credit is due in the main to the Council.

The infectious hospital of the Town Council at Sokólniki is a mass of many buildings, some small, some very large; they are scattered over a great open space, which is divided into walks and planted with trees; there are twelve different sections, each in a separate building, for small-pox, diphtheria, scarlatina, eruptive typhus, recurrent typhus, erysipelas, and other diseases. The use to which some of these buildings are put is occasionally changed according to need, but the section for small-pox is never used for any other disease. There are sometimes a few inmates with non-infectious diseases. Everything in this vast establishment is remarkably clean and orderly. The doctors are assisted by students, who have completed the university course but have not as yet had any practical experience. All the staff live in comfortable quarters, a large double room which serves as sitting-room and bedroom being reserved for each student. There are good bath-rooms with a dressing-room on each side, one for the clothes to be worn outside the hospital and the other for the clothes of inside use. The felsher on duty is well housed in a comfortable room. All the sanitary arrangements are excellent. The passages are broad, and the wards clean, big, and airy. Each section is in this respect separately and adequately equipped with bath-rooms, etc. The operating theatre is well lighted; the slabs are all of glass. Very much money has been spent upon the instruments, the best of which come from England (Weiss & Meyer, of London). The big smiling doctor picks up one instrument which has seen many years' service and is still as sharp as ever. "With this," he says, "I can cut and cut and cut." No expense is spared on drugs. There is a good douche-room. Services are held in the chapel on feast-days, and the chaplain is always ready to administer the last sacrament in the wards. In the crypt is another chapel, where the last rites are performed for the infected dead.

On the road to the Sparrow hills stands a great hospital for those who are more or less permanently disabled. The head doctor, a little brown man with a very pleasant manner, has been here since the hospital was founded, and is all wrapped up in his work, giving to the whole institution a general feel of businesslike capability. He has two assistants, and they and the rest of the staff are well housed in a separate building.

The hospital, with its out-buildings, is all built in the old Russian style of architecture; it stands in a great open space. Everything is clean and pleasant. There are some 1,000 inmates, housed in wards which contain some eight beds, some four, some two, some one; these last are for the more advanced cases. Forty per cent. of the patients have nervous ailments; some few have rheumatism or a weak heart; in one ward I see six of the first category, one of the second, and two of the third. Most of them are in a drowsy condition and very weak. The clean beds are usually surmounted by little ikons. In a broad bay is a pleasant sitting-room commanding a view of woods and open country; from the opposite side the eye travels to a brilliant prospect of Moscow. The baths and other sanitary arrangements are excellent. Some patients go out for work for a time; but the incurables can remain here all their lives. The children's wing is bright and pleasant. The favourite ikon over the beds is the picture of Seraphim. I see here a clever-looking little fellow who was born with one arm; he is being taught how to do some work; there is also a half-witted boy, with bright staring eyes, who will probably remain here for life. The school is pleasant and clean; the schoolmistress is a member of the regular staff, On the balcony outside, a gramophone is being exhibited.

The dining-room has four large pictures of the Emperor, the Empress, and a gentleman and lady who left money to the institution. There is a bandaging-room for small incidental operations. In the well-lighted galleries of the almshouse old men and women are sitting out, and entertaining their visitors to tea. The kitchens are a separate building. The little church is built in the old Russian style, and has been decorated by a nun with some remarkably good paintings. The chaplain is constantly visiting the wards.

In the visitors' book are interesting signatures: "Sergius," in fine narrow characters; "Trépoff," in a bold, easy, masculine hand; "Bulýghin," in puny and rather intricate letters; "Golítsyn," the Mayor of Moscow; and others.

High up on sandy soil, in very large grounds planted with silver birches and oaks, stands the asylum, built on the initiative of Alexéyeff, Mayor of Moscow. He gave a large sum of money himself, and was indefatigable in getting money from others; one rich merchant was obdurate, but Alexéyeff, I am told, said that he would even go down on his knees to him if necessary and actually did so, with the result that he got a large donation. His portrait and those of the other chief benefactors hang in the central hall. One notices Kühn, after whom one section has been named, and the keen clever face of a member of the great and generous family of Morózoff. This institution, which I visited on August 4, 1905, has a vast moral significance, especially in Russia, for it is conducted on the so-called "open door" system. The chief, Dr. Kashchénko, a massive man with florid complexion, rugged beard, and strong steady eyes, is a vital part of the idea which he represents. He was trained wholly in the free atmosphere of the Local Councils, being first assistant at Tver under Litvínoff and then head of an asylum at Nizhny-Novgorod. He was sent to study asylums in England and Scotland, and published an account of his work. There are twelve doctors, all housed in good quarters; one of them went off his head, and had to enter the asylum. In the next house we overhear his wife singing the beautiful song of faith from Glinka's "Life for the Tsar," "Thee the powers of heaven on high shall protect," and one realises in what an atmosphere of effort this work is done. The nurses have to be very carefully chosen. Some try the work and go away after three days; others can stand it quite well, and there are but few breakdowns. Of course, as Dr. Kashchénko tells me, they are more irritated, more strained than is normal, and the nerves are generally brought into play; they are never

allowed to work for more than ten hours at a stretch, and have
a complete holiday every fourth day.   Their uniform is white.

There are 1,000 patients, all insane (imbeciles are housed elsewhere).   The huge main building is very spacious throughout.
There is a large hall in which lectures are given.   A great deal
of wickerwork is done.   From the long corridors open little
rooms for single patients; they are pleasant and orderly, and
give, of course, immeasurably better accommodation than most
of the patients have been used to at home.   In the first section
the inmates are quite quiet, and gather and talk in the corridors.
Our entry arouses a little excitement.   One old lady breaks out
into a flood of narration, very animated but quite peaceable, and
shaded with all sorts of variety of expression.   Another, who
follows us about for something like half an hour, has pinned a
little paper red cross on to her dress, and explains that this is her
" full powers," which she can only hand over to someone else
who is equally plenipotentiary; she does not at all disturb us
with her constant interruptions, and the doctor is never at a loss
for patient answers, which keep her interested and quiet.   One
old lady, of charming manners and prettily dressed, has put up
on the door of her room a notice to announce that she is the
daughter of Alexander II.; she comes up with a long story, to
which the doctor answers, " I will beg you, Mária Petróvna, to
defer this conversation till to-morrow," and he adds to me, " If
we stood and listened to her it would be for an hour, and, as she
is very nice, one could hardly go away in the middle."   He has
similar answers for those who ask him to let them out.   The
garden of this section is a large open space with pleasant walks;
none of the doors being locked, the patients move about freely,
and we see a young girl inmate going out to fill a basin at the
spring.   In the next section, entered only through the first, there
is more noise.   One woman shouts aimlessly and harmlessly.
Another has been born with a skull like a monkey; she is a
diminutive creature, with a most amiable little wrinkled face; she
is petting a doll and a ball.   The doctor calls her up, and half
caresses her little close-cropped head while he explains its exceptional shape; he uses to her endearing diminutives, and says,
" She's very good-hearted"; she nestles her head in his caressing
hands, and then runs away and walks round us cuddling her

doll. The third section is entered through the two others by a
door which has to be unlocked. An insane girl raves ecstatically
through the little garden; a wild woman rushes up and throws
her arms quite nicely round the doctor, calling him "dear papa."
A strange silent nurse seems to show signs of the pressure of her
work. The men, who are more in number, are similarly divided
on the other side of the main building. Those whom we see are
silent and respectful, and show an evident liking for the doctor.
Outside the doors are large gardens, where all the work is done
by the inmates, only one professional gardener being kept. The
little plots are orderly and uniform. Three patients, with a nurse
behind, are wandering at will through the open fields.

We sit on the doctor's balcony with his clever motherly wife
and pleasant children. Before the Zemstva and Town Councils,
he tells me, the ruling principle of all asylums was fear, and it is
still the same where the Local Councils have not yet penetrated.
Dr. Kashchénko has seen the rapid change which has taken place
since the eighties. The old method was sinister: the chief
object was to "shut men up"; in everything there was the
assertion of "authority." Now the buildings are far better, and
the food far more wholesome. The patients are even allowed to
go out to see their relatives; some recover, and are discharged.
The doors are open, and the patients can go away; sometimes,
but not often, they do. Dr. Kashchénko never talks of them
except as "the patients," and the institution is with him, not an
asylum, but a "mind hospital" ("psychiatria"). I ask Mr.
Matvéyeff about the remarkable personality and influence of the
doctor, and he answers, "Yes, of course, without that the
system would be impossible; but it is better to depend on the
doctor than on walls and fences." The doctor tells me that
more and more patients come in every year, not that there is
necessarily more mental disease, but because people did not like
to take their relatives to the old asylums. Most of them die of
general paralysis of the insane some four or five years after it
has developed. There is a great tendency to consumption, and
indeed, the nervous system being the base of everything, their constitutions are generally very weak. What is called "degeneracy"
is less prevalent in Russia than in Western Europe. Even the
Russian Intelligents are notably more free from it. A far more

common cause of insanity in Russia is sheer superstition; the peasants still believe in bogies, witches, and the evil eye : and, nonsense as all this may be, the effects on the mind are very real. Of course very many of the inmates are peasants; and in the still summer evening I hear a number of voices strike up the long-drawn peasant refrain, "Down Mother Volga." Dr. Kashchénko has encouraged lectures to all the employés on the details of their work; he desires that they should all meet together as equals in the study of their common task.

In no place have I felt more strongly the moral importance of the Local Councils. The issue between them and the older system is here quite clear : on the one side fear and darkness, on the other life and light; on the one side paper and neglect, on the other an immense obligation willingly undertaken and sustained.

Near the great park of Sokólniki, a kind of Bois de Boulogne, only more after the Russian or English heart, there stands, on sandy soil, a great mass of town buildings. Amongst them is the Workmen's Home ; the Director, a kindly and simple man, showed me over this institution on July 17, 1905. It is the biggest of its kind in Russia ; at St. Petersburg there is also an important one. It can receive as many as 2,500 inmates, but usually has 1,500. At the time of my visit, owing to the mobilisation, there were but 900; but many more were expected in the autumn, and it would be difficult to find work for them. The inmates have entered, by their own choice, in search of work, and they are free to go when they like. Preference is given (1) to those who have not been here before, (2) to those who have lived in Moscow for two months, and the longer their residence the more consideration is given to their claim ; (3) to those who know a trade, for the institution is partly a business concern, and for these last it is more easy to find work. Inmates who have earned twelve shillings in a month inside the institution will, if there is a pressure of applicants, be asked to go. There is also a section which contains some 500 beggars, mostly old men and old women who are unable to work ; these are sent to the institution whether they consent or not, and remain there permanently ; there is a similar section for children ; and, lastly, there is a hospital, with two doctors and 120 patients from

amongst the inmates. The working inmates sleep in very large
dormitories; the beds are arranged in couples, and there is
very little space between each couple. Each bed has a rough
rug and a mattress. When there is a better standard of living
outside, the accommodation inside will improve correspondingly.
A large number of men are sitting on their beds; I notice one
clerkly-looking man with a sly face, who has evidently been some
kind of a priest. There is a long trough for washing, (again
one must remember that it is better than nothing), and in
each ward there is the totally inadequate provision of two
towels on rollers. The sanitary arrangements, as elsewhere
in all these institutions, are on the English model. The women
sleep in similar wards; all midwifery cases are taken straight
away to the special institution which the Town Council has
provided for them. There are other dormitories for lads and for
children. The behaviour of the inmates to the Director struck
me as somewhat casual. They themselves supply the staff of
the institution, except for the three or four clerks in the office
and the skilled workmen who are paid to teach in each workshop.
Inmates are selected by rotation to keep order in the wards.
The chief punishments are the threat of expulsion and actual
expulsion, which last follows of itself if an inmate gets drunk.
The workshops have plenty to do; their work is all for the
Town Council. They make stanchions for the electric tramways, beds, chairs, shoes, packets for powders for the hospitals,
and book-covers with printed titles for the schools. There are
smiths, painters, and weavers; in one room eighteen looms are
at work on cloth of blue, white, or mixed patterns. The cobblers
and wicker-plaiters are kept busy with orders. There are four
meals in the day, the most important being a midday dinner of
vegetable soup and gruel. The hospital is tolerably spacious
and well ventilated, except in one section. There are, however,
too many beds for the space. The chief patients are old men
and old women; there is no special department for children.
There is a fine theatre, in which are given readings, lantern
lectures, and concerts, which are sometimes offered by the
Moscow Conservatoire.

I have mentioned only a few of the chief institutions; there are
many others, such as other hospitals, a shelter for the destitute,

and a huge white building in which are found quarters for 1,000 destitute widows and widowers. In connection with the establishing of shelters I will mention the name of Professor Guerrier, of Moscow University.

We turn to the work which the Zemstva have done in the development of agriculture. Novotorzhók had to fight hard for the right to keep an agricultural expert. The present Agronom is the third occupant of the post; he is assisted by a deputy, and by a controller of the agricultural depôt. His duties, he told me on August 12, 1905, are now tolerably well defined. The peasants call him out to their land to give advice as to what seeds should be sown, and where and when. They are very intelligent, and often come in to ask him questions, chiefly about manuring.

The Zemstvo houses, in several large sheds, a number of agricultural instruments. It takes a 10 per cent. profit on all goods to go to the extension of its work, and it has almost driven out of the field the old dealers, who claim 40 per cent. It keeps all sorts of mineral manure; it gets its seeds from Holland, Moscow, and other places; it sells them at a somewhat dearer price when they are wrapped up in small parcels, because of the waste involved by sorting. Its machines are mostly from England or from Riga; there is some Swedish iron and a little American. The primitive " sokhá " still exists in some parts, but the plough is driving it out. Specially made ploughs are sold for working the narrowest strips of peasant land; these machines are double, and can be turned round in the smallest space; they cost more than twice the price of the others. The very fact of their existence is an argument against the communal system of property. I see machines for winnowing, and others for grinding and threshing. The peasants have got accustomed to using them, and no longer break them as frequently as they once did. The Zemstvo also makes some of its own machines.

I visited on August 11 and 12, 1905, the depôt of household industries established by the same Zemstvo. A number of clean peasant women with pleasant faces had brought in their books for settlement. Those books which I looked at showed for each worker payments of about three shillings a fortnight, earned in the time which could be spared from household work. The naval badges include emblems of wheels, telescopes, machines, etc., to be worn on the arm by men of different ranks. They are stitched very quickly in dark red thread on the top of a paper design. The patterns for other work are many of them of ancient Russian origin; they are simple, quaint, and fascinating. Leather slippers are stitched out of pieces of quaint shapes and various colours, silk being used to mark the divisions. On these slippers may be stitched designs in rough gold or silver gilt thread. For the lace workers the Zemstvo keeps an album of photographed designs. I saw one old woman in her own house working in silk a curious belt; she had bought her own little loom, a primitive contrivance with a lot of string. Her clean bare feet, by means of pedals, held apart the upper and lower divisions of the machine. I saw her work through the most difficult part of the pattern, and was struck by the method and quickness with which she changed her threads. A little girl doing gold-stitch work seemed equally at home with her task.

In Moscow the Government Zemstvo has established a depôt of the same kind on a much larger scale in a rugged and handsome building of the old Russian style decorated with Slavonic letters. Amongst the peasants, the Director tells me (July 8, 1905), there are many real artists, but they are ignorant. In the six months of winter they have to do something to eke out their earnings from the soil. Many work in their own houses. To help these, the Zemstvo supplies models, trying to direct rather than to dominate the natural taste of the workers. With this object, it has collected into a museum a number of examples of old Russian art, such as hearths, ironwork, and the gold-stitched head-dresses of the wives of ancient Boyars. One of its objects is to revive the old Russian arts, which began to be driven out at the time of Peter the Great. It keeps a staff of artists, whose designs have been photographed both for the peasant workers and for the agents of the Zemstvo in and outside Russia. More than seventy different objects of art are produced in the Moscow Government. In the District of Podólsk alone there are twenty-five. The depôt contains toys of an admirable fancy, notably little figures of men which shut up as boxes inside each other, and also animals of all kinds. Most of the wood-carving comes from the District of Dmitroff. Easter eggs are a special industry. One sees also lace, brocade, chairs, baskets, ikons, and ironwork; £40,000 worth of goods are sold every year. Similar depôts have been established in Nizhny-Novgorod, Vyátka, and Perm. I have seen others at Tver and Ryazán.

Forty years ago Russia was altogether inadequately provided with schools of any kind ; the Local Councils have in this respect changed the face of the country. Their hands have been far more closely tied than in the case of hospital work. Yet the contrast established between the past and the present is their work, and it is astonishing.

Mr. Puzyrévsky, the member of the Moscow Council Board who is responsible for this section, acquainted me with the out-lines of its work. The Council is always busy building new schools. The secondary Town School provides for a class which can hardly secure admission to the Gymnasia and Real schools. The programme is the same in all institutions of this type ; it now includes German and French, but not Latin and Greek. Discipline in the streets is to some extent preserved by a *custos*, who, before and after the school hours, patrols those streets by which most of the scholars go home. For misconduct on the streets the school authorities can punish. In these day-schools detention on feast-days or on Sundays is not in use. A refractory scholar is rebuked, first alone and for the second offence before the whole class ; he may be ordered to write out an intelligent summary of some lesson, by no means corresponding to our "lines." The children are keen and interested in their lessons. For recreation there are certain Russian games, perhaps a few concerts and lantern lectures, and, lastly, excursions with the masters, which are free of railway fares for thirty miles round Moscow.

The working classes are keenly desirous of instruction, chiefly because they hope thereby to earn better wages ; and schooling is now far more within their reach than it used to be. It is impossible to give statistics for the difference which it has made in their general life ; but one district in the Moscow government, where nearly all the women lived by prostitution, has been radically improved by the institution of a school, which was for twenty years maintained by a simple peasant and has now passed into the hands of the Zemstvo.

The secondary Town School of Tver is housed in the chief Gymnasium. It is in the top corner of the building, and occupies one-sixth of the whole. It has 200 scholars and six masters, including a teacher of divinity. The four class-rooms are broad and airy. There are fifty scholars in a class. The library has a haphazard look, but is really very complete. There are several handbooks of divinity, history, geography, mathematics, natural history, and physics; the literary section is peculiarly strong. There are advanced scientific magazines, and text-books for the use of the teachers. One notices a great many numbers of the *Pedagogic Magazine,* and of the great *Historical Review.* The cabinets contain skeletons of men and beasts, designs for drawing, models of machines and electrical appliances. The programme includes the Russian language, history, geography, elementary algebra, mathematics, and natural history. Boys spend five years here, entering between eleven and sixteen and leaving between fifteen and. twenty; of course, this mixture of ages sometimes produces bad results. The headmaster remembers one boy who managed to pass the difficult line of division between Town School and Gymnasium by practically teaching himself Latin and Greek; such a boy would enter the Gymnasium half-way up (the fourth class). Each master, while teaching little more than his own special subject, acts as a tutor to one of the classes, and is consulted by the boys in any of their difficulties. The headmaster has a great belief in games, and, in his previous post, used to organise entertainments for his pupils. The pupils are allowed to form groups for the study of literature or music. The method of punishment is the usual ball system, elsewhere described. There is also detention after class work. The pupils all come from practically the same class of parents.

I receive similar information (July, 1904) from the head of the secondary town school in Káshin; his title is "Teacher-Inspector." This school serves a district in which forty primary schools have been established by the Zemstvo. There are also two private schools, which possess the only two teachers who are specialists.

The better teachers are constantly going off to the neighbouring districts, where the pay is higher. A teacher in a town school is an official, and is free of the peasant's dues and responsibilities. The school has six classes, covering the ages between eleven and sixteen The programme includes practically the same subjects as at Tver, but at the time of my visit no foreign languages were taught. One-third of the pupils are the children of well-to-do peasants ; these are the best workers. A few come from the families of the officials, but most are of the shopmen class. Some go on to the lower technical schools, where the teaching is narrow and practical, and then obtain posts. Very few make the transition to the Gymnasium.

In the matter of schools, the Zemstva have a harder task than the Town Councils. The Zemstvo of Novotorzhók keeps a very interesting depôt of school necessaries. There are many copies of the Russian classics, such as Gógol, and even a complete edition of Ostróvsky, which I had difficulty in finding in a good Moscow book shop. The depôt has very much of a political character. There are special studies of burning questions, such as an extensive work on the epoch of the great reforms, Býkoff's "England and the English," with pictures of political demonstrations, etc., the text of Magna Charta, with a commentary written in a style not easily accessible for the peasants—and pamphlets, such as Danchénko's "Far off Brothers," "From Ignorance to Knowledge," and others on electoral rights, national representation, and the system of budgets in parliamentary States. The seller in charge goes out of his way to say to me : "Don't take that one ; this will interest you more." I find also a brief sketch of the Belgian Constitution, and Marx on "Bourgeoisie, Proletariat, and Communism." Amongst the lighter tales are "Meeting with a Bear," "Unexpected Help," and "The Love Story of a Murderer." (So it is coming there too, is it ?). Also there are postcard portraits of the heroes of the Intelligence, Gorky, Shalyápin, and Chekhoff, and pictures of barely dressed actresses which must have a curious effect on the peasant mind.[1] From these one turns with relief to admirable reproductions of famous views, scenes of foreign life in all parts of the world, and illustrations of the chief

[1] Several peasant members of the Imperial Duma thought the evening dress of court ladies indecent.

events of Russian history. One of the best series of school pictures deals with Bible history. There is about these religious pictures a broad humanity which ought not to be as rare as it is ; and I know of no more sympathetic decoration for the walls of a nursery.

A Government training college for teachers has already been described. At Tver the Zemstvo has one of its own ; and the difference of atmosphere in the two institutions is interesting. The story of the Tver training college was told to me (August 9, 1905) by the Principal, an elderly lady of charming manners, who has travelled in all the chief countries of Europe, and has held her post here for seventeen years. She gave me a clear businesslike narrative, which answered in advance every one of my questions.

The Zemstva have five training colleges in Russia; each has had a different origin and a different history. Near Tver there lived a notable member of the Zemstvo, Mr. Maximovich, a man of keen energy and considerable ambition. In 1869 he proposed to the Government Zemstvo that a training college should be founded ; the idea met with approval, but the funds were not voted. Maximovich, therefore, with the help of a few supporters, set about getting them. He possessed a small estate, and was able to spend a little money. A humble building which no one wanted was engaged ; ladies of the Zemstvo families helped in the work. Next year the members came to visit the institution, saw that it was useful, and voted a subsidy of £10. Maximovich continued to collect funds, to secure the approval of Ministers in St. Petersburg, and to subscribe himself whenever there was a pinch. Mr. Robert, greatly to his pecuniary disadvantage, resigned the headmastership of the Boys' Gymnasium in Tver, and worked here as Director of Studies ; and a most talented lady served as the first Principal. Mr. Robert was later succeeded by Mr. Oldenburg, who is well acquainted with similar work in other countries. The governing board consists of the Principal, the Director of Studies, and representatives of the Zemstva. The Ministry of Public Instruction has a single representative. The support of the Government is thus, to a certain extent, guaranteed; if its representative wishes to object to anything, he is listened to ; if, say, he wishes to

reject a certain candidate for a teaching post, he is asked for
his reasons, and if he shows that the candidate has, say, been
convicted of some offence, the rejection is voted. In other
cases the Zemstvo members can outvote him and act independently. There has been a good deal of trouble with the
Government, though not in the last few years. " This subject,"
says the Government, "must not be taught, or that subject
must be taught differently." There was once a similar school
in Novgorod; but an answer, given by a pupil at the time of
examination, annoyed the Minister of Public Instruction, and
the school was closed. In Tver, too, the Minister was at one
time so hostile to the Zemstvo that he was clearly seeking for
an excuse to stop the work. It would not be difficult to find
one. For instance, there is issued by the Ministry a catalogue of
the books which may be used in such colleges. The Principal
remarked to me, with reasonable annoyance, that if she were fit
to be entrusted with the administration of the college, she might
be depended on to choose the right kind of books; yet, if an
answer in the examination showed that some book which was
not on the list had been read by the pupil, even though the book
had never been recommended by the college staff, the college
might have to die.

The institution was designed for the use of peasant girls between
the ages of seventeen and twenty-five. Most of the first pupils,
however, were daughters of priests. Now half of the pupils are
peasants. The District Zemstva of the Government receive
reports from their village teachers, and, on this basis, are granted
several scholarships of £7 10s. a year, which cover all the cost of
teaching, food, lodging, and washing. There is no special uniform such as one sees in all Government institutions. The girls
wear their ordinary clothes, red, blue, or brown, as they please.
This is to the taste of the Principal, who says, " When God made
flowers of different colours it meant that He liked variety."

There are twenty teachers, all salaried. Twelve of them live
in the house together, and have common meals. There is a very
cordial feeling between them. This feeling is in the air, and
even a visitor must needs be conscious of it. There are no
actual punishments; if an offence is committed, the teacher or
the Principal speaks to the class as a whole, explaining that

conduct of that kind will not do. The girls, who all live very
freely together, have a great distaste for anything like "sneaking."
Many of the girls come from bad homes, and have to learn
character here. One, who had a drunken father and a bad mother
and sisters, committed several small thefts; things were found to
be missing. One girl, who knew who was the culprit, said to her,
"If you want anything of mine ask me, and whatever I have got,
I will give you part of it, only don't take." The thefts went on;
so in the end the pupils, by common agreement, invited the
teacher to help them to persuade the girl that she was doing
wrong.

There are five classes, with thirty-three as the average number
in each class. The programme includes a general scheme of education, thorough instruction in those subjects which the pupils will
later on have to teach, and special training in teaching itself. I
am shown a sketch lesson on the subject "How to explain the
shark." The pupil writes out her idea of what the lesson should
be; next morning she gives the lesson to school children, while
other pupils and the class teacher listen; in the evening the
teacher explains what mistakes have to be avoided. The pupils
enter for the ordinary examination of the Government, and take
the ordinary certificate, which is of a very low standard and, in some
other institutions, carries no guarantee of practical experience.
Students from this institution are, therefore, everywhere preferred as candidates for posts. Six hundred teachers have left
the college. Of these, 300 are married and 300 are teaching
in the Government of Tver. Invitations from other provinces
have to be refused, as all the teachers are wanted here. The
college cannot receive more than one-half of the paying candidates
who apply, and refuses applications for entrance from other
provinces; otherwise the number of pupils could easily be more
than doubled.

I have usually made my country journeys in Russia during the
long summer holidays. I could not, however, escape the evidence
of the work of the Zemstva, which came to me through visits to
many school buildings, talks with many schoolmasters, and the
testimony given alike by gentry, officials, priests, and peasants.
The effects on the peasant life are dealt with elsewhere. The
schoolmasters are, in many places, themselves practically peasants,

but they have an ideal, and they are holding up a light in a dark place.

I take one of the humblest as an example. In a village of the Kashín district (July, 1904), the Zemstvo schoolmaster is an old peasant, with a long solemn face, but shrewd fiery eyes. His young and bright wife has amiable town manners. He was the son of a parish clerk, went to a school, but not to a university, and, in the old days, took some teaching work in the house of the local squire. As a schoolmaster he at first got only £16 a year; now he has from the Zemstva £21, but prices are very much higher than they were. He is quite content to live right away in the country; he can "walk in the woods and see nature," and he has long holidays. He himself reads quite respectable text-books, for instance, of history; and he talks far more intelligently of England than most Englishmen do of Russia. This is a poor district; the people are very rough, and the boys very dull and "blunt." He has none of Pobyedonóstseff's doubt as to the profit of learning. The children do not want it, but the parents want it for their children.[1] It enables them to earn more money, and many of them go to settle in the towns. Unlike most village teachers, he considers the teaching of "religiousness" to be the most important part of his work. In this respect the people here are good, only they are very lazy. Superstition as yet does not seem to diminish; the children grow up in the atmosphere of their parents. His wife wishes me "everything good, after the fashion of our Asia." My host pats his blue-bloused chest and says proudly, "I am a European."

In some other Districts the school statistics show that illiterateness, even amongst girls, is practically disappearing. The change has been wonderfully rapid and complete.

The Ministry of Public Instruction has established a small number of Secondary Schools for peasants in some of the larger villages. The schoolmasters have somewhat similar social responsibilities to those of the servants of the Zemstva, and are not unlike them in manner and intelligence.

One such school, in the Government of Yaroslavl, has five classes, of which the head-master takes the higher ones. The children are quickwitted and interesting. The parents question the

---

[1] In other districts it is exactly the opposite.

value of instruction, but the children themselves have no doubt as to it. Only 7 per cent. stay to the end of the five-year course. One on an average in every year goes on to a higher school; one girl actually went on to a Gymnasium, but that is an exception. There are peasants from this village who have been to universities. Some of them are now teachers and doctors. The school-master gives public readings, and gets up theatrical performances. There is a library, not merely for the scholars, but for the peasants, who read Tolstoy, Pushkin, or even Dostoyévsky.

Out of the employés of the Zemstva and Town Councils,—doctors, lawyers, agronoms, and others,—there has sprung up in the country districts almost a new class, which is known there as the Third Element. These men are not landowners and not peasants. By the present regulations the Zemstvo franchise has no room for them. It is no exaggeration to describe them as missionaries, and the moral privations to which they have submitted will be realised from the preceding notes on schools and hospitals. They have exercised over the peasants an influence stronger even than that of the Zemstva themselves, but being, like the Intelligents of the sixties, excluded from any voice in public affairs, they have for the most part worked in an anti-governmental direction, and this the Zemstva found out to their surprise only in 1906. Practically all of them joined the pro-fessional unions which did so much to give volume to the move-ment of liberation in 1905. While approximating in programme to the Zemstvo Liberals, they contain in their ranks a majority of convinced Socialists, and it is by them that Socialist dogmas are expounded to the peasants. There are many signs to prove that these hard-working Intelligents, who have been put into such close touch with the real life of the peasants, have far more political instinct and are far more practical in their political methods than those other Intelligents who still await the education which can be gained from responsibility. This makes it possible that, given a chance of peaceful development, they may gradually tend more and more to reinforce the middle party; but the very absoluteness of the sacrifices which they have made disinclines them to half-measures, and such acts of the Government as the dissolution of the Duma only confirm them in their desire for a complete reconstruction of the social order.   The destinies of the Third Element still hang in the balance; there are two main political tendencies between which it will be called upon to choose : it can become either more revolutionary or more Liberal, and its choice will have the most far-reaching influence on the future of Russia.

CHAPTER XII.

WHEN the great act of emancipation of 1861 set free from serfdom some fifty millions[1] of Russian peasants, many did not dare to guess to what use the peasant would put his new measure of liberty. When Wallace was writing his great book, the answer to this question was still uncertain. The peasant had got to pass from one system to another, from the morality of the slave, loyal, like a good dog, but lacking in all initiative, to the morality of the free and self-respecting man. Others were far more gloomy in their anticipations than Wallace. Nekrásoff, one of the many friends of the peasant, in his notable poem, "Who can live happy in Russia?" sends a little band of rustics all over the country to answer the question which is asked in the title, and brings them back with no better answer than that the only happy people in Russia are the drunkards, and they only while they are drunk. Indeed, we are told that peasants roamed over Russia crying, "I am free of will; I am free of will," and making no better use of their freedom than to soak themselves in vodka. But the emancipation is one of those towering events which can only be seen in perspective from a distance. All those who dared to believe in human nature could not doubt that the final result must be good. The freedom, which at one time was conceived to have come too early, is now generally considered to have been too incomplete. The use to which the peasant has already put his liberty has far more than satisfied all those of his critics who know anything about him. These may be officials, priests, country gentry, doctors, schoolmasters, or themselves peasants; but their verdict, which I have summarised in the following pages, is always in the main the same. The progress of the peasants, when judged by the methods of the historian, will prove to be the most fundamental factor of Russian history

[1] 47,200,000 (Rambaud, p. 677).

of the last forty years. In some respects, as, for instance, notably
in the matter of morality, the transition from the bond life to
the free is not yet complete ; also in those provinces of Great
Russia which I have so far studied it is evident that some districts
have lagged far behind others ; but though the ratio of improvement has differed in various parts, an upward movement is to
be seen everywhere. This progress has generally taken the
same course. It has been at the first purely economical ; it
will undoubtedly end by being also strongly political. Its rate of
development was remarkable long before the beginning of the
Japanese war ; since then, while slowing down in certain respects,
it has become infinitely more rapid in others.

The fact that the peasants were about 90 per cent. of the population, and were, therefore, the ultimate political basis of any system
of government, has since 1861 been fully appreciated. Everyone
has bid for their goodwill, and therefore everyone has done something for them. The generosity of the emancipation itself can
at least defy all English criticism till we have endowed all
our country labourers with land. When the reaction came,
Alexander III. was peculiarly the peasants' Tsar ; it was amongst
them that he felt most at home : both he and his successor have,
on behalf of themselves and of the State, made very large remis-
sions of the payments due from the peasants, which deserved a far
greater publicity in the Western Press than they received. The
Government, in order that the peasants might at once enter into
the possession of their land, had charged itself with the financial
loss due to the emancipation. There was established in 1883
a Peasants' Bank to advance money at a very low rate for the
acquisition of new land ; and, though there was also established in
1886 a competing institution which gave the same help to the
gentry, the Peasants' Bank has done some good work. Further, the
Government was now more anxious than before to go to the help
of the peasants in years of famine ; and at least the ordinary
English reader is inconsistent if he condemns it for having failed
to do more than half of an obvious duty : we have never gone so
far in the matter of State support.

Amongst the newly established authorities, the temporary "arbitrators" of the time of the emancipation are generally allowed
to have shown both wisdom and generosity in the execution of

their most difficult task of dividing the land between the gentry and the peasants. The short-lived "Justices of the Peace" helped very much to acquaint the Intelligents with the needs of peasant life. The admirable work done by the Local Councils has already been more fully described. Lastly, the country priests, stirred by the general competition to a far greater intelligence and activity, have set a new example to the peasants : they have become far better models of a moral life ; and, as the first small farmers of their respective parishes, they have often been the first to avail themselves of the many improvements put at their disposal by the Local Councils.

But the peasant has done more for himself than others have done for him. The first sign of self-respect and initiative is that the houses are kept cleaner inside. Next, the peasant will set about decorating the outside of his house and carving the projecting wooden beams to curious patterns. By these exteriors one can very well gauge the relative prosperity of a district. In the district of Rostóff I noticed a carpenter's house whose whole exterior was one mass of excellent fretwork, one of the most legitimate advertisements which I have seen. If the peasant's idea of literateness is still narrow, he at least understands that study is a profitable enterprise and will increase his independence. The peasants of a district at first become what is called in Russia "little literates"—that is, persons who merely know how to read and write ; but even this is a notable step forward. From the hospitals, which are before all things educational institutions, the peasant learns the advantage of taking care of oneself, and applies at home those rules of health which he has learned in the wards.

Drunkenness has been a besetting sin of the peasant of Central Russia, and many attempts to diminish it have been made from above. These have perhaps been not more successful than the efforts made in our country. In 1895 the Government tried, in four of the eastern provinces, a system by which the sale of liquor was entirely in its own hands ; and in 1896 was drawn up a law which was gradually applied to the Empire in general. In principle no compensation was given to the former sellers of liquor, but in the West and North-west private rights were, as a matter of fact, bought up. The number of dram-shops and beer-shops was gradually diminished. In the country districts vodka

might not be drunk on the premises or on the street outside ; the
bottles, when sold, are sealed up, but the peasant has his own
speedy way of opening them.   Whilst closing a large number of
liquor shops and limiting the hours during which liquor can be
sold, especially on feast-days, the Government also created and
partially subsidised local Committees of Temperance, which were
charged with the building and improving of tea-rooms to take the
place of the liquor shops which had been abolished.   In 1895
the Government gave £20,950 for this purpose, and by 1900 it
had increased its grant to £258,144.   At first these tea-rooms
were very popular with the peasants, and they are still much
patronised during the winter months.   I have visited several of
them.   In one I find a large room with a stage, and a smaller
room for private conversations ; an enormous musical box plays
you a tune for $1\frac{1}{4}d.$, and I enter to the sound of the " Boulanger
March " ; the library has pictures of Russian writers, Leo Tolstoy
being in the place of honour.   The favourite reading consists of
short stories, religious books (such as the " Lives of the Saints "),
and, especially of late, the best newspapers.   In another the
arrangements are exactly the same ; the rooms look as if they
had been much used.   In a third readings are held, secular or
religious, but I am warned that the institution is no longer a
novelty.   Tea is sold, not only for drinking on the premises, but
for taking home ; a portion which I bought for $1\frac{1}{4}d.$ seemed very
liberal and exceedingly cheap at the price.   It included bits of
lemon and two lumps of sugar.

The Government report of 1899 maintains that the monopoly
has worked well ; it states that the quality of the drink is better,
that there are fewer places of supply, that the prices are uniform,
that cash payment is required, that there is less drunkenness and
therefore less crime resulting from drink, that the Crown income
has all the same been increased, that the peasants of the four
eastern provinces have more money in the savings banks, and that
in three years they have acquitted themselves of nearly £2,000,000
of their arrears of dues for the redemption of their land.   There
is no doubt that this picture is altogether too rosy.   Drunkenness has been driven on to the streets, and has been concentrated
specially on to certain places where drink shops exist, and on
to certain times when drinking is allowed ; very probably the

peasant drinks less, but he now drinks it all at one time; and as he lives on poor food, has a very weak head, and starts drinking with the deliberate intention of getting drunk, he is very soon able to do his business even under the present system. Also there have sprung up all over the country illicit dram-shops, which are able to satisfy his thirst at a somewhat increased price. The Government must be credited with the best intentions; but it would seem that we have not yet the right to say that drunkenness is diminishing in Russia.

Crime, too, if it is diminishing at all, is doing so very slowly. The authority of the police has not gained by the antagonism between it and the new institutions. The police, as we know, complain bitterly of the respect with which they have to treat even habitual criminals. When I ask a small farmer what the peasants think of the police, he replies, "They think that the law prevents the police from touching them." Meanwhile a better public opinion is undoubtedly growing up. It has, of course, long ago condemned those crimes which are a danger to society; but peasant opinion is very lenient when it is a matter of drunkenness or brawling in the streets. Morality was another of the chief subjects of my investigations, and I shall have to report some conflicting opinions. Piety, according to all accounts, remains practically the same in the country districts, even amongst those who have returned from a " go-away " life in the towns.[1] These seem to sink back easily into the old groove of country instincts, which are still in the main far more powerful than the new instincts of town life. But those peasants who permanently transplant themselves into factories, and join the new race of working men, are rapidly losing their respect for religion. The hold which religion, in general, still has over Russia seems to the visitor from the West very remarkable. Peasant life, then, still presents a many-sided picture; but if we have taken due notice of the conditions of the past, we shall not underrate the importance and rapidity of the present progress.

I will take first the worst districts of Central Russia with which I am acquainted.[2] There we shall, at least, see some

---

[1] In this respect there was a noticeable change for the worse in 1905 and 1906.

[2] This chapter deals exclusively with Central Russia.

beginnings of progress. In the best district of all, this progress will be very definite and pronounced. I shall generally let my informants speak for themselves.

RANENBURG DISTRICT, GOVERNMENT OF RYAZÁN (July, 1905).

The Police Colonel :
The number of literates has doubled in the last twelve years. Fifty-two new parish schools have been founded. On the working of the monopoly it is difficult to express an opinion. There is rather less drunkenness ; crime has diminished, but only slightly ; there are fewer brawls, but more thefts, in consequence of the influence of Moscow. A superficial "towniness" of manner and habits has been developed, and the sense of discipline has deteriorated. Some of the "go-aways" succeed in Moscow, and some fail through lack of character. The population has gone up, and the peasant lots are very small. Practically everyone except himself in the district believes that it is time to abolish the communal system, but he looks upon it as an excellent system of poor relief.

A Police Captain :
The monopoly is a great improvement. In one of his villages fourteen men drank themselves to death in three days, but since the monopoly there would be not more than three cases in the year. In every village there are some five illicit drink shops ; it is impossible to prevent them from springing up. The peasants do everything to conceal their whereabouts ; they would rather pay an extra penny for their drink at such a shop than make what may be a long journey to the nearest Crown depôt. Still the influence of these unlicensed shops is not so pernicious as the former all-round encouragement of drinking.

The doctor of the Town Hospital :
The life of the peasant is healthy, but this is a weakly generation. The peasants are not quick to learn the rules of health. They have still their own local quacks, but these are being steadily driven out by the hospitals.

Two peasants (Zimárovo) :
One of them, a big, square-headed man, does not believe that literateness is of any use : it spoils the character, and sets men on

the wrong road, not because it is literateness, but because it is so often taught in a wrong way (literally "against the rules"). The monopoly has done no good; neither drunkenness nor crime has decreased. The other, a keen, thin man, says that instruction has done much good, that it leads to enterprise, and that there must be profit in it; altogether too many people are folding their hands and doing nothing, and they must be roused to a more energetic life. Both men have a good manner of talking; they are simple, intelligent, and respectful.

A cantonal peasant clerk (Pikovaya Ryasa), whose Court-house is very small and dark:

The peasants, before all things, want to buy land; several of them have been to Moscow, and now wear better clothes, which are imitated by the "stay-at-homes." Some of the "go-aways" do well and get rich, but others become spendthrifts and exercise a bad influence on the "stay-at-homes" when they return. The number of literates in this village has gone up by leaps and bounds; it has more than doubled in the last ten years. It is generally what is called "little literateness," but the war has in very many cases turned it into something better. The peasants of course read newspapers; many will also read any book that they can get hold of. This official doubted if it had done any good to their characters, but his information was given in the presence of the Police Captain, who made his own view pretty clear.

Several of the heads of houses of a prosperous village (Babyno) have a talk with me alone. There has been no division of property here for forty years, that is, since the emancipation. One-third of the village land still remains, in principle, divided into communal lots, and the Village Society still exists. The other two-thirds are, in law, recognised as private property, which can be inherited. This security of tenure means that the peasant need not fear to lose the work and the money which he has put into the land, and as a result there is here (as I can see for myself) a much better cultivation and a far more self-respecting spirit than in the neighbouring villages, planted on just the same kind of soil. These peasants are very conscious of their superiority; in other places, as one of them says to me, capital, advanced by the Government for making improvements in the existing holdings, would simply go in drink, but here it would certainly be used to great advantage. One of the most evident signs of this is the number, extent, and good culture of what are called the "plantations," or, as we should say, orchards and cottage gardens. These, under the communal system, are rare, as they demand enterprise, labour, and expenditure, but, once established, they are not subject to the ordinary division. One peasant shows me his plantation; it is exceedingly well arranged; it contains a considerable number of apple-trees, and space has been found for a plot of sunflowers, which he grows "not for oil, but to look at." This shrewd man, who excellently understands his own sphere, explains the various advantages of the system of personal property. The great desire of the peasants is, he says, not to rebel nor even to seize land,—for nothing will be gained in that way,—but to acquire it by some Government scheme of purchase.

I will mention that it is precisely in this province, where the soil is far the richest, that signs of progress are less visible than in other parts which I visited. The peasant expects everything from the land which he takes no trouble to improve. If the harvest fails him, he has no other resource, and he nearly always sits idle throughout the winter months. Yet even in this District I have come upon a cottage with a loom which makes rough cloth for home use or for sale.

KRASNY DISTRICT, GOVERNMENT OF SMOLENSK (August, 1904).

This province is also behindhand, but not because of any innate thriftlessness of the peasants, or any inability to deal with a good soil. The land here is barren, and the period of Polish rule has left its mark on the driven and hunted people. We have not the right to expect here as much enterprise as in Ranenburg, and in some ways we get rather more.

A priest's wife (Khókhlovo) :

The peasants are quite accustomed to their freedom, and have learned to appreciate it. Fifteen years ago there were hardly any literates; now there are amongst the men 30 per cent. These generally can only read, write, and count; the profit which they hope for from literateness is simply better earnings. Some of them think that they are now too good to work in the fields, and seek for paid posts. They read newspapers and religious books; they are as God-fearing as they were: peasants do not go out of the groove of their elders. Possibly there is a little less superstition, and probably there is less drunkenness, but in neither case is the difference great. The monopoly works well on the whole, but it has its disadvantages. Morality is worse than it was; many are now "unbridled." The peasants keep their houses cleaner, but in other matters show too little enterprise. The population has increased, and land has been much subdivided. It is impossible to persuade the Village Society as a whole to adopt any improvements in agriculture, and if the Society fails to move, the individual cannot.

The son of a small farmer, formerly of the townsmen class (Krasny):

He has a good wooden house, of which he places the two reception rooms at my disposal; they are very close, and the windows will hardly open; there are lamps, ornaments, plants, and ikons; the floors are bare but well polished.

He has the fresh mind of a clever child; but he is also shrewd of wit, and pauses to weigh his words carefully. He thinks little of the peasants of this part. Most of them are very poor, but some save money and buy land. The chief trade is in timber. Property is much subdivided, but not much has been done to improve its value, and nothing can be expected of a Village Society. The peasants have become quite accustomed to their freedom. One-third of them are literates, but of these many are "unbridled" and less moral than the rest. In morality few have fought their way through the transition stage. Drunkenness and crime are on the whole decreasing. He follows, with the greatest keenness, my explanations of the battle of Krasny, and asks me to show him over the ground. He will not accept any return for his hospitality.

A large landowner:

The peasants here are not enterprising, but are gradually developing in character; they are fairly honest, but are still addicted to small thefts. Their homes are noticeably cleaner; that of course depends mainly upon the wife: one interior, which he knows, is as clean as if it were all polished. Sometimes one

will see a beginning of decoration outside. Improvements in
agriculture are almost impossible under the communal system.

It is a period of transition, but of levelling up. Out-patients
in local hospitals have very quickly increased from fifteen for
each day of reception to fifty. At first no peasant woman would
allow her child to be vaccinated ; now they all bring them in of
themselves. Peasant drunkenness has hardly been diminished by
the monopoly. The Government revenue from it is the same,
and it cannot be pretended that the educated classes are drinking
more than they used to do. If the peasant would divide his
quantum of liquor it might be better, but he drinks his supply for
the day or the week all at once, till he is under the table. He
helps to conceal the existence of illicit drink shops. Beer has
so far not supplanted vodka.[1] There is however less drinking
on working days, and altogether drunkenness is probably more
irregular. The peasant makes good use of the tea-rooms, even
preferring them where there is a Crown liquor shop in the
village : in the tea-room he will meet many of his fellows, and
will read newspapers. Some tea-rooms want to sell small quanti-
ties of vodka with the food supplied; indeed, the lesson of
moderation would be far the best, but permission has not yet
been given.

DISTRICT OF NOVOTORZHÓK, GOVERNMENT OF TVER (August, 1905).

In entering this district, we pass into a different atmosphere.
But it is more in political interest than in economic progress that
Novotorzhók has taken a lead, and that part of our subject is
dealt with elsewhere. The houses however are in this district
incomparably better built. The neat little gabled attics, built on
to the top of a cottage, have a pleasant appearance. Here the
old " sokhá " has been almost driven out by the Zemstvo ploughs.
Though the crops are not rich, they look as if they were well
attended to.

A landowner :

Many of the men of the older generation are still illiterate;
the younger are nearly all literates. The figure amounts, in

---

[1] Vodka is far more pernicious.

the case of recruits for the army, to 87 per cent. The monopoly, in his opinion, spoils itself by aiming at two objects at once: to diminish drunkenness and to sell more drink. Peasants will sometimes drink for three days on end, till they have nothing left; it is nearly always not beer, but vodka. Perhaps, in some villages, there is now less drinking; but, in general, there are very many illicit drink shops. These sell their liquor dearer, but they also spoil it. As their very existence is not recognised, their profits are in no way under the control of law. Forty per cent. of the males are " go-aways." Some go all over the country as itinerant cobblers, patching shoes in an inn or anywhere; these are often of the most independent spirit. The "go-aways" are the introducers of all new political propaganda. In this district there is a large number of Socialists, but the peasants are getting to understand politics better, and see that they cannot, for instance, simply seize the land of the gentry and expect to be left in possession.

I find here a Co-operative Distributive Society, founded by peasants, about which the caretaker, a clean and capable man, gives me some information. There are ninety members and a committee of six, which meets once in every three months to look through the accounts, and sometimes comes round to inspect; the president is a local schoolmaster. The store sells pretty well everything that the peasant can want; it gives 6 per cent. discount and also a dividend of 6 per cent. to the shareholders. It has not, however, got the better of the competition of private dealers, and, in fact, has failed to secure the confidence of the majority. The older peasants generally go to the private dealers; the younger more commonly buy from the store.

This distinction between the old and the young is in general very closely marked in this district. It implies that a great transition is going on. In the store I see a good example of the contrast. A young, clever-looking man praises the co-operators; a very dirty old peasant, with aquiline features, a spirituous voice, and a great deal of gesture, takes the other side.

A peasant Elder of marked intelligence and ability (Prechístaya Kámenka):

In his canton there are many Zemstvo schools, but only one Church school. A Church school, in his opinion, cannot be properly staffed. Many of the older peasants are illiterate, but all the younger are literate. In this matter, as in that of superstition, there is the sharpest difference between the two generations. Of the younger a large number are masons who have been to St. Petersburg or Moscow, but more especially to St. Petersburg. These will have nothing to do with superstition, but some of the old men still even believe in witches. Peasant piety is, in his opinion, only external, and closely allied to superstition.

The communal system makes good agriculture impossible. It is useless to talk of equality, if the land which one man has improved goes to another who has taken no pains at all, and *vice versâ*. The village agriculture ought to be on an altogether larger plan. The strips are too narrow, and the division of them causes a great many jealousies, some of which are simply stupid. For instance, the older men will object to taking the parts which lie higher up from the valley, whereas they have only to manure these to make a very good profit. The agricultural expert of the Zemstvo has, however, done much to dispel ignorance; and in some parts there has been established the so-called plan of "six fields agriculture," two of the six being left fallow, and the whole going through a regular rotation.

A country driver (or "yamshchík"):

An ignorant man of no great intelligence. He is a loyal soul, serving me well for three days. He has very little sympathy for the claims and programme of the Zemstva. There are fifty of his brotherhood who work in the small town, and others who work in the district. But though they cultivate no land, they belong to a Village Society, which they help by carrying goods from place to place. He himself possesses two portions of land, and pays £2 10s. yearly to the Society. He owns his two horses.

His manner is businesslike and independent. While he is giving me information he interrupts himself to point out a glorious starry sky, and says simply: "What a wonderful night!" The phrasing and the manner are not those which we associate with peasants. He rejoices in having plenty of work. The crops of the district are rye, oats, and a little flax, which are grown in rotation. He describes Novotorzhók as a "good town"; "good," used in this sense, means very much the same as clean and civilised. We pass a country party of students and girls, who

are singing very loudly with unmusical voices. " Rather countrified," he says. He has three children; his boy, of whom he is
very proud, is a great book-lover: "he doesn't care what he
learns." Nearly everyone here is literate. The monopoly has
not stopped drinking, and the illicit dram-shops are everywhere;
there are even more in the villages than in the towns. " Are
people very religious here?" I ask. " Yes," he says, in a
voice that passes by easy modulation from a boast to a sneer,
ending in a kind of crow. When I ask what recruits have been
taken for the war, he says, " Many," in just the same way.

KASHIN DISTRICT, GOVERNMENT OF TVER (July, 1904).

I start with the curious indirect testimony of a thoroughly
reactionary country gentleman; he was set in authority over two
Districts, to maintain the system of Plehwe.

The peasants understand the stick, and nothing else; with
them strict orders are necessary. They have made a great move
forward, and are now nearly all literate, sending with their own
horses to the nearest station for newspapers. I ask: " Are they
the worse or the better workers for that?" His wife[1] quickly
intervenes: " In my opinion worse." He himself qualifies:
" They are lazy; when they drink, they are of no use at all.
The English and the Germans have strong characters; none of
the Slavs are steady: they are fatalists, and say: ' It will all be
good, as God has arranged it.' Russia is behind England,
because there are few people to cope with the needs of great
areas, and those that there are have less grit; thus the upkeep
of roads, for instance, is practically neglected." The peasants felt
little interest in the Russo-Turkish war. They said it was not
their affair. They went because they were told to. In the
Japanese war they have shown far more interest.

Another reactionary country gentleman, who lives much more
intimately with the peasants:

The peasants have got used to their freedom. The conditions
of life are better now: the work is healthy, and the " stay-at-
homes " are as robust as they used to be; but the " go-aways "
are less sturdy. The district " lives on flax," but the portions

---

[1] The country ladies are often more reactionary than the country gentlemen.

of land get smaller and smaller. The big united peasant homes[1]
could afford to keep cattle; the small homes of to-day cannot.
The loss of a worker through illness tells very greatly upon a
small family.

We pass nearer to the peasants, and the evidence becomes
more satisfactory.

A priest of a town parish (Kashin) :

In the country, life is simple and more healthy than in the
town. The Temperance Societies are active and useful; in three
places the Crown liquor shops have been closed on their representations. In the tea-rooms there are always libraries and
country newspapers : in some cases all the peasants subscribe to
buy them; in others some more well-to-do peasant or some landowner pays the cost. The drunkards are always lazy, and are
always losing time; but the sober attend to their business, and
read. There are visible improvements in the peasant's life.

A country priest (Vanchúgovo) :

There are two schools in his parish, a parish school and a
Zemstvo school. When the former was closed during an inter-
regnum between two teachers, the peasants sent their children to
the Zemstvo school, which was a mile and a half further off,
and kept begging him to reopen the parish school as soon as
possible. In winter the children always go on foot. Ten years
ago half his people were illiterates ; now you will rarely find one.

The local flax gets excellent prices[2]; more and more land is
being taken into cultivation. Some peasants go into the town for
small posts. Though this canton has been mobilised, only fifteen
have gone to the war, (July, 1904). There are 400 more who
might be called up.

A country priest :

The peasants have now got thoroughly used to their freedom ;
their progress during the last ten or twenty years has been slow
but certain. Ten years ago half of them were illiterates ; now
they are all literates. They keep their houses better and cleaner,
(I was struck by the particular cleanness of this village), and are
more attentive to the rules of health. They have far more
personal consciousness of what they are after. The younger

---

[1] Two or three generations used to live together in one house.
[2] I have heard the same from a flax-merchant in Dundee.

generation now all laugh at the bogies and goblins in which their elders still believe. They understand much more about this war than about any former one, and take much more interest in it. The appearance of a railway in the District has caused a steady improvement in the peasant life; the railway is a friend. Flax is here very important: the peasants live half off their crops and half off money sent by those who have gone to St. Petersburg.

A country priest (Koy):

Land is much subdivided. Very many go for half the year to St. Petersburg, some for the summer, some for the winter; but very few settle there permanently. Those who stay at home are physically the stronger. The people here are prosperous and contented: "Look at their houses," says the priest; and they are certainly spacious and tidy, far more like farmhouses than like cottages.

A quaint little hairy creature occupies the humble post of care-taker in a peasant Court-house (Súkhodol). He is very dirty and very untidy. We spend the evening alone together, and I wish I could always be sure of as good company. In all that he says there is a touch of shrewd fancy which cannot be reproduced.

He was called out to the Russo-Turkish war, but did not arrive in time for the fighting. This time, eleven have been mobilised in the canton out of a population of 2,000. The Japanese, he thinks, "are playing a very risky game."

Flax spells money; but the lots are so small here, that there is no means of keeping horses and pigs. The large peasant households of old times used on occasions to eat pork and mutton; the present small households regale themselves on tea. He can remember the change coming; it has weakened the peasant's strength.

The Village Society meets as often as once a week at harvest-time. Many go from here to the towns; some get "spoilt," and so have no money to send back to the Society.

Here, as in practically every other village of this district, there is a local school. Of course literateness is clear profit. "How else could it be?"[1] I ask about the priest. "Nothing wrong," he says, "but the Mother is good."

[1] Literally, in the English of Marlowe, "What else."

He wants to know all about my work, and settles down to a series of questions on the practical working of the English Constitution. " But what," he says, "if the House of Commons has passed a law, and the House of Lords won't have it ? What if the House of Commons passes it again ? " " Well, perhaps the House of Lords won't have it again." " But what if the House of Commons passes it *again* ? " Perhaps some reader will suggest the right answer. Anyhow I do not think that we understand as much about his country.

A cantonal peasant clerk with whom I spend an evening (Vanchúgovo) ; he looks clever, but not steady :

He remembers the great reforms ; he was a boy then. He began his lessons in a hut, and then went to the Town School for a year ; this was then almost the only school in the District.   He has no manner of doubt as to the profit of literateness : " It is an obvious gain." Now all the peasants and their children are keen about it, and illiterates get laughed at.   Ten years ago these were half the population ; now you will seldom meet with one.

The peasant's lot is about eleven acres here. For seven years there is still due an annual instalment of 12s. for the redemption of the land.   On each two and a half acres the peasant pays $1\frac{1}{2}d$. in Government taxes, and $8\frac{3}{4}d$. to the funds of the local Zemstva, " a mere trifle." Some peasants are still very lazy, but most of them are much more well-to-do than they were ; more and more land is being brought into cultivation, and prices for timber and flax are much higher than they used to be. Some " play the dandy in fine boots." Formerly many peasants wore no boots at all.   The women wear coloured slippers.   There is no dram-shop very near, and the drinking is much less than it was.

During intervals of silence he occasionally says something about the war, as much to himself as to me. He thinks that the Japanese have too few supplies in Manchuria, as the newspapers say that twenty-seven of their transports have been sunk. " It is quite an unpopular war ; we didn't want it, but the Government required it of us ; it will mean great sacrifices."

Another cantonal peasant clerk (Koy). He is a clever sensible fellow, well instructed and with a kindly persuasive manner. He evidently likes giving information and is a pleasant guest at dinner.

The clerk and the Cantonal Elder have no "rank" ("chin") in the State. He himself has had to add to the very small salary of his assistant. His son is at school in Kashin; he wants to send him on to the Gymnasium, but ignorance of French and German will keep the boy out.

From the canton of Koy one son in every family always goes to St. Petersburg. The father will always be trying to make him send home a larger part of his wage than he can spare, say half of it; but the son has got his own position to keep up. The father will even go to St. Petersburg to worry him, or he will try to work the Village Meeting against him, or he will turn the son's wife and children out of doors, on the ground that they are not paying for their keep; and sometimes the woman will go to the bad altogether. Men expelled from St. Petersburg are first sent home, and then receive passports for other towns, not the capitals. Many of them potter about for odd jobs, and get drunk when they can; there are several such in this village.

There are peasants in the Gymnasia and in the Universities; these often laugh at their village priests, and look down upon them as less educated.

One of the "go-away" peasants, who consents to drive me a long distance in this district:

He seems not to know which world he belongs to, St. Petersburg or the country. At St. Petersburg he is a baker; Feast-days, so far from being days of rest, mean only the more work. He has no time to himself, and, worst of all, he is not his own master. He married young, because, as he says, "that's a bit cleaner," and has six children; but he has to leave his family in the country. When he comes home, however, he finds the rustic folk "coarser," and the food and wages very poor.

He has an over-courteous manner; every woman whom we pass he salutes as "my nice one," and every child as "darling." "Nice little girls," he says, "to go and open those gates for us!" His confident manner, however, seems artificial, and is certainly not appreciated by the passers-by. To everything that I say he answers, "Absolutely right, sir." He makes many mistakes as to the roads; yet he is always wanting to be pointing out something.

RostÓff District, Government of Yaroslavl (July, 1904).

This District is acknowledged to be one of the best in Russia. It has a longer tradition of freedom, energy, and initiative than most others. Ninty-nine per cent. of the males of the whole district are literates. Allowing for differences in the characters of different populations, it is not unfair to imagine that we see in Rostóff a picture of what the Russians of other parts may become. We shall, then, be encouraged to believe that the faint gleam of initiative which we have noticed in Ranenburg, and which has widened out elsewhere into the confusing lights and shades of a partial progress and a partial perversion, will produce in the end, not a frenzy of Socialism or of revolution, but a steady economic advance; and that would be the best guarantee for the political future of the nation.

The Police Colonel:

The peasants have made such an advance in the last ten years that those who knew them before, (and he himself has grown up amongst them), can hardly believe it. He saw a man disgracing himself in a village and said to him: "You're not a peasant"; the peasants said, "You're right, sir: he's a townsman." "Take him away," said the Police Colonel; and the peasants added, "Come again when you're more sober." The District town, though in many ways behind the villages, is not the same as it was ten years ago. The population has increased; prosperity, education, and the instinct of order have all advanced. In the next five years the town is likely to progress still more quickly.

A country priest (Lyeff):

The peasants of to-day are enterprising, and will go for work anywhere. They are self-loving and proud, (he makes a gesture which is suggestive of spitting); they hold their own even in St. Petersburg; and they are no strangers there, because homes are found for them in advance by those who have preceded them. These "go-aways" return every summer to help to cultivate their own market gardens. Certainly they acquire town habits, and some of them perhaps become less moral. Though his parish lies close to Rostóff, the life of this little town has no influence on them. They do not seek their work there. Why should they? They are quite as well off in their own parish. The peasants have been gaining fast in character; they used to wear a hunted look, but now they have been for a long time " working themselves into shape." The change which has taken place in forty years is unbelievable, even to one who has seen it.

The Cantonal Elders of this part are superior men, highly capable and intelligent. They reminded me of the very pick of our own working men. But there was one important difference. The intelligent working man, being a product of town life, holds strongly to theories and general principles, and appeals to a standard of right, real or imaginary, which he believes to be accepted by everyone. The best kind of Russian peasant is essentially a country product; he makes very few assumptions; he has great shrewdness and excellent judgment, he is full of reticences and reservations, he will carefully qualify each of his statements, and he will only speak on subjects which he understands. The information which I derived from such peasants proved to be more accurate than that which I got from men of almost any other class in Russia. These men had a natural dignity of address, a strong sense of responsibility, and often a simple courtesy of a peculiarly graceful kind.

A Cantonal Elder, a clear-headed and capable man (Ugódichi):

The canton runs far inland from Lake Nero; in the back part of it the peasants grow corn. Here it is all market-gardening: leeks, garlic, chicory, potatoes, etc. The village is large enough to make two parishes, and there are two good churches. The young priest enjoys universal respect. The land is exceptionally good. The Elder refuses to explain the local prosperity by any special enterprise of the peasants of these parts : " It cannot be said that it is the peasant who is specially gifted, or that he would be as well-to-do if the land had not helped him."

The communal system, though good as providing for the less capable, is here specially felt to be a great hindrance to initiative. If a certain peasant does not improve his land, it will probably be, not because he is lazy, but because he has no interest in doing so, for here he is threatened with the possibility of a redivision in three years' time.

There are many "go-aways," who generally prosper, and send a great deal of money home. From this place they usually go unmarried; they then return to marry here, but go back without their wives, sending for them as soon as they have established their positions in the capital. Amongst them there are good and bad according as they prosper there. Some " pet themselves " (that is, get unused to country life), and no longer dress as peasants; but in general it is difficult to mark any difference between the " go-aways " and the " stay-at-homes," of whom many are quite as intelligent and as well-to-do.

The neighbourhood of the little town of Rostóff has an influence which is " not good." (I notice that Rostóff is no intermediary between the village and St. Petersburg. If the peasant goes at all, he goes straight into the larger life, and I find intelligence in these villages to be of a much higher standard than in Rostóff.) Practically all here are literates ; of course literateness is a clear gain. As there are a beershop and a spirit depôt in the village, the drunkenness of the district is concentrated here. In the other villages of the canton there is certainly much less drinking than formerly ; and taking the whole canton together, the monopoly may be considered to have diminished drunkenness.

Fifty men have gone to the war out of a population of 2,500 ; they are all serving in the fleet.

A Cantonal Elder (Borzha):

A very businesslike and reserved old man. He offers me tea, and inquires closely into my objects. It is not enough for him that I carry an official letter, or that I state my general aim ; he wants to understand for himself exactly what I am after, and how I propose to work my plans out in detail. I explain, point by point, why a better understanding between our two countries is to be desired, how our Parliament and consequently our Government rest on public opinion, and by what means our public opinion can be better informed. He follows each point closely, and from time to time asks practical questions on matters of detail. He has already a very good idea of the order of things which exists in England. "Here," he says, "we are all sub-jects," which is indeed the whole point of the difference. At the end he says to me very nicely: "Well, God give you good success." He asks, in something of a challenging way, "What do they think of the war in England?" "And what," I ask in turn, "do you yourself think of the war?" The answer comes prompt and determined : "We think we shall go on and win ; it may

be a year or perhaps two ; but if England begins to mix in——"
" The attacks on England in the Russian newspapers must," he
says, " be very unpleasant articles for you ; what do your newspapers say ? Do your peasants read them ? Our peasants read
all ours."

A large and exceptionally prosperous village (Poréchye) :

The clerk, who has held his post for ten years, is a shy-looking
man with bright clever eyes. His clothes are very neat, black but
of a peasant cut, and he has black shining top boots. He sits
and talks while I eat, but will not share my beer, because, as he
says very simply, "he is not equal to it."

The canton consists practically of this one village, and contains
3,000 souls. It suffered great damage from a fire, which burned
most houses to the ground and sent many families roaming.
Much of the land is good ; some is of thin soil, and requires
manure. It is all taken up with the market-gardens of the peasants ;
half of it is devoted to the culture of medicinal herbs, some of
which grow wild here. No corn is sown.

The Village Society expends a good deal of money on the
direct relief of its poor. It dares not even here launch out on
general improvements of agriculture : but if one peasant went,
say, to England and on his return successfully started some new
plan, all would follow his example ; only they will risk nothing
on the common credit. The portions of land are exceedingly
small, but that does not matter. As they become smaller they
demand more and more individual enterprise in cultivation (which
the communal system, in this case at least, does not hamper) ; and
the land is always good enough to repay such enterprise. Besides,
the peasants, by saving up, can always buy land for their own.

There are many "go-aways," who are practically all in a position
to send money home. But those who stay here are more moral
and more religious. The peasants read both newspapers and
books, such as Pushkin, Turghényeff, Dostoyévsky, and Tolstoy.
These books are lent out by the local library. Only two men have
gone from here to the war.

The Cantonal Elder now joins us. He is an easy capable man,
who has served for nine years, having twice been re-elected. I
notice the excellent dignity and courtesy which he maintains with
all those who meet us as we pass through the village. We walk

through some of the market-gardens, the clerk following slightly behind. The Elder asks many questions about England far more intelligent than most educated Englishmen are capable of asking about Russia. When we part, he asks, " Shall we see you again in our *town*? " (I note the word.) " Well, if I come again, I hope I shall find you still Cantonal Elder." "God disposes. Good-bye."

A picked man (Ugódichi) :

A short bearded man, with a lion-like look. He is the best type of a peasant, simple, plain-spoken, and sensible. His little wooden cottage is neat and pretty. The rooms are stuffy, but full of flowers and rustic ornaments. In each of the two main rooms there is a sofa, with quilt bedding. His wide fields are in perfect order, and every foot of them has been utilised ; he has large barns.

His six daughters are all married. Two of his sons are soldiers; two are shopmen in St. Petersburg. They will never come back, as they are now " no use for work " ; they wear town clothes, and lead a town life. But they have not transferred themselves from the peasant class. " I'm a peasant," says their father ; " I have let them out; but, go-aways as they are, they don't go away out of my will." I see on the table two books which may belong to them : one is the ordinary magazine of the educated class, with sentimental stories of love and ladies; the other contains two short stories by Victor Hugo.

Fruits and green-stuffs go as far as seventy miles to market. Dried fruits and vegetables go even beyond the frontier. There were market-gardens here in the time of John the Terrible.

Here the emancipation was not so radical a change as elsewhere, because this district was partially enfranchised earlier. But certainly the peasants have got quite used to their new groove. He remembers that, in his youth, an official came to advise them to found a school. They said that they saw no need for it. "Then come," says he, " and talk it over with me." "But we cannot talk with you ; we are dark" (ignorant) "people." "Then do you wish your children to be dark people too ?" said the official. " You have built your own church ; now put a school beside it ; that too will be a holy work." My host had a good deal to do with the affair ; now there is a school, with two mistresses.

Nearly all the peasants are literates. The children are keen to be taught. Teaching is, of course, sheer gain, "unless weakness of character overcomes you" (that is, unless you are so poor a creature that all improvements will be wasted on you). The peasant learns anything that comes his way. "The weak only read novels" (a word which he himself mispronounces).

The morality of the go-aways depends upon the surroundings into which they fall. There are some of all sorts. Of course, there are many instances of a "second establishment" in the capital. The morality of the stay-at-homes is better, and many of them are both enterprising and contented.

The communal system is good for the worse, bad for the better. It is unlikely that a Village Society as a whole would ever be converted to improvements; yet this one built the school.

The monopoly has, on the whole, done good, but several villages have illicit dram-shops. The Police Corporals know of this, but don't stop it. "Do you mean they are bribed?" "Well, what else?"

In 1882 my host was in Finland. Many go thither from Rostóff as gardeners. He suddenly received an official message, and he thought for a moment that "they were looking for him." The messenger, however, addressed him as "Mr. ——," and gave him a paper, which he had treasured up and showed to me. It was an alphabetical list of thirty-two persons appointed to serve on an Imperial Commission. He was the only peasant; most of the rest were princes or counts. He was sent for by the Minister of the Interior, who, addressing him by his christian and father's names, put his hand on his shoulder and said, "I know all about you, and I have invited you here because I know that you will be useful. Don't bother yourself (limit yourself) because of the other names on the paper; on the Commission they are your colleagues in service." The Commission was to deal with peasants' drunkenness, and with their haphazard and disorderly migrations to Siberia. At the opening meeting he found all very friendly, and ready to advise him as to points of order. Three Ministers were present, and each spoke. The Minister of the Interior told the Commission to find out how they could help the cause of morality. The Minister of Finance agreed, but asked them not to forget the interests of the public revenue. The third Minister said that morality came altogether first; to improve it was a holy work: the State's best riches consisted of good citizens; the revenue would then increase of itself. The Commission, left to itself, chose a President, a Vice-president, and a Committee to draw up the questions to be submitted to the whole body. Each member would be asked to state his views.

Our friend was very nervous. He had no experience in public speaking. "I shall lose myself," he thought, "and then what will happen?" These gentry were nearly all reactionaries; the speeches mostly dwelt on the incurability of peasant drunkenness: the peasants, they said, were naturally a feeble folk, and, by the way, were always in debt. One pointed the interested moral that they ought not to have been freed so soon; they were not ready for it. The speakers were all large landowners, the former masters of the serfs. Our friend felt his isolation and helplessness; but he remembered that he had got to stand up alone for the Russian peasant. He asked leave to express his opinion in writing; he could thus avoid the chance of hostile interruptions and consequent confusion, and at the same time secure much more attention for his opinion.

He had had no practice in writing official reports, which is almost a fine art in Russia. So, to avoid stumbling-blocks, he sought out a small clerk. After some hours of work, he had drawn up, as he told me with evident pride, quite a passable exordium and statement. He first restated in detail the criticisms which had been passed on the peasants. "These gentlemen ought to be ashamed to send to reporters and beyond the frontier such an opinion of those who had been their own peasants. If it was as you said, why did you take no steps to remedy it? You are reviling yourselves, as for centuries you were the rulers of the peasants. You say they are unfit for freedom; when they were yours, we heard of no measures which you had taken to improve them; you never set them free to go to schools or dealt with their drunkenness; and so, if they had remained yours, would it have been for another thousand years. No, the peasants are not of themselves hopelessly bad; on the contrary, everything depends on those who govern them. We in the Rostóff District have our own plans. If a man gets drunk and brawls in the streets, we speak to him; if he does it again, we punish him; and the next time we punish him more sharply. We find that drunkenness is quite curable, and that is why Rostóff is prosperous. As Russians, you should be ashamed to speak ill of the Russian peasant."

One sees the shrewdness of this appeal to a "Russifying" Government; the Minister of the Interior saw it too. He again summoned our friend to the Ministry, laid a hand on his shoulder, and said, "Good lad, good lad! (molodyéts). I knew I was right in choosing you; they have heard what a real peasant has to say; you'll see, they won't revile the Russian peasant any more." Nor did they. The report of the Commission went up to the Council of State, and some years later the monopoly was established.

The good man told his story with very little display of self-consciousness; and even if his memory has dramatised some of the details, his sound sense speaks for itself.

The Emancipation justified itself in many different ways; the most striking proof of its beneficence is to be found in the great increase of the peasant population. But this increase helped to create a new question. The portions of land had to be divided and subdivided. Apart from the great reserves of forest land, which help to constitute the wealth of the State and must not be broken up without careful consideration, there are still vast estates of the Crown, of the appanages of the Grand Dukes, and of the monasteries, whose culture has so far been very ineffective, and there are large private estates of which one may say the same. At the time of the emancipation, many landowners obtained a new hold over the peasants by securing the best of the land and establishing something like an economic tyranny; but even they themselves have in many parts found that they cannot make a profit on farming alone, and have established small industrial enterprises on their estates.[1] The peasant is still more straitened; it is possible that the existing peasant holdings might be sufficient if they were properly developed, but that they cannot be, owing to the retention of the communal system. The so-called "intensive culture" is practically impossible, for the Commune as a rule will not launch out on improvements. The individual holdings are broken up into plots distant from each other, and the strip system is a further inconvenience. Owing to the artificial

[1] Notably in White Russia.

equality which the communal system has established, land passes into the hands of men who are incapable of working it properly, and some strips are abandoned altogether. The constant sub-divisions, by making it difficult to keep cattle, have led to a shortage in manure. The Commune has helped to preserve the old laziness of serfdom ; and in the south centre, where there is good black land, the peasant, after scratching the soil with a wooden plough, sits down to live off whatever the harvest may give him. Thus in a bad year he has no resource, and it was there-fore in these provinces that agrarian riots were most general in 1905-6. But in the so-called grey land of the north centre, where the soil is poor, the peasants, who have a much better tradition of energy, have seen the need of eking out their earn-ings from the soil by profits derived from other sources. The railway brings such facilities within their reach ; but, owing to the restriction of private enterprise, railways have extended through Russia only very slowly. One estate which I know could not for a long time be worked to any profit, because the surplus of a good crop could not be conveyed to the nearest port ; when the railway at last came, the estate was sold on very advantageous terms. Much is hoped from the establishment of lower technical schools in country districts, but this development still lies in the future. Much has been done by the Zemstva to revive the manufacture of local art products, but this is only a partial and limited remedy. In certain parts, notably in the Government of Vladímir, the peasants have of themselves developed some particular industry in a group of neighbouring villages. Thus at Kimry, in the Government of Tver, several villages, all lying close together and counting a population of some thousands, have long been mainly occupied with boot-making; 626 families, or 55 per cent. of the whole, work at this trade. In the Tver Government there are 20,000 workmen who make shoes in their own homes. Further than this, a great number of factories have been established in country districts ; it was hoped that they would be able to give town wages to the peasants, without taking from them the healthy conditions of country life. Many of these factories are still isolated ; they are too far off from their markets, and too ill served by the railways to be able to compete on fair terms with the factories of the towns. But in the Government of Vladímir, owing to the large enterprise of the Morózoffs and other great trading families, there has sprung up a whole factory area. Here the workmen are recruited from the surrounding Village Societies, to which they continue to belong. On the eve of a feast-day they are all to be seen going home, and when they return to their work they bring food with them. Their wages in ordinary times keep the Village Society solvent; and they received in return the support of their fellow-peasants during some of the notable strikes of 1905. But the peasant, who has the old wandering spirit in his blood, has found for himself a more distant way out of his difficulties; this is supplied by the so-called "go-away industries" to which I have so often alluded. Peasants from almost every home in a given district make straight for St. Petersburg or Moscow; there they do the best work of their life; but they still remain members of their Village Societies, and the wages which they send home are the chief source of income for the district. Thus Rostóff lives off market-gardening and go-away industries, and the market-gardener of this district will find a good price all over Russia. He does not come to the capital as a total stranger, for the way has been prepared for him, and he drops at once into a little world composed of his own fellows. Thus, by a regular and systematised operation, the peasant brings into the town an unceasing supply of country vigour, and he himself in his old age often returns to his first home. The men of Rostóff are to be found everywhere in St. Petersburg, holding such responsible posts as are open to their class. Some of them succeed extraordinarily well; there are examples of simple peasants who have risen to great wealth and high honour; these men in many cases refuse to leave the peasant class, although their means and their intelligence have become such that it is almost a farce to call them peasants. Some of their big houses which I have seen are rather country villas than cottages, and they build them, not in places where their origin is unknown, but in the villages where they were born. Imagine a Village Society where there are several such men; one of this kind the local Police Captain compared to a House of Commons. And if the go-away brings the country life into the town, he on his return takes back with him the town intelligence. His natural loyalty and common-sense are enlightened by all that he has learned ; and he is become one of the chief links between the country and the town, that is, between the old Russia and the new.

Mobilisation at Novgorod (July, 1904).

It is the broad spirit of loyalty in the Russian peasant which enables him to act as a moderating influence at the time of great changes. His patriotism is by no means merely the passive obedience of a stupid animal. It is true that he himself does not wish to govern and is ordinarily very willing to leave affairs of state in the hands of the Tsar and his advisers; but he is quite ready to do his own share of public work, which is after all far the most onerous. This is because, however unintelligent and lazy he may have been, he has recognised all through his history a standard of corporate duty. He hated the Japanese war, but almost everywhere his phrase was, " We have got to win." Certainly it was not the Russian soldier who lost that war, and it was not the Russian peasant who demanded an early peace.

I find myself in July, 1904, at Novgorod the Great. This province has a great military tradition : Suvóroff was one of its country gentry; at Krasny in 1812 an old sergeant from Novgorod, declaring that " some day one must finish," rushed alone on to the French bayonets, and opened a way over his body into the enemy's square.[1]

The blow has fallen. Notices posted up in conspicuous places announce (1) that all reservists of the lower ranks, except those excused, must go to their headquarters; (2) that all horses, except those of the Imperial Public Service and those which are used for breeding purposes, must be brought in for the officials to choose from; (3) that an allowance will be made to those who bring with them their winter clothes. The horses all stand round a great open space ; of course it is the best that have been ᛫bought by the Government.

The station is crowded; families are saying good-bye. The women bear up very well; the men keep themselves in hand, but

---

[1] Report of Prince Golítsyn, November 24, 1812.

their eyes are filling; a sheepish peasant walks nervously about trying to be brave; the train moves off, hats are lifted, but there is no shouting, only the greeting, "Till we meet again!" At several stations we pick up more peasants; at one place the whole village have come down in the rain to see them off. The men lift their hats to their departing friends with grave courtesy; a tall bearded man who is losing his son says quite simply to his wife, "God alone! it is what He pleases." All who are going out are quiet and businesslike with their good-byes; they find time for a simple word with each friend, and jump in without hurry as the train moves on. "God grant that you may not be taken," say the women. A fine young fellow, with fair hair and loyal blue eyes, takes leave of a group of relations; his wife runs up and down the platform after him, wildly shrieking; he leaves his good-bye to her till the last, he holds her fondly in his arms for a minute, and then, at the point of breaking down but with set face, he gently disengages himself and jumps in. She rushes after the train with loud piercing cries; he is at the window calm and contained, lifting his hat.

A PEASANTS' REFORM MEETING (August 13, 1905).

In front of the Cantonal Court-house are gathered some one hundred and fifty village representatives, surrounding a table on which stands the cantonal clerk. These men are not a party meeting; they are the legal representatives of the whole canton. The clerk in an easy conversational voice reads extracts from the newspapers, each of which bears on the failure of the existing Ministry. The peasants listen without excitement; there is a bond of mutual understanding between the clerk and his audience. A young peasant now takes charge of the meeting; he reads out a list of peasant demands, for each of which a reason is stated in moderate language. The peasants "have resolved to declare to all those who love their country, who value the interests of the people, and who genuinely want to amend the existing Imperial order of things, that to go on with our former life is impossible." Nine points are read through. (1) The peasants demand that there shall be no obstacles in the way of instruction: "We wish to know more; we want really to teach our children." This point is adopted without discussion. (2) The peasants " demand the

abolition of distinctions of class before the law, the establishment of a common criminal and civil code for all, and the
abolition of the office of Land Captains." All are agreed. (3) They
claim "the abolition of indirect taxes, the return of the payment
for redemption, and the replacing of the land tax by a tax on
income and capital." Many do not understand, but this point is
accepted. (4) The next point demands the nationalisation of
land "for proportionate distribution between the peasants and
all who wish to engage in agricultural work." This, too, is readily
accepted, but without any precise comprehension. (5) "We are
deprived of the right of speaking openly of our needs. Not
wishing to be any longer slaves without a voice, we demand
freedom of word, of meeting, of association, and of the Press."
This is really the programme of the Zemstva, but it is easily
explained and secures a ready acceptance. (6) An eight-hour
day is claimed for the working men. Many of the peasants do
not understand this at all; but they are willing to support their
go-away brothers. (7) "For the regular and speedy satisfaction
of all the above-named needs, we demand the summoning of
national representatives on the basis of universal, equal, direct,
and secret electoral rights." This, too, has to be explained at
length to the meeting, but the point is in the end carried by a
great majority. (8) "We demand the speedy cessation of this
bloody and suicidal war." With this the majority of the meeting
will have nothing to do. The war has hit them harder than
almost anything else, but they will not dictate to the central
Government on a point of foreign policy, nor will they weaken the
hands of the Tsar whilst he is struggling against a foreign
enemy. The point has to be amended. It now reads thus:
"The question of prolonging or ending the war must be left to
the elected National Assembly." This solution seems to satisfy
almost everyone. (9) "Full pardon is demanded for all exiles
and prisoners who have suffered for the rightful cause of the
people." This point is accepted without discussion.

At a kind of committee meeting of the more prominent peasants,
including both go-aways and stay-at-homes, several very sensible
things are said. "As to the troops," says B., a big country
peasant, "the thing to do, if they are quartered on us, is to say,
'Tea is served, dear boy (golúbchik),' and to make your soldier

one of your family." "If we (that is, the National Assembly) say that the war is to go on," says M., "then it will be our affair, and we shall do our best to really make Russia win, and not to find jobs for those who are in favour." "They think," says the rustic and clever-looking P., "that the peasant is not ripe for responsibility; even the Zemstva have this at the back of their heads. The truth is, we have gone past it. So it was in the French Revolution: men thought that the peasants were not ripe, and found them over-ripe." "They don't give us schools," says B., "because we ought to think it right that we should starve and be miserable; what they want to teach us is to have no needs at all." "The Church schools," says S., "only teach us to be good boys. We are to know the names of the famous churches and what is meant by each bit of the priest's dress, and then we shall be little angels." "It is very nice," says W., "to be angels; but our ambitions are not so high as that: they are a little lower to begin with, that is, they are on this earth; we will resign the being angels for the present." "We should like," says J., "to begin the kingdom of heaven here," and using the simile of the Russian dinner, which always begins with relishes eaten at the side board, he adds with a brilliant smile, "We should like to stand up and have a first bite."

It was not possible before 1905 to know of how much the peasant mind was capable when directly applied to public affairs. Those of us who knew a little about the peasants and believed in them were not surprised to find that the peasant members of the Duma, especially those known under the name of "non-party," were some of the shrewdest of all and brought some of the best contributions to the settlement of national questions. This will be seen in a later chapter. Personally I am inclined to see more solid material for political judgment in the shrewd thoughts of the peasant than in the doctrinaire formulæ of the Intelligent; and I believe that some day the peasants, who are fast losing their old indifference, will act as a kind of ballast in the direction of the political destinies of Russia. Already in 1906 there have been many significant indications of this development. All the more then may we rejoice to find that the peasant, while rapidly becoming quicker of intelligence, has not really lost his old instinctive loyalty and sound sense.

CHAPTER XIII.

THE PEASANT IN TOWN—FACTORY LIFE.

WE have brought our "go-away" to the town. He at once finds himself amongst people of his own sort; in Moscow half of the population consists of peasants. Perhaps his father held his town place before him; in any case he is likely to go straight to a part of the town which is occupied by peasants from his own province and of his own occupation.[1] Just as the district of Monte Cassino supplies England with most of its organ grinders, the Swiss canton of Ticino with many of its waiters, and the Bavarian Palatinate with most of the German bands, so also in Russia, in spite of the very long distances, a given country district sends most of its go-aways to a certain great town, to take part in a certain trade. The men of Novgorod go to St. Petersburg, very often as cabmen; the men of Tver and Yaroslavl, although Moscow is nearer to them, go almost without exception to St. Petersburg and have established a very strong hold there. From Tula, Ryazán, and Vladímir, peasants go in great numbers to Moscow. Vladímir supplies carpenters; Smolensk supplies spade work; masons come from Tver, and market-gardeners from Yaroslavl.

In the country the peasant's two chief recreations were the church and the drink shop. Of drink shops, licit or illicit, he will find plenty in the town, but the parish tie is here far more loose; and owing to the exigences of his work, he will perhaps soon abandon all regular practice of religion. Possibly he will fail at his work, and will become simply a town loafer; but, in most cases, the ties of the country will remain very strong upon him. He will probably go home, at least once a year, for a considerable time, for instance after Easter, or in the summer, when the factory machines are under repair. In many occupations, such as cab driving and bricklaying, he is even able to regularly spend half his year in the country. When he is there, instead of

[1] This chapter, like the last, deals almost exclusively with Central Russia.

being a guest, he will resume his ordinary work as a country peasant; in fact, many go home to help in the harvesting. His wife, it will be remembered, he usually chooses from his own village. If he misbehaves himself in the town, it is to that village that he will be sent; and, in any case, he may look forward to a final return to the land when he is grown old. Thus country and town jostle together for predominance in the peasant of Moscow.

Many of the Moscow people are as purely peasants as any that one will see in the country. As you alight at the station of a large town the porter may look after "master darling" as affectionately as if he had been born on your estate, or he may give you a touch of the peasant fancy when he clears out the luggage from your compartment in the early morning and ends with the words "More it won't yield," as if it were a kind of bran tub. The waiter in the hotel comes and tells you all his troubles; and when you go, he says: "Do come back to us, we shall want to work for our old master." The better class of servants look like old country butlers. They will tell you quite simply what they think. "Italy," says a lackey to me, "I prefer for nature, and France for pleasure." "Oh yes," says the guide of a public monument who is also an old soldier, "what they say about a war between England and Russia is all rubbish; we shall settle that affair (the Malacca incident); war there won't be." The Russian habit of addressing people by their christian names ("John son of John") is not merely a habit: it is an expression of a certain kind of nature.

A very large number of the "go-aways" become cabmen. There are far too many for them all to be able to get work. Outside every important building you see long smiling rows of them. They whine like good dogs for a job, and drive after you in the hope of employment, saying: "Let's come for a turn," or suggesting suitable places of entertainment. Everyone can drive here after a fashion; and you see them navigating their homely ramshackle little carts over the stony streets of Moscow, which are amongst the noisiest in the world, like ships in a stormy sea. Past the smaller craft sail triumphantly the so-called "vicious" ones, who ask a higher price and go so fast as to soon wear out their horses. The ordinary cabman seems to sit on nothing; a rope serves him as reins; the whip is a stick, which is hardly ever used to strike, but often to flourish. The morality of hiring a cab is quite simple: you offer half of what you mean to give, and the cabman suggests perhaps four times as much; you then walk straight on, and he drives after you offering less. If you make no arrangement in advance, there will invariably be trouble, and, no matter what you give, he will generally be quite shameless; but if he has accepted your terms, it is very seldom that he will complain, unless you have altered his course. His driving is of a kind which I will describe as the "just missed you" sort; he will go at full pace, shouting to all concerned: "Look out, you." Between him and his horses there is a perfect understanding, conveyed by reproaches and expostulations, whining and wheedling. There is nothing odd in Chekhoff's story of the cabman who has lost his son, wants to tell everyone about it, can find no customer who will listen to him, and finally tells it to his horse. The cabmen are a pleasant folk, and seem to take one's interests to heart. When you come out of a shop to rejoin them, their faces brighten up with a happy joyous smile; they always like to talk, and will tell you all their family histories. Sometimes they will give you the answer which you appear to be asking for, not in any cringing manner, but simply to be polite. "Were you born in Moscow?" I ask one of them. "Born in Moscow," he says. "Do you know any other big town?" "Yes, Warsaw." "Do you know Warsaw well?" "Born in Warsaw." "Can you read?" I ask a big-bearded man. "Oh yes." "What do you read?" "Fairy tales." "Tell me a fairy tale," and he tells me a long rigmarole about a Russian who married a Chinese princess. A dog jumps on to the empty cart of a cabman. "I'm not going to travel with you," he says; "you've got no money on you." You take a new cabman to-day; and, as you pass your man of yesterday, he says with a smile: "You've forgotten me, master." A cabman may enter the employ of a proprietor who has forty cabs; he has to bring in sixteen shillings a month: if there is more, three-tenths of the gain go to the cabman; but the bargain is not a very profitable one. The cabmen foregather in certain public-houses, where there will usually be, as in many of the better hotels, large glorified musical boxes, which will play you airs from Glinka, Rubinstein, or Western comic opera. Sometimes I have found it difficult to stop these organs. "Ah! but we've got so-and-so," says the waiter, and sets the box going again out of sheer enthusiasm. The cabman practically requires no quarters; in his big blue overcoat he is ready to sleep anywhere. It is in pouring rain that I admire him most: one can see that he is soaked through; but it seems to make no difference to him whatsoever.

Many peasants engage in service in shops; these very closely approximate to the class which is described as "townsmen." Booths are erected in certain parts of the towns; and there you can buy pretty well anything that a peasant might want and a good many things which he might not want, such as strange toys of a quaint fancy: a lamb, a rabbit, a pig, or a monkey. I buy a pig and go into a shop to buy a monkey. "Why do you ask 4d. for your monkey when they only ask 2d. for their pig?" "Oh! you will see," and he gives a little demonstration. "This monkey is good work; your pig is no use," and so on. A peasant woman in a toy-shop, after making her bargain with me, says: "Good God! I'll get nothing out of this; it's all because of the war. We've got to simply give things away." Another small shopwoman tells me that she has to work from early morning till 9 p.m. every day. Shop servants are peculiarly dependent: their employers are much more exacting than the gentry. There are many peasants who travel about as pedlars; these are, at least, more free, and this is to be seen in the independence of their opinions.

But the most important of the "go-aways" are those engaged in factory work; more and more of these settle permanently in a given factory, and thus there is growing up in Russia a new factory race which is very largely composed of them; it already numbers some two millions. In my opinion it is utterly unjust to accuse the Government of caring but little for the welfare of the factory workers. A very considerable part of the manu- facturing capital of Russia is in the hands of foreigners; and, even where the employer is a Russian, the Government has no particular reason to prefer his interests to those of his men. On the contrary, a Government which tries to base itself upon the support of the peasants as against the Intelligents will naturally do exactly the opposite. In order that the facts may speak for themselves, I will here give a short summary of the laws which concern the administration of factories.

The Governor presides over a special "Presence" (or committee) for factory administration. It is composed of the Vice-Governor, the Proctor of the Circuit Law-court, the Commandant of the Governor's special police, the Senior Inspector of Factories, and a representative of the employers; the Inspector is the paternal spokesman of the workmen. This system, like all others in Russia, is worked by means of official instructions, and there is no free initiative on the part of the workmen. But, so far from identifying itself with the interests of the masters, the Government has taken infinite pains to safeguard all the interests of the men, and to establish a machinery which will ensure attention for all their complaints.

The Governor's Presence looks after the conditions of work, the health, and the morality of the workmen, investigates violations of the rules, interprets the law, and makes local byelaws.

The Inspectors of Factories, who have very great power, must see that the laws are observed, sanction or amend the rules of each factory, settle disputes between masters and men, and prosecute either party where necessary. Complaints against the Inspectors are judged by the Governor's Presence.

The engagement of a workman is a legal treaty; no workman may contract himself out of the protection of the law-courts. During the term of the treaty, wages may not be raised by the action of the workmen or reduced by the employer. If no term is fixed, either party must give a fortnight's notice. Mutual agreements, stoppage of the works, and other reasonable causes may terminate the agreement. The workman can be summarily dismissed for the following reasons : for unexplained absence from work for three days running or six days in the month, for an unavoidable absence of two weeks, for arrest on a charge which may involve imprisonment, for threats against his employer or bad conduct which injures the interests of the factory, and for infectious disease. He may demand his discharge for blows or insults from the employer or his officials, for violation of the treaty engagement as to food and quarters, for grave danger to his health caused by the nature of his work, for the death of his nearest relations, or if the bread-winner in his country home is taken as a recruit.

Not later than seven days after his engagement the workman

must receive a little book which is, so to speak, his charter.   If children, his own or under his charge, work in the factory, he may let his book serve for them too.   If he loses it, he must pay for a new one.   When checking the entries in it, the office may not keep it for more than a week, unless it supplies the workman with a duplicate.   In this book are entered his name, village, work in the factory, term of engagement, rate of wages, any special extras guaranteed (such as board and lodging), any changes from one kind of work to another, and any alterations made by mutual agreement in the original conditions of his employment; such agreements must be signed by the employer and by the workman.   At the end of the book are registered and dated the payments of wages (including any that are due for extra work), the fines incurred, and the amounts subtracted for goods supplied.   The book also contains a reprint of all the regulations of the Government which apply to workmen and employers.

During a fixed term, payment is made fortnightly ; in default the workman may sue at law for the cancelling of the agreement and may be awarded two extra instalments as compensation.   No payment in coupons or in kind is legal. Deductions are allowed only for wages advanced or for food supplied from the factory shops, and are limited to one-third of the fortnightly pay of bachelors, or one-fourth of that of married men or widowers with children.   The employer may take no interest on loans to the workmen.   The charges made to the workmen for board, lodging, and baths must be approved by the Inspector of Factories.

The hours of work are limited by law.   Children under twelve may not be admitted to work.   Children of twelve to fifteen years of age may work eight hours a day, exclusive of meal-times and school-time ; not more than four hours of work may be done at a stretch ; all their work must be done between 5 a.m. and 9 p.m ; they may not do work which is officially declared to be too exhausting, or harmful to their health.   For three hours a day or eighteen hours a week they must be free to visit the nearest school, which is often in the factory itself.   In cotton, hemp, and flax factories lads of fifteen to seventeen, girls, and women may not work between 10 p.m. and 5 a.m.

For men day-work is limited to eleven and a half hours, and night-work to ten. Night is defined as lasting from 9 p.m. to 5 a.m. If working for any portion of the night, the workman must count his time by the higher night-standard of wages. In day-work there must be at least one interval of an hour during which the workman is free to leave the factory, unless the nature of the work absolutely forbids. He must have an opportunity of eating every six hours.

All exceptions to these rules are carefully defined. The hours of one day's work may be increased in a fixed proportion in cases where the gangs relieve each other twice instead of once in a day, and where the work of one day is therefore not equal to that of the next. Twenty hours must be the ordinary limit of two successive days' work. A man who has worked at night may not be employed again for a certain number of hours. There are similarly regulated exceptions to the ordinary laws applying to children, women, and lads. Damage to the machinery or damage by fire may be repaired at once without regard to the time limit; but the case must be at once reported to the Factory Inspector.

Extra time can only be worked by mutual agreement between master and man; such an agreement may only form part of the original treaty when it is necessary for technical reasons. Extra time may not exceed 120 hours in the year. The Inspector must have word whenever such an arrangement applies to a whole section of the factory. He must see an exact account of all extra time, and must sanction all exceptional arrangements on the subject, which must then be posted in each of the work-rooms in which day-work and night-work are intermingled. Each man who works eight hours a day must have three clear days off in every month, or four if his work exceeds eight hours. In all cases Sundays and fourteen Feast-days must be observed as holidays (for a clear twenty-four hours); but by a mutual arrangement, which requires the sanction of the Inspector, a Sunday may be exchanged for a week-day.

In the factory shop, which sells goods to the workmen, the prices must have the approval of the Inspector.

In mines and in factories where there is danger of accidents, an elaborate system of compensation is enforced. The details fill about a third of one of the workmen's pay-books. Any accident must at once be reported to the police and to the Factory Inspector. An inquiry is held with the assistance of a medical officer. Two records of the inquiry are kept, one by the employer, one by the workman or his family. The employer can be fined £2 10s. to £10 for failure to report or for not observing the other regulations.

If the investigation does not reveal evil intent or gross carelessness on the part of the workman, compensation must be paid. No workman may contract himself out of his right; but an agreement as to the amount may be made after the accident and, if not against the spirit of the law, will be sanctioned by the Inspector.

If temporarily disabled, the workman receives half-pay; if totally disabled for life, he gets a pension of two-thirds of his year's pay, and if partially, less. Pensions to children increase with time according to the normal average of pay for their age. The hospital bills must also be paid by the employer.

In case of death the employer must pay the cost of burial, £3 for each man or £1 10s. for a lad or child. The pension is reckoned by the year's wage of the deceased. The widow gets one-third of it, each child one-sixth till he or she is fifteen, or, if completely orphaned, one-fourth; brothers, sisters, or grandchildren who were formerly supported by the deceased get one-sixth till they are fifteen. There are regulations for the event of remarriage of the widow. The whole sum may not exceed two-thirds of the year's pay. The nearest claims are satisfied first. Claims of children are entrusted to appointed guardians.

The employer must pay 10 per cent. monthly for delays of payment. He must insure for the sum required, against the chance of the stoppage of his business. If the works are sold, and the purchaser will not take over the debts, the seller must pay them.

The special rules of each factory must be sanctioned by the Inspector and posted in each work-room; they must state explicitly, amongst other things, the hours of work and the breaks. Fines may be imposed only for bad work, idleness, and breaking of the laws or the local rules. " Bad work " is defined as negligent workmanship or the spoiling of machines or materials.

In this case the workman, besides being fined, can be condemned in a law-court to pay damages. "Idleness" is defined
as half a day's absence unexplained by accident, fire, overflow of
rivers on the road, personal illness, or death or serious illness of
near relations. "Breach of order" includes disobedience, coming
drunk, introducing games played for money, or, where that is
forbidden by the local rules, introducing strong drink (which, however, may not be confiscated). The fine for "breach of order"
may not exceed a rouble (2s.). The register of fines must be shown
to the Inspector. If all the fines exceed one-third of the current
instalment of wages, the employer may exact no more than the one-
third, but may cancel the engagement; the workman may then
appeal to the law-courts, and, if he wins, will get compensation
for dismissal. Fines must all go to a common fund for relieving
sickness and confinements, and for paying the workmen's losses
by fire and the expenses of their burial.

It will be understood that the laws only define the outside
limits of hours, fines, etc.; those local rules which I saw were much
milder, with the single exception that men who came drunk
were not admitted to work at all.

In the workman's pay-book are also printed extracts from the
general laws of the Empire. The civil laws ordain that children
cannot be employed without the consent both of their parents or
guardians and of themselves, that the workman may not work for
others without the leave of his employer, and that damage done
to the employer must be paid for in money or by continued
service. For leaving work before the expiry of the term the
workman can be imprisoned for one month; for deliberate
damaging of tools or materials he can be imprisoned for three
months; if this last leads to stoppage of the works, he can be
imprisoned for one year.

Strikes are, in consonance with the whole tendency of the
system, direct breaches of the treaty and therefore of the law which
guarantees the treaty. The workmen must trust absolutely to the
Inspectors, and may not act for themselves. For a strike which
has the object of raising wages the leaders are liable to imprisonment for a term ranging from three weeks to three months, and the
other workmen for a term of from seven days to three weeks; if the
works are stopped, the leaders may get four to eight months, and

the others two to four; those who come in at the first demand of the police are not punished. If harm is done to property, the leaders may get eight to sixteen months, and the others four to eight. For violently stopping or preventing others from work there are the same penalties.

If the employer tries to lower wages before the expiry of a term, or to force acceptance of payment in coupons or in kind, he is liable to a fine of £10 to £30, and must pay due compensation to the workmen. If such action of his is repeated, or if it leads to such disturbances in the factory as call for the re-establishment of order by the police, he is liable to three months' imprisonment and the loss of his right to manage a factory for two years.

I may add that the Government has practically compelled the greater employers to found a school, a hospital, and often also a *crèche* in each factory. If the employer is recalcitrant to a demand from the Government, he may lose the right to conduct a factory, which is after all considered to be a favour. Thus, in troublous times, some mills have even had to work on at a loss, in order not to lose the hope of future profits.

The Factory Inspector is the Government official who has to arbitrate in the first instance between master and men.[1] One might fairly say that it is the interests of the men which are especially committed to his charge. He is unlike the ordinary administrative official, for he has been entrusted rather with the charitable functions of government than with the restrictive. At first he was appointed from amongst the ordinary officials; now there is a tendency to give preference to candidates who are engineers; but the Factory Inspector is not likely to be a man who has had any practical experience of running a business. For this reason owners and managers often find him to be unintelligent; they resent so much interference between themselves and their men, with whom they would like to be able to fight out the different issues on the basis of supply and demand. Most of them would, therefore, like to see the Factory Inspectors abolished altogether.

From two Factory Inspectors I received very kindly help. They did not scruple to tell me in what factories they considered the arrangements to be thoroughly bad. One of them gave me

---

[1] I must here specially acknowledge the great kindness of Mr. K., who did everything to facilitate my visits to factories and to Factory Inspectors.

his card to show to employers, but I did not always find that it
secured me admission.   Those who knew him spoke of him to me
with evident cordiality, and he seemed to me a man of considerable
ability.   The other was a big kindly man, not very quick of mind;
for the time he was occupying the post of senior Inspector, but
he was ordinarily in charge of one of the twenty-two Sub-districts
of a given area.   All the big factories, he told me, if they have to
house workmen at all, have good schools and hospitals.   The term
of engagement is usually half a year.   It is therefore unlikely
that all the workmen will have simultaneously arrived at the end
of their respective terms; and, as it is only at the end of the
term that they can ask for more pay, general strikes are legally impossible.   Many, however, are engaged for indefinite terms which
can be ended at a fortnight's notice from either side; such men
can combine to strike without breaking the law.   In practice the
workmen simply take no notice of the law at all in the matter, as
they only think of getting their "needs" satisfied by any means
that come to hand.   Thus, when some factories are striking,
everyone thinks that now is the time to strike too.

   "For the labour troubles of 1905," said the Factory Inspector,
"there is a very real foundation : the food supply is often bad,
and the pay very low, even if one allows for the lower standard of
living in Russia."   Here, in Great Russia, the Jews have but
little influence as agitators.   The agitation comes from two distinct sources : from the students (who for a long time have been
"working" the factories) and in recent years from propagandist
work of the police themselves.   Discontent may be divided into
two kinds.   The workmen of the more prosperous parts are always
the more exacting in their demands, because they have intelligence
and enterprise and claim an altogether new standard of life.   But
there is also the "dark discontent" of the less enlightened parts.
There the workmen simply think that the present time offers
them a good chance of getting something for themselves, and
they strike accordingly.   It is to be desired that the hours of
daily employment should be limited to ten ; the prospect of a
rest is an incentive to better work.   Statistics prove that, in the
months that precede Christmas and Easter, 45 per cent. more
work is done than at other times.   One employer instituted a
ten-hours day, feeling quite sure that he would get better work

and the same or a greater profit; but unfortunately the workmen deliberately tried to work badly, because they now wanted to create an argument for an eight-hours day. Most workmen as yet fail to understand that, when a factory comes to be not worth the working, the employer can transfer the remains of his capital to some other business and leave them standing; they think that, to get, they only need to demand; for instance, in one case they demanded 50 per cent. more wages, and this was simply non-sensical and impossible. Their fundamental demands are always for more pay and for fewer hours of work, but these demands are often complicated with political developments, for instance with the war. The war has greatly altered the conditions of work; and in some places, significantly enough, the employers have established a six-hours day for the simple reason that there is just now very little work to do. The strikes have but little connection with any claim for a Constitution; but it would not be possible entirely to separate the political from the economic, and some of the semi-political claims of the workman are very genuine. He demands, for instance, freedom of education, the legal right to strike, better conditions of life, and a further legal limitation of the hours of work. In the intelligence of working-folk a notable progress is going on. No satisfactory arrangements can be hoped for from above, whether, the Inspector would seem to say, from the employers or from the Government. There is no vitality at the top of things, strong enough to deal with the needs of those below.

In his office, men are waiting about with questions and peti-tions; one shrewd-looking old peasant has come to ask for relief, as the factory in which he works is closed altogether. The Inspector replies that the sum allotted by the Government to pensions in this province came to very little and has all been exhausted, so that for this year nothing more can be done.

COUNTRY FACTORIES.

1. Rostóff District, July, 1904.—Preserved vegetables.
I will start with a very small factory, in which twenty hands are employed. The manager has been in France and Germany, and is going to England. The machines here are English. Local work-men make much more money than they would in agriculture,

and are yet able to live at home ; therefore few of them leave the factory.

The working day is from 6 a.m. to 7.30 p.m. There are intervals for meals at 8 (half an hour), 12 (an hour), and 3.30 (half an hour). Night work lasts from 7.30 p.m. to 6 a.m., with half an hour's interval at 12.30 a.m. Twenty-eight Feast-days are observed as holidays, besides all Sundays. The rules prescribe that clothes must be kept clean, and that "the workman must be faithful, obedient, and respectful to the master and his family, and also to all persons delegated by him." The fines are—for coming late, 1*s.*; for going away without leave, 1*s.*; for coming drunk, 1*s.*; for noisy behaviour, 1*s.*; for gambling, 1*s.*; for not keeping clean, 6*d.*; for carelessness with the furnace, 6*d.*; for disobedience and rudeness, 2*s.*

2. Rostóff District, July, 1904.—High-class cloth for suits.

This factory was founded by foreigners a hundred years ago ; it is quite in the country, ten miles from a small railway station ; the goods are all carried thither by road. The district is marshy, and it would cost a great deal to lay down a light railway. I am told that the relations between master and men have been very much those of landowner and labourers ; there have been no labour troubles.

The manager is a brisk little man, interesting and very ready, but with a rather equivocal manner. A peasant elder has accompanied me hither, and our talk turns upon the value of country factories and a comparison of their workmen with the surrounding peasants. The elder is all for having more lower technical schools, but in the country factory he sees no advantage for the better of the peasants. "In these factories," he says, "morality is, if anything, worse. Some come out and return to agriculture ; these do not compare well with the ordinary peasants; in particular their health is weaker."

The manager takes up the challenge. "Yes," he says, "indoors there is of course less exercise ; but we must distinguish. Some of the hands are loafers, good-for-nothings ; they are those who have been sent home from the capital to their villages ; they are no longer fit to work in the fields ; they want a 'towny' life, and they come into the factory. But others have lived with us from father to son for generations; these have grown up here, and no longer know from what village their family came."

The peasant smiles a pleasant country smile. "Yes," he says, "you are our disinfector: you clear away our waste elements; for that I am very grateful to you. Perhaps some of the factory hands are better off than they would be in the town; they may gain in health and may interest themselves by pottering at a little gardening work; but real peasants have little to get from the factory except wages." "But," says the manager, "think of how they must benefit by being under the control of a fixed discipline; the factory is an educational institution; these good-for-nothings, of whom you have spoken, are at least trained to do this kind of work, even if they could have done no other." The elder, however, holds his own; and, when he goes, his last word is "Disinfectors!"

The manager, relieved of country criticism, now further emphasises his point. The rules are strict. The men learn order and good behaviour; the factory is like a great home to them. We talk to four lads who are strolling along in town costume with cigarettes in their mouths. They play up to the manager, and say that they would not now care for country work. The manager confidently tells each where he comes from, and guesses wrong in nearly every case.

One of his master-weavers, a Belgian, takes me through the long low work-rooms. "There are some good workmen," he says, "but most are lazy." The turbine system is used; the dynamos were made by an English firm in Moscow; there are forty looms. Much of the cloth was such as would go to a good London tailor, but the factory seemed to have regular customers and not to worry itself about extending its trade.

I hear from one of the employed that they are a "good lot"; they live in common quarters, have their own Guild, and are quite at home. They have good food, and eat meat every day. The factory has its own school, which has done a great deal of good; there are entertainments of a spectacular kind, but not concerts. In this factory the men find their amusements on the spot; "in the town you don't know where they would go."

FACTORIES IN A SMALL TOWN.

1. Rostóff, July, 1904.—Syrup.

There are more than one hundred hands. For nine months of work the pay averages 26s. a month, with keep. During two months of every year the works undergo repair, and the workmen go back to their villages.

Most of them have just enough intelligence to do as they are told, but the skilled artisans have enterprise and become "masters," that is, certificated skilled labourers. The manager promotes men who show keenness, but only on the expiry of their terms. He does not believe in fines, and has only fined once in three years; his plan is to reprimand for a first offence, to threaten dismissal for a second, and to dismiss the workman at the end of his term if he remains unsatisfactory. If a man fails to put in an appearance on the morrow of a feast-day, he will on re-engagement be only offered lower work, which means a loss of self-esteem as well as of pay.

The men have common quarters. It is seldom that they quarrel; if the common rest is disturbed, they appeal to the manager. They are all "go-aways," and often end their lives in the country, sending their sons instead; thus they are "better than the townspeople."

There is much less drunkenness since the monopoly. The men deposit their savings with the company, and therefore do not drink, as drinking on credit is now illegal. Eighty per cent. of them are literates; these are in general better at their work, but somewhat lower in their standard of morality.

The workmen have no clubs, but they combine to buy newspapers, which they take their turns to fetch from the town. There have been no strikes here so far.

2. Rostóff, July, 1904.—Flax spinning.

Eleven hundred hands. The manager speaks English; he was in France for three months, and in England for eleven; he will have to go to England again.

The factory is a big building, with three floors; the office is separate, away from the noise; the big engines are English, from Leeds, Bolton, and Glasgow. The first engineer gets £3 10s. to £4 a month, the second £1 10s. to £1 12s.; the mechanics who repair the machines get from £2 to £2 8s. The noise is deafening; every now and then the shriek of a loud whistle gives warning that the bobbins are to be moved. The manager tells me that all this bustle and clamour gets on the men's nerves.

A large room is devoted to heckling by hand or by machine; the better flax undergoes both methods. This work is very unhealthy; ten years of it is "killing work"; after that, few are good for anything. He sometimes transfers an ailing man to another department, but not often, for it does not pay the factory to lose time in teaching the man a new business. The wages here are 1s. 6d. a day for nine hours' work on end, or 11½d. if an interval is taken. The tow is separated off and made into army cloth. Women prepare the flax for spinning at £1 a month; spinning of yarn earns from £1 8s. to £1 14s., and reeling 16s. to 18s.

The regulations are very minute. If the engines stop, those men who are doing piece-work draw half-pay during the stoppage. The hours of day-work are from 6 a.m. to 7 p.m., that is, a full tale is exacted just within the legal limit. The works are closed for twenty-four Feast-days and for Sundays; children have nine extra holidays. Women may not sew at their work, (there is a great deal of lolling about in many Russian factories); men who look after the machines may not wear loose clothes. The door-keepers must see that nothing is ever carried out of the factory, and that no workman goes away without leave during working hours; they are ordered to stop all quarrels among the men, and to pay all courtesy to the inquiries of strangers.

Workmen and their families have the right to medical attendance and medicine gratis; the "felsher" comes every day, and the doctor twice a week. All children of the workmen receive free education in the factory school; there is a free library, with five hundred volumes, mostly novels, which are the favourite reading of the workmen, especially Turghényeff and Danilevsky; in the last year sixty men, forty women, five hundred children, and seventy-five outsiders made use of this library. Every Sunday throughout the winter, priests or factory clerks give free magic lantern lectures to the workmen and their families; the subjects are generally of a moral character, but the management sometimes chooses a subject of present-day interest, say, for instance, "Life in Japan."

Whole families work together here, and live, some round the factory, some in the town. Many will go to a new factory every two years. This migration is bound to lead to a certain intelligence of common interests.

The manager " sees no enterprise in the Russian workmen; they want nothing to do and more pay; that is their ambition." But he carefully separates the " go-aways " from the town-bred men. With the former he never has any trouble; with the latter he is often at loggerheads.

The faces are all white. " Health spoils here," he tells me. But the " go-away " is often called back to the village, to help his father; later he generally returns to the factory. Only a few go back to the country for good in their old age and send their sons instead.

The men buy Moscow newspapers, and, during the war, they paid the advance rate in order to get the paper by quick train on the day of its issue. As families all " pig " together anyhow, morality loses by factory life, but the " go-aways " are much the steadier; also they get drunk much less frequently. Since the monopoly, he has observed that there is less heavy drinking, and much less foul language on the streets; but here beer is not driving out vodka.

FACTORIES IN LARGE TOWNS.

1. Yaroslavl, July, 1904. An ironmaster, with a very large business, and credited with unusual ability.

Big machinery, he tells me, all comes from abroad; to set up works for making it in Russia would be very costly, and a firm which did so would not receive large orders soon enough to repay this expense. Much of the Russian iron trade is in rails; those supplied to the Transcaspian and Trans-Siberian railways were home-made.

Strikes have generally become more frequent since 1901. A strike is usually the work of some three or four leaders. The ordinary workman, when he strikes, generally does not know what he is after; he still imagines that capital is a gold mine, from which unlimited concessions can be extorted.

2. Yaroslavl, July, 1905. A great cotton-spinning factory.

My informant, a member of the firm, is a very smart business man, who gives me a good deal of his time and makes every bit of it valuable to me.

The mill was first used for flax spinning. Since it became a cotton-mill additions have been built on, and it has developed at an ever-increasing rate. As there were not many factories in the district, and no new suburb was springing up, the directors put up a great building to house the workers almost free. Fifty-five per cent. live in this building; the rest find their own lodgings, which are paid for by the factory. It will also lend to the workman £40 or £50 that he may rent land and build a wooden house for himself; 1,000 workmen have availed themselves of this help, and the money is always paid back; such workmen do not, as one might imagine, interest themselves in gardening work. This plan is now preferred to the further development of the barracks system. "We did a great deal in that way for forty years, and were very well pleased with ourselves, but now we see that we were on the wrong road."

The workmen come from all parts. The men of Kostromá are dull; the men of Yaroslavl are smart and self-respecting; the men of Tver are the best of all; the Moscow men seem half asleep, "though they are considered to live in the very centre of Russian culture." There are families which have lived in the factory for three generations; many of the workmen were born there, and will die there. A new factory race is fast springing up.

The barracks system means too much responsibility. There, under the charge of the directors, live 10,000 persons, that is, 5,000 workmen and their families. This is an abnormal state of things. For so great a number there must be a strict discipline. The workmen feel that they are "under the stick." If they shout, they are told to stop. This goes on day by day, drop by drop; they get to hate it. Then, too, there are certain rules which are inevitable, if one is dealing with so large a number. Stealing is far too easy; thieves must be sent away at once, and with them go their families. This, say the workmen, is unjust. So, too, if the children play with matches and set fire to the building while their parents are at work, then they must be turned out, and their parents will go with them; but, after all,

one cannot sit down and let the barracks burn. The factory is
ruled by a council of managers and heads of departments ; there
is a special manager of the barracks, and at every daily meeting
he has some three or four questions of this kind to bring up. In
other words, the barracks system takes up far too much time.
In England the managers are not bothered with such questions,
and have all their time free for questions of trade. The barracks
are like one great magnetic organism : an idea, once started, goes
through the whole body.[1]

All the men are paid by the piece. Food and wages are
certainly much worse than in England, even if one allows for the
difference in the rate of living.

There is a hospital with three doctors. There are 300 out-
patients every day. The workmen will only trust the doctors as
far as they see them. If they are cured, they will be grateful;
if not, they will say, "In the hospital they cut you about." In
every year 1,000 midwifery cases have to be attended to, and so
the doctors are kept too busy; the women insist on getting up
after five days instead of nine, and therefore women's diseases
are very common. Serious operations are impossible, and such
cases are taken to the town hospital. One of the doctors was a
trained gynecologist, but he was, (very inappropriately), sent off to
the war. Most of the children are weakly. The health and the
physique of the workmen are generally declining; perhaps that is
because more weaklings survive. The birth-rate is much better
than it was; but the best of the present generation are not so
hardy as the "old heroes" of the last. Lung diseases are the
most common.

There is a large *crèche* maintained at the expense of the factory.
The working families used to be allowed to engage girls of sixteen
or seventeen to look after their children, and to live in the factory;

---

[1] A labour member of the Duma, Mr. Savélyeff, of Moscow, explained to me that
this aspect of the barracks system has two sides to it. "Certainly," he said, "it
is easy for an idea to pass right through the barracks, but, on the other hand,
there is an atmosphere of constant fear. One has to remember that 'perhaps So-
and-so will talk.' A group of men who are discussing organisation must break off,
if an outsider comes up." This is all very true, as the Yaroslavl manager has himself
testified; but it only means that, when once the workmen are united, their victory
will be all the more complete. In many places, not only the workmen, but also the
peasants, have already reached this stage.

but it was found that these had come to number 900; this seemed ridiculous, and therefore the *crèche* was founded. The workmen look upon it with disfavour; their wives are at work in the factory, and the nurse-girl, whose time was free, used to cook their meals.

The factory has its own school; it is also visited by three priests who have parishes in the town. To this manager the religiousness of the workmen seems only superficial; and he notices no difference, in this respect, between the "go-away" and the man whose home is in the factory. There is a large theatre, and once a week throughout the winter there are evening readings with lantern slides, or even concerts. The factory used to have its own band, but the practices spoilt work, and as work is paid by the piece, they also diminished the earnings. Now the military band plays in the factory park for a fixed fee during the summer.

The men do not live as well as English workmen, "who have two rooms for a family, which means that they are already a cultured people." The workman marries at the age of seventeen or eighteen, and is "much less immoral than you would think." But morality is getting worse. The chief evil is syphilis; it is the troops that carry it everywhere. A medical friend told the manager that near Moscow 40 per cent. of the cases of disease are of this kind.

By the system of the Factory Inspectors the Government has "taken all factories under its wardenship." This is a bad plan. To no one is freedom of speech and of person so well guaranteed as to the Englishman. The manager is a moderate Conservative; but he says: " The most important of all things is the right of initiative."

Ten years ago there were labour troubles in the factory because one manager, a man of academic mind, tried to make a difference in payment between the easy work done with the new machines and the hard work done with the old ones. The workmen all imagined themselves to have a grievance; they said that their pay was being decreased, and they struck. This year the directors have anticipated the introduction of a new law by diminishing the hours of work from eleven and a half to ten, at the same time giving an increased rate of pay for an hour's work; but some of the men have put glue in the machines in order to delay work and to get more for overtime. The men are silly, and do not understand how a factory can be worked; they want a day of eight hours; they think that they have only to ask in order to get. Their demands are always for more pay and for less hours. In purely political questions they have no interest, except so far as these questions nearly affect their life; but of course the war has been precisely a question of this kind. One, for instance, has had a father taken, another a brother or a son. Lately the managers seized 1,000 copies of a manifesto from the Northern Social Democrats; it described factory owners as " drinkers of blood "; it urged the men to secure an eight-hours day and more pay. These were the chief points, but at the end came a short sentence suggesting also the demand for freedom of Press, conscience, and meeting, and the establishment of a check upon the Ministers, (in other words, the Zemstvo programme).

3 A labour leader from the Lower Volga.

Mr. Aládin was born of peasant parents in the government of Simbírsk. He not only passed through the secondary school system, but also studied in the university of Kazán; he engaged actively in labour propaganda, and took a leading part in the organisation of several strikes. These strikes were not based on theoretical or even on political grounds; on the contrary, the claims made were in each case very special and related to some undesirable feature in the management of the factory concerned. For instance, Mr. Aládin would have protested against the waste of life which was acknowledged to me by the manager of the hemp-factory in Rostóff. One strike of his organising was a protest against the carelessness of a certain employer, who in his unwillingness to spend a little money on improvements allowed the constant escape of certain gases which were ruinous to the health of the workmen. By picking his ground and making sure of his facts Mr. Aládin was able to direct more than one successful strike; but he himself had a larger policy and was anxious to call the attention of the working men to the need of bettering political conditions. In this he was less successful, for it was not till the great movement of 1905 that the workmen began to definitely connect their economic demands with political claims. Aládin was threatened with administrative arrest and exile to Archangel; this fate he avoided by a timely escape. In Paris he for some time manufactured "antiques"; then, refusing an invitation to America, he repaired to Belgium, where he made himself something like an expert in engineering. In Belgium he learned English from the *Daily Chronicle*, and passing over to our country, he spent some four years here, doing any work that came to his hand; towards the end of this time he made a little money by lecturing. His English, which is that of a superior English working man, is better of its kind than that of almost any other member of the first Duma. Aládin returned to Russia at his own risk at the end of 1905, was elected to the Duma, took a most prominent part in the organisation of the Labour Group, and was one of its most effective spokesmen. He has the greatest respect for the English working man, and, in spite of the very demonstrative and agitating character of some of his speeches in the Duma, he has done much to restrain his comrades from precipitate action against the Government.

Factories in Moscow.

There are large factories in the Moscow and Vladímir Governments which are amongst the most important in Russia, but which are planted in country districts. Such are the establishments of the Morózoff family, which has numbered amongst its members men whose intelligence and generosity would be remarkable amongst the merchant princes of any country. The late head of one of the Morózoff firms was a man who far exceeded the demands of the Government in the sums which he expended on the schools, the hospitals, and the general comfort of his workmen. The arrangements of this kind at his factory are considered to be one of the best models in Russia, and in Moscow itself his influence was a great moral force. He recently died in his prime, disappointed both by a Government which refused to listen to reasonable remonstrances, and by a working class which took all the benefits showered upon it as a simple excuse for asking for more.

1. The Moscow factories are all situated in the environs, and the sky, even in their neighbourhood, is generally smokeless. Some

of these environs are even attractive, and none are as squalid as those of our own manufacturing towns. At the south-east end of the town I obtained admission to the great cotton-spinning works of Messrs. Zindel (July, 1905). The manager was a young man with a very pleasant manner, who seemed to call all his employés, especially the children, by the term "golúbchik" (literally "little pigeon"). There are 2,400 of them, including 400 women and 400 lads; most of them are peasants; they go home for three weeks at Easter, whilst the machines are being repaired, and whenever they are convalescent after illness.

The buildings are all pleasant, clean, and airy. Each dormitory in the new barracks is large and roomy, and has, say, thirteen spacious windows. Each contains ninety-two beds, arranged in couples side by side. The factory supplies a good mattress to each workman, but he brings in his own rug and pillows. The Russian loves colour, and the room is a medley of variegated quilts and of pillows, pink, red, or white, piled upon each other sometimes four high. The factory gives one ikon to each room, and those of the workmen are ranged along shelves which run round the walls; they most of them are small, but some look quite expensive. In the summer, orders are given to keep the windows open. Some of the men we see resting on their beds. I am next shown the old barracks, of which the manager says with reasonable pride: "Some factories would wish that they had anything as good." Of course all comparison between this accommodation and that which the peasant has to put up with at home is altogether impossible. On each landing stage is a huge urn of hot water for making tea at odd times. The sanitary arrangements are quite creditable.

The married quarters are separate; they are really excellent little rooms with broad windows; there is space enough to entertain guests. Some of these quarters are called "one and a half"; and some of the better-paid families have two rooms each. The public dining-room is spacious and clean; there are separate tables for the women.

In the hospital there are twenty-two beds, four of which are for cases which require isolation. The staff consists of two doctors and two female "felshers." The most common ailments are stomach trouble, lung trouble, and women's diseases. For the women there is a small separate ward. The hospital has a small dispensary, a bandaging room, and a kitchen of its own. The doctor tells me that here in Moscow far more can be done than in the isolated country hospitals to teach the peasants the ordinary rules of health. They have no longer any kind of suspicion, and come in for every trifle. In the course of the year 14,000 visits are made by patients. In the country, on the contrary, far more hospitals and doctors are required; but the peasant is a much stronger and healthier man than the townsman.

The school is a good new building, with broad passages and exits; the class-rooms and teachers' room are pleasant. The workmen come to evening classes, but the school is of course chiefly for their children. Much use is made of the library, and the workmen read all the Russian classics, such as Pushkin, Lérmontoff, Gógol, and Dostoyévsky. Some books the Government does not allow the factory to buy. A theatre holding four hundred is attached to the school; the manager intends to hand it over to a professional provider of entertainments, as he thinks that will be cheaper, simpler, and better. There are frequent lantern lectures; for theatrical performances he generally selects farce, as he is sure that the workmen enjoy laughing better than anything else. The factory has a good deal of open space for amusements, and there is a band composed of workmen, who are supplied with instruments at the expense of the factory. The playground for the children is rather severe in design.

The manager talks very frankly of the labour question. In January, 1905, he had three troublesome days. The impetus undoubtedly came from outside; in fact, a great crowd surrounded the building and compelled the men to strike, which they did at once. Inside there are some fifty Social Democrats; these are some of the better workers. The men made fifteen demands, of which thirteen were quite unimportant; for instance, they claimed, as a right, that certain benevolent institutions, which do not exist at all in some other factories, should be further improved. Thus there is a doctor always on duty to treat workmen gratis, but they demanded that he should be in the hospital day and night. The two chief demands were, of course, for less hours and for more pay. Some of the claims could not possibly be allowed, but the hours of work will probably be diminished.

At present the men work for ten and a half hours a day, with more than an hour's interval for dinner, and there is no night work. He asked to be allowed to delay his answer till July 20, and will soon have to meet the men again.   Some of the men stand up loyally for the masters, but these are not chosen as representatives of the others, and, in fact, they are restrained from speaking out, presumably by threats.   Anyhow, he is convinced that the majority of the men are hostile.   The leaders are generally new-comers, who are put forward by those who have more to lose. The pension for twenty years' service is at present 6s. to 30s. a month for the ordinary workman, and 60s. to 150s. for the best of all.   When the workman has reached his fiftieth year, a shorter term of service qualifies for the pension.   Bonuses for good work are also given by the factory.

The men, without exception, have less of political instinct than the workmen of Germany ; they still think that they can demand anything of capital, and at Ivánovo they attacked a firm which was strong enough not to give in.   Still, strikes are, in any case, awkward.   When so many factories are closed, trade goes to those who continue work ; and, as this means big profits, the masters are ready to make certain concessions rather than lose the opportunities of the time.   He is not a believer in the system of Factory Inspectors ; he would prefer trade unions, and, in fact, would welcome them, as giving the masters someone with whom they could treat.

2. One of the chief businesses in Moscow is that of Baron Knoop. He is also a member of many other of the largest houses in Russia, and some of them are practically under his control.   By his courtesy I was able to see over his own cotton-spinning mill, which lies in one of the poorer quarters in the south of Moscow (July, 1905).

These vast works are under the charge of two managers, one for the spinning department and one for the printing.   One of these, a foreigner, showed me over.   Practically all the big machinery comes from England.   " When you lose a piece," said the manager, " Mather & Platt will send you exactly the part that you write for ; from other countries you may get something which is an inch out."   He had heard that in England and in America one man could manage two looms, or even three ; but there the mind is better developed, and the food and physique are also superior ; he tried the experiment, and found that, if one man managed two looms, the looms went wrong. Now he sets a man to two looms for a month, but after that the man's health seems to suffer, and he will be put for one month on to a single loom.[1] The huge, noisy printing rooms were full of streams of cotton of the brightest colours, folding themselves away, so to speak, into the floor. Different provinces, I am told, have their own special fancies in the matter of pattern ; and these fancies have to be satisfied by the factory. A bright purple is peculiarly admired. The peasants of Novgorod favour a flowery design, like a wall-paper ; others, in the same province, have better taste, and prefer an excellent design of which a strap is the *motif*. Wares are made to meet the taste of the Caucasus and even of Persia. The fire engines, which are particularly fine, come from Worthington, of America ; they act with extraordinary rapidity, and an artesian well keeps the factory always prepared with water for immediate use. The firemen are chosen from amongst the workmen.

There are ordinarily some 5,000 hands, of whom many live in quarters provided by the factory. In the older buildings a low dormitory houses forty-two persons. Much trouble has been taken with the ventilation, but the result is by no means wholly satisfactory. It is hard to get the workmen to make a proper use of the sanitary arrangements. A kitchen is attached to the build-ing. In some other barracks, the married live in small dormi-tories which each contain four couples, separated into little cabins. The inmates of this part apparently keep their rooms very untidy, but at least the accommodation is far better than that which they would have at home. One thousand live in this single building. The workers are allowed to have small gardens, but often quarrel about them. "One would like," says the manager, "to do anything to make them more like men and less like pigs." He is a man with a very drastic manner, and, as a foreigner, he is inclined to despise the Russians. The workmen, who do not look very intelligent, are stirred into a kind of spasmodic activity by his quick approach, and obey him with alacrity. At the stores which supply the workmen with cheap food I am shown a sample of everything. There are three

---

[1] This statement, which was confirmed by all my other informants, has a consider-able bearing on the academic claim for an eight-hours day with increased wages.

different qualities of meat, black bread, rings of white rusks on string at $2\frac{1}{2}d.$, sugar at $4d.$ a pound,[1] and bitter kvas (a non-alcoholic drink made from bread) of two kinds, strong and weak. Each workman has a book in which is entered the amount of credit given to him. When provisions are sold on credit, the Factory Inspector has to define the prices, and the stores are, as a whole, run at a loss.

Higher up the hill there is a hospital with several wards containing about five beds each. There is also a separate lying-in hospital, well ventilated, and with bath-rooms attached. One doctor is in charge of both. The *crèche* is also a separate building, and houses three nurses and at times eighteen babies. There is also a school.

Six times in the last year—so the manager tells me—a crowd of strikers has approached the works. Once he sent out to ask from whom they came, and they replied: "From the Revolutionary Committee." But his own men would not go out and join them; and Cossacks and police had time to arrive and disperse the demonstrators.

Here are some opinions on the labour troubles of 1905.

An electrical engineer,—an able, masterful man,—gives me his opinion of the Russian workmen. He thinks them poor workers as compared with foreigners, but not as compared with the Russian peasants. Everywhere in Russia, in factories as in offices, but little work is got through in the day.[2] Factory hands smoke cigarettes whilst at their business. To knock off one and a half hours from the working day would make but little difference to them. He himself served his apprenticeship in the United States; there he worked for ten hours daily, and he and others struck to reduce this to nine and a half; they all knew very well how much that half-hour would mean to them, but here men would never do a real hard day's work, whatever they were paid. They don't understand that capital expects a profit. To one old peasant woman he gives a penny a day, and it is all

[1] The price of sugar, which, in consequence of indirect taxation, is sometimes much higher, has been one of the most common grievances of peasants and of workmen in 1905 and 1906.

[2] I have heard the same story from officials, employés of the Zemstva, and business men; and I have often seen how true it is.

charity; another is cheaper to him at two shillings. He admires the Ivánovo masters for making no concessions; they were too strong to be touched; the strike did not mean ruin to them, but the workmen starved. It is always the best-treated workmen who strike first.

Another gentleman has a large factory in the Valdai district, right in the country. He and his brother are the two managers. There are families who have worked here for three or four generations. The factory has a school and a hospital. Horses or cows lost by the workmen are often replaced for nothing by the masters. The Factory Inspectors always want to show their power, and take the side of the men. This stirs up trouble. Some students came to the factory and persuaded the men to strike. One of the managers spoke to them as follows : " We can't give you more without ruining the business; if we transfer our capital to something else, we live, and you starve." The strikers begged pardon, caught four of the students, and knocked them about.

Another factory owner of whom I was told saw that his mill was going to fail. An expert, whom he consulted, said to him : " You are ruined ; the only way to save yourself is to share all profits with the workmen." This advice he took. He established a council of master-workmen to regulate and control the profits ; this council was always ready to accept his guidance in the policy of the factory. Inside the walls all matters of discipline remained in his hands, and, with this degree of public control, the factory has since worked well for several years.

" The workmen," said another gentleman, " are much more developed than they were. This is evident when you compare them with the other peasants, but they do not understand that by constant strikes they can kill a factory altogether." In a tallow factory at Kazán the men made the most unreasonable demands ; their employer said : " Very well, I'll strike too, and I'll live on the interest of my capital, and you will starve." The men at once returned to work.

Of another factory in the Ryazán Government I am told, at second hand, the following story. Some sixty strikers came from Moscow. " You must strike," they said. " Why ? " asked the workmen, " We see no reason." " Why, because everyone else is striking." "Then what for?" "For an eight-hours day, and, if you don't, we will burn your factory." To this the workmen said, " No," and the agitators passed on to a neighbouring factory, which they did actually set on fire. At this the men in the first factory struck, apparently because they realised that the burning of the factory would deprive them of a livelihood. They were asked what they struck for; they replied: " For an eight-hours day." " All right," said the employer, " I will give you an eight-hours day," and on examination it turned out that, on account of the slackness of trade, they were already working for less than eight hours. The men thereupon sent a deputation saying: " Please let it be as it was."

In 1905 several of my informants alluded to labour propaganda of a violent kind carried on by the police themselves. One Factory Inspector, it will be remembered, frankly divided the agitators into two classes: students and police. Another gentleman, connected with trade, told me that a letter from the Minister of the Interior was at this time one of the poorest introductions which one could have ; a factory owner would cross himself and say, " Good heavens! who is this man? " Very probably these suspicions were too general, but unfortunately official documents leave no doubt that there was a foundation for them. Something has already been said of Mr. Witte's factory laws, of the undignified struggle between Mr. Witte and Mr. Plehwe, and of the noxious activity of Zubátoff, who had the support of many high-placed reactionaries, including General Trepoff. Whereas his successor at the head of the Moscow police, Count Shuváloff, seems to have favoured the Intelligents and to have been very severe with the working men, Trepoff appears to have thought that the workmen could really be won over to the side of the Government. Anyhow Zubátoff received encouragement to organise public lectures, and to suggest to the workmen that, if they demonstrated against their employers, they would have the support of the Government and of the local officials. The factory owners, as obviously the sufferers by Zubátoff's scheme, became very bitter against the police. Zubátoff had some measure of success in Great Russia. There were disorders in the Goujon and Danilevsky factories, and a demonstration of 50,000 persons was arranged for the purpose of laying a wreath on the monument of Alexander II. A Society of Independent

Working Men was founded in Odessa, and a Club of Russian Working Men in St. Petersburg. In many places, the workmen eventually saw through Zubátoff's idea and his attempts at agitation completely failed. But in Odessa the application of these methods led to serious results. This town was always prone to political excitement; it is a great centre of industrial activity, and it is peopled by the hot-headed "Little Russians" and very many Jews. In April, 1903,—so writes the senior Factory Inspector of the government of Kherson,[1]—Unions of working men were organised by the Gendarme Vasílyeff, head of the detective department, and a young Jew named Shayévich; the latter was recommended to the Gendarme by official instructions from St. Petersburg. There followed a series of strikes for the most senseless objects, in which the Unions compelled other workmen to join. The acting City Prefect, so far from hindering the strikers, received a deputation of them and expressed his sympathy. In June, 1903, Shayévich extended his propaganda to the seamen and stokers of the merchant fleet and to the dock labourers and tramway servants. The efforts of the senior Factory Inspector to dissuade the strikers were fruitless. In July the dock labourers and the tramway servants struck work. At a great meeting of the strikers on July 17, speeches against the Government were made and revolutionary manifestoes were distributed. The crowd unanimously demanded freedom of meeting and of the Press, and some kind of a Constitution; but it protested against any diminution of the autocracy, and speakers who had not been selected by the promoters were badly handled. On this day a general strike broke out all over the town. Even hotels, restaurants, bakers, and haircutters were forced to stop work. Forty factories and in all 6,000 workmen were on strike, and only the official newspaper could publish, and that with the greatest difficulty. The police, so far from resisting the strikers, in some cases advised the factory owners to send their men out at once. One Police-Master himself escorted the strikers, and there is evidence of a very serious kind to the effect that he rescued some of them from the troops. Shayévich was seen leading the rioters. In the presence of these demonstrations, both

---

[1] His report was published in the Conservative " Russkoë Dyelo," in July, 1905.

masters and men had to consent to shut their factories without
any attempt at resistance. The Factory Inspector attempted to
secure immunity for those who wished to go on working, but in
vain. In some cases, after the rioters had gone away, the workmen came back of themselves and asked leave to resume work,
but these were compelled by a new demonstration to desist.
Attacks were made by the strikers on the water supply and on
the slaughterhouses; when attacking the electric station, the
crowd threw stones at the soldiers, five of whom had to be taken
to hospital: a few discharges in the air were the only reply, and
the electric light was soon cut off. From threats the crowd soon
passed to blows. There was no doubt that Shayévich and his
friends had for the time lost all control: he quite failed to get a
hearing, and the strikers went their own way without him.
Bread had risen to two or three times its normal price. On
July 18, the City Prefect gave notice that all disorders would be
repressed by armed force, but his instructions to the Police-
Master were not carried out. Dock labourers and sailors of the
volunteer fleet were compelled by force to join in the strike. The
City Prefect himself drove about the town and did his best to
restore order; more troops were now brought into the town, and
gradually Odessa began to resume its normal appearance. A
last attempt of the strikers to stop the bakers from working was
defeated by the soldiers. Many strikers, when arrested, maintained that they had simply been egged on by the assertions of
their leaders; these had told them that the troops and the town
authorities had instructions from St. Petersburg to take their
side and to help them to better their lot; they now expressed
contrition for their conduct and were ready to resume work.
The City Prefect, having obtained leave from the Minister of
the Interior, wished to arrest Shayévich, but the Police-Master
and Vasílyeff alleged that this would lead to an acute renewal of
the disorders. At the same moment arrived a telegram from the
Director of the Department of Police in St. Petersburg, advising
that the strikers should be divided into groups according to their
trades and should elect deputies to present their demands, which,
if possible, should be satisfied. The City Prefect replied that this
was impossible, as the strikers had so far made no definite demand,
and that most of them had been compelled to stop work by threats

and violence; at the same time he telegraphed once more to the Minister of the Interior for leave to arrest Shayévich. On this day Shayevich, speaking from a balcony to a great meeting, bade the strikers desist from further disorders, announced the temporary dissolution of the Unions which he had established, and invited each section of strikers to make its own demands, which, he said, would certainly be satisfied. Clearly he had been informed of the telegram from the Police Department. The demands were thereupon drawn up and distributed to the strikers, and were presented the next day to the City Prefect. They included an enormous raising of wages, to as much as 200 per cent., a reduction of the working day to eight, nine, or ten hours, more courteous treatment by the managers, and so on. In some factories the workers claimed a share in the profits, no dismissal without consent of one's fellow-workers, the discharge of certain foremen, etc. The City Prefect took no notice of these demands, and the owners, at a common meeting, declared that their workmen were really quite contented, and that the demands, having been inspired from outside, did not need to be considered. On July 19, Shayévich was, by order of the Minister of the Interior, arrested and sent away from Odessa; the City Prefect had insisted that the Police-Master should, under his own eyes, make all dispositions for this arrest. During the next four days all the factories resumed work; some employers, with the consent of the Factory Inspectors, diminished the working day by half an hour or a quarter, or slightly raised the pay of certain classes of workers. "I think it my duty," the senior Inspector continues, "to state that the conditions of working men in the factories of the town of Odessa,—their pay, their working hours, and their relations to their masters,—are quite satisfactory, and could not have called forth disorders of this kind." The temporary closing of the factories involved a trade loss of £60,000.

The Factory Inspector, as will be remembered, is a Government official appointed to look after the interests of the men; he is the authorised expert on his subject. Than an official report of the senior Inspector no better evidence can be asked for, and I have confined myself to quoting his statement throughout. We have, however, the further confirmation of a special memorandum addressed by the Minister of Finance to the Emperor, which happens to have passed under my eyes. The Minister asserts that the first attempts of the police to organise the working men were made in 1901 from the Ministry of the Interior; he mentions General Trepoff as one of the champions of this scheme; his own protests were, he says, flouted by the Minister of the Interior and by Mr. Pobyedonóstseff. The police, he says, tried to direct the working men because it looked upon them as unable to cope with their employers; but he maintains that the result has been exactly the opposite to that which was intended. Revolutionary propaganda, so far from being arrested, have thrown out far wider roots; and the whole movement has simply led to disorder. The wording of the memorandum, from which I have made the above analysis, is strong but restrained throughout.

Such intrigues, though by no means confined to Odessa, are, let us hope, exceptional, and peculiar only to the last years of the Reaction. At least the Russian Government may be said to have done as much for the men as it did for the masters. As the whole development of industry has come later in Russia than in England, the working men have still much less understanding of the conditions of a struggle between capital and labour. They have been encouraged by theorising outsiders to ask for an eight-hour day; but most of them do not know for what they are asking, and the more discontented amongst them still ask for anything which they think they have a chance of getting. An eight-hour day in Russia may easily mean a no-hours day; physique is so low and laziness is so general, that many a factory will be compelled to put up its shutters sooner than make this concession. On both sides it has been a battle of might, not of right; and we can hardly expect to turn factories into charitable institutions to be run at a loss, largely by amiable foreigners, for the benefit of Russian working men. The Government, which, as I have said, cannot be accused of acting on the principles of any broad trade policy, has tried to interpose its own academic mediation in favour of the men. If reform never meant anything more than charity, we could reasonably say that the care of the Government for its poorer subjects has accomplished greater things than that mass of convictions, moods, and interests which makes up public opinion in free countries. The workman has a school and a hospital for nothing; in his pay-book

he carries the charter of his rights.   But, if the students are not
the right leaders for the working men, they have at least taught
them to desire instruction and to seek it in their own way.   Some
of the workmen have developed a keen political sense, and have
even, as I am told by a competent English critic, made speeches
of which the leader of a great English party might be proud.
This gentleman, who had many conservative instincts, regretted
that the Emperor could not understand how much political ability
there is in these men, and how naturally it might be used as a
support for a Government which united the two principles of order
and freedom.   But the Government of the Reaction has feared
initiative more than anything else.   What the workmen ask, and
what the Government will not concede, is the right to fight out
their own questions freely with their employers by the means
customary in other countries, that is, by trade unions and strikes ;
but to give up its claim of wardenship seems to the Government
like an abnegation of one of the first principles of autocracy.
Here, too, then it is in direct conflict with the demands of the
times, and that, too, on a point of principle.   The new factory
race will grow faster and faster ; trade interests will assume
greater and greater political importance ; the old system of
hedges and ditches will inevitably go down, and the men will
be left more free to fight out their questions for themselves.   It
does not follow that they will at once be better off ; it is more
than probable that many of them will regret the old system of
tutelage ; but, though they are likely to pass through such a
temporary depression as was the result of the Emancipation, one
cannot doubt as to which is the right side to take in the great
duel between initiative and wardenship.   Under normal circumstances, initiative, when once triumphant, is likely to provide the
remedy for its own ailments.   The working men will learn to
appreciate far better what work really is.   If the present régime
were to be eternal, the industrial advance of the country would
be practically impossible ; but, when the barriers are down, the
natural ability of the Russian peasant, which has already brought
him to the town in the search for better conditions of life, will,
one may feel sure, carry him on over this new great transition.
Such a transition cannot be easy ; in Russia it was some years ago
hardly to be thought of.   The industrial race is still in the making ;

the war came, and gave an immense vogue to the doctrines of the Social Democrats ; authority was disorganised, and now was the time to make any demand with impunity ; but already the working men, after a short experience of politics, are keen to throw off also that other wardenship, the intellectual tutelage of theorising students. They joined willingly in a general strike of a non-party kind to champion the principle of reform ; this strike resulted in the Manifesto of October 30, 1905. But when another general strike was proclaimed in the cause of the eight-hours day, the workmen themselves confessed that it was a mistake to use such a weapon for the removing of special grievances. With admirable good sense, their delegates requested that those Social Democrat members of their committee who were not working men should leave them to deal with their own interests. With a simplicity which is natural in Russia, the Social Democrats left the room, and the real working men, left to themselves, then settled to stop the strike.

I add a few comments of Englishmen and others on Russian trade.

An Englishman resident in Russia :

Factory owners have the greatest difficulties to contend with. Capital, which would elsewhere be sufficient, is here inadequate ; there must be a considerable reserve. Results are not immediate ; thus the smaller businesses are often not able to last, and the foreign investor is not willing to launch good money after what he considers as money lost; if he came and saw how great are the opportunities and how great is the need of a large outlay at the start, he would think differently. A factory must be ready for every kind of stoppage or breakdown ; a great supply of fuel must be kept on the spot; and, as all of it is wood, it takes up a lot of room. The machines must be the very best, for they cannot be repaired on the spot, and it takes a long time to order anything new from England or elsewhere. The railways are not to be depended on ; they are a monopoly conducted without business principles : for this reason cotton mills would prefer to get their raw material from the Americans, who will at least send it in good time, rather than from Tashkend, which can never keep its engagements, and may excuse itself by the fact that some bridge has broken down. The demands of the Government for the insurance of workmen and for hospitals, schools, and barracks are a further embarrassment to capital. The labour troubles have accentuated all difficulties. Some factories have to pay for the protection of the troops, and then do not get it. Small businesses go down at such a time. The larger businesses either let them die, or, by advancing money, practically secure the control of them for the future. The workmen are paid quite as much as they are worth; labour, anyone will tell you, is just as dear here as elsewhere, because it takes two men to do the job of one. Russian factories cannot yet do the finer kinds of work.

A trade expert :

There are great possibilities in the country; they are only very partially developed. The Ural district is full of ores, but there is no coal; so wood has to be used as fuel. It is the same on many of the railways, including all those of Siberia; for instance, from Moscow to Yaroslavl coal is used, and from Yaroslavl to Archangel only wood. Apparently there is plenty of wood left in the country. The coal of the Dónets region is poor, and means of transport are so bad, that it is as expensive in North Russia as the far superior coal of Newcastle. The Russians are beginning to make some of their own big machinery. All cotton goods for peasant wear are Russian-made. Englishmen would be wrong in thinking that there are insuperable obstacles to the starting of English businesses in Russia. Russian workmen are well suited for certain kinds of work : they are strong and hardy, and they are used to hardships. But they have not much initiative or perseverance, they do not keep steady, and they do not much care how little they earn. He puts down the labour troubles chiefly to the students; but he thinks them artificial. The officials dare not stop them (1905). In Moscow most of the men did not want to strike, but crowds of demonstrators came round and fetched them out by force.

An English trader :

The big spinning machines are still bought in England, but large machinery of other kinds is now made in Moscow and Tula. The great Lancashire and Yorkshire firms once had a great business here, and where there is no need to strike out a new line their trade still holds good; but in general, English trade is declining : it is being supplanted, not by Russian, but by German businesses. Englishmen will not trade in a sensible way: they expect everyone to speak English; they quote all their prices in pounds and shillings; they do not know the cost of carriage of goods, and therefore before giving estimates they always say: "We must consult the firm." A German is ready with all these figures in advance. On the other hand, Englishmen would find plenty of trade if they only knew how to work it; the laws of the country are by no means a fatal bar to the establishment of businesses by foreigners.

A German lecturer in a Higher Technical School:

Some time ago Russia had no respectable text-books of engineering work, and there were but few magazines which dealt with the subject; thus the engineer had to know foreign languages; this gave an advantage to foreigners when applying for posts. But there has been a great change, and now very many of the engineers are Russians. The country has great possibilities. There is plenty of unworked coal, and Russia will some day supply it to all the world. Russia still buys most of her spinning machines from England, and much of her larger machinery from America; there are also large importations from Germany; but she is now beginning to make big machinery for herself. There was a great deal of trading enterprise before the war; it has been temporarily arrested (June, 1905); but when peace is made it is sure, he thinks, to develope faster than ever.

The natural resources of Russia are not to be confused with the financial credit of the Russian Government. Even the Government, with the help of foreign loans, has been able to live through an exhausting war and exceptional internal disturbances. It has often been prematurely declared to be on the verge of bankruptcy; but its position is now critical, and, as in the case of the old French Monarchy, it is this factor that augurs best for the development of the powers of the Duma; Count Witte may, from one point of view, be described as one of the last of the Comptrollers of Finance, called in to deal with the imperative need of getting money. But we must avoid the common mistake of our ancestors of 1792, who all seem to have imagined that France was being ruined by the Revolution. The opportunities of trade must indeed be immense in Russia, or foreign capital would not have continued to exploit them under the disadvantageous conditions of a very unpractical régime. All the best-informed Russian traders are agreed that trade has surmounted the wave of political troubles with an astonishing vitality. The prospects for the future are far brighter. All that is needed is the removal of a kind of extinguisher which is at present imposed on all enterprise. When once it is removed, the immense resources of Russia will develope almost of themselves, and we may even anticipate a period which will recall the beginning of railways in England. That time, when it comes, will offer a vast field to foreign enterprise. Much as Russian industry has developed of late years, it is not likely to be equal to all the new opportunities; and, if Englishmen are ready to do something to recover and extend their trade connections with Russia, they will have a unique chance of doing so. Only it is essential that preparation should be made in advance. Englishmen who are to enter into trade-relations with Russia must be equipped with the Russian language, and must have a reasonable acquaintance with the trading conditions of the country.

PART IV.

CHAPTER XIV.

——✦——

I.

The Claim for the "Freedoms" and a National Assembly.

THE Eleven Points adopted by the Zemstvo Congress of November 19 to 21, 1904, mark an epoch in Russian history.[1] The document bore throughout the impress of Mr. Shipóff's loyalty to tradition and respect for the throne. Personal freedom from the arbitrary control of officials and the calling of some kind of national assembly were put forward, not as demands, but as requests, and the Government was left to settle all details. At the same time the principle that the Emperor must be brought into touch with his people was stated with a simple frankness, and it was clear that behind that modest petition stood practically the whole mass of the educated classes.

Soon after the Congress the Emperor called a meeting of his chief counsellors. Of this meeting we as yet have only one account. It represents that, when the question of reform was raised, Mr. Pobyedonóstseff told the Emperor that he had not the right to infringe the principle of autocracy, that his position as Head of the Church would not allow of it. Mr. Witte is said to have answered that an autocracy which had no power to make changes would not be an autocracy at all. In any case it is clear that the reactionaries won the day. Prince Mirsky asked leave to resign, and though his request was not at once granted, his power was already gone.

When, in the spring, the "Liberators" had attempted to organise a public banquet, they had found the war mood too strong for them. But on December 3 meetings were held in many towns to celebrate the fortieth anniversary of the reform of the Law-Courts. Many of these meetings took the form

[1] See p. 88.

of public dinners. In St. Petersburg a dinner was arranged for
December 2. It was postponed in consequence of a collision
between the public and the police, but on the next day
600 guests met in the Pavloff Hall under the presidency of
a well-known Liberator, Mr. Korolyénko; a resolution which
followed closely on the lines of the Eleven Points was adopted
and signed. In Moscow, on the same day, similar dinners ending
with similar resolutions were held by the lawyers and by the
Justices of the Peace; on December 4 lawyers, professors, and
journalists met at a dinner in the Hermitage.   On December 4
the lawyers of St. Petersburg organised a demonstration of protest
against the postponement of a banquet arranged by them.
Banquets were also held in the provinces; at Sarátoff the
guests numbered 1,500. In Russia members of the professions
could under certain conditions meet to discuss professional
subjects. The reformers had the tactical instinct to seize upon
this means of making themselves heard. Doctors met presumably to discuss medical matters, and one of them would rise to
say : " We cannot discharge our duty as doctors in Russia unless
we have freedom of person, freedom of conscience, freedom of the
Press, freedom of assembly, freedom of association, and a national
assembly." In other words, the vast majority of intelligent opinion
formed itself into line under the banner of the Eleven Points.
The very fact that the professional unit could thus be used, that
all doctors or all lawyers could be unanimous on a political
question, made it all the more evident that the Government was
quite out of touch with the nation.   On December 18 there
was a banquet of engineers in St. Petersburg, with a resolution
on the needs of Russian industry ; on December 27 there was a
great dinner in honour of the Decembrists of 1825.   The
Government prevented some of the meetings ; more frequently it
punished the owners of the restaurants at which they had taken
place. This led to important street demonstrations in St. Petersburg on December 11, and in Moscow on December 19. In the
latter case the students came into conflict with the police.

On December 13 the Zemstva received the adhesion of
another most important ally. The Town Councils, being elected
largely from the merchant class, had so far been backward
in the cause of reform ; but in Moscow, at the last election,

many Intelligents had been elected as representing important corporations, such as the University. The new Moscow Town Council, in the presence of a numerous audience, unanimously decided to telegraph to the Minister of the Interior that the "real obstacle to the further development of civic economy was to be found in those conditions which had been imposed by law upon the community"; the Council definitely adopted the principles of the Eleven Points; other Town Councils too followed the example of Moscow. Meanwhile the Zemstvo deputies had returned to their respective Zemstva, which proceeded in some cases to ratify what had been done at the Congress. Even the Marshals of the Gentry, elected as they were only by the large landowners, had met to make a moderate plea for reform, and one of them, Mr. Mukhánoff, who was also president of the local Zemstvo, carried through the Zemstvo Assembly a bold repetition of the Eleven Points. This address was telegraphed to the Emperor, and reached him in the midst of the congratulations on his name-day. Those who were present say that they never saw him so angry; on the margin of the telegram he wrote the words "Impudent and tactless." But the voice of public opinion was too powerful to be resisted, and on December 25 there was issued an Imperial Edict which spoke of reforms.

In this decree the Emperor desired to distinguish between "what really corresponded to the interests of the people" and the "faulty and temporary accidents of a gust of aspirations." He was not unwilling to make material modifications in the laws if it were really necessary; peasant questions would be attended to. For the rest, the officials would be compelled to observe the law; the Local Councils would have their jurisdiction extended as far as possible; the Law-Courts would be unified and made more independent; workmen would be insured by the State; the administrative ordinances would be revised and their sphere of action limited as far as possible; the edict of toleration of March, 1903, would probably be extended; and the law of aliens would be modified. Superfluous restrictions on the Press would be abolished. The Committee of Ministers would be invited to suggest how these principles should be applied; that is to say, the bureaucracy was to undertake the

reform of itself. The Official Communication which was
issued two days later accused the popular leaders, such as Mr.
Shipóff, " of trying to bring confusion into the life of society and
of the State. . . . Their efforts had resulted in a series of noisy
conventions which put forward various inadmissible demands,
and in mob demonstrations on the streets, with open resistance to the appeals of the authorities." Such phenomena were
declared to be " alien to the Russian people, which was true to
the ancient principles of the existing Imperial order, though an
attempt was being made to give to the above-named disturbances
the unwarranted significance of a national movement." The
leaders, " blinded by delusive fancies, did not realise that they
were working not for their country, but for its enemies." Conventions of an anti-governmental character would be stopped by
all means that legally pertained to the authorities. The Zemstva
and Town Councils were ordered to return within the limits of
their jurisdiction, and not to touch those questions which they
had no legal right to discuss. Their presidents were threatened
with punishment if they permitted such discussion, and the
newspapers were ordered " to restore peace in the public mind,
which had lately deviated from its proper direction." Clearly this
pronouncement was hopelessly below the level of the situation.
It is possible to explain the remarkable difference between the
two twin documents, the Decree and the Communication; the
second was to serve the purpose of a keeper ring; at the
moment when the Government found it necessary to make concessions to a united public opinion, it reasserted its own supremacy.
But this was not the way to secure the confidence of the people ;
on the contrary, the gap between it and the Government was now
more visible than ever. At the beginning of January the
Technical Congress in Moscow and the Natural Science Congress in Tiflis were closed, but these were trifling victories. At
the other end of the Empire General Stoessel surrendered Port
Arthur to the Japanese, before the means of resistance were
exhausted and against the advice of his council of war.
Scarcely less significant of the demoralisation of the army was
the shot fired against the Emperor on January 19 from the
fortress of Peter and Paul. Nicholas left his capital, not to
return for more than a year; and he was from this time

onward more than ever cut off from all knowledge of his people.

So far, the movement of reform had been in the hands of the Zemstva and the professional classes. Suddenly the whole area of political interest was widened by the events of January 22. The propaganda of Zubátoff amongst working men had already in some cases resulted in the spread of revolutionary opinions. Amongst the adherents of the equivocal Zubátoff was the priest Gapon, whose objects it is still more difficult to define. By his own account, Gapon became a priest in order to take part in the Zubátoff movement, and received money from Zubátoff. Naturally he had not the sympathy of the Social Democrats. From one point of view, his successful organisation of the working classes may be regarded as one of the first attempts to draw them into a purely economic movement, independent of the revolutionary theories of propagandist Intelligents. What political direction he meant to give to this movement we cannot say. He was a man of very great personal magnetism, but excitable and uncertain of temperament ; perhaps he himself did not see his way clearly. His very numerous followers were divided into sections, each of which elected an " Elder." The Elders formed a kind of central committee; they were implicitly obeyed by their electors, and were themselves completely under the influence of Gapon. To them he seems to have communicated only his tactical directions. The labour troubles in the Caucasus had produced a great impression in Moscow and St. Petersburg. The great Putíloff factory in St. Petersburg struck work ; and a deputation, headed by Gapon, demanded better economic conditions. The manager gave an evasive reply, and the strike continued ; but there was no resort to violence. The example of the Putíloff men was followed by one factory after another, and the demands were almost always identical. On January 19 was established a strike committee which represented the workmen of many factories ; relief was organised on a large scale. Meeting with no success with the employers, the committee decided on the characteristically Russian step of presenting a mass petition to the Emperor. The petition, which was drawn up by Gapon, may be divided into two halves : side by side with the economic claims there was a résumé of those political demands

which had been put forward by the Zemstva and professional
classes. In all probability, even Gapon's own followers were at
that time almost exclusively interested in the economic claims.
Certainly it was so with most of the outsiders who joined in
during the march to the Winter Palace. The working classes at
this time had no common political programme; if they had had
one, it would not necessarily have been that of the Zemstva.
By including the Zemstvo minimum in his petition, Gapon probably meant to consolidate the claims of the whole people; but
the Emperor could easily have dissociated the economic demands
from the political. If he had met the demonstrators and had
told them that he himself would preside over a Commission to
deal with their grievances, probably even Gapon and his Elders
would from that moment have counted for nothing, and the
petitioners would have gone home satisfied. But it is reported
on credible authority that, when asked what he would do if the
Emperor refused all the demands, Gapon declared that he would
wave a red flag and try to secure the Emperor's person, presumably in order to "free him from his advisers." Under such
circumstances, we cannot wonder that the Emperor did not come
at all.

Speaking on January 21, Gapon told his followers to come
without any arms, as they were "not robbers, but citizens." He
secured from them a promise to "die, if need be, in the holy
cause." The chief factories of St. Petersburg lie on the outskirts
of the city. On January 22 bands of workmen marched in
orderly processions converging from the suburbs towards the
Winter Palace; they invited the numerous onlookers to join
them. Troops were posted at all points round the city; they
broke up the processions, in some cases by firing upon them.
Gapon himself never got near the Winter Palace, but fell under
the body of a workman who was just in front of him; he was
eventually rescued by his friends. Several of the demonstrators,
when the processions were broken up, passed separately into the
city and walked up the Nevsky Prospekt; these and the
onlookers who had joined them reached the square in front of
the palace, but were pushed back towards the Moika Canal,
where troops fired upon them; this crowd received the fire with
the roar of a wild beast surprised. In the Alexander Garden,

little boys who had climbed the trees to watch what was going on were shot down like birds. No resistance was made, but a few officers who were driving down the streets were violently handled. In the Basil Island, to which many of the workmen retired, a half-hearted attempt at self-defence was made behind hastily constructed barricades. In the afternoon and evening, prominent Liberal writers conducted meetings of protest in the Public Library and at the Free Economic Society. Gapon was present in disguise at one of these meetings, and was afterwards smuggled across the frontier. The Russian revolutionaries in Switzerland received him with a mixture of sympathy and suspicion. Later on he visited England and Monte Carlo, and only returned to Russia after Count Witte became Premier. He then again entered into relations with the Government, but his political significance was at an end. The organisation which he had created was almost crushed out of existence by the events of January 22.

That day was, in many ways, one of the landmarks of the liberation movement. General Trepoff, a policeman and the son of a policeman, was hastily summoned from Moscow. His father was a foundling, who had risen to high rank as a guardian of the life of the Tsar; he himself was a man of narrow intelligence and little education. As Head of the Moscow Police he had carried out the ultra-reactionary policy of the Grand Duke Sergius, and had stood fire more than once in the cause which he had chosen. Himself free from all mercenary motives, he honestly believed that police machinery could save his master. The policy of prohibition, so long as it was a simple question of giving orders, was carried out by him in the most whole-hearted way. He was now appointed, first, Governor-General of St. Petersburg, with extraordinary powers, and later Assistant Minister of the Interior, with a jurisdiction over all the police of the Empire and the right of acting independently of the Minister, Mr. Bulýghin. Mr. Bulýghin himself had been the coadjutor of the Grand Duke Sergius in Moscow, but his name stood for bureaucratic correctness and moderation. The practical independence allowed to General Trepoff established another dualism in the heart of the Government.[1] The Governors of

[1] See p. 156.

provinces all over Russia were now in a very awkward position : they could not know what instructions the local Gendarmes might have received from St. Petersburg, and yet, as will be remembered, their own local police were bound to co-operate with the Gendarmes without asking for any reasons ; the Assistant Minister was their real master, and could not be checked by the Minister. One of them, Prince Urúsoff, Governor of Tver, wrote to explain that he could not approve of the policy of Trepoff, and resigned office. In nominating Trepoff, the Emperor practically confessed himself to be at variance with the vast majority of his subjects.

Trepoff at once proceeded to forbid all street gatherings, and arrested even the leaders of the Liberals, who could only be indirectly associated with the petition of January 22. It would seem that, identifying in the usual way reformers with revolutionaries, he believed in the existence of a provisional revolutionary Government, of which he supposed Maxim Gorky, a man of no political ability or importance, to be the head. Gorky was amongst the arrested, but the list also included some of the most honoured of the Moderate Liberals. After a short confinement these prisoners were set free. It was thought worth while to organise a bogus deputation of workmen, who were received by the Emperor, treated to a good dinner, and allowed to admire the beauties of the Palace gardens. Two Government Commissions, appointed to inquire into labour questions, failed one after the other. That of Senator Shidlóvsky never got to work at all ; and that of the Minister of Finance, Mr. Kokóvtseff, never carried out the prescribed condition of admitting representatives of the employers. Gapon's clubs were suppressed, and a large number of workmen were deported to their country homes. Nothing contributed more than this to the spread of revolutionary principles in Russia.

The Social Democrats, some of whom had joined at the last moment in the processions, now claimed to have shared in the initiative of the march, and were able to secure very many new adherents throughout the Empire. The echoes of the struggle of the Putíloff men aroused a series of strikes all over the country, and more especially of course in those western and southern districts where the population was mostly alien, where industry was strongly developed, where the Jews were an important factor, and where the Social Democrats were most numerous. Some of these strikes went on into the late summer; the most important were those of Oryékhovo-Zúyevo and Ivánovo-Vosnesénsk. In the last-named place, which is in the heart of Great Russia, the workmen were drawn from a large number of peasant villages, and it was the resources of agriculture which enabled the strike to last for more than two months. Thus the contagion spread from the workmen to the peasants. Russian workmen had as yet but little idea of combination and only a vague sense of their needs. In many cases it would seem that the men simply seized the opportunity of the prevailing disorder to ask for anything they could get. It is notable that, whereas the houses of managers were sometimes wrecked, the men never laid hands on the factory itself, recognising it as the means of their livelihood. In this chaos the Factory Inspectors found themselves buffeted about between masters and men. The protection of the troops was sometimes sought, but the soldiers, whilst causing great expense to their clients, were of little service; in fact, masters and men had an opportunity of fighting out their own battles, and this state of things rapidly developed amongst the working classes the idea of Trade Unionism.

The events of January 22 and the results which they produced amongst the working classes gave a very much wider scope to the public interest in the question of Reform; but, now that many new questions had been raised, it was far more difficult for any one organisation such as that of the Zemstva to lay down a common programme. During the next few months, each of the many units which claimed Reform was feeling its own way and raising questions rather than answering them; but in many cases the quick Russian mind found the right tactical word for the moment, and the Russian genius for standing together like one great family made organisation a very much easier matter than it would otherwise have been. Thus was maintained a kind of unity between workers of widely different kinds; at least all were united against the dictatorship of Trepoff, and many were only too hasty in their altruistic efforts to realise the claims of other classes than their own. The Government still possessed the railways, the post, and the telegraphs;

and the immense distances made it almost impossible for the movements in any two areas to coincide in date. Thus Russia for a long
time presented the spectacle of an enormous field in all parts of
which intermittent bonfires were burning at different times, and the
Government still had the means of extinguishing them one by one ;
but the very persistence, with which the bonfires kept lighting up
again, showed how deep and how general was the discontent of
the people. The disorders of course took different forms. In one
place there would be an abortive public meeting, in another signs
of revolutionary violence, and in a third some attack upon students
or schoolboys, which would be interpreted by the reactionaries as
a kind of national vengeance, but in fact was often traceable to
the promptings of the police. The most common form of all was
the strike, for, when force was the chief weapon of the other side,
it was safest and wisest to limit oneself to something in the nature
of a passive resistance. It was very easy for people to drift into
this programme, and it was impossible for the authorities to deal
effectively with great movements of this kind, recurring as they
constantly did at almost all points of the Empire. The harassed
Governor had hardly reported that the strike of the bakers in
A. had been suppressed, when the strike of the tramway men
had begun in B. The strikers were themselves surprised and
excited at their success, and many employed the means which
had come into fashion to ask for anything they might like to have ;
thus there were strikes not only of factory hands, not only of whole
trades in a given area, but even of schoolboys and of domestic
servants. Everyone was striking against somebody else. The
working men were at issue with their employers ; the peasants
began to present claims to the country gentry, and especially
claims of land ; the servants of the Zemstva, the so-called
Third Element, also held their meetings, and sent their
demands to their employers. The students were more or less
directly engaged against the Government ; but the schoolboys
followed the general fashion by putting forward a demand for the
abolition of compulsory Greek. The nursemaids might come
out on the cry "One nurse, one baby." It would, then, be quite
impossible to see in every strike the expression of some real and
special grievance. Much of the agitation was simply fishing in
troubled waters, and we can easily foresee that such a social chaos

would lead to the formation of a class of professional malcontents, who would later be excellent material both for the revolutionary Fighting Organisations and for the reactionary "Black Gangs." Yet, if there was not always a special grievance, there was always a general one : all alike found their social life made intolerable by that system of sheer prohibition which had been developed during the Second Reaction and had now culminated in the dictatorship of Trepoff.

We have seen that the alien parts of the Empire had most ground for complaint against the Government. In almost every such district there were special causes of discontent. Often class quarrels were made infinitely more bitter by racial differences. Thus in the Caucasus, as soon as the weakness of official control was apparent, Mussulmans and Armenians flew at each other's throats. The Poles indeed never attempted any general rising ; but with them the claims of Polish nationality helped to complicate the exceedingly critical questions of industry. The Little Russians of the Ukraine had a vague tradition of independence ; and here too industrial questions were very acute. Races which had for centuries been in economic bondage, such as the Lithuanians, the Letts, and the Ests, being naturally anti-governmental, dreamed of establishing little local republics; the Tartars had religious and racial grievances to settle. The Russians of Siberia had long, for economic reasons, desired a greater measure of freedom from home control. But if the spectacle of disorders was confusing to the eye, in each case, if one cared to analyse, one could distinguish a common grievance and a common remedy. All alike were protesting against the rigid control of the bureaucracy. Even in the Caucasus, where it was the Russian Government that had kept the peace between warring peoples, the bureaucracy had made the ruinous mistake of identifying its interests with one of those peoples, the Orthodox Georgians. All alike claimed the extension of local self-government. The bureaucracy had failed to satisfy the needs of every corner of the Empire, and the same Liberal programme of decentralisation which was put forward by the Zemstva would satisfy all the aspirations of the alien races and religions. It can be positively stated that not a single fraction demanded separation from the Empire.[1]

[1] Conversations with representatives of each of these fractions in the Duma.

Now that we have traced the general picture of the Empire in the summer of 1905, we can with better advantage follow the record of the main events. In the beginning of February, were held the annual sittings of the local Zemstva and of the Assemblies of the Gentry. They sent to the Emperor addresses in which they urged him, sometimes with self-restraint, sometimes with insistence, to call together a National Assembly. Such was also the content of addresses from factory owners of the Moscow and St. Petersburg areas. Some Zemstva, declaring that work was impossible under the existing conditions, adjourned their sessions. The Universities and Higher Schools, in which the professors and the students were now acting in concert, took the same step. On January 31 there were street disturbances in Tomsk (Siberia). Eight days later three Polish provinces and three Districts of the Caucasus were put under martial law. In December members of the Zemstva had been badly handled in the streets of Tamboff; in St. Petersburg students were wounded in a street conflict after January 22, and in Moscow on February 17; in Kazán on February 19 students were pursued down the streets; in Pskoff on the 20th, and in Kursk on the 25th, the police came into conflict with bands of schoolboys. Such were the beginnings of the Black Gang organisation; and there were priests in Moscow, Uralsk, and Sarátoff, who incited their parishioners to take vengeance on the Intelligents. On February 19, Armenians and Mussulmans attacked each other in Batúm and in Bakú (Caucasus), and many were killed. In Georgia, which had been in disorder for three years, there was a general rising. More and more provinces were placed under martial law. Perhaps the most ominous symptom was that the peasants of Russia Proper were now developing their demand for more land.

There had been a series of political murders in the Caucasus. On February 10, an attempt was made on the life of the Police-Master of Mohilyéff; on February 17, a blow was struck which bereaved the sovereign himself. The Grand Duke Sergius, who was the Emperor's uncle, was one of the most convinced reactionaries in Russia. He had not hesitated to express the opinion that "this people wants the stick." As Governor-General of Moscow, he had been peculiarly hostile both to the Jews and to the students. Morózoff, a public-spirited merchant who had sent immense supplies to the Red Cross Society, came to complain to him that these goods were being sold in the streets of Moscow; the Grand Duke, instead of punishing the peculators, vented his anger on Morózoff. The *Moscow Gazette* was his organ; and, as we know, this paper was always inveighing against aliens, foreigners, students, and the Zemstva. It would seem that to the public causes of his unpopularity there were added many others which were purely personal. The revolutionaries had recently declared that, though they were not going to touch the Emperor, whose indecision they considered to be very useful to themselves, they would remove, one by one, his most reactionary advisers. The assassination of Sergius was announced to him in advance, and was undertaken by one Kaláyeff, a young man with the conviction and resolution of the fanatic. As the carriage of the Grand Duke passed out of the dark gateway of St. Nicholas into the Kremlin Kaláyeff stepped forward, launched his bomb, and without attempting to escape stood gazing awestruck. The Grand Duke was blown into fragments. The population made no pretence of indignation or of regret. The appointment of Prince Mirsky as Minister after the murder of Plehwe had lent colour to the popular idea that bombs were the only argument to which the Government would listen. The murder of the Grand Duke Sergius was followed on March 3 by an Edict which definitely promised some kind of a National Assembly. We cannot but contrast the attention paid to the bomb of Kaláyeff with the reception accorded to the requests of the Congress of Shipóff. But, apart from this, the words in which the new concessions were announced were very ill chosen. The Emperor issued three kindred documents: a Manifesto in which he reasserted his authority and an Edict and a Rescript in which he promised reforms. Any other course would have been unworthy of him so soon after the murder of his uncle. But he adopted a wording which suggested that he still identified the Reformers with the Terrorists.

The Manifesto, after stating that "Divine Providence had visited the country with grievous trials," accused the reformers of "raising confusion, to the joy of our enemies" at the moment when "the most illustrious sons of Russia" were fighting in the war. "Blinded by pride, the evil-intentioned leaders of a movement of riot impudently lay hands on the fundamental principles of the Russian Empire, sanctified by the Orthodox Church and confirmed by the laws; they propose to break the natural tie with the past, to destroy the existing Imperial order, and in its place to found a new government of the country on principles alien to our fatherland." Meanwhile, in the Edict of the same date, the Council of Ministers is ordered to "consider any views, submitted by private persons or by institutions, on questions which touch the perfecting of the Imperial order and the improvement of the national well-being." The Rescript to Mr. Bulýghin, after thanking public bodies for their congratulatory addresses on the birth of an heir to the throne, proceeds as follows: "Their readiness to come at my call, to work with me for the realisation of the changes which I have proposed, has entirely answered to the wish of my heart. Continuing the Imperial task of my crowned ancestors, I have decided for the future, with God's help, to invite the worthiest persons, invested with the confidence of the people and chosen from the population, to share in the preparation and discussion of legislative proposals." The Emperor foresees the difficulty of carrying through great changes and at the same time preserving the foundations of the Empire ; and he orders a special conference, under the presidency of the Minister, to discuss the best ways of realising his intention. By an order to the Senate, the country is invited to declare its opinion on Imperial questions.

The public interested itself most in the important passage which invited persons and institutions to send in their "views and proposals." This invitation was turned to good account. Town Councils and Zemstva elected special commissions for drawing up their suggestions as to the National Assembly. The chief result of the invitation was that parties began to define themselves. A few reactionaries of no great standing organised themselves in the defence of absolutism. The vast mass of the people was in favour of a National Assembly ; but many Conservatives desired that its functions should only be consultative and stood out for indirect election. Shipóff, while preserving throughout his own independence, was inclined towards this view. The Zemstvo Constitutionalists, who had formed the majority of the first Zemstvo Congress, met at the beginning of March to discuss their position, and adopted the precise formula of universal, equal, direct, and secret suffrage. Some of them were for disregarding the Commission of Mr. Bulýghin, but a considerable majority insisted that representatives of the Zemstva elected, not nominated, should be admitted to the discussion of the proposals, with full freedom of speech; it is interesting to note that this view was shared by General Trepoff.[1] The majority were in favour of a Second Chamber, consisting of deputies chosen by the Zemstva and Town Councils when the latter should have been reorganised on a basis of universal franchise. This conference decided almost unanimously in favour of the increase of peasant holdings, and of the compulsory sale of some of the land of private owners. About the same date, deputies from different Town Councils met for the first time and came to very similar conclusions.

The Zemstvo Constitutionalists were the natural link between the Zemstva and the professional classes. These last welcomed with special alacrity the invitation to send in their views to the Minister. From January to May they were rapidly organising themselves. Professional conferences of all kinds met in the capitals and in the chief towns, and each profession showed its unanimity on political questions by forming itself into a union. One of the first unions to form itself was that of the Engineers and Technicians. Its foundations were laid at the banquet of December 18, 1904. The Academic Union, consisting both of professors and students, was formed on the lines of a programme drafted by Professor Vernádsky, of Moscow,[2] at the end of December. The Office Clerks and Book-keepers formed their union on March 12, the Teachers and Workers in Primary Education on March 25, the Medicals at the beginning of April, the Lawyers and the champions of Full Rights for Jews at the same time, the Pharmacists on April 15, the Writers on the 18th, the advocates of Full Rights for Women on May 9, and the Secondary School Teachers in the same month. One of the last and most important of the unions was that of the Railway Servants. From this list it will be clear that the unions embraced the mass of professional intelligence; to take an instance, nearly every doctor belonged to the Union of Medicals. Some amongst them, such as the Unions of Lawyers, Writers, and Advocates of Women's Rights, represented the more irresponsible section of the Intelligence,

[1] Conversation with the late Prince S. N. Trubetskóy.
[2] Later Vice-Rector of the University.

but others, such as the agricultural experts, the doctors, and the primary teachers, had a direct connection with the work of the Zemstva and Town Councils, which had done so much to put the educated classes in touch with the needs of the peasants and workmen. The engineers, who were always to the fore in the movement for reform, had secured in other ways a practical experience of the national needs. Many of the Russian Intelligents are not far removed by instincts and associations from the labouring classes, and in the Union of Railway Servants we see an instance of how it was possible for both Intelligents and working men to organise themselves on very similar lines. This union was a beginning of more definite organisation amongst the labouring classes. Later there were formed several other unions, including even a Union of Officials for the reform of officialdom and a Liberal Union of Policemen. The programmes of all the unions were practically identical, and were developed from the original minimum requests of the Zemstvo Congress of November : they claimed a National Assembly elected by universal, equal, direct, and secret suffrage, inviolability of person, and freedom of speech, of the Press, of association, and of meeting. The unions met in various buildings, as opportunity offered, and submitted suggestions to the public or to the Minister. Such were, for instance, the note of 198 engineers on the needs of Russian industry (December 18), the note on the needs of education drawn up by the Academic Union, the resolution of the doctors (December 31st), the note on the necessity of abolishing the restrictions on the Jews (March 9), the note of the primary teachers (March 25), and the note on the needs of Secondary Schools. Many of these notes were the original programmes of the unions concerned.

Towards the beginning of this movement Professor Milyukóff, a "Liberator" in close touch with the Zemstva, and one of the most acute politicians in Russia, had conceived the idea of massing all the unions into a Union of Unions. The meeting of protest on January 22 furthered the idea. A few persons constituted themselves as a central committee, and invited deputies from each union. So far they acted only as an intelligence department, and Professor Milyukóff never intended to swamp the individuality of each union in any central body. Many of the unions were themselves still in process of formation ; but when the Congresses of the unions had enabled men to acquaint themselves more nearly with political questions and with each other, Milyukóff's idea became capable of execution. On May 21, delegates from fourteen unions met in Moscow. Here was established a loose organisation, which left absolutely free the action of each union. All were, however, declared to be conducting a struggle for the political liberation of Russia on the principles of democracy. A second Congress was held on June 4 in Moscow, after the battle of Tsushima. Without committing itself to any definite tactics, the Union of Unions made suggestions founded on the common experience of the several unions, and, by a vaguely worded resolution, recognised all means of combating the bureaucracy. Certainly one of the most effective of these means was suggested by the central committee itself. When, in June, some persons were prosecuted for belonging to the Union of Engineers, their fellow-members filled up and forwarded to the police the following declaration : " In view of the prosecution of some members of the Union, in accordance with article 126 of the Criminal Code, for belonging to the Union, I declare that I belong to the Union, and if belonging to it is a crime within the meaning of article 126, then I am equally guilty with the persons who have been prosecuted, and am under the same responsibility." So many engineers signed this formula that the authorities, overcome by the hopelessness of the task, set free those who had been arrested. The policy of Milyukóff, then, was one of passive resistance; but the resolution which approved of all methods was easily interpreted to cover political assassination. Milyukóff himself was always opposed to such methods; but he had no business to tamper with the question. In presence of the overwhelming material resources of the bureaucracy, he was certainly bound to secure allies amongst the general public ; but he ought never to have deferred to the views of the Terrorists. In so doing, he sought his allies in the wrong place ; and thus put upon the beginnings of the new Liberal party a taint of opportunism and worse, which was later to weaken the claims of the first Imperial Duma.

The Union of Unions continued its activity throughout the summer ; but obviously its value was only temporary. In the country, a doctor might find himself isolated from most other members of his union, and his natural affinity would be with the schoolmaster who was working in the same village. There was no reason why all the doctors in Russia should have one set of political views and all schoolmasters another. As a means of asserting the opinion of the professional classes, the unions had been of immense service ; but their members now began to wish for more frankly political organisations. Milyukóff, who had foreseen this, tried to restrain the central committee from compromising itself by too many definitions; but after his imprisonment in the autumn the Union of Unions passed into the hands of irresponsible doctrinaires; and though it continued to exist, its pronouncements were no longer representative. The more moderate section of its members passed into the Cadet party ; the more extreme section took some part in the abortive Moscow rising of December. The working men had by that time made themselves independent of the Union of Unions; and, as it now represented only a very small party, it failed to have any very sensible influence on the elections for the Imperial Duma. In the summer was founded the last of the unions and far the most important, that of the peasants. Though in loose connection with the main body, it had its own programme, and must be studied as a separate development.

The work of drawing up schemes of reform was not confined to the Zemstva and the unions. Obedient to the Imperial command, the Committee of Ministers, assisted by the officials of the different Ministries, plunged into the business of lawmaking; and in the course of five months, from January to June, there were published more new Acts than had before been produced in the course of years. The bureaucrats, who were themselves closely akin to the Russian Intelligents, had even more of a liking for report writing ; but the very atmosphere of bureaucracy gave a nerveless character to much of this work. Much energy and time was spent on it, but there was a lack of humour which prevented the authors from seeing that their activity was belated, and a lack of seriousness which made the public think, in many cases very unjustly, that the whole work was insincere. Some measure of freedom of religion was given to the Old Believers on April 30, to alien confessions on May 14, and to the Jews on July 8; Edicts of April 13 and May 19 aimed at bettering the conditions of peasant life. The whole Ministry of Agriculture was hastily remodelled ; certain vague and inadequate regulations dealt with the publishing of laws and with the modification of some of the Press laws. The one measure which could have quieted the country was the definite summons to a National Assembly. Over and over again the Government has offered concessions which might have given satisfaction three months before. The bureaucracy was now in that disordered state of mind which history has attributed to the Duke of Newcastle : it seemed to have lost half an hour in the morning, and to be hurrying all day in a vain attempt to catch it up. Its activity at least showed that it too was being driven by public opinion and was reluctantly submitting to the necessity of making concessions. But its conversion, if such it could be called, was only the result of the stress of events and lacked all conviction; the bureaucrats were therefore the last people who could be expected to make any practical settlement of the questions which were at issue.

The real leadership of the movement for reform was still in the hands of the Zemstvo men. The two parties which had formed themselves at the November Congress were now more precisely defined ; but far the more numerous was that which followed the lead of the Zemstvo Constitutionalists. This party had very much the views of English Liberals, while the minority, under Shipóff, represented the best instincts of English Conservatism. The Liberal leaders, on the initiative of Mr. Golovín, president of the Moscow Zemstvo, had established an Organising Committee. At the beginning of May this committee summoned another Zemstvo Congress. This time some of the delegates sent by the local Zemstva were formally elected ; but others still came by invitation of the committee, or represented no more than the progressive groups in their respective Zemstva. The Congress, by an overwhelming majority, decided that the National Assembly must be not merely consultative, but legislative. The formula of universal suffrage adopted by the Zemstvo Constitutionalists and their attitude towards the commission of Bulýghin were ratified by a large majority. The Zemstvo Conservatives held a separate Congress under the presidency of Shipóff; here a greater proportion of the members came simply by invitation. This too was the moment when the Town Councils also entered the political arena as a corporate unit. So far they had been disunited. Some of them had sent respectful addresses which vaguely reflected the general feeling of the people; some had addressed petitions to the Council of Ministers. Some Town Councils, like that of Sarátoff, had put forward the most modest requests as to the constitution and functions of the National Assembly, but a large number had accepted the lead of the Town Council of Moscow. Moscow adopted the formula of universal suffrage; Stavropol spoke boldly of a Constituent Assembly; Erivan even raised the questions of women's suffrage, land nationalisation, and the municipalisation of economic enterprises. Members of Town Councils began to get into touch with the Organising Committee of the Zemstvo Congresses.

The Government, discredited at home, had more need than ever of a success in the war. The Emperor's last manifesto and the *Moscow Gazette* had spoken in one breath of the enemies without and the rioters within. It was indeed possible that a Russian victory in the far East would silence the more timorous of the claimants for reform; but success required something more than the mere wishing. Kuropatkin, it would seem, had more than once been pressed to advance towards Port Arthur at all costs. The rest of the Russian fleet had been despatched on a voyage the difficulties of which far exceeded those of the transit by railway. The task had already proved to be too great both for the bureaucracy and for the naval resources of Russia. Some of the so-called armour plates were made, not of steel, but of wood.[1] A large proportion of the crews consisted as usual of Finns, who could hardly be expected to be content with the Government. As the best men had been used up, there were left only inferior elements. The commander of a torpedo boat informed an English officer that he had never in his life been on a ship of this kind before. At Libau some of the improvised sailors had been driven on to their ships at the point of the bayonet.[2] One captain, addressing his men, told them that they were going to certain defeat, and that the best that they could promise would be that all would go down fighting; this pledge was kept to the letter by his crew in the final battle. The strange conditions of their task quite unhinged the nerves of both officers and men, and their wild shots at the English fishermen in the North

---

[1] So says an English naval expert who tapped them.
[2] Evidence of the army officer who drove them on.

Sea created a new danger which was not likely to restore their composure. The first detachment made a long halt in Madagascar, others were despatched without any adequate equipment, and long before the voyage was over Port Arthur had fallen. As far as the central control was concerned, it would be hard to imagine a worse-managed expedition. Admiral Rozhdestvensky several times complained that his advice was disregarded. He viewed his mission in the spirit of the words of Villeneuve, "I go to make a painful experiment." Criticism was early at work in Russia. Before the November Congress had raised the courage of all reformers Captain Kládo, who had stayed behind to put the Russian case at the Paris Commission, openly condemned the whole enterprise. The Government arrested him; but one newspaper in a clever article explained that Kládo could not be touched even by the Government, that his veracity could not be impugned because Russia depended upon it for her justification as to the North Sea incident; and indeed Kládo was soon set at liberty. Before the conclusion of the voyage, Russian public opinion had been developed by the events at home which have already been described. It was into almost a new world that there fell the thunderbolt of the news of Tsushima. Putting his head down and trusting to luck, Admiral Rozhdestvensky had tried to force the narrow passage to the Sea of Japan, and his fleet had been practically annihilated. He himself was taken prisoner, and his colleague Admiral Nebogátoff surrendered almost without fighting. The number of homes bereaved by Tsushima was legion.

For some days the Government postponed the publication of the news. In other cases, this plan of letting the worst details filter out only gradually had sometimes succeeded in diverting attention to events which were still to come. But here the expectation had been too long, and the blow was final. A chorus of indignation rose all over Russia. Just as in the Crimean war, the word "bureaucrat" became the popular term of abuse. For instance, a workman in a railway carriage by refusing to give up his ticket gathered all the staff of the station round him, and then said, "You dirty bureaucrats!" There had already been several murders of policemen, but now the police became marks for the chance shots of anyone who had grievances to avenge. The police had been on a kind of pedestal; they still remained in this position, but it now exposed them to daily attacks. Their enemies welcomed this novel and exciting opportunity; a witty journalist described the police murders as a "new kind of sport." Of course they were most frequent in the Jewish pale, and in Poland. From this time, hardly a newspaper but contained the news of some crime of this kind. The murders were more often than not the work of Jews, and one Jew even claimed for his people the whole credit of them and maintained that they were a sign of Jewish pluck.[1] Most of them were committed in the most cowardly way from behind corners and at night. The police had never been remarkable for their patience with the public, and the strain which was now placed upon it was intolerable. After Tsushima, there was a culmination of all the local disorders which I have described elsewhere. The workmen, after failing in the great strike of Oryékhovo-Zúyevo, now engaged in the long industrial struggle of Ivánovo-Voznesénsk, which ended in bloodshed. Poland and the Caucasus were in complete disorder; and the Nationalist Poles themselves began to protest against the industrial disturbances. The threatening apparition of peasant discontent loomed large all over the south, the west, and the Baltic provinces. The last hope of the Government lay in two forces, the peasants and the soldiers. There is no doubt that the peasant discontent, through the medium of the reservists, powerfully contributed to bring about the military riots in Sevastópol. In the Black Sea fleet, where the officers were lazy and arbitrary, the sailors had developed amongst themselves a revolutionary organisation such as is only possible where men with the same instincts and the same grievances are in close daily touch with each other. It was arranged that, when the fleet reached Odessa for the summer manœuvres, an outspoken protest should be made. The crew of the *Prince Potyémkin* anticipated their fellows by presenting a list of grievances against the discipline and the food. The man who handed in the petition was shot dead by an officer; the men overpowered the officers, and killed or threw overboard nearly all of them. They then landed the body of their dead comrade at Odessa, and, by the threat of cannonading the town, frightened the local authorities into allowing a public funeral to pass without resistance. When

---

[1] Conversation with the author.

the rest of the ships came up, their crews, though not joining in the revolt, were unwilling to fire on the *Potyémkin*, and Admiral Krüger faced about for Sevastópol. The *Potyémkin*, after ravaging the coasts of the Black Sea, consented to be interned in Roumania. Again the news was suppressed in Russia, and the suppression led to exaggerations. The revolt was followed by disturbances in Odessa, which the soldiers did not hesitate to put down, but its general effect upon the morale of the army was such as to shake the confidence of every official. These were some of the later results of the battle of Tsushima. But long before the revolt of the *Potyémkin*, authority was breaking down at point after point of the Empire. General Trépoff continued to issue prohibitions, and Mr. Bulýghin continued to map out a National Assembly; but the Government almost seemed to have disappeared, and the further issues were left to be disputed between the Reformers and sheer anarchy.

The Reformers rose to the height of the occasion. Directly after Tsushima the Organising Committee of the Zemstvo Liberals called a Congress for June 6 in Moscow. The Zemstvo Conservatives were invited, and came; invitations were also accepted by the Marshals of the Gentry, and, what was more important, by representatives of the Town Councils. A bold address to the Emperor, speaking with a freedom to which he was as yet a stranger, was laid before the Congress. Shipóff and his friends carried certain emendations suggested by their respect for the principle of authority, but they did not rob the address of its resolute and decisive tone. The final draft speaks of the " criminal neglect and abuses " of the Emperor's counsellors "; ·of the " vices of a hateful and ruinous bureaucratic system "; of the non-fulfilment of the promises contained in the manifestos; of the absolute need of summoning at once national representatives " elected equally and without distinction by all subjects " of the Empire. The address ends, " Do not delay, Sire. At the terrible hour of national trial, great is your responsibility before God and Russia." The Congress elected fourteen persons to lay the address before the Emperor; three of them were Town Councillors, and the rest were Zemstvo Liberals. Shipóff, not having suggested the address, did not join the deputation; but the deputies were expected to represent to the Emperor the opinion, not of a party, but of the Congress as a whole. Thus the Zemstvo Liberals had again consented to accept a minimum which would secure the adhesion of all, and the Zemstvo Conservatives continued to give their moral support to the movement of reform. The deputation was received by the Emperor on June 19. As its spokesman it chose Prince Sergius Trubetskóy. This choice was another proof of the moderation and practical unanimity of the reformers. The Prince, who came of one of the oldest families in Russia, could hardly be identified with any political group. He was a wise man, and his earnest desire was that bureaucratic anarchy should be replaced by a genuine sovereign authority, resting on the support of the nation. Amongst the deputies he was perhaps the least likely to put himself forward, but his colleagues all felt that he at that moment represented the best instincts of the united nation as no one else could have done. The Emperor, we are told, entered with an appearance of irritation. Prince Trubetskóy did not speak like a demonstrator; he came quite close up to the Emperor, and talked in a low conversational voice. One who was present describes his manner as that of a wise father reasoning with a wayward child. He explained with simple firmness that the principle of order was itself in danger, and that the threats of anarchy were directed against all who were called masters. He said very plainly that there were but few amongst the Emperor's counsellors who were able to enlighten him as to the state of opinion, and that the Emperor must be put in touch with his people without delay. As he spoke the face of the Emperor changed, and the answer which he made to the speech had perhaps not been anticipated even by himself. After making the inevitable reassertion of his power and of his goodwill, and explaining that there could be no break with the past, he said: "Throw aside your doubts; my will, the will of the Tsar, to call together representatives from the people, is unchangeable. Their labours will be regularly applied to the work of the Empire; I every day follow and stand for this work. You may tell this to all who are near to you, living whether in the country or in the towns. I hope you will co-operate with me in this task."

Prince Trubetskóy had not written out his speech, but he and his colleagues put it on paper directly after the reception, and they also recorded with more exactness the answer of the Emperor.

When the speech and the answer were made public there was a chorus of approbation in which even the reactionary *Svyét* took part. Most Russians felt that at last the voice of the people had been heard in the palace; one old man of moderate opinions told me that he thanked God that he had been able to live to see this day. But immediately afterwards the dissensions began again. Mr. Tatíshcheff obtained the suspension of the Liberal newspaper *Rus* for publishing the speech and answer with daring comments. On the other hand, the Union of Unions was only with difficulty restrained from passing a vote of censure on the deputation for its moderation, and the deputation itself, when later asked to explain its attitude, made no claim to have put forward the full demands even of the Zemstvo Liberals. The Organising Committee of the now united Zemstva circulated lithographed copies of the speech and of the answer all over the country; and the Land Captains received orders to confiscate these copies wherever they could find them.

On June 15 the mayors of some large towns met in conference in Moscow, and established an organising committee after the model of that of the Zemstva. This committee called together on June 28 a Congress at which eighty-six provincial towns were represented. The Congress was held in the Town Hall of Moscow, and adopted a resolution claiming the well-known "freedoms" and a National Assembly. Already there had been published details of Mr. Bulýghin's as yet unfinished scheme for a National Assembly, and it was quite clear that the Minister aimed at producing only a show of public opinion, and allotted to the Assembly a *rôle* hardly superior to that of a bureaucratic "college" after the model of Peter the Great. The Congress therefore demanded the freedoms in advance and condemned the scheme of Mr. Bulýghin. It adopted the rival scheme proposed by the Zemstvo Liberals, who advocated a parliament with two chambers and universal suffrage, including women. It also decided to join with the Zemstva in calling another Congress which should represent both the Zemstva and the Town Councils.

This General Congress met on July 19 in Moscow. Invitations were sent to all Russian Zemstva and Town Councils; but these did not in all cases definitely elect their deputies, and no plan had as yet been devised for the representation of alien provinces where Zemstva did not exist. For all that, this Congress marks a great

advance in the movement. It was a part of the policy of the
Zemstvo Liberals to widen further and further the area of representation; thus at each congress there were men who had not
yet met together, and who came in order to be enlightened as to
the objects of the movement; and in each case the tact and self-
restraint of the Organising Committee[1] enabled it to send back to
the provinces so many more convinced adherents. The Governor-
General of Moscow, Mr. Kozlóff, had, on instructions from St.
Petersburg, published a notice warning the deputies that they
would not be allowed to meet. Some members of the Organising
Committee went to him and represented that the meeting of the
Congress was awaited by the nation, that it was the natural
antidote for disorder, and that the intentions of the committee
were both loyal and orderly. Mr. Kozlóff seemed to share their
views; but on Saturday, July 15, the committee was interrupted in its deliberations by a visit from a Police-Master. This
official asked who had given leave to the committee to meet and
discuss public affairs. Mr. Golovín, making a clever use of the
Imperial answer to Prince Trubetskóy, stated that the permission
came from the Emperor himself; they had been ordered to tell
those who were near to them, living whether in town or country,
of the kindly intentions of the Emperor and to co-operate with
him in the task of reform; clearly the Zemstva were the best
representatives of the country, and the Town Councils were the
best representatives of the towns. It was now the turn of the Police-
Master to say from whom his own orders came. A telephone message to the Governor-General elicited the reply that Mr. Kozlóff
knew nothing about the matter, and the official in the end had to
fall back on the City Prefect of Moscow and General Trepoff. The
discussions were resumed in the presence of the Police-Master,
who was invited to make any record of them which he thought fit.
He carried back to his superiors a statement of the committee
acknowledging the receipt of the message and giving its reasons
for not obeying. On July 19 the *Russian Gazette* published
the scheme of the Constitution which was to be laid before the
Congress. Like other papers of the capitals, it enjoyed the
right of printing anything at its own risk and answering for it

[1] This Committee now consisted of representatives both of the Zemstva and of
the Town Councils.

afterwards. On the same day the Congress met in the house of Prince Paul Dolgorúkoff. Of the three hundred deputies expected, two hundred and thirty-five had been able to disregard the Government prohibition. Count Heyden, a Conservative Reformer, whose age, family, and career could exact the respect of the Court itself, was elected president. Soon after the opening of the Congress the police penetrated into the hall. There was a moment of confusion, and then Prince Paul Dolgorúkoff, in a quiet conversational voice, told the Congress that it had no reason to be angry with officials who were discharging their duty, but that, as it had more important affairs on its hands, it had better proceed with its deliberations. The police remained as interested spectators of the scene. They drew up the usual protocol, stating that they had executed their instructions, and Mr. Golovín added in writing the answer of the Congress. He asserted that they were meeting by the express invitation of the Emperor, and protested that the entry of the police into a house in which nothing disorderly was going on made the peaceful course of life impossible. The blame for disorder was therefore put upon the police, who did not seem to take it very seriously; and this amiable scene was commemorated by a snapshot photograph.

The Congress, which sat for three days, subjected the scheme of Bulýghin to severe criticism and declared it impracticable. It then made its one notable mistake by discussing whether a Bulýghin parliament should be boycotted or not; but returning to saner counsels, it decided to leave the Government to digest its vote of censure, without committing itself to any dangerous tactical step. It did not, however, limit itself to mere criticism, and the Constitution printed in the *Russian Gazette* was now discussed in detail. This draft had been prepared long in advance by a few of the "Liberators," of whom Mr. Kokóshkin was one of the most notable. Both he and his colleagues had an intimate knowledge of constitutional precedents all over Europe. They made no attempt to abrogate existing institutions wholesale; on the contrary, they took for granted those fundamental laws of the Empire which guaranteed to the Emperor the control of the succession and of the army. The draft was a very capable piece of work, embodying in precise and restrained language the main traditions of English political life, though of course the English

House of Lords was not taken as a model for the Russian Second Chamber. The grip of the authors only relaxed when they reached comparatively unimportant questions of detail, such as the manner in which elections were to be conducted. The Constitution represented the claims of the Zemstvo Liberals, who had throughout taken the initiative in the movement for reform, and were later to have the almost exclusive control of the first Imperial Duma.[1] It was, however, not put forward as a final enunciation of absolute principles, but rather as an object-lesson by which the nation could know what kind of thing it was asking for when it claimed a Constitution. The Congress was anxious to establish English precedents in Russia as opposed to German, and, by the acute suggestion of Professor Múromtseff, the draft was carried in principle " at the first reading " without discussion of detail. There was a special reason for this expedition, for the Congress did not yet know that its deliberations would not be cut short by the arrival of troops. Desiring to stand on the widest possible national basis, the Congress invited discussion of its scheme in local meetings all over the country, and asked that the decisions of such meetings should be reported to its Organising Committee. It had already issued a kind of Grand Remonstrance, recapitulating in moderate language the instances in which the Ministers had failed to observe the principles enunciated in the Imperial decrees ; and it followed this up with a shorter address to the people, which was full of the best spirit of English tradition. The address was another example of the remarkable unanimity of parties. It was originally drawn up by the veteran Liberal leader Mr. Petrunkyévich, and was submitted for revision to the tactful hand of Professor Múromtseff. The final draft was simple and restrained. "We will then," it concluded, "with united strength go forward towards our common object; we must quietly and openly assemble, consider our needs, and express our desires, having no apprehension as to whether anyone whosoever will prevent this. It is fully lawful that the population should consult together as to how it can best deal with that change which lies before it. . . . If all decide together what is to be

---

[1] "Liberators," "Zemstvo Constitutionalists," "Zemstvo Liberals," " Constitutional Democrats," and "Cadets" are terms which all describe the same tendencies and often the same persons at different stages of political organisation.

done, then their views will have such a strength as no arbitrary power or lawlessness will be able to withstand. The path which we have pointed out is the path of peace; it is to lead the country to a new order of things, without great convulsions, without bloodshed, and without thousands of unnecessary victims." The address was signed by all the deputies except seventeen Zemstvo Conservatives. Measures were taken to widen the representation in future congresses. After some discussion as to what measure of opposition to the authorities should be sanctioned by the Congress, it was decided that the deputies should " stand for their natural rights, using all peaceful means and refusing to submit to official orders which violated them."

Following the Address into the country, I was present at some local meetings at which the respective Zemstva endeavoured to get into touch with the people. These meetings, even in minute points of detail, bore the strongest family resemblance to the Moscow Congress. As at Moscow, extreme measures were suggested only to be refused; and the general attitude was that of unanimous insistence on claims which appealed alike to all.

Mr. Golovín, directly after the Congress, journeyed to St. Petersburg and laid the resolutions before General Trepoff. The General seemed to find no reply to this open disregard of his commands. A revising senator, Mr. Postóvsky, was despatched to Moscow, where his investigations were facilitated by the frankest confidence on the part of the Liberal leaders. The Government took no action against them, but, on the other hand, it made no adequate modification of its own scheme of a parliament. On August 19 this scheme was issued in the form of an Imperial Decree.

The old division of the population into three classes has ceased to be efficient, but the decree retained this distinction and made it the basis of the electoral system. Each class was to have a separate electoral body to choose its own representatives; thus the district landowners, the town electors, and the representatives of peasant cantons were all to meet separately. Amongst those excluded from the franchise were—men under twenty-five, the police, soldiers on active service, nomad aliens, and persons who were under prosecution for any criminal offence. Women with property might be represented by their male relations; fathers might be represented by their sons.

The district landowners consisted (*a*) of men who satisfied the high gentry franchise for the Zemstva, and (*b*) of representatives of the lesser gentry and of the landed priests, chosen at a preliminary assembly. In towns which did not elect separate members this category also included the owners of considerable real property and of industrial concerns, and persons who paid the higher tenants' rates. Each peasant canton was to elect from the local peasantry two representatives. In towns which had separate members the franchise was the same as in the smaller towns, except that owners of real estate in the capitals had to pay in rates twice as much as elsewhere. These towns were divided into wards.

The conduct of the elections was entrusted to the Governor or the City Prefect, assisted by a Government Commission formed in the ordinary way. The Marshals of the Gentry and the mayors of the smaller towns were to preside over the local electoral assemblies. Lists of voters were to be published six weeks before the election, and a fortnight was allowed for the challenging of votes. The voting was to be by ballot. The candidates, who were to be balloted separately, had to obtain, except in the towns, more than half of the votes of all present. Protests might be made against the validity of an election. By the process thus described the voters would choose those who were finally to elect the members of the Duma.

The electors would now meet together in the chief town of the province. Here the peasant electors would first choose amongst themselves one peasant member; then all the electors together would choose the remaining members for the province. In the election of town members all would be chosen at once. Members who held salaried Government posts would have to resign those posts. No person ignorant of the Russian language could be elected. The Senate had power to annul elections.

It will be noticed that there were three stages of election for the peasants and smaller landowners, and two stages for all others; the workmen were disfranchised altogether. At the final election, a majority of one would be enough to determine the choice of all the members from the province or town. Officials had an extensive control over the elections. The Duma, when it at last met, was to be divided into sections, and most of the work was to be done in these sections. It had no effective control over the Ministers, and it had to submit all measures to the Council of State, that is to an Upper House, not based on the principle of hereditary nobility, but composed of former officials. The rules of procedure were so clumsy as to postpone indefinitely the carrying through of even the simplest law. On the other hand, the final draft of the scheme allowed the Duma to name its own presidents, general and sectional; and the tenants' rate admitted to the franchise a certain number of the Intelligents of the towns who had hitherto been unclassified.

Such was Mr. Bulýghin's answer to the almost universal discontent with which the first details of his scheme had been received. As at the Moscow Congress, so in local meetings all over the country, the question had been raised whether it would not be wisest for the people to boycott such a Duma altogether. The most advanced sections were determined only to use the Duma in order to transform it into a Constituent Assembly. In the end nearly all parties decided to accept the Duma and use it as the weapon to get something better.

The war still dragged on, but there seemed to be no chance of success, and the position of the Russian army in Manchuria looked very critical. The Emperor could hardly continue to struggle against Japan and against his own people at the same time. He proceeded to treat with Japan. It is possible that the determining factor in the negotiations was the final refusal of prominent Americans to lend any more money to Japan. Mr. Witte made an adroit use of his opportunities, and was credited with a diplomatic victory. Some disheartened bureaucrats, realising how little ability they had on their side, had already suggested that Witte should receive correspondingly full powers to deal with the Russian people.

On September 8, the Government took steps to satisfy the special claims of the students; Prince Trubetskóy had been invited to report to the Emperor on the question, and now the universities were declared to be autonomous. They were to choose their own Rectors, and could hold meetings of their own members within their own walls. The official Inspectors were subordinated to the Rectors and lost all importance. Moscow chose for her first freely elected Rector the man who

had given her autonomy, Prince Trubetskóy ; but not long afterwards, while on a visit to the Ministry of Public Instruction in
St. Petersburg, where he was pleading for a further extension of
freedom, the Prince suddenly died of heart disease. He left a
great gap in Russia, and his funeral in Moscow was the signal for
a remarkable demonstration of the affection of his fellow-citizens.
In the autumn Professor Milyukóff was imprisoned for some
time. Deprived of his able leadership, the Union of Unions was
now becoming more and more doctrinaire, and less and less
representative. Milyukóff, who throughout the summer had been
doing all that he could to temper the excitability of its members,
had already taken steps to carry the majority of his followers
into a wider and stronger organisation. From the start, the
Reform movement had been largely the result of an understanding
between the Zemstvo Liberals and the more responsible of the
Intelligents. In July Milyukóff had proposed to the Zemstva a
closer co-operation with the Union of Unions. Naturally the
Zemstva, which alone could claim a representative character, did
not wish to sink their individuality in the Union or to take the
position of a simple professional body, such as the Union of
Lawyers of the Union of Doctors. Conservative reformers, such
as Count Heyden, were alienated by that resolution of the Union
of Unions which had declared all means to be permissible. But
the Zemstvo Liberals and Mr. Milyukóff were too necessary to
each other to leave the matter as it was. Gradually the
foundations of a new party were being laid.

On September 25, another General Congress of the Zemstva
and Town Councils was held in Moscow; one hundred and ninety-
four deputies were present. The police made no protest, and a
representative of the Governor-General attended the sittings.
The circle of political education and political support had been
further widened. Three of the Zemstvo Liberals had visited
Poland, conferred with the leaders of the Polish National party, and
agreed to insert the chief Polish claims in the general programme.
The Congress therefore included representatives not only of the
Zemstva, but of districts where there were no Zemstva. There were
present Poles, Lithuanians, Don Cossacks, and Siberians.

The reports from the country meetings read at the first sitting
practically pledged the Zemstvo Liberals to enter the Duma and

to there demand universal suffrage at once ; that is to say, they were to take part in the elections only in order to further widen the Government scheme. The Congress adopted a programme including the effective realisation of the " freedoms," a legislative parliament, local autonomy, rights of nationalities, and other claims, of which the chief was the extension of local government. Some of these questions had been discussed by previous congresses ; but the report of Mr. Kokóshkin on the question of autonomy and several speeches suggesting Home Rule all round called forth vehement opposition from the Zemstvo Conservatives, under the leadership of Mr. A. Guchkóff. A resolution in favour of Home Rule for Poland was adopted with only one dissentient ; but the claims of other racial units for Home Rule met with stronger opposition. The majority of the Congress, in view of the conspicuous success of the Peasants' Union and the need of capturing the support of the peasants, welcomed certain suggestions which looked not unlike Socialism. State land and even some private land was to be expropriated in favour of the peasants, and the principle was put forward that the extent of the holding should be determined according to the working power of the holder. However, these questions and others which concerned the working men were postponed for further deliberation.

Mr. Milyukóff had almost completed his arrangements for the formal constitution of a great Liberal party ; and to the first meeting of this party, which was now sure to embrace the majority of the Zemstvo Liberals, was committed the drawing up of an electoral programme. In April, when the " Liberators " had met in Moscow, they had already contemplated the formation of such a party, but were not able to clearly define its fundamental principles. The majority insisted on the control of the executive by the Legislature and on universal suffrage, including women. This last point had nearly led to a rupture, and the final constitution of the party had thus been delayed. The idea had again been taken up at the fourth Congress of the Liberators in August, and a joint committee of the Zemstvo Liberals and the Liberators, many of whom belonged to both bodies, had been at work on the programme. Representatives of both these groups were summoned to a meeting on October 25. This meeting took place during the general strike of October, and it was impossible for more than one-fourth of the delegates to attend. The party was indeed constituted, but everything was referred for ratification to a fuller Congress. The more advanced Liberals, (that is, those who were not identified with the Zemstva), proved to be in a minority. The debates were very animated; the discussion of women's suffrage was indecisive. Twice the debates were adjourned in order to deal with questions of the moment. The Congress "sympathised with the general strike," but desired that it should be " peaceable." On the last day but one arrived the new Manifesto of October 30; this gave even greater predominance to moderate views; a resolution criticising the Manifesto was indeed adopted, but the Radicals were dissatisfied with the Congress, and a large number of them abstained from joining the party. The new political party, which was the first in Russia to deserve this description, called itself "the Constitutional Democrats," a title which was soon shortened to " K.D.'s " or " Cadets."

The other chief development of the autumn was the growth of the Peasants' Union. Up till now, the Union of Unions had represented a compact majority of educated opinion and certain trade organisations of the working class. But men of all views realised that they could not hope for success unless they could capture a really considerable proportion of the peasants. It was the Socialist Revolutionaries who had done most to conduct propaganda amongst the peasants. The ablest of them were well aware that the peasants would not rise to establish a new form of government. The peasants never pretended to have the same interests as the professional classes; a Peasants' Union was formed during the summer, but it carried no real weight and served only to give an appearance of completeness to the organisation of the Union of Unions. In the autumn, however, this Union quite suddenly became an important factor in politics. Dr. Stahl, of Moscow, and some other Socialists, dropping their hopeless propaganda against the Imperial form of government, laid down a programme entirely economic, of which the chief feature was the principle that "the land should belong to those who laboured." The number of active members of the Union did not greatly increase; but whole villages, using the old-fashioned and nonparty machinery of Village Meetings, adopted the new formula. The Union recognised these village voters as its members; and so great was its success that it was able to count as many as 200,000 adherents, at which point it stopped counting. We can estimate the strength of the Union by the fact that during the subsequent repression 12,000 of its members were imprisoned. The leadership of the Union remained with the Socialist Revolutionaries. Some few of them took part in agrarian riots; but in general the riots took place in those districts which lay on the fringe of the activity of the Union, and were conducted by ignorant disturbers of the peace, who were reduced to silence as soon as the Union obtained a strong hold. The importance of this development can hardly be overestimated, and will be as interesting a subject for historical study as the local federations of 1789 in France.

The disorders of the past year had brought the students into much closer touch with the working men of the towns. The series of strikes had lasted through the summer. The students, after obtaining academic autonomy on September 8, had, in spite of the opposition of some of their professors, conducted a series of open meetings within the walls of the universities. Scholars of Secondary Schools had been drawn into the movement, and in South Russia the Jews and the revolutionary element had become bolder and more aggressive than ever. The funeral of Prince Trubetskóy had been marked by a great demonstration and a collision with the police, who continued to make impossible the realisation of the "freedoms" promised by the Emperor. Street meetings were of common occurrence; and on the other side, amongst the floating population of the towns there was a rapid development of hooliganism. In July a Black Gang attacked a crowd of demonstrators in Nizhny Novgorod, with the result that a peaceable Liberal, Mr. Heintze, was killed and mutilated. In August at Sarátoff one of the most eminent public men in Russia, Mr. N. N. Lvoff, with members of the local Zemstvo, was flogged by Cossacks before the eyes of the Governor while endeavouring to allay a street disturbance.[1] At Nizhny the police and the Vice-Governor had been incriminated in a Black Gang affair, and at Sarátoff the Archbishop Hermogen had committed

---

[1] The Governor, Mr. Stolýpin, did what he could to stop such attacks; but the Cossacks had got out of hand. Later, as Prime Minister, he showed what he thought of Mr. Lvoff by trying to persuade him to join his Ministry.

himself in print to an appeal for similar disorders. Bishop Nikon, of Moscow, was a member of a Black Gang committee, and in October the Metropolitan Vladímir preached a sermon inciting to violence. Poland and the Caucasus were in the usual disturbed condition ; the army in the far East was showing discontent ; a famine increased the restlessness of the central provinces of Russia. In the midst of these disorders the Government attempted to carry through with a high hand the first elections to the Imperial Duma.

In the middle of October the delegates of the Congress of Railwaymen in Moscow were arrested. This led to a general railway strike, beginning with the railways of the Moscow area and the south, and extending to almost the whole Empire. Tactically the railways were all-important to the system of Government control. The railway strike immobilised a large number of industries, and those who found themselves deprived of work thought they might as well have the credit of striking too. The printers were amongst the first, and were soon followed by the tramwaymen, the chemists, the doctors,[1] the lawyers, and the teachers. The Higher Schools were already closed; the secondary schools stopped working too. Thus almost the whole people drifted into a great national strike, which, though it was too vast to have been prepared in advance, yet gave an extra-ordinarily unanimous expression to the protest against mis-government. Public life practically stopped ; persons laid in stores of food as if they were under siege ; the general strike, coming as it did in the winter, cut off the whole supply of light ; the mere absence of all newspapers powerfully impressed the imagination ; the sick could not be attended to; supplies of oxen reached St. Petersburg only on foot and almost unfit to eat. On the Exchange stocks fell rapidly, and thus another of the last fortresses of the Government was endangered. It was necessary to yield, but to whom ? The first real political party in Russia was not yet formed, for the Constitutional Democrats were still discussing their organisation in Moscow ; but if there was not a dominant party, there was at least a generally accepted programme. For a time the Emperor appears to have thought of establishing a frankly military dictatorship in the hands of General Trepoff, who now issued his famous order "Don't spare

---

[1] The participation of the doctors was later generally condemned.

the cartridges "; but for the moment concession was inevitable. In any case, the Government had to proclaim its definite acceptance of the programme first promulgated at the November Congress; Russia had to become a constitutional State. In any case the reactionary Ministers had to resign. But the reconciliation between the Emperor and his people could not be complete unless the sovereign chose as his new counsellors men who commanded the confidence of the nation. Nicholas II. had lived for nine months in practical seclusion from his people. He consented to dismiss his incapable Ministers, but he knew nothing of the chief men of the Reform movement and recognised as the only possible alternative the leaders of the Opposition within the bureaucracy itself. Amongst these the only eminent man was Count Witte, who had succeeded in making an advantageous peace after his rivals had been responsible for a most ruinous war. Count Witte was an able administrator, but in no sense a statesman; whether rightly or wrongly, he was distrusted as much by the Court as by the leaders of the reformers; in fact, the hardest things said against him have been said by reactionaries, some of whom have even thought fit to accuse him of aiming at the crown. But he enjoyed a European reputation, had been strongly opposed to the war, and possessed a special ability for arranging foreign loans. Foreign capital was now more than ever necessary to the Government. Count Witte had many friends at Court, and had the chance of representing himself as a person who would be acceptable to the reformers. He was allowed to draw up a Manifesto in which the Emperor went to the furthest limit which his instincts of autocracy would allow. He himself was appointed to the new-made post of Prime Minister, and in the control which he was to have over his colleagues Russia might perhaps recognise the first beginnings of constitutional government.

There can hardly be any doubt that the Emperor at this crisis ought to have sent for one of the leaders of the national movement. Mr. Shipóff would probably have been the best choice. The principle which was then, and is still, the main issue in Russia, was the principle of Ministerial responsibility. Mr. Shipóff, without being a leader of the Cadets, would have been accepted as Minister by them; and this solution would have allowed the main question to remain for a time in abeyance. But the Emperor was not wrong in thinking that it was on this ground that the last battle of autocracy was to be fought, and he did not wish to treat at all in the matter. He thus debarred himself from choosing a Prime Minister from amongst the real leaders of the nation. In appointing Witte, he, after all, accepted a man and not a principle, and this might well seem to him the lesser evil of the two. Witte, knowing what was the extent of his credit with the nation, would be no more anxious than himself to raise the obnoxious question. And, lastly, the Emperor might naturally, at a moment of transition, prefer a man with Ministerial antecedents, and in whom the bureaucracy might recognise its master. For all that, the mistake was a bad one: The new Premier had imposed himself upon an unwilling sovereign by an adroit use of the national discontent, and now, as the nominee of his sovereign, he endeavoured to impose himself upon an unwilling people. As a politician who felt in himself the ability to govern, he was perhaps entitled to his triumph. But his victory was a personal one, and his continuance in office depended upon his success in securing support. It was soon evident that he could neither win the reformers nor restrain the reactionaries, and later his nominal control over his own colleagues was derided even by himself.

II.

The Claim for Ministerial Responsibility.

The Manifesto of October 30 expresses the Emperor's affliction at the spread of disorder. It proceeds : " The welfare of the Russian sovereign is inseparable from the welfare of the people, and the sorrow of the people is his sorrow." Fears are expressed for the integrity of the Empire : " The great vow of service as Tsar orders us to strive with every power of our mind and of our authority to set an early term to such dangerous disorders." The Government is directed—(1) " to give to the population the immutable foundations of civil freedom, on the principles of effective inviolability of person and freedom of conscience, of speech, of meeting, and of association " ; (2) without delaying the elections, to enfranchise as far as possible those classes of the population which are at present totally deprived of the suffrage, "leaving to the newly established order of legislature" the further development of the principle of universal suffrage; (3) "to establish, as an unalterable rule, that no law can have any force without the consent of the Imperial Duma, and that the representatives of the people may have guaranteed to them an effective share in the inspection over the legality of the acts of our officials." The new Prime Minister is ordered to "take measures to unite the action of the Ministers." At the same time was published a report of the new Premier written at the command of the Emperor. The report declares that the disorders "cannot be regarded only as the effect of merely partial imperfections in the Imperial and social order, or as the result of the organised action of extreme parties. The roots of these disorders, without doubt, lie deeper: they are to be found in the destruction of the balance between the ideas and aspirations of a thinking society and the external forms of its life. Russia has outgrown a certain form of order; she aspires to a legal order on the foundation of civil freedom." The realisation of the "freedoms" must be the first task of the new Government. The next task is to establish "such principles of legislation as would answer to the expressed political idea of the majority of Russian society." The economic policy must be directed towards the welfare of the widest masses of the people. These principles involve a great deal of legislative work and a consistent plan of administration. This work, it is declared, cannot all be done at once, as the Empire cannot at once accustom itself to a new order. An essential condition is " the uniformity of the composition of the Government and the unity of the object which it pursues." The ideas of this united Government must also be the ideas " of all the agents of authority, from the highest to the lowest." The Government must adopt " the unchangeable principle of absolute non-interference in the elections for the Imperial Duma," and, " amongst other things, must make a genuine effort to substantiate the measures announced by the decree of December 25th." It must " take trouble to preserve the prestige of the Duma, and show confidence in its labours." " It must follow the idea expressed by Your Majesty, that the constitution of the Duma is subject to further development according as time may reveal imperfections in it or may raise new questions "; the Government must bring forward such questions, " guiding itself, of course, by the ideas which prevail amongst the majority of society." " It is extremely important to reform the Imperial Council on the principle that an elective element should take part in it, for only on this condition can we expect normal relations between this institution and the Imperial Duma." " Efforts must be made to do away with exceptional legislation ; measures of repression against actions which clearly do not threaten society or the Empire must be rescinded; but actions which are clearly threatening must be opposed on the ground of law, and in a spirit of harmony with the reasonable majority of society. We have got to believe in the political tact of Russian society. It is impossible that Russian society should wish for anarchy, which, apart from all the horrors of conflict, threatens to dismember the Empire." This report is a very clever piece of work. It draws the Emperor as far as possible on to the path of Reform; without really guaranteeing full political control, it proclaims the main principles of the Reform movement; it definitely declares war against anarchy ; and it invites the mass of the nation to trust itself to Count Witte. The one serious defect is the absence of all control of the people over the Prime Minister ; and this means that he will not be supported.

Five days before the Manifesto, while other influences still prevailed, the very strictest regulations had been issued with the aim of making the holding of public meetings as difficult as possible. General Trepoff had issued instructions which could hardly fail to lead to street conflicts. Whereas the reactionaries were allowed to make electoral demonstrations, the meetings and processions of both the reformers and the revolutionaries had been dispersed with the use of arms. More than that, the Black Gang movement, which had been developing throughout the summer, had now taken definite shape. In Kharkoff, hooligans ransacked the gunsmiths' shops, and the troops when called out, instead of dispersing the hooligans, fired on the crowd of onlookers. The students erected a barricade near the University, but after a little fighting order was re-established. The Manifesto, when it came, was received with scepticism. In Revel, there was an unprovoked demonstration of hooligans of almost exactly the same kind. Again the police were absent, but two days later a peaceful meeting of protest near the Town Hall was fired upon by the troops. In Minsk, the Governor sent troops with orders to fire on a somewhat disorderly public meeting. In Libau, the strikers offered to resume work if martial law were removed, but General Trepoff sent instructions that even the Manifesto had not changed the situation, and, in spite of the recommendation of the local Governor, martial law was retained. In Kieff and Odessa, there had been a series of disorderly meetings and processions, and the revolutionary red flag was to be seen everywhere; but there had not been any bloodshed. The news of the Manifesto, so far from bringing tranquillity, led to the opening of direct hostilities by the Black Gangs. With every sign of organisation by the police, crowds of hooligans fell upon the Jews, and in both places were allowed to go on robbing and even killing for three days on end. The time limit of these "pogroms"[1] had been known in advance; the hooligans had been supplied with revolvers by the police; disguised policemen took part in the rioting; even higher authorities refused protection to peaceable persons if these were Jews; the plunder was carried to the police stations. In Kieff the Police-Master, Tsikhótsky, and one of the chief military officials, Major-General Bersónoff, gave their public sanction to the rioters; and in Odessa the City Prefect, Mr. Neidhardt, did the same. Certainly, in no case were all local officials involved in this criminal work; but the impunity of persons so highly placed showed quite clearly what was the answer of the reactionaries to Count Witte's plea "for the unity of authority." The Premier sent to the scenes of the "pogroms" revising senators, that is, Government investigators of the first class; their reports put the responsibility of local officials beyond all doubt, and the chief offenders were removed from office.[2] But Count Witte was not able to know that at this very time inflammatory appeals for wholesale risings against the Jews were being sent out from the Police Department itself, where a Gendarme, Komisároff, had been supplied

[1] This word, which has been applied to the work of the Black Gangs, means a "smash."
[2] The above account of the "pogroms" of Kieff and Odessa is based exclusively on the senators' reports.

with house-room and a secret printing press for this very purpose. In St. Petersburg and in Moscow, though the evidence of organisation was not so convincing, the Manifesto was followed by a number of street conflicts.

The first general strike had come of itself, and had been almost universal. But there were already signs that the working men were organising themselves specially as a class, after the manner of the Peasants' Union. Trade Unions had begun to show their power during October; and passing very quickly through this stage of development, the working class now began to form a vast organisation common to all trades. In one way this was much to be desired: if the working men united on the basis of an economic programme, they might, like the peasants, defer ulterior questions concerning theories of government, and bring their great weight to the support of those simple principles upon which practically the whole nation was agreed. But if this was to happen, it was necessary that the struggle should not be accentuated by the passions of a moment. Every direct conflict with the Government was likely to give the Socialist bodies a fresh chance of imposing their theories upon the working men. The organisation of Gapon had had an economic character rather than a political. There still remained relics of this body, which the events of January 22 had helped to purify from the taint of connivance with the police. But when the idea of such a general organisation was resumed, the chief mover was a strong Socialist of peasant origin and of great ability, Mr. Khrustalyéff (Nosar[1]), who as a lawyer had lived in close relations with working men. During the general strike, the servants of different railways had taken common action. They held a Congress on October 24, and sent a deputation to the Minister of Ways and Communications, Prince Khilkoff, and to Count Witte, "adopting as their only motto" the proclamation of political guarantees of freedom, and of the summons of a Constituent Assembly on the basis of universal, equal, direct, and secret suffrage. So far the programme was that of the Zemstvo Liberals. On October 27 there met in St. Petersburg a common council, representing the working classes, which claimed the direction of the whole strike. This claim was

---

[1] Often a revolutionary lives under two names.

allowed, not only by Unions of working men, but even by
professional Unions. The Council threatened employers with
the destruction of machinery and stores; on October 30 it
arranged to organise district staffs, to compel all businesses to
stop work. It suggested that working men should not pay rent
until after the strike, and hinted to their landlords that this
temporary loss would have to be accepted. It was at this
moment that the Manifesto was published. On November 1
the Council included one hundred and thirty-two deputies, representing seventy-four businesses and four Unions. It decided to
stop the strike, "in order to organise as well as possible and to arm
for the final struggle, that a Constituent Assembly might be summoned . . . to establish a democratic republic." On November 3
the strike stopped everywhere in Russia; of course many more
moderate claimants had been comparatively satisfied by the
Manifesto. On November 8, the sailors of Kronstadt rose;
though at first successful, they used their liberty to plunder
and get drunk, and the revolt was easily suppressed. The leaders
were threatened with the death penalty. At the same time
Poland, which was as usual full of disorder, was placed under
martial law. On November 16, the Council of Working Men's
Delegates declared a second general strike, as a protest against
death sentences and against martial law in Poland; but the first
great movement had been of a far more national character, and
general strikes were a weapon which it was unwise to use too
often. The public was exhausted, and the new war-cries aroused
no enthusiasm. The second strike, then, failed almost completely,
and on November 20 the Council put an end to it. Other
general strikes were attempted, such as that which demanded
the eight-hours day, and that which appealed to the public on
behalf of the special interests of the servants of the post and
telegraph. The Council was becoming dictatorial; it invited the
workmen not to pay taxes. It was openly described as "the
Workmen's Government," and it was suggested that it would be
easier for Khrustalyéff to arrest Count Witte than for Count
Witte to arrest Khrustalyéff. Witte attempted to appeal to
the workmen by the memory of the factory laws; but his appeal
to them as "brothers" elicited the answer that they would be
ashamed to have him for a brother, and one of his messages

brought the reply, " We have read it, and we strike." All the attempts at general strikes failed, some of them ignominiously. This policy was condemned by Gapon, who had returned to Russia and was now entering into relations with Count Witte. Struve, the editor of *Liberation*, declared that " the summons to senseless and ruinous strikes was either light-headed or criminal, and would ruin the Russian revolution." On December 20, another general strike was proclaimed, and was unsuccessful. Khrustalyéff and some of his comrades had already been arrested, and his removal left a great gap in the Council. The places were filled up by inferior men, and later the whole of the remodelled Council was imprisoned. This event led to the equally abortive rising of December in Moscow.

Count Witte, then, had to deal with the "pogroms" and the strikes together. His task was further complicated by a series of naval risings in Kronstadt, Vladivostók, and Sevastópol, and of military revolts in Kieff, Vorónezh, Bobrúisk, Ekaterinodar, Novorossísk, and Moscow. Most of these risings began with purely economic demands, for instance for the improvement of the food, but political influences from outside could be traced in many cases. In Moscow the chiefs were in the end surrendered. In Sevastópol Lieutenant Schmidt was at one time in command of a rebel fleet and engaged the forces of the Government. He ultimately surrendered, and, in spite of many efforts to save him, suffered the death penalty. At one moment, the Manchurian Railway itself was in the hands of insurgents.

Finland had been the last part of the Empire to lose its liberties. There the political instinct was far more highly trained than elsewhere. The Finns made an able use of their opportunities ; and, by a great corporate movement which suggested what could be done by a united Russia, they without violence rendered the position of the Russian Governor-General untenable. The Government thought it best to treat with Finland, and restored the old rights. The example of Finland did not fail to inspire Russia ; and later the Russian Liberals had only to make a few hours' journey from St. Petersburg in order to voice their demands with the utmost freedom. In Finland, where opinions are more Radical than in England, many raised the cry for further reform,

and many drastic changes were indeed adopted ; from time to time
the Finnish and Russian publics were agitated by the reports of the
prowess of Captain Kock, the " commander of the Red Guard."
Kock, however, was little more than a talker, and his futility was
later, in the summer, exposed by his share in the abortive rising
at Sveaborg. Towards the end of November, the Lettish peasants
of the Baltic provinces began a chaotic movement which, both
politically and economically, was purely revolutionary. These
peasants hated their German masters even more than they hated
the Russian Government. Their grant of emancipation had not
been accompanied by endowment with land, and they were still
in economic dependence on the squires, being a subject race, with
practically no gentry of their own. They were republican ; and
the Government had at one time winked at the spread of their
propaganda, in its desire to degermanise these provinces. The
rising of the Letts, which resulted in the sacking of private
estates and even in the establishment of a little revolutionary
Government, so frightened both the authorities and the German
squires as to make their cause a common one. The rising was
suppressed by punitive columns. One of its results was that
very few Germans were elected to the Imperial Duma. In
Poland a similar class-war, was in progress. Mr. N. N. Lvoff,
who travelled through the country at this time, witnessed open
fighting between the Polish Nationalists and the Polish Socialists ;
for here too the landowners, though adhering to all their national
claims, found it necessary to combat revolution.

Count Witte had also to reckon with the peasants of Russia
Proper. The sacking of estates had become more and more
frequent. On November 16, a Manifesto of the Emperor dealt
with the redemption dues still owing for the land allotted at the
Emancipation ; it reduced them to one-half for the year 1906,
and abolished them altogether from January, 1907. This
enormous lightening of the peasants' burden did not put an end
to the agrarian riots. The promise contained in the Manifesto
that the operations of the Peasants' Bank should be extended was
received with derision. The riots were purely elemental and the
product of what is called in Russia ignorant discontent. Three
flying columns were sent down to the country, and fired without
discrimination on houses and villages. General Sákharoff, the

commander of one of these columns, was killed by the peasants ; but at least they were cowed and reduced to silence. Very naturally, the Government was especially severe towards the Peasants' Union, which it seems to have considered as the chief source of the trouble. Thousands of the members were imprisoned ; and several villages which had accepted the programme of the Union asked leave of the central committee to take back their decisions. It was only later, when the memories of this month were becoming fainter, that the Union began to recover its former hold ; but it found it necessary to change its tactics. It had begun with meetings of whole villages, and had organised district, provincial, and regional assemblies. Several districts had driven out the Land Captains and the Elders imposed upon them by the Government ; one had even made itself practically independent, and, while acknowledging the Emperor, had formed itself into a kind of municipal republic, possessing its own newspaper. Shcherbák, the founder of this republic, was thrown into prison, and his republic came to an end. After the repression, the Union went to work in another way. It enrolled not whole villages at a time, but individual members ; and from March onwards these became more and more numerous.

Count Witte thus failed to find a base for his power amongst the working men and the peasants, and also had to deal with disorders in the alien provinces. He worked night and day as few men could have done, and defied with the utmost courage the symptoms which told him that his physical strength was coming to an end. Distrusted by the Court and disliked by the people in general, he had all the more need to conciliate at least the more moderate leaders of Reform, and from the first he tried to secure the support of the Zemstva. The party of the Cadets was still in process of formation ; Witte therefore made his appeal to those whom he recognised as the leaders in the Zemstvo Congresses. He summoned by telegram representatives of the last Congress. The deputation which went to him consisted of Mr. Golovín, Mr. Kokóshkin, and Prince G. E. Lvoff. They demanded the early summons of a Constituent Assembly on the basis of universal suffrage. Meanwhile the horrors of social chaos were impressing on the more moderate reformers the need of supporting any force which made for order. On November 19, the last Zemstvo Congress

met in Moscow. The formation of the Cadet party had by now
given compactness to the Liberal majority, but the Conservative
Reformers, or, as they preferred to call themselves, the Moderates,
were rallying round the principles expressed in the Manifesto of
October 30. Here, as at other times, we notice that the excesses
of despotism on one side and the excesses of disorder on the other
were gradually hammering out the great nucleus of a central party;
this party was unanimous for reform, but was divided by the
question of methods and degree into two sections, which respectively represented the ordinary tendencies of English Conservatives
and those of English Liberals. At the Congress some insisted
on the need of materialising the reforms, while others pointed out
the necessity of combating the extreme revolutionary elements.
But the two needs were really identical. As to points of detail,
there were many divisions. Some were for direct suffrage, some
for indirect; some claimed constituent rights for the new Duma,
and others did not. The Liberal majority, under the influence of
Milyukóff, who, though not a Zemstvo man, had been admitted to
the Organising Committee, put forward a softened expression of
their programme, asking that the "national representatives might
formally receive constituent functions for drawing up, with the
approval of the sovereign, a Constitution for the Russian Empire."
This formula secured an enormous majority. The Congress, with
practical unanimity, declared " that the Ministry of Count Witte
could reckon on the help and support of wide groups of the Zemstva
and Town Councils, so far as it carried out the constitutional principles of the Manifesto regularly and consequently." The Congress adopted an appeal for an amnesty and for the abolition of the
death sentence. It unanimously condemned the pogroms, and
demanded equal rights for Jews. On the question of Poland the
division was more serious. Mr. A. Guchkóff sturdily opposed the
idea of complete Home Rule. This was, however, accepted by a
great majority, and was accompanied by a demand for the abolition
of martial law in Poland. A deputation was chosen to confer with
Count Witte. The Congress selected some of the chief leaders
of the Liberal party: Mr. Múromtseff, Mr. Kokóshkin, and
Mr. Petrunkyévich. Count Witte was now in no hurry to receive
them, and when he did so, they realised that he was committed to
the Emperor not to go beyond a certain point. The Liberals, as

committed to the principle of Ministerial responsibility, could make no further concessions.

The Conservatives, or moderate reformers, were not yet an organised party; but they perhaps represented at this moment almost as important a section of the whole people as the Liberals. Their leaders, Mr. Shipóff, Mr. Stakhóvich, Count Heyden, and Mr. Guchkóff, were all men who had played a prominent part in the Zemstvo Congresses, and had from time to time put in their plea for calmness and good sense on points of detail. Though their claims were in the main not unlike those of the Liberals, they put them forward in a different spirit. The Moderates claimed not so much rights as responsibilities; that is, they asked for reform not because the people desired it, but because the people needed it, and because without responsibility there could be no living loyalty and no national conscience.[1] As they could hardly as yet be called a party, Count Witte was free to treat with them separately, which he began to do soon after he became Prime Minister. Mr. Shipóff took now, as at other times, a line dictated solely by honour, without regard for the prevailing storm of voices. While himself keeping independent of the Liberals, he referred Count Witte to them as at present representing the majority of expressed opinion.[2] Negotiations with Mr. Guchkóff and Mr. Stakhóvich also came to nothing, and Count Witte was left alone to face the increasing difficulties of his position.

Nothing that had happened since October 30 was calculated to confirm the public confidence in the Government. The series of general strikes had completely exhausted the working classes, but at the same time had further embittered them. Rumours of a new general strike were in the air, and the Government met them with a policy of sheer repression. On November 29, shortly after the second Congress of the Peasants' Union, the whole committee of the Union was arrested in Moscow. On December 5, the committee of the Post and Telegraph Union was also arrested in Moscow. On December 9, Khrustalyéff was arrested in St. Petersburg. On December 15, eight St. Petersburg papers were closed. On December 16, almost the whole of

---

[1] Conversations with three of the above-named leaders.
[2] This advice was consonant with Count Witte's own declaration in his pronouncement after October 30.

the Council of Workmen's Deputies, numbering 190 persons, was arrested while sitting at the Free Economic Society in St. Petersburg. A general strike was now declared at St. Petersburg. It was quite unsuccessful; but again were to be seen the evil effects of the old system, by which one part of the country was isolated from another and a healthy public opinion was made impossible. The revolutionary leaders in Moscow, ill-informed, ill-supported, unprepared, and disunited, thought it was their duty to act with decision. Their supplies of arms were not ready. They were all quarrelling amongst themselves; the Social Democrats were as usual jealous of the Socialist Revolutionaries, and the Peasants' Union, though still strongly represented in Moscow, was hardly consulted. The proclamation of the strike and some street demonstrations led to conflicts with the troops and the erection of barricades, and a comparatively small number of persons drifted into open revolt. The fighting was practically limited to the north-west quarters; the centre of the city was almost untouched. Small fighting bodies had been organised in various wards, but there was no unity of command, and the number of combatants was so small as only to show up the neutrality of the mass of the inhabitants. Some of the infantry had been quite demoralised by the recent military outbreak; the Dragoons did not act with decision, and, as elsewhere, the Cossacks, with sudden charges from behind street corners, bore the brunt of the fighting. More troops were marched in from the Government of Tver, and as the revolutionaries never made any serious attempt to seize and hold the railway from St. Petersburg, the Semyénoff regiment of the Guard reached Moscow and put the balance of force on the Government side. The so-called barricades were often only thin lines of wire, which were hardly defended at all. The revolutionaries, however, managed to irritate the population by their exacting demands. They would enter a house, fire from its windows, and then leave it to the mercy of the troops. Cannon was employed against some houses, and the revolt was gradually driven back on to the factory of Messrs. Prókhoroff, in the north-west suburbs. Here, after a more desperate resistance from the local workmen assisted by a few volunteers from outside, the movement was stamped out. The fighting, grossly exaggerated by some newspaper correspondents, created a great sensation in Europe. Its effects in Russia

were quite as important, but very different. Both Moscow and the
country in general had now seen the revolutionaries at work, had
realised what improper agents they were for the transformation of
the order of government, and were utterly disgusted with them,
their programmes, and their methods. A great movement to the
right took place all over the country ; and the party of Radicals,
which represented the more extreme section of the Intelligents
and the later and more dogmatic committee of the Union of
Unions, was caught in the process of formation and practically
dissolved. The workmen, as they had already done during one of
the previous strikes,[1] began to protest against the leadership of
revolutionary theorists. The chances of a Radical Duma were gone.[2]

All this of course militated in favour of the lately formed Liberal
party known as the Cadets, but the matter did not stop here.
Count Witte practically lost from this time the control of the
Government itself. He was indeed retained as a bid for the good
opinions of Europe, and especially as the man who could secure
foreign loans ; but, in spite of the new principles of Cabinet control,
the real administrative power now passed into the hands of his
Minister of the Interior, Mr. Durnovó. Witte, seeking for support on all sides, had nominated Durnovó as the one man who
could give a definite direction to the work of the police. Durnovó
was another of the watchdogs of the throne ; he was in touch
with General Trepoff, who, as commandant of the Imperial Palace,
became once more the chief source of real power. Admiral
Dubásoff, the Governor-General of Moscow, was a man of the
same school ; and the principle of repression was now defined more
boldly and applied more extragavantly than at almost any previous
period. The country sank into a kind of inertia, and turned its
half-interested attention to the coming elections. The Socialists
had boycotted these elections ; the Peasants' Union was neither
able nor willing to play a prominent part in them. The first
elections were conducted in a hole-and-corner way under the stress
of administrative restrictions ; but there was always the chance
that the country might still make its voice heard, and the very
violence of the repression made it certain that, if any opinions

---

[1] See p. 483.
[2] The above account is largely based on the evidence of Revolutionaries and
Radicals.

were expressed at all, such parties as seemed to stand near to
the Government would share in the unpopularity of Mr. Durnovó.
This meant the ruin of the Octobrists or Moderates.[1] Thus, by
a curious double stroke, the Cadets found themselves triumphing
over their rivals on the left and on the right.

These tendencies were strengthened by the events of January
and February. At this time the assistant Minister of the Interior
was, as so often before, a man the very opposite of his chief.
Prince Urúsoff, who had always combated the policy of Trepoff,
had taken office with the object of bringing order into the administrative system. Letters which reached the Ministry spoke of
" appeals " circulated broadcast in the south and west of the
Empire, and calling for armed attacks upon the Jews. In Gomel
the local Chief of Gendarmes, Count Podgorecháni-Petróvich, had
himself distributed revolvers to the hooligans who looted Jewish
houses. In this case the pogrom could not be traced to any other
origin than the initiative of the Chief of Gendarmes. The report
of a Government investigator sent down to the spot gave the most
damning details.[2] The similar Government reports on the events
of October in Kieff and Odessa had been equally conclusive.
Prince Urúsoff and others managed to avert a further extension
of the pogroms, which were not resumed until the summer. But
at the same time it was discovered that the Gendarme Komisároff
was circulating appeals wholesale from a secret press in the Central Police Department at St. Petersburg; this officer had boasted,
" A pogrom we can make for you, if you like for ten persons, if
you like for ten thousand." Count Witte had here a last chance
of capturing public opinion by plainly denouncing to the Emperor
the pogrom organisation and its promoters. It was a question on
which morality did not admit of two views. But Count Witte
knew that he had no support in the nation, and that persons who
were not Ministers were stronger than himself at the Court.
Exhausted with all his labours, he was seized with an attack of
nervous asthma when the new discovery was announced to him.
He dismissed Komisároff, but did not prevent him from living at
large under an assumed name. Witte remained in office, allowing

[1] " Octobrists " and " Moderates " are terms used at this time to describe the
Conservative Reformers.
[2] Actual Councillor of State Sávich. His report contains the confession of
Podgorecháni-Petróvich.

the matter to drop. Prince Urúsoff resigned his post, and later became the accuser of the policy of pogroms as member for Kaluga in the Imperial Duma. Though all this was not as yet known, public opinion, exasperated by the pogrom of Gomel, flew instinctively to a tolerably correct view of the matter, and even designated the names of those courtiers whom it saddled with the responsibility.

Count Witte had had a last success during the Moscow revolt; it was of the very greatest importance. On December 18 the Government had issued a " Communication" condemning the actions of the revolutionary parties. It had, however, also formulated a scheme which quite remodelled the elections to the Duma. This scheme represented the last concessions which the representations of the Prime Minister could extract from the sovereign. It was for a time held in reserve, and was launched only when the Moscow revolt had seized on the attention of the country (December 24). It made a really strong appeal to the intelligence of the working men, but the moment of its publication was a most unfortunate one. Amongst the mischief done by unscrupulous newspaper work, not the least harmful was the exaggeration of a piece of street fighting conducted by men destitute of all constructive ability, and the comparative suppression of an Edict which completely altered the character of the first Russian Parliament. The decree has been summed up by a Liberal critic as, " within the limits of the Manifesto of October 30, really satisfying all demands and admitting to the elections every single important class of the population, at least in the person of its chief representatives." The decree of August 19 had excluded from the franchise the middle and lower classes of the towns, a few of the smaller landowners, and those workmen who had ceased to be peasants. The franchise was now accorded, in the towns to all payers of taxes and tenants' rates, and to all who received salaries or pensions for paid work; in the country, to all holders of land or real property, to all managers or leaseholders of estates, and, as in the towns, to all who were doing paid work. The workmen were to meet in their factories and choose by indirect election representatives who were to share in the election of members for the Duma. It is true that the very smallest factories were still disfranchised, but this was due to the difficulty of creating an electoral unit for them at such short notice, and at least the intentions of the Government were in this case beyond criticism. The holders of the tenants' franchise in sixty provinces were increased from 18,876 to 2,000,000. The franchise was now withheld only from workers in factories which employed less than fifty persons, small craftsmen, casual labourers, and peasants without property. The Government further announced that the Duma would itself have the right of discussing the extension of the franchise. On January 11, another " Communication " pledged the Government to aim at fixing the earliest possible date for the meeting of the Duma, and, with this object, voters were advised to register themselves at once and to help to preserve order. The vast changes made by this decree realised as far as was practicable the demand for universal suffrage put forward by all parties of the Left, from the Liberals to the Revolutionaries. But the importance of these measures was overlooked in the noise of the Moscow rising and in the general bitterness against the subsequent repression. Whilst official violence was daily witnessed, men looked upon the decree as mere words; thus the dual Government was its own worst enemy, and Durnovó wrecked the last appeal of Witte. Even Moderates criticised the new edict, and the working classes, quite failing to see what immense power it had given to them, still persisted for the most part in their resolve to boycott the Duma altogether.

But for those who could see it a great opportunity was opened up. The political ability of Russia was largely concentrated within the ranks of the Cadets. This party had been the first to constitute itself with a definite programme. It had been consistent in its negotiations with Count Witte; it was the only section of public opinion which did not lose heart under the lash of Durnovó. It was excellently disciplined, contained some of the most illustrious names in Russia, and had in Mr. Milyukóff a leader of remarkable acuteness, tact, and resource. It established local committees all over the country. Being the last unit to the Left which the Government would tolerate, it freely circulated its propaganda in the most active way, and in some peasant villages its papers were even imagined to carry, like other papers, the sanction of the authorities. It established relations with every organised section of opinion which was aiming at similar objects.

Thus, concordats were made with the National Democrats of Poland, who, while combating revolution, desired to obtain Home Rule, with other Nationalist sections, and notably with the Union of Full Rights for Jews, which, as a Liberal body, was opposed to the revolutionary Jewish Bund. It was arranged in detail which of the contracting sections should name the common candidates for common support in given towns and provinces. By recognising a so-called " Left Wing of the Cadets," the Liberals were able to draw within their ranks a large number of Radicals or peasant members who would ordinarily have formed separate groups. The further education and closer organisation of the party itself was proceeding at the same time; but, in face of the difficulties caused by disturbances and by distances, this task could not be accomplished till the elected deputies should all meet in St. Petersburg. Still the Cadets had an immense advantage as being the one organised party. Their object was to create a practically unanimous Duma ; for they realised that even such a Duma would still have the greatest difficulty in gaining a control over the Ministry and over the official world. Their grave fault was that, in the limited sense of the word, they were altogether too clever. They were ready to defer to almost everyone, to treat with almost everyone. They thus signed bills which they would later have great difficulty in meeting.

The exceptional cleverness which the Cadets brought to their task found no answer in the Government. The officials could not understand the working of the system which they had themselves established. There was always the same division within the camp. Durnovó was for repressive measures at the time of election ; Witte was opposed to them. The question in the end settled itself ; the Government proved to be quite unprepared, and it was soon obvious that the country had a chance of expressing its real opinion. The Cadets supplied the needed backbone of programme and organisation. When it was seen that a Liberal Duma was sure to be elected, the voters took heart ; repressive measures became impossible and were indeed abandoned; and even those who had boycotted the Duma, though their party leaders still persisted in this foolish policy, came forward in whole masses to swell the majority. The absurd plan by which all the electors of a given province met to choose by common vote all the

representatives for that province, made it possible for an organised
majority of one to secure practically the whole representation.
Even where the Cadets and their friends did not possess an
absolute majority, they had to deal with a disorganised mass of
conflicting rivals, and thus were able to secure even in such districts, by local compacts or otherwise, a far greater measure of
success than they had a right to expect.

Of course they were not able to do everything at once. Electoral
campaigns could be conducted in the towns, that is, at the town elections and before the final choice of all the members for a given province; but in the country districts they were almost impossible,
and the peasants, when they chose their own electors in the first
instance, judged rather by personalities than by political opinions.
In some cases these elections went almost by chance; in one case,
and possibly in more, the peasants drew lots. Even the workmen
of Moscow thought of doing the same; they imagined that each
member would present a written list of grievances from his constituents, and that each list would be attended to in turn.[1] Of
course many peasants thought that the Tsar would sit in the Duma.
The Cadets only had time to deal with the existing political
organisations; and a large number of the peasants elected refused
to be classified, and composed a mass of non-party members. But
the "non-party" were certainly not without definite tendencies
of their own. They represented, in the first place, the peasant's
habit of non-committal; they were by instinct deeply Conservative, but they, as much as anyone else, had grievances against the
officials, and they quite realised the need of better administration.
Though they never published a programme, they were all for the
allotting of more land, the removal of Land Captains, and freedom
of education. Their attitude can best be illustrated by a very
shrewd remark made to me by one of them. "There are four
parties," he said: "the Moderates, the Cadets, the Labour Group,
and the Non-Party. Each party has its secret; that party which
keeps its secret longest will win. I think that the Non-Party will
keep its secret longest, and that it will win." In a word, the
peasants quite realised that everyone would be trying to capture
their goodwill, and, as they knew what they wanted, they were
not going to sell themselves to anyone.

[1] Conversation with Mr. Savélyeff, Labour Member for Moscow.

Each party exaggerated its numbers in the Duma; several persons belonged to two groups at once ; but the constitution of the Duma may be roughly outlined as follows :—

There were seven reactionaries who had no leader of any eminence, and seldom dared to oppose the majority in speech or in voting. There were some fifty Moderates, of whom the nucleus consisted of some sixteen Octobrists. This was a group of persons of similar instincts rather than a party. It had, however, a most able and distinguished leader in Count Heyden and a fervent and convincing spokesman in Mr. Stakhóvich. Mr. Shipóff, the natural leader of this group, failed to secure election, and became one of the new elected members of the Council of State. The Non-Party finally numbered between seventy and one hundred. There were several small racial groups, which generally sided with the Cadets or the Labour Group in the hope of obtaining local self-government. Such were the National Democrats of Livland (2), of Esthonia (2), and of Lithuania (5), the Ukraine Democrats (2), and the Mussulmans (6). More Conservative, though still quite opposed to the Government, were the Polish representatives, who as the Polish Socialists had boycotted the elections, consisted almost exclusively of nobles and a few peasants. The two Polish parties in the Duma, the National Democrats of Poland proper (19) and the Constitutional Catholics or Polish nobles of Lithuania (8), had slightly different programmes, but both were sure to draw closer to the Moderates as soon as their demand for self-government had been satisfied. All these racial units joined to form a group known as the Autonomists. Just before the elections was formed a small party representing Liberal views rather more moderate than those of the Cadets. It called itself the Party of Democratic Reforms, and amongst its four members it counted two men who were always listened to by the Duma, Professor Kovalyévsky and Professor Kuzmín-Karaváyeff. Next to this party, and in the centre of the Assembly, sat the mass of the Cadets, who numbered nearly two hundred. Amongst them were most of the notable men of the movement of liberation : Petrunkyévich, Ródicheff, Múromtseff, Prince Peter Dolgorúkoff, Prince Shakhovskóy, Kokóshkin, N. N. Lvoff, and Nabókoff. Professor Milyukóff had been excluded from the Duma by an unworthy trick: by the Duma law, persons under prosecution were ineligible; he was accused of a small Press offence of which he was later acquitted. For all that, he was the real ruler of the House, and every important step was referred to him by his party for decision. The Left Wing of the Cadets included Professor Shchepkin, a vehement speaker, and others who chafed under the control of Milyukóff. To the left of the Cadets sat the Labour Group ; this party was formed after the elections. By March the Peasants' Union had begun to recover from the repressive measures of Mr. Durnovó. However, as a body, it boycotted the elections, and it was only half-way through them that its members began to act with effect. In Sarátoff some of its leaders shook themselves clear of the domination of the Cadets, and, refusing a contract which would have allotted to them three of the nine seats, managed to win six. The most able of the labour leaders, Zhilkin, Aládin, and Aníkin, came from the Lower Volga. On their arrival in St. Petersburg they set about organising a Labour Party; the members of it they proposed to capture from the Cadets and from the Non-Party. A similar attempt was being made by the reactionaries ; Mr. Yeróghin, one of the few reactionaries elected, made arrangements to house many of the non-party members in a far corner of St. Petersburg close to the Duma. At one time over seventy members were living in Kírochnaya 52. A country priest who had been elected was quartered in amongst them ; every attempt was made to discipline them, and they were at times invited to sign so-called minority resolutions counteracting those decisions of the Duma which they had not dared to oppose publicly. But Yeróghin's machinations worked to the profit of his adversaries. Aládin and his friends soon found their way into Kírochnaya 52, and possibly Yeróghin now regretted that he had gathered together so many members to be an easy prey for the labour organisers. Some moved from their new quarters ; others still more disobligingly accepted Cadet or Labour leadership, but remained in the enemy's camp. The organisation of the Labour Group, so far from being opposed by the Cadets, was actually helped forward by them. About a hundred members still remained non-party ; most of the other peasants were now Labour men. The Labour Group was never homogeneous; but it was disciplined with remarkable ability by Mr. Zhilkin, it possessed an effective agitator in Mr. Aládin, and in Mr. Aníkin it had a speaker of impressive simplicity and deep conviction. The Labour Group was like the Peasants' Union: it allowed each of its members to propagate his own views, but it refused to advocate any formula of a system of government; it left that question to be settled by representatives of the nation elected on manhood suffrage. It adhered to the resolutions of the Cadets without ever becoming dependent upon that party; its programme was practically summed up in the formula of the Peasants' Union, "All the land for those that labour."

The workmen had boycotted the elections more completely than the peasants. In the later elections some few of them had been chosen, chiefly by the goodwill of the Cadets. These represented the less uncompromising of the Social Democrats. They had no leaders of any force, and generally concurred in the decisions of the Labour Group; but they received an accession of strength from the elections in the Caucasus and in Siberia, which were not completed until long after the Duma had met. But for the dissolution, they might have begun to take a prominent part; but the character of their speeches did not suggest that they would make any serious contribution to the work of the Assembly.

The Emperor, when he consented to issue the decree of December 24, had tried to think with Count Witte that this great enlargement of the franchise would secure for him a Duma which would work with the Government. The elections falsified this hope; and meanwhile on March 5, 1906, was issued a series of fundamental laws strictly defining the limits of the competence of the new Assembly. The Upper House (the Council of State) might play an important part; and, in order to give it a more national character, the nominated members were to be reinforced by an equal number of members elected by the clergy, gentry, Universities, Zemstva, Town Councils, and other bodies. The Council was declared to have the same rights of legislation as the Duma. No law could be passed without the approval of both bodies. During recesses or after dissolutions the Ministers could act independently, but were bound to submit their enactments to the assemblies later on. The Council and the Duma were to be summoned yearly; the fundamental laws were excluded from discussion. Bills passed by both bodies, but not approved by the Emperor, could not be brought in again during the same session. The subjects which the Duma could discuss were again clearly stated.

The Ministry of Count Witte had long outlived its usefulness. The Premier was retained in office until he had succeeded in obtaining by foreign loans as much money as was immediately necessary for the expenses of government ; he was then dismissed somewhat unceremoniously ; Mr. Durnovó left office at the same time. No one seemed to have any idea as to what would happen when the Duma met ; and the task of government was committed to men of the second order, whose political opinions were almost colourless, and who represented, if anything, the intention of the Court to give the Duma a chance of showing what it was like. Mr. Goremýkin, the new Premier, was a mildly Liberal bureaucrat of eminently respectable antecedents ; Mr. Stolýpin, the Minister of the Interior and the one really strong man in the Cabinet, was known at once for his firmness and for his respect for law. As much cannot be said for Mr. Stishínsky, the Minister of Agriculture, who would have to meet the Duma on the difficult ground of the land question. His assistant, Mr. Gurko, was a typical champion of all those instincts of bureaucracy which were most irritating to the outside world. The fundamental defect of this Ministry lay in the well-known fact that it did not really handle the reins of power. The actual leaders of the oligarchy did not care to expose themselves to an open conflict with the Duma, but they remained encamped around the throne and made any understanding impossible.

During the sittings of the Duma, all parties observed a kind of unwritten truce. The Terrorists abstained from terrorising ; and on the other side the Government accorded an unwonted measure of liberty to the Press. The weekly *Právo* (Right) had long championed the cause of reform. In February the Cadets started their organ *Rech* (Speech), a daily under the editorship of Miluykóff and Hessen, which soon enjoyed a circulation of over fifty thousand copies. Struve founded a short-lived daily, *The Duma*, which published the debates every evening. *Straná* (the Country), edited by Kovalyévsky and representing the Party of Democratic Reforms, had for a time a large circulation. The Socialist organs could now appear freely ; most of them took this occasion to show their insipidity; the only one which was really formidable to the Government was issued under several different names by the Labour Group; it printed letters from the peasants and votes of Village Societies. Constitutionally, these votes of whole villages were the proper legitimisation of its policy, and the Government suppressed this organ time after time. It did the same to the other Socialist newspapers; we must suppose that it failed to observe the increasing moderation of their tone; otherwise it would hardly have once more put upon them the premium of secrecy.

The Duma met on May 10, 1906. The Emperor, who had not visited his capital since the attempt made upon his life in January, 1905, in a firm and vigorous voice expressed his hope that the labours of the Assembly would be conducive to the welfare of Russia. The Duma, when it had met in the palace prepared for it, elected its President, Vice-Presidents, and Secretaries. There was no contest; nearly all were chosen from the ranks of the Cadets. All the prominent leaders of different parties had at one time or another been under the displeasure of the Government, and Professor Gredyéskul, a man of no particular eminence, was appointed Vice-President simply because he had been one of the last to suffer persecution. The Assembly made an admirable choice of a president : Professor Múromtseff is a trained lawyer of great distinction, whose nice legal sense and keen and conscientious discrimination would do credit to the English bench. His noble presence gave dignity to the Assembly ; and his untiring concentration of mind, though it visibly aged him during the sittings, maintained throughout the debates the control of the spirit of law. In his absence Prince Peter Dolgorúkoff was an able and business-like chairman. Prince Shakhovskóy was a capable secretary.

The Emperor's Speech from the Throne had not contained any programme of legislation, nor did the Ministers suggest any. Of this great mistake the Duma took immediate advantage. We might say that the Emperor wanted a German Parliament, and that the Duma intended to be an English one. It decided to take the initiative by putting forward a whole programme in its "Address to the Throne." This was a policy which would help to keep the Assembly united ; for the minimum demands of all sections could be expressed together. The Address was very cleverly drafted. The abruptness of some of the demands was masked by the loyal and moderate tone adopted throughout. The needs of the peasants held a prominent place ; the more radical demands of the workmen received less recognition, but then the workmen had by their boycott practically excluded themselves from the Duma, and the object of the Cadets was to secure the unanimity of those present. The debates were animated ; a leading part was taken by the Labour Group, which was still in process of formation. The Labour leaders adopted the wise policy of leaving their more extreme claims unexpressed, supporting the Cadets in all their disputes with the Moderates, and trying to secure the most decisive wording which could be passed unanimously. The Address was read three times ; at the second reading it was debated sentence by sentence. Discussion centred chiefly round the land question, and the demands for an amnesty for political prisoners and for the abolition of the death penalty. Count Heyden, standing for wise moderation, used his excellent debating power to keep the demands within reasonable bounds. On the land question the Moderates, who more than anyone else represented the country gentry, showed their public spirit by accepting the principle of expropriation of land ; the measure of compensation was left to be decided later. Realising the numerical weakness of his party, Mr. Stakhóvich reserved his effort for the question of the amnesty. In two great speeches, which came straight from his heart and would have carried conviction to any who were not hopelessly prejudiced, he demanded that the amnesty should be two-sided, and that the Duma, while condemning the death penalty as inhuman[1] and demanding the immediate release of political prisoners, should in the name of the country frankly express its opinion that murders of officials should cease from that day. No more just or more eloquent claim was heard during the sittings of the Duma. The country gentry had not pleaded for themselves ; they spoke in the cause of the police, with whom they had nothing in common. Mr. Stakhóvich had seized the exact moment when, with only one dissentient, the Assembly had decided on the abolition of the death penalty. But the Cadets, who always kept their eyes fixed

[1] It has long been abolished for all except political crimes.

on the extremists to the left of them, and, in their tactical mani-
pulation of the votes, failed to appreciate the great mass of opinion
outside, now made their first crucial mistake ; and Mr.
Ródicheff was put up to oppose the amendment of Stakhóvich. Turning
his back on the Left, and adopting an almost threatening manner
towards the Octobrists, he gradually worked himself up into a
rhetorical piece of special pleading, in which he maintained " that
the time was not yet come for moderation, that it would come
only after the victory." The Labour Group applauded, and on a
division Mr. Stakhóvich found himself in an insignificant minority.
But the Duma had lost its best chance[1]; Mr. Lvoff one of the
most able and honest of the Cadets, soon afterwards left the party.
    The Address was piloted throughout the debate by Mr. Nabókoff.
In a voice under whose soft inflection lay the suggestion of a great
reserve of strength, he over and over again gave matter-of-fact
and convincing answers to the objections of individual members.
When he was not speaking, it was often more interesting to watch
him than to follow the debates : he would rise in a casual way
from his seat, move through the assembly much as an English
gentleman might pass through the smoking room of his club,
seat himself beside the terrible Aládin of the Labour Group, and
work out with him some formula which could be accepted by
that party. This, after very outspoken discussion, would at
last be achieved, and Nabókoff, with his little slip of paper in his
hands, would walk straight across to Count Heyden, the Conservative leader, with whom the same process would be repeated. It
was to be noticed that almost anything proposed by Nabókoff
was passed unanimously. The time came for the third reading.
Heyden, Stakhóvich, and a few others,[2] being unable to accept
certain phrases, retired to avoid breaking the unanimity of the
House. At 3 a.m. the final draft was accepted in a full House
by all present.
    The Address expressed a number of general principles and

---

[1] Of the many members with whom I talked immediately afterwards on the
subject, nearly all admitted that it was a mistake. It would seem, then, that the
action of the Cadets was decided for them by their leaders. It was well known
that Petrunkyévich, Nabókoff, etc., were utterly opposed to the methods of Terrorism.
Why, then, did the party submit to this disgrace? Soon afterwards a gentleman
sent to Mr. Ródicheff an open letter couched in these terms : "Dear Sir,—I have
made a plot to kill you. Will you kindly ask for an amnesty for me in advance?"
[2] Less than ten.

suggested legislation on each. It was far more easy for the Government to break up the unity of the Duma than for Milyukóff to maintain it. Formally, the Address was simply an answer to the Emperor's speech; it remained that each demand contained in it should be turned into a separate Bill. If the Government were still so lacking in initiative as not to produce any Bills of its own, it might leave the Duma to go on with this work in the full assurance that there would sooner or later be divisions inside the Assembly. There was one way of keeping the Duma united against the Government, and that way was adopted by the Ministers. An unnecessary fuss was made as to the way in which the Address should be received by the Emperor. The Duma was ordered to send it to him, not directly, but through the Marshal of the Court. This made a very bad impression, as publishing to the nation the fact that the Emperor was isolated from the Duma. But the Ministers did not stop here : they solemnly came down to the Duma to pronounce a kind of judgment on the Address. The Premier, Mr. Goremýkin, read out a long statement in which, while suggesting certain mild reforms, he characterised the chief demands of the Duma as "inadmissible." Above all, he strongly repudiated the policy of expropriation, which he declared to be anti-social. His manner was that of a schoolmaster reading a lesson, yet it was well known that he was not the real possessor of power. His remarks were listened to without the slightest interruption and in a painfully breathless silence. When he sat down, Mr. Nabókoff mounted the tribune. Speaking very simply and quietly, like a man who was thoroughly at his ease, he expressed the disappointment of the Assembly, and proceeded in a matter-of-fact way to move a vote of censure on the Government. Thus thrown upon their defence, the bureaucratic Ministers proved utterly incapable of meeting outspoken criticism. In their own Ministries they could order any critic out of the room; but here was a situation which they had never had to face before. They sat there bowing beneath the storm as one speaker after another drew instances from the vast store of official abuses, and catechised them point-blank on questions both of principle and of detail. Kovalyévsky asked whether the Emperor Alexander II. acted anti-socially, when he emancipated the serfs and endowed them with land. Kokóshkin, in defence of certain English principles to which the Duma had appealed, suggested that the maintenance of order was rather more successful in England than in Russia. One Minister, Mr. Shcheglovítoff, rose to almost apologise for the Government, very much to the chagrin of his colleagues. One can imagine how this scene would lower the prestige of the Government in the eyes of the average non-party peasant. After standing the racket for some time as best they might, the Ministers withdrew; and the vote of censure, which had the support of the Moderates, was carried without any opposition.

The Duma now settled down to its work of discussing separate Bills. The family atmosphere, which is so noticeable in Russia, was here peculiarly strong. The Assembly, having complete control of its own house, turned it into something like a vast caravanserai. The beautiful hall soon came to be regarded, even by the peasant members, as a kind of home. The long side lobbies were furnished with great tables covered with green baize, at which peasants and Intelligents sat down indiscriminately to write letters to their families. A constant stream of members was always passing through these rooms; and all congregated from time to time in the great noisy corridor. Here the chief leaders walked up and down arm in arm; and isolated peasants, Russian, Cossack, or Polish, sat about on the different benches and were quite ready to converse with any stranger. Members and correspondents gathered without distinction at the buffet and in the restaurant, and little groups of acquaintances wandered through the pleasant gardens outside. The building contained its own postal and telegraph office. If the Duma did nothing else, it brought together for the first time representatives of every class and of every interest in Russia. It was of course far more Imperial than any other European Parliament. It would be difficult to imagine a more picturesque gathering. Each man wore the costume of his class. The country gentry of the Intelligents dressed very simply, but there were Russian priests with long beards and hair, a Roman Catholic bishop in skull-cap lined with red, finely accoutred Cossacks from the Caucasus, Bashkirs and Buryats in strange and tinselled Asiatic dress, Polish peasants in the brilliant and martial costumes of their people, and a whole mass of staid, bearded, and top-booted Russian peasants. Strangers easily obtained admittance; and amongst the most picturesque visitors were the so-called "walking deputies" who were sent by peasant constituents to look after their members, and others who had tramped for hundreds of miles to ask the Duma to settle their private disputes. Groups of members and non-members formed in the corridor to discuss without reticence any question of the moment. Small party conferences, sitting in the committee-rooms, seemed in no way disturbed by passing strangers. Milyukóff, in the simple dress of an English country gentleman, walked up and down the corridor receiving the suggestions of various party leaders, which seldom induced him to deviate a yard from the tactics upon which he had determined. One noticed that the Cadets as a body quite failed to get hold of the non-party members. These peasants, who would not sink their individuality in any party formula, expressed the most fresh and interesting opinions of all. Count Heyden could often be seen discussing matters with them; he understood them, and they understood him; but Milyukóff was hardly ever to be seen talking to a non-party man. At one time it appeared that Kovalyévsky and Kuzmín-Karaváyeff might capture a considerable section of the Cadets; but the Cadets arranged that every member should register his seat in the House, and this made it more difficult to pass from one party to another. The Labour Group, which continued its organisation throughout the sittings, tried in every way to absorb the Non-Party, but without success.

Bills were introduced into the Duma guaranteeing freedom of conscience and the inviolability of the person. The discussions were not very interesting; everyone was agreed as to these main principles, little more than the principles was expressed in the Bills, and almost as much had been said in the Emperor's manifestos. A month's delay had to pass after the notice of introduction, before the Assembly could deal effectively with any proposed measure. The Duma was allowed to discuss the franchise, and it of course declared in favour of the well-known formula "universal, direct, equal, and secret." The debate on women's suffrage excited a lively interest. On this day the corridor was invaded by an active band of suffragettes, who evidently thought that they could give the necessary lessons to the non-party peasant. It was amusing to watch the peasants dealing with these young ladies. One very typical peasant admitted that it was most unfair that women should receive lower pay than men for similar work. "We will put that right for you," he said; "let us get on our legs first, then we will give you some rights." But the young ladies wanted not to receive, but to take, and claimed that women ought to be sitting in the Duma. "Look here," said he, "I will tell you what: you go and marry! You will have a husband and children, and your husband will look after you altogether." "Look after, indeed!" said the young ladies; but the peasant would not promise anything more. Equally interesting was the attitude of the Non-Party group towards the Jews: they spoke without any ill-will, but remarked: "Even without rights, the Jews are on the top of us." They were therefore almost the only dissentients on both these questions.

All these Bills were not really practical politics, for not a single measure of the Duma became law except a vote of credit to the Government to relieve peasant distress; they were rather appeals for popular support. Realising from the first that the bureaucracy was definitely hostile to it, and that no frank reform could successfully pass through the various stages ordained by the Government, the Duma naturally set itself to secure strength from elsewhere. With this object, it deliberately turned itself into a machine for propaganda. "The tribune," said one Labour member to me, "is the only part of this House that counts." Nearly every newspaper published the fullest reports of the sittings, and these were eagerly devoured in distant villages all over the country. Immobilised in its legislative work, the Duma put a number of carefully but firmly worded interpellations to the various Ministers. The abuses of the administration were thus brandished before the eyes of the country. This was already war, but it would be difficult to say which side had first declared it. Ministers, severally or together, continued to visit the Duma, to make explanations or to answer interpellations. Each such visit naturally led to a scene; when the Duma had, with one dissentient, abolished the death sentence, the Government sent down General Pavloff to explain that it refused this measure. Pavloff was generally believed to have hurried on the execution of certain death sentences contrary to law, and the Labour Group interrupted him with cries of "Murderer!" The President even had to adjourn the sitting. Aládin, who spoke with far more vehemence inside the Duma than amongst his own party, suggested that it was very amiable of the Ministers to continue to come down to the House after they had been told that the country did not want them. The situation was in fact an entirely false one for all concerned. The only Minister who knew how to face it was Mr. Stolýpin. He answered interpellations with the utmost moderation, but with the utmost firmness; and once, when the Labour Group tried to shout him down, he turned on them and addressed the rest of his speech to them in a voice which rose loud and strong above all their clamour. He was the one Minister who was ever cheered by any member of the Duma. But Mr. Stolýpin, though universally credited with honesty and courage, had to meet the strongest charges of all: he had to answer for the faults or omissions of his predecessors in office. On June 21 he had just replied to an interpellation on the "pogroms," when Prince Urúsoff rose to make his memorable speech on the official circulation of appeals to murder, and the malignant activity of Komisároff. The Prince spoke in so low a voice as to be almost inaudible; many of the peasant members in no way realised the importance of his speech; but it was published in full in most of the newspapers, and dealt to the Government by far the most crushing blow which it had yet received. The speech was exemplary in its moderation and loyalty; Prince Urúsoff in no way inculpated the existing Ministry: the only inference which he drew from his disclosures was that the dualism within the Government itself must be abolished without delay, and that the Emperor must be put into real touch with his people. But to make his meaning clear, he had to attack "those obscure forces which," he said, "are arming against us." This was a more open declaration of war between the Duma and the unofficial advisers of the Crown.

Rumours of dissolution had been in the air ever since the passing of the Address. The Cadets desired to use every day to the full, in order to make the position of the Duma so strong in the country that dissolution would become practically impossible. This is why they gave such prominence to the land question, and

why their Bill bore so pretentious a character. Mr. Milyukóff
might almost be compared to the gambler in the famous opera of
Pushkin and Chaikóvsky. Three cards will, he believes, give him
fortune, and he dreams that the numbers have been revealed to him:
he calls the three, (the three autonomies), and wins ; he calls the
seven, (the seven freedoms), and wins ; he calls the ace, and the
card produced is the Queen of Spades ; pique—mort. The Queen
of Spades was the land question.

The Land Bill of the Cadets was in many ways much less
objectionable than it seemed. The principle of expropriation is
in itself not revolutionary in Russia ; it had been accepted by
almost every section of public opinion, including the Conservative
representatives of the country gentry ; indeed, some reactionaries
had blamed Mr. Goremykin for publicly opposing it. The
Cadets were all in favour of compensation to the landowner,
and were only divided on the question as to what would be a fair
price ; naturally, many objected to the artificial prices produced
by the operations of the Peasants' Bank. Though the Cadets
accepted the principle of the Labour Group that there should be
a legal limit to the extent of estates, they fixed this limit so
high as to rob the principle of all its force. The Cadets also
agreed with the Labour party in declaring that land should be
State property ; but the long leases which they proposed knocked
the life out of this declaration. Certainly Mr. Heŕtzenstein, the
chief authority of the Cadets on this question, was not so much
a land expert as an expert on land values, and his views were
chiefly dictated by theories of almost a socialistic kind.[1]
Certainly nothing but theory could explain the assumption that
Russia would prosper only on the basis of limited holdings. But
leading Cadets themselves suggested in conversation that the
Bill would come out of committee robbed of all its disagreeable
characteristics. This is itself the sum of their condemnation.
As it was they who had drafted the Bill, the pretence of Socialism
in the original draft can only be looked upon as a hardly ingenuous
piece of tactics, designed to preserve the unanimity of the Duma,
and to capture the votes of the Labour Group. For all that, the
Labour men introduced a separate Bill of their own. Their Bill
was really that which the Cadet Bill only pretended to be, but the

[1] Conversation with Mr. Hertzenstein.

very similarity between the two justified the general opinion that
the Cadets were almost Socialists. Beyond this, the Cadets had
altogether misjudged their public. If I may trust the common
conclusions of peasant members from almost every part of the
Empire, only the least enterprising of the peasants were still in
favour of the communal system of land tenure, though all wished
to retain the Village Society. The most cherished dream of the
intelligent peasant was that of personal property in land. The
first land debates were ruled by the tactics of propagandism.
Almost every peasant was encouraged to speak. Nearly all read
their speeches; the speaker would afterwards proudly despatch the
draft to his constituents. Thus the debate was rambling in the
extreme. Next an enormous Commission was chosen to represent every section of the Duma; it was hoped that now the
peasants would be willing to wait a little longer for the land; the
Commission did not propose to hurry itself.

But the Government was getting ready to move. The recent
pogrom in Byelostok, though presenting no signs of collusion
with St. Petersburg, was undoubtedly in large part due to the
neutrality or worse of local officials. The Duma sent its own
investigators to the spot, and they accepted without due examination any evidence offered to them so long as it was hostile to the
police. It was now proposed, with the hearty concurrence of the
Labour Group, to constitute in the country small committees to
investigate the land question in each locality; in other words, the
Duma was making a bid to gradually become the Government of
the country. The tension between the representatives of the
people and the Ministers was too severe to last.

More than once voices were raised even at the Court suggesting an accommodation. This could only be obtained by the
resignation of the Ministers and the appointment of men who
commanded the support of the Duma. Amongst those who were
said to advocate this step the public were surprised to see the
name of General Trépoff. The Ministers, it may be imagined,
were not unwilling to retire from their exceedingly disagreeable
position. From the appointment of a Cadet Ministry certain
results were practically sure to follow. There would inevitably
be an open conflict between the new Ministers and the so-called
camarilla, or unofficial Court clique; but at the same time the

Cadets would be forced by their new responsibilities to sever their connection with the Labour Group and to move more to the right; there would then be some kind of a split in the Cadet party itself, and thus there would be constituted inside the Duma a real Opposition. The governing Right Wing of the Cadets would be compelled to lean for support on the Moderates, and this new party of the Right would include nearly all those members of the Duma whom the Zemstva had trained in practical work. It could hardly have failed to take a tinge of class interests from the country gentry and the more responsible section of the middle class. The new Ministry, once in power, would be on its defence; every measure which it brought forward would be severely criticised, and men who had shown ability in opposition would now have to prove that they were more capable in administration than the bureaucracy. As the number of able Cadets was limited, and as they had been trained after all only in the sphere of local government, they could not have dispensed with the support of a certain number of the more Liberal bureaucrats. Such men would have to be retained both in the *personnel* of officialdom and in the Ministry itself. Any failure of the Cadets would help to develope in the public mind a natural movement of moral reaction which was already in process. For the Government, one of the strongest arguments in favour of a Cadet Ministry was that for once Russia possessed a Duma in which the strength lay near the centre. This phenomenon is comparatively rare even in constitutional assemblies of long standing; in Russia it was the artificial result of circumstances already explained; but it made for the formation of a great middle term between the sovereign and his people, and it was something to be seized upon and used to the utmost. Anyhow, the Court was half prepared to compromise; twice Mr. Shipóff was summoned to Peterhof, but as one who had failed to enter the Duma, and whose supporters in it were only a small and unorganised group, he once more refused office. There was much talk of a Ministry which should include both Mr. Múromtseff and Count Heyden. It was definitely resolved to invite Mr. Múromtseff to Peterhof that he might suggest the names of possible colleagues; but a small disturbance in the Preobrazhénsky regiment of the Guard led to a Court panic, and the step was deferred. Mr. Múromtseff, admirable as the President of the Assembly, would perhaps not have

made a strong Prime Minister ; and the Cadets seemed inclined
to refuse to serve under any but their recognised party leaders.
Certainly they represented the spirit of opposition in the country,
and had given so many pledges to the public that they could hardly
sink the individuality of their party in a coalition. But for
these very reasons the personality of Mr. Milyukóff was highly
distasteful to the Court. Not once during the session had the
President been invited to Peterhof except as one of many guests
at a Court banquet. If he had possessed a right of claiming inter-
views with the sovereign, or if there had been in the Assembly a
responsible person in touch with the majority who reported the
daily debates to the Emperor, the Court would have possessed
more detailed knowledge of the actual political atmosphere.
Anyhow all the chances of an accommodation came to nothing.

Meanwhile the Ministers could not but realise that the Duma
was undermining their prestige amongst the people. The Land
Bill was the most extreme bid of the Assembly for support against
the Government; the Ministers drew up their own alternative
measure, and, in a circular which they officially published all over
the Empire, they condemned the principles of the Cadet Bill, thus
making a direct appeal to the country against the Duma.

So far the propagandism of the Duma had been indirect ; the Duma
was precluded by law from issuing a direct address to the people ;
but such action had been equally illegal when these same Cadet
leaders had carried their appeal through the Moscow Congress of
July, 1905 ; and the fervour of the Labour Group and of the Cadets
of the Left was not likely to be daunted by this formality. It was
now that patience snapped on both sides. The Land Commission
was the body specially attacked by the Government circular. All
parties were represented on it; but its office-holders were not the
chief leaders of the Cadets, and Milyukóff, as not being in the Duma,
was of course excluded from it. At the Congress of July, 1905,
a prominent part had been taken by Kuzmín-Karaváyeff, who in
the name of legality and order had begged the Congress to proceed with the greatest circumspection. This gentleman had played
a prominent part in the Duma ; he was supposed to be more
Conservative than any of the Cadets ; a speaker of remarkable
grace and fluency, he always commanded attention. He now
proposed to the Land Commission that it should send out to the

country a weakly worded appeal asking the constituents not to believe in the Government circular, and to trust the Duma to make an effective Land Bill. The Commission, as representing all parties, adopted the address, and presented it for the acceptance of the whole Duma. The debate on this address was very remarkable. Late at night Mr. Lednítsky, sitting amongst the Cadets of the Right and also representing the Autonomist group, in vigorous language denounced the appeal as both feeble and irritating; he was loudly applauded both by the Moderates and by the Labour Group. But party discipline was strong amongst the Cadets; and the Labour Group preferred to compromise their rivals by a weak appeal rather than have no appeal at all. After pleading for the insertion of a stronger wording at certain points, they supported the address, and it was carried at the first reading by an immense majority.

On the next day there was no sitting, but in the evening there was a party meeting of the Cadets. Milyukóff and others of the leaders looked upon the address as a bad tactical mistake; they might be ready to appeal to the country, but this was neither the right time nor the right way. Many of their followers seemed inclined to break loose from them. However, the leaders in the end triumphed, and on the succeeding day Mr. Petrunkyévich rose at the second reading to suggest an entirely different wording of the whole address. This he moved by way of amendments to each paragraph. The Labour Group saw itself defeated on those points which it had most at heart, and the Cadets, in opposing the Labour amendments, had the support of the Moderates; finally the Labour Group left the hall *en masse*, and decided to draw up a more abrupt appeal of its own. After its departure, the Moderates contested the whole measure, and for the first time a proposal of the Cadets was passed only by a small majority. The suggestion that the address should be officially printed in the *Official Messenger* could not be discussed at all, because it was found that at this late hour the House did not possess the necessary quorum.

The wording of Petrunkyévich was far superior to the original draft. But the Duma had definitely decided to disregard the fundamental laws. Far more important was the obvious fact that the Duma and even the Cadet party were no longer unanimous. It seemed strange that a measure adopted almost unanimously by the Duma should be radically altered at the next sitting because a given party had decided to give it a different character; and an appeal to the people was precisely the measure which, of all others, most required firmness and solidarity. Naturally one asks why the Cadet members of the Land Commission originally adopted the first draft without ascertaining the will of their party. There had been similar mistakes before, as when Professor Petrazhítsky had risen apparently to introduce the Land Bill and had proceeded to condemn it. Tactical unity was hardly to be expected in the first Russian Parliament, and it is immensely to the credit of Milyukóff that he was ever able to keep the Duma united for so long. But now the Duma had published its dissensions before the world, and this was the moment which the Government might choose, if it desired a dissolution.

At Peterhof the counsels of General Trépoff were opposed by Mr. Stolýpin, the only Minister who had followed the later debates in the Duma. Stolýpin's view was clear and consistent; he recognised Russia as having passed into a constitutional régime: that is to say, there would always be a Duma to join in the work of legislation; but he refused to concede the principle that the Ministers should, as a matter of course, be selected from the party prevailing in the Assembly. He was against the formation of a Cadet Ministry, because it would be compelled by its pledges to surrender almost all the power of the administrative system in a single day. The Duma was at war with the Government; if the Government would not make way for a Cadet Ministry, the only step left for it was to dissolve the Duma.[1] The discussion of the two views at Peterhof was long; but by the evening of Saturday, July 21, the view of Mr. Stolýpin had prevailed, and the Emperor had signed the decree of dissolution. The decree expressed in no uncertain terms the Emperor's disappointment at what he regarded as the factious spirit of the Duma. It was read out in churches and posted up in public places all over the Empire; Stolýpin himself accepted office as the new Prime Minister.

The dissolution of the Duma was the victory of a single strong-minded man. How he understood the difference between Constitutionalism and Parliamentarism was at once apparent: almost every newspaper in St. Petersburg was stopped except the

---

[1] This is a summary of a conversation which I had with Mr. Stolýpin soon after the dissolution.

Official Messenger. The public was stupefied and bowed beneath the yoke ; it again felt the paralysing weight of an overwhelming governmental force hostile to the vast majority of expressed opinions. However, the Cadets and the Labour Group acted with a remarkable unanimity. They at once made their way to a common rendezvous at Vyborg, in Finland. Here a large majority of those members who had still remained in St. Petersburg[1] discussed the drafting of a far more bold address to the people ; Heyden, Stakhóvich, and Lvoff, came out to confer with the majority, but were not able to join with it. Some forty of the Cadets, led by Hertzenstein, were against any strong expression of policy ; but these were persuaded to make common cause with the rest, and a draft was discussed, accepted, and eventually signed by over two hundred members. In forcible language it invited the people to refuse recruits and the payment of taxes until there was a new Duma. The Cadets and the Labour Group could hardly have believed that isolated peasant communities would take the lead in resisting the Government with arms in their hands, and the Labour Group proposed the establishment of a central committee to represent the late Duma and to organise the resistance. This proposal, however, fell through in consequence of the attitude of the more moderate of the Cadets. A more effective article of the Vyborg manifesto was that which, in the name of the nation, refused responsibility for future foreign loans made to the Government; but the programme of a resistance to the Government all over Russia broke down when the Cadets, accepting the dissolution as final, practically retired into private life. Stolýpin was expected to arrest all the members returning from Vyborg, but he was too clever to make this mistake. The Cadets continued to hold party meetings, but after making their great appeal for the support of the nation they themselves failed to take any action whatsoever. They were now looked upon as neither one thing nor the other; even the murder of Mr. Hertzenstein, which might have restored to them the sympathies of public opinion, resulted in nothing but a rather fussy expression of irritation. The artificial character of their tactical victory at the elections now became more and more apparent.

Once more, then, a premium was put upon the political activity

---

[1] Several had gone down to their constituents before the dissolution.

of extremists on both sides; the Parliamentary Labour Committee resigned, and was replaced by men who represented more
definitely revolutionary ideals. To the revolutionaries two policies
were possible. They might adhere to the programme of passive
resistance represented by the strikes of the winter months; but
for this it was necessary that they should command a strong
support of public opinion outside their own ranks. A strike was
indeed announced by them with all the usual publicity, but the
people were tired of such exhausting methods. There was the
usual disagreement amongst the revolutionaries themselves. The
Social Democrats, always the most obstinate theorists, decided
to carry out the strike alone, and it ended in a complete
fiasco. The Committees of all the revolutionary bodies joined
in an appeal to the nation for something more effective than
a strike, that is, for an armed rising. But the revolutionary
organisations were in no way ready. This appeal invited the
peasants to head the rising; the army would then follow, and
later on the working men. But the writers of the appeal themselves knew that the peasants would take no such wholesale
action; a few days later, hearing of a small military rising at
Sveaborg, in Finland, they countermanded their first instructions,
and suggested that the army should move first. The Sveaborg
rising was easily stamped out, and the same fate attended other
abortive military risings at Kronstadt, Oránienbaum, and elsewhere. Those Labour members who had taken part in the
risings were arrested and punished. As to the country in general,
it took no part in these movements, and still lay under the stupe-
faction caused by the dissolution of the Duma; but while visiting
some country districts at this time, I came upon several very
striking symptoms which showed that the peasants were not as
they were a year before. Agrarian rioters were universally condemned by all the more solid of the peasantry; no peasants of
any consequence had the slightest intention of marching out with
pitchforks for the conquest of a new constitution; but some
of them were ready enough to expel any Land Captains or
nominated Elders who might attempt to interfere in the local
affairs of their communities, and for the first time within my
knowledge voices were freely raised on the village green in
criticism even of the dynasty itself. In one village church where

the decree of the dissolution was read out, the peasants interrupted the priest with the words, " That will do, Father ; we know as much about it as you do." When the priest continued to read the decree, a large part of his congregation left the church, as if it had been profaned.

Mr. Stolýpin's position was one of extreme difficulty. He had convictions of his own, but he stood almost alone in them. He definitely dissociated himself from the reactionaries ; he publicly pledged himself to keep the officials within the spirit and letter of the laws. But this was not enough. Ministerial responsibility is not necessarily a law of divine origin, but it is a practical way of doing business. When we are discussing it, we have to ask, What is the alternative ? In Russia the alternative was the supremacy of the Court clique. Mr. Stolýpin was not a member of the clique ; he owed his appointment to its fears ; the better he succeeded in restoring tranquillity, the less necessary he would be to it. This was very soon made clear. The Moderates had not signed the Vyborg manifesto ; in a pronouncement which they published they submitted to the dissolution as quite constitutional, and invited their supporters to help in the maintenance of order and to take an active part in the next elections. Some newspapers described their advice by the ironical epithet of " bread pills " ; but Mr. Stolýpin might be expected to take advantage of their favourable attitude. It was no longer a question of the accession of Shipóff; on the news of the dissolution this notable patriot had resigned his seat in the Council of State ; but several of the Moderates were consulted by Mr. Stolýpin and invited to take part in the government. Professor Vinográdoff, an eminent public man, who was living abroad, was offered the Ministry of Public Instruction. He had very much the opinions of Mr. Shipóff; his conditions of acceptance were that legality should be observed in all measures of the Government, that a new Duma should be summoned, that a kind of Habeas Corpus should be granted, and that restrictions on the Jews should be abolished. The other chief Moderates, who were at this time trying to organise a strong Conservative party, also plainly put forward their conditions. These, it would seem, were accepted by Mr. Stolýpin, and were to be embodied in the form of an Imperial decree ; but it appears that the Prime Minister, while fighting the people single-handed, had not enough credit at the Court to obtain the promulgation of this decree.

Stolýpin, however, continued to go his way with integrity and with courage. As he explained at this time, he was compelled to present two fronts : while strongly opposing revolution, he would use all his powers to make legality the controlling force in public life. In contrast with his predecessors, he intended to take the initiative in legislation, to deal as best he could with administrative questions, and to submit his work to the criticism of the next Duma. Much in the way of reform, he said, could legally be done by the Government itself. The land question required real attention. Meanwhile he had issued a circular to the officials demanding the observance of the law, in order to show that the Government "has parted company for ever with the old police system of administration."[1] He at once proceeded to allot a large portion of the appanage land to the peasants; later he made drastic changes in the communal system. With exceptional moral courage, he did not allow a brutal attempt upon his own life, which inflicted cruel injuries upon one of his children, to deflect him from the path which he had marked out. But the difficulties which surrounded him did not really decrease. From time to time the enforced silence was broken by murders and robberies; these criminal tactics of the revolutionaries obtained a new and artificial consequence from the complete suppression of the voice of the people. At the same time it was to be noticed that several of the victims were taken from amongst the unpunished abettors of pogroms.[2] The Black Gang clubs freely interpreted the dissolution as a condemnation of constitutional government. Enjoying a freedom of expression which was not permitted to the extremists on the other side, they now showed their heads everywhere. There was a new great pogrom in Sedlce, and others seemed imminent in Odessa and elsewhere ; Mr. Stolýpin again had to openly express his hostility to such methods. Meanwhile, the establishment of courts-martial all over the country and the frequency and severity of their sentences seemed to prove that

[1] Conversation with Mr. Stolýpin.
[2] Police-Master Sheremétyeff was gravely implicated in the pogrom at Byelostok. Von der Launitz gave his signature to a provocative "appeal." Count Ignatyeff was generally believed to be largely responsible for the policy of pogroms.

the good intentions of Mr. Stolýpin, like those of other Ministers before him, were being drowned in a multitude of exceptional ordinances. There were further embarrassments within the Ministry itself. The Minister of Finance, Mr. Kokóvtseff, was curiously indiscreet first in sending to him a memorandum threatening the Government with bankruptcy, then in allowing this important document to be stolen, and lastly in acknowledging its authenticity after it had been disavowed by the Prime Minister. Serious charges were brought by a Moderate, Mr. Stakhóvich, against the new Minister of Agriculture, Mr. Gurko; it became evident that the contract for the relief of famine-stricken districts had passed into improper hands, and that a large part of the sum voted by the Duma had gone astray. The Moderates had now split up into two groups; Guchkóff, Volkónsky and others, retaining the old name of Octobrists, were drawing closer to the reactionary "Union of Russian People," which had taken a prominent part in the organisation of the pogroms; while the more important section, which was now known as the "Party of Peaceful Renovation," and included Shipóff, Heyden and Stakhóvich, declared itself dissatisfied with the Government. Even Professor Kovalyévsky, leader of the Party of Democratic Reforms, saw his paper closured for a time, and was later thrown into prison for a Press offence. All these parties were more Conservative than the Cadets, who had formed the centre and the majority in the late Duma. The Cadets, themselves, in spite of some overtures which they made to the Government, were considered by Stolýpin to be so hostile to order that their clubs were closed, and they were refused legalisation as a party. This meant that they could hold no meetings, distribute no electoral literature, and propose no parliamentary candidates. It was as if the right of electoral organisation were refused at our next General Election to the whole of our existing parliamentary majority. Such measures turn an electoral campaign into a vast conspiracy. Of course, the Cadets determined to put forward their own candidates, even if they had to seek cover by posing as a section of the unorganised and non-party opinion of the country; it was precisely in this way that many Labour members had secured their seats in the first Duma. If the elections were to be practically simultaneous, it was almost impossible for the

Government to provide for repression everywhere; if it succeeded in doing so, it would simply rob the new Duma of all practical value; nor would it be able to impose on foreign opinion and secure foreign loans by so transparent a device. It would be more consistent to frankly assert that the Russian people is so vicious that it is unworthy of all control of its own affairs and must remain under the tutelage of those official or unofficial advisers of the Emperor who were responsible for the Japanese war.

Russia had reached a new turning-point in the movement for liberation. There was no question that the people, educated by the events of the last few years into an interest in public affairs, were slowly beginning to find their feet in the new world of politics, and that extremes both of reaction and of revolution were becoming more and more distasteful to them; but as there was now no central and controlling formula, the tension became greater, and violence became more and more possible. The army, daily more and more traversed by the propaganda of the revolutionary parties, seemed to them to be not far from the moment of general explosion; but that moment is probably still distant; military revolts would at the most lead to nothing more decisive than civil war. The question of finance suggested a more threatening danger, but here too the danger was not necessarily imminent. In Russia, where the social instinct is so strong, men would naturally refrain from reckoning up even their own powers until they could judge of the intentions of their fellows. In the absence, then, of a free Press, the next moment of decision was deferred till the elections which were to constitute the second Duma. It was probable that the Conservative party would be both stronger and better organised in this new Assembly; but if repression were extensively employed at the elections, the Duma, being deprived of all national authority, would become useless, and if there were no repression it seemed more than probable that the Assembly, as a whole, would prove more Radical and more intractable than the last.

After the dissolution of the first Duma one foreign correspondent, who did not know Russian, made the ingenuous remark: "I have been reading it all up in Carlyle's 'French Revolution,' and I don't see where this comes in." It is all-important that we should realise the difference between the two great movements. "By the rules of the game," Russia ought at this point to have given us a Tennis-Court Oath. She did not, and many who sympathised with her were disappointed. But it does not follow that the Russian movement is the worse for that. We English, with our traditions of consequent development, are at least the last people who should think so. It was said of the Duke of Wellington by a French historian : "He was not the man to conquer the Peninsula in one campaign, but he was the man to conquer it in several." This might justly be applied to the Russians of 1904–6. Even at the cost of ridicule, the leaders of reform have over and over again drawn back from extreme steps ; and this is only in consonance with the slow, painful, and persistent march of Russian history in general.

Russia is not going to disappear from the earth before our eyes. She exists for some better purpose than to supply us with melodrama. Despite the ominous pronouncements of a number of untrained correspondents, who have by their exaggerations almost killed public interest in this great country, the crops go on growing and life goes on developing. What we have to watch is the gradual formation of a middle term between despotism and revolution. This has been in progress for more than forty years, and the last few years in particular have made it impossible for the country to finally go backward into the unnatural groove from which it is now issuing.

It is no business of mine to suggest in detail what should be the lines of the ultimate settlement. I have only to claim attention for the most momentous of all the changes now proceeding in Europe and to indicate the issues at stake.

Autocracy is a conceivable principle of Government, but it requires certain conditions. These have not existed in Russia during the reign of Nicholas II. The moral forces of the system have disappeared ; the country has outgrown the old order of things. Even without political convulsions, industry at least must ultimately emancipate itself. The real reactionaries are not five per cent. of the population ; in the first Duma they numbered seven members out of five hundred. The revolutionaries are weak in numbers and still weaker in political ability. It is only reaction that keeps revolution alive; the first Duma while it lasted was making revolution more and more improbable. Similarly, the reactionaries have now no hope except in the excesses of the revolutionaries. On the other hand, the Reformers are incomparably stronger in ability, prestige and character than the extremists on either side of them. The Duma made several mistakes but, in spite of the far greater difficulties of its position, it made none worse than have been committed in the course of the last two years by the two chief political parties in England. The average of political ability amongst the Liberal and Conservative leaders will quite sustain comparison with that of either of our Front Benches of the last two years. In political tact and in toleration of secondary differences, the Reformers have done better than we have. No complaint can be made as to the volume and intelligence of public interest on the main questions. The Government will have to make peace with the people. It can still do so with comparative ease. A single public trial of one of the officials who has joined in pogroms would be an immense step in the right direction; but this is precisely the kind of step which the Government is not likely to take. On the other hand, the Reform Movement will be almost invincible from the day when its adherents publicly and universally condemn the methods of Terrorism. Apart from more important considerations, how is the Emperor to be expected to get to know his people, if Terrorism is to confine him, from generation to generation, within the walls of his palace?

A vast moral change has taken place in Russia, but, in the sensational sense of the term, there has never as yet been any Russian Revolution. This was conclusively proved by the sequel of the dissolution of the Duma. It may be long before there is one. But for all that the Government is losing countless opportunities which it will, perhaps, never be able to recover. It is not by isolating the peasants from the educated class that it is going to pacify the country. Day by day, the intelligence of the individual is outstripping the measure of responsibility allowed to him by the authorities. Thus, day by day many Russians become more anti-governmental. But to this grave fact the bureaucracy, though composed in the main of honest and well-meaning officials, seems indifferent. Otherwise it would surely have taken more trouble to show that it could in no way be identified with the acts of a Podgorechani, or a Komisároff. It is this indifference that offends all our most Conservative instincts ; for we cannot but see that the prestige of authority is being recklessly squandered. It is only a change in this attitude that can avert quite unnecessary convulsions.

With or without convulsions, the Reform Movement is certain to sooner or later have its legitimate results. Underneath, the great main factors are slowly but surely changing, and Russia will eventually issue on the path of a renewed life, with loyalty to the past and with confidence in the future. So far from being weakened, she will be better able to take her natural part in the common affairs of Europe. This is a prospect which we in England can welcome. For a hundred years England and Russia have been alienated from each other, not only by Imperial jealousies, now happily decreasing, but still more by a contrast and even an antagonism in the very principles of government which has made a mutual understanding between the representatives of the two countries almost impossible. The establishment of a frankly constitutional regime in Russia will be like the establishment of a common language, in which England and Russia can converse freely. The questions which separate the two nations will still, of course, have to be dealt with separately and in detail ; but the very fact that the two countries are become more intelligible to each other may be expected to sweep half these questions out of existence and to give a reasonable chance of settling the rest.

INDEX.

THE END.